solutions@sy

With over 1,000,000 copies of our MCSE, MCSD, CompTIA, and Cisco study guides in print, we have come to know many of you personally. By listening, we've learned what you like and dislike about typical computer books. The most requested item has been for a web-based service that keeps you current on the topic of the book and related technologies. In response, we have created solutions@syngress.com, a service that includes the following features:

- A one-year warranty against content obsolescence that occurs as the result of vendor product upgrades. We will provide regular web updates for affected chapters.

- Monthly mailings that respond to customer FAQs and provide detailed explanations of the most difficult topics, written by content experts exclusively for solutions@syngress.com.

- Regularly updated links to sites that our editors have determined offer valuable additional information on key topics.

- Access to "Ask the Author"™ customer query forms that allow readers to post questions to be addressed by our authors and editors.

Once you've purchased this book, browse to

www.syngress.com/solutions.

To register, you will need to have the book handy to verify your purchase.

Thank you for giving us the opportunity to serve you.

SYNGRESS®

WINDOWS 2000
CONFIGURATION WIZARDS

SYNGRESS®

Syngress Media, Inc., the author(s), and any person or firm involved in the writing, editing, or production (collectively "Makers") of this book ("the Work") do not guarantee or warrant the results to be obtained from the Work.

There is no guarantee of any kind, expressed or implied, regarding the Work or its contents. The Work is sold AS IS and WITHOUT WARRANTY. You may have other legal rights, which vary from state to state.

In no event will Makers be liable to you for damages, including any loss of profits, lost savings, or other incidental or conscquential damages arising out from the Work or its contents. Because some states do not allow the exclusion or limitation of liability for consequential or incidental damages, the above limitation may not apply to you.

You should always use reasonable case, including backup and other appropriate precautions, when working with computers, networks, data, and files.

Syngress Media® and Syngress® are registered trademarks of Syngress Media, Inc. "Career Advancement Through Skill Enhancement™" is a trademark of Syngress Media, Inc. Brands and product names mentioned in this book are trademarks or service marks of their respective companies.

KEY	SERIAL NUMBER
001	XWPL2C94AS
002	877QZXC555
003	PLTX32AZ12
004	VBM6742DAZ
005	865XXCV214
006	DFW234CXVB
007	MNB3451AWQ
008	678VCXQW21
009	AQW234ZX45
010	78YTXXV234

PUBLISHED BY
Syngress Media, Inc.
800 Hingham Street
Rockland, MA 02370

Windows 2000 Configuration Wizards

Copyright © 2000 by Syngress Media, Inc. All rights reserved. Printed in the United States of America. Except as permitted under the Copyright Act of 1976, no part of this publication may be reproduced or distributed in any form or by any means, or stored in a database or retrieval system, without the prior written permission of the publisher, with the exception that the program listings may be entered, stored, and executed in a computer system, but they may not be reproduced for publication.

Printed in the United States of America

1 2 3 4 5 6 7 8 9 0

ISBN: 1-928994-08-3

Copy edit by: Beth Roberts
Technical edit by: Paul Shields
Index by: Robert Saigh
Project Editor: Julie Smalley

Proofreading by: Ben Chadwick
Page Layout and Art by: Emily Eagar and Vesna Williams
Co-Publisher: Richard Kristof

Acknowledgments

We would like to acknowledge the following people for their kindness and support in making this book possible.

Richard Kristof, Duncan Anderson, Jennifer Gould, Robert Woodruff, Kevin Murray, Dale Leatherwood, Shelley Everett, Laurie Hedrick, Rhonda Harmon, Lisa Lavallee, and Robert Sanregret of Global Knowledge, for their generous access to the IT industry's best courses, instructors and training facilities.

Ralph Troupe and the team at Rt. 1 Solutions for their invaluable insight into the challenges of designing, deploying and supporting world-class enterprise networks.

Karen Cross, Kim Wylie, Harry Kirchner, John Hays, Bill Richter, Michael Ruggiero, Kevin Votel, Brittin Clark, Sarah Schaffer, Luke Kreinberg, Ellen Lafferty and Sarah MacLachlan of Publishers Group West for sharing their incredible marketing experience and expertise.

Peter Hoenigsberg, Mary Ging, Caroline Hird, Simon Beale, Julia Oldknow, Kelly Burrows, Jonathan Bunkell, Catherine Anderson, Peet Kruger, Pia Rasmussen, Denelise L'Ecluse, Rosanna Ramacciotti, Marek Lewinson, Marc Appels, Paul Chrystal, Femi Otesanya, and Tracey Alcock of Harcourt International for making certain that our vision remains worldwide in scope.

Special thanks to the professionals at Osborne with whom we are proud to publish the best-selling Global Knowledge Certification Press series.

From Global Knowledge

At Global Knowledge we strive to support the multiplicity of learning styles required by our students to achieve success as technical professionals. As the world's largest IT training company, Global Knowledge is uniquely positioned to offer these books. The expertise gained each year from providing instructor-led training to hundreds of thousands of students worldwide has been captured in book form to enhance your learning experience. We hope that the quality of these books demonstrates our commitment to your lifelong learning success. Whether you choose to learn through the written word, computer based training, Web delivery, or instructor-led training, Global Knowledge is committed to providing you with the very best in each of these categories. For those of you who know Global Knowledge, or those of you who have just found us for the first time, our goal is to be your lifelong competency partner.

Thank your for the opportunity to serve you. We look forward to serving your needs again in the future.

Warmest regards,

Duncan Anderson
    President and Chief Executive Officer, Global Knowledge

Contributors

Brian M. Collins (MCNE, CNI, MCSE, MCT, CTT) is a technical trainer for Network Appliance Inc., a premier provider of Network Attached Storage, as well as a consultant and trainer through his own company, Collins Network Engineering. Brian is an 18-year veteran of technology industries and has worked as a network engineer, trainer, software developer and consultant for government, Fortune 500 companies, and small business. His hobbies include hiking, golf, and operating systems. Brian lives in the redwood forest of Boulder Creek, California, 30 miles from California's Silicon Valley.

Stace Cunningham (CCNA, MCSE, CLSE, COS/2E, CLSI, COS/2I, CLSA, MCPS, A+) is a Systems Engineer with SDC Consulting located in Biloxi, MS. SDC Consulting specializes in the design, engineering, and installation of networks.

Stace has participated as a Technical Contributor for the IIS 3.0 exam, SMS 1.2 exam, Proxy Server 1.0 exam, Exchange Server 5.0 and 5.5 exams, Proxy Server 2.0 exam, IIS 4.0 exam, IEAK exam, and the revised Windows 95 exam. In addition, he has coauthored or technical edited 19 books published by Microsoft Press, Osborne/McGraw-Hill, and Syngress Media.

He was an instrumental force in the design and engineering of a 1700 node Windows NT network that is located in over 20 buildings at Keesler Air Force Base, Mississippi. He also assisted in the design and implementation of a 10,000 node Windows NT network also located at Keesler Air Force Base and received a quality initiative award for his remarkable contribution to the project.

His wife Martha and daughter Marissa are very supportive of the time he spends on the network of computers and routers located in his house. Without their love and support he would not be able to accomplish the goals he has set for himself.

Martin Weiss (MCSE, MCP+I, CCNA, CNA, CIBS, A+, Network+, i-Net+) is a Senior Information Management Specialist with ACS Government Solutions Group, which is a recognized leading company in providing broad-based information technology solutions for client organizations. Marty lives in New England and can be contacted via e-mail at castadream@hotmail.com.

Technical Editor

Paul Shields (MCSE) currently works as a network engineer for a major telecommunications company. He has been working with, supporting, and writing about Windows NT for the last five years. His current projects revolve around the design and implementation of enterprise-class servers in a mixed platform environment. He is also working on the roll-out of Windows 2000 to the corporate desktop. Paul can be contacted at pshields@applelinks.com.

Contents

Part I Installing Windows 2000 — 1

CHAPTER 1 Preinstallation — 3
Introduction — 4
Before You Begin — 4
    Upgrading versus New Installation — 6
    Hardware Requirements — 7
    Hardware and Software Compatibility — 8
    Hard Disk Partitioning — 10
    Choosing a File System — 10
    Licensing — 11
Per Seat Licensing — 11
Per Server Licensing — 11
    Determining Advanced Setup Needs — 12
Domain or Workgroup? — 12
Choosing Components — 12
Networking — 13
    Final Preparations — 16
Summary — 16

CHAPTER 2 Windows 2000 Setup Wizard — 19
Introduction — 20
Before You Begin — 20
    The Purpose of this Wizard — 20
    Information Needed to Work with this Wizard — 20
The Initial Installation Process — 21
Windows 2000 Server Setup Wizard — 23
Summary — 26

PART 2 Configuring Windows 2000 — 27

CHAPTER 3 Windows 2000 Configure Your Server Wizard — 29
Introduction — 30
Before You Begin — 30
    The Purpose of this Wizard — 30
    Information Needed to Work with this Wizard — 31
Windows 2000 Configure Your Server Wizard — 31
Configure Your Server Program Overview — 37
Summary — 38

CHAPTER 4 Active Directory Installation Wizard   41

Introduction   42
Before You Begin   42
    The Purpose of this Wizard   42
    Information Needed to Work with this Wizard   43
The Active Directory Installation Wizard   43
Uninstalling Active Directory   54
Summary   58

CHAPTER 5 Network Connection Wizard   61

Introduction   62
Before You Begin   62
    The Purpose of this Wizard   62
    Information Needed to Work with this Wizard   62
The Network Connection Wizard   63
    Launching the Network Connection Wizard   63
    Dial-Up to a Private Network   64
    Dial-Up to the Internet   68
    Connect to a Private Network through the Internet   79
    Accept Incoming Connections   81
    Connect Directly to Another Computer   88
Summary   90

CHAPTER 6 Managing DHCP Servers   93

Introduction   94
Before You Begin   94
    The Purpose of this Wizard   94
    Information Needed to Work with this Wizard   94
Add DHCP Server   95
The Create Scope Wizard   95
The Create Superscope Wizard   105
The Create Multicast Scope Wizard   108
Summary   112

CHAPTER 7 Create A New Zone Wizard (DNS)   113

Introduction   114
Before You Begin   114
    The Purpose of this Wizard   114
    Information Needed to Work with this Wizard   115
The Create A New Zone Wizard   115
Summary   124

CHAPTER 8 Routing and Remote Access Configuration Wizard — 127

Introduction	128
Before You Begin	128
The Purpose of this Wizard	129
Information Needed to Work with this Wizard	129
The Routing and Remote Access Configuration Wizard	129
Configuring Routing and Remote Access	136
Summary	143

CHAPTER 9 Create Shared Folder Wizard — 145

Introduction	146
Before You Begin	146
The Purpose of this Wizard	146
Information Needed to Work with this Wizard	146
The Create Shared Folder Wizard	147
Summary	153

CHAPTER 10 Add Printer Wizard — 155

Introduction	156
Before You Begin	156
The Purpose of this Wizard	156
Information Needed to Work with this Wizard	156
The Add Printer Wizard	157
Local Printer	157
Network Printer	162
Summary	167

CHAPTER 11 Internet Information Services (IIS) Wizards — 169

Introduction	170
Before You Begin	170
The Purpose of this Wizard	170
Information Needed to Work with this Wizard	170
The FTP Site Creation Wizard	171
The Web Site Creation Wizard	176
The New SMTP Virtual Server Wizard	182
The Virtual Directory Creation Wizard (Web and FTP)	184
The New Domain Wizard (SMTP Virtual Server)	188
Summary	191

CHAPTER 12 Windows Component Wizard — 193
Introduction — 194
Before You Begin — 194
    The Purpose of this Wizard — 195
    Information Needed to Work with this Wizard — 196
The Windows Component Wizard — 196
Adding a Component — 196
Removing a Component — 201
Summary — 204

CHAPTER 13 Windows 2000 Resource Kit Setup Wizard — 207
Introduction — 208
Before You Begin — 208
    The Purpose of this Wizard — 208
    Information Needed to Work with this Wizard — 208
The Windows 2000 Resource Kit Setup Wizard — 209
Adding Resource Kit Support Tools — 209
Removing, Adding, or Reinstalling Resource Kit Support Tools — 214
Summary — 219

CHAPTER 14 Add/Remove Hardware Wizard — 221
Introduction — 222
Before You Begin — 222
    The Purpose of this Wizard — 222
    Information Needed to Work with this Wizard — 222
Add/Remove Hardware Wizard — 222
    Adding a Plug and Play Device — 223
    Adding a Non-Plug and Play Device — 228
    Removing Hardware — 239
Summary — 244

CHAPTER 15 Internet Connection Wizard — 245
Introduction — 246
Before You Begin — 246
    The Purpose of this Wizard — 246
    Information Needed to Work with this Wizard — 246
The Internet Connection Wizard — 247
Optional Advanced Parameters — 250
Summary — 260

CHAPTER 16 Connection Manager Administration Kit Wizard — 263
Introduction — 264
Before You Begin — 264
    The Purpose of this Wizard — 264

Information Needed to Work with this Wizard	264
The Connection Manager Administration Kit Wizard	265
Summary	289

CHAPTER 17 Create New Dfs Root Wizard — 291

Introduction	292
Before You Begin	292
The Purpose of this Wizard	292
Information Needed to Work with this Wizard	293
Create New Dfs Root Wizard	293
Summary	298

CHAPTER 18 Delegation of Control Wizard — 299

Introduction	300
Before You Begin	300
The Purpose of this Wizard	300
Information Needed to Work with this Wizard	300
The Delegation of Control Wizard	300
Summary	308

CHAPTER 19 Create Partition Wizard — 311

Introduction	312
Before You Begin	312
The Purpose of this Wizard	312
Information Needed to Work with this Wizard	312
The Create Partition Wizard	312
Summary	320

CHAPTER 20 System Maintenance Wizards — 321

Introduction	322
Before You Begin	322
The Purposes of these Wizards	322
Information Needed to Work with these Wizards	323
The Scheduled Task Wizard	323
The Disk Cleanup Wizard	333
The Scheduled Synchronization Wizard	335
Summary	340

CHAPTER 21 Environment Configuration Wizards — 343

Introduction	344
Before You Begin	344
The Purposes of these Wizards	344

Information Needed to Work with these Wizards ... 344
The Create Shortcut Wizard ... 345
The Customize This Folders Wizard ... 348
New Taskpad View Wizard ... 355
Summary ... 360

CHAPTER 22 Accessibility Wizard ... 361
Introduction ... 362
Before You Begin ... 362
   The Purpose of this Wizard ... 362
   Information Needed to Work with this Wizard ... 362
The Accessibility Wizard ... 362
Summary ... 383

CHAPTER 23 Send Fax Wizard ... 385
Introduction ... 386
Before You Begin ... 386
   The Purpose of this Wizard ... 386
   Information Needed to Work with this Wizard ... 386
The Send Fax Wizard ... 386
Summary ... 394

CHAPTER 24 Backup and Recovery Wizards ... 395
Introduction ... 396
Before You Begin ... 396
   The Purposes of these Wizards ... 396
   Information Needed to Work with these Wizards ... 396
Backup Wizard ... 396
Restore Wizard ... 409
Emergency Repair Disk Wizard ... 416
Summary ... 417

CHAPTER 25 Microsoft Windows 2000 Registration Wizard ... 419
Introduction ... 420
Before You Begin ... 420
   The Purpose of this Wizard ... 420
   Information Needed to Work with this Wizard ... 420
The Microsoft Windows 2000 Registration Wizard ... 421
Summary ... 427

INDEX ... 429

Part I

Installing Windows 2000

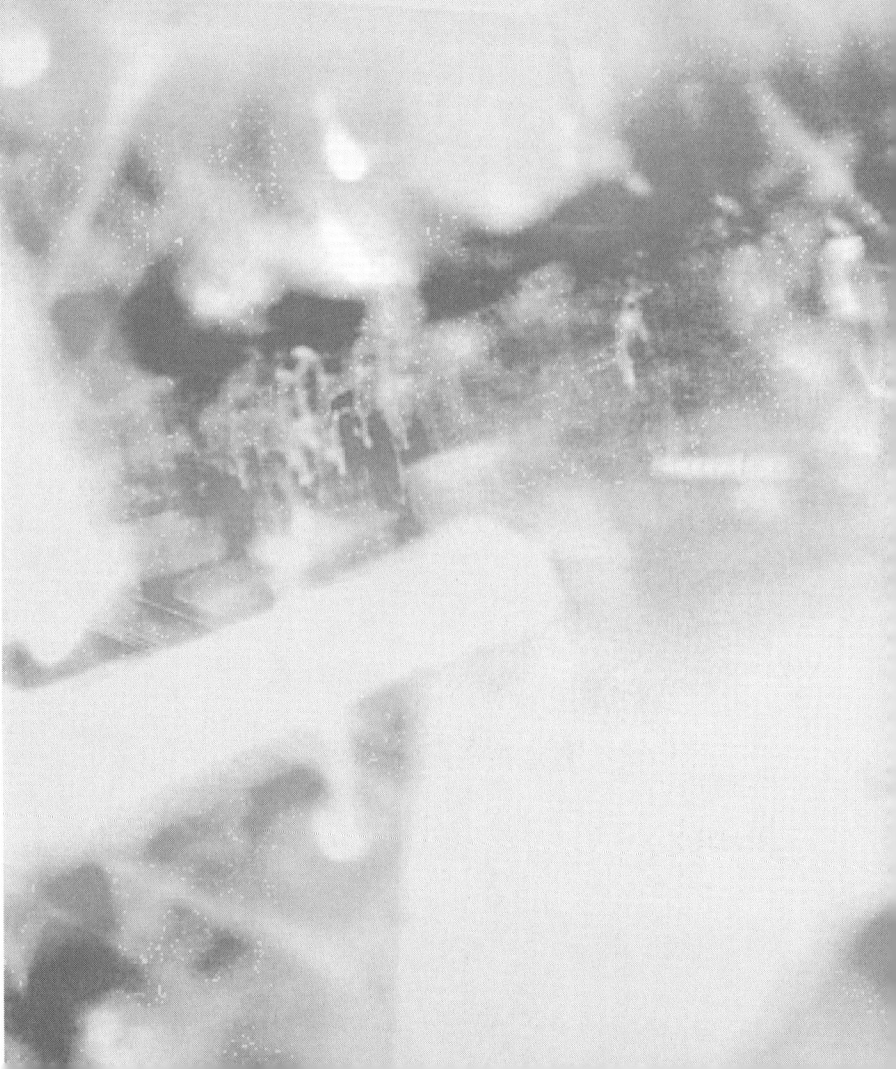

Chapter 1

Preinstallation

Introduction

Before beginning the process of upgrading your current Windows NT servers and Workstations to Windows 2000, it is important to take some time and understand the system requirements and upgrade process. Many System Administrators may be surprised to find that the system requirements for Windows 2000 exceed many of their current system configurations.

Another important consideration is the introduction of Active Directories and their impact on network design. Administrators should take time to understand how Active Directories compare to the traditional Domain model. Before upgrading, you will need to decide how you will upgrade to Active Directories and, if necessary, how you will handle the interoperability issues. Since Windows 2000 represents a significant change in the design of Windows networks, System Administrators should plan upgrades carefully. These plans should include testing of upgrades on low-risk systems and ensuring that complete and reliable backups are available in case of a problem.

By the end of this chapter, System Administrators should have a basic understanding of the system requirements for Windows 2000, the fundamental differences from Windows NT, and have a complete backup of systems scheduled to be upgraded.

Before You Begin

It is important that you familiarize yourself with Active Directory before installing Windows 2000. Active Directory is without a doubt the biggest, most important, and most significant change to Windows 2000. One of the reasons Active Directory is capable of scaling so well is because of the *domain tree*. While Windows 2000 still uses the term *domain*, as does Windows NT 4.0 and earlier, the concepts and structures are actually quite different. Active Directory is a set of one or more domain trees. A domain tree is composed of domains that share a common configuration and form a contiguous namespace. Each domain is further subdivided into organizational units (OUs) for administrative purposes. Unlike Windows NT 4.0 and earlier, a Windows 2000 domain can grow to contain over 10 million objects! Figure 1.1 illustrates a domain tree with OUs.

A *forest* is another term that you should also be familiar with. As the name implies, a forest is a set of one or more trees. The primary difference with a forest is that trees within a forest do not form a contiguous namespace. To better illustrate why a forest might exist in your network, imagine two completely separate and well-known companies. Now suppose that they merge, yet because of their client base and name recognition, they still want to maintain separate identities. Such a situation is ideal for the creation of a forest.

Figure 1.1 A Windows 2000 domain tree contains domains, which in turn contain organizational units.

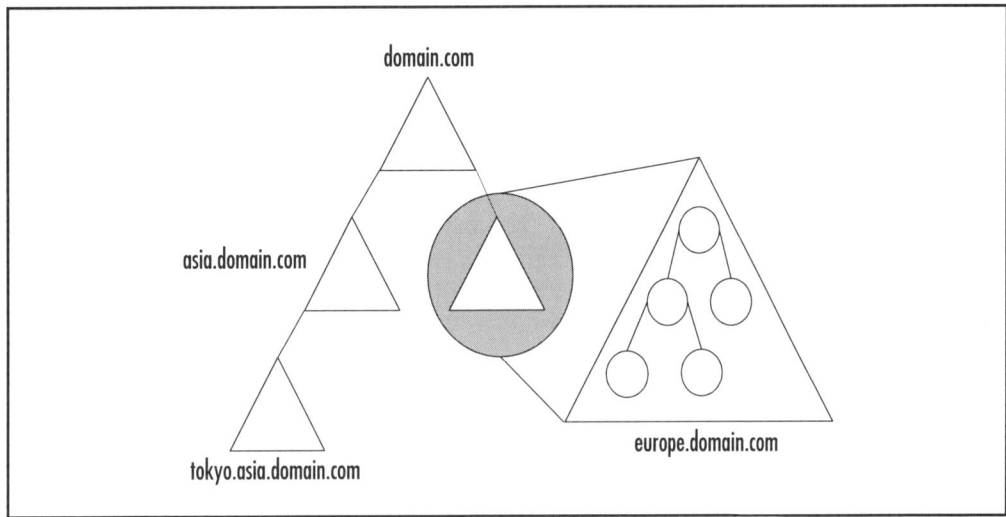

Because of the vast differences in domain models between Windows NT and Windows 2000, you may be wondering if the two can coexist—the answer is yes. Windows 2000 domains and pre-Windows 2000 domains operate in *mixed mode*. In mixed mode, all down-level servers and clients are unaware that the Primary Domain Controller (PDC) is now an Active Directory Server. When all of the Backup Domain Controllers (BDC) have been upgraded or removed, you can switch over to *native mode* and take advantage of additional Windows 2000 features. Native mode provides for added security group functionality. For example, Windows 2000 operating in native mode has the ability to nest groups. Figure 1.2 illustrates the stages of an upgrade from Windows NT domains to Windows 2000 native domains.

Once you have familiarized yourself with the key features of Windows 2000 and the changes Active Directory brings, you can begin preparing for the actual installation of Windows 2000. The key to a successful upgrade or installation of Windows 2000 is proper preparation. What follows are various factors that must be taken into consideration before running the setup procedures. Additionally, you should review the files located on the root directory of the Windows 2000 CD. These files contain important notes and last-minute information that may be critical to the success of your installation.

Figure 1.2 Moving domains from Windows NT to Windows 2000.

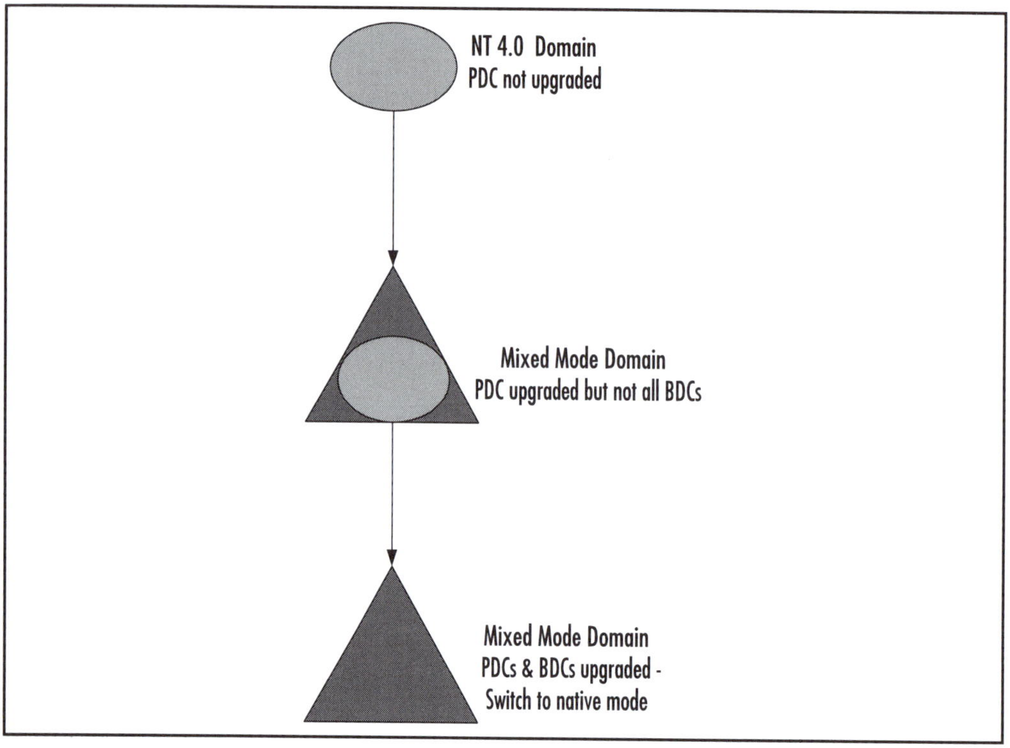

[Diagram showing three stages: NT 4.0 Domain PDC not upgraded (circle) → Mixed Mode Domain PDC upgraded but not all BDCs (triangle with circle) → Mixed Mode Domain PDCs & BDCs upgraded - Switch to native mode (triangle)]

Upgrading versus New Installation

A decision that needs to be made before running the Windows 2000 Setup is to determine whether to upgrade your existing operating system (see Table 1.1 for supported upgrade paths) or perform a new installation. Generally, a new installation will require many more decisions to be made prior to the procedure, which are discussed later in this chapter. An upgrade, on the other hand, is usually straightforward and requires mostly that certain precautions be met, which are also discussed further on.

Upgrading simply means installing Windows 2000 on a system, in the same partition that already has an operating system that can be upgraded. Alternatively, a new installation will remove the previous operating system, or will install onto a partition without an already existing operating system.

> **NOTE**
>
> Versions of Windows NT earlier than 3.51 cannot be directly upgraded to Windows 2000. You can, however, upgrade these systems to NT version 3.51 or 4.0, and then upgrade to Windows 2000.

Table 1.1 Windows 2000 Upgrade Paths

Old Versions	Can Be Upgraded To
Windows 95/98	Windows 200 Professional
Windows NT 3.51/4.0 Workstation	Windows 2000 Professional
Windows NT 3.51 Server	Windows 2000 Server Windows 2000 Advanced Server
Windows NT 3.51 Server with Citrix	Cannot be upgraded
Windows NT 4.0 Server	Windows 2000 Server Windows 2000 Advanced Server
Windows NT 4.0 Terminal Server	Windows 2000 Server Windows 2000 Advanced Server
Windows NT 4.0 Enterprise Server	Windows 2000 Advanced Server Windows 2000 Datacenter Server
BackOffice Small Business Server	Cannot be upgraded

Hardware Requirements

Before deploying a new operating system, many are initially concerned with the minimum hardware requirements. This is one of the most frequently asked questions, yet it largely depends on the individual circumstances. For example, if your only need is to become acquainted with the user interface of Windows 2000 Server on your computer at home, you can feasibly install the operating system on a Pentium 133 with the minimal amount of RAM. Although this may serve your needs, using this system in a production environment would only serve at best as a space heater.

The hardware requirements for Windows 2000 are rather steep, and it is highly recommended that you take into account your plans for the system. For example, if you plan to use a Windows 2000 Server as domain controller supporting several thousand users, you will likely want to exceed the listed requirements. Generally speaking, however, you should ensure that your system meets the recommended minimum hardware requirements shown in Table 1.2.

Table 1.2 Minimum and Recommended Requirements for Windows 2000

Component	Professional	Server
CPU	133 MHz or higher Pentium-compatible processor	133 MHz or higher Pentium-compatible processor
Memory	64MB or more	256MB or more (128MB supported)
Hard disk	2GB with a minimum of 1GB free space on the partition that will contain the system files	2GB with a minimum of 1GB free space on the partition that will contain the system files
CD-only Install	El Torito compatible CD-ROM drive	El Torito compatible CD-ROM drive
Floppy and CD Install	High-density 3.5-inch disk drive and CD-ROM drive	High-density 3.5-inch disk drive and CD-ROM drive
Network Install	Network adapter and access to the network share containing the setup files	Network adapter and access to the network share containing the setup files
Accessories	Keyboard and mouse or other pointing device	Keyboard and mouse or other pointing device

Hardware and Software Compatibility

Before attempting to run Windows 2000 Setup, you should ensure that your hardware is compatible. Although a Hardware Compatibility List (Hcl.txt) is located in the Support directory on the Windows 2000 CD-ROM, it is recommended that your review the most current list, which can viewed at www.microsoft.com/hwtest/hcl (Figure 1.3). Before running setup, it is also probably a good idea to contact the vendors of your hardware devices and obtain the latest drivers. Be sure to pay special attention if you have any mass storage controllers (e.g., SCSI, RAID). A common problem with unsupported controllers is receiving an error after the initial Setup phase, indicating that there is an inaccessible boot device.

Also available from Microsoft's Web site is an easy-to-search directory of applications that are known to work with Windows 2000. To help ensure third-party software reliability and performance with Windows 2000, Microsoft has created the following three classifications for applications:

- **Certified**. Microsoft provides a Windows 2000 Applications Specification, which specifies uses of advanced Windows Technology. Any Independent Software Vendor (ISV) who uses these advanced specifications is eligible for this level of classification.
- **Ready**. This classification is provided to software that has been tested for compatibility with Windows 2000.
- **Planned**. This classification is assigned to software in which the vendor is working on a compatible version to meet the Ready or Certified level.

During the installation, Windows 2000 Setup will check your hardware and software, and identify any possible conflicts. Nevertheless, verifying the Hardware Compatibility List and software compatibility before running Setup may save you a lot of time later on. Additionally, verifying this list is critical if you will be purchasing new systems to install Windows 2000 on. You would not want to spend thousands of dollars on new systems only to find out that they cannot run Windows 2000!

Figure 1.3 The HCL list from Microsoft's Web site makes it easy to search for your hardware and contains the latest information.

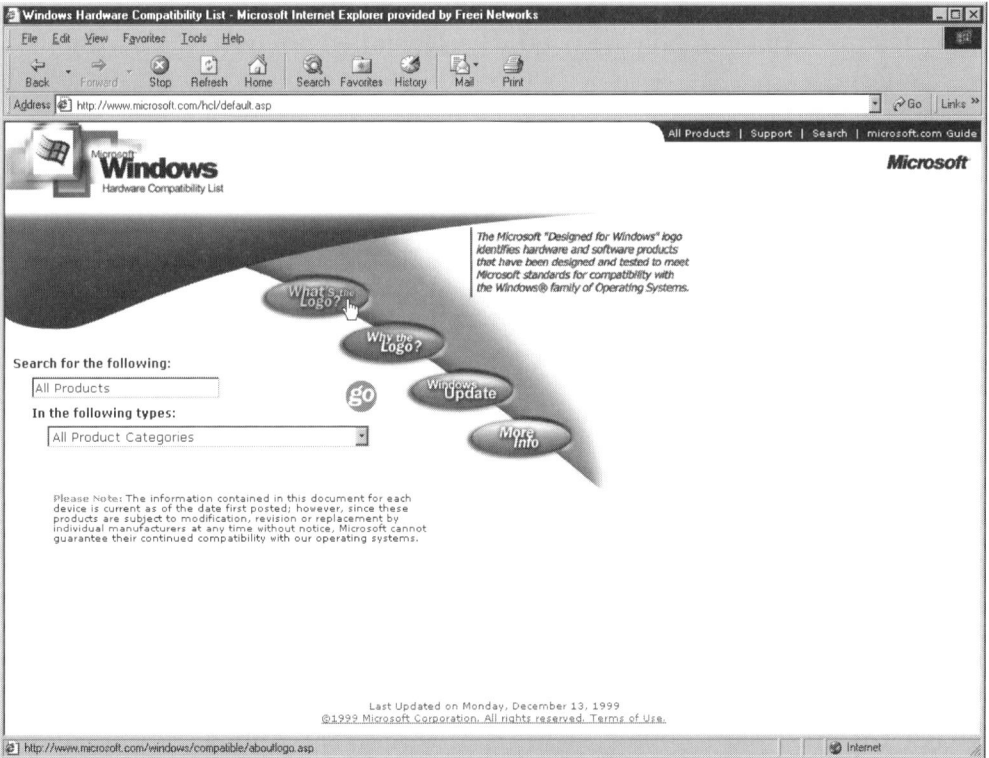

Hard Disk Partitioning

If you are performing a new installation of Windows 2000, you will need to consider how you will partition your hard disks; an upgrade will not require this because an upgrade will use your already existing partitions. Partitioning allows you to divide your hard disk into one or more isolated sections that can be formatted for a particular file system such as FAT, FAT32, or NTFS.

If you do not already have a partitioning plan, it may be a good idea to seek out further information relative to your specific needs before performing Setup. If you plan to use multiple partitions, it is important that you allow enough room for the data that will be grouped on the individual partitions. For example, the requirements in Table 1.2 indicate that you need at least 1GB of free disk space on the partition that will contain the system files. You should, however, plan for future growth and allow more space than what is needed at the time.

Choosing a File System

Before installing Windows 2000, you should also determine the type of file system you require (e.g., NTFS, FAT, FAT32). If you are familiar with previous versions of Windows NT, you may recall that NTFS is the preferred file system—even more so with Windows 2000. The following is a brief list of the many features that can only be used when installed on an NTFS partition:

- Active Directory
- Domain support
- File-level security
- File encryption
- Sparse files
- Disk quotas
- Disk compression
- Increased scalability

> **NOTE**
>
> If you do not format the partition as NTFS during the installation process, you can easily convert from FAT or FAT32 later by using the Convert command from within Windows. Type **convert /?** at a command prompt for more information.

For the most part, a file system other than NTFS should be considered when you have a need to run a dual-boot computer. Other operating systems cannot gain local access to files located on a Windows 2000 system formatted with NTFS. A FAT partition allows local access through MS-DOS, Windows NT, Windows 2000, and OS/2. A FAT32 partition allows local access only through Windows 98 OSR2, Windows 98, and Windows 2000. Another consideration when determining the file system is possible disk sizes. For example, a FAT partition only supports volumes up to 4GB in size. Although FAT32 supports volumes up to 2TB, Windows 2000 will only allow you to format a FAT32 drive up to 32GB.

> **NOTE**
>
> A Windows NT 4.0 system with Service Pack 4 or higher that resides on a FAT partition can access files locally on an NTFS partition but only with limited access.

Licensing

Licensing plays a critical role in the Windows 2000 Setup process. Determining your needs is critical before running Setup, as you will see shortly. When running a server operating system, each client connection to the server will require some type of license. This Client Access License (CAL) allows connections to the server to access network services, shared folders, and other resources. The Windows 2000 Server licensing options are the same as those in previous versions of the operating systems. From Setup, you will have the option of selecting either Per Seat or Per Server.

Per Seat Licensing

Per Seat licensing requires each connection to have a CAL. Per Seat allows any computer with a CAL to access any number of servers on the network, which is why this is the most common choice for larger companies, or those with more than one server. On the other hand, for smaller organizations or those with only one server, Per Server licensing may be a better option.

Per Server Licensing

Per Server licensing assigns CALs to the individual server instead of the client connections. Therefore, each connection to the server will require the server to have a CAL for each concurrent connection. Assume you operate an organization with 20 employees and you have one server. If you purchase 15 CALs for the server, you can have 15 connections to the server; thus, your server has a fixed number of allowable connections. Of your 20 employees, if you expect that not of all of them will need to be connected concurrently, purchasing fewer than 20 licenses might be a good idea. Keep in mind, however, that once you have reached your maximum allowable connections, no other connections can be made until one or more connections terminate.

> **NOTE**
>
> If you choose Per Server, you are allowed to change your mind at any time and switch to Per Seat without incurring any additional charges, but only once! You will not be allowed to convert back to Per Server.

Determining Advanced Setup Needs

There are several concepts you will need to be conscious of when determining your setup needs.

Domain or Workgroup?

You will be prompted during installation to select the type of security group your computer will join. The available options are joining a domain, which will require a domain name, a computer account, an available domain controller, and a DNS server; whereas, joining a workgroup only requires a name of a new or existing workgroup. It is common to join a workgroup only in a small network or if you plan to later join a domain. Joining a domain can also be done after Windows 2000 has been set up.

> **NOTE**
>
> If your computer is the first one installed on the network, you will have to first join a workgroup and then create and join the domain after installation.

Choosing Components

In addition to the components installed automatically by Windows 2000 Setup, there are a number of other components that you are given the option to install in order to further extend the functionality of Windows 2000. Keep in mind, however, that if you choose not to install any of these additional components, you can always install them later using the Add/Remove Programs option located in the Control Panel. It might be helpful to determine ahead of time which of these components you may require. Remember that components that are not needed will only take up extra disk space. Table 1.3 provides a list of the available options and a brief description of each.

Networking

Before installing Windows 2000, you may wish to give thought to various issues if you plan on being networked. TCP/IP is the most common protocol in use today. It is the protocol of the Internet, and the protocol used on most servers. In addition, Windows 2000 uses TCP/IP natively and is optimized for this protocol.

TCP/IP uses an IP address as an identifier for a device on the network. Additionally, these addresses are used to route messages over the network. An IP address is a 32-bit numerical address, part of which identifies the network, and the other part identifies the specific node. In addition, if you are connected to the Internet, you must use registered IP addresses, which are assigned by the InterNIC or acquired from your Internet Service Provider (ISP). Table 1.4 explains the three primary classes of IP addresses, and Figure 1.4 illustrates a simple TCP/IP network with a network address of 198.168.0.0.

You have the option to configure TCP/IP during the installation process, or you may elect to configure it after installing Windows. Either way, you will need to think about and address the issues of IP addresses and name resolution. TCP/IP requires that an IP address is assigned to the system, and name resolution allows these IP addresses to be resolved to names that are easier to remember and more user friendly.

Depending upon your existing environment or future plans, there are numerous ways to approach IP addressing. The following list outlines these methods:

- Automatic Private IP Addressing is a feature of Windows 2000 that will automatically assign an IP address for a limited number of systems. For example, if you have five networked systems, and each is given the same subnet mask, each will be assigned an IP address automatically and able to communicate.
- Dynamic Host Configuration Protocol also allows for the automatic assignment of IP addresses. The DHCP server, however, must be assigned a static IP address, and it will then assign IP addresses from a specified pool of available addresses. This is commonly found on networks where there are multiple subnets.
- If you plan to provide access to users from the Internet, you will need to assign a static IP address to the server. You will thus need to obtain a network address from either your ISP or the InterNIC.

Table 1.3 Components That Can Be Selected from Windows 2000 Setup Routine

Component	Description
Certificate Services	Provides authentication support for smart cards, e-mail, and Web services.
Internet Information Services (IIS)	Provides Web site management support. Also includes NNTP, FTP, and SMTP support.
Management and Monitoring Tools	Provides tools for monitoring and managing the network, as well as a Novell Directory Service migration tool.
Message Queuing Services	Provides support services for messaging needed by distributed applications.
Microsoft Indexing Service	Allows users to search document text or properties for documents stored on disk.
Microsoft Script Debugger	Provides support for script development and debugging.
COM Internet Services Proxy	Provides support for distributed applications that use Web service to communicate through IIS.
Domain Name System (DNS)	Provides name resolution support.
Dynamic Host Configuration Protocol (DHCP)	Provides support to dynamically assign client IP addresses.
Internet Authentication Service	Provides dial-in user authentication.
QoS Admission Control Service	Provides support to control application bandwidth use on the network.
Simple TCP/IP Service	Provides support for tools such as Echo, Quote of the Day, and Daytime Discard.
Site Server LDAP Services	Provides support for telephony applications.
Other Network File and Print Services	Provides added support services for Macintosh and UNIX.
Remote Installation Services	Allows for remote setup of client computers.
Terminal Services	Allows clients to run applications from the server.
Terminal Services Licensing	Must be installed with Terminal Services. Allows for the management of licenses for Terminal Server clients.
Windows Media Services	Provides support for delivering streaming multimedia content over a network.

Table 1.4 Properties of IP Address Classes

Class	Format	First Octet (8 Bits)	Hosts Supported	Networks Supported
A	Net.Node.Node.Node	1-127	16 million	127
B	Net.Net.Node.Node	128-191	16 thousand	65 thousand
C	Net.Net.Net.Node	192-223	254	2 million

NOTE

Static IP addresses are required for some types of servers that cannot be assigned dynamic addresses. Examples include Web, mail, DNS, and DHCP servers.

Windows 2000 Server uses the Domain Name System (DNS) to resolve numerical IP addresses to host names. If you elect not to install DNS, it will be automatically installed if your computer becomes a domain controller. In addition to using DNS, you may also need to install Windows

Figure 1.4 A simple network with a Network ID of 198.168.0.0.

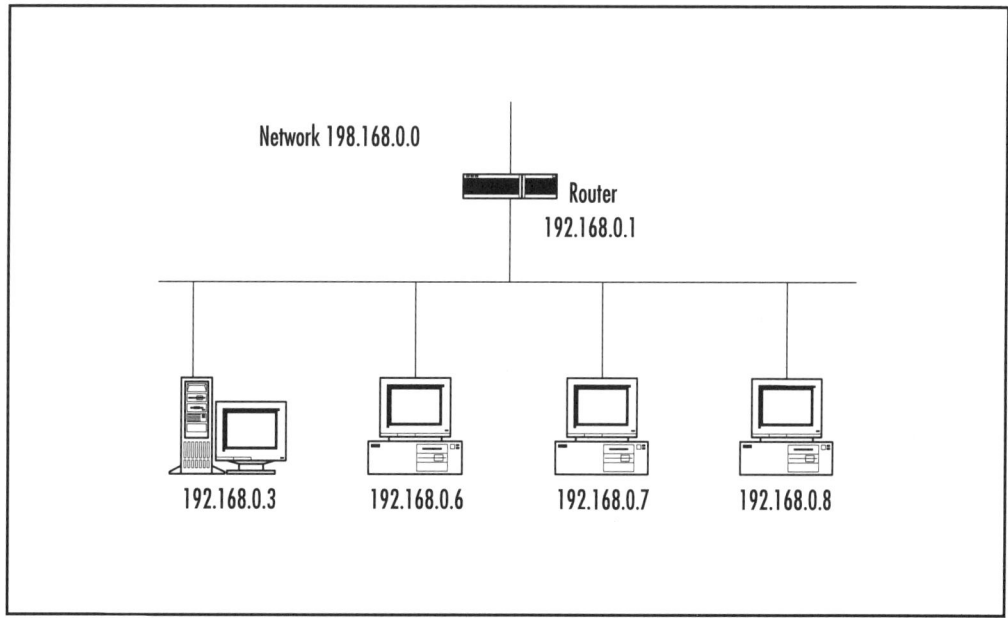

Internet Name Service (WINS) to support any clients running earlier versions of Windows.

Final Preparations

After you have planned your installation and are ready to install the new operating system, you should take the time to perform some basic steps that will prepare your system for Setup. Additionally, if you are performing an upgrade, be sure to also review the release notes on the CD-ROM and ensure that you have disabled or removed any applications specified before running Setup. The following tasks should be performed before running Setup to ensure a smooth installation of Windows 2000:

> **Perform backups.** Unless your system does not have any files, you should always perform a backup of your existing files before any major changes. The importance of this simple task cannot be overstated. If for some reason, something goes wrong, you should then have an easy way to restore your previously existing data. Additionally, you may want to use a product such as Norton Ghost to make an exact copy of a critical server onto another system to serve as an additional fallback.
>
> **Disable disk mirroring.** Before installing Windows 2000, be sure to disable disk mirroring if it is running on the computer. You may then reenable it after the upgrade or new installation is successful.
>
> **Disconnect UPS.** Uninterruptible power supplies (UPS) oftentimes create problems during the detection phase. Because Windows will try to detect any devices connected to serial ports, be certain to disconnect the serial cable if you are using a UPS.

> **TIP**
>
> While added reliability and stability are two of the key benefits of Windows 2000, you may want to consider running test installations in a test lab. If you are operating on a large network, this could prove critical to ensure interoperability with other systems.

Summary

Before installing Windows 2000, it is important to consider the changes in the operating system and how they will apply to your organization. One of the biggest and most significant changes in Windows 2000 is the Active Directory directory structure. Because of the vast differences between

Windows 2000 and previous versions of the operating system, you will need to consider various factors before installing Windows 2000.

Windows 2000 requires significantly more powerful hardware than Windows NT. If you are planning to run Windows 2000 Server in a production environment, it is recommended that you consider a Pentium II system with at least 128–256MB of memory. Although this chapter provides you with minimum and recommended guidelines, it is critical that you take into account your current and future needs.

In addition to ensuring you have enough power to run Windows 2000, you will also need to ensure that your hardware and software is compatible with Windows 2000. Microsoft provides an up-to-date and comprehensive database that you can search to ensure that your hardware and software is compatible.

Installing Windows 2000 will require that you make decisions such as which partition to install the operating system on, which file system to use, and which licensing method to use. Additionally, you will need to consider other issues that relate to your needs. For example, will you join a domain or a workgroup? It is also a good idea to determine your server needs, so that you can easily select the components to install that will be required by your organization. Finally, Windows 2000 offers you the option to customize your network configuration during a new installation; therefore, having a firm understanding and knowledge of your existing or proposed network is important.

As a final preparation to installing Windows 2000, you will need to perform some simple, yet important, tasks to ensure a smooth installation. These include performing backups, disabling disk mirroring, and disconnecting any UPS attached to the system. Proper preparation before setting up Windows 2000 will help ensure a smooth and successful installation.

Chapter 2
Windows 2000 Setup Wizard

Introduction

The first step in working with Windows 2000 is the installation process. The process and wizards are similar to those in Windows NT 4.0, but offer a number of new features and options. On most systems, you can boot from the CD-ROM to begin the installation process. The first step is to select a partition and copy over the installation files. The interface used is not a traditional wizard, but does walk you through the process step by step.

The next phase begins after you reboot. Windows 2000 will load and run the initial Setup Wizard. This wizard contains the bulk of the basic Windows 2000 setup process and is very similar for both Server and Professional versions of Windows 2000. By the end of this chapter, you should have a fully functional Windows 2000 system.

Before You Begin

Before you install Windows 2000, ensure that you have considered the various factors discussed in Chapter 1, "Preinstallation." Additionally, ensure that you have backed up your files and disabled disk mirroring and UPS devices before you begin. Although the installation is divided into two phases, there are actually four stages to the Setup routine. These include running the Setup program, running the Setup Wizard, installing Windows networking, and completing the Setup program.

The Purpose of this Wizard

Although the following steps are geared toward the installation of Windows 2000 Server, the installation process for Windows 2000 Professional is nearly identical. The initial installation process and the Server Setup Wizard provide a friendly and step-by-step method to install Windows 2000 on a computer system. Figure 2.1 illustrates the basic steps involved when installing Windows 2000 Server.

Information Needed to Work with this Wizard

To perform the initial installation process and follow-on wizard, ensure that you have the following:

- Windows 2000 CD-ROM
- Networking information. If you prefer, you may use the default settings and then further customize networking components once Windows is installed.

Figure 2.1 These steps are involved for Windows 2000 Setup.

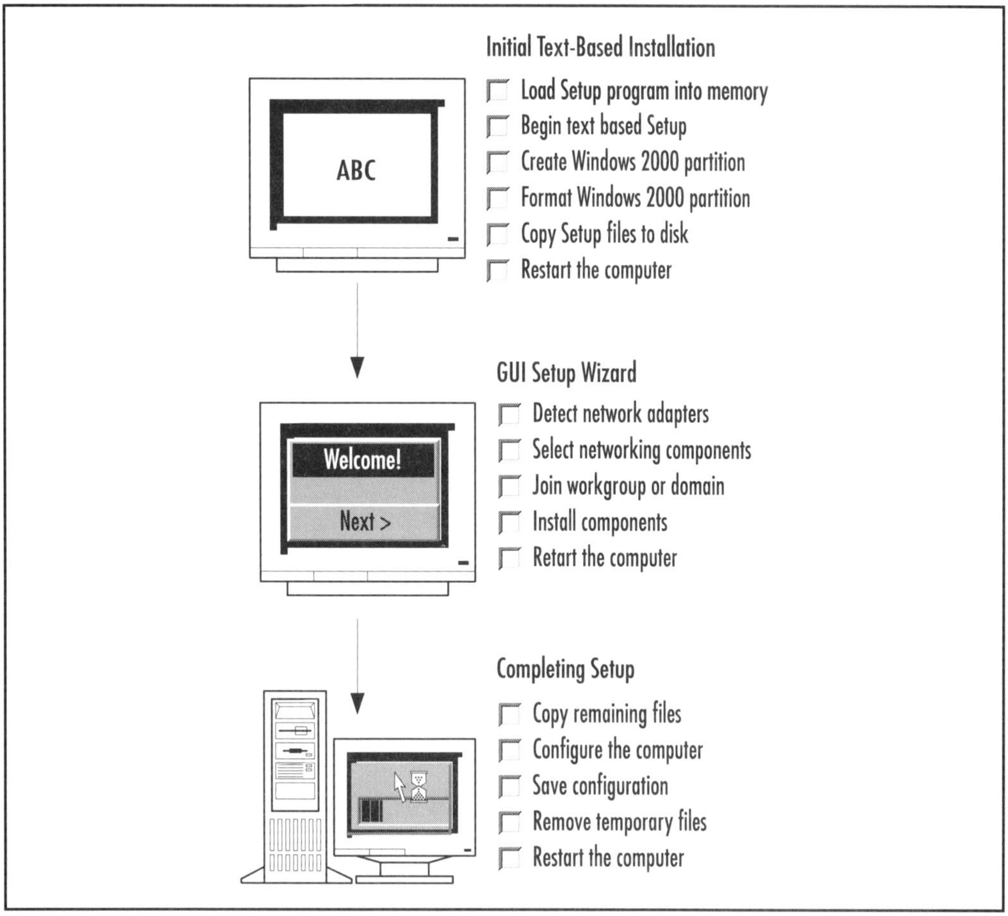

```
Initial Text-Based Installation
    ☐ Load Setup program into memory
    ☐ Begin text based Setup
    ☐ Create Windows 2000 partition
    ☐ Format Windows 2000 partition
    ☐ Copy Setup files to disk
    ☐ Restart the computer

GUI Setup Wizard
    ☐ Detect network adapters
    ☐ Select networking components
    ☐ Join workgroup or domain
    ☐ Install components
    ☐ Retart the computer

Completing Setup
    ☐ Copy remaining files
    ☐ Configure the computer
    ☐ Save configuration
    ☐ Remove temporary files
    ☐ Restart the computer
```

The Initial Installation Process

➢ STEP 1

To initiate the Setup routine, you can use either the Setup boot disks or the CD-ROM, if your computer supports booting from a CD-ROM drive. To start from the CD-ROM, simply insert the CD and turn on or restart your computer. To start from the boot disks, insert Setup Disk 1 into Drive A and turn on or restart your computer.

If you are performing an upgrade, you cannot boot from the CD-ROM. To perform the upgrade on most systems, simply insert the CD-ROM while running your current operation system, and if the auto-run feature is enabled, Setup will display a dialog box to begin the installation (Figure 2.2). Alternatively, you can execute winnt.exe from the I386 directory on the Windows 2000 CD-ROM.

Figure 2.2 The Windows 2000 Server setup dialog box.

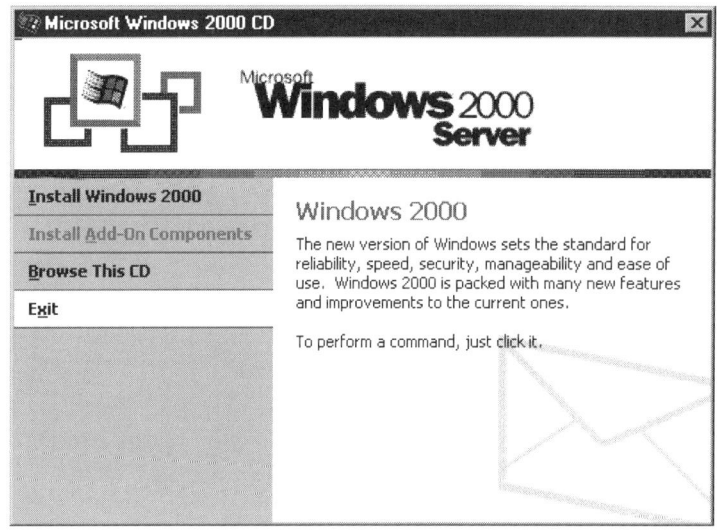

> **NOTE**
>
> To make the Setup boot disks, run the makedisk utility from the bootdisk directory on the CD-ROM. Remember that boot disks created from the Windows 2000 Server CD cannot be used with Windows 2000 Professional and vice versa.

➤ STEP 2

After booting from the CD-ROM or boot disk, enough of Windows 2000 is loaded into memory to start the text-based portion of Setup. Read the license agreement that appears. To accept the terms of the license agreement, press F8.

➤ STEP 3

This step allows you to create and delete partitions. You are prompted to select an installation partition. You may select an existing partition, or you can create a new partition by using unpartitioned space.

> **WARNING**
>
> If you are performing a new installation on a partition that contains another operating system, this operating system will be overwritten. Additionally, deleting a partition will also delete any existing data.

➤ STEP 4

Next, you need to select a file system for the partition, which Windows will then format using the specified file system. After formatting the partition, Setup will copy files to the hard disk and then save the configuration information. Setup will then restart the computer and start the Windows 2000 Server Setup Wizard. This wizard is the graphical user interface (GUI) portion of Setup, which will continue with the setup of Windows 2000.

Windows 2000 Server Setup Wizard

➤ STEP 1

The first step in the GUI portion of Setup is to select your regional settings. Here you can set your system up to use multiple languages and regional settings by customizing the language and locale settings.

➤ STEP 2

Next, you will personalize your copy of Windows 2000. Enter the name of the person and the company for which Windows 2000 is licensed for use.

➤ STEP 3

You will then be prompted to choose your licensing mode. If you are upgrading, the mode is already selected based on your existing configuration. As discussed in Chapter 1, you have the option of selecting Per Server or Per Seat licensing. If you select Per Server, you will need to enter the number of Client Access Licenses (CALs) purchased for this server. If at the time of installation you are still unsure which mode to use, be sure to select Per Server, since you are allowed to change from Per Server to Per Seat for free.

➤ STEP 4

Next, enter your computer name. Keep in mind that Windows operating systems earlier than Windows 2000 will only recognize the first 15 characters of the name. You are, however, able to enter a computer name up to 63 characters. Ensure that you enter a unique name.

➤ STEP 5

Windows 2000 creates a user account called Administrator, for which you are prompted to enter a password. The password you enter can contain up to 14 characters. After you have entered your password for the Administrator account, you will need to enter it again to confirm the password.

> **TIP**
>
> Remember to always choose a complex password. It is recommended that you choose a password that consists of numbers, symbols, and uppercase and lowercase letters.

➤ STEP 6

You are able to choose among many components that provide added functionality to Windows 2000. See Table 1.3 in Chapter 1 for a list of available components. In addition to the components discussed earlier, you will also find the Accessories and Utilities component, which provides accessory programs such as Calculator, WordPad, Games, and others.

➤ STEP 7

Next, select your corresponding time zone and adjust the current date and time. Finally, you have the option of specifying if you want Windows 2000 to automatically adjust for daylight savings time by clicking the check box.

➤ STEP 8

Setup will next begin installing the Windows networking components. First it will detect any network cards that may be installed. If it detects a network card, it will configure the card, and then Setup will next try to determine if a DHCP server is running on the network. You will be prompted to select networking components, which can use the

typical settings, or you may elect to customize them individually. If you select the typical settings, the following will be installed:
- Client for Microsoft Networks
- File and Printer Sharing for Microsoft Networks
- TCP/IP

You may, depending on your existing network, elect to install other clients, services, and protocols such as NetBEUI, AppleTalk, and so forth. Keep in mind that there is no harm in keeping the typical settings. You may make any changes to your networking configuration after Windows 2000 is installed.

➢ STEP 9

Setup will display the Workgroup or Computer Domain page. Here you specify if you want the computer to join a workgroup or a domain.

> **NOTE**
>
> Choosing to join a domain allows you to only join an *existing* domain. If you wish to create a new domain, you should first join a workgroup. After the installation, you can create a new domain by using the Active Directory Installation Wizard, which is discussed in Chapters 3 and 4.

➢ STEP 10

Windows 2000 will automatically perform the following final installation steps:

1. Copy remaining files to the system.
2. Apply and save the configuration settings.
3. Remove temporary files copied during installation.
4. Restart the computer (be sure to remove the Setup floppy disk or CD-ROM).
5. Windows 2000 Server will display the Configure Server Wizard after you log on, which allows you to easily perform further configuration of the system.

NOTE

After logging on to the system for the first time, if any additional peripherals are detected, Windows may launch the Found New Hardware Wizard.

Summary

Installing Windows 2000 is comprised of a text-based initial installation and a graphical portion. Together there are four stages: running the Setup program, running the Setup Wizard, installing networking, and completing the Setup program.

To install a fresh copy of Windows 2000, you can use either the supplied startup disks or the CD-ROM, if your system supports booting from the CD-ROM drive. After booting the system from the CD-ROM or setup disk, Windows 2000 is copied into memory and the Setup program starts. Installing Windows is comprised of a series of steps, which include accepting the licensing agreement, selecting a partition, and an appropriate file system. The Setup program then copies necessary files to the hard disk, saves the configuration information, restarts the computer, and then initializes the graphical Windows 2000 Setup Wizard.

After starting the Setup Wizard, Windows 2000 will prompt you to provide various bits of information. You will need to confirm your language and locale, and the name and organization for whom the software is licensed. Next, Windows Setup prompts you to select either a Per Seat or Per Server licensing mode, and then asks you to specify a name for the system and an Administrator account password. After providing the password, you have the opportunity to specify a number of additional components that you wish to install.

After specifying additional components, the installation of Windows 2000 networking begins. Setup will determine and configure any network cards attached to the system, and you are then asked to use typical or customized networking settings. Finally, Windows Setup will configure the networking components you selected after specifying whether Windows will join a domain or a workgroup.

Finally, Setup will copy any remaining files, and then apply and save the configuration settings. After it deletes any temporary files used during the installation process, Setup will restart the computer. Assuming a smooth installation, the Windows 2000 logon prompt will appear. After entering the Administrator password and logging on to Windows 2000 Server, the Configure Your Server window will appear.

Part II

Configuring Windows 2000

Chapter 3

Windows 2000 Configure Your Server Wizard

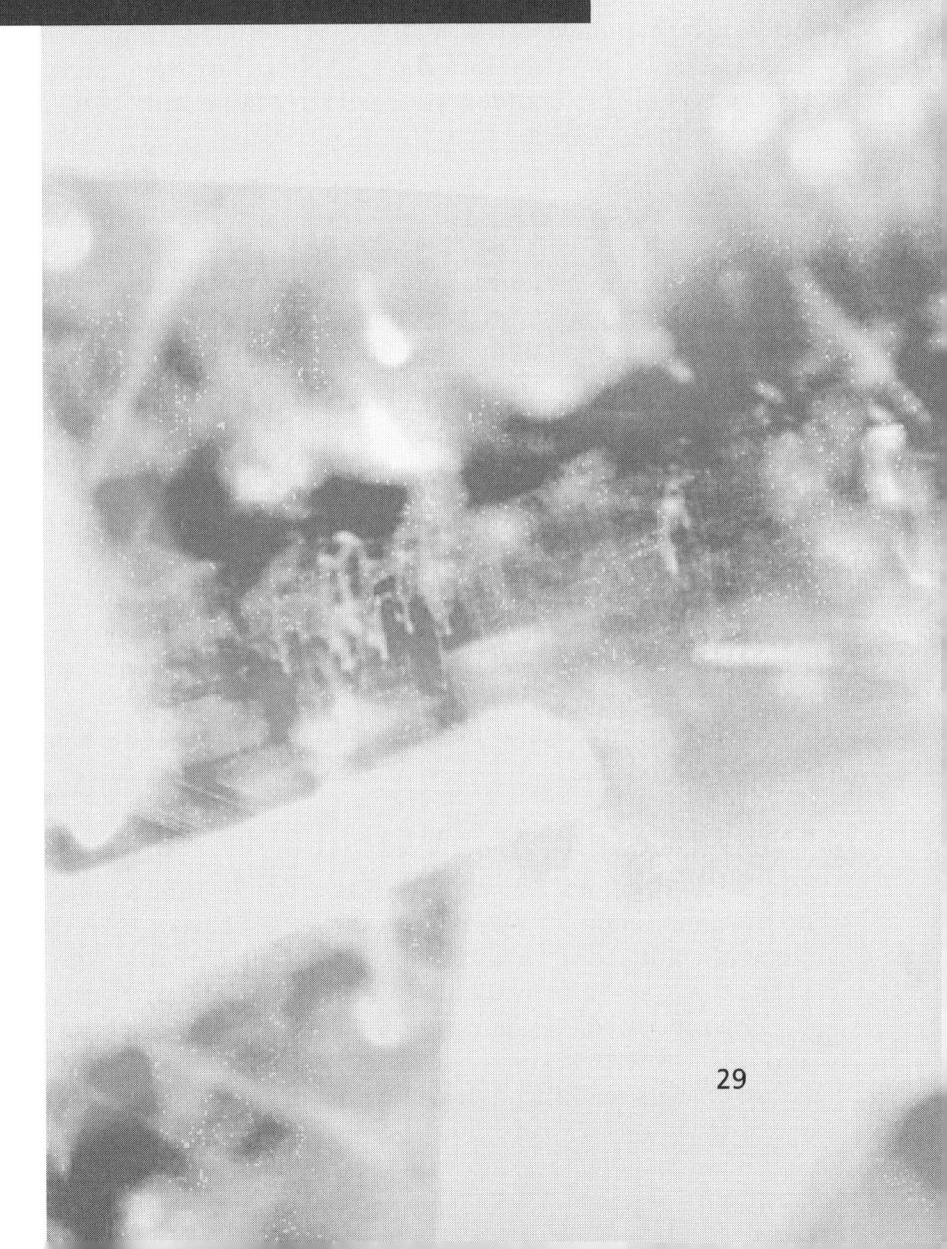

Introduction

Once the setup program has configured Windows 2000 for your specific hardware, the next step is configuring the server for the network. The Configure Your Server Wizard walks the Administrator through the process of configuring the machine either as a stand-alone server or as part of a domain.

One of the other things most new installations require is a series of passes through the Add New Hardware Wizard. For those Administrators familiar with Windows 95/98 plug-and-play technology, this wizard will seem familiar. Windows 2000 adds plug-and-play capabilities to the underlying Windows NT kernel. When installed, new hardware will be automatically detected, and the Add New Hardware Wizard will launch. By the end of this chapter, your server will be fully configured and functional on the network.

Before You Begin

Before using the Windows 2000 Configure Your Server Wizard, it is first important to understand the difference between a member server and a stand-alone server. A Windows 2000 member server is part of a domain, but it is not a domain controller. Although a member server does not store a copy of the directory database, as do domain controllers, member servers can still allow users to access resources located on the server. On the other hand, a Windows 2000 stand-alone server is not part of a domain at all; thus, it can only process requests using its own local user database.

Although later in this chapter, the various components of the Configure Your Server utility will be discussed, the process of configuring the server demonstrated applies only to a stand-alone computer that is currently the only server in the network.

To perform the following tasks, ensure that you are logged on as an Administrator.

The Purpose of this Wizard

The Configure Your Server Wizard is a great launch point to configure the many components of Windows 2000. This chapter takes you through the steps of configuring the first server on your network, and introduces you to the many options available from Configure Your Server.

The process of configuring the first server in the network is a simple and quick way to set up the core services needed for a Windows 2000 network. This walkthrough will transparently configure Active Directory,

Domain Name Service (DNS), and Dynamic Host Configuration Protocol (DHCP) on the system. This process will create a new domain tree, domain, and make the server the first domain controller in the network.

Information Needed to Work with this Wizard

Before beginning, you should ensure that you have the following:

- Windows 2000 Server CD-ROM
- A name for the new domain
- Public domain name, if applicable

Windows 2000 Configure Your Server Wizard

➤ STEP 1

After completing the Windows 2000 installation and logging on to the system as an Administrator, the Configure Your Server program (Figure 3.1) appears. Choose from the following options, and click **NEXT**:

- **This is the only server in my network**.
- **One or more servers are already running in my network**
- **I will configure this server later**.

The first option is the basis of this walkthrough. If you select the second or third radio button and click Next, the window shown in Figure 3.2 will appear, instructing you to use the menu on the left-hand side to manually configure the server.

➤ STEP 2

Click **NEXT** to continue configuring your server (Figure 3.3). Windows will install the server as a domain controller, and will also install the following components:

- **Active Directory**. The Windows 2000 directory service.
- **DHCP**. Provides for the dynamic assignment of IP addresses.
- **DNS**. Provides TCP/IP name resolution.

To learn more about any of these components, click the hyperlinks at the bottom of the screen.

Figure 3.1 After completing the Windows 2000 Setup, you can easily configure your server.

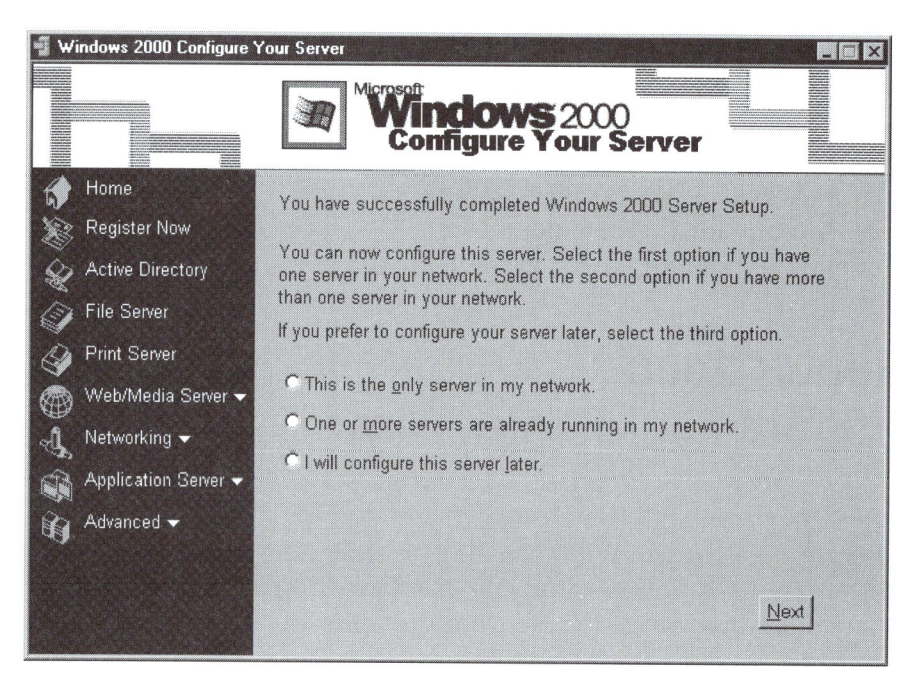

Figure 3.2 Customize your server using the menu on the Configure Your Server program.

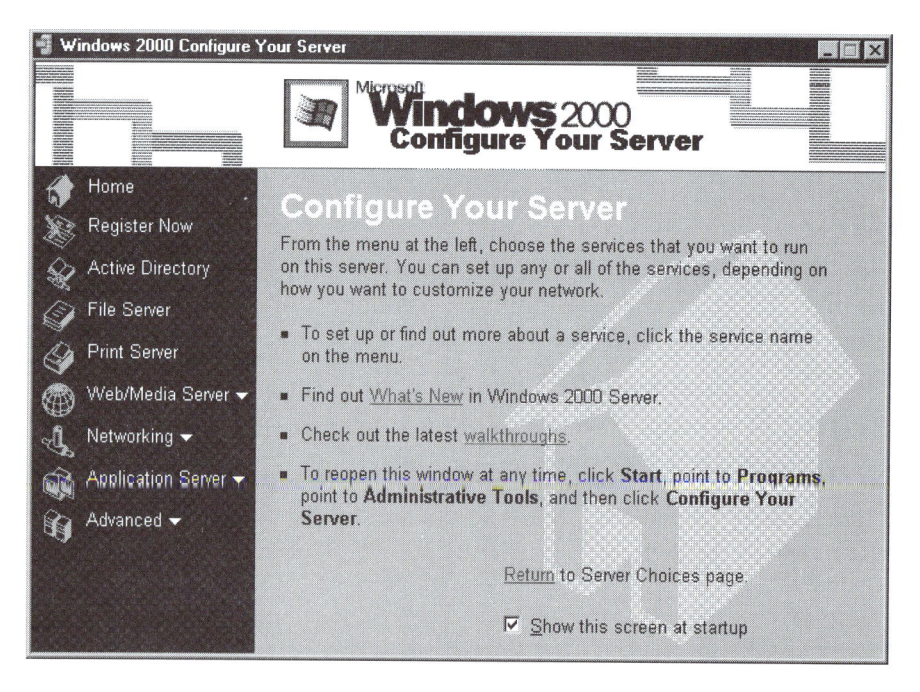

Figure 3.3 The Configure Your Server program will install Active Directory, DHCP, and DNS.

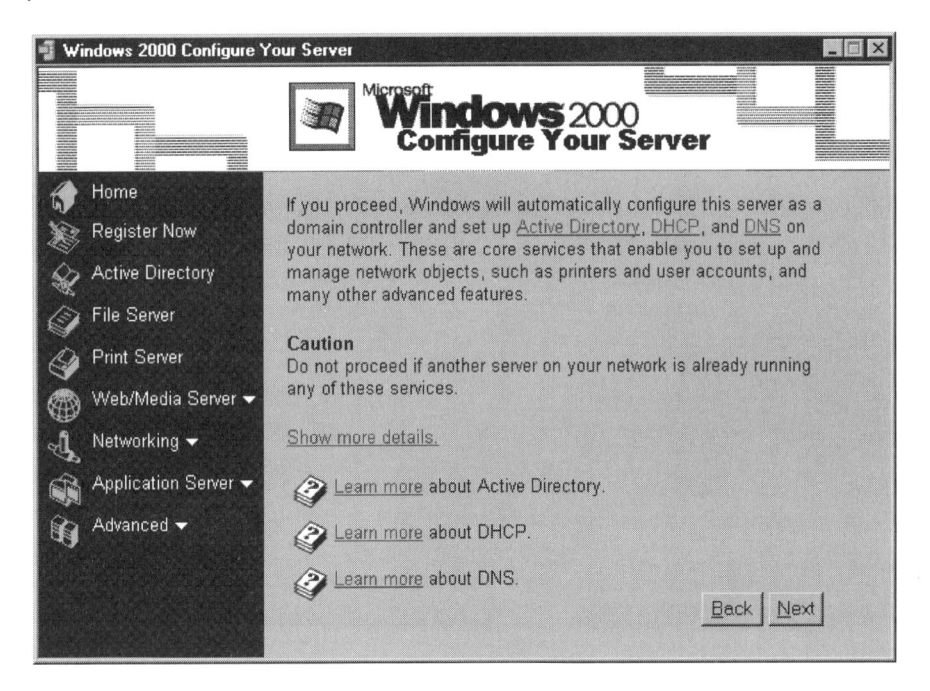

➢ STEP 3

If you did not previously configure TCP/IP with an IP address, you will see the screen show in Figure 3.4, indicating that Setup will configure your server with a private static IP address. This is acceptable for a private network; however, once you have an assigned IP network address, you will need to reconfigure your server.

NOTE

A static IP address is an assigned address that is associated with a system, and is not expected to change. Static IP addresses are usually managed by an Administrator, whereas dynamic IP addresses are managed by a DHCP server. When using the Configure Your Server Wizard, the system will use a static IP address because DHCP is also being installed and requires a static IP address, as it cannot dynamically assign itself an IP address.

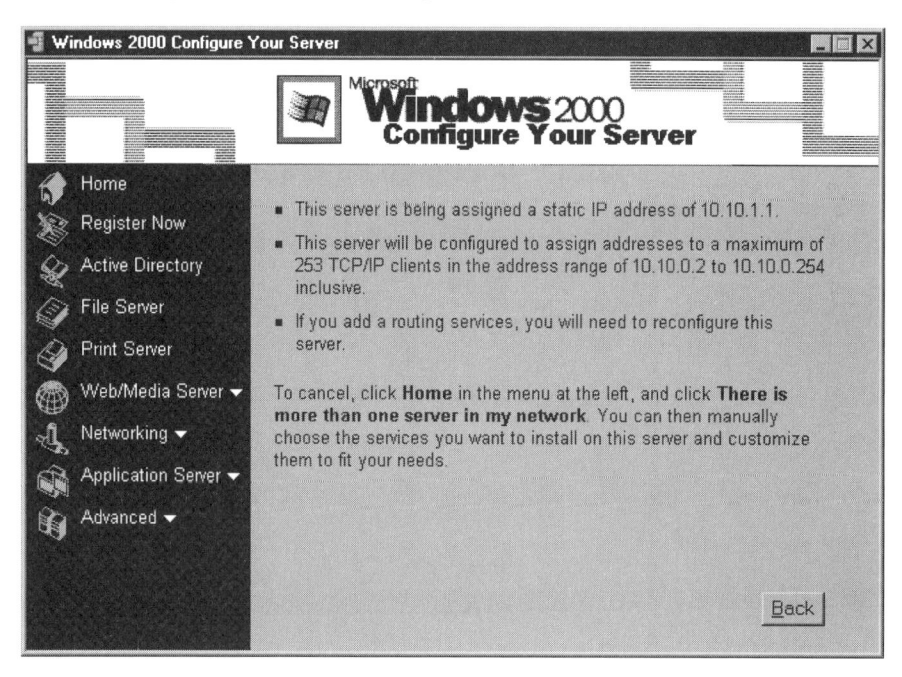

Figure 3.4 Configure Your Server assigns a static Private IP address.

➣ STEP 4

This step configures a domain name for the server.

- Enter the name of the new domain you will be creating followed by the domain name you have registered on the Internet, or you can enter **local** if you do not have a public domain name (Figure 3.5).
- Click **NEXT** to continue.

A preview of the Active Directory domain name will automatically appear as well as the NetBios name for compatibility with non–Windows 2000 systems.

➣ STEP 5

Configure Your Server informs you that the process is ready to begin and may take several minutes (Figure 3.6).

Click **NEXT** to continue.

Figure 3.5 Specify your new domain and domain name.

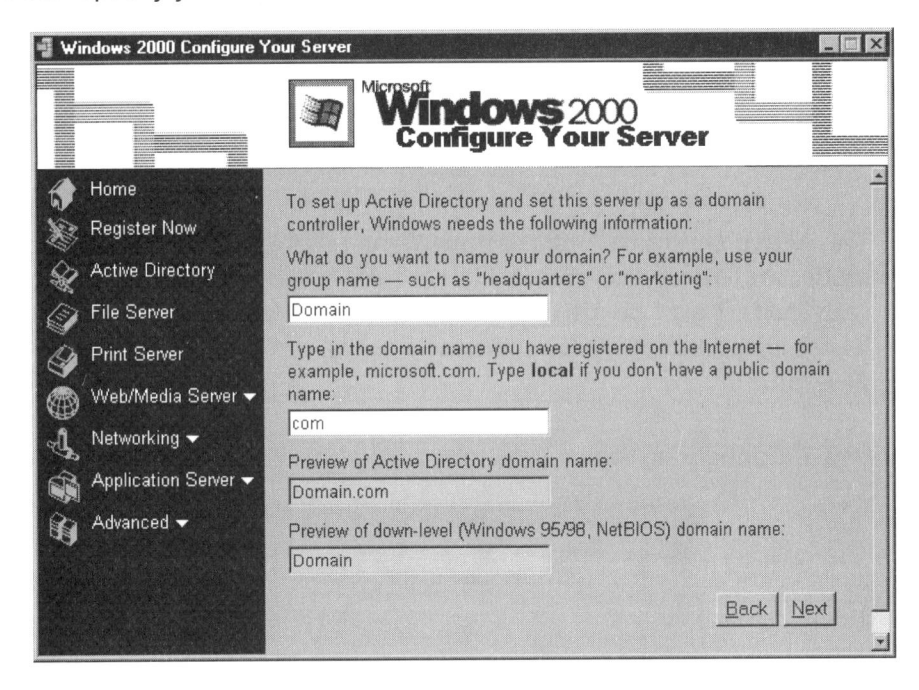

Figure 3.6 Configure Your Server is ready to begin the actual setup.

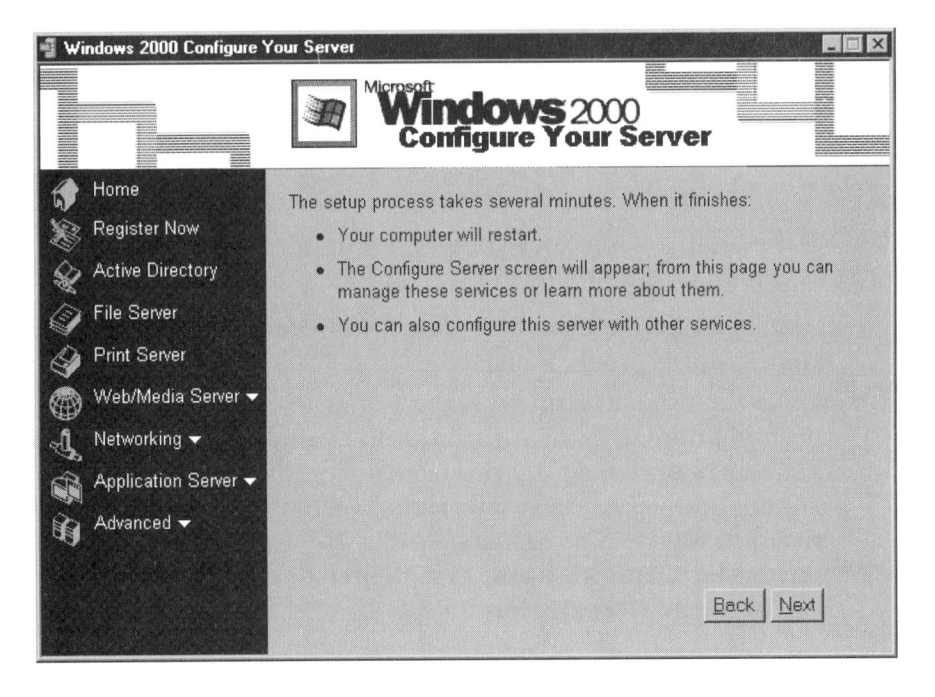

➤ STEP 6

The system will begin to configure additional components, and may prompt you for the original media to be inserted.

- If you are prompted to insert the original media, place the Windows 2000 CD-ROM in the drive, and click **NEXT**.

The process will begin configuring Active Directory (Figure 3.7). The Active Directory Installation Wizard will then run in unattended mode, and when the process is complete, the computer will automatically restart and be a fully functional server on the network. To configure additional services, continue using the Configure Your Server program.

Figure 3.7 Configuring Active Directory dialog box.

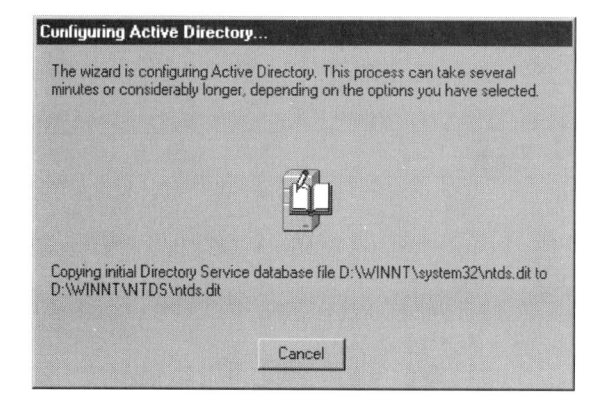

➤ STEP 7

To view the changes made to your system and designate a description for this system, do the following:

- First, open Active Directory Users and Computers from the Administrative Tools menu.
- Notice the domain icon with the name of the new root domain you just created. Beneath that, find the folder called Domain Controllers and view the properties of your server by right-clicking and selecting **Properties**. The Server Properties box shown in Figure 3.8 appears. Notice the full DNS name given to your system. You may optionally enter a description for the system in the **Description** field.

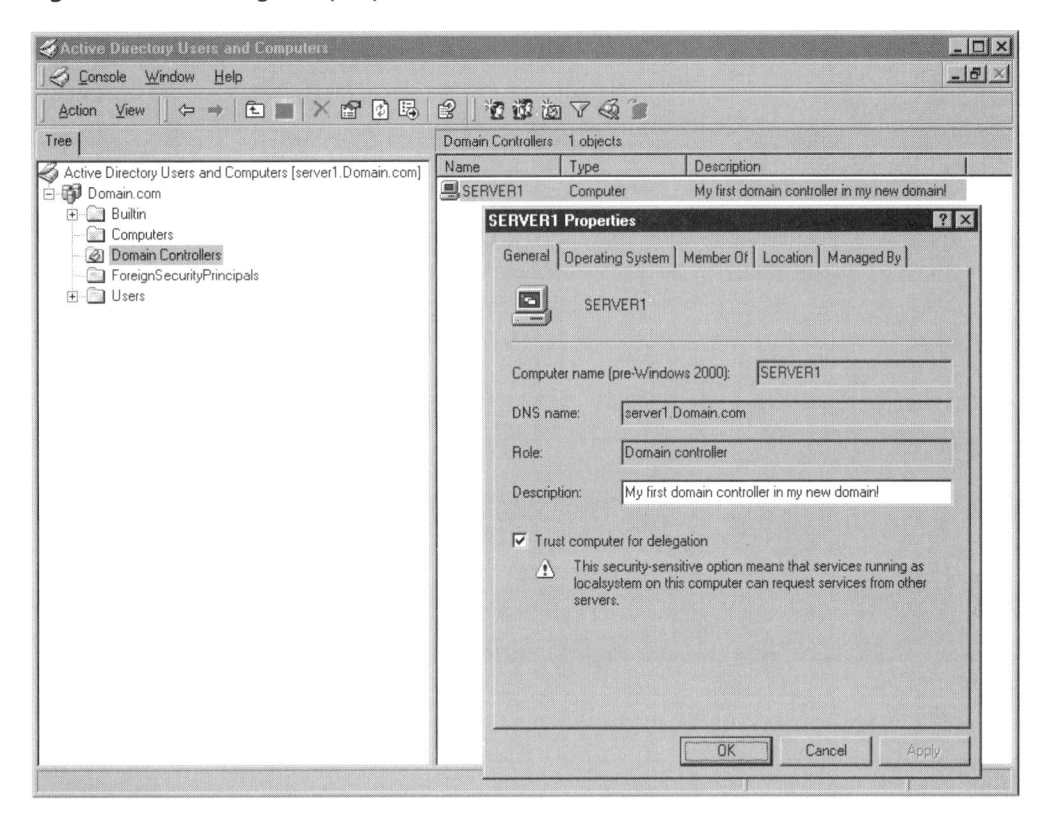

Figure 3.8 Viewing the properties for a domain controller.

Configure Your Server Program Overview

If the Configure Your Server program does not automatically appear when you start your computer, it can be accessed from the Administrative Tools menu. To disable the utility from appearing when the computer starts, de-select the check box next to **Show this screen at startup** located on the **Home** page of the utility (Figure 3.9).

The menu on the left provides an easy method to perform tasks and configure additional components on your server. Table 3.1 outlines the links available on the left-hand side, and presents a brief listing of the elements that can be accessed.

Figure 3.9 You can customize your network using Configure Your Server.

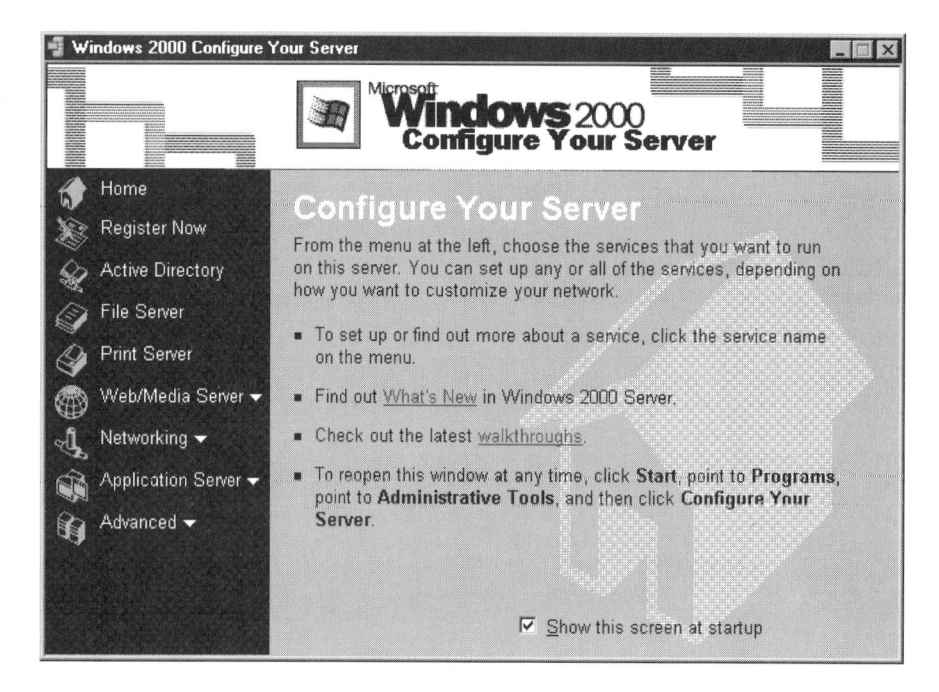

Table 3.1 Elements of the Configure Your Server Program

Link	Elements
Register Now	Registration Wizard
Active Directory	User accounts, domains, server roles, permissions, security
File Server	Shared folders and network resources
Web/Media Server	Web sites, multimedia sites, FTP sites
Networking	DNS, DHCP, Routing and Remote Access
Application Server	Component Services, Terminal Services, database server, and e-mail server
Advanced	Message queing, Resource Kit, other optional components

Summary

After installing Windows 2000 Server, and logging on as an Administrator, the Windows 2000 Configure Your Server program loads. This utility provides a convenient way to configure the many components of Windows 2000.

The initial page provides an option to quickly set up the core services if the server is the only server in the network. Selecting this option will install Active Directory, DHCP, and DNS, which will result in a fully configured and functional server.

To begin the process, you must provide a name for the new domain being created, such as "headquarters." Next, provide a domain name registered on the Internet, such as "Domain.com." If you do not have a registered name, or do not want to be connected with the Internet, you can enter **local**. After providing this information, Windows will begin the process of setting up the core services, and will restart automatically when completed. The Windows 2000 Server will then be configured as a domain controller in the new domain.

The Configure Your Server program will continue to load on startup until the **Show this screen at startup** check box is cleared. As an Administrator, you may continue to configure additional components from this program by clicking on the appropriate links from the pane on the left side, which include the following:

- Home
- Register Now
- Active Directory
- File Server
- Print Server
- Web/Media Server
- Networking
- Application Server
- Advanced

Additionally, these components can also be configured using the tools located in the Administrative Tools folder. Finally, you may always return to the Configure Your Server program by clicking **Configure Your Server** from the Administrative Tools menu.

Chapter 4

The Active Directory Installation Wizard

Introduction

In Windows 2000, Active Directories replace domains as the method for defining and managing Windows-based machines. Active Directories offer more scalability and better performance compared to their domain predecessors. Configuring Active Directories is one of the more complex tasks associated with Windows 2000 installation. Make sure that you take time to study and understand Active Directories before you begin the configuration process. By the end of this chapter, you will have established the domain controllers for your Active Directory and begun placing servers in the directory.

Before You Begin

Before you begin the Active Directory Installation Wizard, be sure that you are familiar with the concepts of Active Directory. Additionally, you will want to be familiar with the specific terms mentioned during the process, such as:

- **Additional domain controller**. A peer domain controller installed into an existing domain. Provides redundancy and reduces the load of other domain controllers.
- **Child domain**. A domain located in the namespace tree directly beneath another domain name, which is referred to as the *parent* domain.
- **Domain tree**. The hierarchical tree structure that is used to index domain names.
- **Forest**. A set of one or more trees that do not form a contiguous namespace.

To install Active Directory, you need a partition formatted with the version of NTFS used in Windows 2000. To convert your file system, open a Command Prompt window and enter

```
convert [drive:] /fs:ntfs
```

When the server is rebooted, the file system will be converted to NTFS.

The Purpose of this Wizard

You can easily promote a member server or stand-alone server to a domain controller using the Active Directory Installation Wizard, and demote a domain controller to a member server or stand-alone server.

Information Needed to Work with this Wizard

To perform any of these functions, ensure that you have the sufficient network credentials needed to create or remove a domain. Specifically, you will need to log on as an Administrator.

Additionally, ensure you have the following information:

- Full DNS name of any existing domains
- Name that will be given to any new domain
- Known location for storing the database and log files
- Known location for storing the SYSVOL folder

NOTE

The database and log files are stored by default in the ntds folder of the systemroot; however, it is recommended that these be placed on separate hard disks within the system. The SYSVOL folder uses the SYSVOL folder of the systemroot as its default location. You can, however, locate this folder anywhere in the computer as long as it's on a partition or volume formatted with NTFS.

The Active Directory Installation Wizard

➢ STEP 1

To start the Active Directory Installation Wizard, enter **dcpromo** at the command prompt, or the Run dialog box located in the Start menu (Figure 4.1). You can also click **START** from the Active Directory pane of the Configure Your Server program.

Figure 4.1 Using dcpromo.exe to start the Active Directory Installation Wizard.

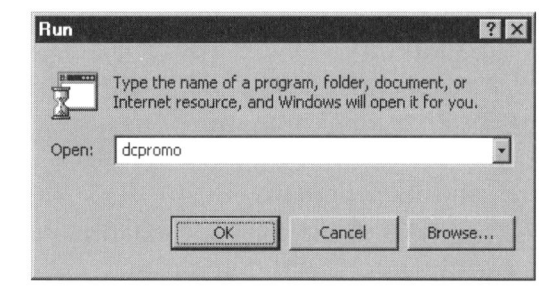

➤ STEP 2

The Active Directory Installation Wizard welcome page appears (Figure 4.2). Click **NEXT** to continue.

Figure 4.2 The Active Directory Installation Wizard welcome page.

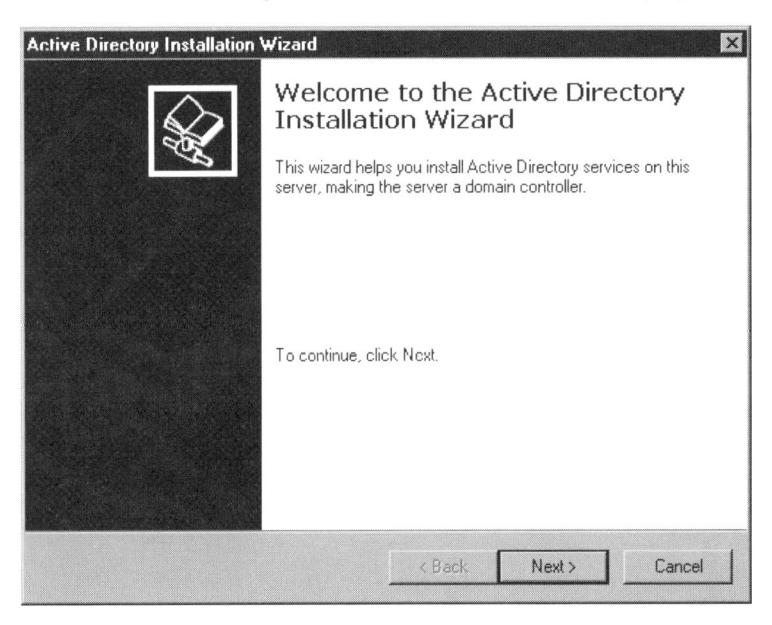

➤ STEP 3

Select the type of domain controller to install from the Domain Controller Type page (Figure 4.3). You may choose either of the following options:

- **Domain controller for a new domain**. This option allows you to create a new child domain, new domain tree, or a new forest.
  - Click **NEXT** to continue.
- **Additional domain controller for existing domain**. Select this option if you have an existing domain and you want this server to become an additional domain controller. This is usually done to improve availability and reliability within the domain.
  - To create an additional domain controller in an existing domain, you will need to provide an authorized username, password, and user domain.
  - Enter the full DNS name for your existing domain that you want to add the additional domain to.
  - Proceed to Step 8.

Figure 4.3 The Domain Controller Type page.

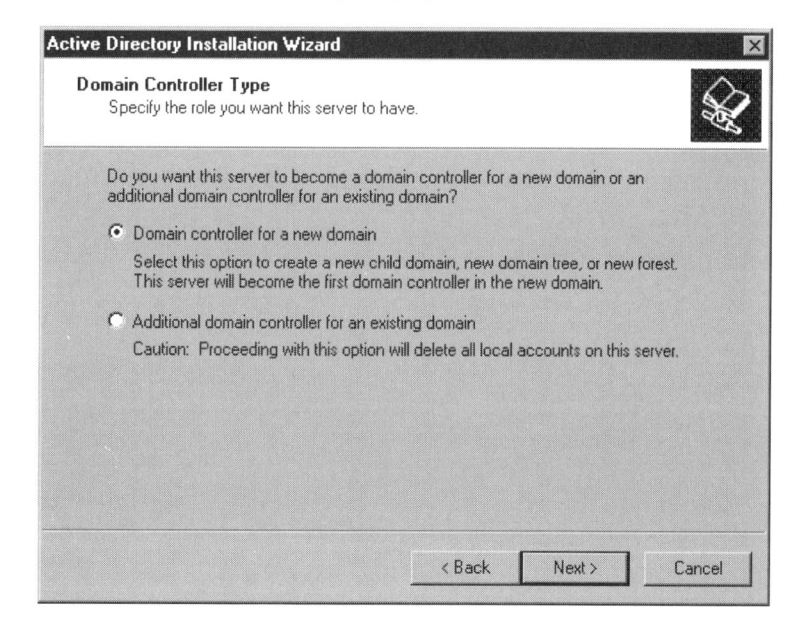

STEP 4

By choosing to create a domain controller in a new domain, you can select from one of the following options listed on the Create Tree or Child Domain page (Figure 4.4):

- **Create a new domain tree**. This will create a new domain tree, which can be placed in an existing forest, or you can choose to create a new forest.
  - Click **NEXT** to Continue.
- **Create a new child domain in an existing domain tree**. This option will create a new child domain beneath an existing domain.
  - To create a new child domain in an existing domain tree, you will need to provide an authorized username, password, and user domain.
  - You will need to enter the full DNS name of the existing domain that will be the parent to this domain. For example, if you want to create a new child domain beneath "domain.com," enter "domain.com."
  - Now enter the name of the new child domain, such as "childdomain." The parent name will be added to this name to create the full DNS name, "childdomain.domain.com."
  - Proceed to Step 8.

Figure 4.4 The Create Tree or Child Domain page.

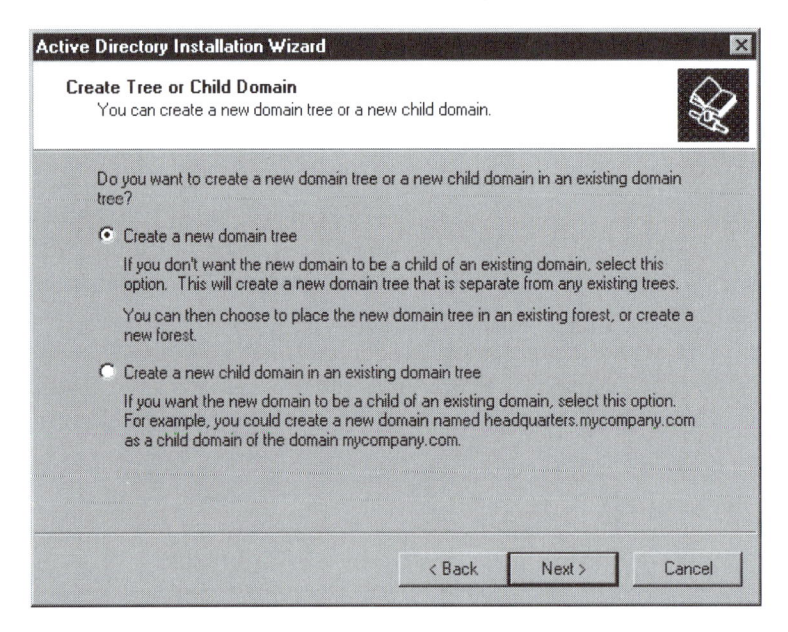

> ## STEP 5

When creating a new domain tree, you can select from one of the following options listed on the Create or Join Forest page (Figure 4.5):

- **Create a new forest of domain trees**. If this is your first domain, you must select this option. If you want to create a new domain tree that is independent of your current forest, you would also select this option.
  - Click **NEXT** to continue.

- **Place this new domain tree in an existing forest**. Select this option to create a new domain tree that will be part of an existing forest. This allows access to resources within the other trees.
  - To place this new domain tree in an existing forest, you will need to provide an authorized username, password, and user domain.
  - Enter the full DNS name of the forest root domain; for example, "rootdomain.domain.com."
  - Enter the full DNS name of the new tree; for example, "newtree.domain.com."
  - Proceed to Step 8.

Figure 4.5 The Create or Join Forest page.

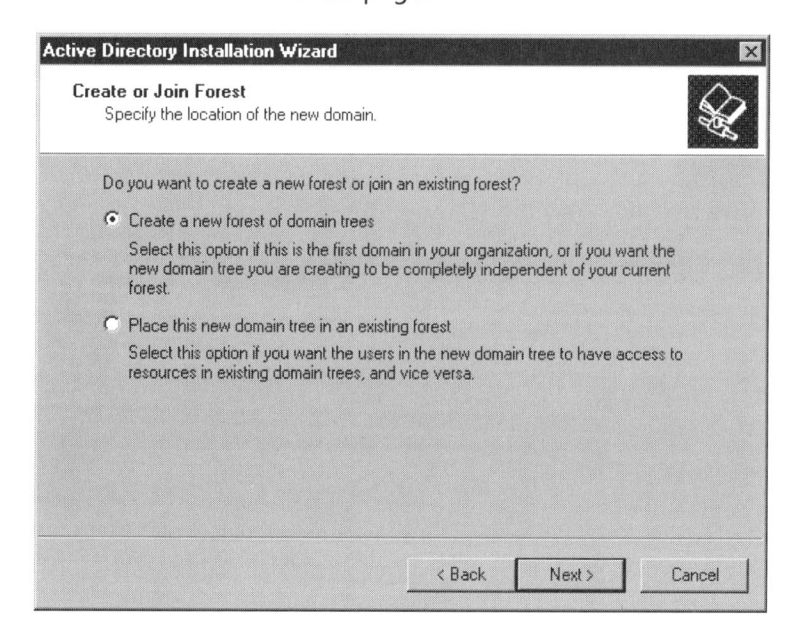

➢ STEP 6

If you chose to create a new forest, enter the full DNS name for the new domain in the New Domain Name page, and click **NEXT** to continue (Figure 4.6).

Figure 4.6 The New Domain Name page.

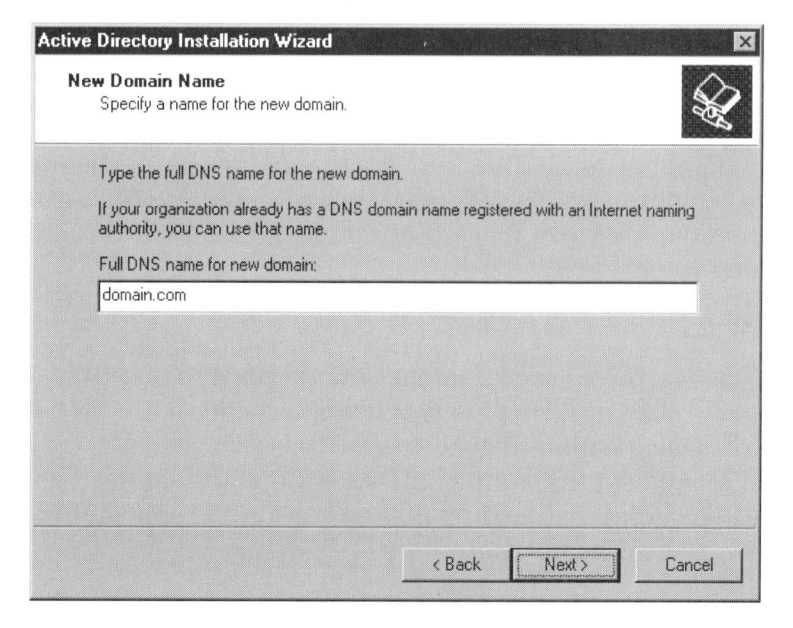

➤ STEP 7

The next step is to configure a NetBIOS name for compatibility with older versions of Windows. A default name will automatically appear in the **Domain NetBIOS name** field of the NetBIOS Domain Name page (Figure 4.7). Click **NEXT** to continue, or you may specify a different name.

Figure 4.7 The NetBIOS Domain Name page.

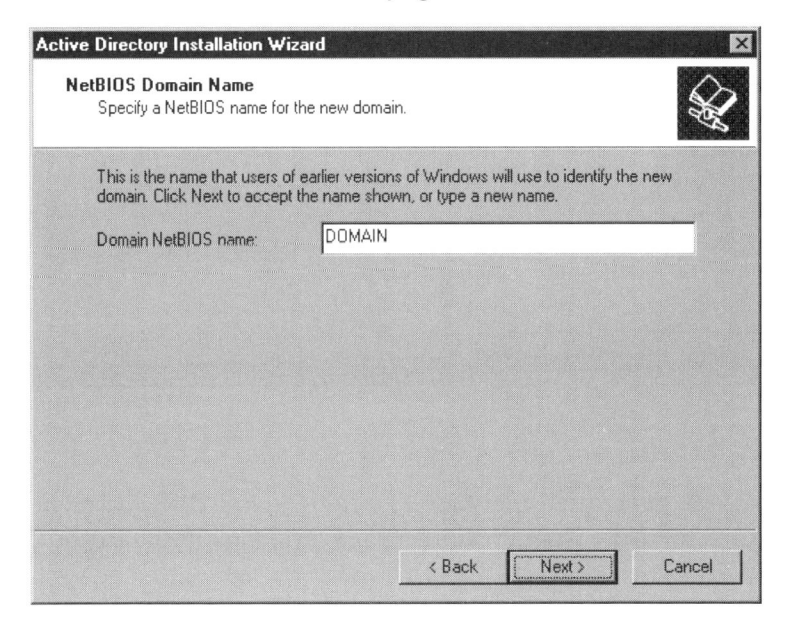

➤ STEP 8

At the Database and Log Locations page, click **NEXT** to select the default locations of the database and log files, or enter a location, or click **BROWSE** to identify a new location (Figure 4.8).

The database is the directory for the domain, and the log file is used to temporarily store changes that are made to the database. It is recommended that you place these on separate hard disks for increased performance.

➤ STEP 9

Click **NEXT** on the Shared System Volume page to accept the default locations of the SYSVOL folder, or enter a location, or click **BROWSE** to identify a new location (Figure 4.9).

The shared system volume stores scripts and Group Policy objects. This folder is used by file replication to replicate information among various domain controllers.

Figure 4.8 The Database and Log Locations page.

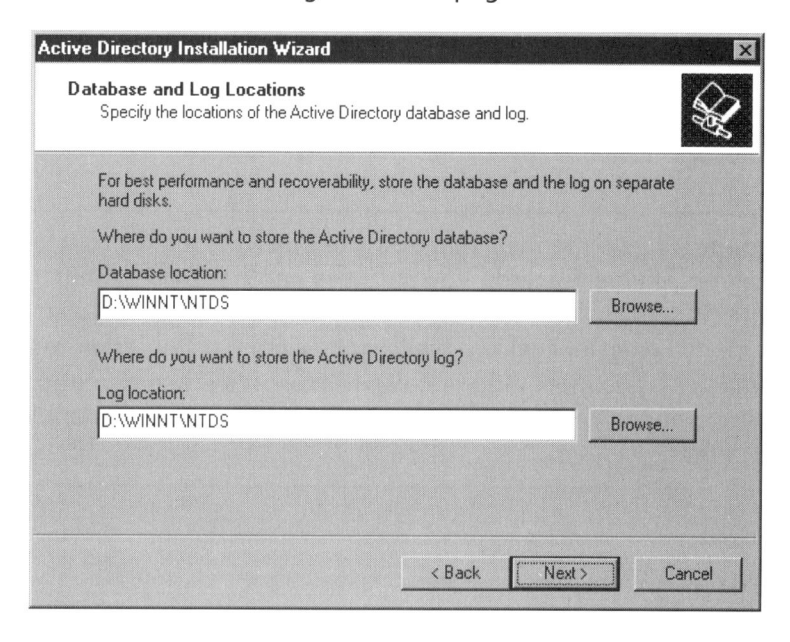

Figure 4.9 The Shared System Volume page.

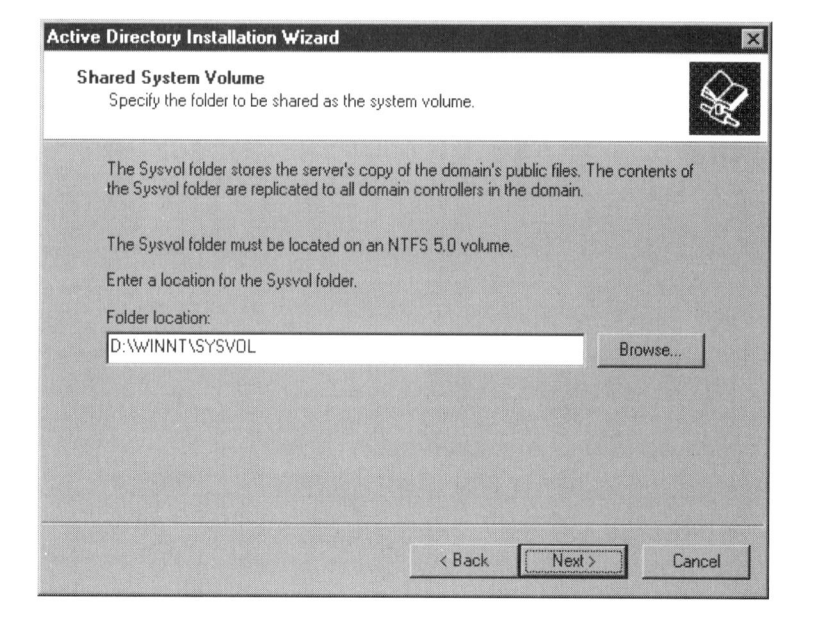

➤ STEP 10

If DNS is not already available on the network, you can choose to have the Active Directory Installation Wizard install and configure DNS on the computer (Figure 4.10). Then, click **NEXT**.

> **NOTE**
>
> Although it is recommended that you use Microsoft's DNS to take advantage of added features, you may use another DNS system. Windows 2000 DNS is specifically designed to take full advantage of Active Directory. It uses multimaster replication, while non-Microsoft DNS servers use a single-master replication. Additionally, Microsoft's implementation of DNS complies completely with Internet standards; thus, it is compatible with any other operating system.

Figure 4.10 The Configure DNS page.

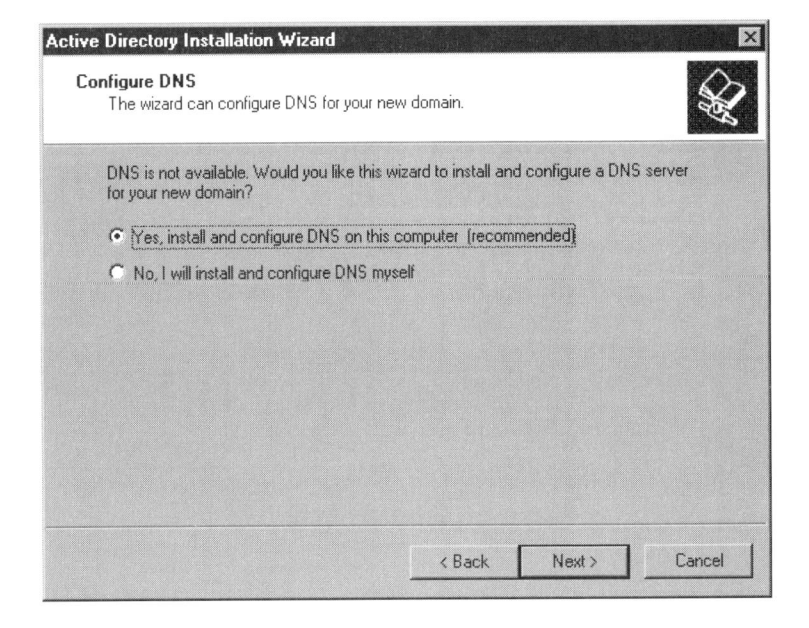

➤ STEP 11

From the Permissions page (Figure 4.11), select one of the following default permissions for user and group objects, and click **NEXT**:

- **Permissions compatible with pre-Windows 2000 servers**. If you run server programs such a Remote Access on pre–Windows 2000 systems, you may want to select this option.

- **Permissions compatible only with Windows 2000 servers.** Select this option if you do not have any pre–Windows 2000 systems, or if you only run server programs on Windows 2000 servers.

Figure 4.11 The Permissions page.

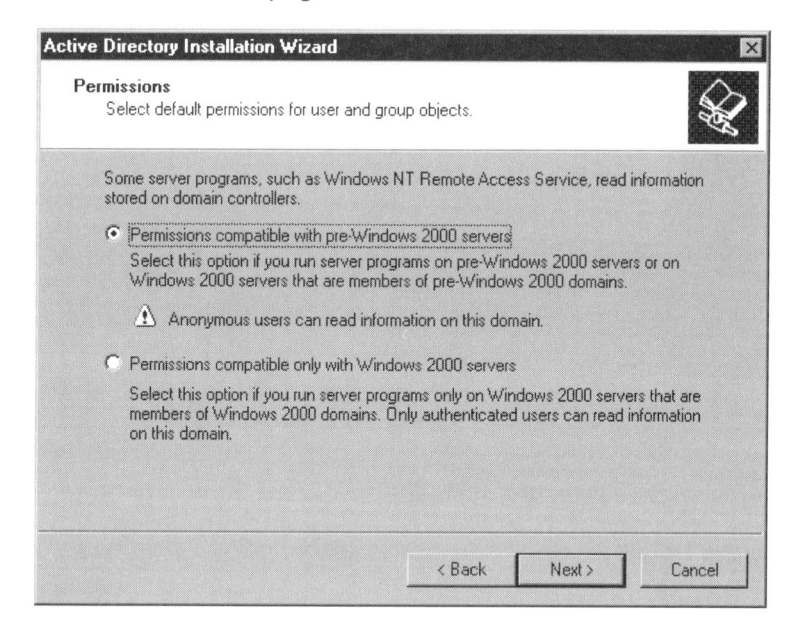

➤ STEP 12

Enter and confirm a password, and click **NEXT**. This password will allow access to the Directory Services Restore Mode (Figure 4.12). The Directory Services Restore Mode allows for the restoration and maintenance of Active Directory and the SYSVOL folder.

➤ STEP 13

Click **NEXT** from the Summary page to begin installing Active Directory (Figure 4.13). This page identifies the options you have selected. If you need to make changes, click **BACK**.

➤ STEP 14

After confirming the options, the system will begin to configure Active Directory (Figure 4.14).

Figure 4.12 The Directory Services Restore Mode Administrator Password page.

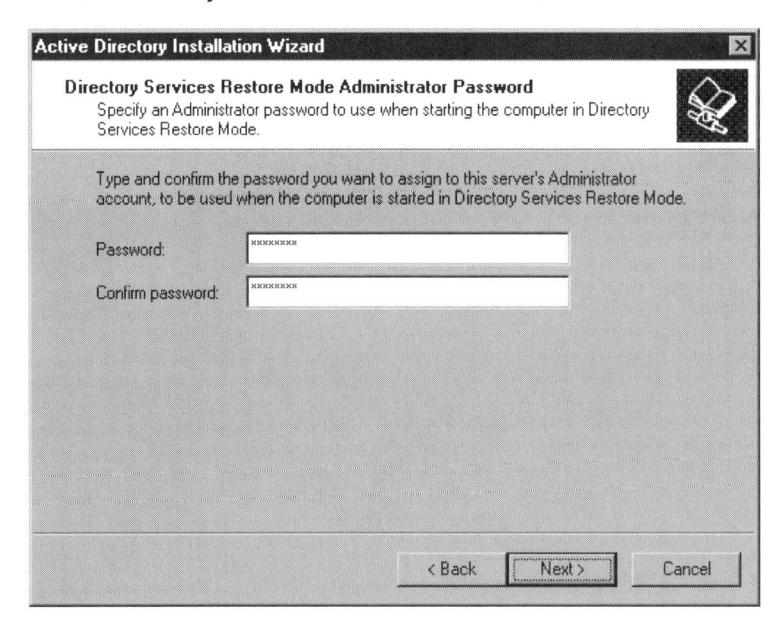

Figure 4.13 The Active Directory Installation Wizard Summary page.

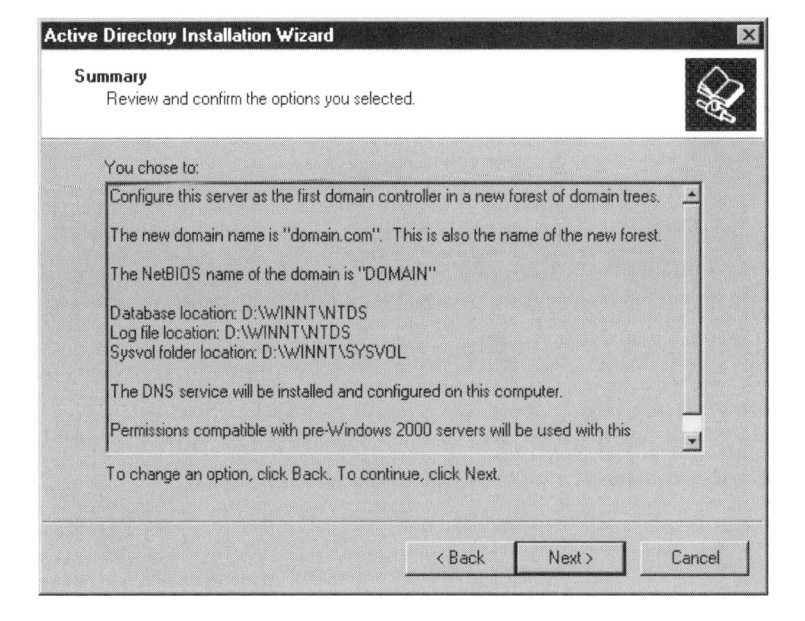

Figure 4.14 Configuring Active Directory dialog box.

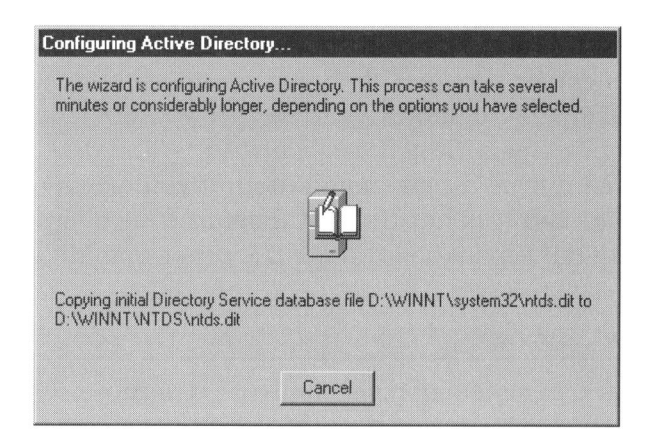

➢ STEP 15

The Active Directory Installation Wizard completion page appears (Figure 4.15). Click **FINISH** to close the wizard.

Figure 4.15 The Completing the Active Directory Installation Wizard page.

Uninstalling Active Directory

Uninstalling Active Directory will demote the domain controller to either a stand-alone or member server. This process removes the system from any forest and from DNS. By demoting a server, you remove Active Directory and all security principals, which are replaced by the default security database installed during a new installation. If you are demoting a domain controller, and it is not the last domain controller in the domain, it will perform a final replication among the other domain controllers.

> **TIP**
>
> If an attempt to demote a domain controller is unsuccessful, you will need to manually remove the metadata from the directory by using the Ntdsutil.exe utility. For further information on using the Ntdsutil.exe utility to remove Active Directory, see article number Q216498 in the online Microsoft Knowledge Base.

➤ STEP 1

To uninstall Active Directory, start the Active Directory Installation Wizard as shown earlier in Figure 4.1.

➤ STEP 2

The Active Directory Installation Wizard (Figure 4.16) will tell you that the computer is already an Active Directory domain controller, and proceeding will remove Active Directory. Click **NEXT** to continue.

➤ STEP 3

From the Remove Active Directory page (Figure 4.17), specify whether this is the last domain controller in the domain, and click **NEXT**.

Place a check mark next to **This server is the last domain controller in the domain** if there are no more domain controllers in the domain and you want to convert this server to a stand-alone server.

Leave the check box empty if this is not the last domain controller in the domain and you wish to remove Active Directory from this computer. Doing so will demote the server to a member server.

➤ STEP 4

To remove Active Directory, you need to enter the account details of an account with Enterprise Administrator privileges to the forest (Figure 4.18), and click **NEXT**.

Figure 4.16 The Welcome to the Active Directory Installation page for a computer with Active Directory already installed.

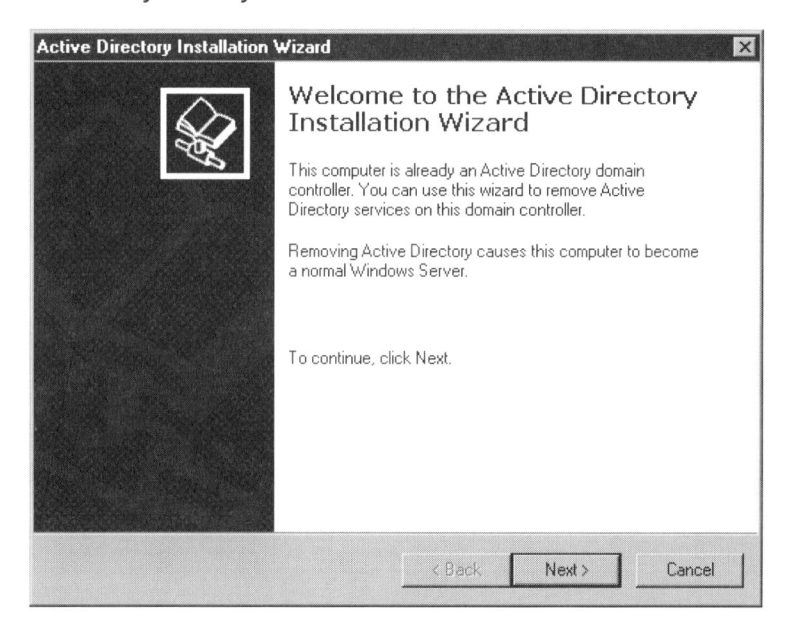

Figure 4.17 The Remove Active Directory page.

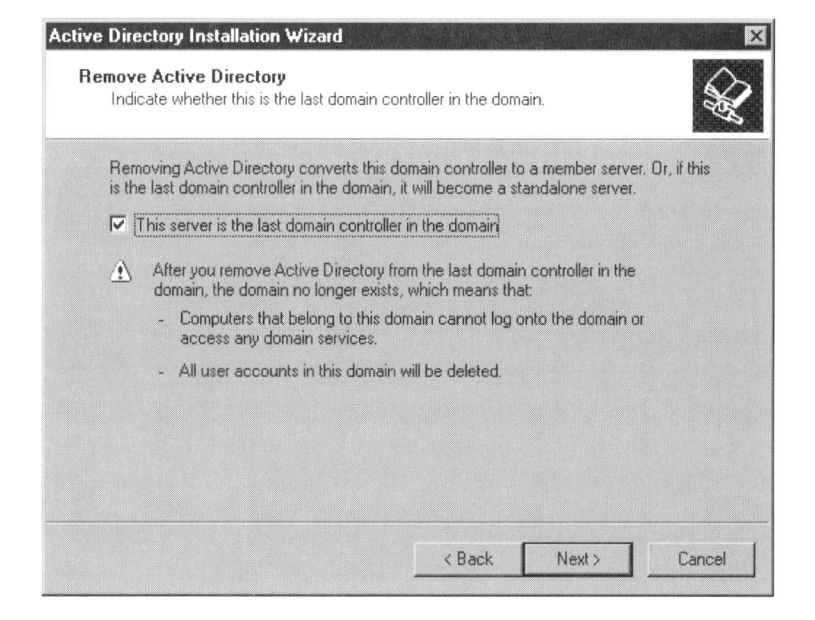

Figure 4.18 The Network Credentials page.

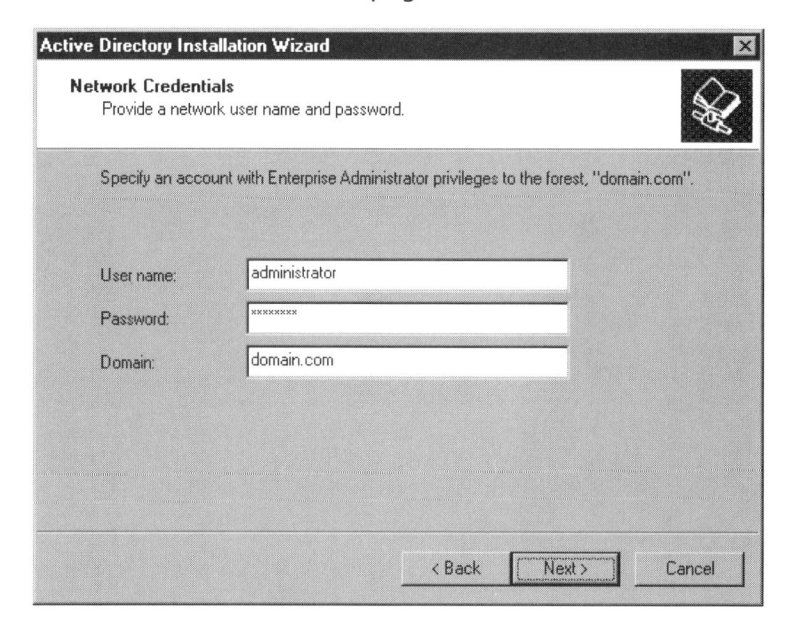

> **STEP 5**
>
> Enter and confirm an Administrator's password, which will be used once the server has been demoted (Figure 4.19).

Figure 4.19 The Administrator Password page.

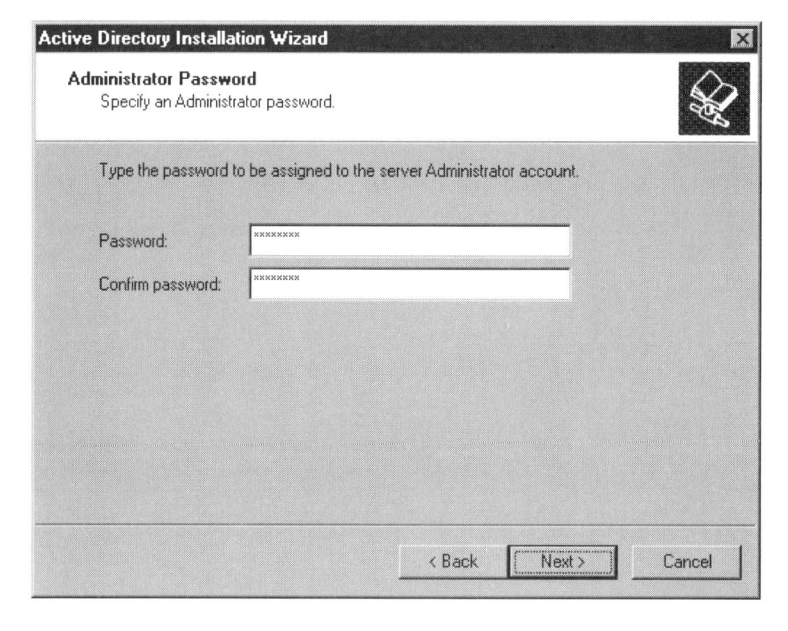

➤ STEP 6

Review and confirm the details by clicking **NEXT** on the Summary page (Figure 4.20).

Figure 4.20 The Summary page for removing Active Directory.

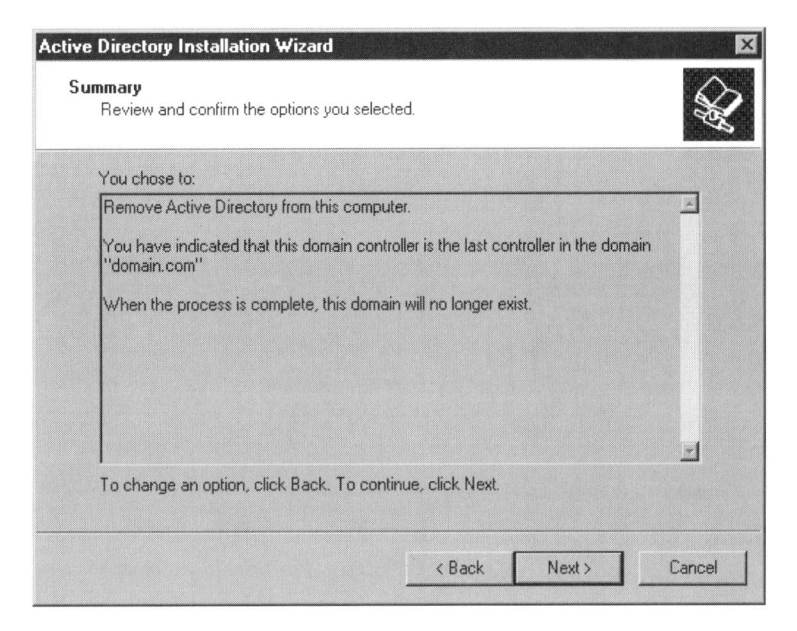

➤ STEP 7

The Active Directory Installation Wizard will begin the demotion process of removing Active Directory and returning the system to a member or stand-alone server status (Figure 4.21).

Figure 4.21 Configuring Active Directory for removal dialog box.

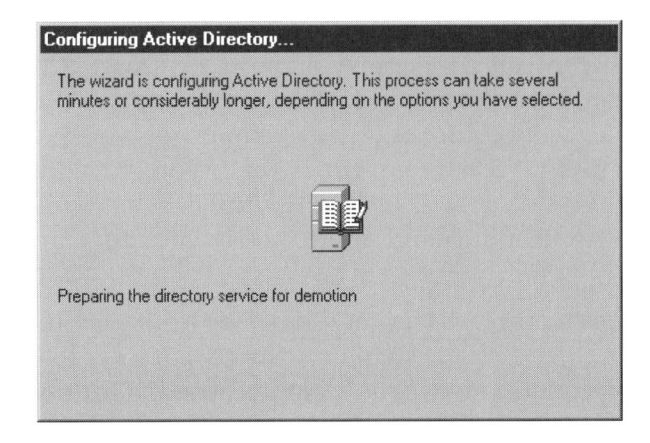

➢ STEP 8

Click **FINISH** from the Completing the Active Directory Installation Wizard page to close the wizard (Figure 4.22). You must restart your computer for the changes to take effect.

Figure 4.22 Completing the Active Directory Installation removal page.

Summary

The Active Directory Installation Wizard can be used to install Active Directory (promotion) or remove Active Directory (demotion). The command-line utility used to start the wizard is dcpromo.exe; it will add or remove Active Directory depending on whether it is already installed.

After starting the wizard on a member or stand-alone server, you can create a domain controller for a new domain, or create an additional domain controller for an existing domain. Selecting to create an additional domain controller will require that you have proper credentials and that you provide the full DNS name of the domain you are adding the new domain to.

Some points to keep in mind about Active Directory promotion include:

- By creating a new domain controller for a new domain, a decision needs to be made on whether to create a new domain tree or create a new child domain beneath an existing domain.

- Choosing to create a new child domain will require the Administrator password, and the full DNS name for the parent will need to be entered. Finally, a name must be provided for the new child domain.
- Choosing to create a new domain tree will allow either the creation of a new forest of domain trees, or allow the new domain to be placed in an existing forest.
- If the new domain is placed in an existing forest, you will need to provide the proper credentials and enter the full DNS name of the forest root domain. Finally, the full DNS name of the new tree must be entered.
- Choosing to create a new forest will require the full DNS name for the new domain.

Regardless of the method selected, you will need to provide a location to store the database and log files, and the shared system volume that will be created. By default, the database and log files are placed in the *%systemroot%\winnt\ntds* folder, and the system volume is placed in the *%systemroot%\winnt\sysvol* folder.

Use the Active Directory Installation Wizard to remove Active Directory from a domain controller. If you demote a server, and there are other domain controllers on the network, the server will become a member server in the domain; whereas, if you remove Active Directory from the last domain controller in the domain, the server will become a stand-alone server.

Chapter 5
Network Connection Wizard

Introduction

Windows 2000 offers support for one or more network connections. These can be either LAN connections or dial-in connections. During the installation process, a single LAN connection was configured if a network interface card (NIC) was detected. As you add new NICs or want to dial out to other networks, you will need to add new network connections.

You can also configure a Windows 2000 server to accept incoming connections. These connections can be through either dial-up modems or a Virtual Private Network (VPN) across the Internet. By the end of this chapter, you will be familiar with the Network Connection Wizard.

Before You Begin

To perform most of the following task, you will need to have an Administrator account.

The Purpose of this Wizard

The Network Connection Wizard allows you to configure outbound connections and host incoming connections from a single location.

Information Needed to Work with this Wizard

A variety of tasks can be performed from the Network Connection Wizard. What you need will depend on the specific task you choose. Some things to remember include the following:

- Connecting to a private network
    - Telephone number
- Connecting to an Internet Service Provider (ISP)
    - Phone number
    - User account name and password
    - DNS address
- Establish an Internet mail account
    - Display name
    - E-mail address
    - Mail server type
    - Incoming and outgoing mail server name
    - User account name and password
- Connecting to a VPN
    - Host name or IP address.

The Network Connection Wizard

Launching the Network Connection Wizard

➤ **STEP 1**

To start the Network Connection Wizard, right-click **My Network Places**, click **Properties**, and then double-click the **Make New Connection** icon. The Network Connection Wizard page will appear (Figure 5.1). Click **NEXT**.

Figure 5.1 The Network Connection Wizard.

➤ **STEP 2**

Next, you will see the Network Connection Type page (Figure 5.2). Several options are available, depending on the specific networking needs. From this page, you can configure outbound and incoming connections. By using the wizard, all protocols and services that are needed are automatically configured.

Dial-Up to a Private Network

The "Dial-up to private network" option allows you to connect from your telephone line to a computer or network such as an ISP to establish an Internet connection, or to a modem, which connects you to a private network. This is most commonly referred to as a Remote Access Service (RAS) client.

➢ STEP 1

From the **Network Connection Type** page (Figure 5.2), ensure that **Dial-up to private network** is selected, and click **NEXT**.

Figure 5.2 Network Connection Type page.

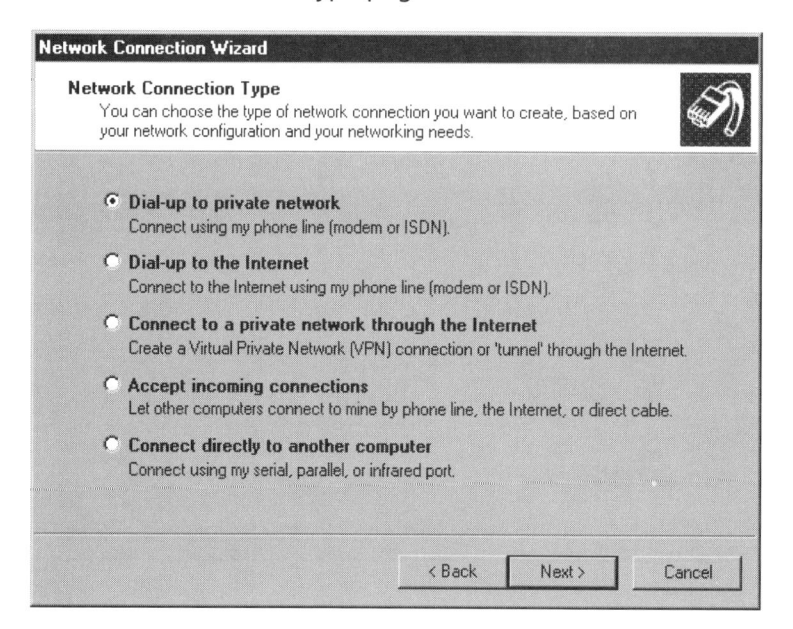

➢ STEP 2

- Enter the telephone number of the computer or network that you wish to connect to (Figure 5.3).
- Select the **Use dialing rules** check box if you wish to use dialing rules, which can be configured using the Phone and Modem Options in Control Panel.
- Click **NEXT**.

Figure 5.3 Phone Number to Dial page.

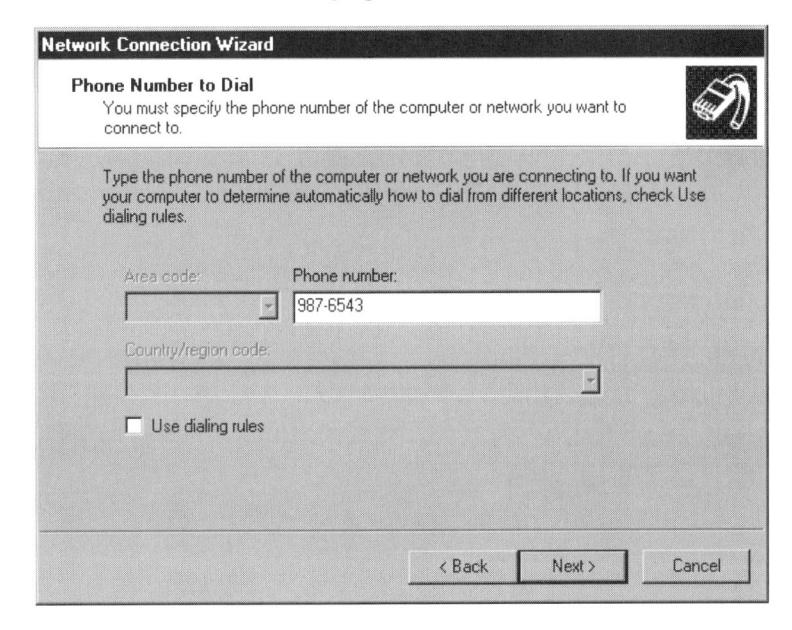

➢ STEP 3

Specify who can use this connection—only you, or all other users (Figure 5.4).

- Ensure **For all users** is selected if you want this connection made available to other users of this computer and/or other systems.
- Select **Only for myself** if you want this connection to be used only by the user currently logged on.
- Click **Next**.
- If you selected **For all users**, proceed to the next step; otherwise, go to Step 5.

➢ STEP 4

By choosing to make your connection available to others, you are also given the option to allow other computers access to the dial-up connection (Figure 5.5).

- To allow other computers on your local network access through this dial-up connection, select the **Enable Internet Connection Sharing for this connection** box.

- Additionally, you can check **Enable on-demand dialing**, which will cause the computer to automatically dial the connection when another computer tries to gain access to external resources. For example, if a user from another system attempts to load an external Web page, a connection will automatically be dialed from the sharing computer. To allow on-demand dialing, you must first enable Internet Connection Sharing.
- Click **NEXT**.

Figure 5.4 Connection Availability page.

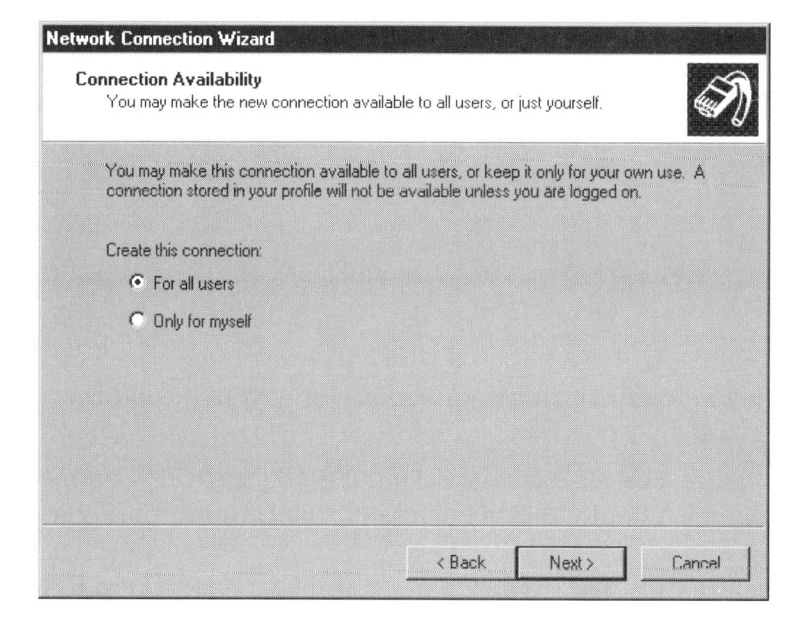

➢ STEP 5

- Finally, enter a name for this connection (Figure 5.6). This will conclude the wizard and save the connection in the Network and Dial-up Connections folder.
- You can optionally create a shortcut for this connection on your desktop by selecting the **Add a shortcut to my desktop** box. Click **FINISH** to close the wizard.

TIP

To connect using X.25, right-click the connection you just made and select **Properties**. Next, select **X.25** from the Option tab to configure the X.25 connection.

Figure 5.5 Internet Connection Sharing page.

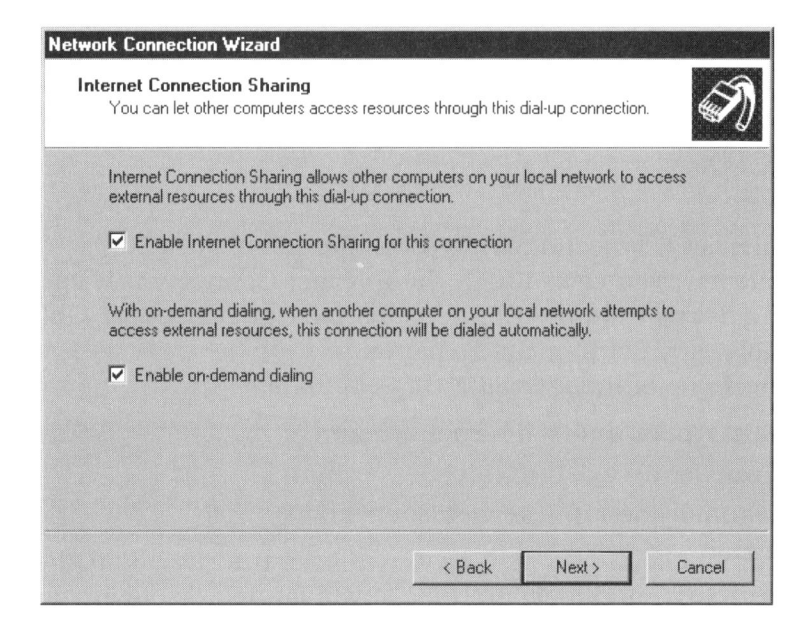

Figure 5.6 Completing the Network Connection Wizard.

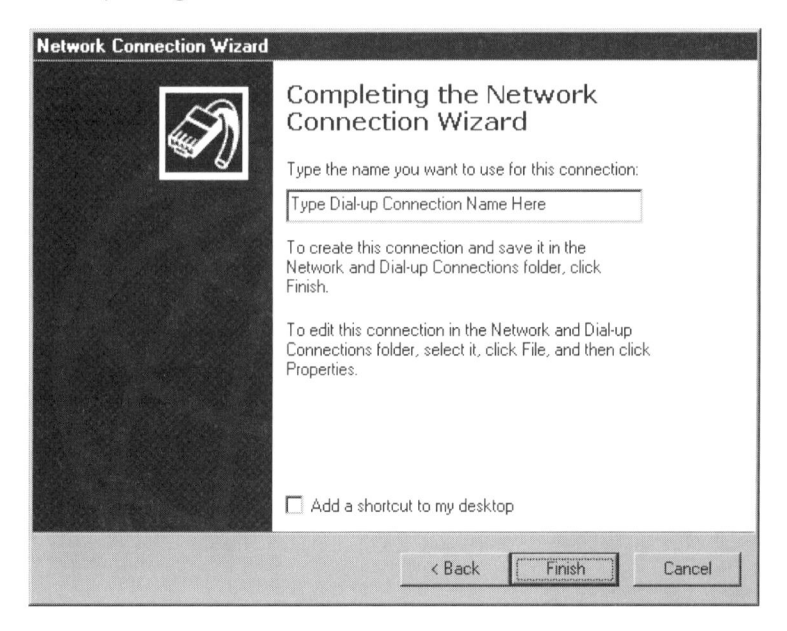

Dial-Up to the Internet

➤ STEP 1

From the **Network Connection Type** page (Figure 5.2), ensure that **Dial-up to the Internet** is selected, and click **NEXT**.

➤ STEP 2

The Internet Connection Wizard will launch (Figure 5.7). Alternatively, you can launch the Internet Connection Wizard by clicking **Setup** from the Connections tab under Internet Options in the Tools menu of Internet Explorer.

Select one of the following three options:

- Sign up for a new Internet account
- Transfer an existing Internet account
- Manually set up Internet Connection

Additionally, if you wish to view a brief tutorial about the Internet, click **TUTORIAL**, and a separate page will launch displaying a brief introduction to the Internet.

Figure 5.7 Welcome to the Internet Connection Wizard page.

➤ STEP 3

Of the available three options, the first two options will cause the Wizard to dial a referral service telephone number (Figure 5.8), which will then attempt to retrieve a list of available ISPs in your area.

Figure 5.8 Selecting an Internet service provider page.

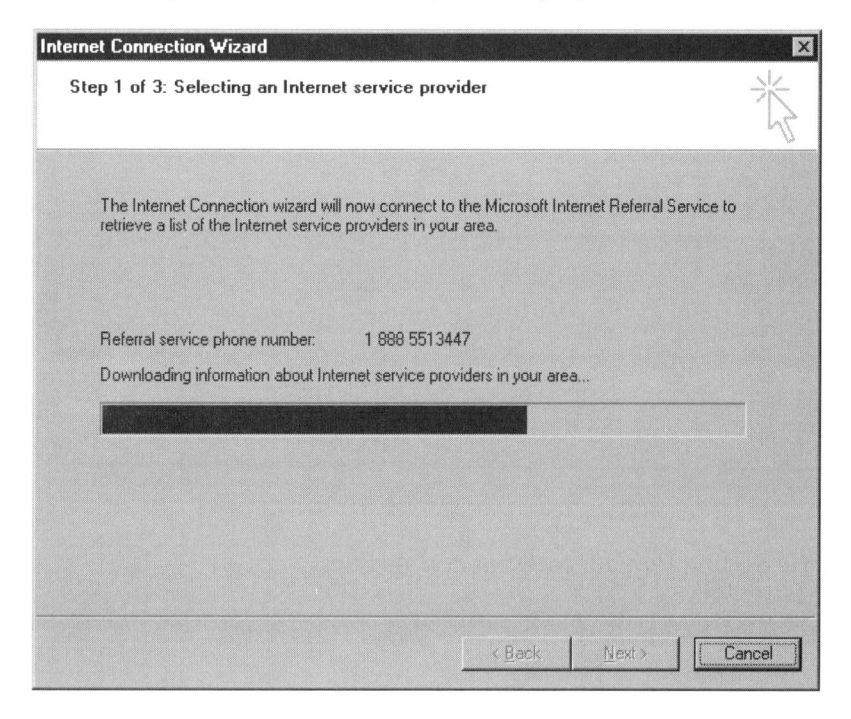

If you select the second option to transfer your existing account, you will be given a list of available providers in your area that support automatic configuration of Internet settings (Figure 5.9). If your existing provider is not listed, select **My Internet service provider is not listed**, and click **NEXT** to manually set up your Internet connection.

➤ STEP 4

If the automatic configuration feature is not supported by your ISP, or if you choose to manually configure your Internet connection, you need to specify how you want to connect to the Internet (Figure 5.10). Available options include:

- Connecting to an Internet provider via a telephone line and a modem
- Connecting through a local area network (LAN).

Figure 5.9 Selecting your Internet service provider page.

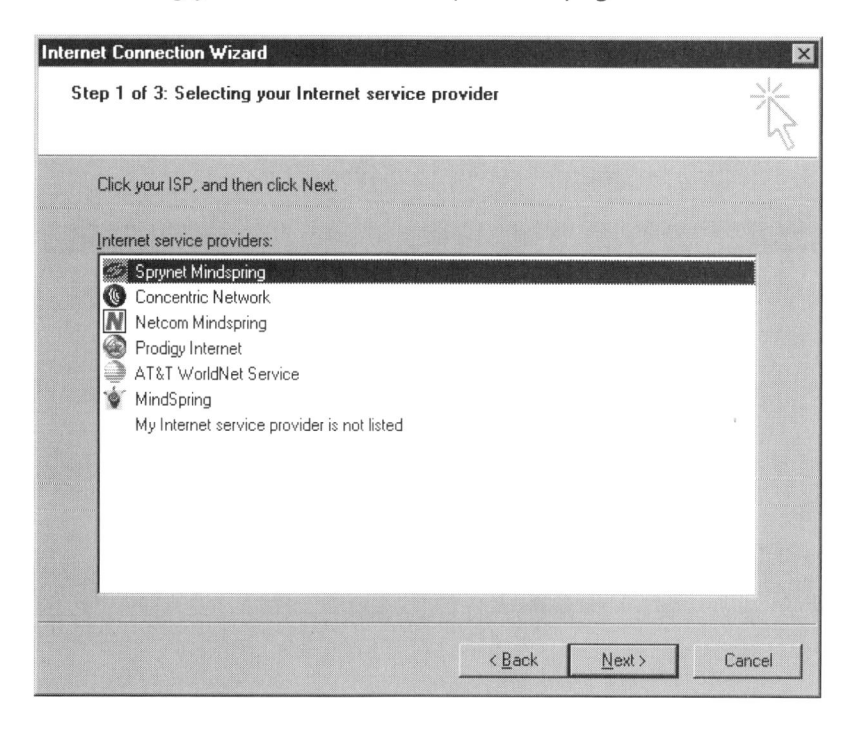

Figure 5.10 Setting up your Internet connection.

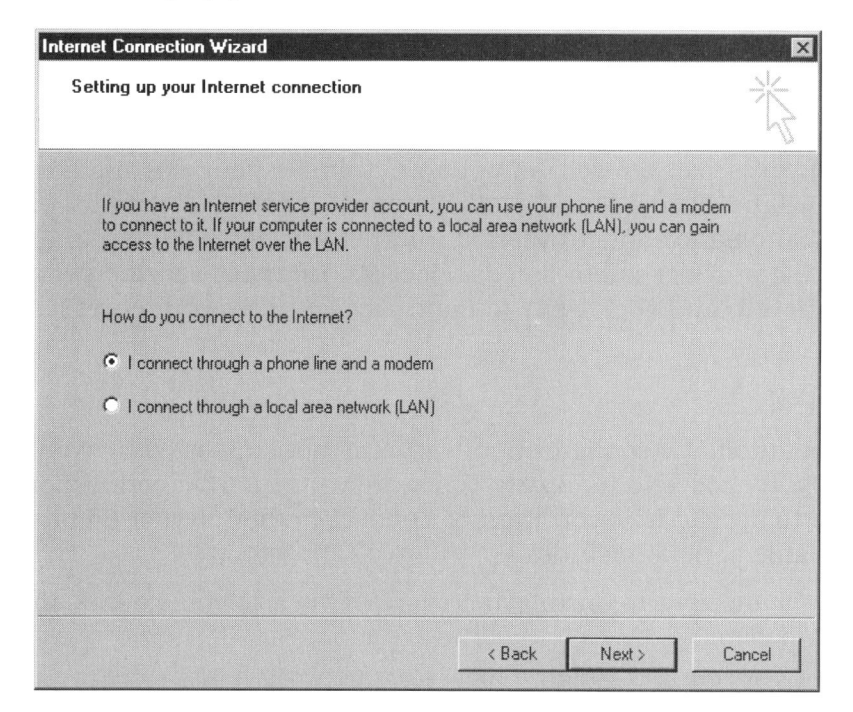

Select a connection preference, and click **NEXT**.

➤ STEP 5

- If you choose to connect through a telephone line and a modem, enter your ISP's telephone number (Figure 5.11).
- If you choose to connect through a LAN, then proceed to Step 8.
- Click **ADVANCED** only if your ISP requires that you manually input the connection type (Figure 5.12) and address (Figure 5.13).
- Click **NEXT**.

NOTE

The majority of ISPs dynamically issue client IP addresses upon connection to the service; however, if an IP address needs to be entered, select **Always use the following**, and enter the IP address assigned to you. If your ISP does not automatically provide a DNS address, you can manually specify a primary and secondary DNS by selecting **Always use the following**, and then enter the DNS addresses assigned to you by your ISP.

Figure 5.11 Internet account connection information page.

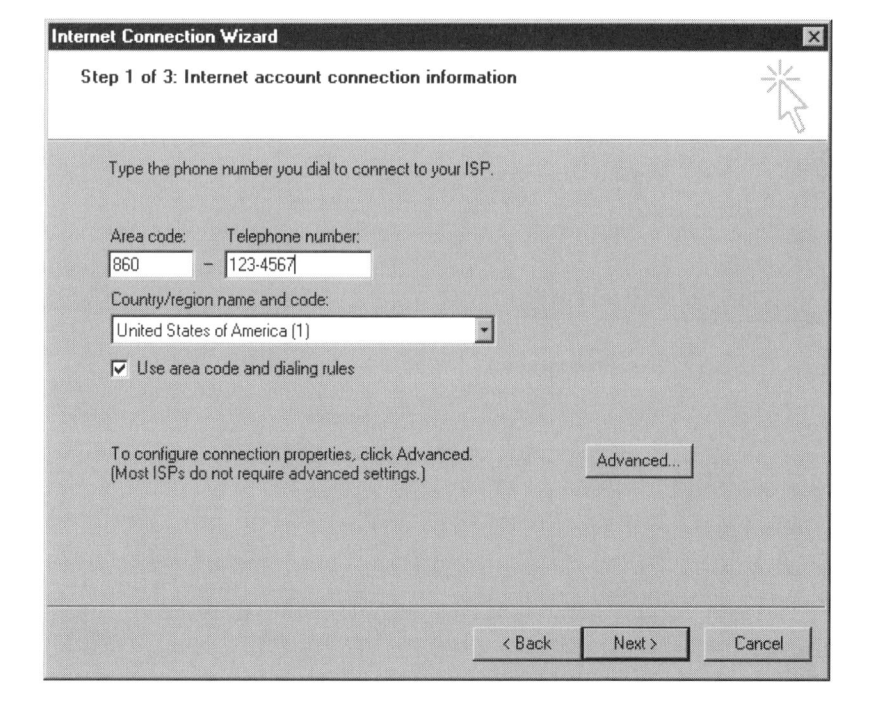

Figure 5.12 Connection tab of the Advanced Connection Properties.

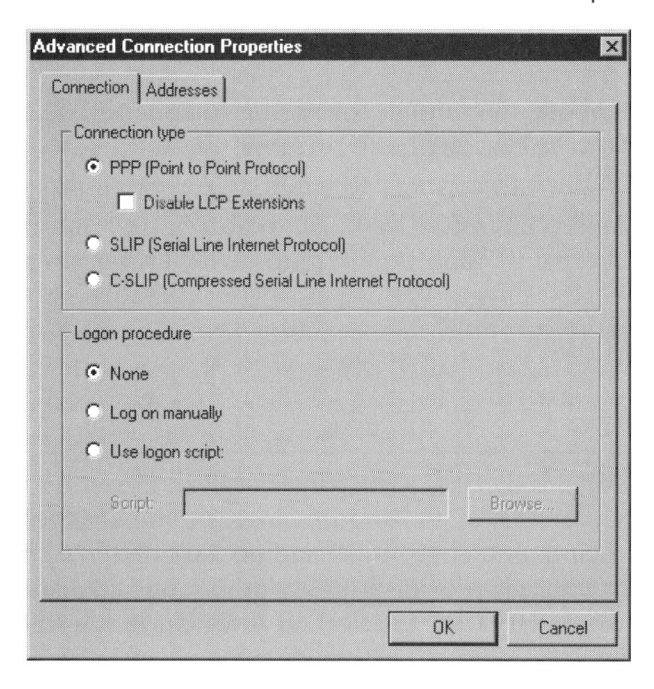

Figure 5.13 Addresses tab of the Advanced Connection Properties.

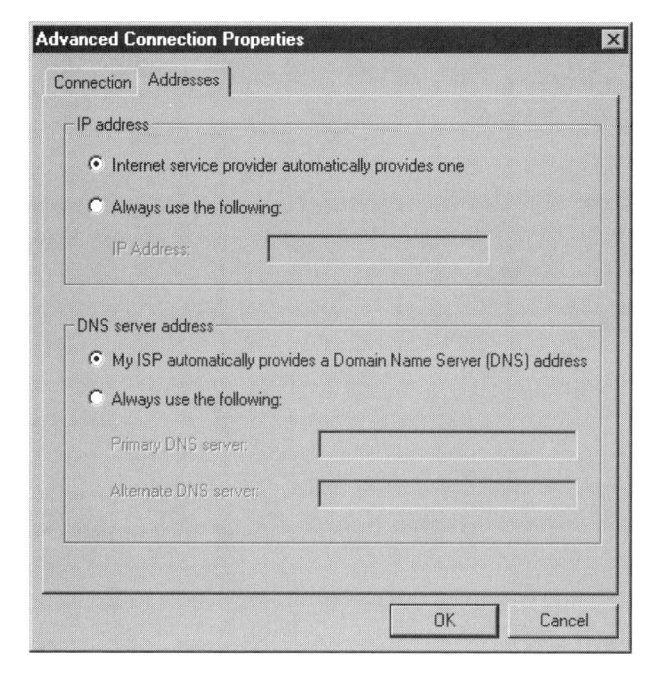

➤ STEP 6

Enter the username and password that was assigned by the ISP, and click **NEXT** (Figure 5.14).

Figure 5.14 Internet account logon information page.

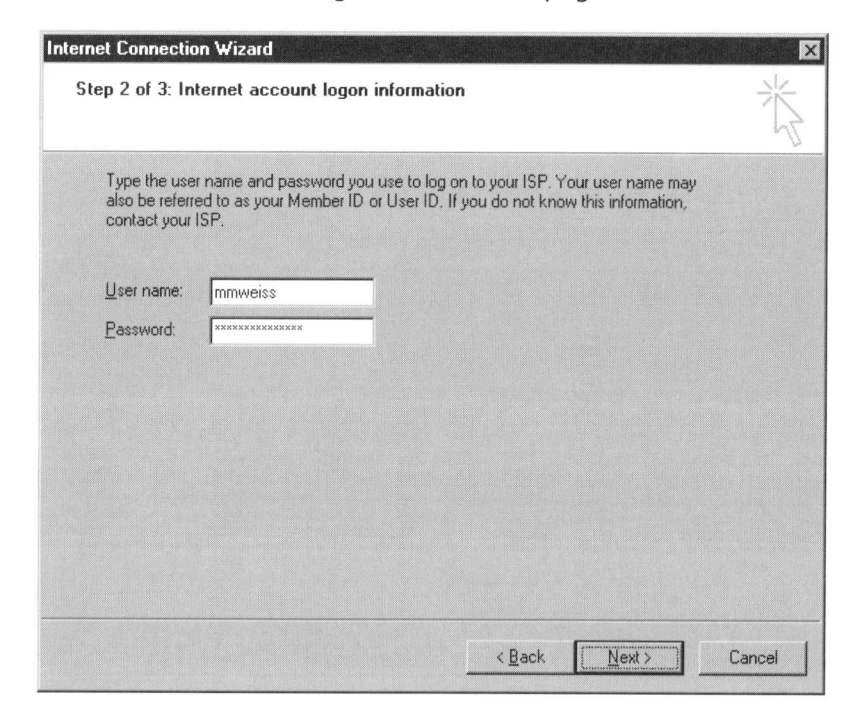

➤ STEP 7

Enter a name for this connection under **Connection name** (Figure 5.15). This name can be any name you choose, and is only used to identify this particular dial-up connection. Click **NEXT** and proceed to Step 10.

➤ STEP 8

The Local area network Internet configuration page appears (Figure 5.16) only if you chose to connect to the Internet via a LAN. If you chose to connect via a dial-up connection, proceed to the next step.

You can select an automatic configuration, or you can elect to manually specify the proxy. Click **NEXT** to continue.

Figure 5.15 Configuring your computer page.

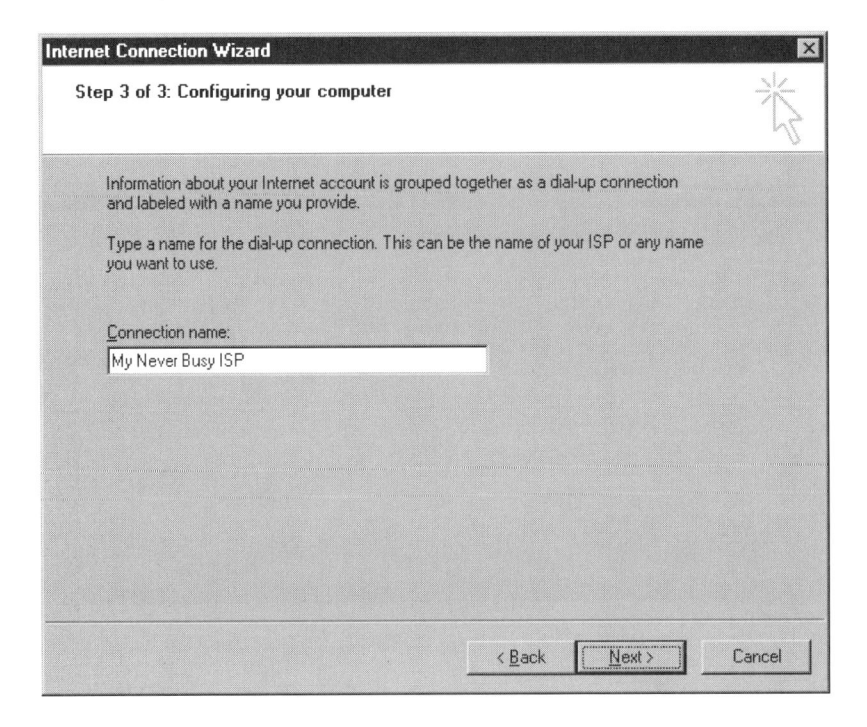

![Internet Connection Wizard - Step 3 of 3: Configuring your computer. Connection name: My Never Busy ISP]

> **NOTE**
>
> Many LAN environments with a connection to the Internet use a proxy server. A proxy server filters information and improves performance. The proxy is the middleman between the client (e.g., Web browser) and the Internet Server (e.g., www.syngress.com). Through a process called *caching*, the proxy first checks to see if it can fulfill the client's request locally to improve performance. A proxy server can also filter requests and deny client access to a specific Internet resource.

➢ STEP 9

The wizard will walk you through the process of configuring an Internet e-mail account (Figure 5.17).

If you do not want to set up an Internet mail account, select **No**, and proceed to Step 14.

To set up an Internet mail account, select **Yes**, and click **NEXT**.

Figure 5.16 Local area network Internet configuration.

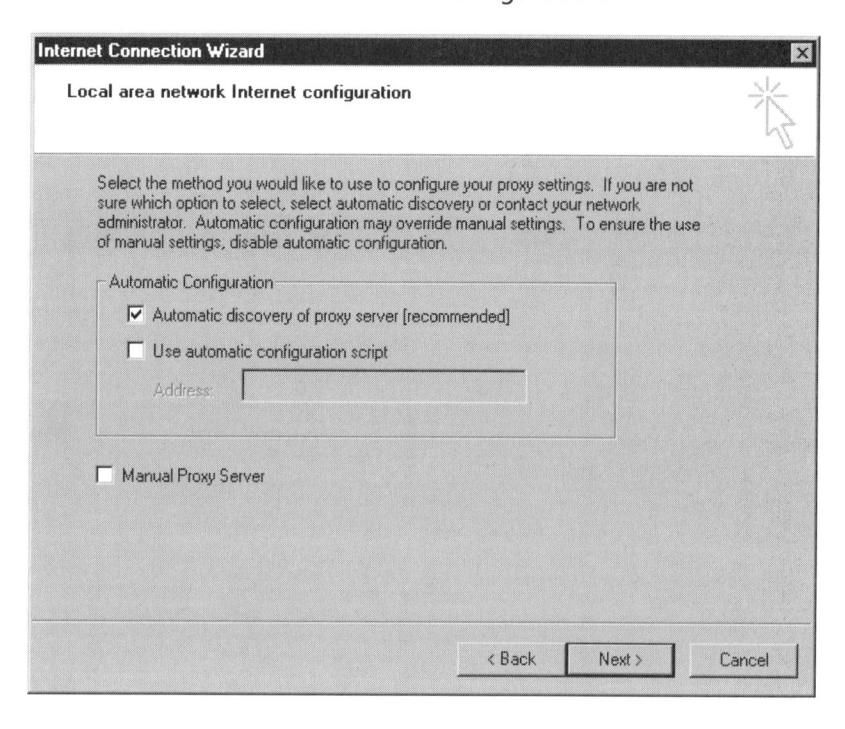

Figure 5.17 Set Up Your Internet Mail Account page.

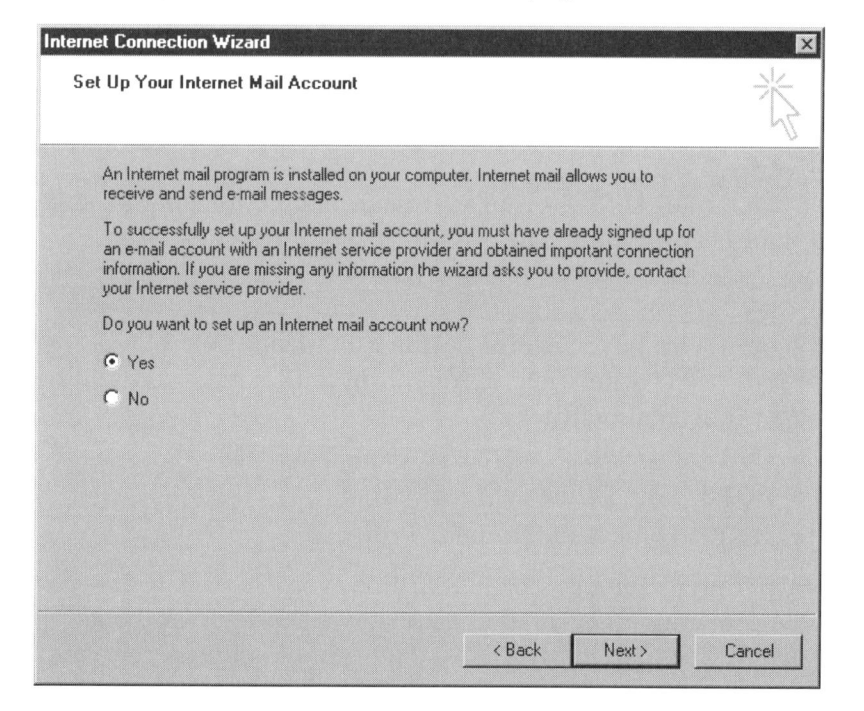

➣ STEP 10

Enter a **Display name** (Figure 5.18). This name will appear in the From field of all outgoing messages that you send from this account. Click **NEXT** to continue.

Figure 5.18 Your Name page.

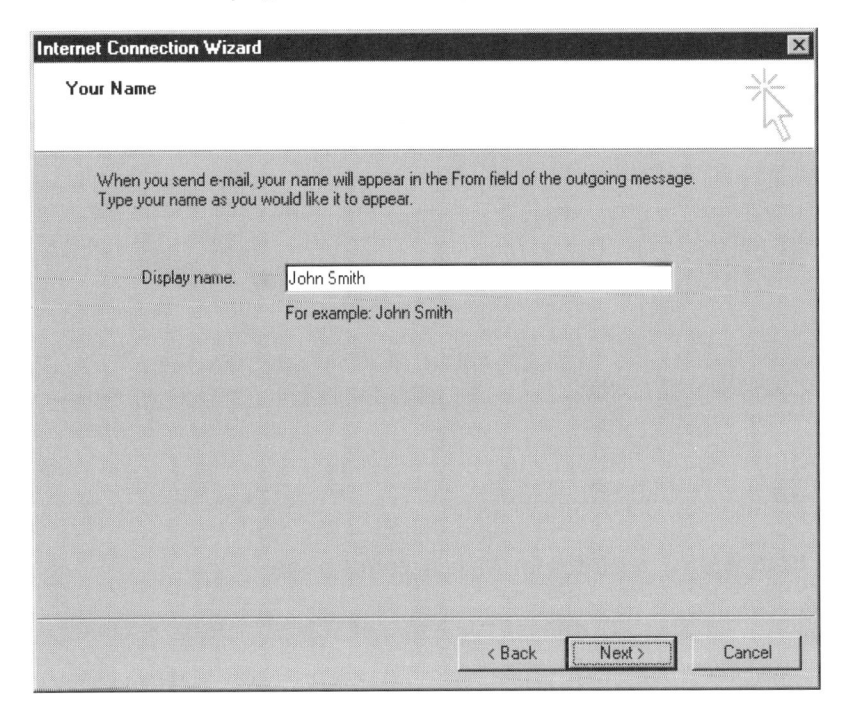

➣ STEP 11

Enter the e-mail address that you wish people to reply to, when you send mail from this account (Figure 5.19), and click **NEXT**.

➣ STEP 12

In this step, you have several options (Figure 5.20).
- First, select what type of incoming mail server you will be using. Your choices include:
  - **IMAP**. Internet Message Access Protocol
  - **POP3**. Post Office Protocol v.3
  - **HTTP**. Hypertext Transfer Protocol

Many e-mail servers use POP3; however, the use of the newer IMAP is growing. HTTP mail is generally used for Web-based e-mail if supported. Because many Web-based e-mail services rely on advertisements for revenue, most do not allow for this method of mail retrieval.

Figure 5.19 Internet E-mail Address page.

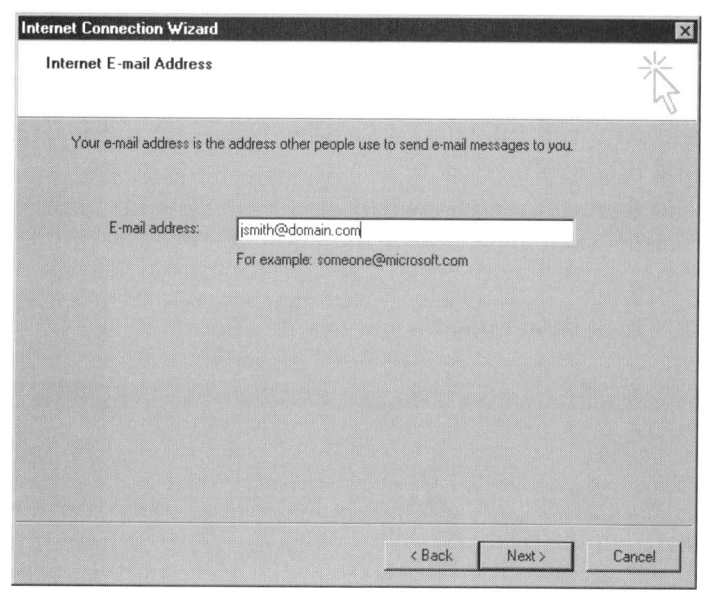

- After selecting the server type, you need to specify the server name under **Incoming mail server**, and specify an **Outgoing mail (SMTP) server**. If you do not know the addresses to enter here, contact your mail administrator.
- Click **NEXT** to continue.

Figure 5.20 E-mail Server Names page.

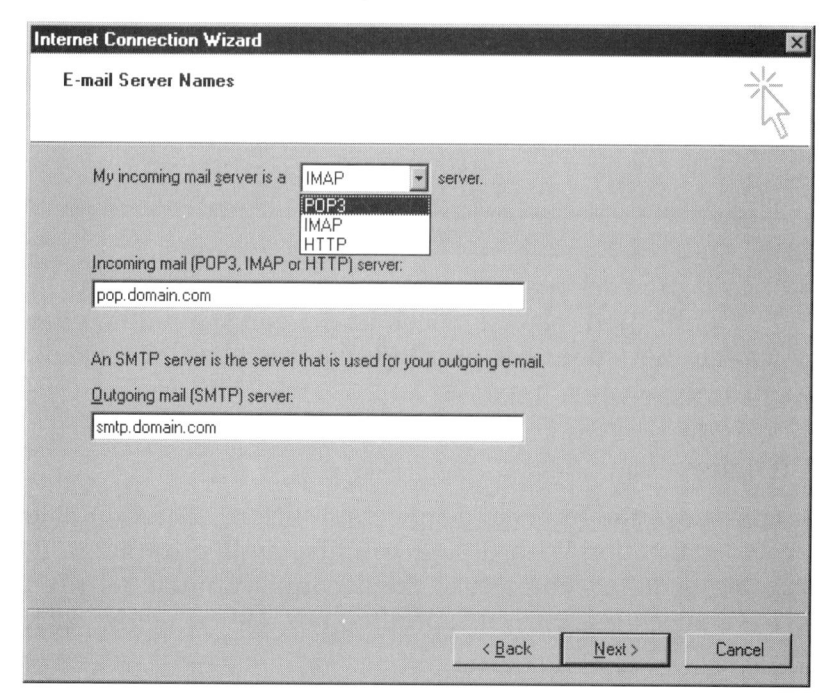

➢ STEP 13

You may have previously entered an account name and password for your Internet account; however, your mail account will usually require a separate account name and password.

- Enter the required information under **Account name** and **Password** (Figure 5.21).
- Select the **Remember password** check box if you do not want to have to enter your password each time you connect to get your mail.

Figure 5.21 Internet Mail Logon page.

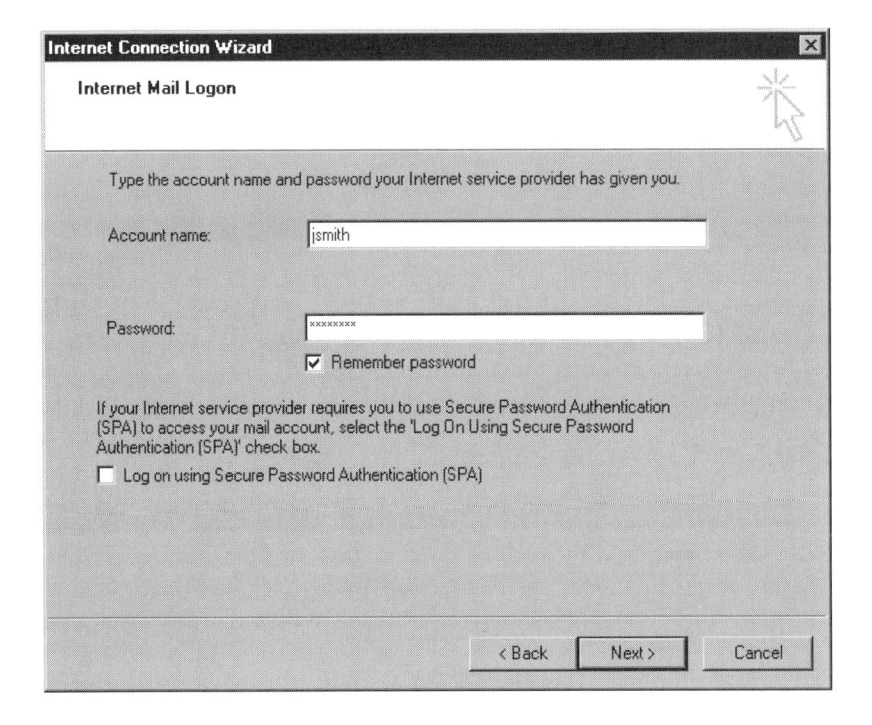

- If your provider requires you to use Secure Password Authentication, place a check in the corresponding check box. If you are not sure, it is best to leave this box unchecked.
- Click **NEXT** when finished.

➢ STEP 14

This concludes the Internet Connection Wizard. The Completing the Internet Connection Wizard page will display (Figure 5.22). If you wish to immediately connect to the account you just set up, be sure to place a check mark in the specified box. When ready, click **FINISH**.

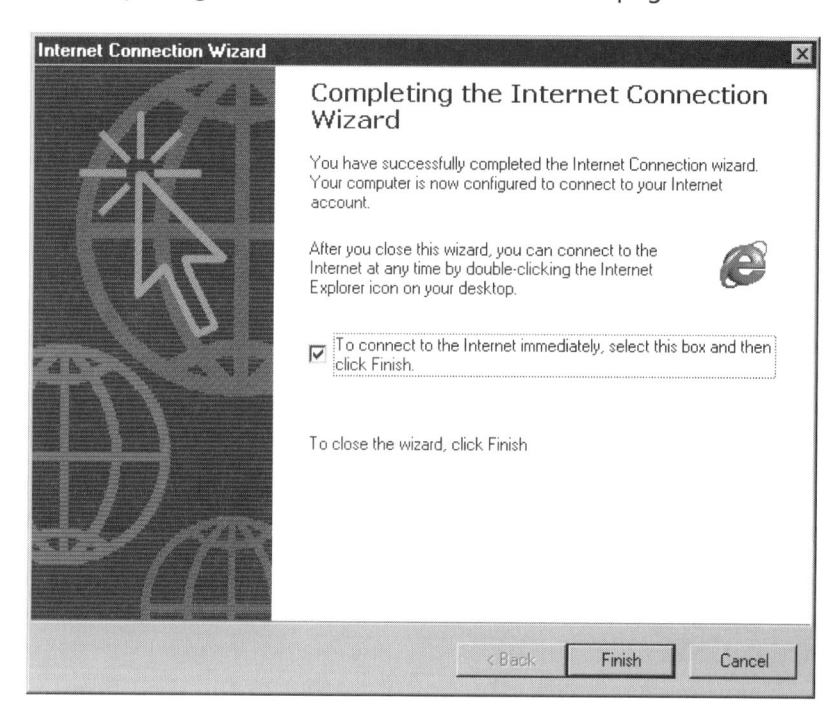

Figure 5.22 Completing the Internet Connection Wizard page.

Connect to a Private Network through the Internet

Windows 2000 has built-in Virtual Private Network (VPN) support. A VPN uses public wires such as the Internet to securely connect two or more nodes (Figure 5.23). In order to safely transport information over a public network, a VPN uses tunneling protocols such as point-to-point tunneling protocol (PPTP) or layer two tunneling protocol (L2TP). Microsoft Windows 2000 makes it easy to connect to a VPN via the Network Connection Wizard.

➢ STEP 1

From the **Network Connection Type** page (Figure 5.2), ensure that **Connect to a private network through the Internet** is selected, and click **NEXT**.

➢ STEP 2

Enter the destination address of the computer or network (Figure 5.24). You may use the host name such as domain.com, or the numerical IP address of the VPN that you want to connect to. Click **NEXT** to continue.

Figure 5.23 A VPN connects two systems via a virtual tunnel through the Internet.

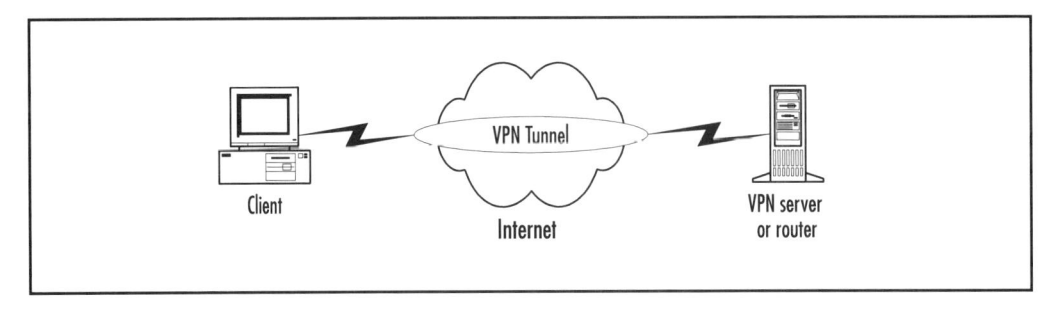

➢ STEP 3

- Specify who can use this connection (Figure 5.4).
- Ensure **For all users** is selected if you want this connection made available to all users.
- Select **Only for myself** if you want this connection to be used only by the user currently logged on.
- Click **NEXT**.
- If you selected **For all users**, proceed to the next step; otherwise, proceed to Step 5.

Figure 5.24 Destination Address page.

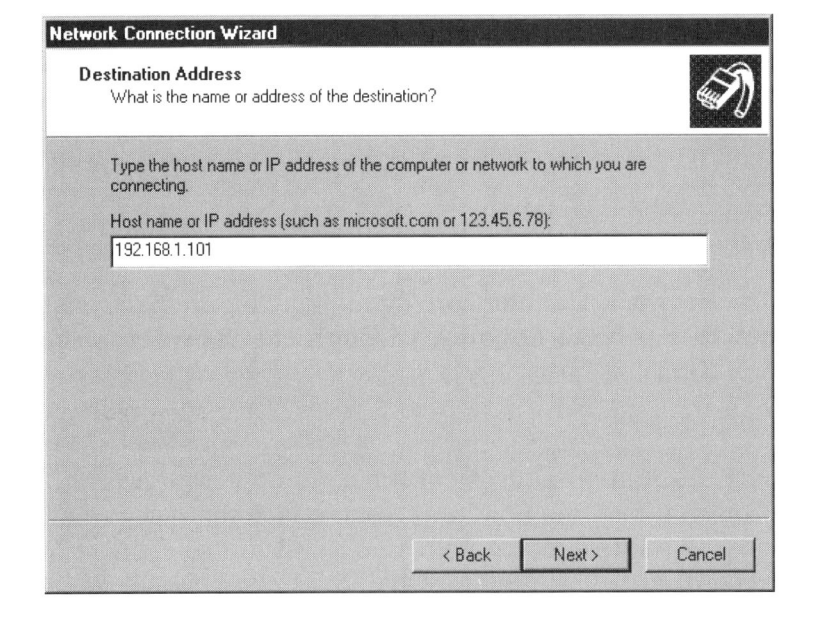

STEP 4

By choosing to make your connection available to others, you are also given the option to allow other computers to access the dial-up connection (Figure 5.5).

- To allow other computers on your local network to access through this dial-up connection, select the **Enable Internet Connection Sharing for this connection** box.
- Additionally, you can check **Enable on-demand dialing**, which will cause the computer to automatically dial the connection when another computer tries to gain access to external resources. To allow on-demand dialing, you must first enable Internet Connection Sharing.
- Click **NEXT** to continue.

STEP 5

- Enter a name for this connection (Figure 5.6). This will conclude the wizard and save the connection in the Network and Dial-up Connections folder.
- You can optionally create a shortcut for this connection on your desktop by selecting the **Add a shortcut to my desktop** box. Click **FINISH** to close the wizard.

Accept Incoming Connections

By allowing incoming connections, you can authorize specific individuals to be able to gain access. The following steps show you how to allow a stand-alone server the ability to accept incoming connections. Keep in mind, however, if you wish to configure incoming connections for a computer that is a member of a domain, use the Routing and Remote Access Configuration Wizard discussed later in Chapter 9, "Create Shared Folder Wizard."

STEP 1

From the **Network Connection Type** page (Figure 5.2), ensure that **Accept incoming connections** is selected, and click **NEXT**.

STEP 2

- A list of devices available for incoming connections will be displayed (Figure 5.25).

Figure 5.25 Devices for Incoming Connections page.

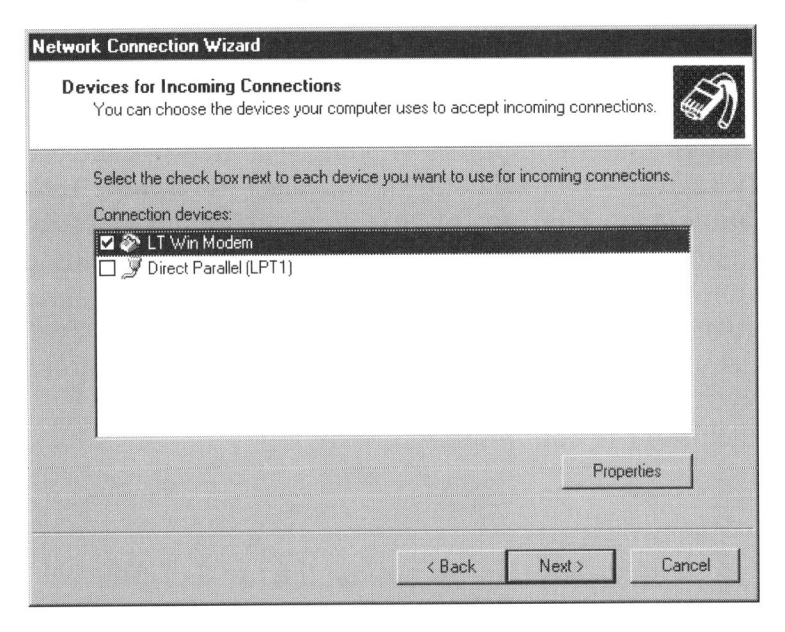

- Select the devices you wish to use by placing a check in the available box.
- Some devices may allow additional configuration via the wizard. To configure the connection device from within the wizard, right-click **PROPERTIES**. If you cannot configure the specified device at this time, a dialog box will alert you that you must configure the individual device after the wizard has completed.
- Click **NEXT**.

➤ STEP 3

Specify if you want to allow incoming connections to create a VPN connection to this computer (Figure 5.26). Select the appropriate radio button under **Choose whether to allow virtual private connections**, and click **NEXT**.

➤ STEP 4

- Place a check mark next to the accounts that you want to grant access for incoming connections (Figure 5.27).
- In this example, there are only two available accounts, but your system may have many more. If you want to add and delete accounts, click **ADD** and **DELETE**, respectively.

Figure 5.26 Incoming Virtual Private Connection page.

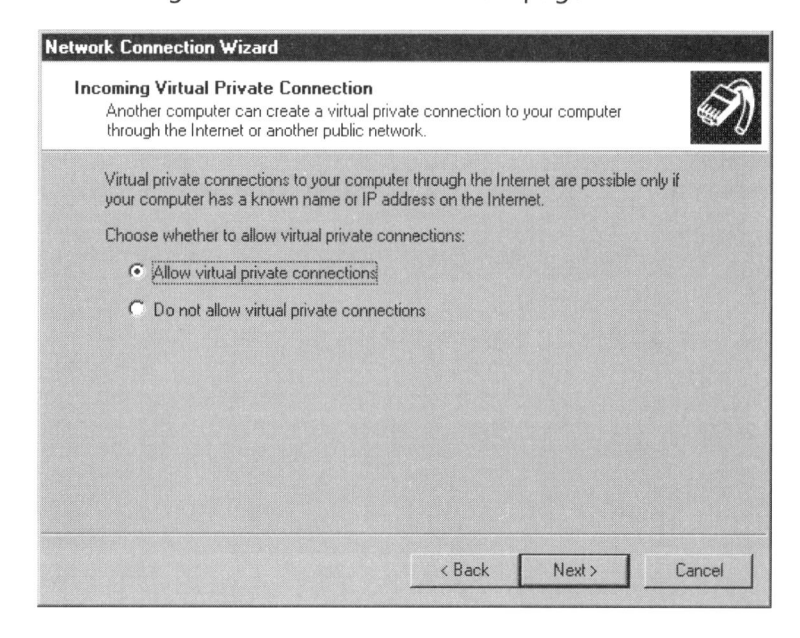

Figure 5.27 Allowed Users page.

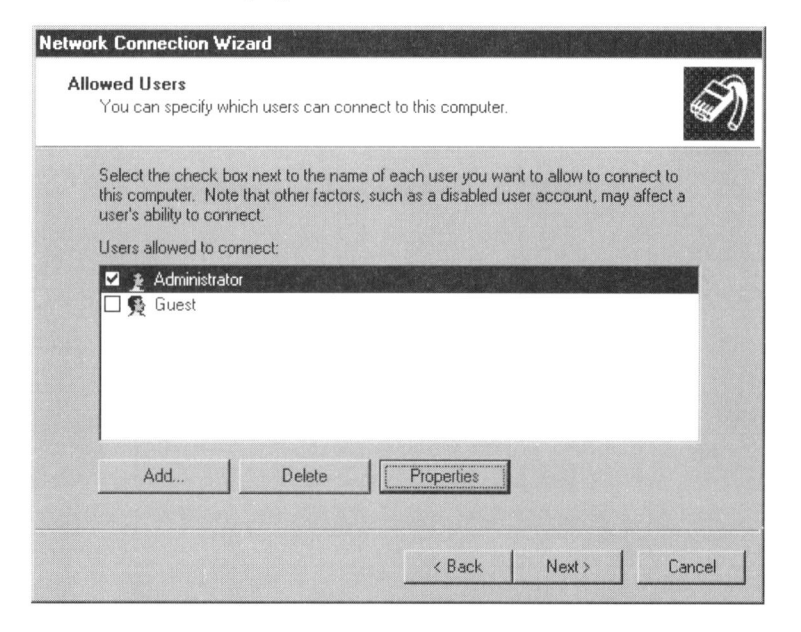

- To configure the properties (Figures 5.28 and 5.29) for each user, highlight the user and click **PROPERTIES.**
- After returning to the Allowed Users page, click **NEXT**.

Figure 5.28 General tab of user properties.

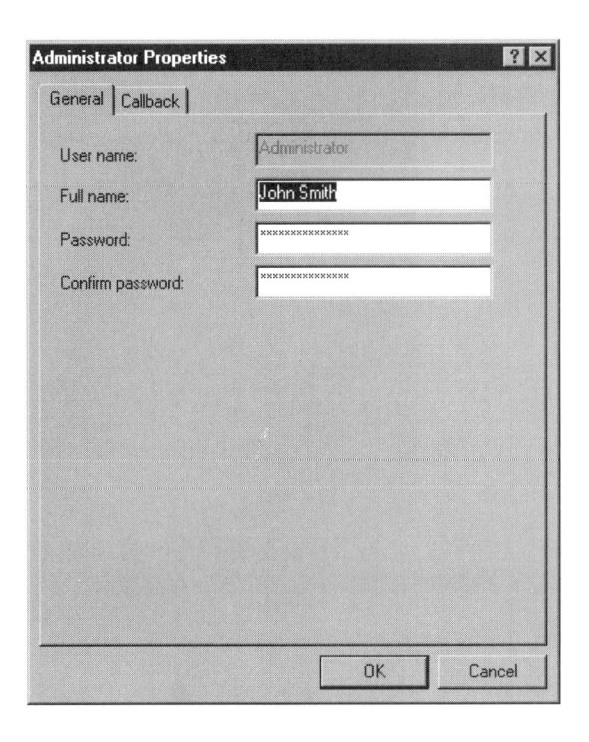

Figure 5.29 Callback tab of user properties.

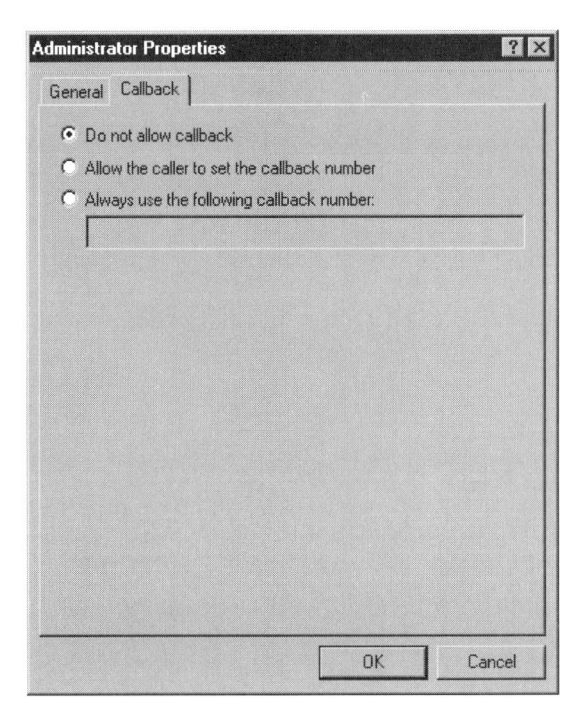

Figure 5.28 shows the available properties from the General tab of the allowed users properties. The username is grayed out and cannot be changed. You may, however, enter the Full name and incoming password for the user. Click **Ok** to return to the **Allowed Users** page.

Figure 5.29 shows the available properties from the Callback tab of the allowed user properties. The three choices include:

- **Do not allow callback** is the default choice.
- **Allow the caller to set the callback number** adds security by having the computer call back the user attempting to gain access at a number specified by the user.
- **Always use the following callback number** also adds security by having the computer call back the user attempting to gain access; however, this selection does not allow the user to specify a callback number. Rather, the callback number is set to one location. An example would be an employee who telecommutes, but the only place he or she dials in from is home.

Click **Ok** to return to the **Allowed Users** page.

➤ STEP 5

In addition to allowing dial-in users access to the dial-up server, you can also use the Networking Components page (Figure 5.30) to select networking components that you want to enable for use by incoming calls.

Figure 5.30 Networking Components page.

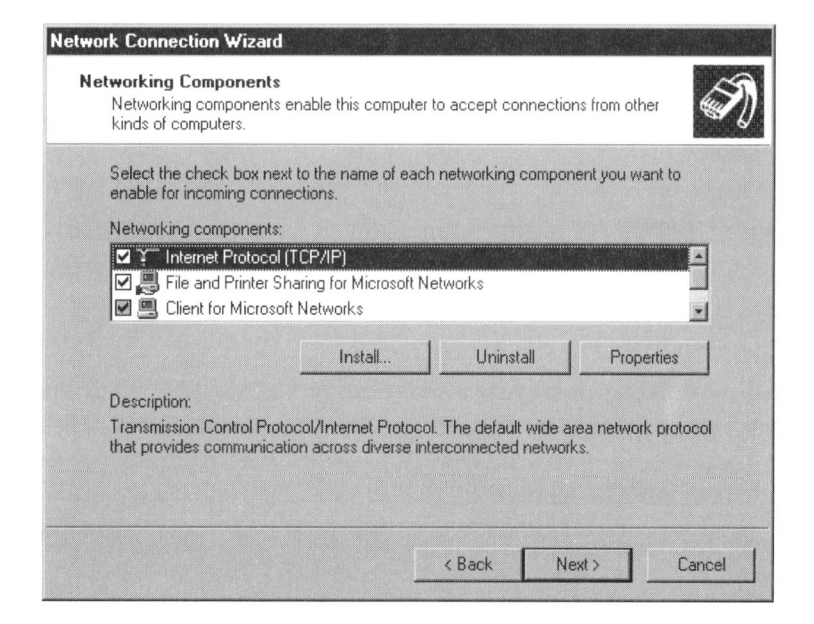

- To configure the individual properties of the networking component, click **PROPERTIES**. The property sheets for TCP/IP and File and Printer Sharing for Microsoft Networks are shown in Figures 5.31 and 5.32.
- When you have finished configuring the networking properties, click **NEXT**.

Figure 5.31 Incoming TCP/IP Properties.

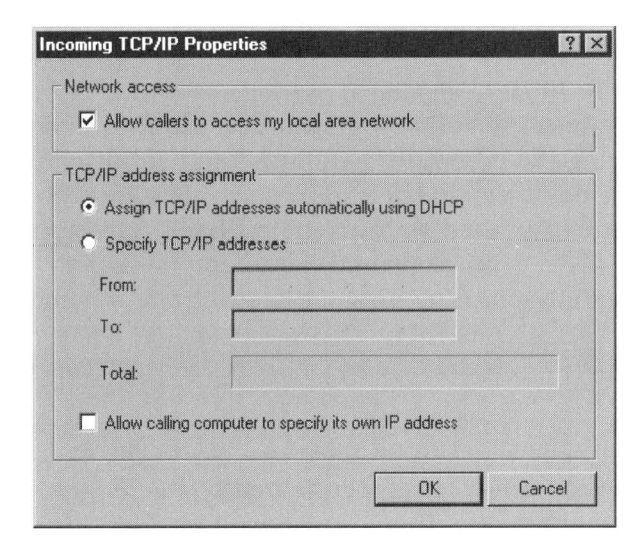

From the TCP/IP Properties page, you can allow dial-in users to gain access outside of the dial-in server to the LAN by selecting **Allow callers to access my local area network**.

Next, configure the TCP/IP address assignment by selecting one of the following:

- **Assign TCP/IP addresses automatically using DHCP**. This will allow a DHCP server to automatically assign users a temporary IP address.
- **Specify TCP/IP addresses** allows the connecting hosts to be assigned an IP address from a pool of addresses based on a base IP and mask address.
    - Enter available IP addresses in the From and To boxes
- **Allow calling computer to specify its own IP address** permits users to specify the IP address they will connect with. You might consider this if you have a dial-in user who has a predefined address on the network.

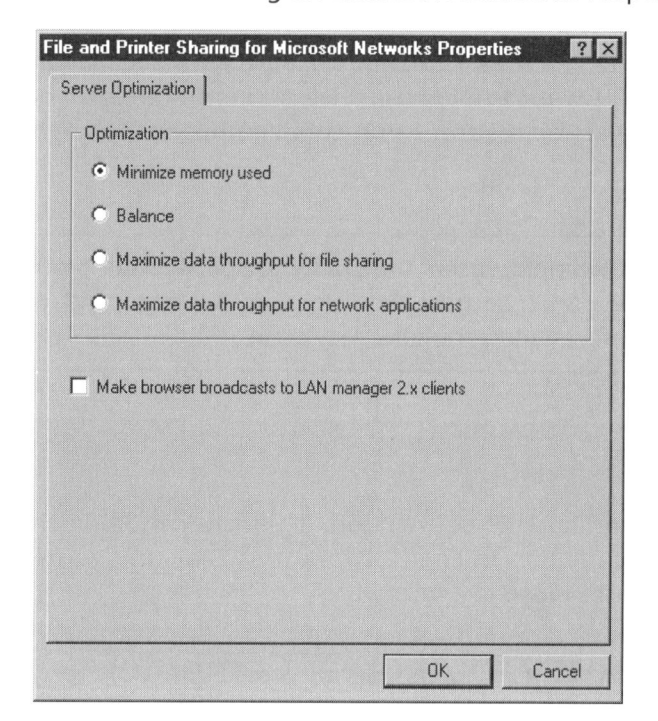

Figure 5.32 File and Printer Sharing for Microsoft Networks Properties.

WARNING

If you select "Assign TCP/IP addresses automatically using DHCP" and a DHCP server is not present on your network, Windows 2000 will automatically assign an address in the 169.254.xxx.xxx range by using the Automatic IP addressing feature.

The property sheet for File and Printer Sharing for Microsoft Networks (Figure 5.32) allows you to optimize the connection for dial-in users. You can choose from four choices:

- **Minimize memory used**. Best used for a small number of clients.
- **Balance**. Best used for file sharing, print sharing, and other services, and when serving as a workstation at the same time.
- **Maximize data throughput for file sharing**. Best used for file and print sharing.

- **Maximize data throughput for network applications**. Best used for distributed applications such as SQL.

Finally, check **Make browser broadcasts to LAN manager 2.x clients** if you want LAN Manager 2.x clients on your network to be able to browse for resources on this computer.

> **NOTE**
>
> Be careful of assigning users the ability to specify their own IP address. If the user enters an IP address that is already assigned and in use on the network, conflicts and problems may arise.

➣ STEP 6

Enter a name for this connection. This will conclude the wizard and save the connection in the Network and Dial-up Connections folder. Click **FINISH** to close the wizard.

Connect Directly to Another Computer

Use the Network Connection Wizard to create a direct (cable) connection to another computer.

➣ STEP 1

From the **Network Connection Type page** (Figure 5.2), ensure that **Connect directly to another computer** is selected, and click **NEXT**.

➣ STEP 2

When creating a direct cable connection, you have the option to specify the role of the system (Figure 5.33). You may select one of the following two options, and click **NEXT** to continue:

- **Host**, if this computer has the information to be accessed
- **Guest**, to access information on a host computer.

> **NOTE**
>
> If the system is a member of a domain, you cannot use this wizard to host a direct connection. You must use the Routing and Remote Access Service.

Figure 5.33 Host or Guest page.

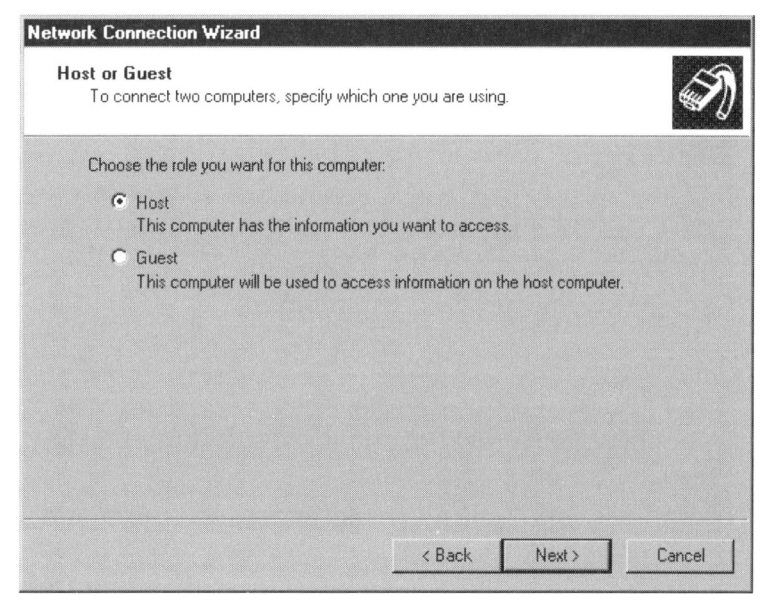

➤ STEP 3

Next, select a connection device from the **Select a Device** page (Figure 5.34). Many direct cable connections use a serial port (COM1 or COM2) via a null modem cable. Click **NEXT** to continue.

Figure 5.34 This is the device that will be used to make the connection page.

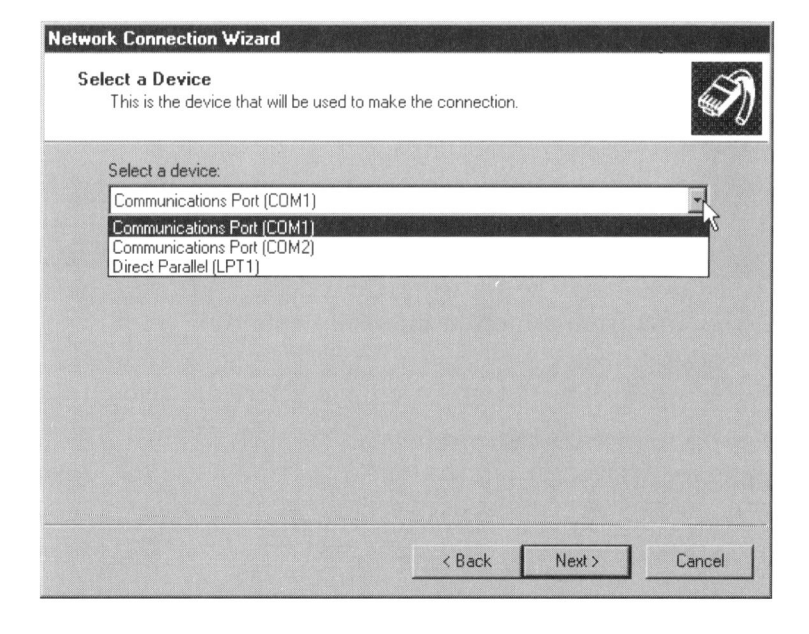

➤ STEP 4

- If you selected **Host** in Step 2, skip to Step 5.
- If you selected **Guest**, you need to specify who can use this connection.
  - Ensure **For all users** is selected if you want this connection made available to other users of this computer and/or other systems.
  - Select **Only for myself** if you want this connection to be used only by the user currently logged on.
- Click **Next**, and proceed to Step 6.

➤ STEP 5

- Place a check mark next to the accounts that you want to grant access for incoming connections.
- If you want to add and delete accounts, click **Add** and **Delete**, respectively.
- To configure the properties for each user, highlight the user, and select **Properties.**
- After returning to the Allowed Users page, click **Next**.

➤ STEP 6

Finally, enter a name for this connection. This will conclude the wizard and save the connection in the Network and Dial-up Connections folder. Click **Finish** to close the wizard.

Summary

Windows 2000 can support multiple network connections. The Network Connection Wizard allows you to easily set up inbound and outbound connections with minimal protocol and service configuration. To create a network connection, start the Network Connection Wizard. The wizard has multiple options from which to choose, depending on your configuration and networking needs.

From the Network Connection Type page, there are five choices:

- Dial-up to private network
- Dial-up to the Internet
- Connect to a private network through the Internet
- Accept incoming connections
- Connect directly to another computer

Dialing up to a private network connects your telephone line to an ISP or to another modem to gain access to a private network. Dialing up to a private network primarily involves entering a telephone number for the network or system you are connecting to. In addition, you can also elect to configure the connection for multiple users and allow others to share your connection.

Dialing up to the Internet actually launches a second wizard called the Internet Connection Wizard. From this wizard, you can sign up for a new Internet account, transfer an existing account, or set up your connection manually. Signing up for a new account or transferring a current account will cause the wizard to dial the toll-free Microsoft Internet Referral Service, which will download information about ISPs in your area. After you finish setting up the Internet account, the wizard will then walk you through the process of setting up your Internet e-mail account. To set up an e-mail account, you will need information such as your logon name and password, e-mail address, type of mail server, and incoming and outgoing address. If you do not have this information, you will need to contact your provider.

The Network Connection Wizard also allows you to make a connection to a Virtual Private Network. A VPN is most commonly used to securely connect two or more networks over the Internet. The process of connecting to a VPN is very much like the previous wizards; the primary difference is that you will need to enter either a host name or IP address of the VPN destination.

Although most of the options available from the Network Connection Wizard are for outgoing connections, you can also use the wizard to allow incoming connections. You have the option to designate which users are allowed to connect, as well as specify additional security options such as callback. Within this wizard, you will also specify the networking components to enable for incoming connections, and configure the method in which clients are assigned IP addresses.

Finally, you can use the Network Connection Wizard to create a direct cable connection to another system. This process involves selecting the role (i.e., guest, host), and finally selecting the device used to make this connection.

Chapter 6
Managing DHCP Servers

Introduction

DHCP is an excellent way to conserve IP addresses, but it requires the presence of a DHCP server. To configure Windows 2000 as a DHCP server, you must first define a scope of addresses that the server will service. By the end of this chapter, your Windows 2000 server will respond to client DHCP requests based on the scope configurations you create.

Before You Begin

Before beginning, first ensure that you are logged on as an Administrator, and that the DHCP Service is installed. To install the DHCP Service, use the Add/Remove Programs. DHCP is a component of Networking Services located under Add/Remove Windows Components. Finally, you want to ensure that the computer you are configuring as a DHCP server has a statically assigned IP address.

The Purpose of these Wizards

To provide support for DHCP in Windows 2000, use the wizards provided to create scopes, superscopes, and multicast scopes. The wizards provide a quick way to configure the needed scopes to deliver automatic IP addressing and other features.

Information Needed to Work with these Wizards

Before working with any of the scope wizards, ensure that you have the following information ready:

- Creating a scope:
    - A name and a description to assign to the scope
    - Start and end IP address range
    - Subnet mask if one other than the default is required
    - IP addresses to be excluded
    - Default Gateway (router) IP address
    - DNS Server address
    - WINS Server address
- Creating a superscope:
    - A name to assign to the superscope
- Creating a multicast scope
    - A name and a description to assign to the scope
    - Start and end IP address range
    - IP addresses to be excluded

> **For IT Professionals**
>
> ### What Is DHCP?
>
> Dynamic Host Configuration Protocol (DHCP) helps reduce the complexity of manually administrating IP addresses and other TCP/IP configurations. On a network, every client workstation must be assigned an IP address. For large networks, managing these addresses can become a nightmare, as each number must be unique and there is a set amount of addresses available to work with.
>
> For small networks, manually assigning a static IP address may not be a problem; however, larger networks and networks with limited available addresses may want to consider the use of a DHCP server. In addition to being able to automatically assign client IP addresses, a DHCP server provides several benefits, including the ability to specify the client subnet mask, default gateway (router), DNS servers, and WINS servers.
>
> Windows 2000 Server provides a DHCP service you can use to manage IP client configuration and automate IP address and assignment on your network. To learn more about DHCP, RFC 2131 is the latest Request for Comments covering the Dynamic Host Configuration Protocol.

Add DHCP Server

With Windows 2000, you can manage many network services remotely from any other server on your network. The DHCP manager provides a simple method to help locate and connect to other Windows 2000 DHCP servers on your network.

To add additional DHCP servers to the DHCP manager on your Windows 2000 server, first open the DHCP manager from the Administrative Tools Menu, right-click the DHCP icon, and select **Add Server**. From the Add Server window, click **Browse**, and then click **Ok** once you have found the server you want to add (Figure 6.1).

The Create Scope Wizard

A *scope* is a range of IP addresses from which DHCP clients can automatically be assigned an IP address.

Figure 6.1 Adding a DHCP server from the DHCP manager.

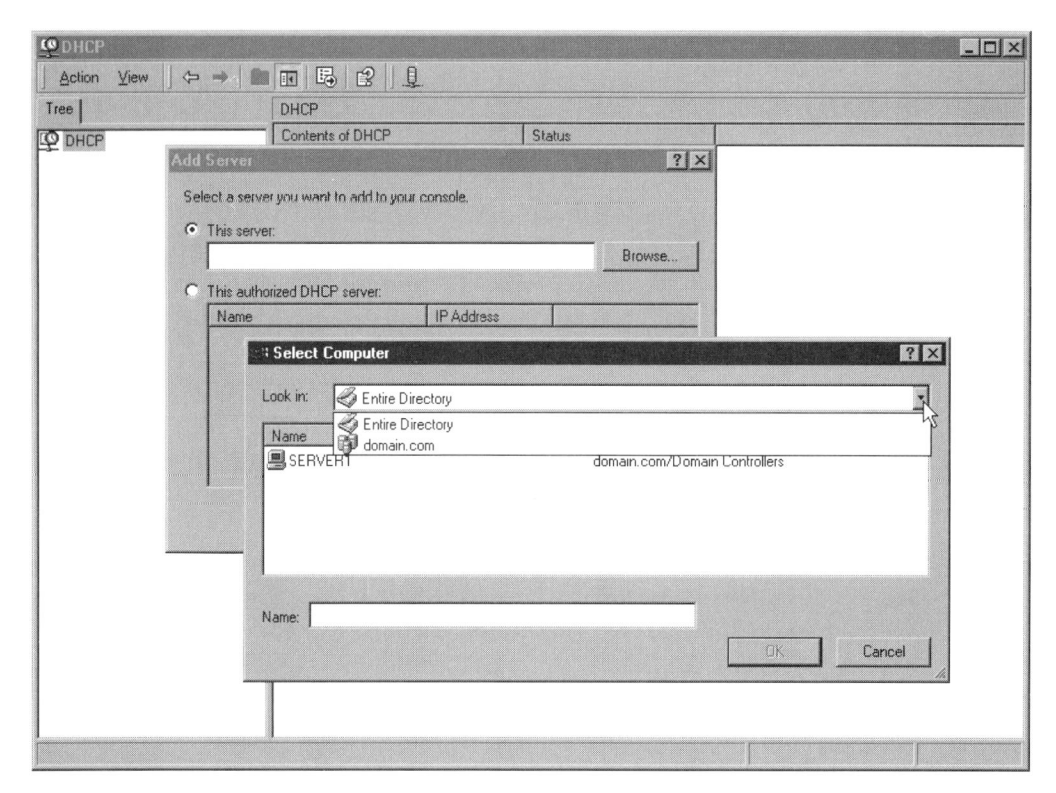

➢ STEP 1

To start the New Scope Wizard, right-click the DHCP server from the DHCP manager, and click **New Scope** (Figure 6.2).

➢ STEP 2

The New Scope Wizard welcome page appears (Figure 6.3). Click **NEXT** to continue.

➢ STEP 3

Enter a name and description to identify this scope (Figure 6.4).

➢ STEP 4

Enter a start and end IP address that can be assigned to a DHCP client from this scope in the **Start IP address** and **End IP address** fields. The **Subnet mask** field is automatically filled in; however, you may modify the subnet mask by changing the **Length** field (Figure 6.5). Click **NEXT**.

Figure 6.2 Starting the New Scope Wizard from the DHCP manager.

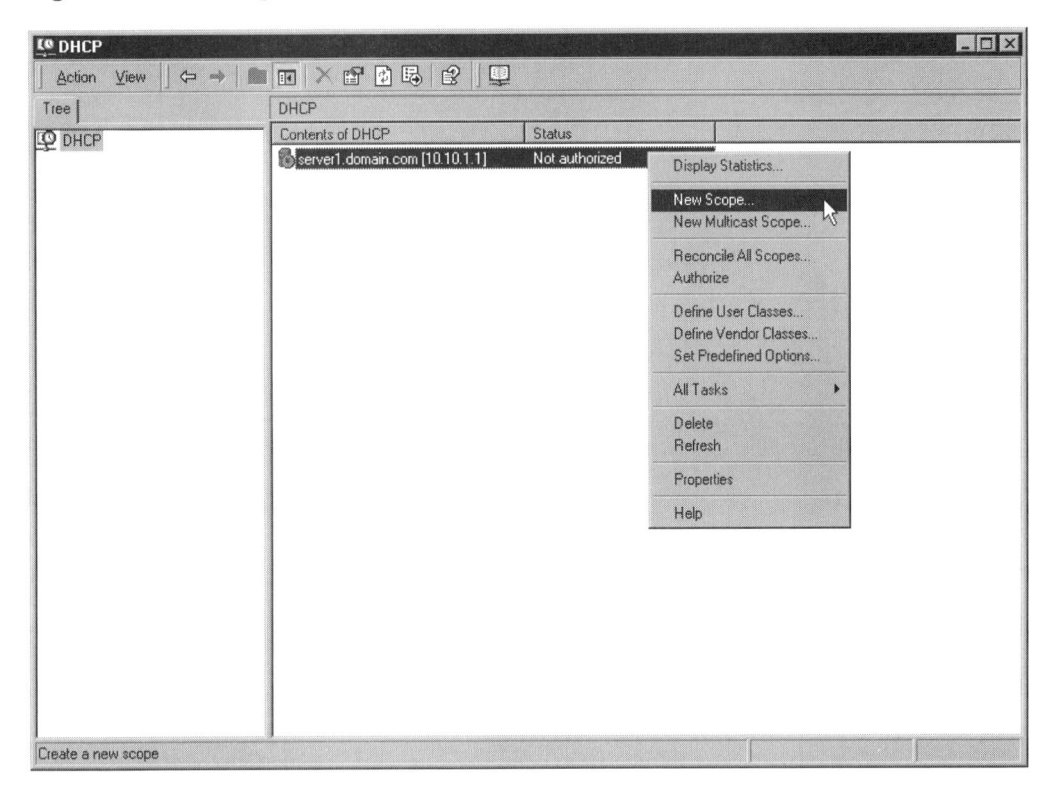

Figure 6.3 Welcome to the New Scope Wizard page.

Figure 6.4 Specifying a name and description from the Scope Name page.

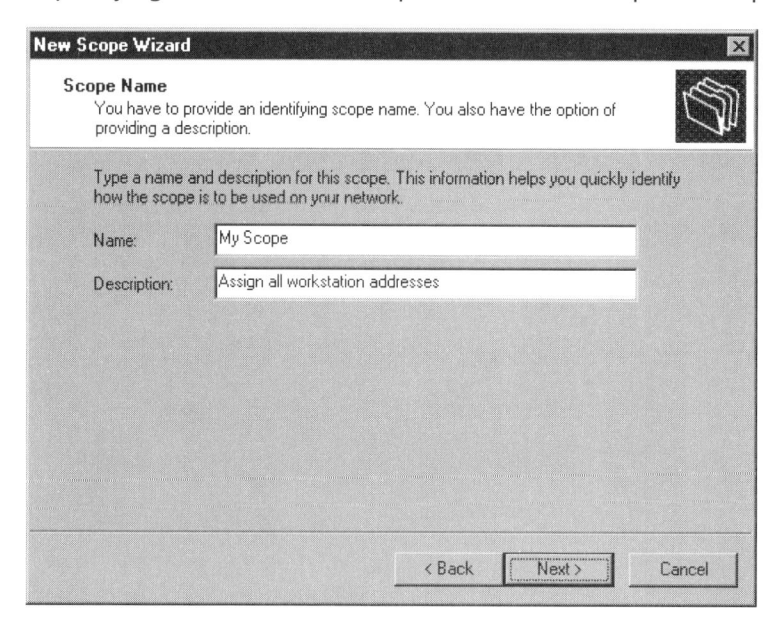

> **TIP**
>
> There are three classes of IP addresses. An address consists of a network and host ID portion. Each class, combined with a subnet mask, defines these portions. Additionally, each class has a default subnet mask that may be modified to provide what is called custom "subnetting." The three IP classes and their default subnet masks are listed in Table 6.1.

Table 6.1 IP Address Classes and Their Default Subnet Masks

IP Address Class	First Octet Range	Default Subnet Mask
Class A	1–126	255.0.0.0
Class B	128–191	255.255.0.0
Class C	192–224	255.255.255.0

Figure 6.5 Defining the Scope IP address range from the IP Address Range page.

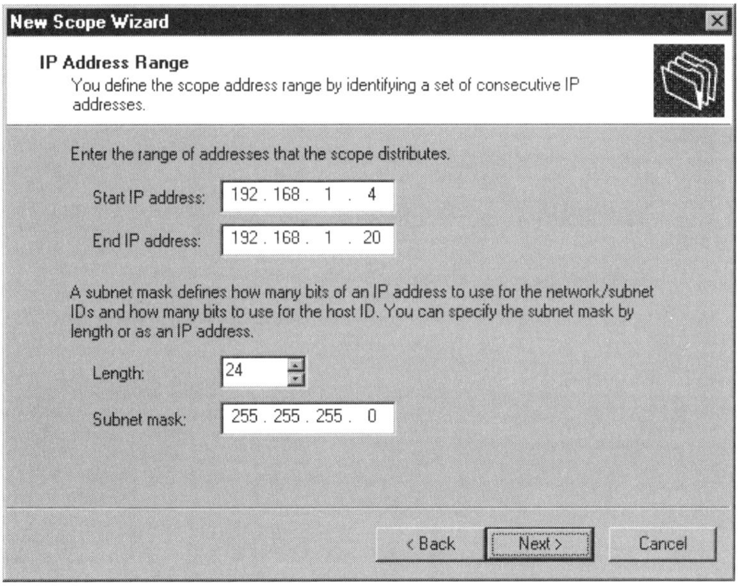

➢ **STEP 5**

Enter a start and end IP address to specify a range of addresses to exclude in the **Start IP address** and **End IP address** fields, and click **ADD** (Figure 6.6). To remove an excluded range, highlight the range in the **Excluded address range** box, and click **REMOVE**. Click **NEXT** to continue.

Addresses included in the exclusion list will not be assigned to DHCP clients. This is important if you have static IP addresses configured on systems not utilizing DHCP. Examples of a system that might not act as a DHCP client and must be added to the exclusion list include routers, file and print servers, DNS servers, and servers requiring a static address for remote connectivity purposes.

➢ **STEP 6**

Specify the amount of time (lease duration) that you want a client to be able to use an IP address before having to request a new one (Figure 6.7), and click **NEXT**.

Figure 6.6 Adding address exclusions on the Add Exclusions page.

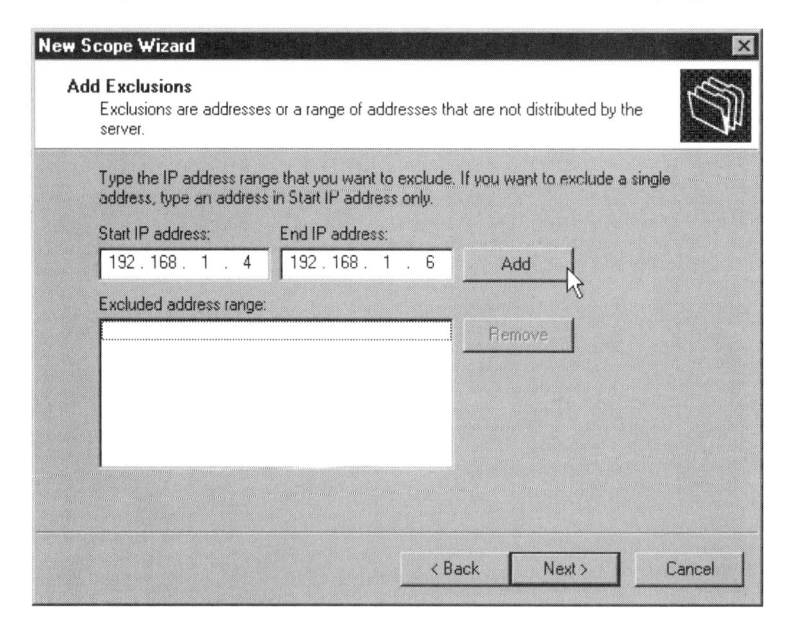

> **NOTE**
>
> You may want to consider reducing the lease duration for certain clients such as dial-up clients, and increasing the lease duration for large and stable networks (assuming you have plenty of IP addresses to go around).

➣ STEP 7

From the Configure DHCP Options page (Figure 6.8), specify if you want to configure additional options.

- Select **Yes, I want to configure these options now** if you would like the wizard to walk you through the process of providing DHCP clients with additional information, such as the address of default gateways and DNS and WINS servers. Click **NEXT** to continue.

- Select **No, I will configure these options later**, and click **NEXT** to complete the New Scope Wizard. Before clients can receive addresses, however, you will need to first specify any options and activate the scope.

Figure 6.7 Limiting IP address duration on the Lease Duration page.

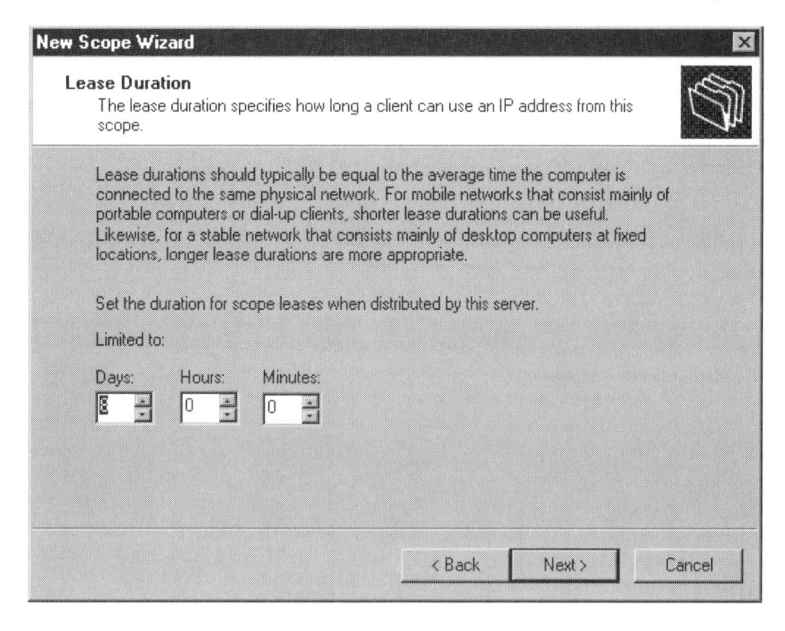

Figure 6.8 Configure additional options from the Configure DHCP Options page.

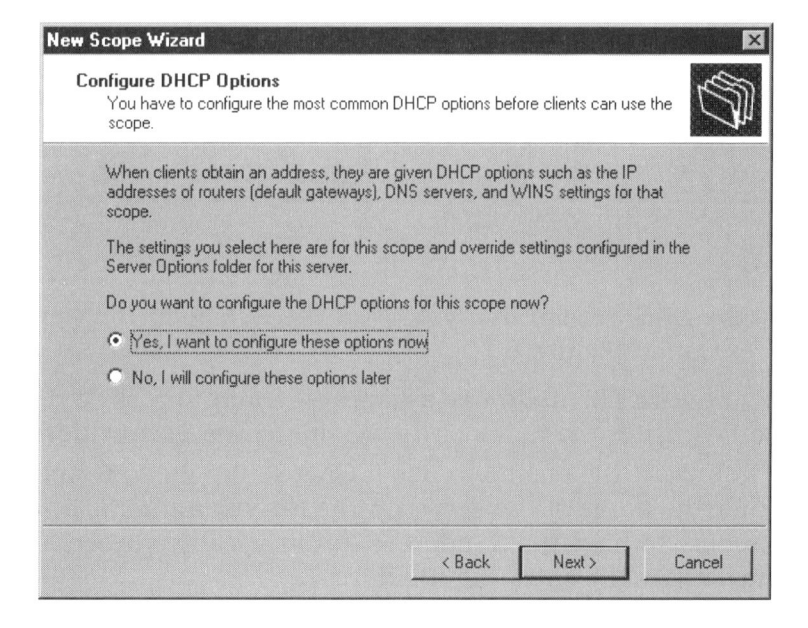

➤ STEP 8

If you choose to configure additional options, the wizard prompts you to specify the Router or the default Gateway address (Figure 6.9).

Enter one or more IP addresses, and click **ADD**. If you specify more than one default gateway, you may click **UP** or **DOWN** to specify the order in which clients use them. Click **NEXT**.

Figure 6.9 Specify one or more default gateways from the Router (Default Gateway) page.

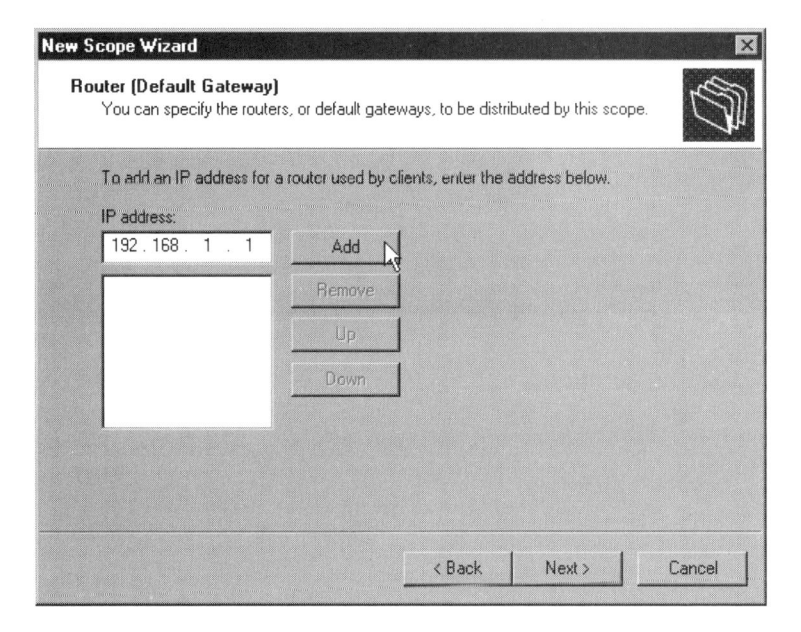

➤ STEP 9

Specify the DNS servers that you want the DHCP clients to use for name resolution (Figure 6.10).

- If you want clients to use a parent domain to resolve domain names, enter the name of the parent in the **Parent domain** field.
- If you want the clients to use a DNS server on your network, enter the name of the server in the **Server name** field, and click **RESOLVE** to have the IP address automatically entered, or you may optionally enter the IP address.
- You may add more than one DNS server by clicking **ADD**. If you specify more than one DNS server, you may click **UP** or **DOWN** to specify the order in which clients use them.
- Click **NEXT**.

Figure 6.10 Specify DNS servers from the Domain Name and DNS Servers page.

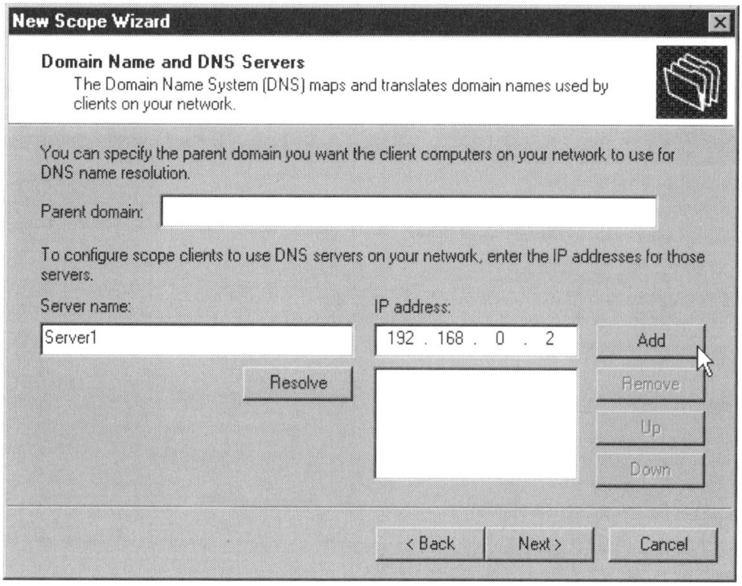

> ## STEP 10

Specify the WINS servers that you want the DHCP clients to use for name resolution of NetBIOS names to IP addresses (Figure 6.11).

Enter the name of the server in the **Server name** field, and click **RESOLVE** to have the IP address automatically entered, or you may optionally enter the IP address of the WINS server. You may add more than one WINS server by clicking **ADD**. If you specify more than one WINS server, you may click **UP** or **DOWN** to specify the order in which clients use them. Click **NEXT**.

NOTE

WINS (Windows Internet Naming Service) is a used by Windows NT Server for associating a computer's host name with its address. While Windows 2000 supports WINS for compatibility reasons, it being replaced by DNS, the name resolution method used on the Internet.

> ## STEP 11

At this point, you must activate the scope (Figure 6.12). The scope must be active before clients can start receiving address leases. If you decide not to activate the scope now, you can do so later by selecting the scope and clicking **Activate** from the **Action** menu in the DHCP manager. Click **NEXT**.

Figure 6.11 Specify WINS servers for DHCP clients from the WINS Servers page.

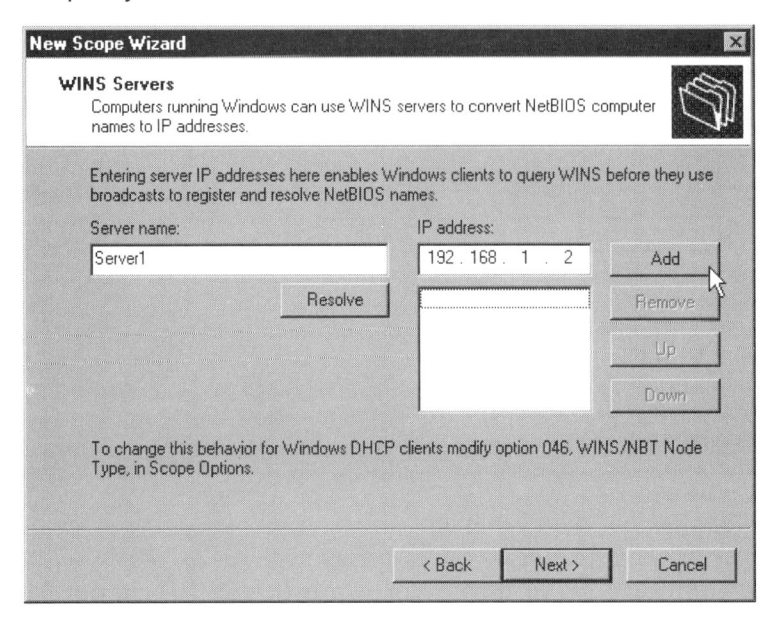

Figure 6.12 Activate the DHCP scope from the Activate Scope page.

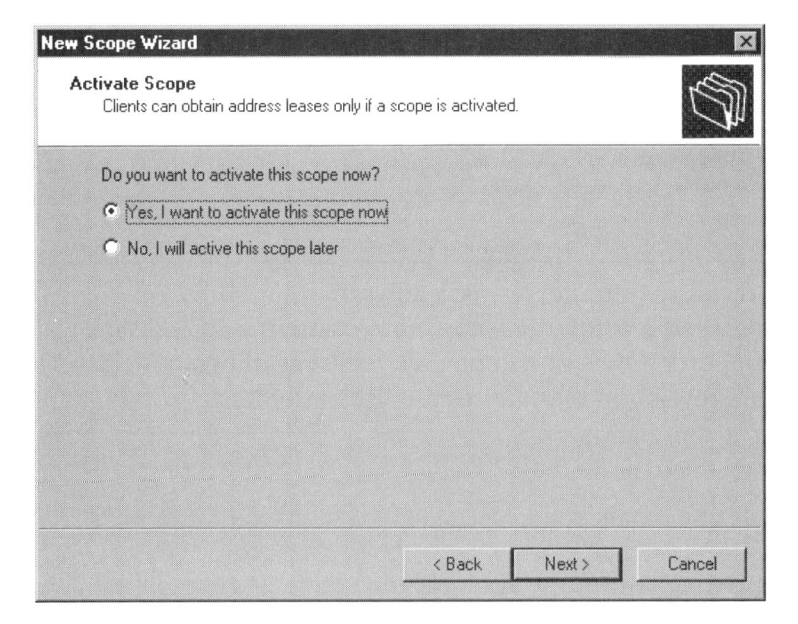

➤ STEP 12

Click **FINISH** to close the New Scope Wizard (Figure 6.13).

Figure 6.13 Completing the New Scope Wizard page.

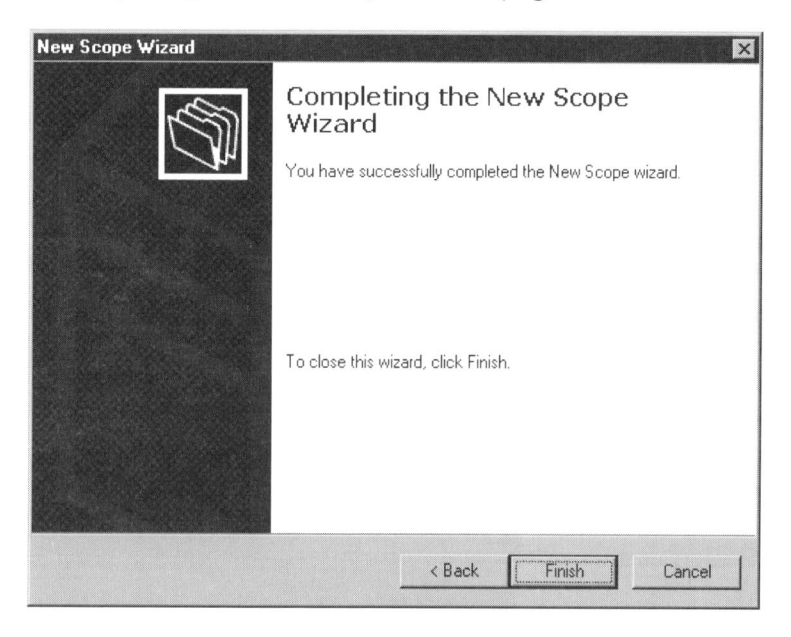

The Create Superscope Wizard

With Windows 2000, you can create superscopes; that is, you can assign IP addresses from multiple logical subnets to DHCP clients on one physical network. In Windows NT, IP addresses for clients are limited to one logical subnet per physical network.

➤ STEP 1

To start the New Superscope Wizard, right-click the DHCP server from the DHCP manager, and click **New Superscope**. The New Superscope Wizard page appears (Figure 6.14). Click **NEXT**.

➤ STEP 2

Enter a name to identify your superscope (Figure 6.15), and click **NEXT**.

➤ STEP 3

To create a superscope, select the scopes you want to add from the Available scopes box, and click **NEXT** (Figure 6.16).

Figure 6.14 New Superscope Wizard welcome page.

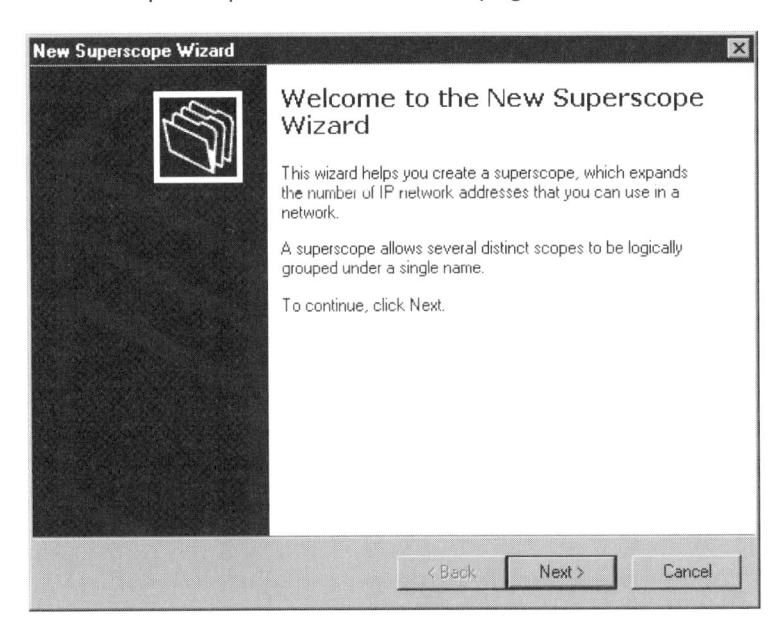

Figure 6.15 Identify the superscope from the Superscope Name page.

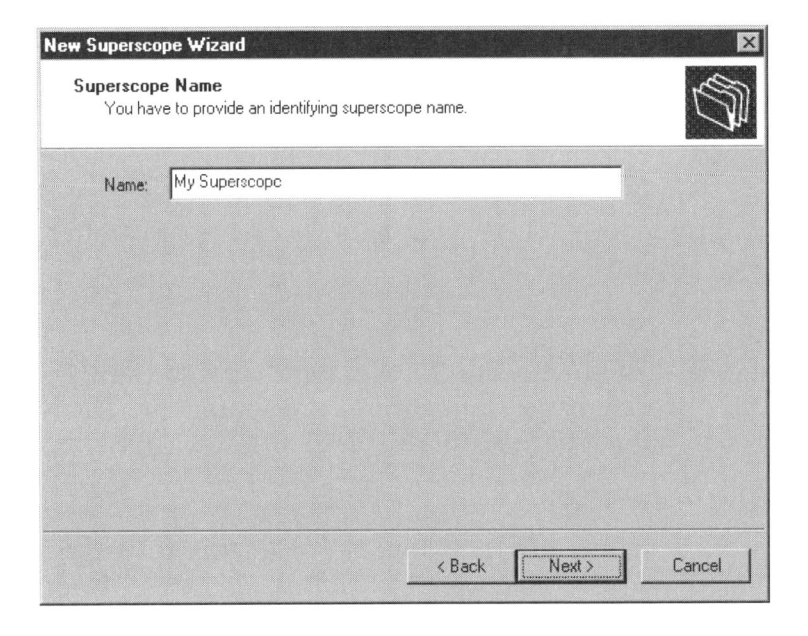

➤ STEP 4

Click **FINISH** to complete the New Superscope Wizard (Figure 6.17).

Figure 6.16 Add scopes from the Select Scopes page.

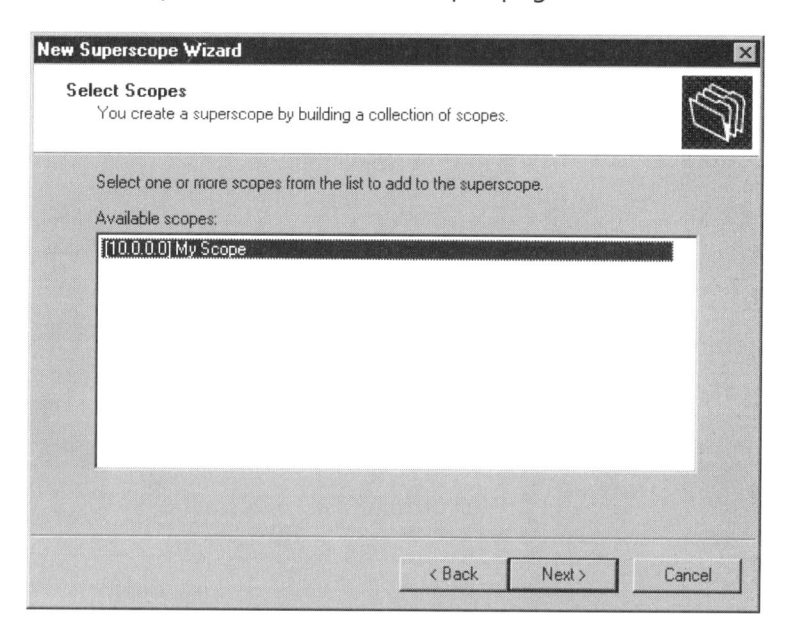

Figure 6.17 Completing the New Superscope Wizard page.

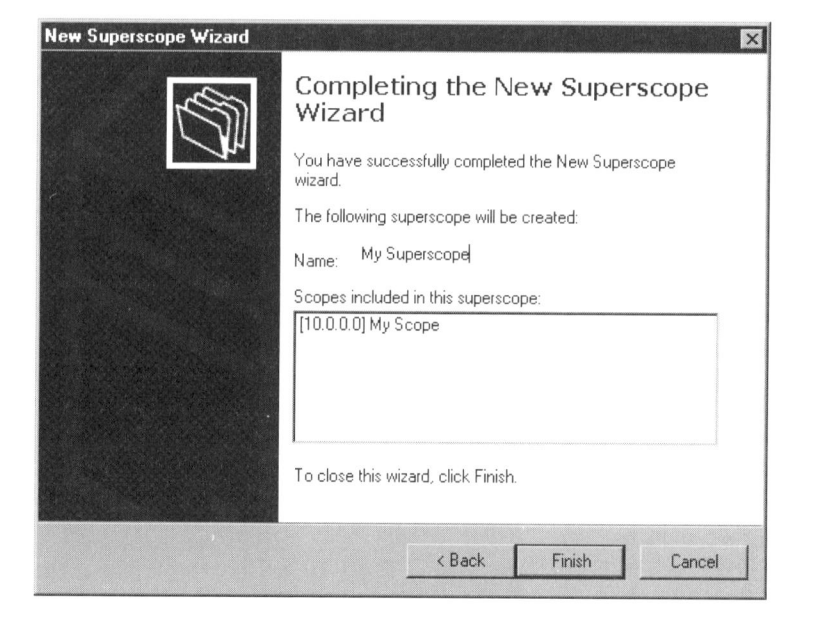

The Create Multicast Scope Wizard

A *multicast* is the process of sending a message simultaneously to more than one destination on a network. Multicast DHCP (MDHCP) is used to support dynamic assignment of multicast addresses on the network. Windows 2000 supports MDHCP via multicast scopes.

➤ STEP 1

To start the New Multicast Scope Wizard, right-click the DHCP server from the DHCP manager, and click **New Multicast Scope**. The New Multicast Scope Wizard page appears (Figure 6.18). Click **NEXT**.

Figure 6.18 The new Multicast Scope Wizard welcome page.

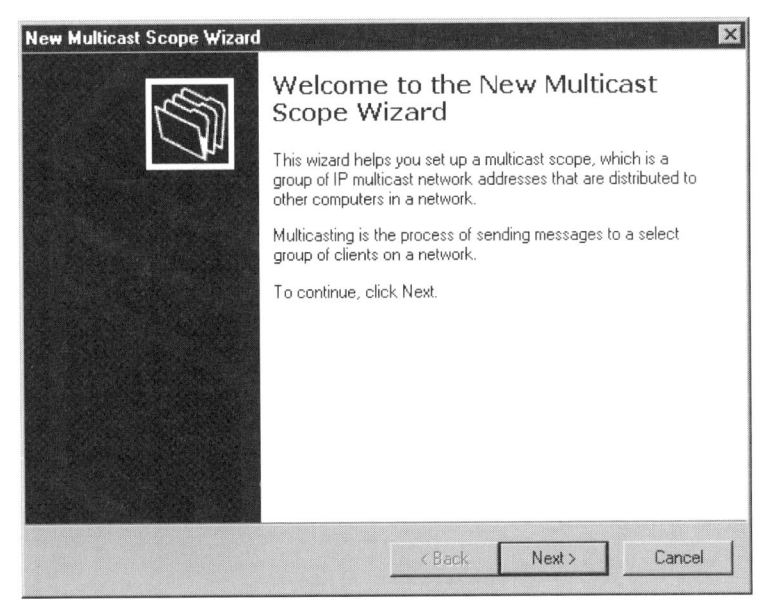

➤ STEP 2

Enter a name and description to identify the multicast scope (Figure 6.19), and click **NEXT**.

➤ STEP 3

- Enter a start and end IP address to specify a range of addresses in the **Start IP address** and **End IP address** fields (Figure 6.20).
- Specify a Time to Live in the **TTL** field. A TTL is a timer value, which is included in packets sent over a network that indicates how long to hold the packet before discarding it. The TTL number for the multicast scope specifies the number of hops the multicast data will take before being dropped.
- Click **NEXT**.

Figure 6.19 Identify the multicast scope from the Multicast Scope Name page.

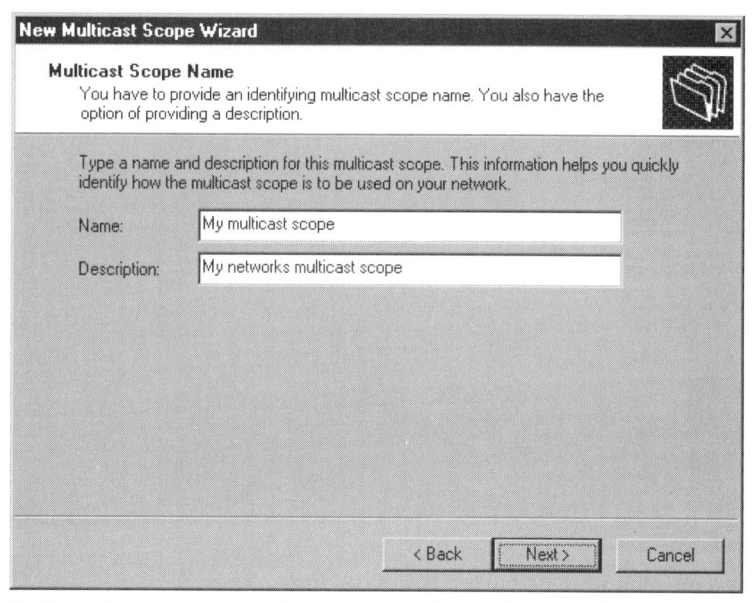

Figure 6.20 Specify the range of addresses from the IP Address Range page.

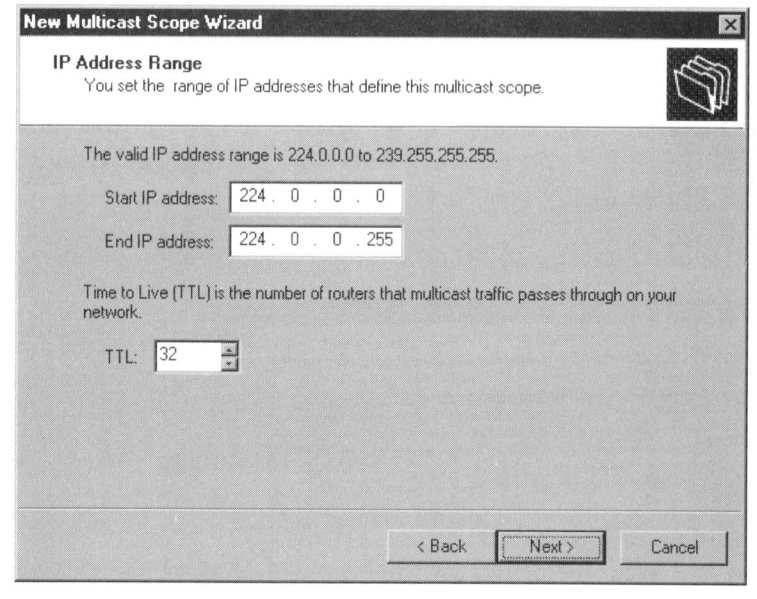

➢ STEP 4

Enter a start and end IP address to specify a range of addresses to exclude in the **Start IP address** and **End IP address** fields, and click **ADD** (Figure 6.21). To remove an excluded range, highlight the range in the **Excluded addresses** box, and click **REMOVE**. Click **NEXT**.

Figure 6.21 Adding address exclusions from the Add Exclusions page.

➤ STEP 5

Specify the amount of time that you want the clients to be able to use an IP address from this multicast scope (Figure 6.22), and click **NEXT**.

➤ STEP 6

Select whether you want to activate the scope (Figure 6.23). You must first activate the scope before clients can start receiving address leases. If you decide not to activate the scope now, you can do so later by selecting the scope and clicking **Activate** from the **Action** menu in the DHCP manager. Click **NEXT**.

Figure 6.22 Limit IP address duration on the Lease Duration page.

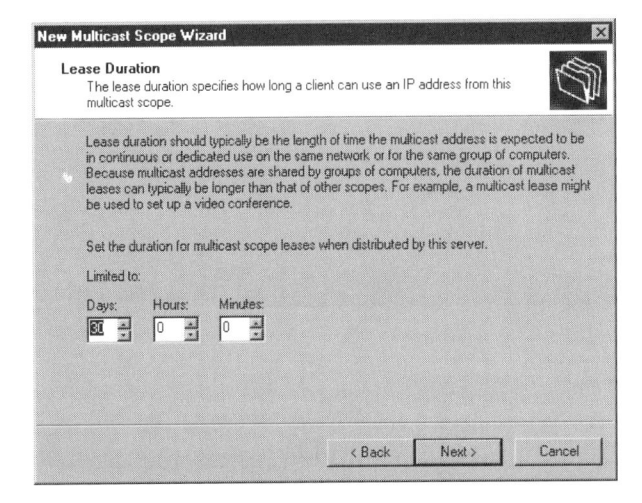

Figure 6.23 Activate multicast scope from the Activate Multicasat Scope Page.

> ## STEP 7

Click **FINISH** to complete the New Multicast Scope Wizard (Figure 6.24).

NOTE

The valid IP address range for a multicast scope must be within the Class D IP address range of 224.0.0.0 to 239.255.255.255.

Figure 6.24 The Completing the New Multicast Scope Wizard Page.

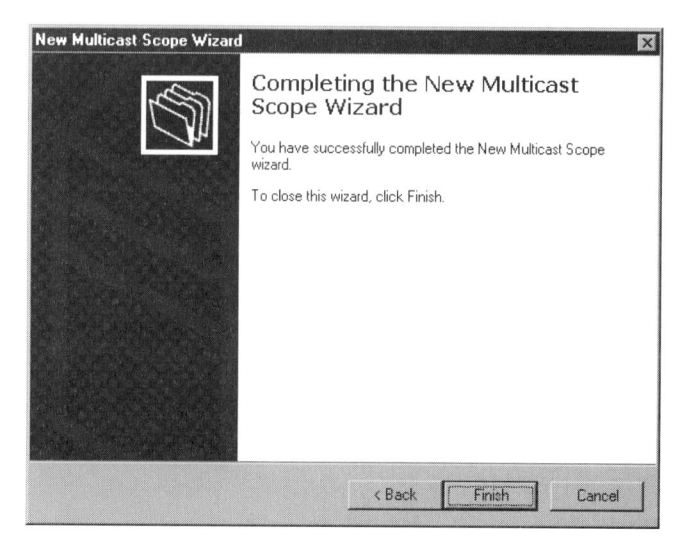

Summary

Windows 2000 provides an easy way to manage IP address assignment via the DHCP manager. Additionally, Windows 2000 provides added support for superscopes and multicast scopes. Using the wizards provided, you create any of the following three types of scopes:

- Scope
- Superscope
- Multicast scope

A scope is a range of IP addresses that can be assigned to DHCP clients. A superscope allows scopes to be grouped to provide IP addresses from multiple logical subnets to clients on a single physical network. A multicast scope provides support for Multicast DHCP.

Additional DHCP servers can be added to the DHCP manager and managed remotely. To configure a scope on any of the DHCP servers, first start the New Scope Wizard. To start any of the wizards, right-click on the selected server from the DHCP manager and select the available options to create one of three scope types. Keep in mind that you will not be able to create a superscope until you have already created one or more scopes.

To create a scope, start the New Scope Wizard, which will walk you through the steps to create the scope. First, you will need to provide a name and description to identify the scope. Next, you provide a range of addresses from which clients will be assigned an IP address. Additionally, if there are any devices that require a static IP address, you can add exclusions so that certain IP addresses will not be distributed. You can also set the duration for the scope that specifies when a distributed IP address will expire. The wizard also allows you to configure additional options that allow clients to obtain an address of a default gateway, DNS server and WINS server, when they obtain their IP address.

To create a superscope, start the New Superscope Wizard. After providing a name to identify your superscope, you then select from a list of available scopes to add to the superscope. For this reason, you will need to first create one or more scopes.

Creating a new multicast scope is much like creating a regular scope. Start the New Multicast Scope Wizard, and enter a name and description to identify the multicast scope. Next, enter a valid IP address range and any exclusions; multicast addresses must fall within the Class D IP address range.

After creating the scopes, they will appear in the DHCP snap-in, and your server will be ready to respond to client DHCP requests.

Chapter 7

Create A New Zone Wizard (DNS)

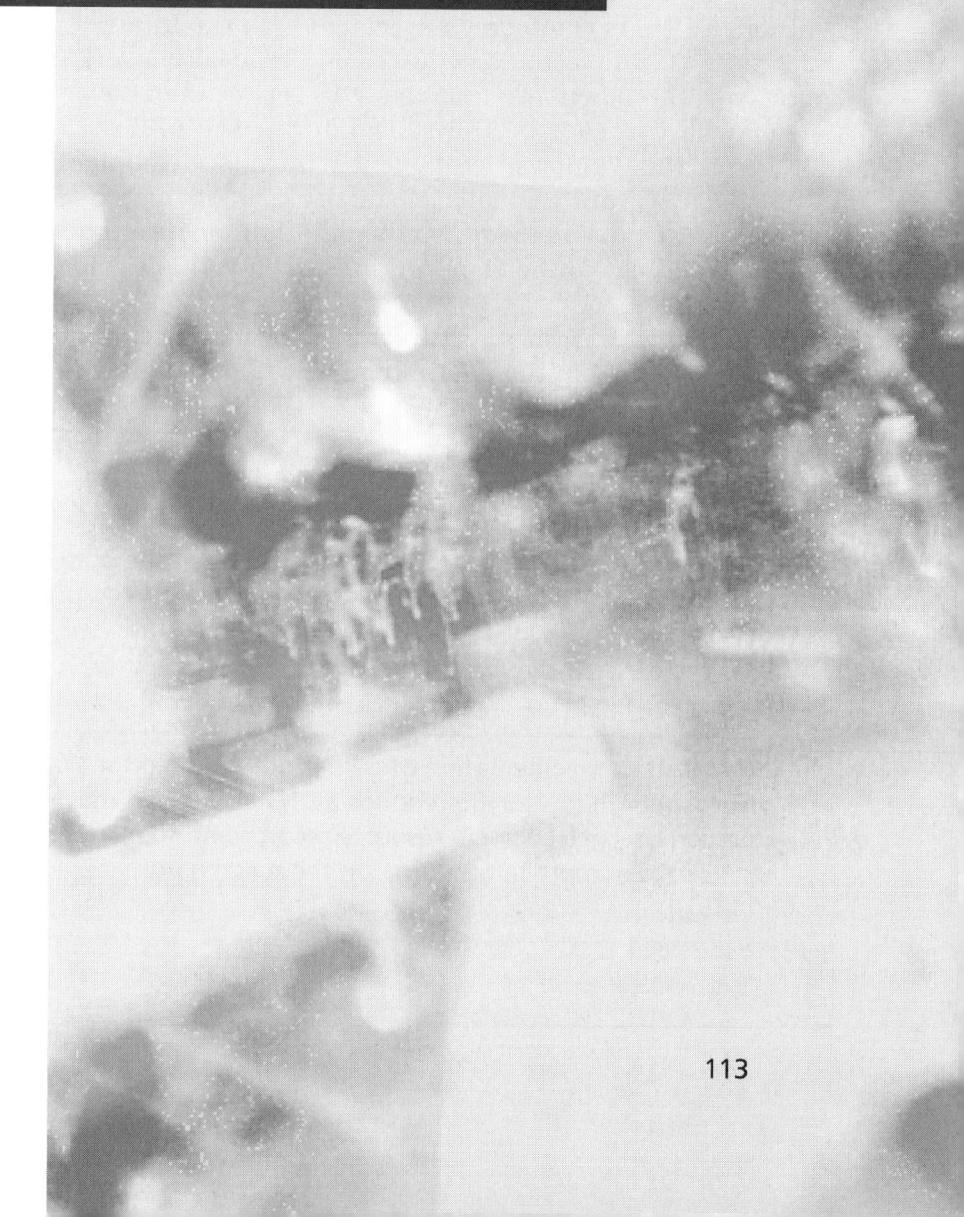

Introduction

As part of making the server a domain/Active Directory server, Windows 2000 prompted you to specify a DNS server. If one for the domain was not available, you were offered the option of making the domain controller a DNS server. Using the Create a New Zone Wizard, you can add new DNS zones to that DNS server or another Windows 2000 DNS server on your network.

Before You Begin

Although DNS is commonly associated with the Internet, Windows 2000 also uses DNS to locate computers on the local network. Before beginning, you should ensure that the DNS service is installed. The DNS service may have already been installed during setup. If not, you can install DNS from the Windows Component Wizard (see Chapter 12, "Windows Component Wizard"). Finally, if you are using dynamic assignment of IP addresses on your network, you should first ensure that you assign a static IP address to the computer on which you are going to install and configure DNS.

Working with DNS is relatively new for many who have only worked with Windows NT in the past. Therefore, it is recommended that you review the Requests for Comments (RFC) about DNS and Dynamic DNS (DDNS): RFCs 1034, 1035, 2136, and 2137.

The Purpose of this Wizard

This wizard walks you through the process of configuring forward and reverse lookup zones. The purpose of these zones is to provide name resolution for resolving host names to IP addresses, and vice versa.

> **NOTE**
>
> Microsoft's implementation of DNS is not required for Windows 2000. Although Windows 2000 requires a DNS server, you may use any server that supports Service Location resource records and the Dynamic Update Protocol. For more information on these standards, see RFCs 2052 and 2136.

Information Needed to Work with this Wizard

To create zones for a DNS server, you will need the following:

- Creating a forward lookup zone
  - Names for the zones you create
- Creating a reverse lookup zone
  - Names for the zones you create
  - Your network's ID

The Create A New Zone Wizard

➤ STEP 1

Start the New Zone Wizard.

- Open DNS in the Administrative Tools menu.
- Right-click the server for which you want to create a new zone (Figure 7.1).
- Select **New Zone** from the pop-up menu.

Figure 7.1 Right-click on the server for which you want to create a new zone.

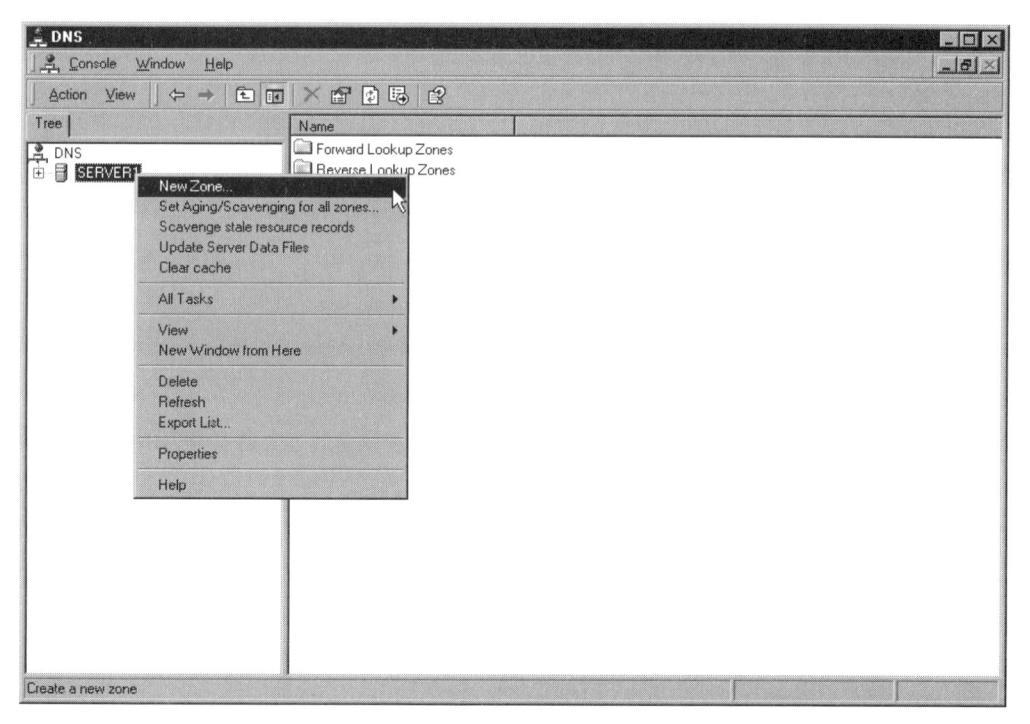

➣ **STEP 2**

Click **NEXT** at the New Zone Wizard welcome page (Figure 7.2).

Figure 7.2 The New Zone Wizard welcome page.

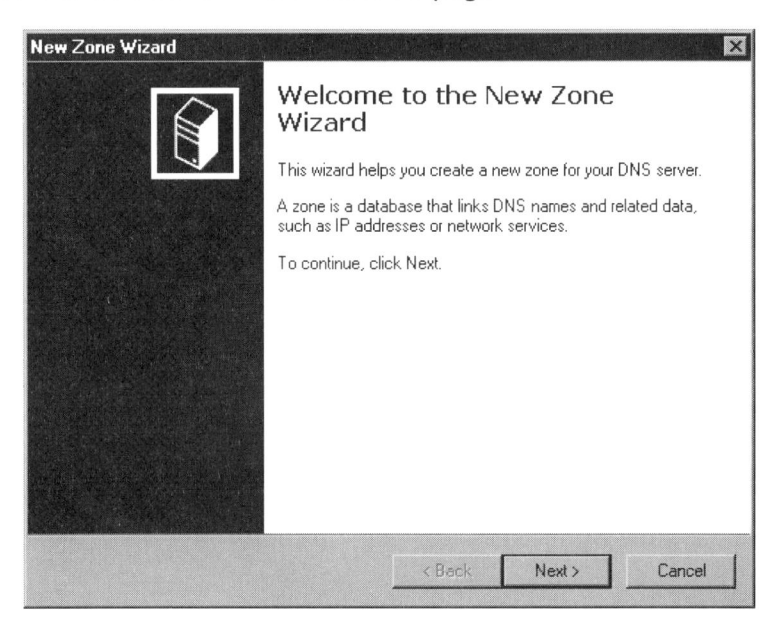

➣ **STEP 3**

Select the type of zone you want to create from the Zone Type page (Figure 7.3), and click **NEXT**. You can select from one of the following three types:

- **Active Directory-integrated**. Instead of storing zone data in standard files, you can store the data within Active Directory. There are several benefits from choosing this method, including:
    - Multimaster dynamic update
    - Secure dynamic updates
    - Additional fault-tolerance support
- **Standard primary**. This creates a standard zone text file. To take advantage of the many features of Windows 2000, it is recommended that you select the Active Directory-integrated zone.
- **Standard secondary**. This type of zone only creates an additional copy of an existing zone to provide for load balancing. Selecting this zone type allows you to browse for other zones from which you can copy.

Figure 7.3 The Zone Type page.

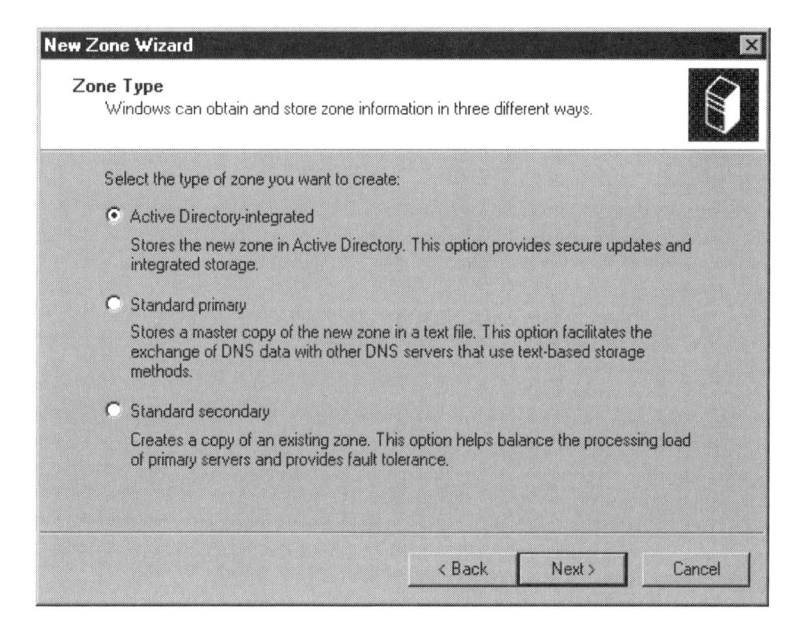

> **NOTE**
>
> To take advantage of the data storage and replication engine provided by an Active Directory-integrated zone, you must run a compatible DNS server located on a domain controller.

➤ STEP 4

Select from one of two types of lookup zones (Figure 7.4).

- A **forward lookup zone** resolves host names to IP addresses.
- A **reverse lookup zone** resolves IP addresses to host names. If you select this option, proceed to Step 7.

> **NOTE**
>
> You must configure at least one forward lookup zone for DNS. Reverse lookup is not required for Windows 2000 and Active Directory, but it can be useful for diagnosing various networking problems.

Figure 7.4 Forward or Reverse Lookup Zone page.

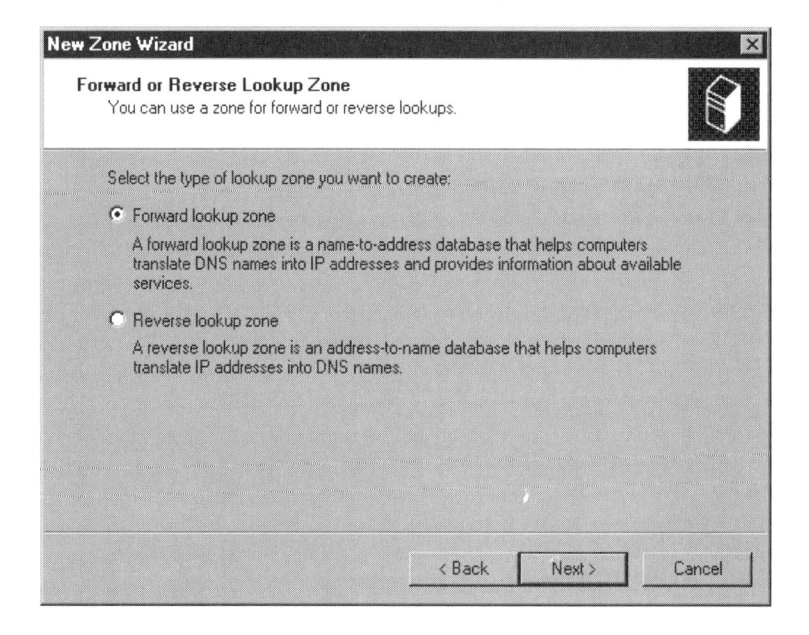

➢ STEP 5

Enter a name for the forward lookup zone, and click **NEXT** (Figure 7.5). If you previously chose to create an Active Directory-integrated zone, proceed to Step 9 after entering the zone name.

A zone name is normally named after the highest domain that the zone has authority over. For example, a zone name of domain.com would cover domain.com and marketing.domain.com.

If you chose to create a standard secondary forward lookup zone, you can click **BROWSE** to find a zone to copy (Figure 7.6).

➢ STEP 6

Select the zone file that you want to use from the Zone File page from one of the following two choices (Figure 7.7):

- **Create a new file with this filename**. This option will create a new file with a default name based on the name of the DNS zone entered earlier. Alternatively, you may enter a new name.
- **Use this existing file**. This option allows you to use an existing file. To select this option, you must have first copied the existing file into the %SystemRoot%\system32\dns folder.

After making your selection, click **NEXT** and proceed to Step 9.

Figure 7.5 Forward Zone Name page.

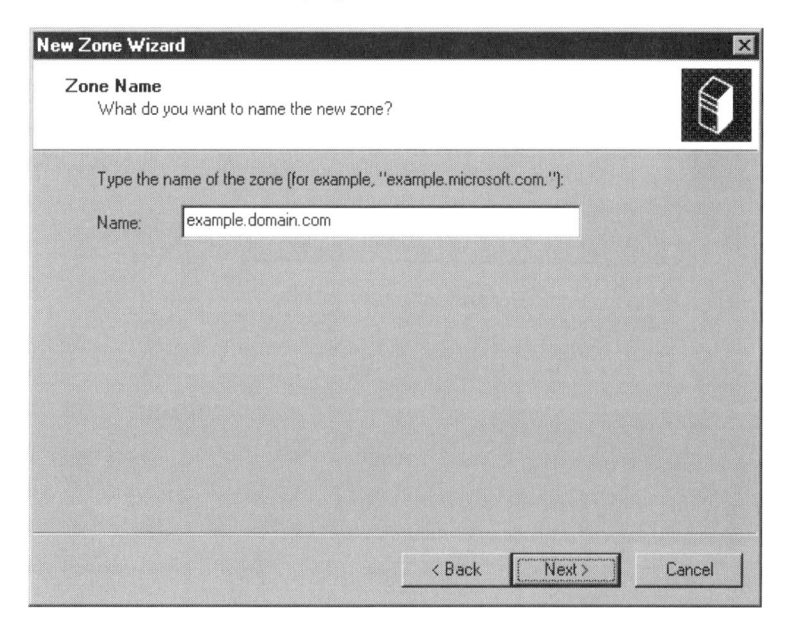

Figure 7.6 Click BROWSE to search for a forward lookup zone object type.

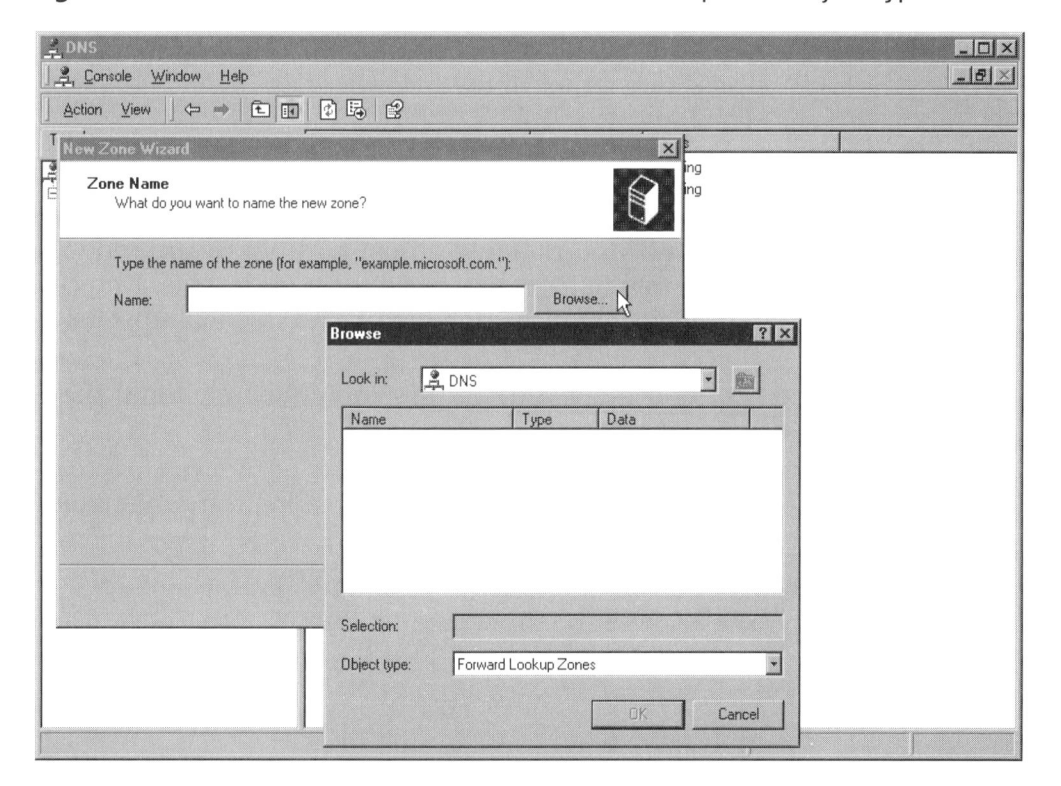

Figure 7.7 Forward Zone File page.

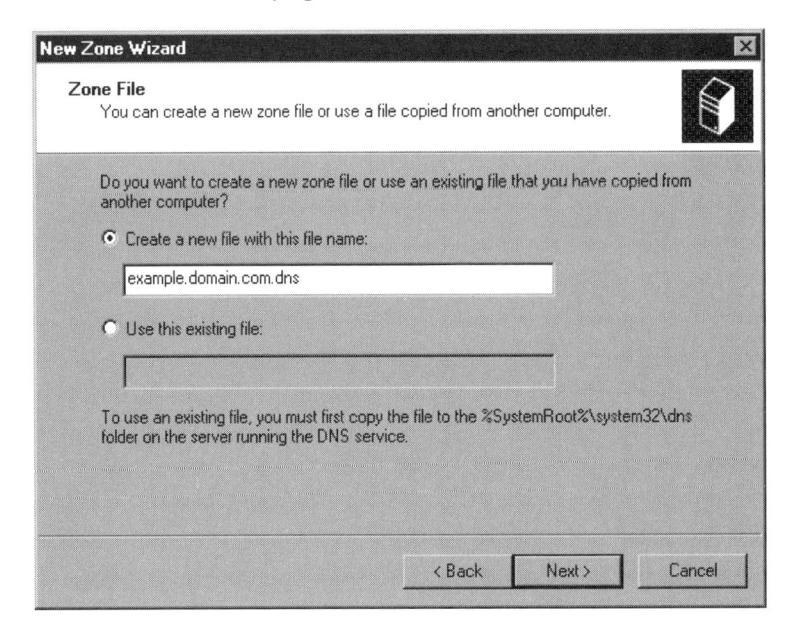

➤ STEP 7

- Identify the reverse lookup zone (Figure 7.8). You may specify the zone by selecting either of the following:
  - Network ID
  - Reverse lookup zone name
- If you select Network ID, enter the **network ID**. An IP address consists of a network portion and a host portion. By entering a network ID, you are omitting any of the host addresses. Entering a network ID will automatically create the reverse lookup zone name.
- If you did not enter a network ID, you can optionally input the reverse lookup zone name.
- Click **NEXT**. If you previously chose to create an Active Directory-integrated zone, proceed to Step 9 after entering the zone name or network ID.

If you selected to create a standard secondary reverse lookup zone, you can click **BROWSE** to find a zone to copy (Figure 7.9).

Figure 7.8 Reverse Lookup Zone page.

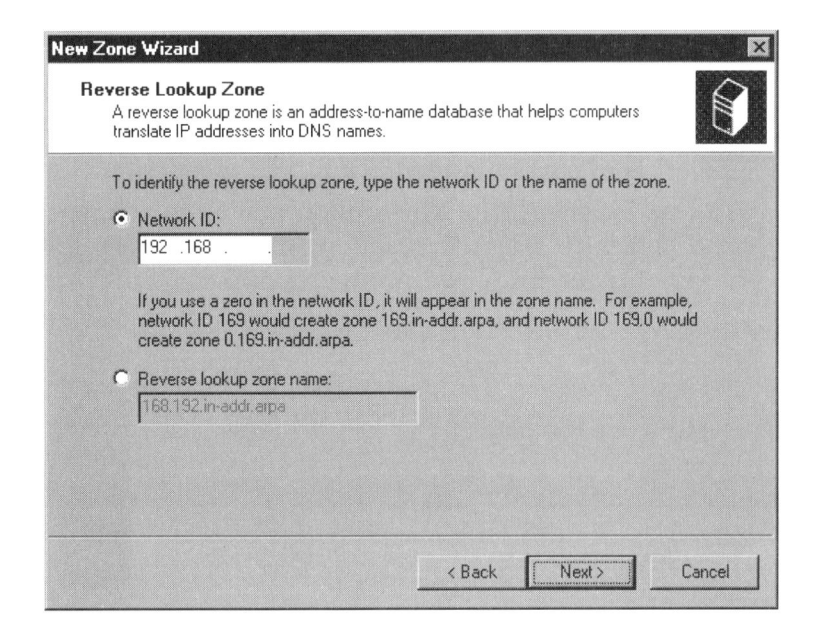

Figure 7.9 Click BROWSE to search for a reverse lookup zone object type.

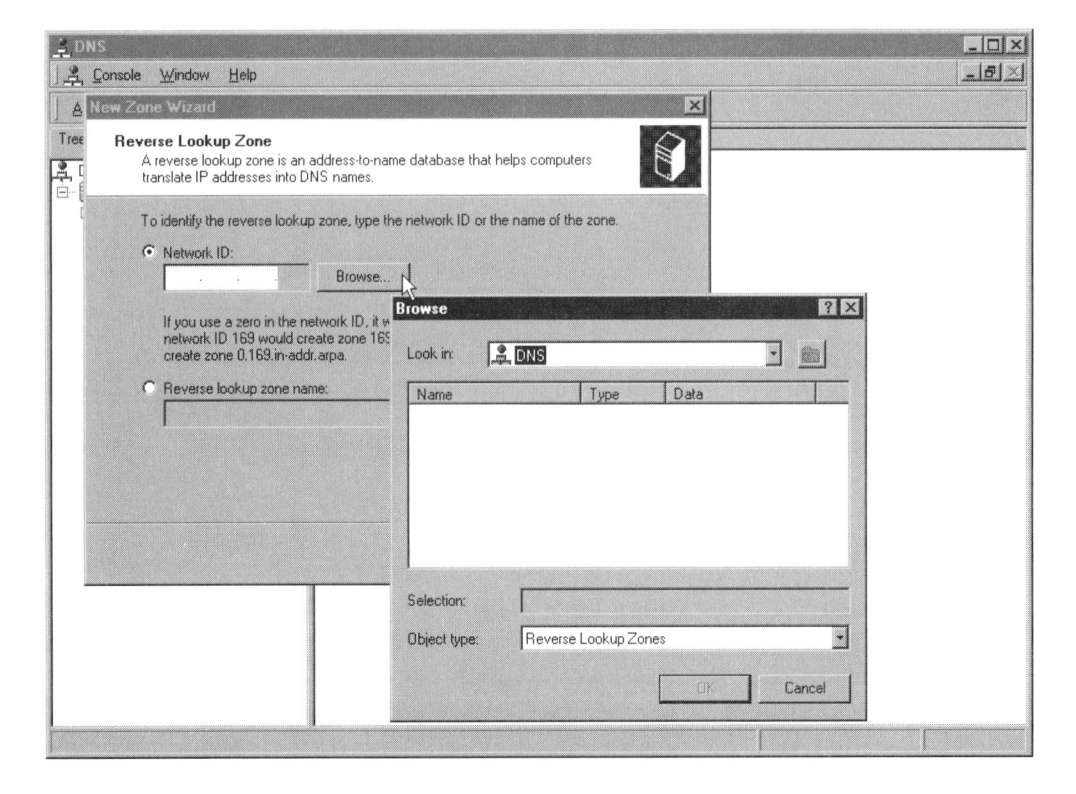

➢ STEP 8

Select the zone file that you want to use from the Zone File page from one of the following two choices (Figure 7.10):

- **Create a new file with this filename**. This option will create a new file with a default name based on the name of the DNS zone entered earlier. Alternatively, you may enter a new name.
- **Use this existing file**. This option allows you to use an existing file. To select this option, you must have first copied the existing file into the %SystemRoot%\system32\dns folder.

After making your selection, click **NEXT**.

Figure 7.10 Reverse Zone File page.

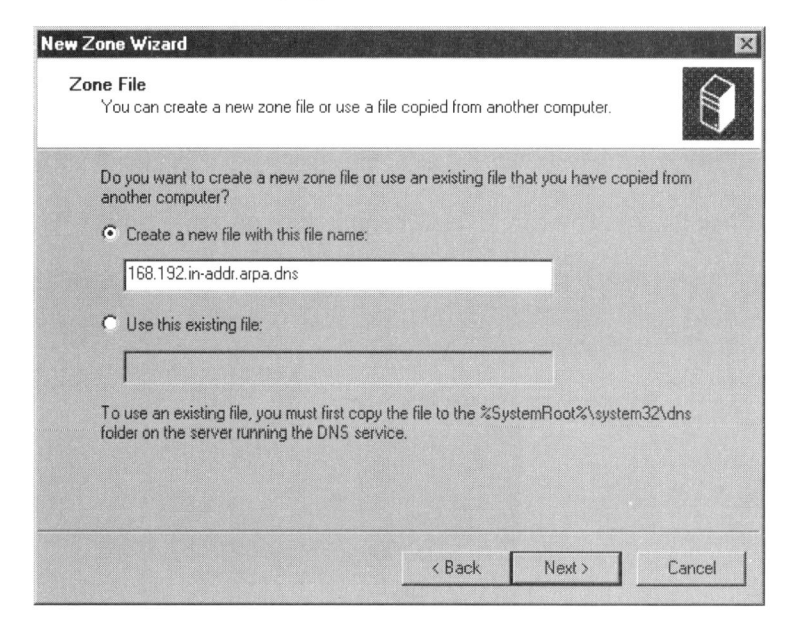

➢ STEP 9

The Completing the New Zone Wizard page will display a summary of what was completed (Figure 7.11). Click **FINISH** to close the New Zone Wizard.

When you create a zone, two resource records are automatically added underneath the zone: the Start of Authority (SOA) and the Name Server (NS). To add additional resource records, use the DNS manager, right-click the zone for which you want to add additional resource records, and click **NEW**. Numerous types of records can be added. Table 7.1 lists the most common resource records and their descriptions.

Figure 7.11 Completing the New Zone Wizard page.

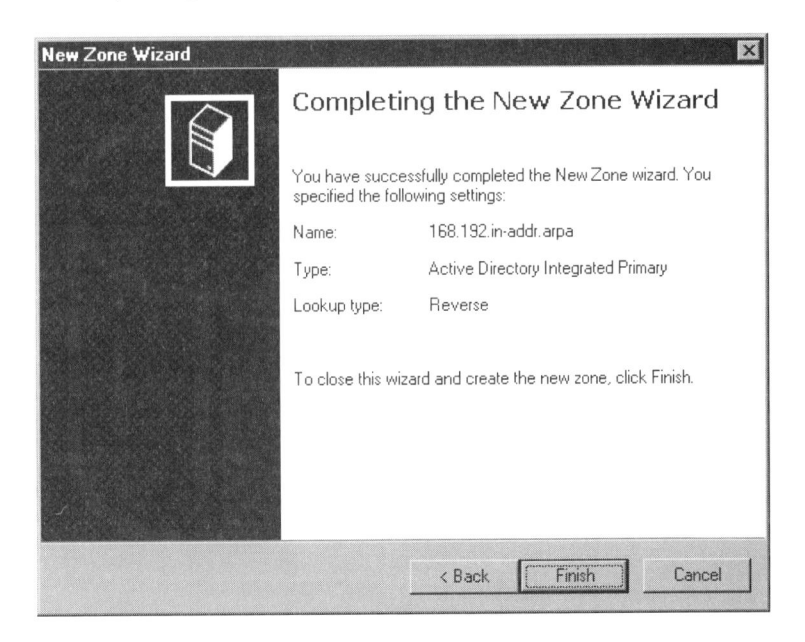

Table 7.1 Common Types of Resource Records

Resource Record	DNS Manager Name	Description
SOA	Start of Authority	Marks the beginning of a DNS zone and identifies which name server is authoritative.
A	Host	Match domain names to IP addresses.
CNAME	Alias	Specifies an alias or another name for the specified host. Use a CNAME to map more than one name to a single IP address.
PTR	Pointer	Points to another location in the domain namespace. Used to construct the in-addr.arpa domain for converting IP addresses to domain names.
NS	Name Server	Supplies the domain name of a name server for the zone.
MX	Mail Exchanger	Identifies the mail exchanger for a specific domain.

A feature of Microsoft's implementation of DNS is its support for *dynamic updates*. As described in RFC 2136, dynamic updates allow clients to dynamically update their resource records when changes occur. An obvious benefit of this is decreased administration. If you create an Active Directory-integrated zone, Windows will default to secure dynamic updates. If, however, you create a zone, you can still enable dynamic updates by opening the properties for your zone and selecting **Yes** from the **Allow Dynamic Updates** pull-down list (Figure 7.12).

Figure 7.12 Allow dynamic updates via a zone's properties.

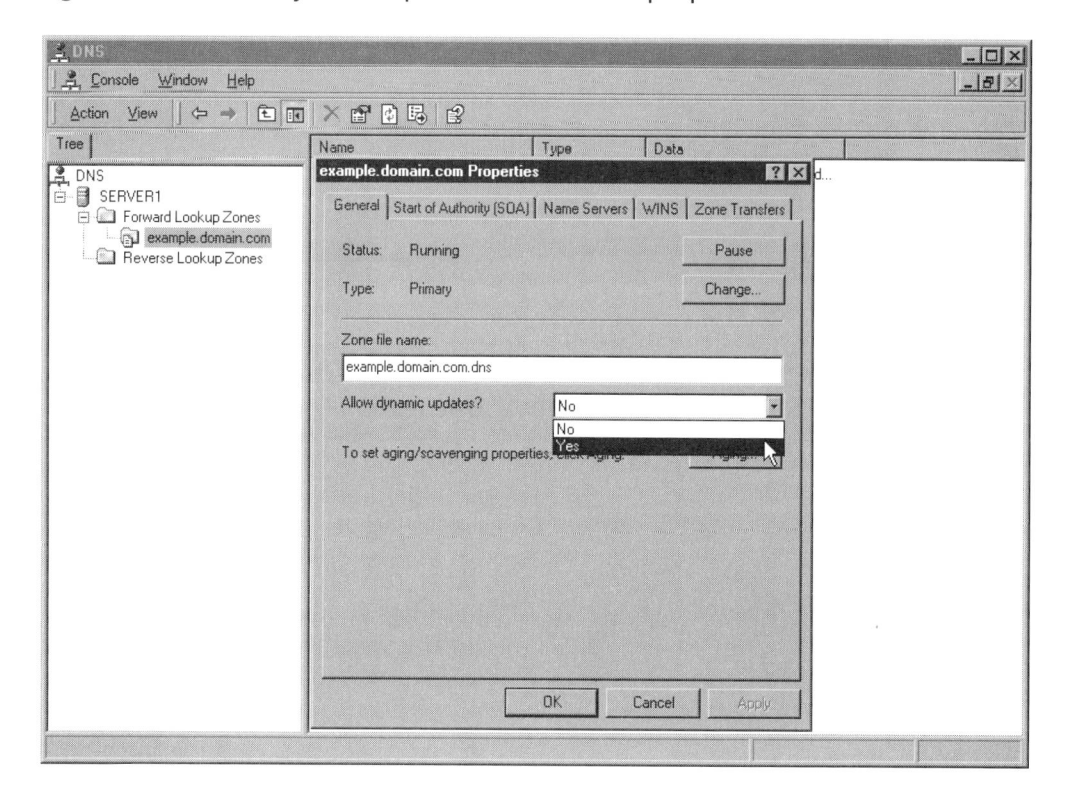

Summary

The DNS Manager (DNS snap-in) allows you to configure and manage DNS in Windows 2000. Before you can use DNS, however, you will need to create a forward lookup zone. Additionally, you can also create a reverse lookup zone.

Using the Create New Zone Wizard, you can create forward lookup zones and reverse lookup zones. A forward lookup zone resolves names to IP addresses, whereas a reverse lookup zone resolves IP addresses to names. The wizard allows you to create a forward lookup or reverse lookup zone based on the following three types:

- Active Directory-integrated
- Standard primary
- Standard secondary

Choosing to create an Active Directory-integrated zone is the preferred method in Windows 2000, primarily because of the secure, dynamic, and integrated features this method provides. You may, however, also create a standard primary zone, which stores a master copy of the zone in a text file, or you may create a standard secondary zone, which creates a copy of an existing zone to provide load balancing and fault tolerance.

After selecting the type of zone you want to create, you need to provide a name for the zone. Choosing to create an Active Directory-integrated zone will cause the zone name to be integrated within Active Directory. On the other hand, a standard zone will create a file based on the name you enter.

The Create New Zone Wizard configures the DNS service by creating the new zones; however, you can use the DNS Manager to add additional resource records, as well as configure the dynamic properties of DNS.

Chapter 8
Routing and Remote Access Configuration Wizard

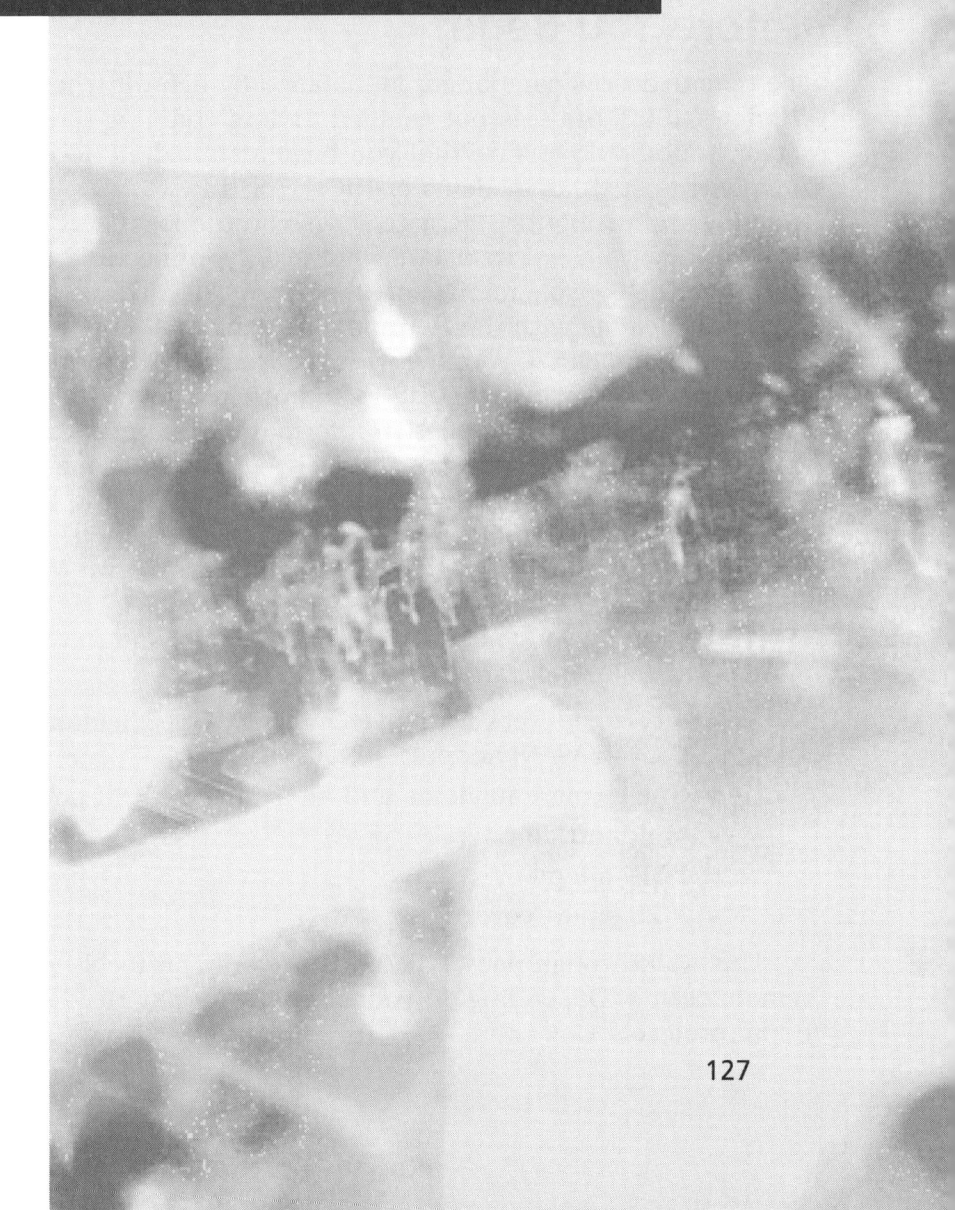

Introduction

Windows 2000 Server can act as a remote access server, allowing your users access to the company network via either dial-up connection or direct connections over the Internet. In order for remote access services to work, the Windows 2000 server must route between the remote connections and the company network. Routing can also be applied to a server with two or more network interface cards (NIC). By the end of this chapter, you will have configured Windows 2000 for remote access clients and as a router.

Before You Begin

The remote access component is installed by default when you install Windows 2000, but it is not enabled. Before enabling the remote access server, you should ensure that you have installed all necessary hardware components such as modems or NICs. For this wizard, we will be enabling and configuring remote access on the local server. The local server is always listed by default; however, you may add additional servers to the console management screen if needed.

Before dealing with the Routing and Remote Access Server Service, you should familiarize yourself with the Remote Authentication Dial-in User Service (RADIUS). RADIUS is an authentication server that provides authorization and authentication information to a network server to which a client is attempting to connect. Windows 2000 can act as a RADIUS server, RADIUS client, or both. RFCs 2138 and 2139 provide detailed information about RADIUS.

To configure the Routing and Remote Access Server Wizard, you must be logged on as an Administrator.

Depending on your network and your needs, you may require one or more of the following hardware devices:

- A certified Network Driver Interface Specification (NDIS) network (LAN or WAN) adapter
- One or more modems and an available COM port
- Multiport adapter
- ISDN adapter
- X.25 smart card

This walkthrough uses TCP/IP as the only protocol needed for the remote clients. Depending on your needs, you may need to install additional protocols.

The Purpose of this Wizard

The Routing and Remote Access Server Wizard allows you to configure your system as a dial-in or Virtual Private Network (VPN) server to accept incoming connections. Earlier, you saw that you could use the Network Connection Wizard to also configure inbound connections; however, you can only use that wizard if your computer is not a member of a domain. The Routing and Remote Access Server is a powerful tool for configuring inbound connections, and is used when the computer is a member of a domain.

> **NOTE**
>
> Routing and Remote Access Service (RRAS) also functions as a software-based router. This Windows 2000 router should only be used by those already familiar with routing protocols and services.

Information Needed to Work with this Wizard

Before performing the following tasks, ensure you have the following information:

- Start and end IP address range. You may use DHCP. In this walkthrough, we also show you how to specify from a pool of IP addresses.
- Primary and Alternate RADIUS Server address.
- RADIUS shared secret password.

The Routing and Remote Access Configuration Wizard

➢ **STEP 1**

Start the Routing and Remote Access Server Setup Wizard.

- Open **Routing and Remote Access** from the Administrative Tools menu.
- Right-click the server for which you want to configure RRAS (Figure 8.1).
- Click Configure and Enable Routing and Remote Access from the pop-up menu.

Figure 8.1 Right-click on the server you want to configure and enable for RRAS.

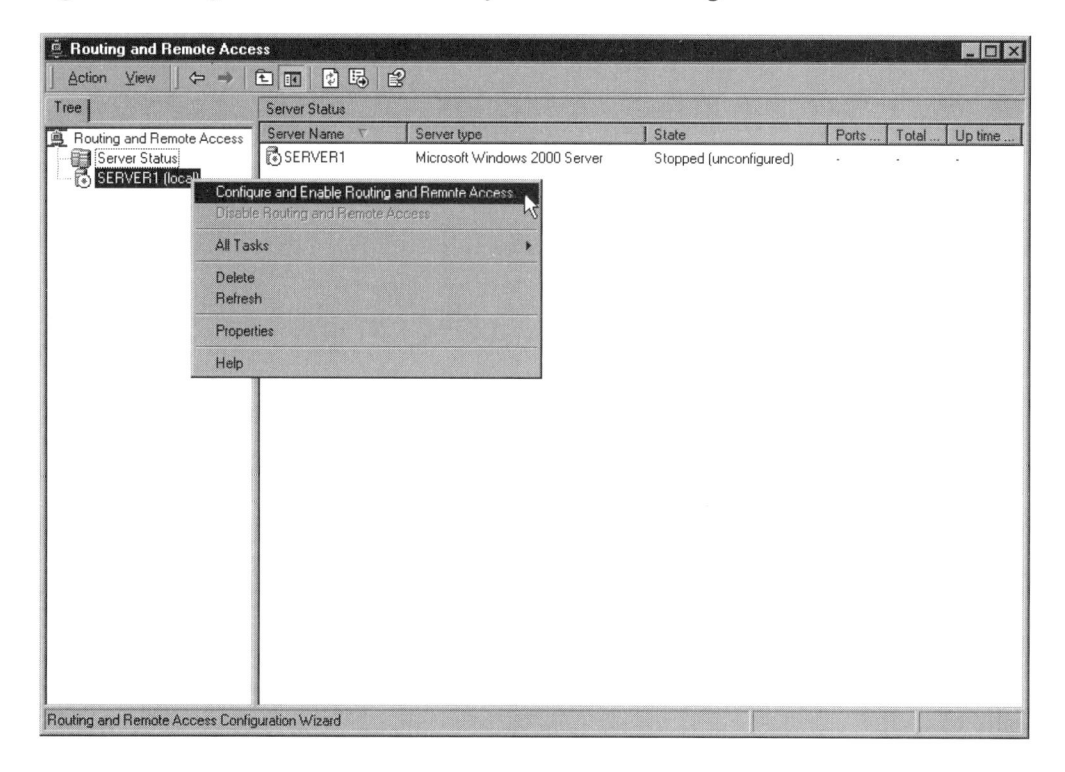

➤ **STEP 2**

Click **NEXT** at the Routing and Remote Access Server Setup Wizard welcome page (Figure 8.2).

➤ **STEP 3**

There are several options available from the Common Configurations page (Figure 8.3). Although each of the choices will walk you through the same steps, depending on your selection, the wizard will transparently configure and enable the needed services and protocol.

To continue with configuring the remote access server, select **Remote access server**, and click **NEXT**.

NOTE

Once you perform the remote access server setup, you will be unable to perform any of the other options from within the wizard unless you first disable routing and remote access. This wizard focuses on the initial setup of the remote access server; however, after configuring the remote access server, you can access the options available to configure the other features via the Properties of the remote access server.

Figure 8.2 The Routing and Remote Access Server Setup Wizard welcome page.

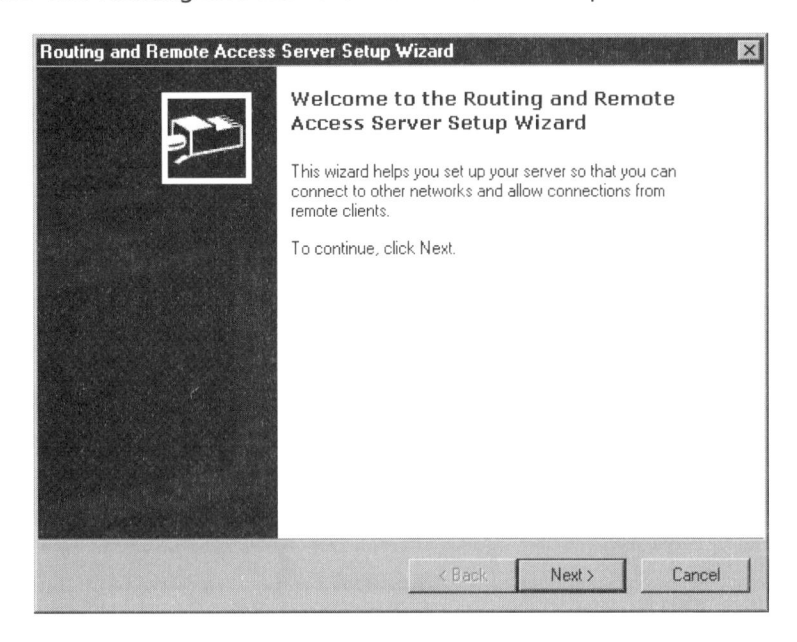

Figure 8.3 Common Configurations page.

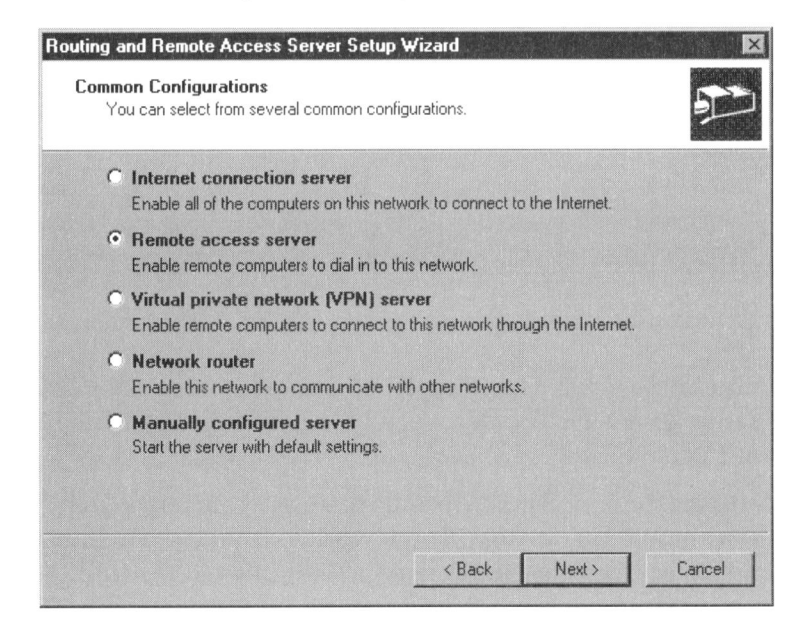

➣ STEP 4

Ensure the required protocols are available on your server (Figure 8.4). The most common protocol in use today is TCP/IP.

- If the required protocols are listed, ensure **Yes, all of the required protocols are on the list** is selected, and click **NEXT**.
- If the required protocols are not listed, select **No, I need to add protocols**. When you have finished installing the needed protocols, restart the wizard.

Figure 8.4 Remote Client Protocols page.

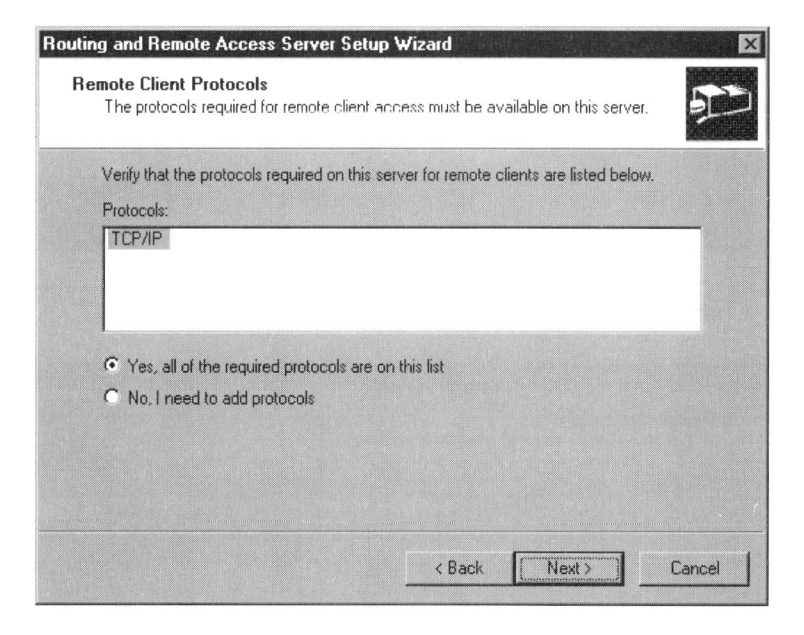

➣ STEP 5

Select the method for assigning IP addresses to remote clients. You may specify to assign IP addresses by selecting one of the following choices (Figure 8.5):

- **Automatically**. Select Automatically if you use a DHCP service to automatically assign IP addresses. If you select Automatically, and do not have a DHCP server, Windows 2000 will automatically assign an address using the Automatic IP addressing feature. If you select this option, proceed to Step 7.
- **From a specified range of addresses**. Select this option to specify in the next step a range of IP addresses that the server will automatically assign to clients.

Figure 8.5 IP Address Assignment page.

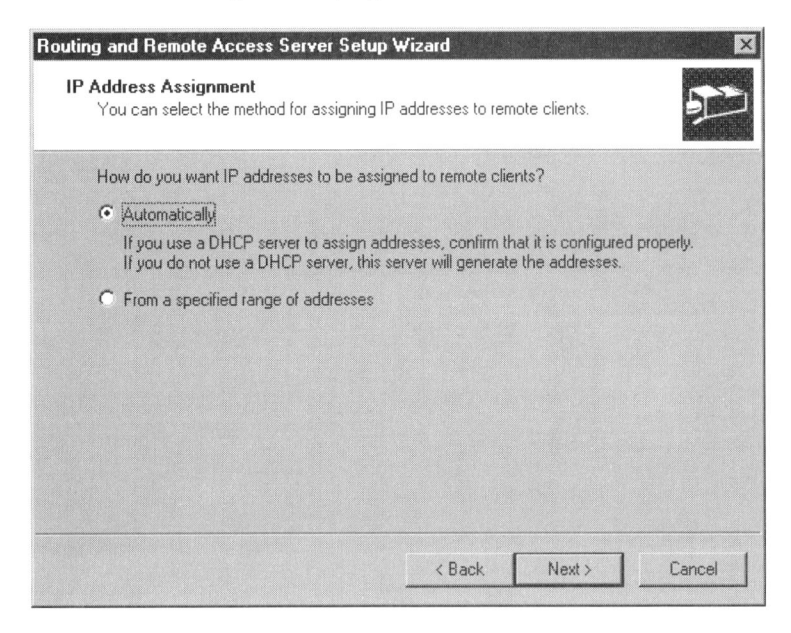

➢ STEP 6

If you choose to apply IP addresses from a specified range, you will need to perform the following procedures from the Address Range Assignment page (Figure 8.6):

- Click **ADD**.
- Insert a Start IP address and an End IP address.
- Click **OK** to close the New Address Range dialog box, and click **NEXT** to continue.

➢ STEP 7

The next step is to decide if you want to use a Remote Authentication Dial-In User Service server (RADIUS) to manage multiple remote access servers (Figure 8.7).

- If you have an existing RADIUS server that you would like this remote access server to use, select **Yes, I want to use a RADIUS server**, and click **NEXT**.
- If you do not want to use a RADIUS server, select **No, I don't want to set up this server to use RADIUS now**, click **NEXT**, and proceed to Step 9.

Figure 8.6 Entering an address range from the Address Range Assignment page.

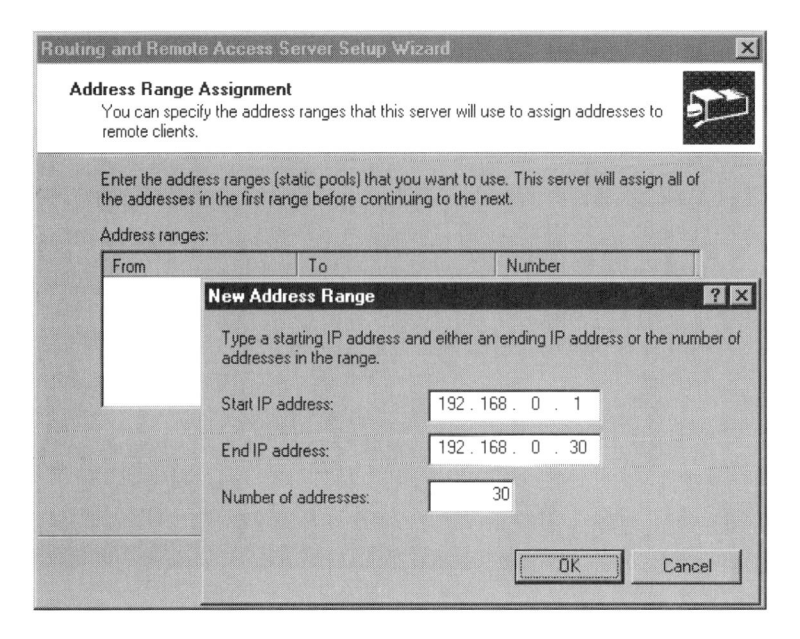

RADIUS is an industry-standard protocol that provides services for distributed dial-up networking. RADIUS servers are primarily used by ISPs and corporate remote access users. These servers take connection information from a RADIUS client, which is usually a dial-up server, and then authenticate and authorize the client request.

➢ STEP 8

If you selected to use a RADIUS server in the previous step, you will need to specify the RADIUS server (Figure 8.8). If you selected to not use RADIUS, proceed to the next step.

- Enter the name for a primary RADIUS server and an alternate if you have one.
- Enter the shared secret password to connect to the RADIUS server.

➢ STEP 9

You have finished setting up Routing and Remote Access (Figure 8.9).

- If you want to display help about managing the remote access server, select the available check box.
- Click **FINISH** to close the wizard.

Figure 8.7 Managing Multiple Remote Access Servers page.

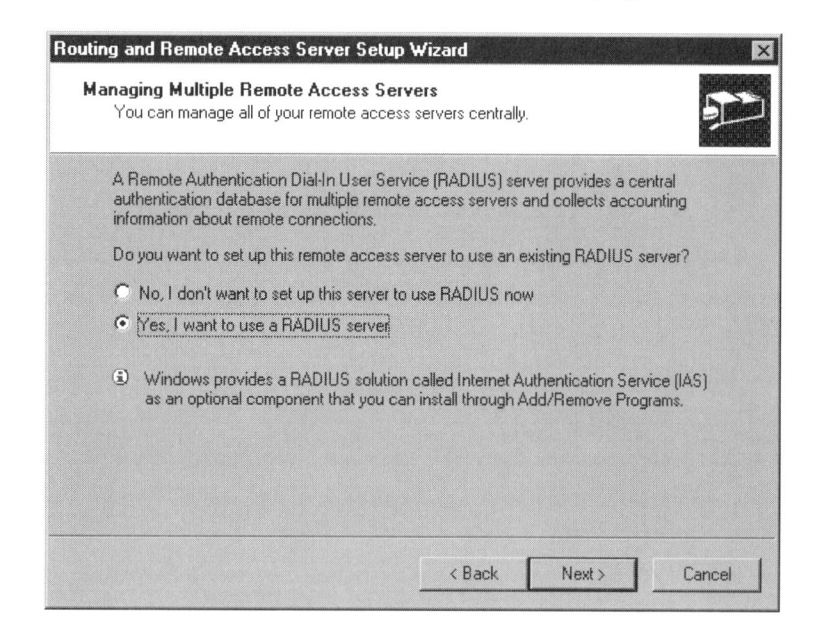

Figure 8.8 RADIUS Server Selection page.

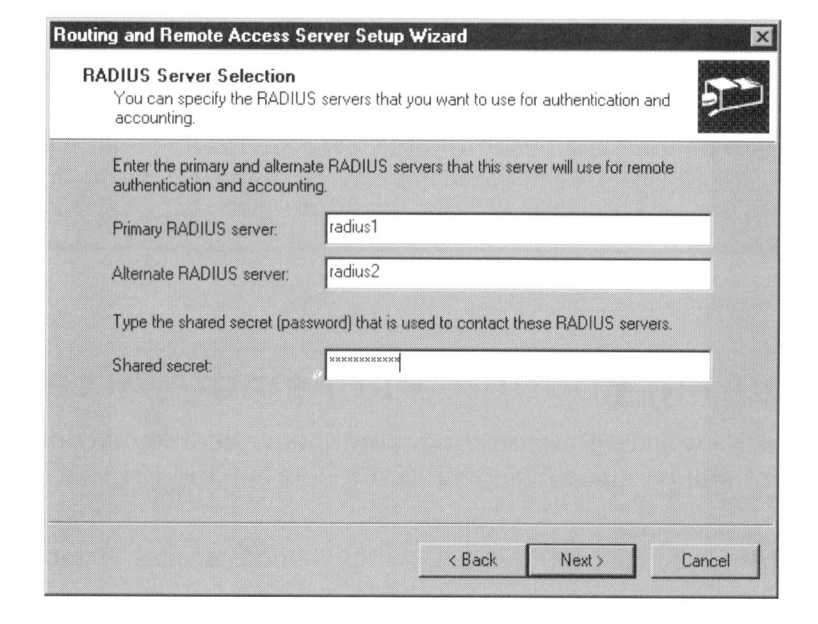

Figure 8.9 Completing the Routing and Remote Access Server Setup Wizard page.

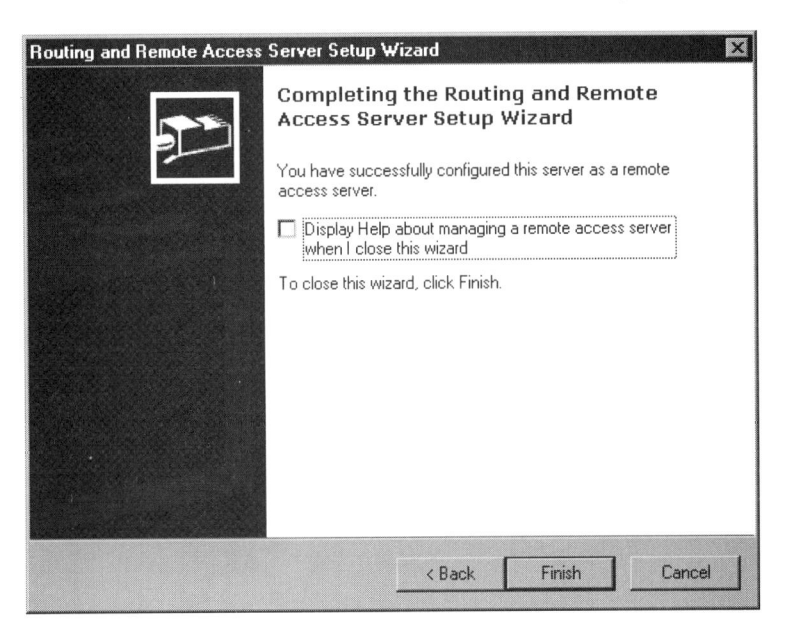

> **NOTE**
>
> After proceeding once through the wizard, you are no longer able to repeat the wizard on the same server for other services. Use the Routing and Remote Access manager to configure user accounts, set permissions, and configure advanced remote access options.

Configuring Routing and Remote Access

Once you have worked through the wizard, many additional configuration changes can still be made from within the Routing and Remote Access manager.

- After completing the Routing and Remote Access Wizard, open **Routing and Remote Access** from the Administrative Tools menu.
- Right-click the server icon, and select **Properties** (Figure 8.10).

Figure 8.10 To configure the RRAS server, select Properties.

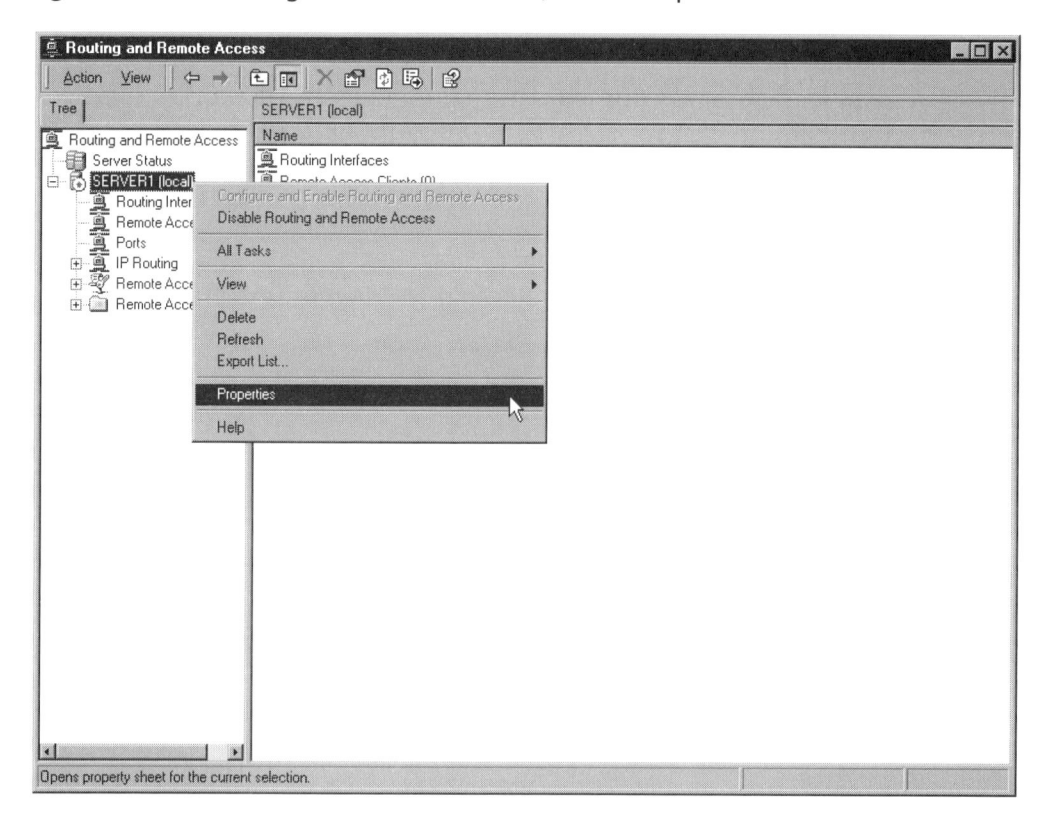

➢ STEP 1

From the server Properties, there are five tabs from which you can configure additional properties (Figure 8.11):

- General
- Security
- IP
- PPP
- Event Logging

If you performed the wizard earlier in this chapter, the box enabling this system as **Remote Access Server** from the **General** tab should be checked. This indicates that the computer is enabled as a remote access server, and is ready to support dial-up or VPN connections. In addition, you can also select **Router**, which will enable the server to forward network traffic between networks. If you select to enable the computer as a router, you need to choose one of the following types of routing the server will perform:

- **Local Area Network (LAN) routing only** configures the server as a LAN-only router, and does not allow demand dial or VPN connections.
- **LAN and demand dial routing** configures the server as a LAN and demand dial router, which will support VPN connections.

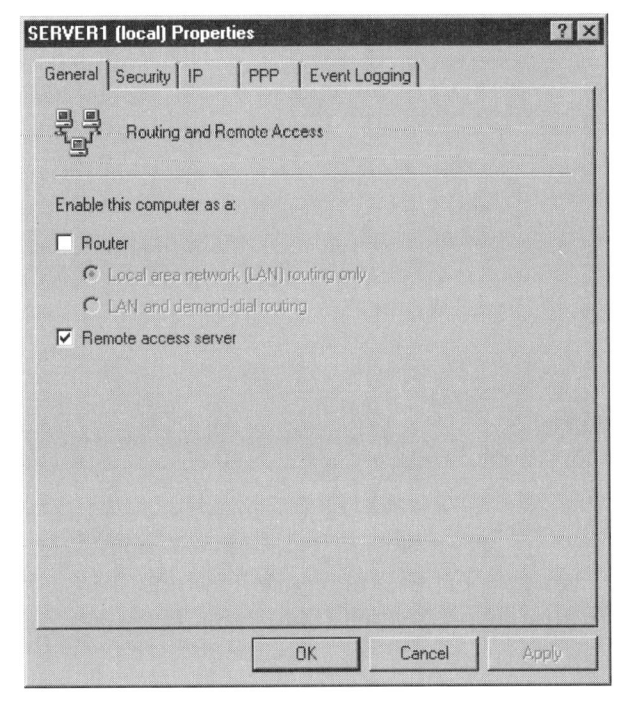

Figure 8.11 General properties tab for Routing and Remote Access.

> **STEP 2**

From the **Security** tab (Figure 8.12), you can configure the authentication and accounting provider for your server. Depending on whether you are using a RADIUS server, you can configure authentication and accounting for either Windows or Radius. From the Authentication Provider pull-down list, you can select one of the following:

- **Windows Authentication.** A Windows account database is used to authenticate connections.

- **RADIUS Authentication**. A RADIUS server is used to authenticate connections.

Click **Authentication Methods** to select the methods by which the server will authenticate remote sessions or to allow allowed connections not requiring authentication. Table 8.1 outlines the various authentication protocols supported.

Table 8.1 Authentication Methods Available in Windows 2000 RRAS

Authentication Method	Description
Extensible Authentication Protocol (EAP)	Uses the Extensible Authentication Protocol (EAP) for authentication. EAP supports various authentication schemes such as Generic Token Card, MD5-Challenge, Transport Level Security (TLS) for smart card support, and S/Key.
Microsoft Encrypted Authentication Version 2 (MS-CHAP v2)	Uses Microsoft Challenge Handshake Authentication Protocol (MS-CHAP) version 2 for authentication. This method provides stronger encryption and is required (or version 1) for encrypted Point-to-Point (PPP) or Point-to-Point Tunneling Protocol (PPTP) connections.
Microsoft Encrypted Authentication (MS-CHAP)	Uses the Microsoft Challenge Handshake Authentication Protocol (MS-CHAP) for authentication. This method (or version 2) is required for encrypted Point-to-Point (PPP) or Point-to-Point Tunneling Protocol (PPTP) connections.
Encrypted Authentication (CHAP)	Uses the Message Digest 5 (MD-5) Challenge Handshake Authentication Protocol (CHAP) for authentication. This challenge-response authentication protocol uses an industry-standard hashing scheme for encryption.
Shiva Password Authentication Protocol (SPAP)	Uses the Shiva Password Authentication Protocol (SPAP) for authentication. This method is more secure than plaintext, but less secure than CHAP or MS-CHAP.
Unencrypted Password (PAP)	Uses the Password Authentication Protocol (PAP) for authentication. Passwords are sent in plaintext. Typically used only when two systems cannot negotiate another method.

Finally, you can select one of the following accounting providers, which maintain a log of connections.

- **Windows Accounting.** Maintains log files located in the Remote Access Logging folder available from the RRAS console.
- **RADIUS Accounting.** Maintains log information, which is stored on a RADIUS server.

Figure 8.12 Security properties tab for Routing and Remote Access.

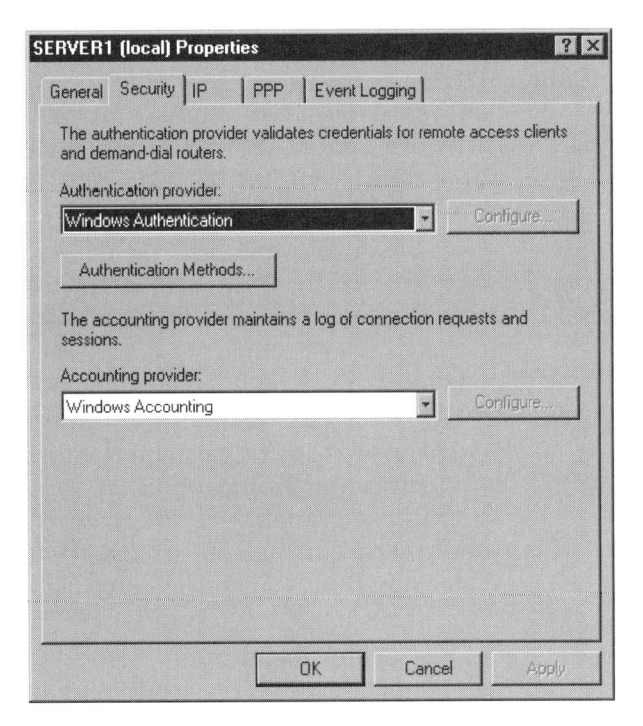

> **STEP 3**

From the **IP** tab, you can make IP configurations to your RRAS server (Figure 8.13). You can select from the following:

- **Enable IP routing** allows packets to be forwarded from one routing interface to another. This must be enabled for remote access clients to access the entire network, or they will only be able to access resources on the server.
- **Allow IP-based remote access and demand-dial connections** permits IP-based remote access demand-dial connections.
- **IP address assignment**

- **Dynamic Host Configuration Protocol (DHCP)** allows clients to be dynamically assigned IP addresses from a DHCP server.
- **Static address pool** allows clients to be dynamically assigned IP addresses from a specified static range of addresses.

Figure 8.13 IP properties tab for Routing and Remote Access.

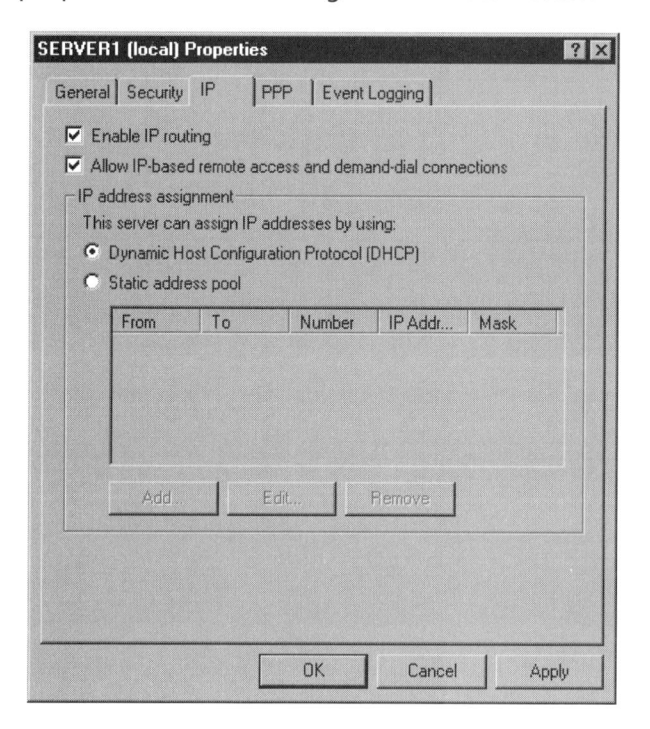

➤ STEP 4

From the **PPP** tab, you can specify the server to use the following point-to-point protocol options (Figure 8.14):

- **Multilink connections** allows remote clients and demand-dial routers to combine more than one physical connection into one logical connection.
  - **Dynamic bandwidth control using BAP or BACP** permits the server to use Bandwidth Allocation Protocol (BAP) and Bandwidth Allocation Control Protocol (BACP) to control multiple physical clients for remote clients and demand-dial routers. These protocols can control bandwidth by dynamically deleting and adding physical connections.

- **Link control protocol (LCP) extensions** allows LCP to send Time-Remaining and Identification packets, as well as request callback during negotiation.
- **Software compression** allows data sent to be compressed.

Figure 8.14 PPP properties tab for Routing and Remote Access.

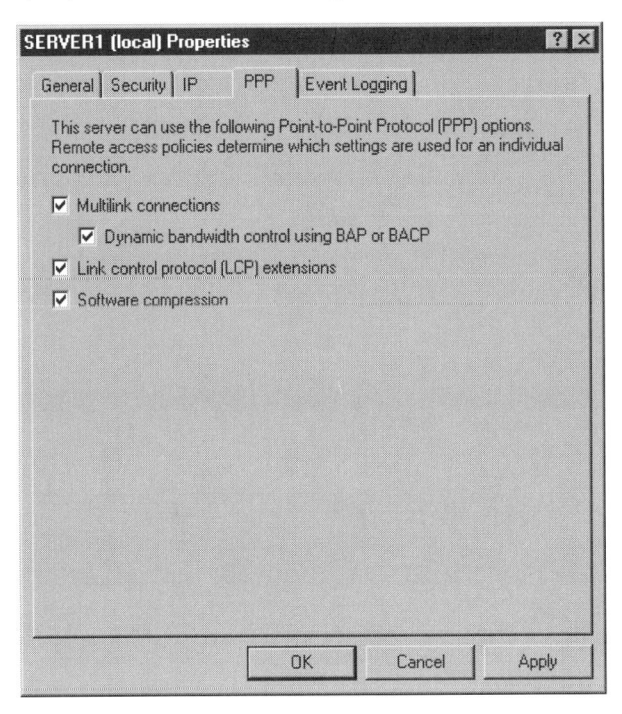

➢ STEP 5

From the **Event Logging** tab, you can specify how logs and warnings are written to Event Viewer using the following options (Figure 8.15):

- **Log errors only** will log only errors in the System Log.
- **Log errors and warnings** will log errors and warnings in the System Log.
- **Log the maximum amount of information** will log everything in the System Log.
- **Disable event logging** will not make any log entries in the System Log.

Additionally, you can check **Enable Point-to-Point Protocol (PPP) logging** so connection establishment events are written to the Ppp.log file in the Tracing folder of the systemroot.

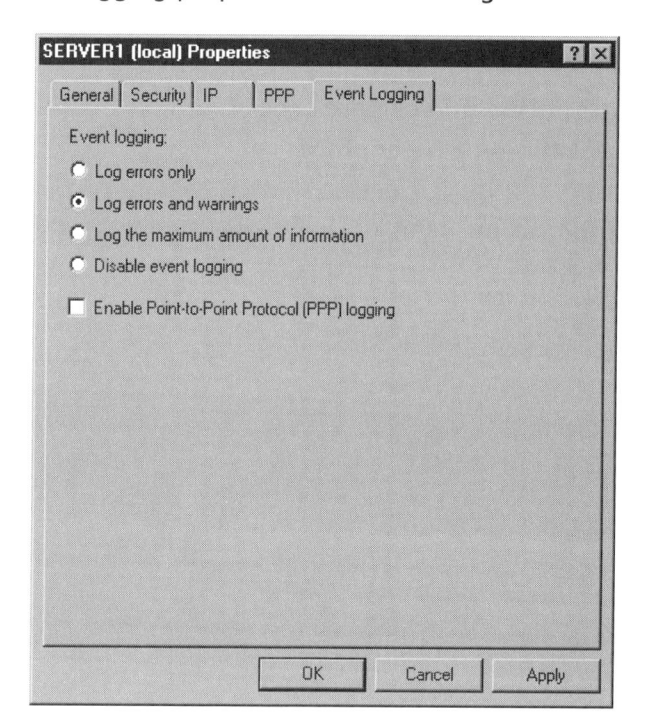

Figure 8.15 Event Logging properties tab for Routing and Remote Access.

Summary

Routing and Remote Access Services for Windows 2000 provide powerful functionality for enabling a server as a router or remote access server. Remote access allows dial-up communication services and VPN services for users to access the server and even the network. In addition, RRAS provides routing services over LAN and WAN environments.

Routing and remote access is managed via the Routing and Remote Access snap-in, but first it must be configured and enabled. Once the service has been started, you cannot repeat configuration via the wizard without first disabling the remote access service; therefore, this chapter concentrates on the remote access server option, from which all other options can later be configured manually.

After launching the Routing and Remote Access Server Setup Wizard, proceed with the Remote access server option. After selecting the required protocols, you can specify how IP addresses will be assigned to remote clients. Remote access also allows a RADIUS server to be used as a central authentication and accounting database for more than one remote access server.

Once remote access has been set up, it can be further configured via the RRAS manager. The manager provides many options for specifying additional options, including:

- General routing and remote access
- Authentication and accounting
- IP routing and assignment
- Point-to-Point protocol
- Event logging

Chapter 9

Create Shared Folder Wizard

Introduction

Sharing data is one of the fundamental reasons we create networks and servers. Sharing data in Windows 2000 is similar to Windows NT, although the addition of a wizard makes the process simple and straightforward. By the end of this chapter, you will have shared a folder of data with other users on the network.

Before You Begin

Before you make data available from your Windows 2000 workstation or server, you should have a thorough understanding of fundamental security issues. These would include any organizational policies that might be in place, corporate security issues surrounding the data you intend to share, and any other security issues pertinent to your organization. You should also understand Share security, and NTFS File System security models and how to use them.

Understanding these issues will allow you to confidentially allow users who need access to your data to do so, while protecting your files from access by unauthorized users, accidental deletion, and other catastrophes.

The Purpose of this Wizard

The Create Shared Folder Wizard allows you to provide access to folders on your system's disk from across the network. In Windows 2000 Advanced Server, this type of operation might be performed by a System Administrator as part of the process to set up a File Server computer.

There are also times when the user of a Windows 2000 Professional workstation might want to make certain folders available to others, such as when sharing files with department members that are common to a given project.

This wizard is available on both Windows 2000 Advanced Server and Professional

Information Needed to Work with this Wizard

- An existing folder to share, or the location on the drive to create one.
- Who should have what kind of access to the data. You should know if it is acceptable for Administrator accounts to have full access to the data in the folder, and what type of access user accounts should have (Read, Full Control, or None).

- A name for the shared folder and a short description of what it holds.

The Create Shared Folder Wizard

Sharing a folder is a two-part process. You need to first identify the folder that is going to be shared and give it a share name. The second step is to set security on the share, thereby determining who can do what to your folder when coming across the network.

➤ STEP 1

After starting the wizard, the Create Shared Folder window appears. First, identify the folder to share and give it a name (Figure 9.1). The Computer field will display the name of your computer, or the computer you are working on if you are running the wizard on a remote machine

- In the **Share name** field, enter the name that you want to use for this share. This is the name that people will see when they browse the network, or want to connect to this folder using a UNC name. In this case, the UNC name for this share would be \\ENGINEERING\NetRoot.
- In the **Share description** field, enter an optional description of this share. You might enter information about what files can be found here, what project the share relates to, or the share's owner.
- Click **NEXT**.

➤ STEP 2

The second part of the process to share a folder is to set security on the share (Figure 9.2).

> **NOTE**
>
> The security settings here are for controlling access to data from the network. They are separate from, and work in conjunction with, NTFS file system security. Restricting users from accessing or modifying data here will not have an impact on their ability to access the data in this folder if they are able to log on to the machine locally.

Figure 9.1 The Create Shared Folder form.

You may select one of the predefined, typical security settings:

- **All users have full control.** Selecting this option allows all users to read and change any data in the files located in this folder.
- **Administrators have full control.** This option allows all Administrators (local, domain, and members of Administrative groups) to read and modify data in this folder. All other users have only read access.
- **Administrators have full control; other users have no control.** This option allows all Administrators (local, domain, and members of Administrative groups) to read and modify the files in the folder; all others are denied access.
- **Customize share and folder permissions.** This selection will allow you to grant access by users and group to this share. If one of the above permission models fits your needs, you may click FINISH and you are done. If not, select this option, and click CUSTOM.

TIP

If you have specific security requirements other than those provided in the wizard, you should take the time to understand the interaction between Share security and NTFS security. Read up on it in the Help system—search on "Best practices for access control."

Figure 9.2 Setting security on the share.

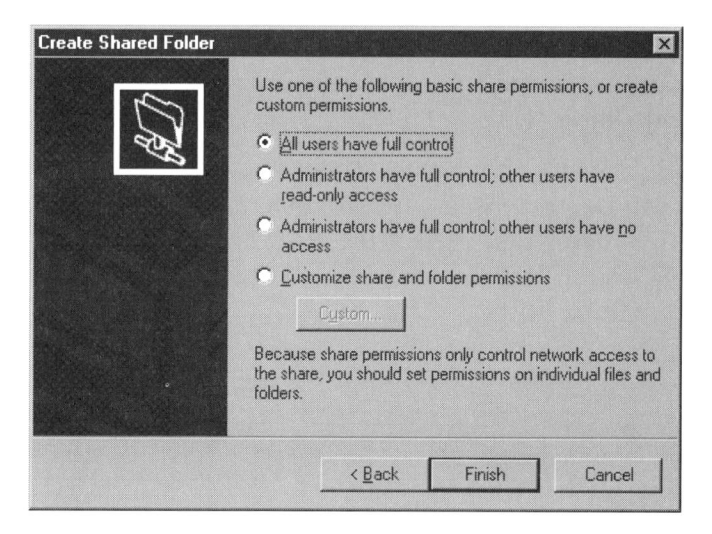

> **STEP 3 (OPTIONAL)**
>
> If the predefined permission sets do not meet your needs, you may decide to grant permissions to specific users or groups. If you have selected Custom in the security portion of the Create Shared Folder Wizard, you will be presented with the Customize Permissions dialog box (Figure 9.3).

Figure 9.3 The Customize Permissions dialog box.

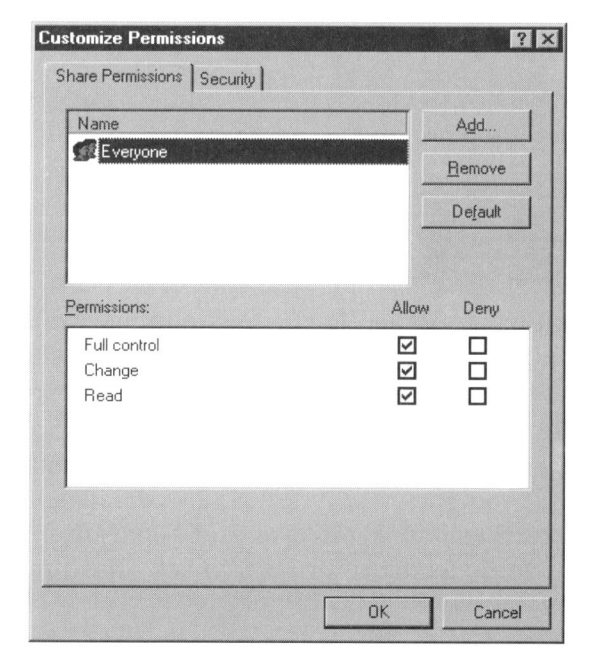

This dialog lists the users and groups that have been granted custom permissions on this folder. Note that by default, the Everyone group has Full control permission.

The following steps will allow you to create a custom permission entry in this list:

- In the Customize Permissions dialog box (Figure 9.3), click **ADD**.
- You will be presented with the Select Users, Computers, or Groups dialog box. Select the user or group you wish to add to your Custom Permissions list for this share, and click **ADD** (Figure 9.4).

Figure 9.4 The Select Users, Computers, or Groups dialog box.

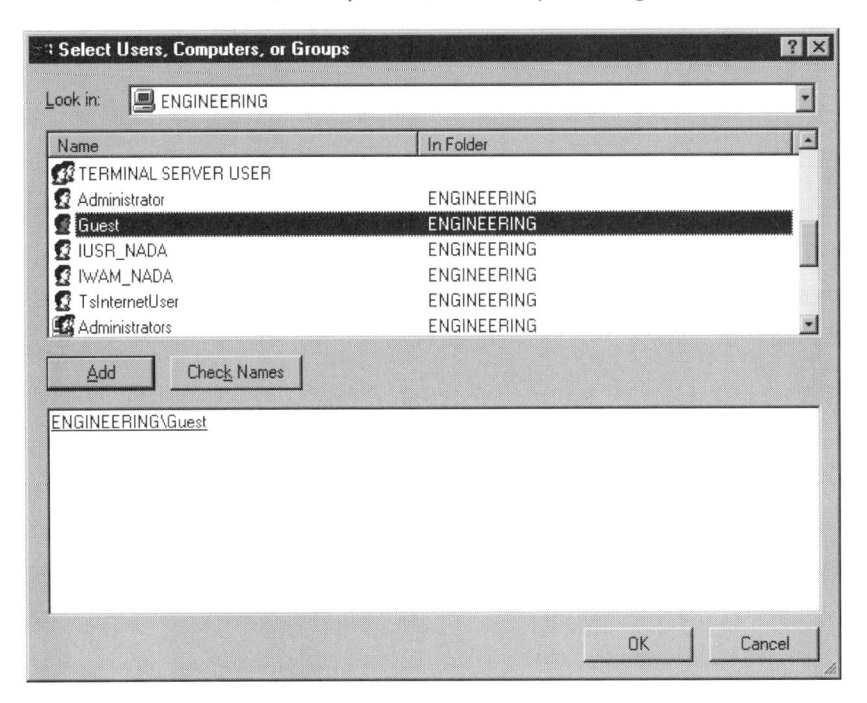

- When you are returned to the Customize Permissions dialog box (Figure 9.5), the user or group you selected will be on the list; you may now select the appropriate check boxes to create the custom permission.
- If you select the Security tab from the Customize Permissions dialog box, you can modify the NTFS permissions on a folder. Notice that these are related to, but separate from, the share permissions. Refer to Figure 9.6 to see an example entry in this list.

Create Shared Folder Wizard • Chapter 9   151

Figure 9.5 Back to the Customize Permissions dialog box after adding a user account.

Figure 9.6 Setting NTFS permissions from the Customize Permissions dialog.

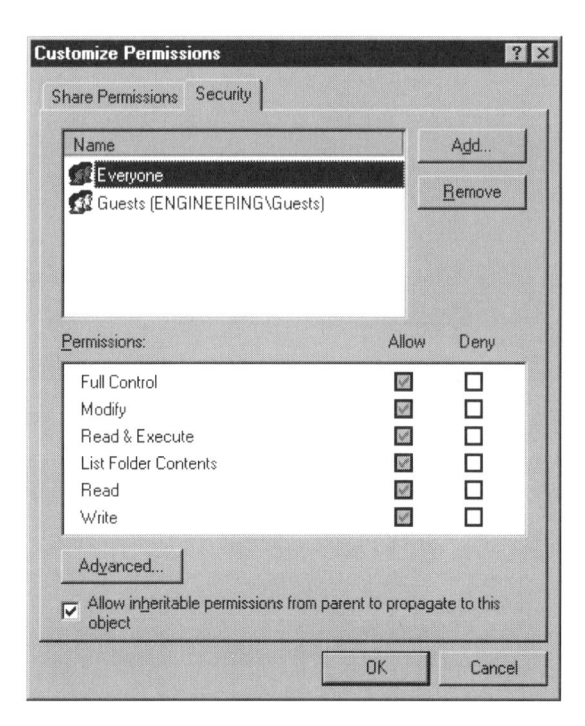

NOTE

The Security tab (Figure 9.6) shows the parameters that are available to you.

- The **Allow inheritable permissions from parent to propagate to this object** check box is selected by default.
- NTFS permissions will trickle down through the directory tree structure and be included in calculating a user or group's final NTFS permission set in this folder.
- Click **ADVANCED** to set up advanced NTFS options such as file system auditing and ownership (Figure 9.7).

Figure 9.7 Advanced NTFS settings.

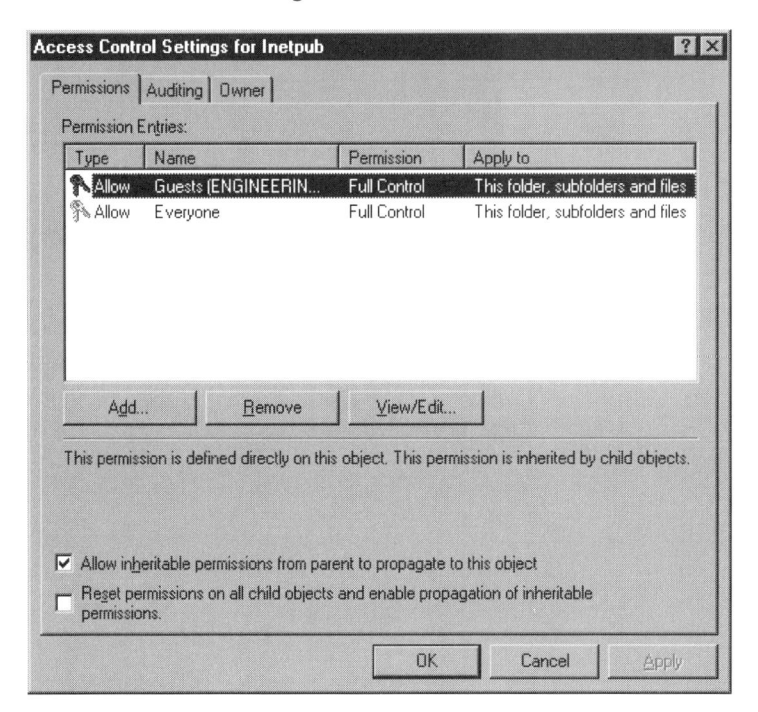

Summary

Using the Create a Shared Folder Wizard, you have shared a folder for other users to access via the network. You started the wizard, pointed to an existing folder, gave it a share name, and set security on the share.

Access to both the Share permissions and the NTFS permission settings are available through the dialog boxes presented via the Custom security option. These can get complicated quickly, so make sure you need these custom settings before going down this path.

Chapter 10

Add Printer Wizard

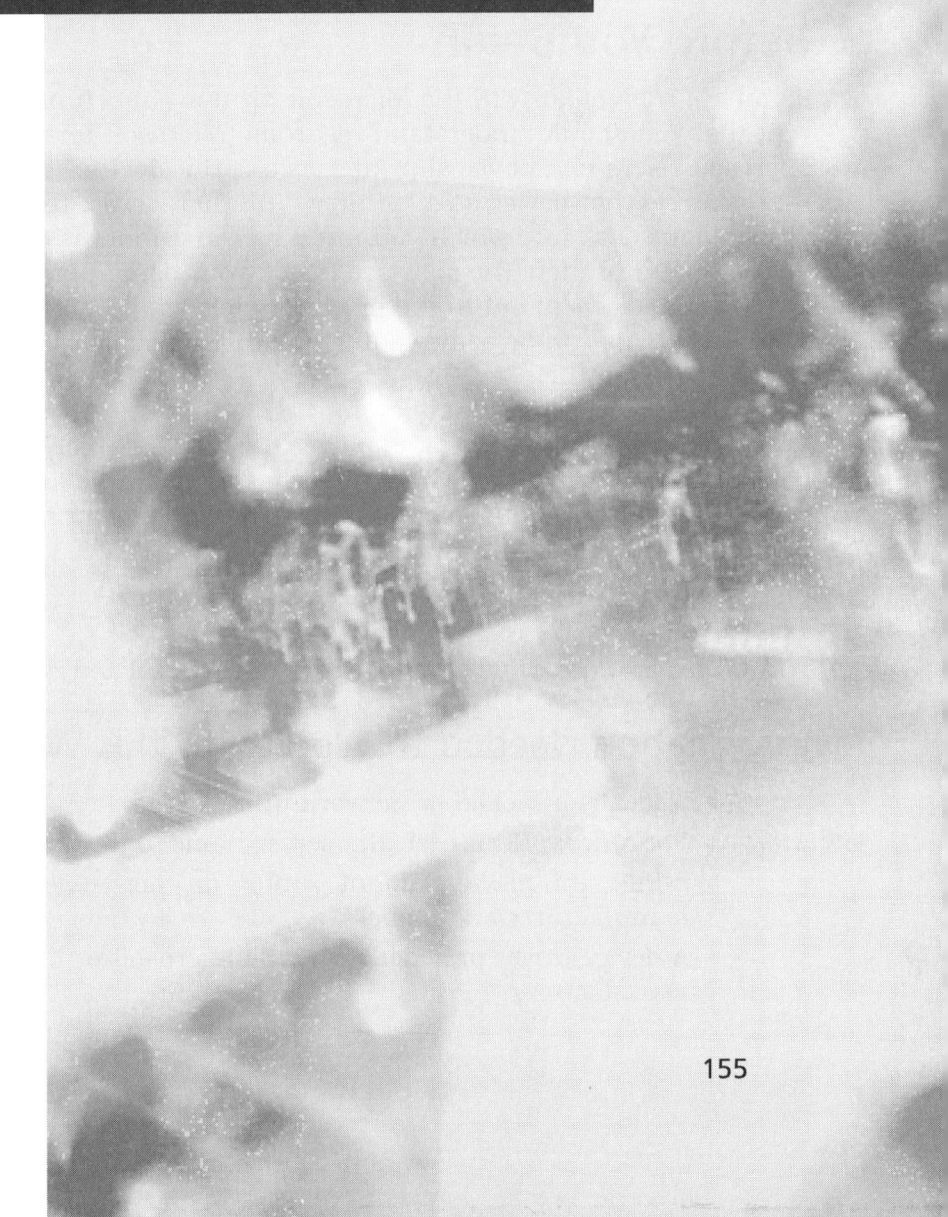

Introduction

Adding and sharing printers is a common function of Windows 2000 System Administrators. Similar to sharing data folders, sharing printers has a place in both the server room and the workgroup. Windows 2000 offers several enhancements to the print server functions in Windows NT, including support for connection to printers via the Internet. By the end of this chapter, you will know how to add local and network printers to your Windows 2000 machine, and share those printers with other users on the network.

Before You Begin

If you are unfamiliar with the Microsoft print architecture, there is a concept that you should understand regarding Microsoft terminology. Microsoft refers to a physical printer as a "print device," and the software that controls that device as a "printer." In other words, the machine sitting on your desk into which you put paper and toner is called a "print device," not a printer. The software inside your computer that holds print jobs and sends them out to the print device is what Microsoft refers to as a "printer." This can be somewhat confusing to people who are used to putting paper in their "printers."

The rather logical explanation for this is that the Microsoft architecture assumes nothing about the physical device to which you are sending data for output. This device could be what most people call a printer; it could also be a fax, a modem, a plotter, or any other output device that makes sense in this context.

The Purpose of this Wizard

This wizard provides a quick way to share or add local and network printers.

Information Needed to Work with this Wizard

- A locally attached or network print device
- For a network printer, the server name and printer name
- A Plug and Play compliant printer, or knowledge of the printer's manufacturer and model
- A device driver provided either by Microsoft or the printer manufacturer

The Add Printer Wizard

Local Printer

➣ STEP 1

When you start the Add Printer Wizard, you will be presented with a screen (Figure 10.1). This screen simply tells you that you are about to install a printer.

- Click **NEXT**.

Figure 10.1 Starting the wizard.

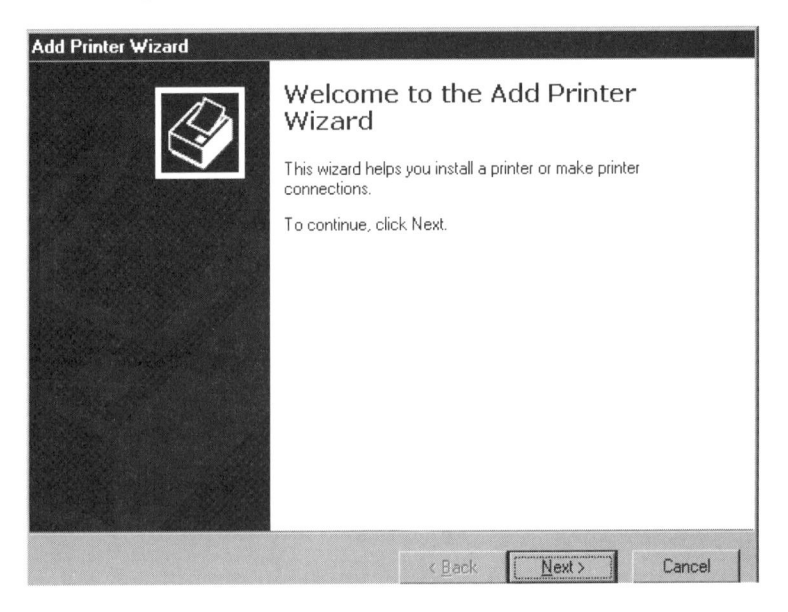

➣ STEP 2

In this example, we are going to connect a local printer to our system. Figure 10.2 shows the second screen of the Add Printer Wizard. The steps to fill out this form are as follows:

- Select **Local Printer**.
- If the printer supports Plug and Play, select the **Automatically detect and install my Plug and Play printer** check box.
- Click **NEXT**.
- If Plug and Play detects your printer successfully, proceed to Step 5.

Figure 10.2 Selecting either a local or network printer.

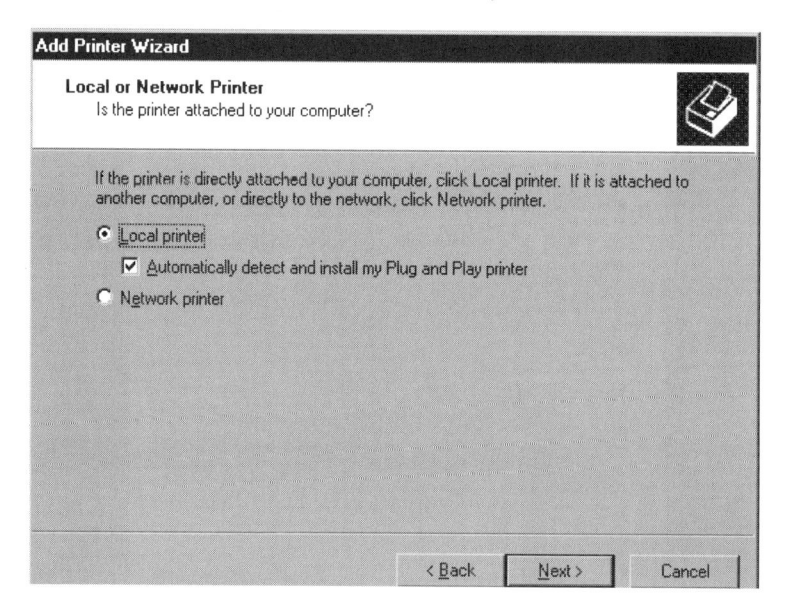

➤ STEP 3

Again, if you are configuring a Plug and Play printer, you may jump ahead to Step 5 of this section. Otherwise, you will need to know the port identifier to fill in the next form. This is most likely going to be LPT1, but may be different depending on your computer manufacturer and model, type of printer, and other peripherals you may have connected to this machine.

The form to tell Windows 2000 where this printer is connected is shown in Figure 10.3. You should fill it out as follows:

- If the printer is attached directly to the computer via a physical interface, select **Use the following port**, and select the physical port that connects the printer.
- If the port is not listed, or this is a TCP/IP connected printer, select **Create a new port** and provide the IP address of the printer, or the name of a port to create.

NOTE

When creating a printer for a locally attached device, the majority of the configuration can be done from the existing list of ports.

Figure 10.3 Selecting the local printer port.

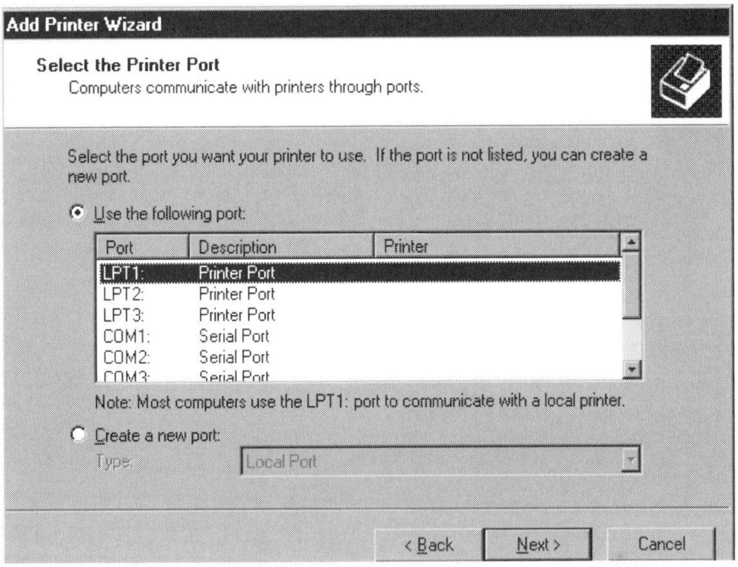

➢ STEP 4

For non–Plug and Play printers, you will need to know the manufacturer and model of your print device. Figure 10.4 is an example of selecting a Hewlett-Packard Color LaserJet.

If you are connecting a print device that is not supported directly by Windows 2000, click **HAVE DISK** to install a third-party driver.

➢ STEP 5

Enter the printer name (Figure 10.5).

➢ STEP 6

The Printer Sharing window of the Add Printer Wizard allows you to share the printer with others (Figure 10.6). From the users' perspective, it will be a networked printer. There are two options available to you:

- **Do not share this printer**. This will prevent this printer from being available to network users.
- **Share as**. This will make your printer available for others to use. In this case, you must provide a share name for your printer. This may be different from the name you gave it in Step 5, but will default to the name entered in Step 5.

Figure 10.4 Select the manufacturer and model of your printer.

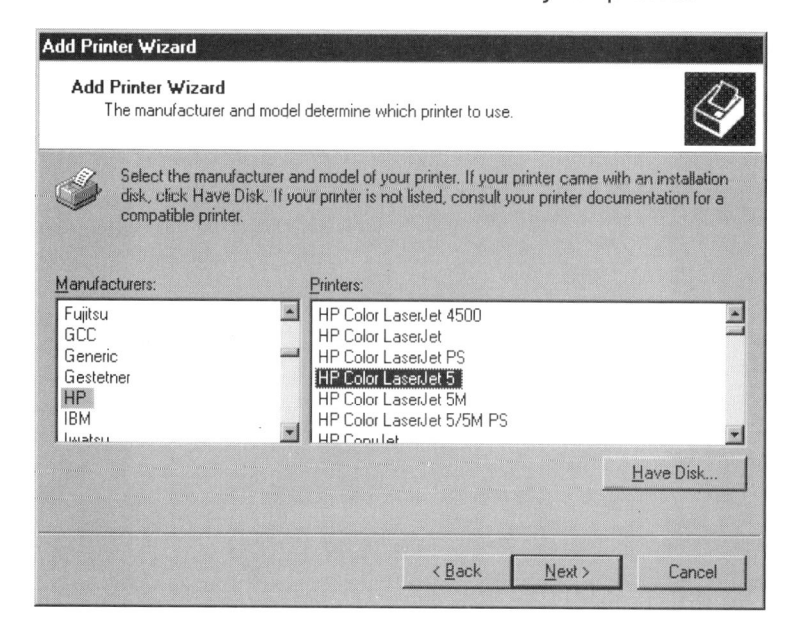

Figure 10.5 Naming the printer.

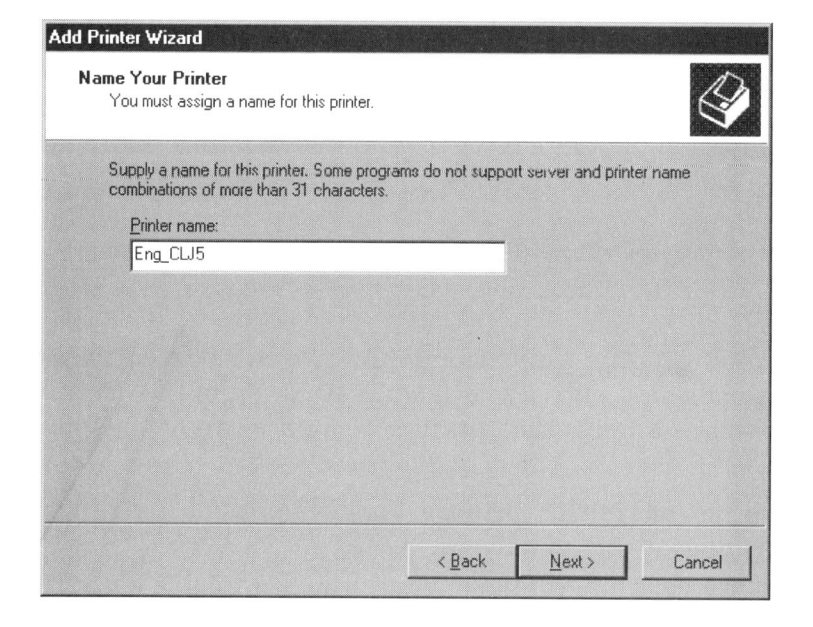

Figure 10.6 Sharing a printer.

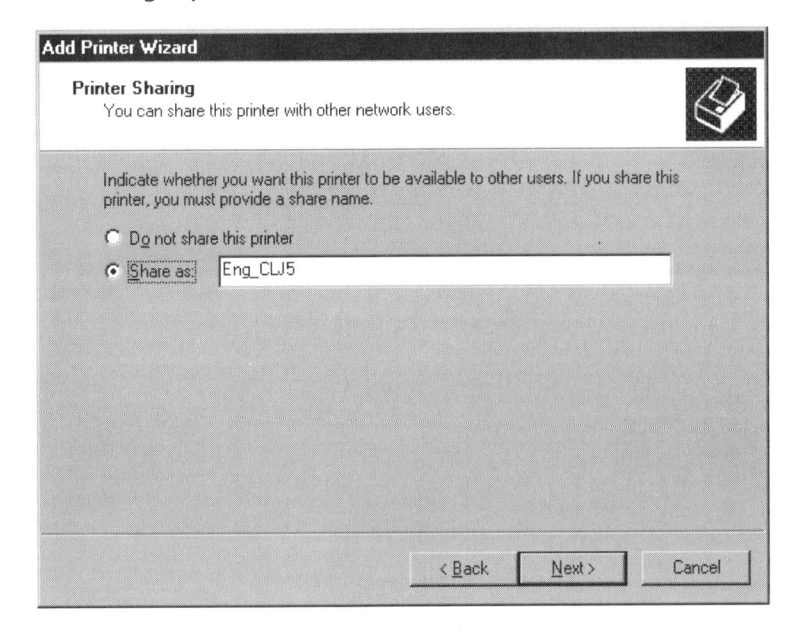

➢ STEP 7

Next, enter a location and comment for your printer (Figure 10.7). Both of these fields are optional and may be left blank.

Figure 10.7 Location and comment.

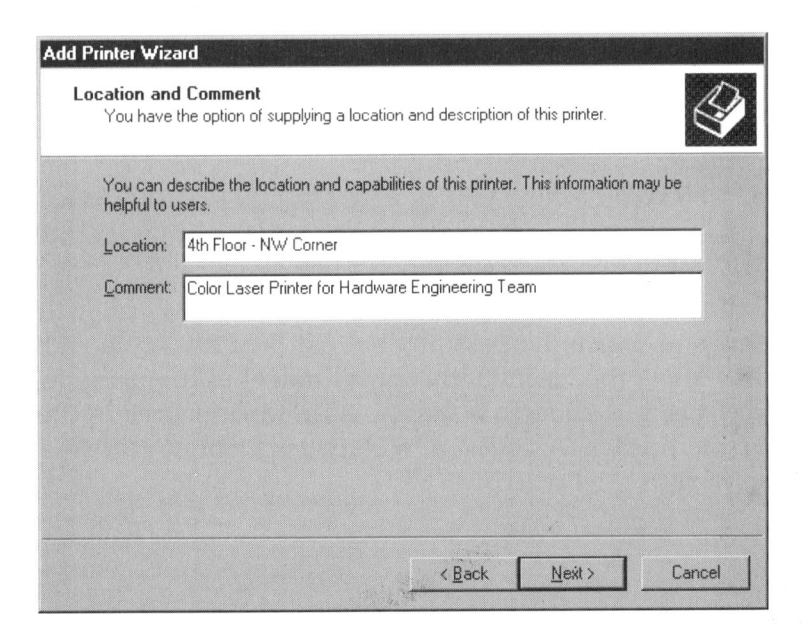

STEP 8

Almost finished! The last decision to make is whether to print a test page (Figure 10.8). Unless there is a very specific reason, such as the printer is not yet physically attached, choose **Yes**. This will test all of the plumbing between the computer and the paper.

Figure 10.8 Print a test page?

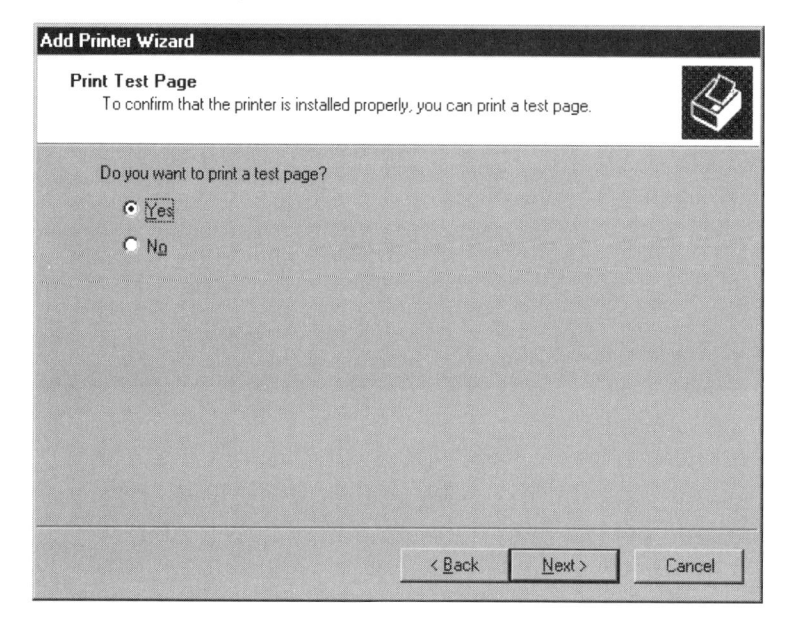

STEP 9

The last step is a review of the settings (Figure 10.9). If everything looks correct, click **FINISH**.

Network Printer

STEP 1

Believe it or not, connecting to a network printer is easier than creating a new one. Since the person who installed the printer initially needed to know the manufacturer and model of the print device, all you really need to know to attach to a network printer is the network name of the printer. To add a new Network Printer, start the **Add Printer Wizard** (Figure 10.10).

Figure 10.9 Reviewing the settings and finishing the wizard.

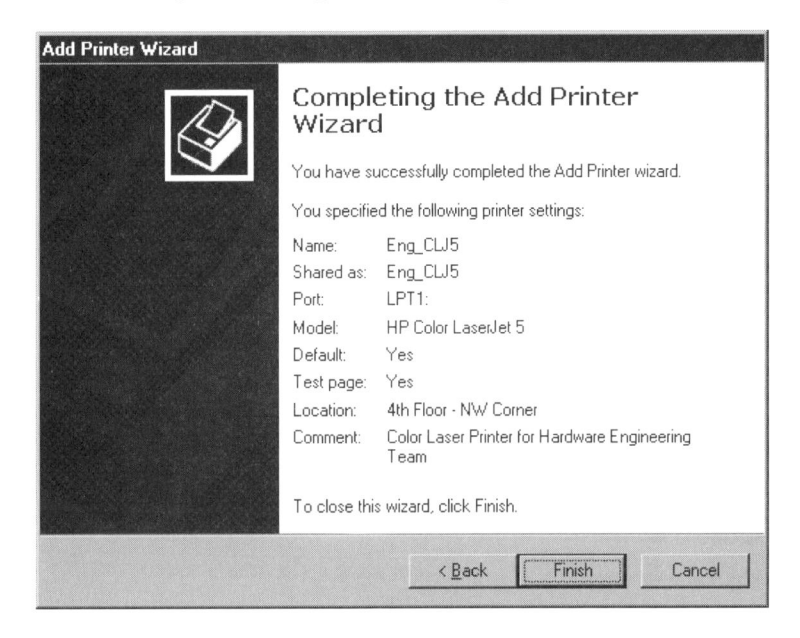

Figure 10.10 Starting the Add Printer Wizard.

➣ STEP 2

Since we have determined that this printer is on the network, when the Add Printer Wizard dialog (Figure 10.11) appears, select **Network printer**.

Figure 10.11 Selecting the Network printer option.

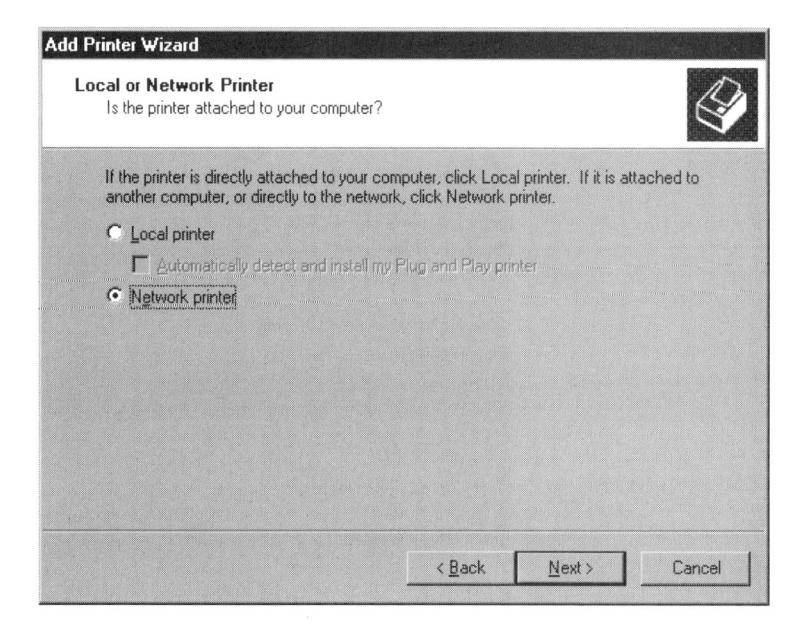

➣ STEP 3

There are two options in the Locate your Printer dialog box (Figure 10.12).

- If printing to a printer on the Internet, select **Connect to a printer on the Internet or on your intranet** and enter the URL of the printer here.
- If the printer is on your organization's network, select **Type the printer name**, or click NEXT to browse for a printer. In this example, the UNC name for a printer has been filled in. If this field is left blank and you click NEXT, you will be taken to the Browse For Printer dialog (Figure 10.13).

➣ STEP 4

Figure 10.13 is an example of browsing for a printer on the network. A printer attached to the server named ENGINEERING has been selected. The printer is called ENG_CLASER.

Figure 10.12 Locate Your Printer dialog box.

Figure 10.13 Browsing for a printer on our network.

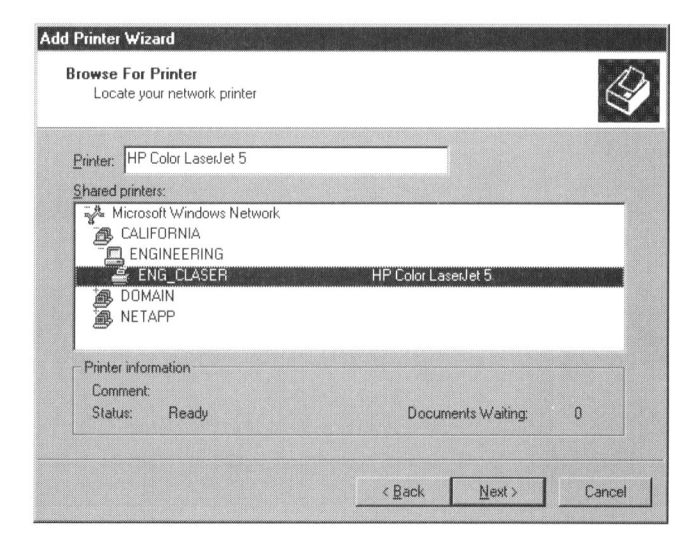

➢ STEP 5

Notice that Windows 2000 did not ask about the printer manufacturer and model! This is because in the Windows printing world, a printer is software. As such, the printer has already been configured for the print device. Just point to the printer and go!

The last configuration item is to tell Windows 2000 if this to be the default printer. In the screen shown as in Figure 10.14, select **Yes** to have this printer used unless the user explicitly selects another.

Figure 10.14 Answering the default question.

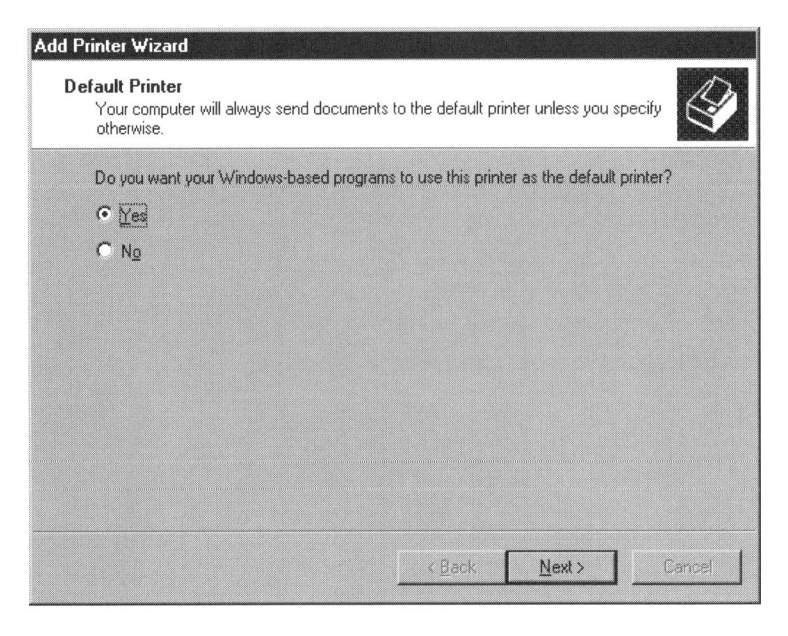

➢ STEP 6

The wizard presents a summary sheet (Figure 10.15). If everything looks okay, click **FINISH**.

Figure 10.15 Completing the Add Printer Wizard.

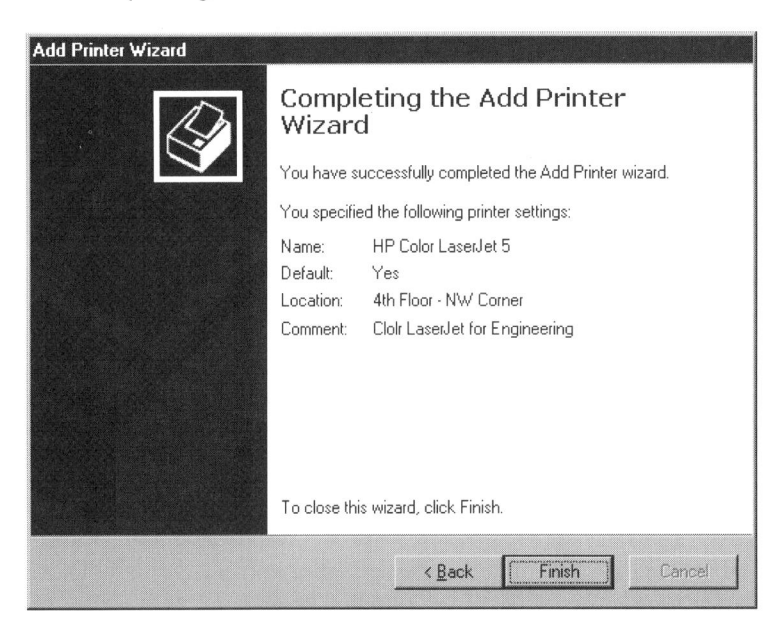

Summary

In this chapter, we learned how to connect a local print device by creating a new printer, and how to connect to a printer that is shared on the network. Unlike many network print environments, it is much easier to connect to a network printer than to create a new local printer.

If the local printer is Plug and Play compliant and supported directly by Windows 2000, creating a local printer is very easy. If not, you must know the manufacturer and model of your printer, and perhaps provide driver software from the manufacturer.

When connecting to a shared network printer, all you really need to know is the name of the machine on which the printer is running, and the printer's name.

Always print a test page to make sure that the printer is working correctly.

Chapter 11
Internet Information Services (IIS) Wizards

Introduction

Internet Information Services (IIS) consists of several components, including an FTP, Web, and SMTP server. Each offers a service creation wizard that allows Administrators to create additional virtual servers to their IIS server. By the end of this chapter, you will be able to use these wizards to add new IIS services.

Before You Begin

To say that the Internet has changed the way businesses work is a huge understatement. Behind all of the Web pages, e-mail, and other objects in Cyberspace are servers. Internet servers, be they Web servers, File Transfer Protocol (FTP) servers, SMTP (mail) servers, or others, make up the internal organs of the Net.

Administering these servers can be a daunting task. The wizards provided by Windows 2000 help a great deal in the management of these critical Internet components. While the wizards will assist in the mundane tasks of server management, they do not make design or implementation decisions. Before creating a new server site, the Administrator should have a good understanding of what the underlying technologies are. Any good book that provides an overview of Internet services and their architecture would be, at minimum, a good primer to read prior to putting up new services.

The Purpose of these Wizards

The wizards described here are not available on Windows 2000 Professional. They are used to configure the services of Internet Information Server (IIS) which is Microsoft's all-purpose server designed to deliver high-performance Internet services to small workgroups, companies, and the world. As such, only Windows 2000 Server and above provide these wizards.

Information Needed to Work with these Wizards

- DNS names for any servers that are to be created
- IP addresses of the server and services that are to be installed
- Domain names for Web, SMTP servers that are to be created
- Security requirements for the data that is to be made available
- A thorough, functional understanding of the differences among the HTTP, FTP, and SMTP protocols

> **NOTE**
>
> All of the wizards shown in this chapter can be launched from the Internet Information Services Manager shown in Figure 11.1.

Figure 11.1 The Internet Information Services Manager.

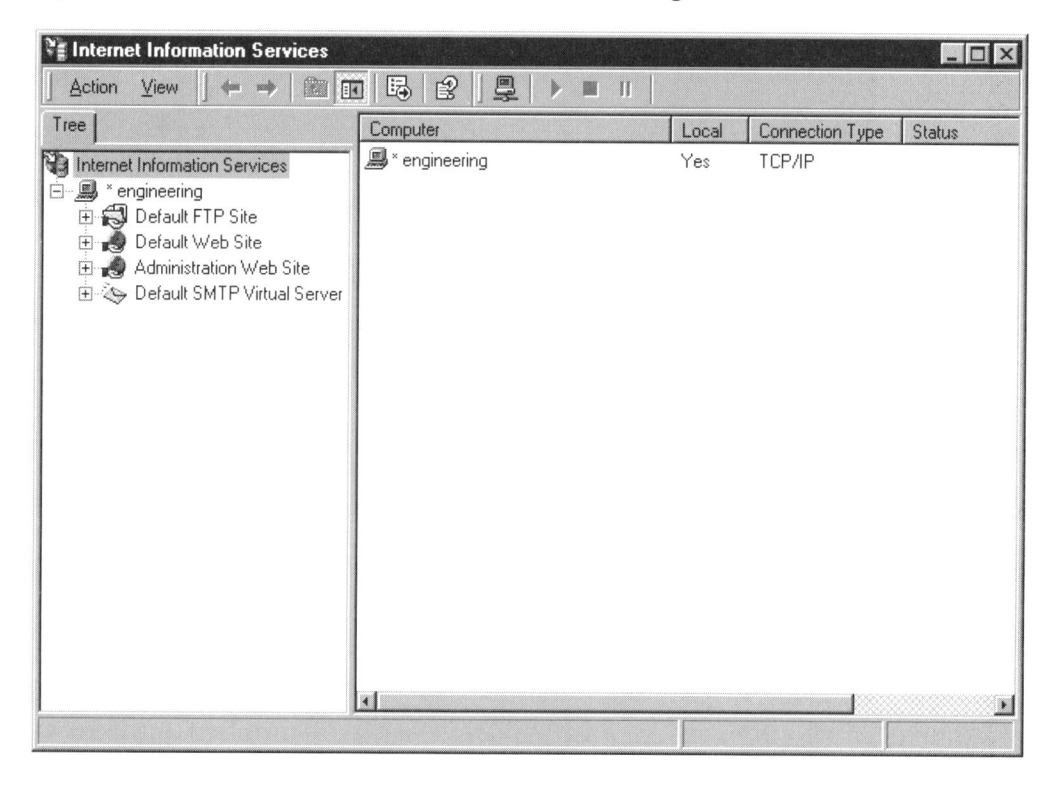

The FTP Site Creation Wizard

➢ STEP 1

When launched, the FTP Site Creation Wizard displays a welcome screen (Figure 11.2).

- Click **NEXT**.

Figure 11.2 The FTP Site Creation Wizard welcome screen.

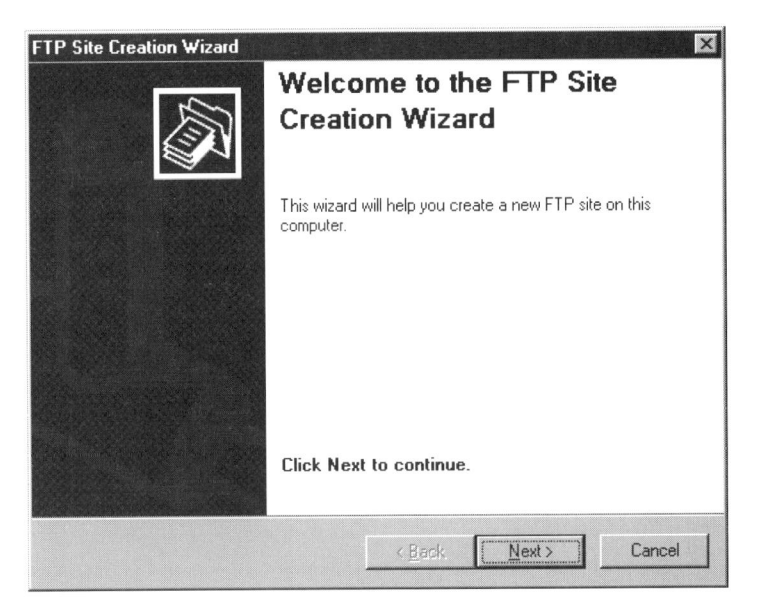

➤ STEP 2

The first parameter that the wizard needs is a description for the new site (Figure 11.3). This description is what is displayed when managing the site. The users of the FTP site will never see this.

- Enter a short description about the FTP site in the Description field.
- Click **NEXT**.

➤ STEP 3

The next step is to assign an IP address and port number to the new FTP site (Figure 11.4).

- Select one or all IP addresses to use for this site.
- Enter a value for the TCP port, or accept the default.
- Click **NEXT**.

> **TIP**
>
> One of the strengths of the IIS FTP server is that it allows direct selection of the IP addresses to which it will respond. This works in conjunction with the Microsoft TCP/IP stack, in which you can bind one or more IP addresses to a single card. Using these two features together allows a single machine, with a single network adapter, to behave as if it were several machines. Each machine can have its own entry in the Domain Name Service (DNS). With this technique, FTP and Web sites can appear to be completely unrelated as different companies, organizations, or departments, when in actuality they are all housed on a single machine.
>
> Notice that the IP address field is completed as a pull-down menu. This menu gets its entries from the IP addresses already configured on the machine. Any legal value may be entered in the TCP port field; the default value is 21.

Figure 11.3 FTP Site Description dialog box.

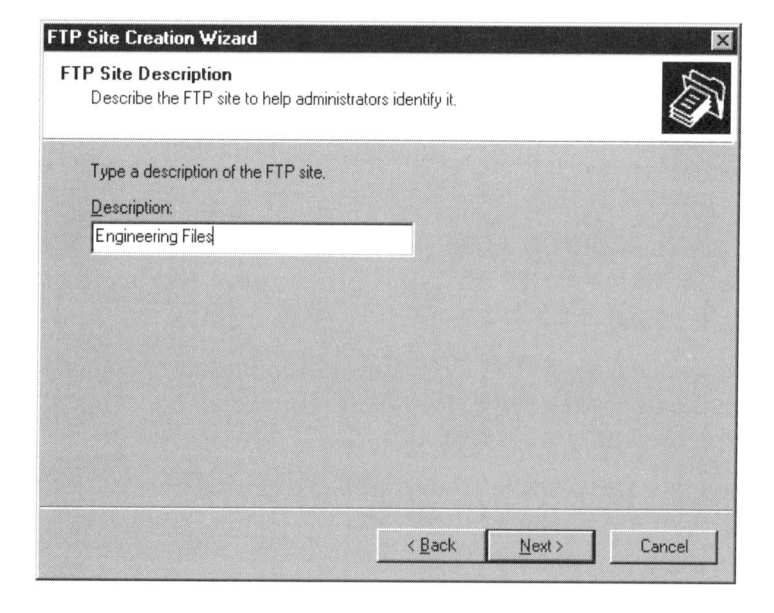

Figure 11.4 The IP Address and Port Settings dialog box.

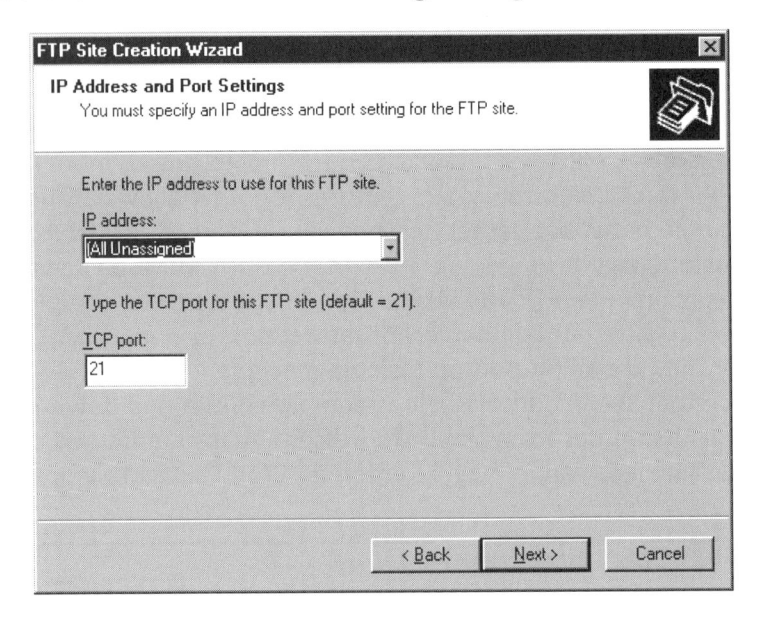

➤ STEP 4

The path to the root of the new FTP site must be provided in the FTP Site Home Directory dialog box (Figure 11.5). This is the directory that FTP users will be taken to when connecting to the site. All other directories for this FTP site will appear as subdirectories of this point of the file system. FTP users will not be able traverse up the file system tree from this directory.

- Enter the fully qualified path to the directory that is to be the root of the new FTP site, and proceed to Step 5.
- Click **NEXT**.

If the exact path to the FTP site's home directory is not known, or for the sake of convenience, BROWSE may be clicked to open a directory browse window (Figure 11.6).

- Navigate the browse tree, highlighting the desired folder to be used as the FTP root directory.
- Click **OK**.

➤ STEP 5

The final step of the FTP Site Creation Wizard is to define permissions to the FTP site. User-level permissions can be applied to the FTP site by requiring authentication from the users when logging on to the site. The permission set here as shown in Figure 11.7 will override any user-level permissions and limit all users to read or write access. If both read and write permissions are granted here, the user's permissions as defined at the NTFS file system level will be applied. The read and write check boxes here limit the maximum available rights to the FTP site.

Figure 11.5 The FTP Site Home Directory page.

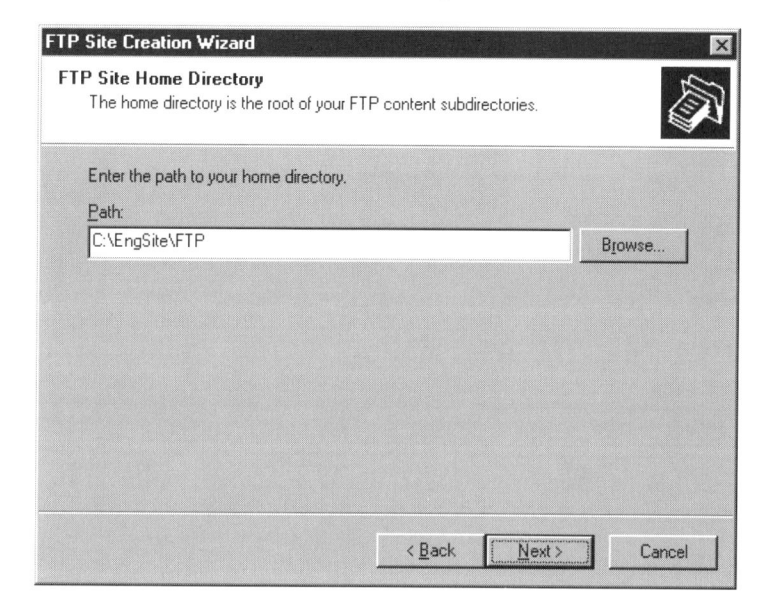

Figure 11.6 Browsing for a directory.

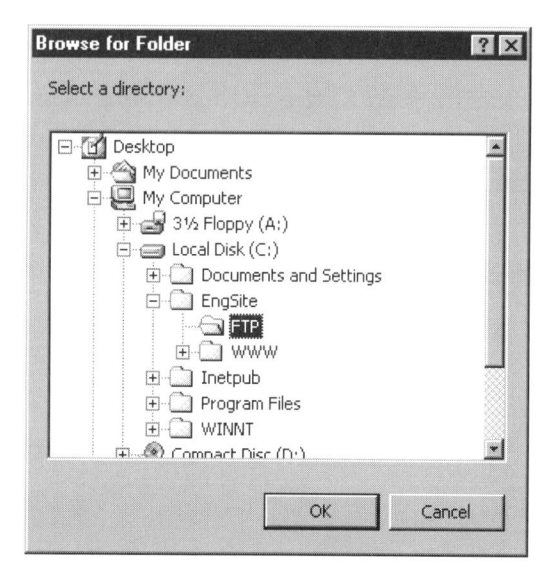

For example, if the Read permission is selected, and the user has adequate NTFS permissions, then reading will be allowed. If Write permission is checked here, and the user has NTFS write permissions to the FTP directory, then uploads will be allowed.

- Check the maximum permissions that should be available to all users.
- Click **NEXT**.

Figure 11.7 Setting permissions on the FTP site.

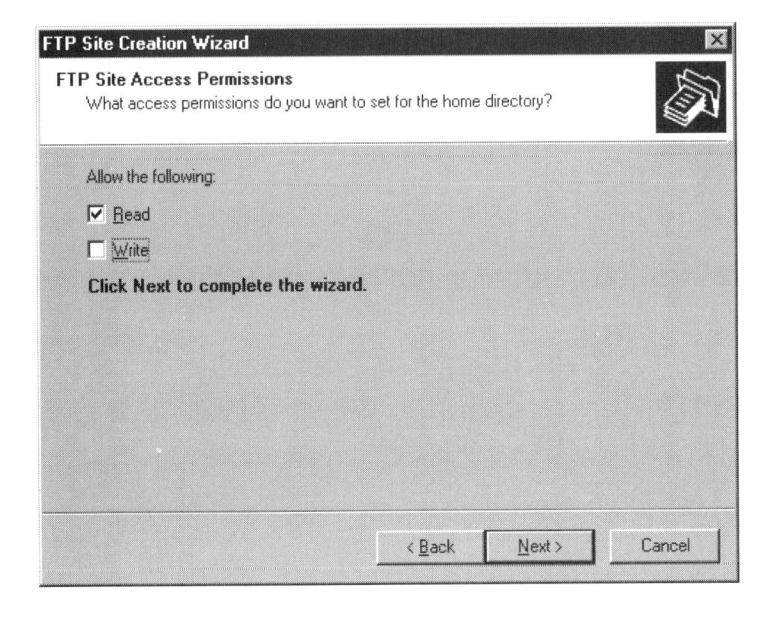

> STEP 6

After clicking NEXT in Step 5, the wizard displays the successful completion screen (Figure 11.8).

- Click **FINISH** to complete and exit the wizard.

The Web Site Creation Wizard

> STEP 1

Launch the Web Site Creation Wizard. The wizard will present a welcome screen (Figure 11.9).

- Click **NEXT**.

Figure 11.8 The FTP Site Creation Wizard completion dialog.

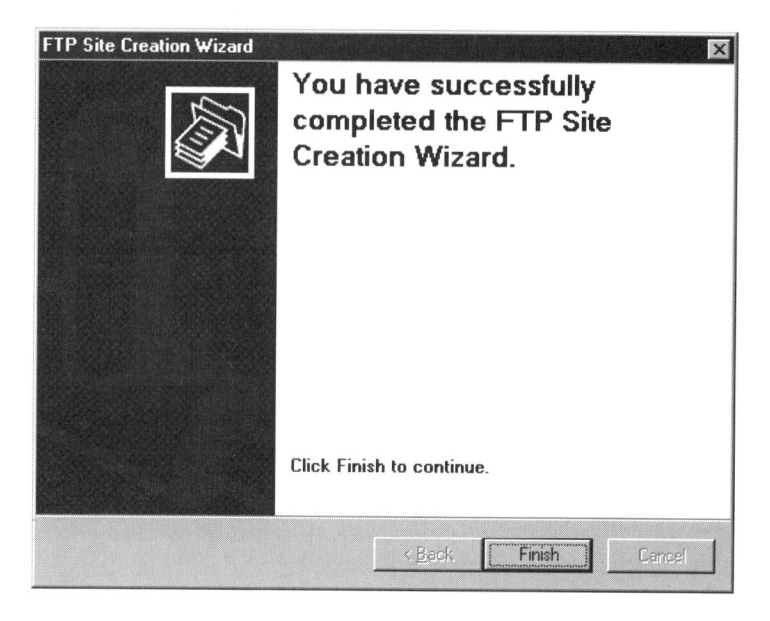

Figure 11.9 The Web Site Creation Wizard welcome screen.

➤ STEP 2

The first data entry screen of the Web Site Creation Wizard is shown in Figure 11.10. This screen is used to provide a description of the new Web site. This description will be displayed in the IIS Manager tool, and used to help identify the site to Administrators.

- Provide an administrative description of the new site in the Description field.
- Click **NEXT**.

Figure 11.10 Web Site Description page.

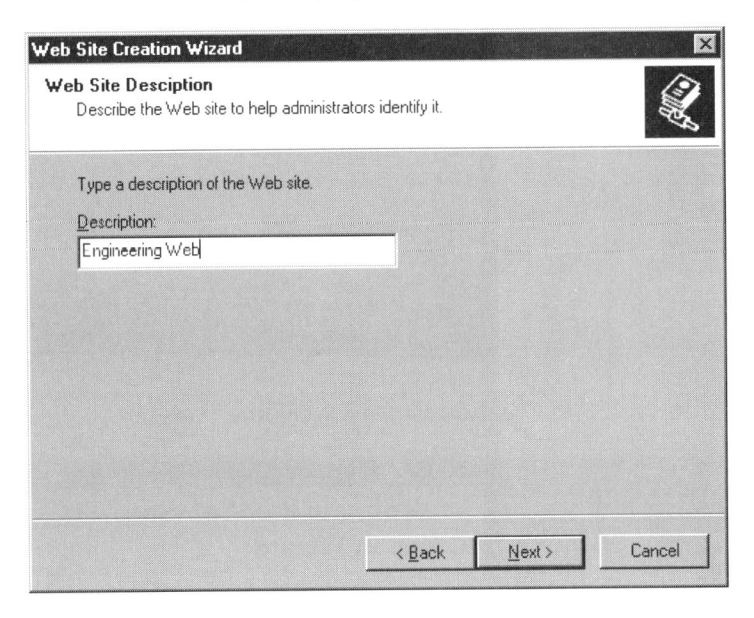

➢ STEP 3

Like other IIS services, unique IP addresses can be assigned to different sites. The IP Address and Port Settings dialog box (Figure 11.11) is used to assign any or all of the IP addresses active on the Windows 2000 server to the newly created Web site. Additionally, a unique port address may be assigned to this site. The Host Header field defines header information that will be sent to client browsers. If Certificate Services are available, the Secure Sockets Layer (SSL) may be enabled and a port value assigned.

- Select one or All Unassigned IP addresses in **Enter the IP address to use for this Web site**.
- Enter a value to use in the TCP port field, or accept the default of 80.
- Enter an optional Host Header string.

- If applicable, provide an SSL port number for Secure Sockets Layer to use.
- Click **NEXT**.

Figure 11.11 The IP Address and Port Settings dialog box.

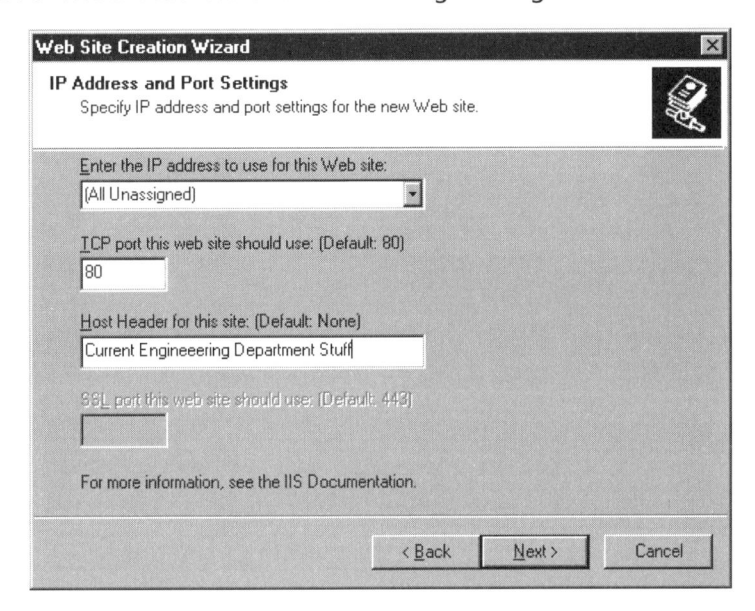

➤ STEP 4

The new Web site needs a root directory from which all other directories will become descendants. This root directory is the physical path to a default folder used when the client browser connects to the site (Figure 11.12).

If users should be allowed to access this site anonymously, be sure to check the "Allow anonymous access to this Web site" check box.

- Check or clear the **Allow anonymous access to this Web site** box.
- Enter the path to the folder that will be the site's root directory and continue to Step 5, or click **BROWSE** to open the Browse for Folder window (Figure 11.6).
- Click **NEXT**.

Figure 11.12 The Web Site Home Directory dialog box.

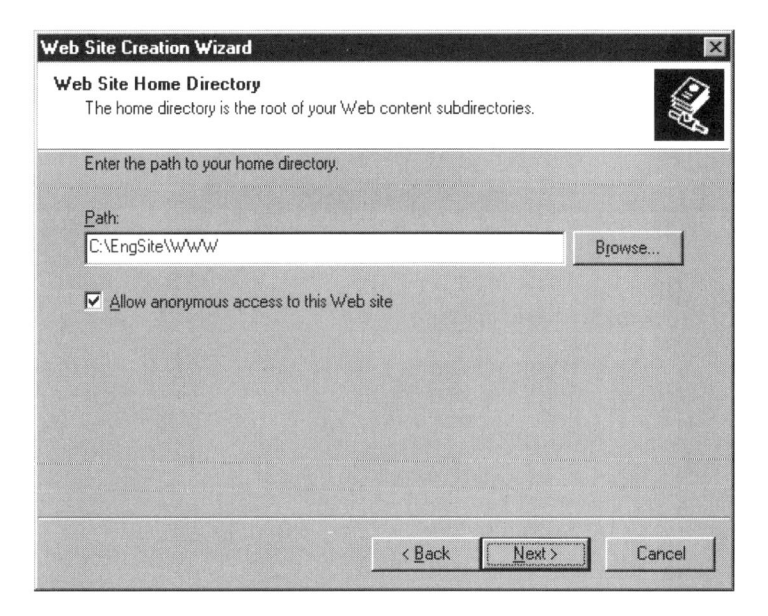

> STEP 5

Setting permissions on the Web site in effect means setting maximum permissions available on the site. If users are authenticated when accessing the site, their permissions on the site will determine what actions they can take while connected to the site, up to but not exceeding the Web Site Access Permissions (Figure 11.13).

The Web Site Access Permissions should be set as follows:

- **Read**. Allows users to read pages from the site.
- **Run scripts (such as ASP)**. Allows users to receive ASP pages, VBScript, and JavaScript code from the Web site.
- **Execute (such as ISAPI applications or CGI)**. Allows users to execute server-side code created as ISAPI extensions or CGI applications.
- **Write**. Allows users to write into the Web site.
- **Browse**. Allows users to browse a raw directory listing.

Using these permissions, the dialog box should be completed as follows:

- Set the desired maximum available permissions using the check boxes next to each permission.
- Click **NEXT**.

Figure 11.13 Setting access permissions on the new site.

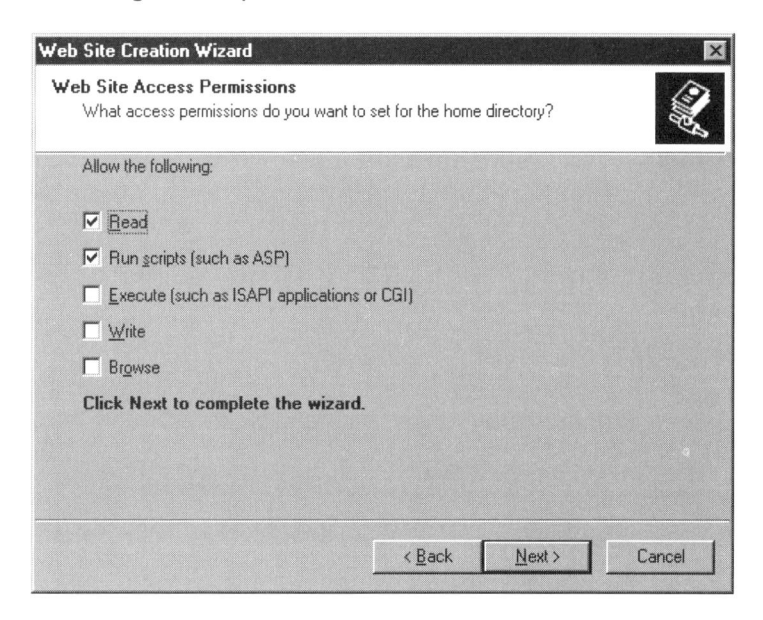

➢ STEP 6

The last screen of the Web Site Creation Wizard is shown in Figure 11.14. It simply states that the wizard has completed successfully and is ready to exit.

- Click **FINISH** to exit the wizard.

Figure 11.14 The Web Site Creation Wizard completed screen.

The New SMTP Virtual Server Wizard

➤ STEP 1

Another IIS service that can have virtual identities is the SMTP, or Internet mail server. After launching the wizard, a screen will appear, asking for an administrative description of the virtual server (Figure 11.15).

- Enter a description in the **SMTP virtual server description** field.
- Click **NEXT**.

Figure 11.15 New SMTP Virtual Server Wizard welcome screen.

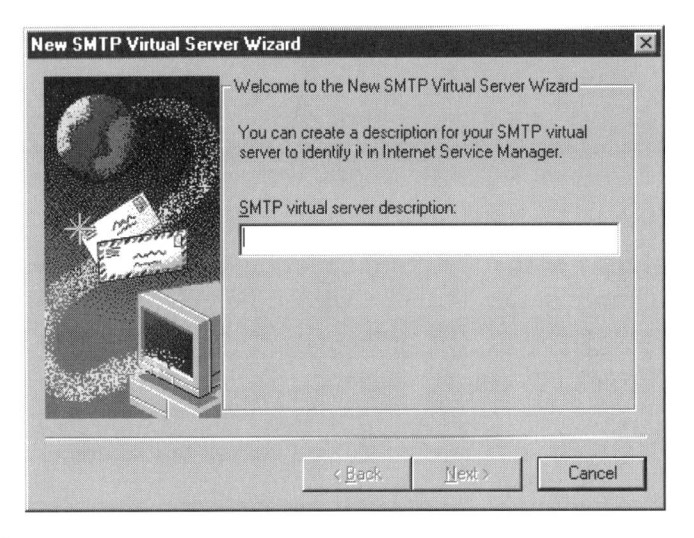

➤ STEP 2

Since a single Windows 2000 server can have multiple IP addresses regardless of the number of network interfaces installed, the SMTP Virtual Server Wizard needs to know what address or addresses should be used for this site. The Select IP Address dialog box is shown in Figure 11.16. This dialog box allows the selection of an address or addresses to use.

- Select **an IP address**, or **All Unassigned addresses**.
- Click **NEXT**.

➤ STEP 3

The SMTP Virtual Server requires a folder in which to store its data files. The next step (Figure 11.17) allows for either manual entry of a path to this directory, or using BROWSE to select a path.

Internet Information Services (IIS) Wizards • Chapter 11   **183**

- Enter the path where the new SMTP Virtual Server should keep its files, or click **BROWSE** to select the path visually.
- Click **NEXT**.

Figure 11.16 Select IP Address.

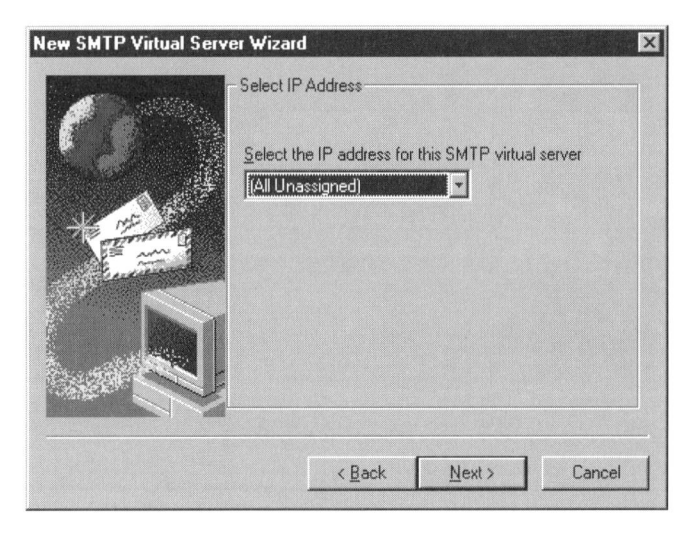

Figure 11.17 The completed SMTP Home Directory dialog box.

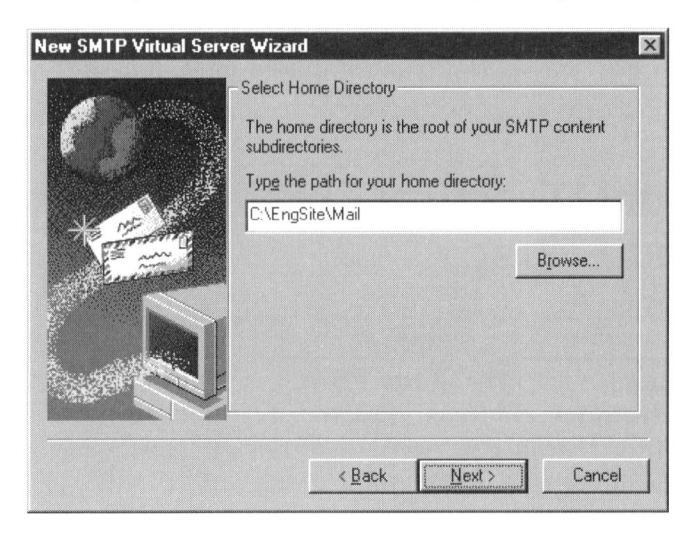

➢ STEP 4

The last step in the SMTP Virtual Server Wizard is to define the domain that this SMTP server will serve (Figure 11.18).

- Enter the fully qualified domain name (FQDN) that this mail server will service.
- Click **FINISH** to complete the wizard.

Figure 11.18 Entering the domain that will be served by this mail server.

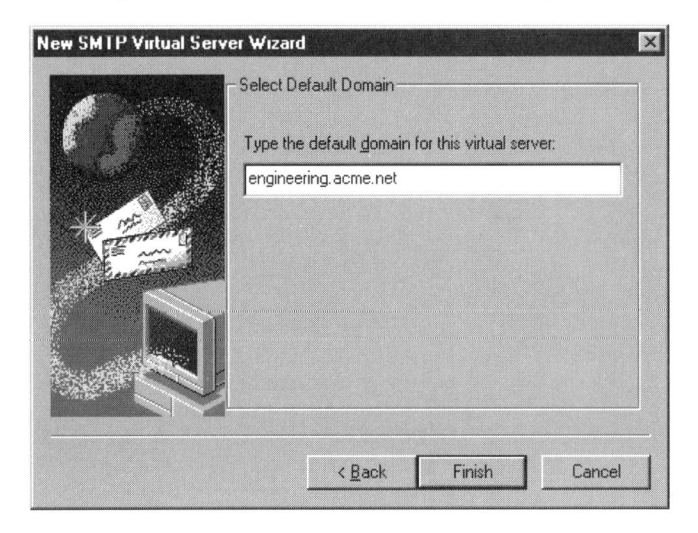

➢ STEP 5

The IIS manager will now show the newly created SMTP virtual server (Figure 11.19). Notice that the administrative description assigned in Step 1 is used to identify the server in the IIS Manager.

The Virtual Directory Creation Wizard (Web and FTP)

➢ STEP 1

One of the nice features of the IIS Web server is the ability to create virtual directories. A virtual directory is a folder containing Web objects (.htm, .html, .jpg, .asp files) that appears to be a descendant of the root directory for the site. In actuality, the physical location of the directory may have nothing to do with the directory hierarchy from the root, and may have a different name on disk than is presented to the client browser. This is a handy way to place directories under the root of the server virtually, without having to change the physical name or location of the folder itself.

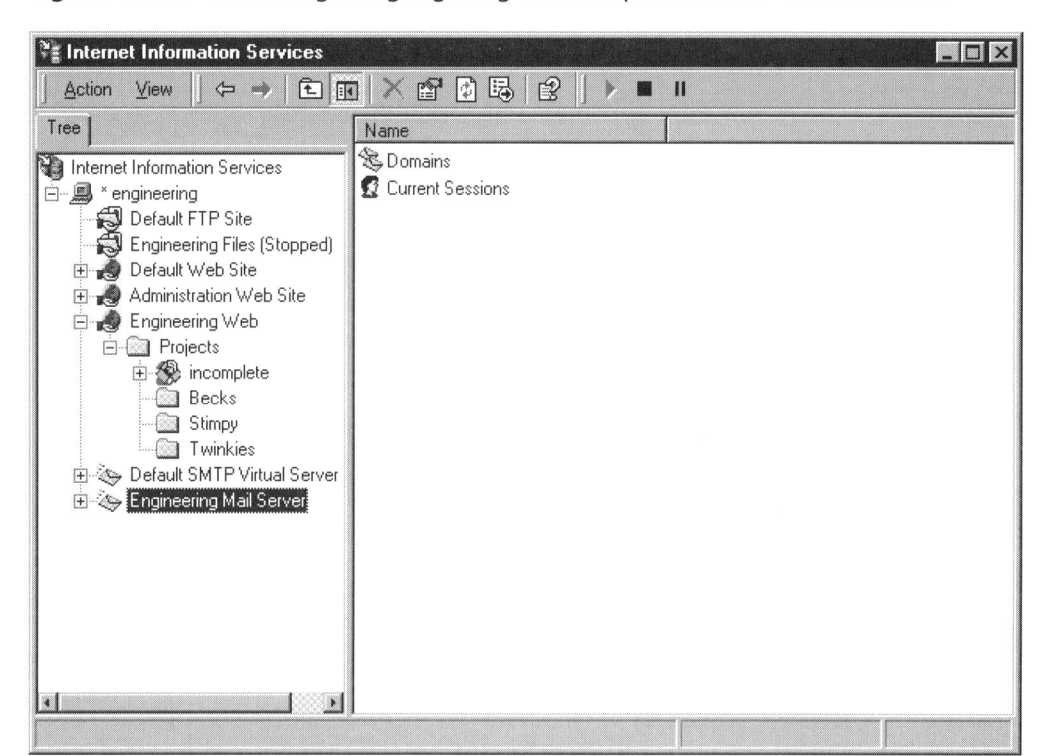

Figure 11.19 IIS Manager highlighting the completed SMTP virtual server.

Administrators use the Virtual Directory Creation Wizard (Figure 11.20) to create these virtual directories.

- Click **NEXT**.

➣ STEP 2

A virtual directory's alias is the name that will appear to users when they navigate your Web site. To the client browser, the alias name of the directory will appear as a descendant of the root directory. The next step is to provide a virtual directory alias (Figure 11.21).

- Enter the directory name as it is to appear to users in the Alias field.
- Click **NEXT**.

➣ STEP 3

The next step is to associate a path with the alias that was assigned in the previous step using the Web Site Content Directory dialog box

(Figure 11.22). The Directory field may be filled in manually, or if BROWSE is clicked, the path may be selected visually.

- Enter the path to the physical directory into the Directory field, or click **BROWSE** to select the path visually.
- Click **NEXT**.

Figure 11.20 Starting the Virtual Directory Creation Wizard.

Figure 11.21 Virtual Directory Alias dialog box.

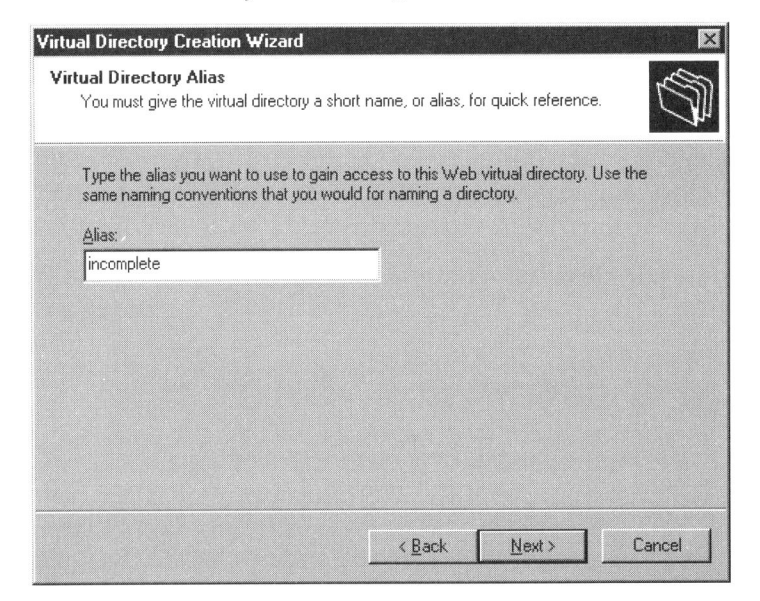

Figure 11.22 The completed Web Site Content Directory dialog box.

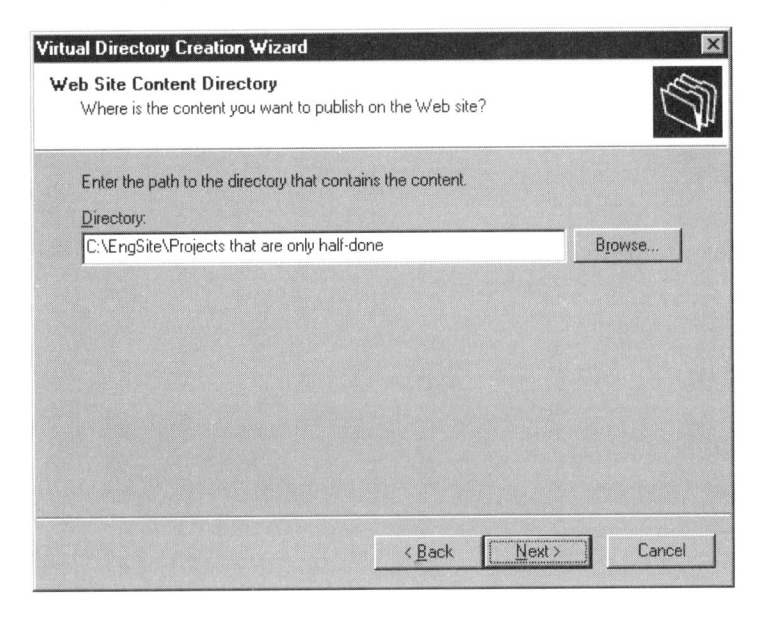

> **NOTE**
>
> It is worth mentioning again here that the alias given to the virtual directory and the physical directory name need not have anything in common. Here, the engineers have a directory called "Projects that are only half-done." This is presented as a virtual directory called "incomplete." This ability to have unrelated names can be both an Administrative convenience, as well as give one the ability to maintain common naming conventions.

➤ STEP 4

Just as with the root directory for a Web site, the new virtual directory can be assigned maximum permissions. As with the root, the actual permissions can be determined by authenticating users when accessing the directory. The permissions assigned here (Figure 11.23) are maximum permissions that will not be exceeded even through the use of greater user permissions.

- Select the desired maximum permissions using the check boxes.
- Click **NEXT**.

Figure 11.23 Assigning permissions to the virtual directory.

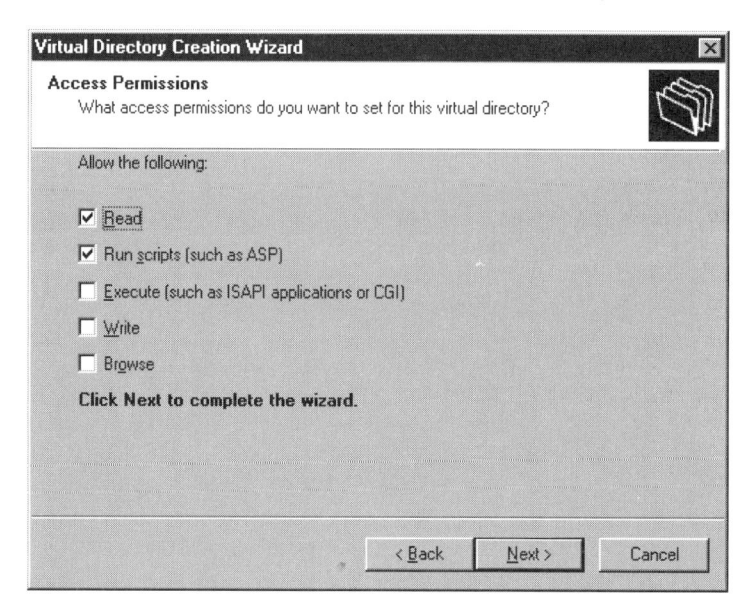

> **STEP 5**

The last screen of the Virtual Directory Creation Wizard (Figure 11.24) is to confirm the creation of the virtual directory. Upon successfully completing the wizard, the virtual directory will be created and can be referenced from the Web site.

- Click **FINISH** to create the virtual directory and exit the wizard.

The New Domain Wizard (SMTP Virtual Server)

> **STEP 1**

Like virtual Web servers, there may be a need to create virtual SMTP servers. Virtual SMTP servers are used in one of two ways:

- A virtual server may represent a remote mail server. That is, the virtual server sends mail on behalf of another domain.
- A virtual server may be an alias for an existing server. This might be the case if a company was renamed and needed to maintain SMTP services for both domains

Figure 11.24 The Virtual Directory Creation Wizard completion screen.

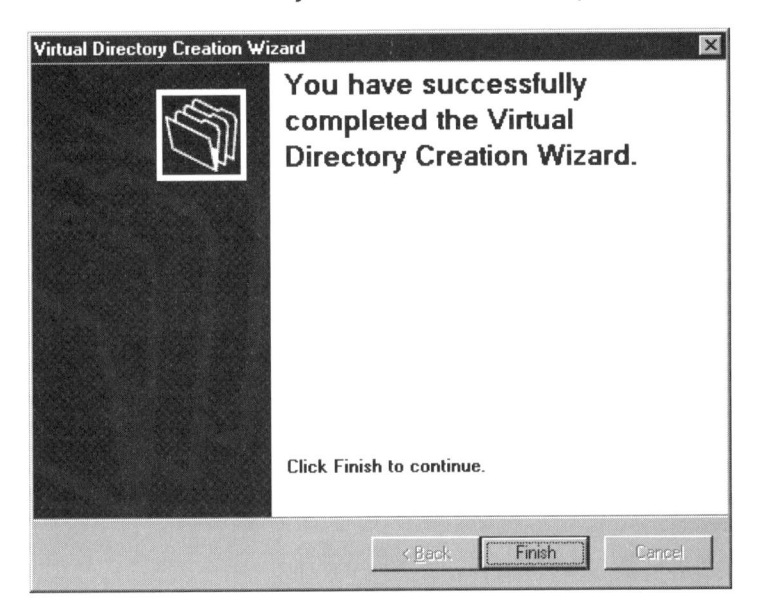

> **NOTE**
>
> In the following example, a virtual SMTP server will be created for a remote SMTP domain. The process for either an alias or a remote virtual SMTP server is the same.

Launch the New SMTP Domain Wizard from the IIS Manager (Figure 11.25).

- Highlight the Domains object.
- Use the right mouse button to display the pop-up menu.
- Select **New**, **SMTP Domain**.

➤ STEP 2

From the opening screen of the New SMTP Domain Wizard (Figure 11.26), the virtual server type is selected.

- Specify either Remote or Alias virtual server.
- Click **NEXT**.

Figure 11.25 Launching the IIS new SMTP domain wizard.

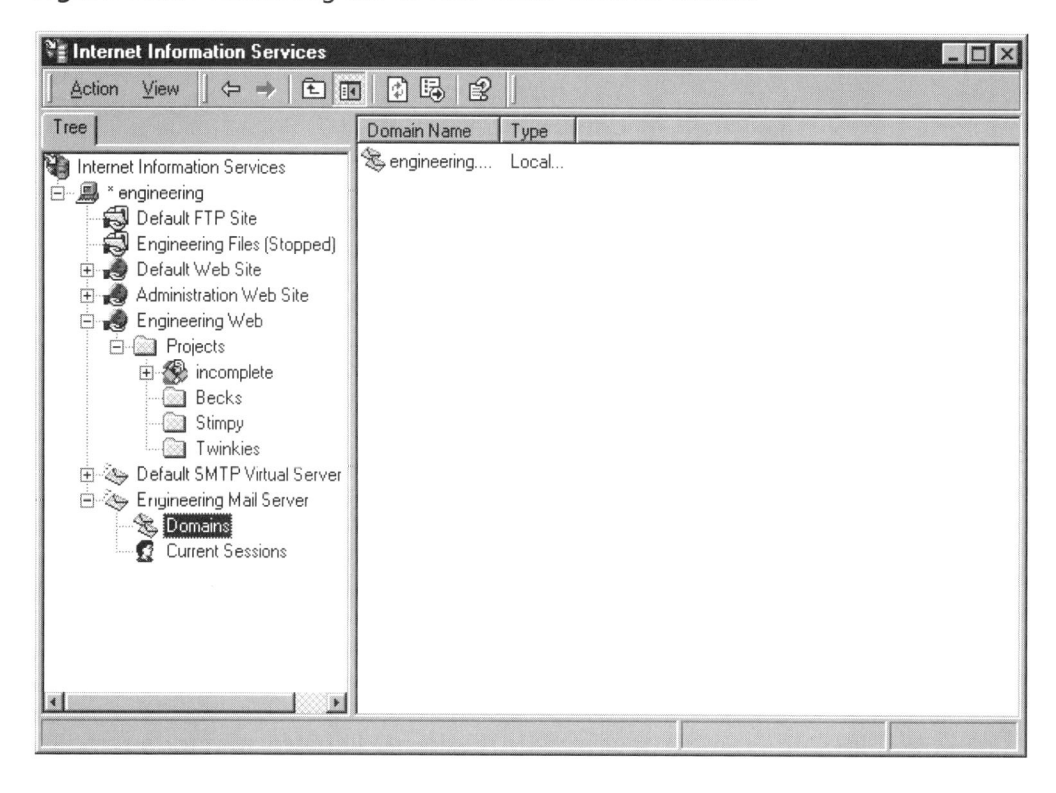

Figure 11.26 Specifying the type of SMTP domain.

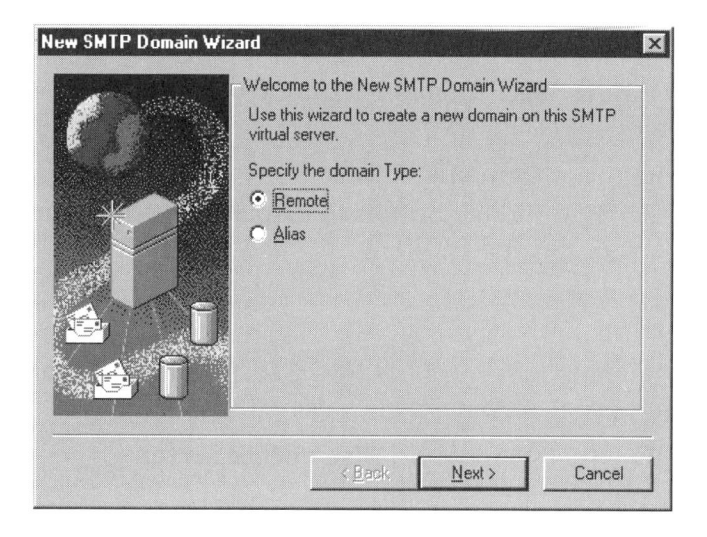

> STEP 3

The only other parameter the wizard needs is the name of the virtual domain. This is specified in the Select Domain Name dialog box (Figure 11.27).

- Enter the name of the virtual domain in the Name field.
- Click **FINISH** to create the virtual SMTP domain and exit the wizard.

Figure 11.27 Select a domain name for the virtual server.

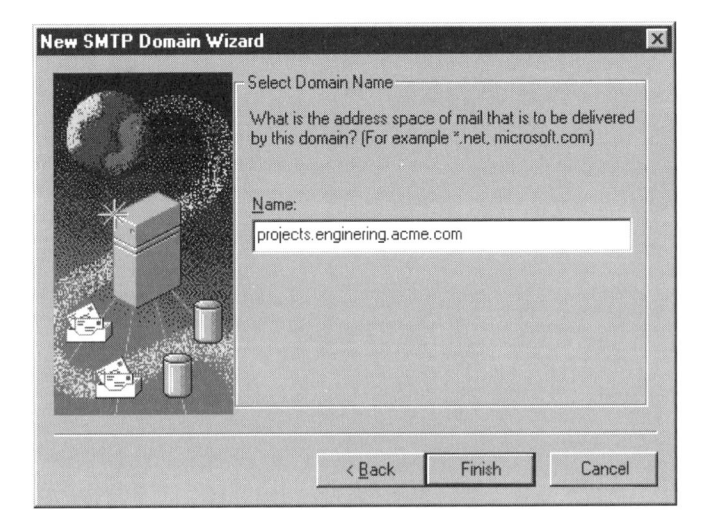

Summary

Microsoft's IIS server is a multiprotocol Internet services server. The wizards provided with Windows 2000 go a long way toward reducing the tedious configuration process of setting up these services.

The FTP Server service can be configured to respond to any installed IP address, on any port, and can be given defined, maximum rights. The Web Server service also allows selection of IP address and port, and includes provisions for security through both maximum rights assignment and SSL. Virtual directories may be created to allow the abstraction of the relationship between descendant directories and their physical location. The SMTP Server service allows the creation of SMTP mail servers that respond to different IP addresses for different domains. Using virtual SMTP domains, one can create alias SMTP domain names, or allow a Windows 2000 server to act on behalf of other, remote domains.

Chapter 12

Windows Component Wizard

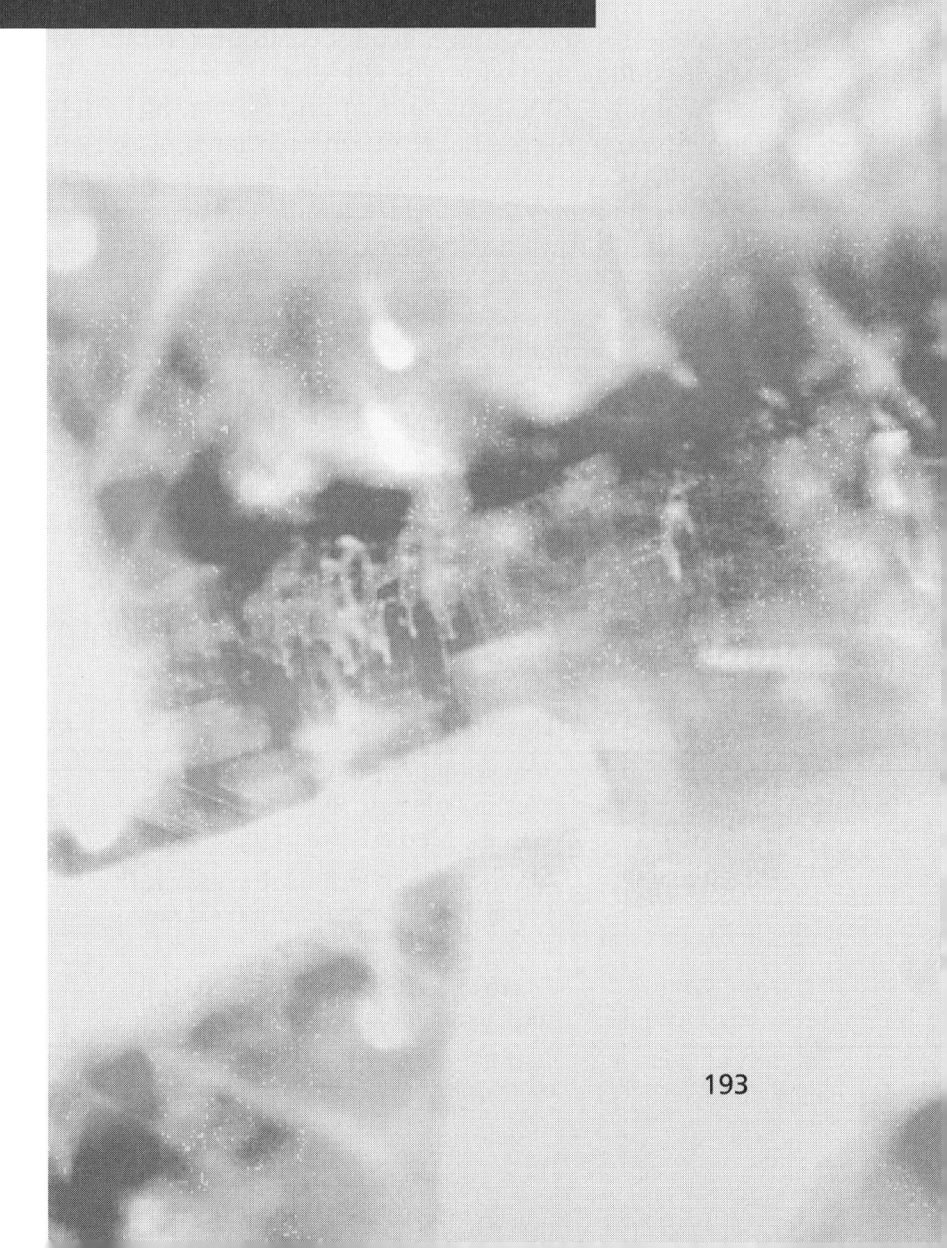

Introduction

Depending on your needs, you may decide to install additional Windows 2000 system components, or remove some of those installed by default. To change the components installed, Windows 2000 provides the Windows Component Wizard. From here, you can select which components to add or remove. By the end of this chapter, you will know how to change the operating system components currently installed.

Before You Begin

Before you get started, it is a good idea to understand what component you are installing and why. The Windows Components Wizard is available in both Windows 2000 Professional and Server, although some services or components are only available on one platform or the other (Table 12.1). For example, Certificate Services or the Cluster Service cannot be installed on Windows 2000 Professional. These services are specialty services that should run on the Windows 2000 Server platform.

Some services are going to place more load on a machine than others. For example, Terminal Services will require at least a Quad-processor Pentium Pro running at 200 MHz with 500MB of RAM to support approximately 30 heavy users of this service. Is the machine in question up to such a task? Other components, such as the Script Debugger, require very little disk space and only minimal system resources when running.

Some components are dependent on each other. A good example of this is Terminal Services. It makes little sense to install Terminal Services Licensing if Terminal Services is not installed.

Table 12.1 Overview of the Components Available in Windows 2000 Server and Professional

Name	Description	Server	Professional
Accessories and Utilities	Accessibility options, Wallpaper, Mouse Pointers, HyperTerminal, Games, Media Player, etc.	X	
Certificate Services	Makes the server a CA for use with Public Key Infrastructure (PKI) services	X	
Cluster Service	Microsoft Cluster Server (MSCS) for highly available applications	X	
Indexing Service	Fast location of files	X	X

Continued

Name	Description	Server	Professional
Internet Information Services (IIS)	Web and FTP server	X	X
Monitoring and Management Tools	Network Monitor, SNMP, Connection Manager	X	X
Message Queuing Services	For loosely coupled network communication services	X	X
Networking Services	DNS, DHCP, WINS, and other network support services	X	X
Other File and Print Services	File and Print for Macintosh, Print Services for UNIX	X	X
Remote Installation Services	Install Windows 2000 Professional on remote boot clients	X	
Remote Storage	Hierarchical Storage Management	X	
Script Debugger	Helps find errors in scripts	X	X
Terminal Services	Terminal Services Server to run Windows applications and manage the server remotely	X	
Terminal Services Licensing	Create a terminal services licensing server to allocate client licenses	X	
Windows Media Services	Stream media services to clients	X	

The Purpose of this Wizard

As the name implies, the purpose of this wizard is to enable the user to add and remove Windows 2000 components and subcomponents. The reason there is a wizard to do this is that very complicated relationships exist between some components and services. By having a wizard to assist in the addition and removal of these components and services, the user is shielded from having to understand many of these complex relationships.

An example of this might be the Management and Monitoring Tools components, which we will use as an example in this chapter. The Management and Monitoring Tools include Network Monitor tools. These tools have deep hooks into the processes of Windows 2000 that allow it to communicate on a network. Registering these components and making other tools and processes aware that they have been installed is a potentially detailed undertaking. By incorporating these complex details into a wizard interface, all the user needs to know is that the tool is to be installed—the wizard takes care of the rest!

Information Needed to Work with this Wizard

Before installing or removing Windows 2000 components, the following should be understood:

- What components are to be installed or removed.
- What dependencies might exist between components.
- What additional resource load or licensing requirements might result from adding components.
- What impact the addition or removal of the component might have on other users or machines on the network.
- Have the distribution media available, including any service packs that might need to be reapplied.

The Windows Component Wizard

There are two distinct modes involved when using this wizard. The interface is essentially the same, but you would use this same wizard when installing or removing a component. The first example illustrates installing Management and Monitoring Tools. In the second example, we will show how to remove a subcomponent of the Management and Monitoring Tools.

You can start the Windows Component Wizard in a variety of ways. Figure 12.1 illustrates launching the wizard from the Configure Your Server application found in the Administrative Tools program group.

Adding a Component

➤ STEP 1

After starting the Windows Component Wizard, a list of available components is displayed (Figure 12.2). In this example, we are going to install the Management and Monitoring Tools component. This is indicated by selecting the check box next to the component.

- Check the box next to Management and Monitoring Tools.
- Notice the Description text below the main window. This shows a brief explanation of what this component does.
- Total disk space required to install the component and space available on the disk is shown at the bottom of the window
- If there are subcomponents associated with the component, **DETAILS** will be active. This button will be covered in more detail in the *Removing a Component* section later in the chapter.
- Click **NEXT**.

Figure 12.1 Launching the Windows Components Wizard.

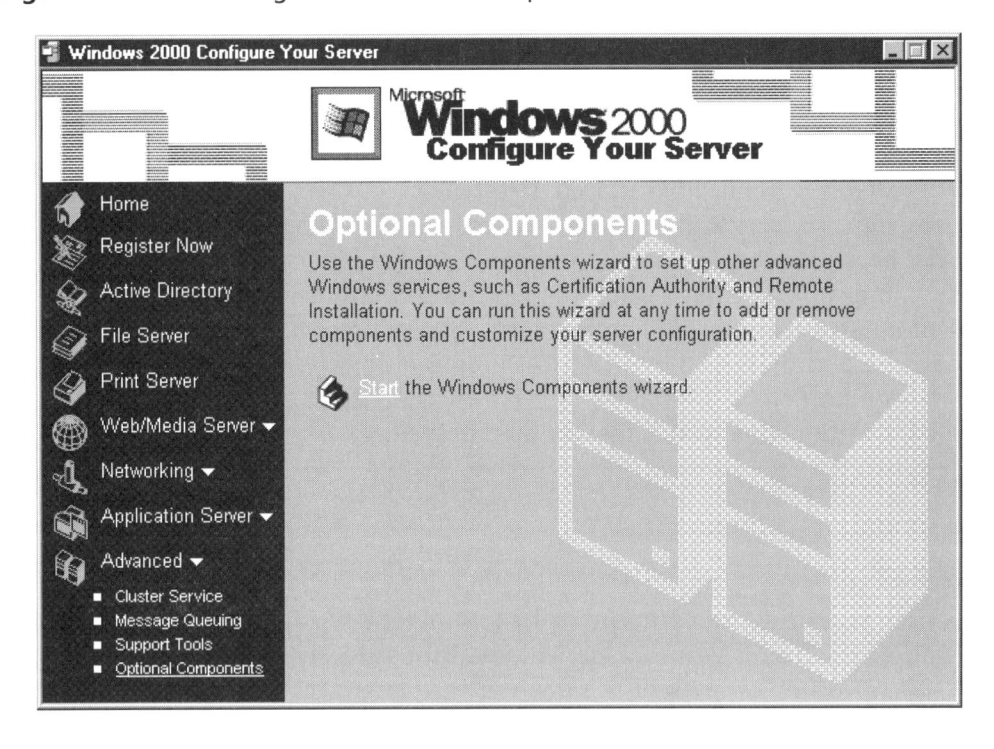

Figure 12.2 Selecting Windows Components to install.

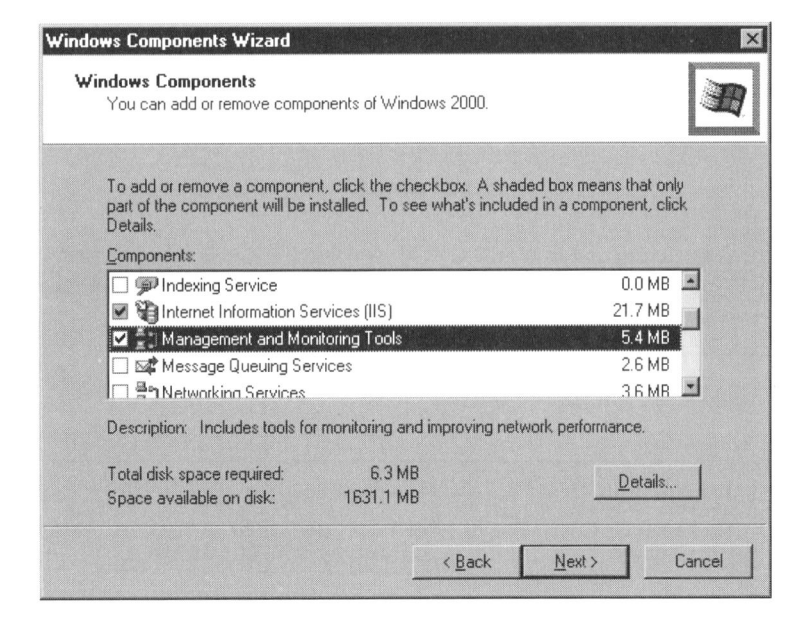

NOTE

The check boxes at the first level of the Windows Components Wizard shows the current status of the component. It can be in one of three states; cleared, checked, or checked and grayed. If the component's box is cleared, that means it is currently not installed. If it is checked, then that component and any subcomponents (if any) are installed. If it is checked and grayed, then it has been installed, but not all of the subcomponents have been installed.

An example of this can be seen in the default installation of the Internet Information Services (IIS) component. All subcomponents except the NNTP Service and the Visual InterDev RAD Remote Deployment Support subcomponents are installed. This is why the Internet Information Services (IIS) component appears checked and grayed.

➢ STEP 2

After selecting the component to install, the wizard begins the installation process (Figure 12.3). This will most likely involve configuring several other aspects of the system that seem to have no connection to the component you are installing. As the Status bar moves, you may see messages indicating the following:

- Files are being copied.
- COM+ is being configured.
- IIS Services are being stopped or started.
- Any number of other configuration activities.

➢ STEP 3

In some instances, the wizard will require files that are not on the system disk. In these cases, a dialog (Figure 12.4) will appear and request the location of the distribution files. If it asks as it did in this case, follow the instructions by inserting the CD-ROM, and click **OK**.

TIP

Many System Administrators like to either mount the CD on a centrally located machine, or copy the contents of the \i386 directory to a file server. Then, when installing a component or making other system configuration changes, you don't need to go looking for the original CD-ROM. This works great for drivers, application software, or any other files that might be commonly needed when doing system maintenance.

Figure 12.3 The Configuring Components status dialog.

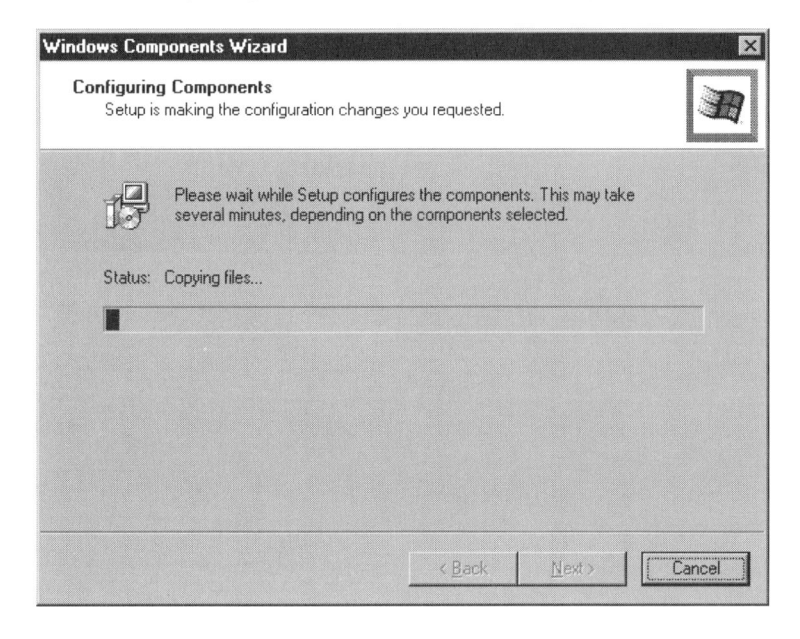

Figure 12.4 The Insert Disk dialog box requesting the Windows 2000 CD.

➢ STEP 4

After providing the wizard with the location of the distribution files, it continues configuring and copying files (Figure 12.5).

➢ STEP 5

The last step is the easiest. If the wizard completed successfully, it will present a dialog as shown in Figure 12.6.

- Observe any messages indicating success or failure of the wizard.
- Click **FINISH**.

Figure 12.5 Continuing to copy files and configure the system.

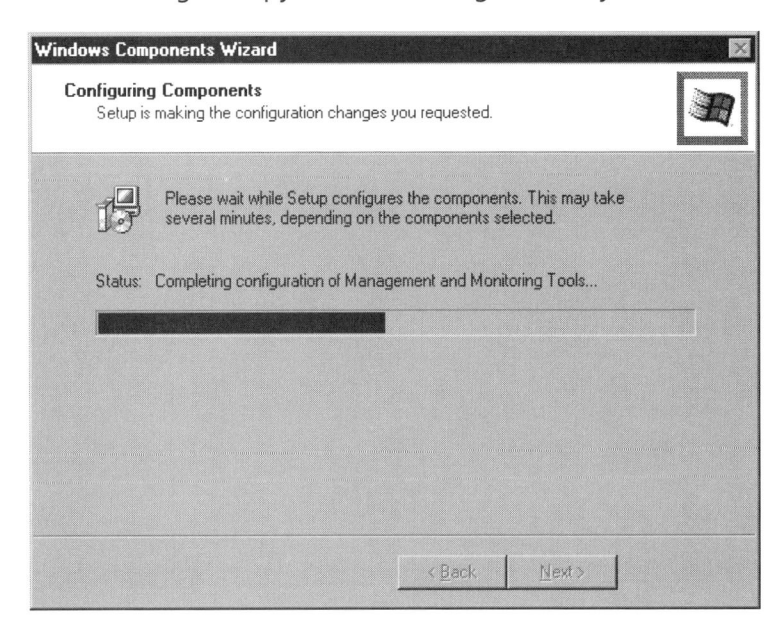

Figure 12.6 Completing the Windows Components Wizard.

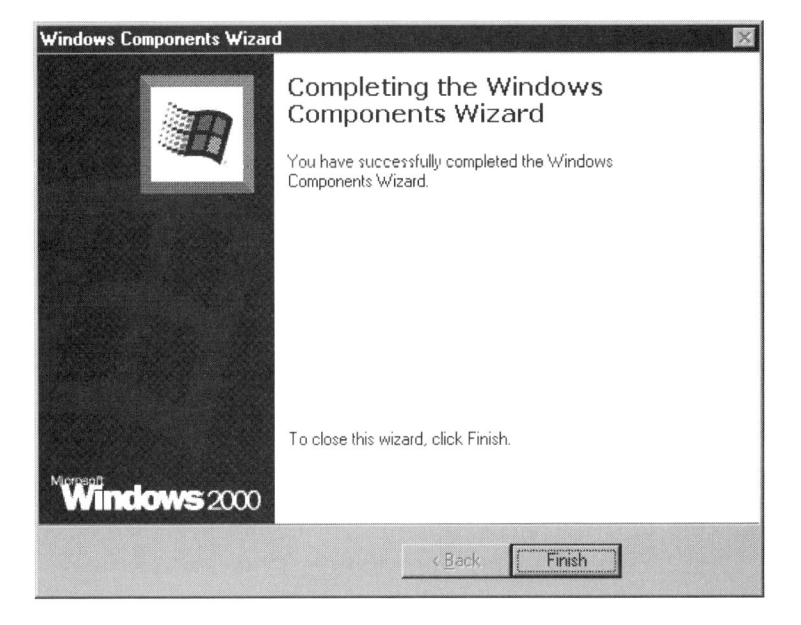

Removing a Component

Removing a component follows essentially the same steps as installing one. The only difference is that the component's check box should be unchecked to indicate that it is to be removed.

➤ STEP 1

In the next example, we will remove a subcomponent of the Management and Monitoring Tools called the Simple Network Management Protocol (SNMP). To do this, we start the wizard (Figure 12.7) and select the Management and Monitoring Tools component. Some things to notice here are:

- The Description, Total disk space required, and Space available on disk fields.
- The Management and Monitoring Tools check box is checked.
- DETAILS is active.
- Click **DETAILS** to continue.

Figure 12.7 Preparing to remove a subcomponent of Management and Monitoring Tools.

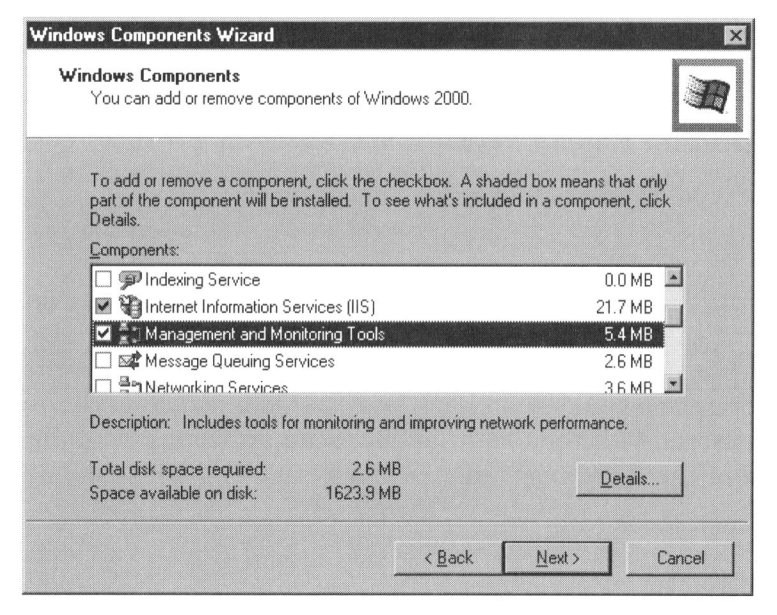

➤ STEP 2

The wizard presents a list of subcomponents to the Management and Monitoring Tools component (Figure 12.8). In this list, individual subcomponents can be added or removed.

Figure 12.8 Management and Monitoring Tools subcomponents.

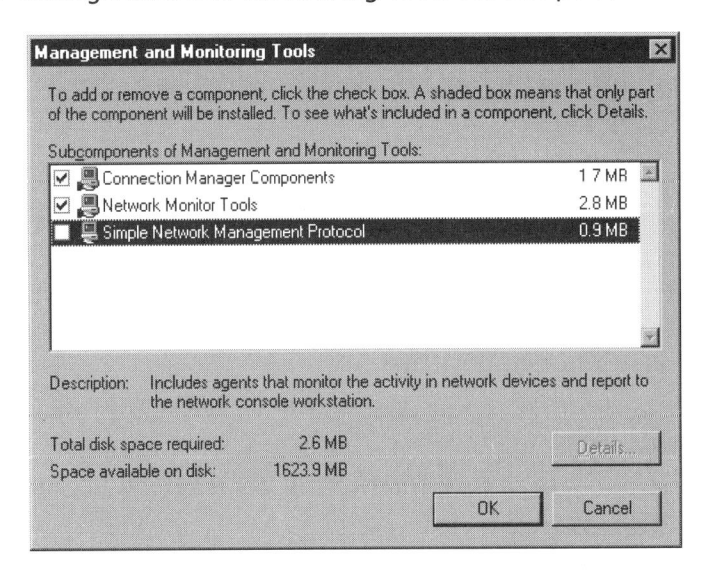

Notice that the form is the same as in Step 1, including the Total disk space required, Space available on disk, and Description fields. There is also a DETAILS button here to accommodate yet another lower layer of components.

We will tell the wizard to remove the Simple Network Management Protocol subcomponent by clearing its check box.

- Clear the **Simple Network Management Protocol** check box.
- Click **Ok**.

➤ STEP 3

Next, the wizard returns one level up in the Components list (Figure 12.9). In this case, that returns us to the main Windows Components dialog box. Notice here that the Management and Monitoring Tools component now shows a check box that is checked and grayed. This is consistent with the idea that there are subcomponents below, and not all of them are selected.

- Click **NEXT**.

➤ STEP 4

Again, the wizard starts running, removing files, and making configuration changes (Figure 12.10).

Figure 12.9 Returning to the main Windows Components dialog box.

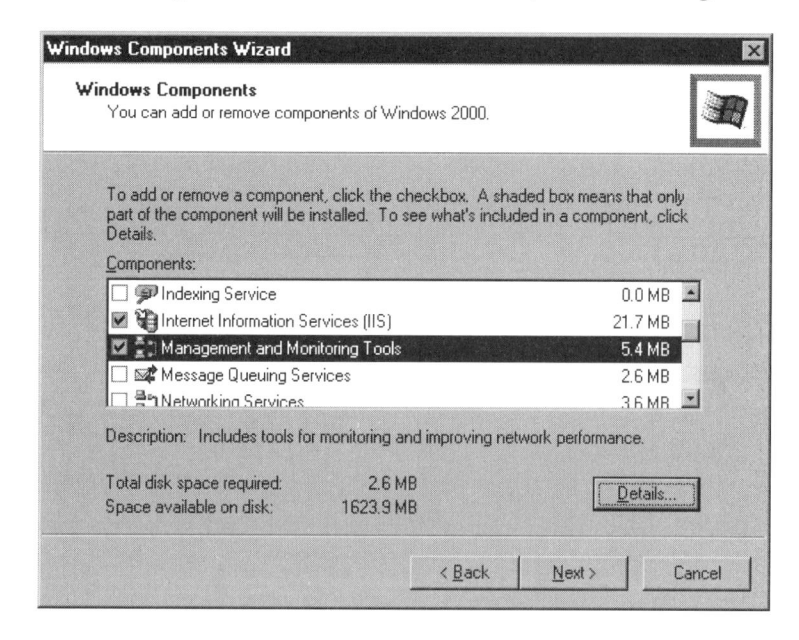

Figure 12.10 The Configuring Components dialog box running while removing components.

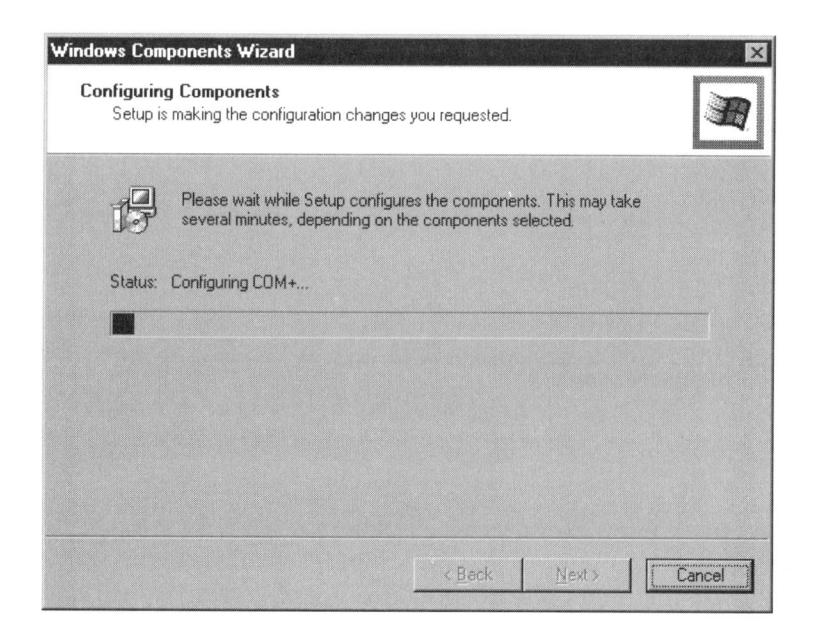

> **WARNING**
>
> Clicking CANCEL here will stop the copy, remove, or configure process, but could leave the system in an indeterminate state. If you click CANCEL for whatever reason, make sure you go back and rerun the wizard to make sure everything is changed correctly.

➤ STEP 5

Figure 12.11 shows the final dialog box in the Windows Components Wizard. If all has gone according to plan and there were no errors, the removal is complete.

Figure 12.11 Windows Components Wizard finished after removing a component.

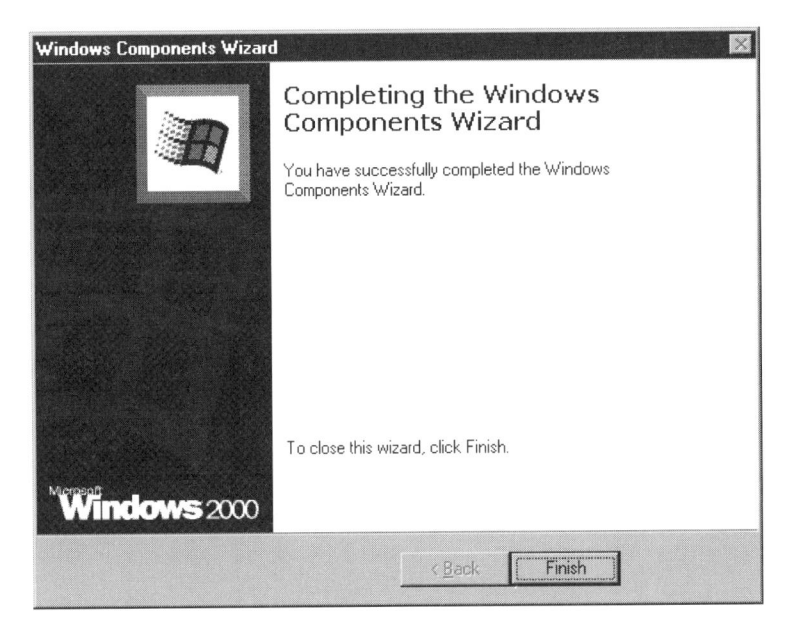

Summary

The Windows Components Wizard provides a simple way to add and remove features on a Windows 2000 Server or Professional workstation. The underlying mechanics of component placement, registry updates, and communication with other system services are hidden from the user. Many components are common between the different versions of Windows 2000, although some are only available where it makes sense, on higher-end systems.

Make sure that licensing and resource requirements are met when adding services to a system. Placing a resource-intensive service on an underpowered machine could result in less than desirable performance.

Unless absolutely necessary, do not interrupt the add or remove process once it starts running. If this is unavoidable, run the wizard again. If the last dialog displayed indicates that the Windows Components Wizard completed successfully, then it did. Any other message indicates that the system might not be configured as intended and the wizard should be run again.

Chapter 13
Windows 2000 Resource Kit Setup Wizard

Introduction

The Windows 2000 Resource Kit contains an extensive set of add-on tools designed to make administering and troubleshooting your Windows 2000 system easier. Most Administrators will want to add the Resource Kit to critical servers and those desktops heavily used for managing the network.

Before You Begin

Windows 2000 is a very comprehensive and complicated operating system. Even so, not all contingencies can be designed into a product even as complex as this. The Windows 2000 Resource Kit was developed to meet the occasional (and sometimes frequent) special needs of Windows 2000 Administrators and users. Anyone who has more than a casual involvement with Windows 2000 will find the Resource Kit a must-have tool. The Windows community as a whole will often make the comment "it's in the Resource Kit" when discussing an elegant solution to a nasty problem.

The Purpose of this Wizard

The Windows 2000 Resource Kit can be installed in both Windows 2000 Advanced Server and Professional. It includes some tools, however, that will only help server administration. The following are some of the included tools in the Resource Kit:

- **Reg**: Allows registry changes on the local or remote computers via the command line.
- **ApiMon**: Monitors calls to the Windows API.
- **Kill**: Terminates processes from the command line.
- **Dumpel**: Exports Event Log to a file for import into analysis tools.
- Several Active Directory utilities
- **DHCP Locator**: Locates DHCP servers on the network.
- Several documents relating to tools and utilities not included in the standard help files.

Information Needed to Work with this Wizard

The only requirement to install the Windows 2000 Resource Kit is a copy of the Resource Kit distribution files. It might be a good idea to look at the Readme file to get an understanding of the included tools. If only one tool or group of tools is needed, there is no need to install the entire Resource Kit; only the tools needed for a specific task need be loaded.

The Windows 2000 Resource Kit Setup Wizard

The Windows 2000 Resource Kit Setup Wizard facilitated both the installation and removal of the tools in the kit. The following processes demonstrate how to add Resource Kit tools to the system. A separate section describes how to selectively add, delete, or reinstall components from the kit.

Adding Resource Kit Support Tools

➤ STEP 1

The first step in the process of adding Resource Kit tools to a system is to launch the Windows 2000 Resource Kit Support Tools Setup Wizard (Figure 13.1).

- Click **NEXT**.

Figure 13.1 The Windows 2000 Resource Kit Support Tools Setup Wizard startup screen.

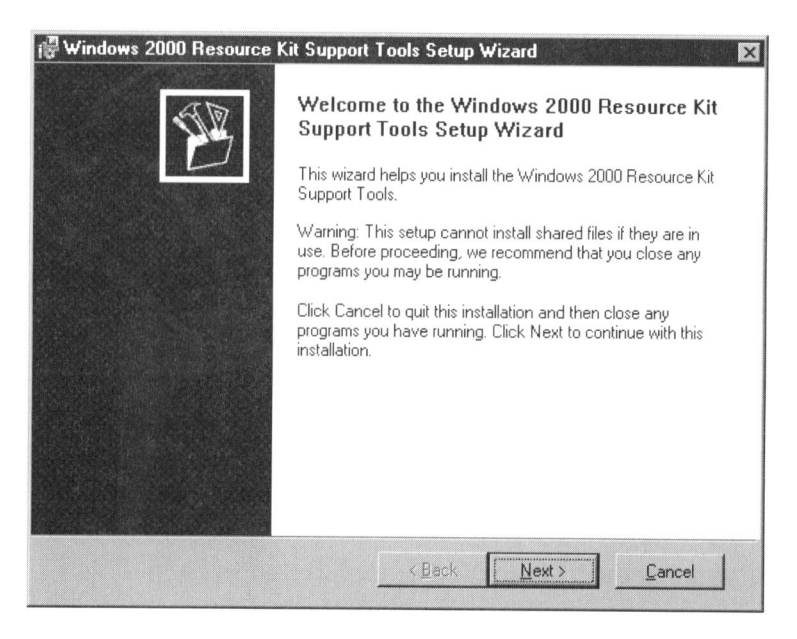

➤ STEP 2

The next step is to fill in the User Information dialog box (Figure 13.2). As with most Microsoft applications, the Name and Organization fields take their defaults from the information provided when Windows 2000 was installed.

- Verify/change Name and Organization information.
- Click **NEXT**.

Figure 13.2 User Information dialog box.

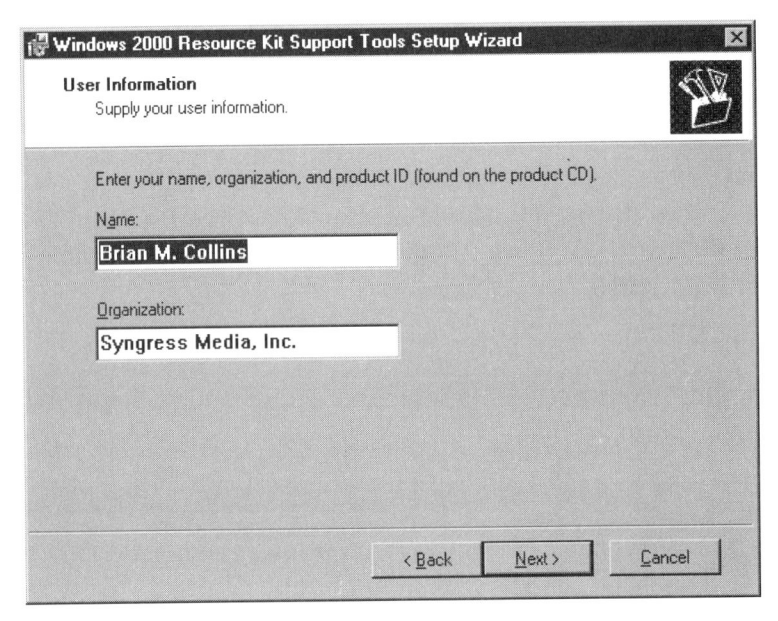

> ## STEP 3

The next dialog box lets the Administrator select the type of installation. The radio buttons provide options to install a Typical, Custom, or Complete installation. The Typical installation provides tools and utilities that are most commonly used, Custom launches a dialog box that allows the selection of individual tools or groups of utilities, and Complete installs the entire Resource Kit (Figure 13.3).

- Select **Typical**, **Custom**, or **Complete**.
- Click **NEXT**.
- If you selected Typical or Complete, go to Step 4.

If the Custom option was selected, the Custom Installation dialog box is displayed. This dialog box has an expandable tree in the main panel used to selectively mark groups of tools, individual tools, or documentation for install (Figure 13.4).

Figure 13.3 Select An Installation Type dialog box.

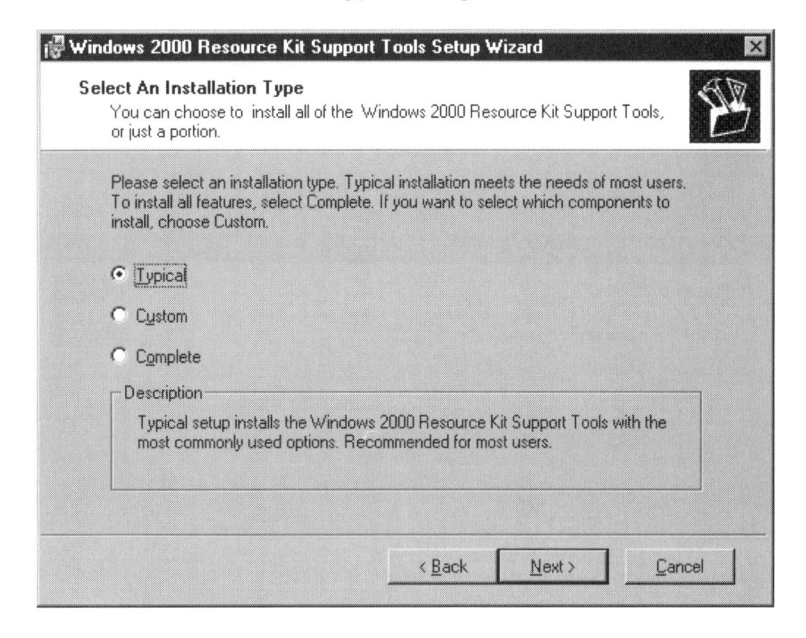

Figure 13.4 The Custom Installation dialog box.

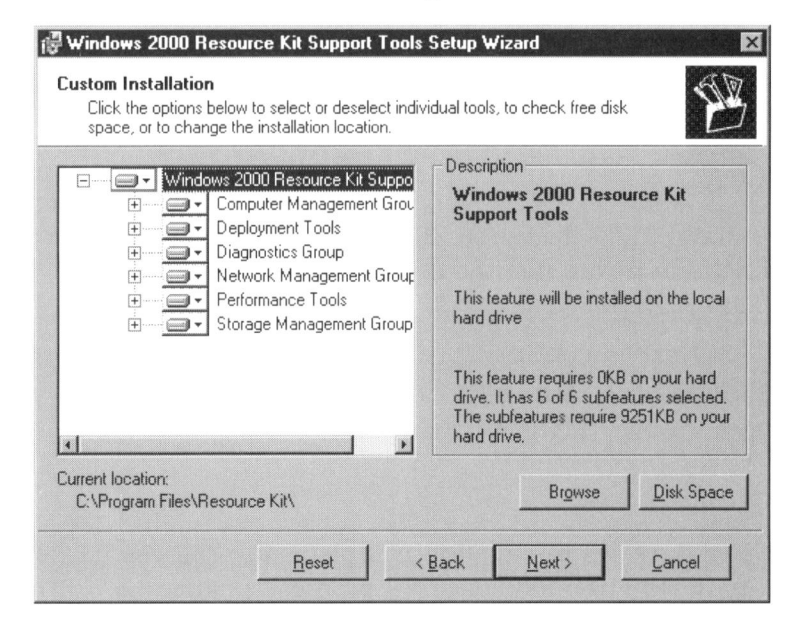

By clicking the expand symbol (+), the individual tools that relate to that group are displayed. Clicking the group name or the tool name allows the installation status of an individual tool or group to be changed. In Figure 13.5, the Sysdiff tool in the Deployment tools group has been marked as "Do not install."

Figure 13.5 Setting the Sysdiff tool to not be installed.

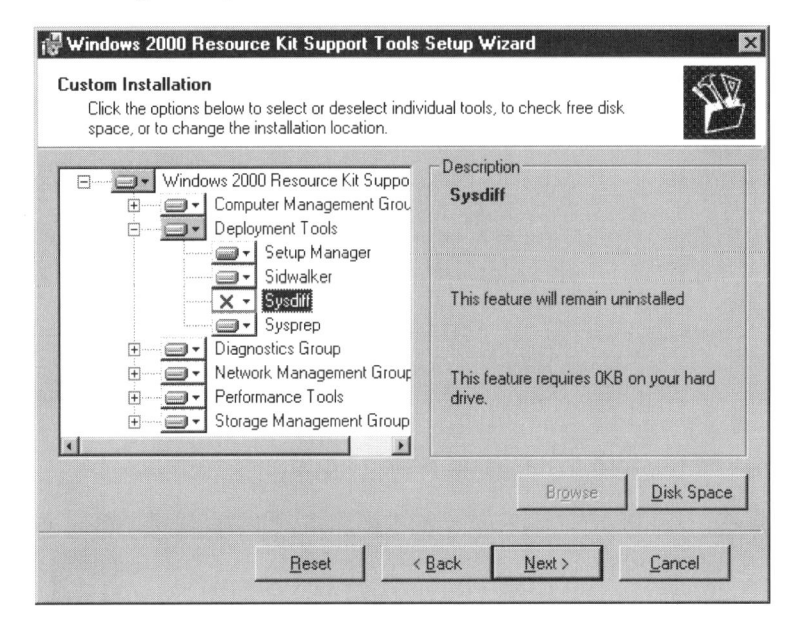

> STEP 4

The Windows 2000 Resource Kit Support Tools Setup Wizard will ask for verification before modifying the system by installing or removing tools (Figure 13.6).

- Click **NEXT** to continue.
- Click **BACK** to change the installation.
- Click **CANCEL** to abort

> STEP 5

As the Resource Kit installation completes, a progress bar is displayed indicating the installation's progress (Figure 13.7). There may be messages displayed detailing copy status, registry updates, and so forth as is appropriate for the tool being installed.

Figure 13.6 Confirmation before installing.

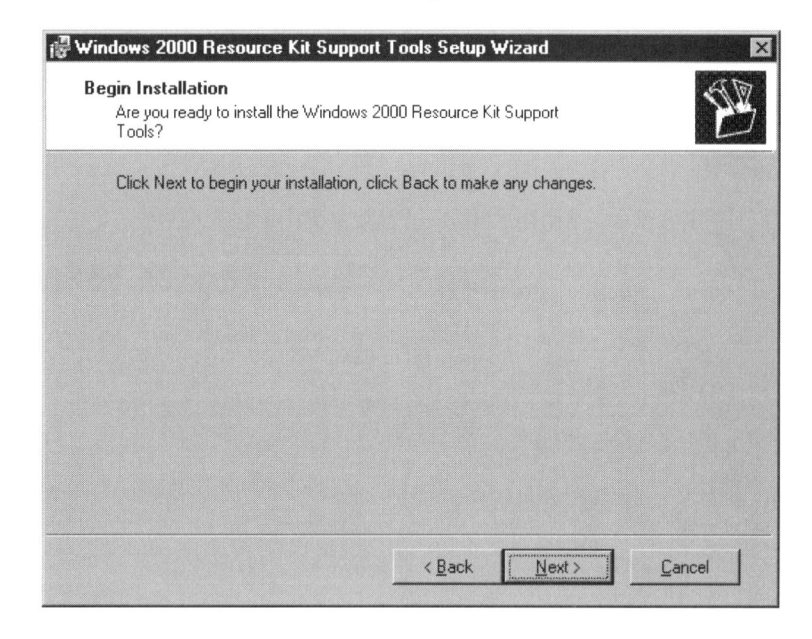

Figure 13.7 Installation progress.

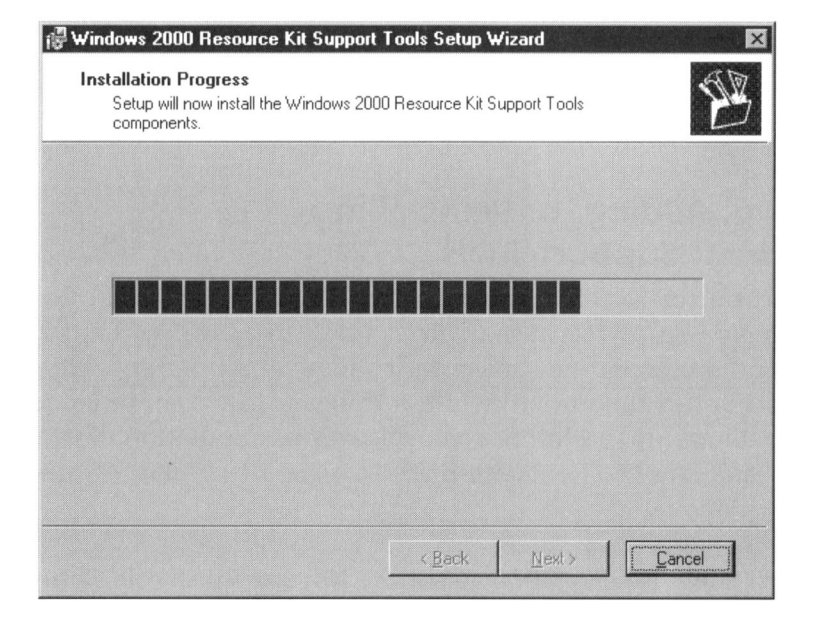

➤ STEP 6

The last task in the installation of the Resource Kit tools is to acknowledge the successful install screen (Figure 13.8). If all went well, the wizard will display the message shown.

- Click **FINISH**.

Figure 13.8 The Resource Kit installation wizard finish screen.

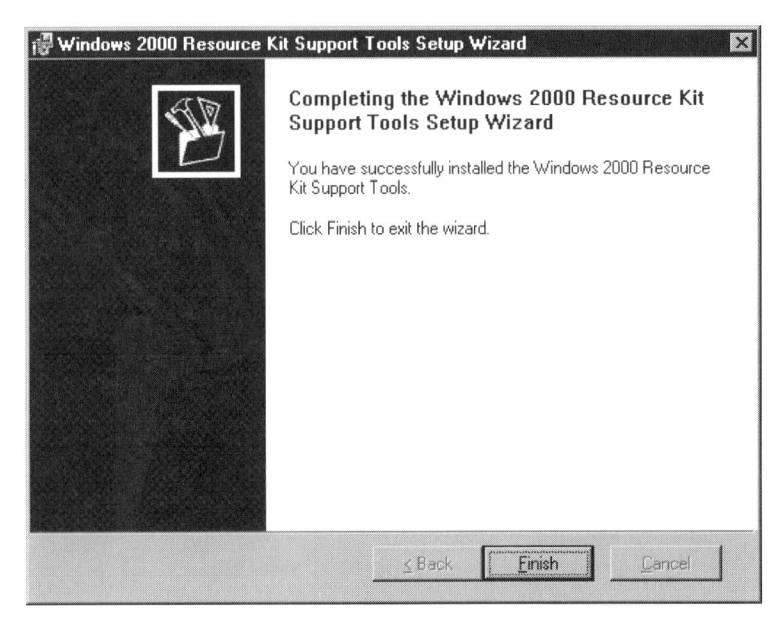

Removing, Adding, or Reinstalling Resource Kit Support Tools

After the Resource Kit has been installed, the Windows 2000 Resource Kit Support Tools Setup Wizard may always be run again. When it is run after the initial installation, however, it takes on a different role. When the wizard is run after the initial install, it appears in a maintenance mode. This mode allows the addition, removal, and reinstallation of the various tools that make up the Resource Kit.

➤ STEP 1

Launch the Windows 2000 Resource Kit Support Tools Setup Wizard. The welcome screen appears (Figure 13.9).

- Click **NEXT** to continue, or **CANCEL** to abort.

Figure 13.9 Windows 2000 Resource Kit Support Tools Setup Wizard welcome screen.

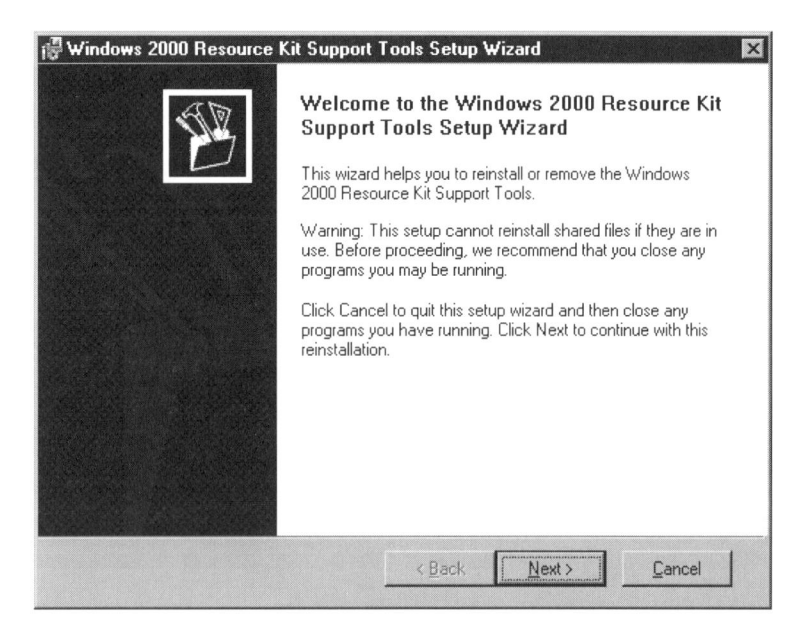

➢ STEP 2

The second screen (Figure 13.10) is where the difference between the preinstallation and post-installation behavior of the wizard becomes evident. The options are very different from when the wizard was run the first time. The options presented in this dialog box allow for maintaining the Resource Kit installation rather than performing a fresh install.

The options presented allow the following configuration changes:

- **Add/Remove** will add or remove individual tools or tool groups.
- **Remove All** will completely delete the Resource Kit from the system.
- **Reinstall** will copy all of the installed tools back onto the system.

For this example, a group of tools will be removed from the system. This may occur if a set of tools was installed for a particular project, test, or operation, and are no longer needed.

- Select **Add/Remove**.
- Click **NEXT**.

Figure 13.10 Setup options displayed when the wizard is run post-install.

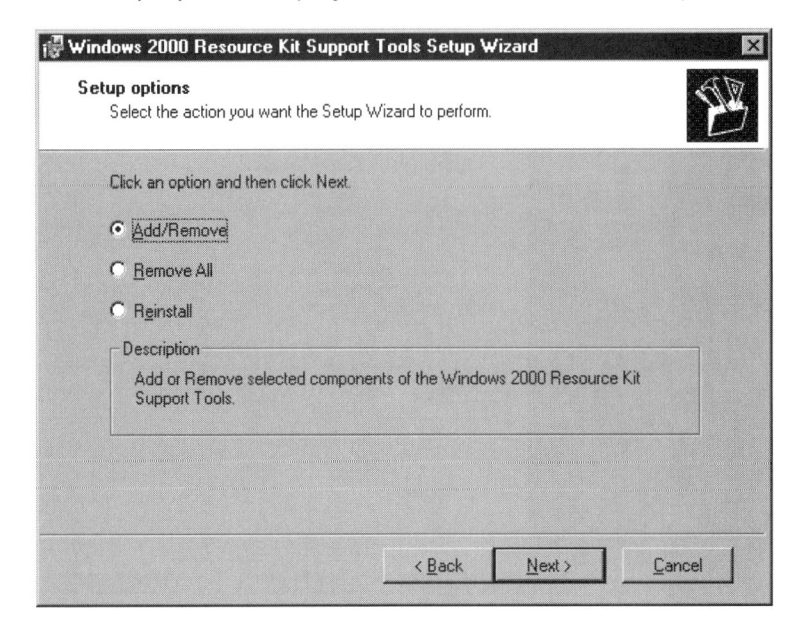

➤ STEP 3

The Custom installation screen seen previously in the section *Adding Resource Kit Support Tools* is displayed again (Figure 13.11). As was the case earlier, individual tools or tool groups may be flagged to be added or removed. In this case, the Deployment tools will be removed.

- Right-click the **Deployment Tools** group and mark it for removal.
- Click **NEXT** to continue.

➤ STEP 4

Again, the Begin Installation message is displayed. The term "Begin Installation" will be used regardless of the operation being performed. In this case, a whole tool group is being removed, but the confirmation box still refers to this as an installation (Figure 13.12).

- Click **NEXT** to continue.

➤ STEP 5

The Installation Progress screen (Figure 13.13) will display various messages describing the operations being performed. When removing a tool or tool group, you will see brief messages stating that files are being removed, as well as other messages such as the one in Figure 13.13.

Figure 13.11 Marking the Deployment Tools for removal.

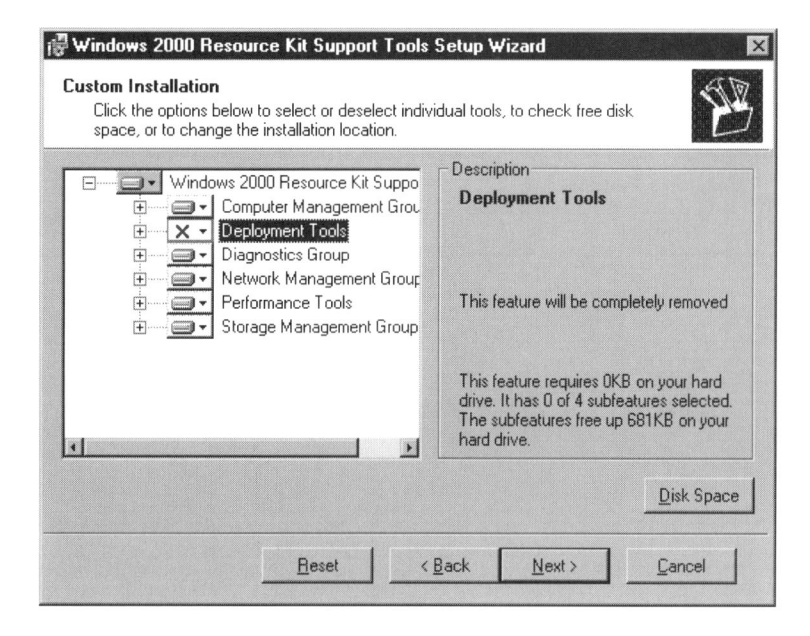

Figure 13.12 Confirming the operation.

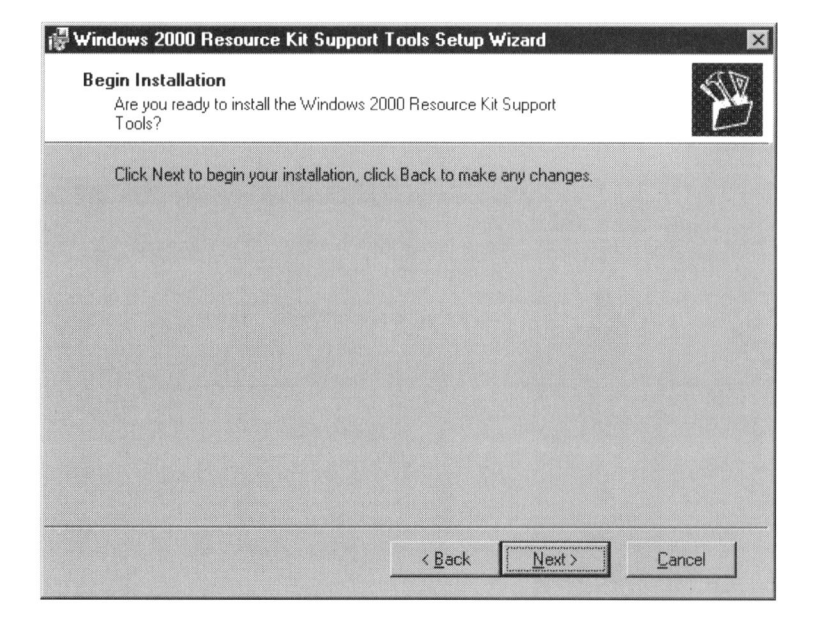

➢ STEP 6

The last step in the Add/Remove operation is validating that the operation was successful and exiting the wizard. The screen shown in

Figure 13.14 states that the operation went as planned and the wizard has removed the tool group.

Figure 13.13 The Installation Progress screen running while removing a tool group.

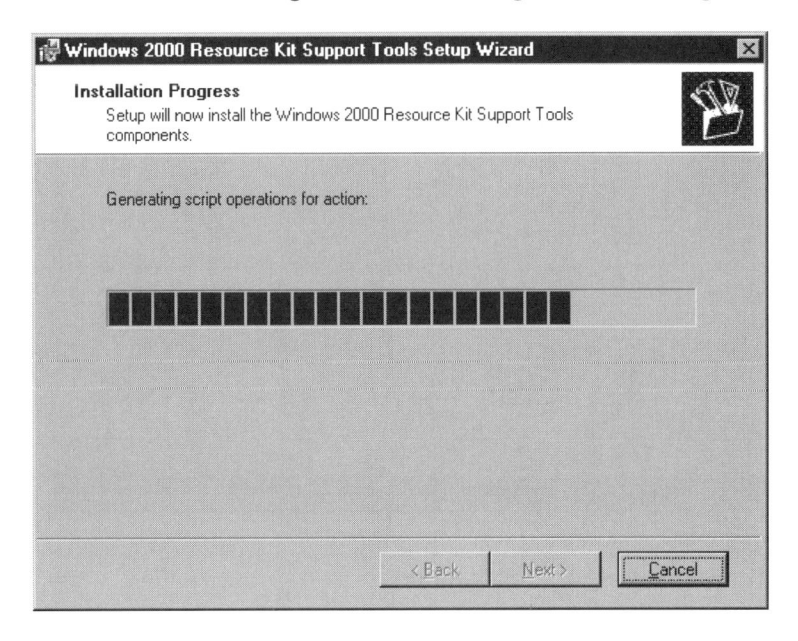

Figure 13.14 The Completing the Windows 2000 Resource Kit Support Tools Setup Wizard screen.

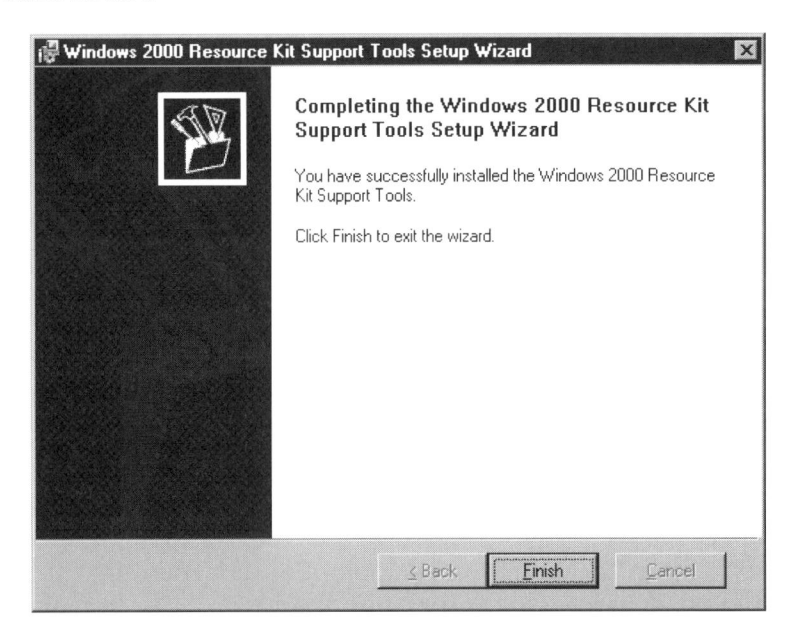

Summary

The Windows 2000 Resource Kit contains a wealth of tools and documentation to support special administrative, troubleshooting, and corner-case solutions that are not included in the Windows 2000 software itself. These include tools to manage networks, deploy software, documentation on Windows 2000 internals, and much more.

The Windows 2000 Resource Kit Support Tools Setup Wizard provides a cohesive, uniform method of managing the installation, removal, and modification of the many tools in the Resource Kit. When run the first time, three install options are provided: Typical, Complete, and Custom. The Custom option allows the System Administrator to select individual tools or groups of tools to be installed. When the wizard is run after the initial installation of the Resource Kit, it takes on a maintenance role that allows the addition or removal of some or all of the tools in the Resource Kit, or the freshening of the tools already installed.

Chapter 14
Add/Remove Hardware Wizard

Introduction

Even with Plug and Play support, it may be necessary at times to manually add or remove hardware. Some hardware devices do not support Plug and Play functionality. By the end of this chapter, you will know how to use the Add/Remove Hardware Wizard to add and remove devices from your Windows 2000 system.

Before You Begin

When working with hardware, it is generally a good idea to be aware of Electrostatic Discharge (ESD) procedures. One should never handle circuit boards or other sensitive components without observing proper grounding and handling guidelines. These guidelines should be documented with the hardware device packaging.

Unless otherwise noted, hardware devices should only be inserted or removed from a system when the system is powered off. Some high-availability components are specifically designed to be inserted or removed while the system is running. It should be assumed, however, that this is not the case.

The Purpose of this Wizard

The Add/Remove Hardware Wizard provides a uniform, complete, and consistent method of adding and removing hardware from a Windows 2000 system. It can also be used to check the status of a hardware device, or to temporarily disable a device.

Information Needed to Work with this Wizard

Any information pertaining to the hardware device that is going to be added to the system should be included with the device. If it is not, consult the person or organization that provided the hardware device for this information.

If the hardware device supports Plug and Play, it will be mostly self-configuring. If not, hardware value parameters will be needed to complete the installation. Again, these should be provided with the hardware product.

Add/Remove Hardware Wizard

The Add/Remove Hardware Wizard can be launched from the Control Panel (Figure 14.1).

Figure 14.1 Starting the Add/Remove Hardware Wizard.

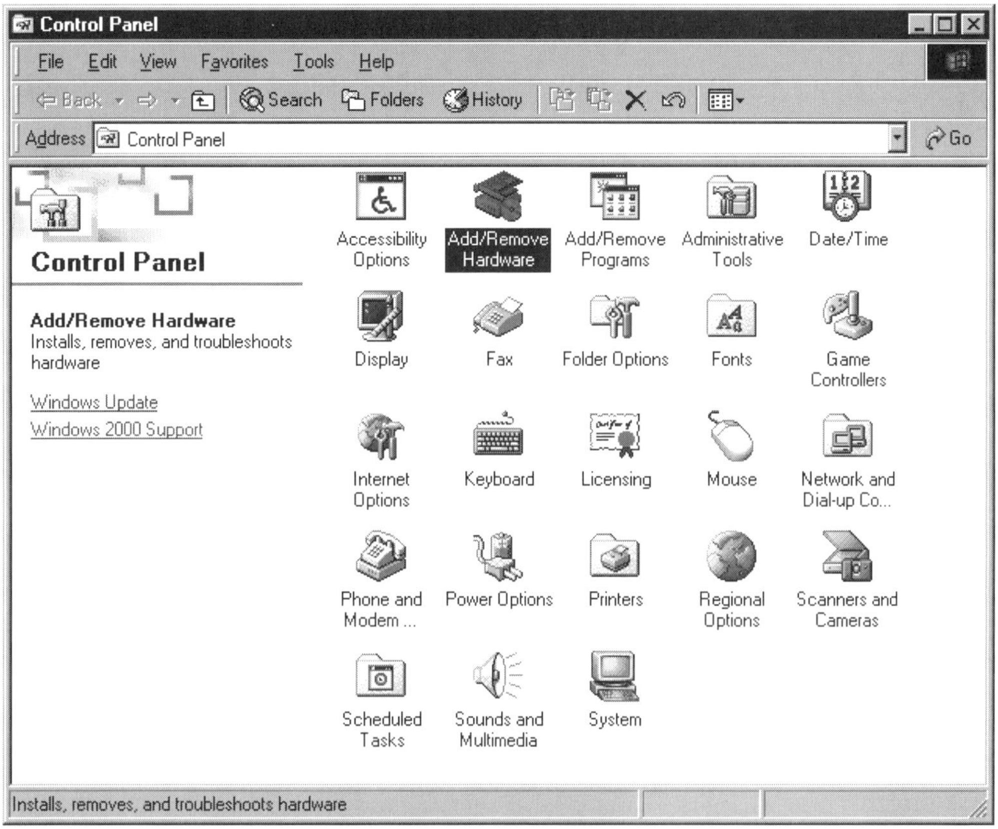

Adding a Plug and Play Device

➢ STEP 1

After the Add/Remove Hardware Wizard is launched, a welcome screen is displayed (Figure 14.2).

- Click **NEXT** to continue.

➢ STEP 2

The Add/Remove Hardware Wizard has two basic branches. One branch allows the user to add a new device or troubleshoot an existing device. The other branch is used to uninstall a device or unplug a Plug and Play device. The dialog box in Figure 14.3 shows the Choose a Hardware Task screen with the "Add/Troubleshoot a device option" selected.

- Select **Add/Troubleshoot a device**.
- Click **NEXT**.

Figure 14.2 The Add/Remove Hardware welcome screen.

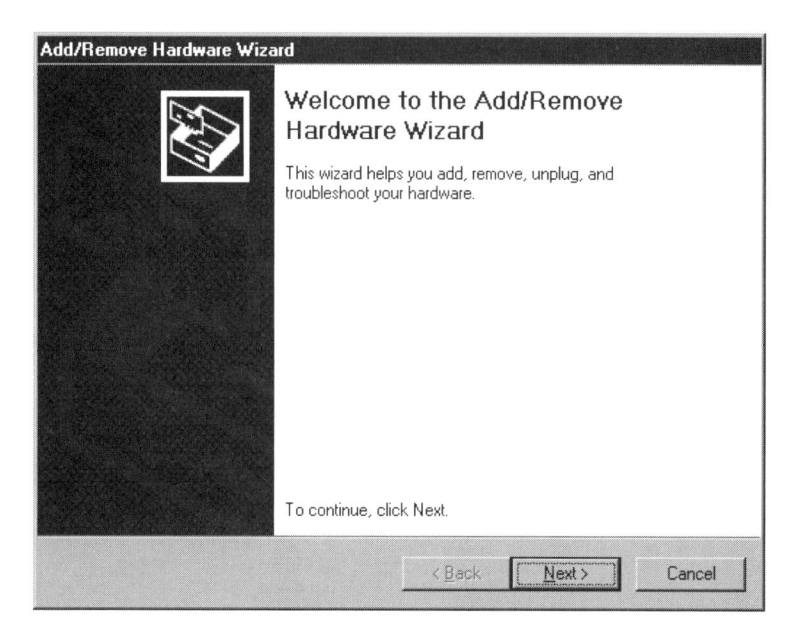

Figure 14.3 Selecting Add/Troubleshoot a device from the Choose a Hardware Task screen.

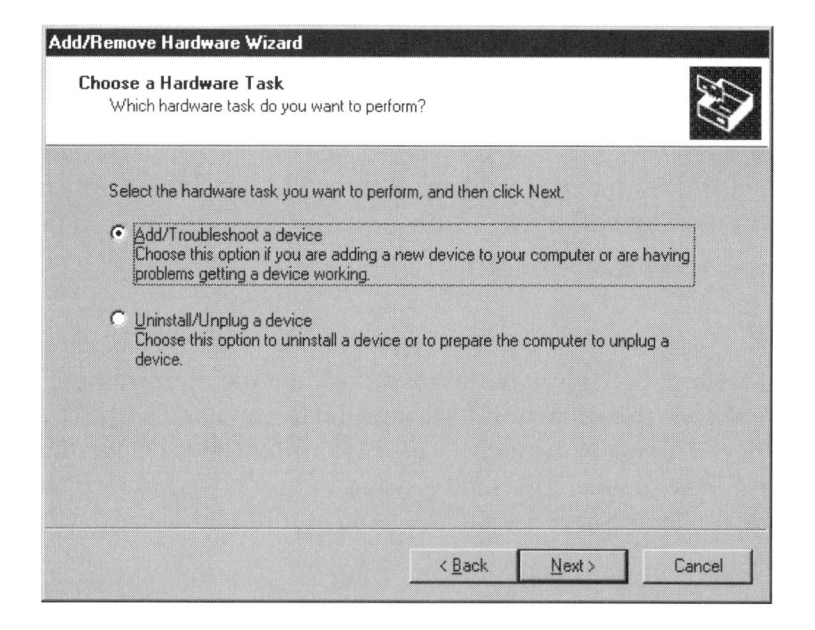

➤ STEP 3

The wizard will search for Plug and Play hardware already installed in the system (Figure 14.4).

Figure 14.4 Detecting devices in the system.

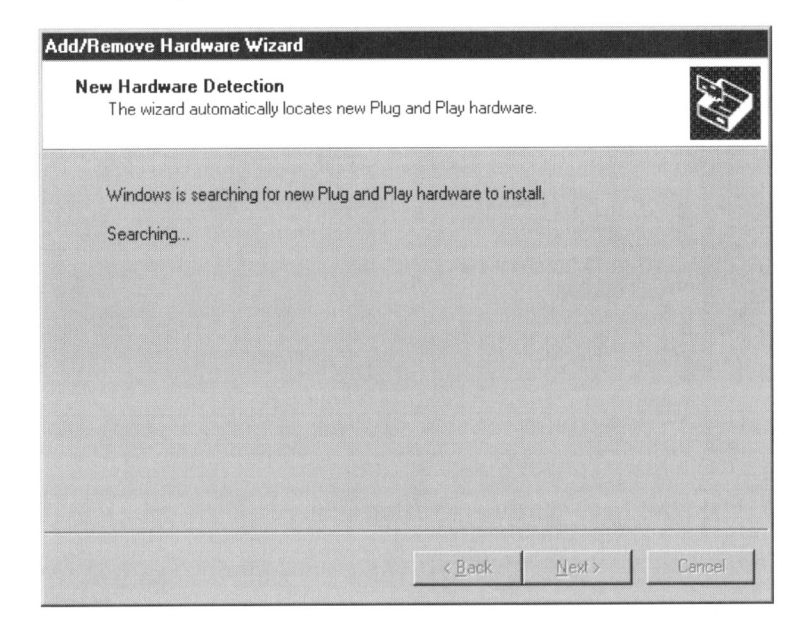

➤ STEP 4

After autodetecting new hardware, the wizard will display a list of previously installed hardware that it has identified (Figure 14.5).

- Select **Add a new device**.
- Click **NEXT**.

➤ STEP 5

It is best to let Windows 2000 search for and detect hardware automatically. This way, the chance of human error is greatly reduced. The option to have Windows 2000 find your new hardware is selected by default. If a previous attempt to identify the new hardware failed, the option to select hardware from a list of supported devices is available from this dialog. To request that Windows 2000 locates new hardware, select **Yes, search for new hardware** in the Find New Hardware dialog box (Figure 14.6).

- Select **Yes, search for new hardware**.
- Click **NEXT**.

Figure 14.5 Choosing a hardware device to work with.

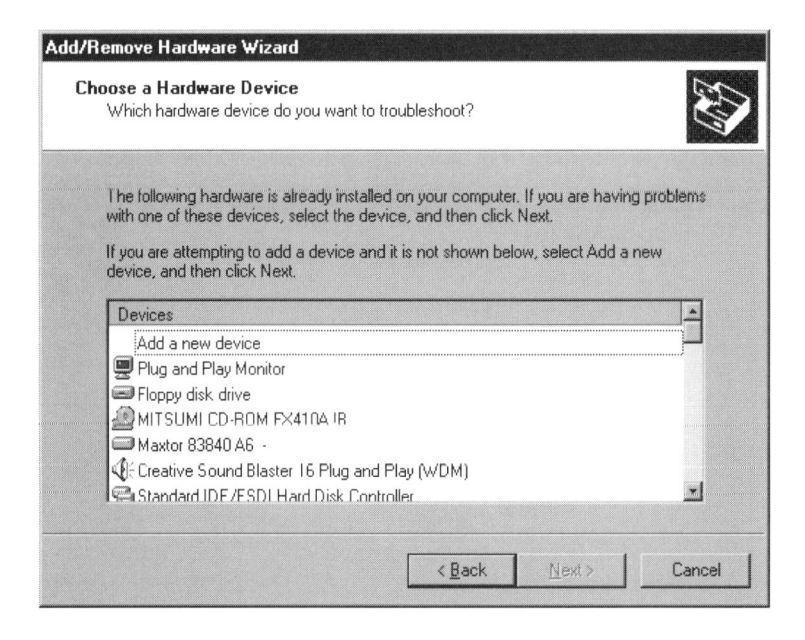

Figure 14.6 The Find New Hardware dialog box.

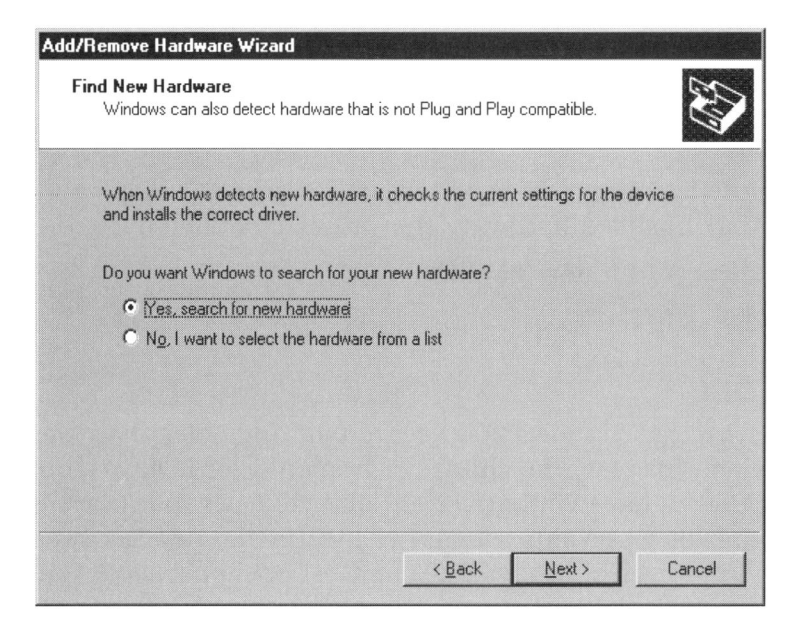

➢ **STEP 6**

The Windows 2000 Add/Remove Hardware Wizard will search for Plug and Play hardware, as well as hardware that is not Plug and

Play compatible but is listed in the Hardware Compatibility List (HCL). These hardware components have driver support included with the Windows 2000 package (Figure 14.7). This can take several minutes.

Figure 14.7 Windows 2000 searching for new hardware.

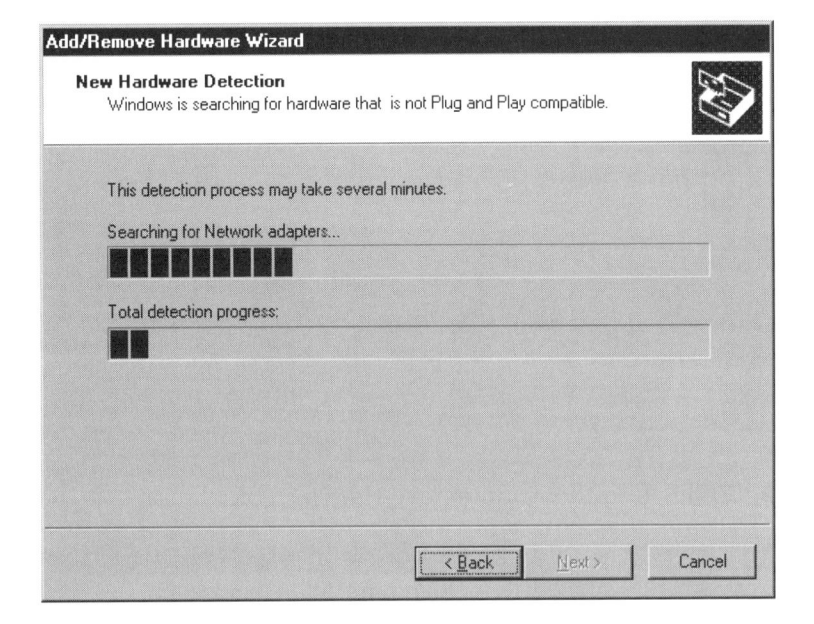

➤ STEP 7

The wizard has successfully detected a Plug and Play device. In this case, the device that has been found is a monitor (Figure 14.8).

- If the new hardware was found, click **NEXT**.
- If the new hardware was not found, click **BACK** and use the **No, I want to select the hardware from a list** option as outlined in Step 6.

➤ STEP 8

Since the new hardware was Plug and Play compatible, the wizard is finished. Configuration for the hardware, including port addresses, interrupt values, and other settings, is automatic. The last screen of the Add/Remove Hardware Wizard indicates that the hardware has been successfully detected and installed (Figure 14.9).

- Click **FINISH** to complete installation of the new hardware.

Figure 14.8 A new Plug and Play monitor detected.

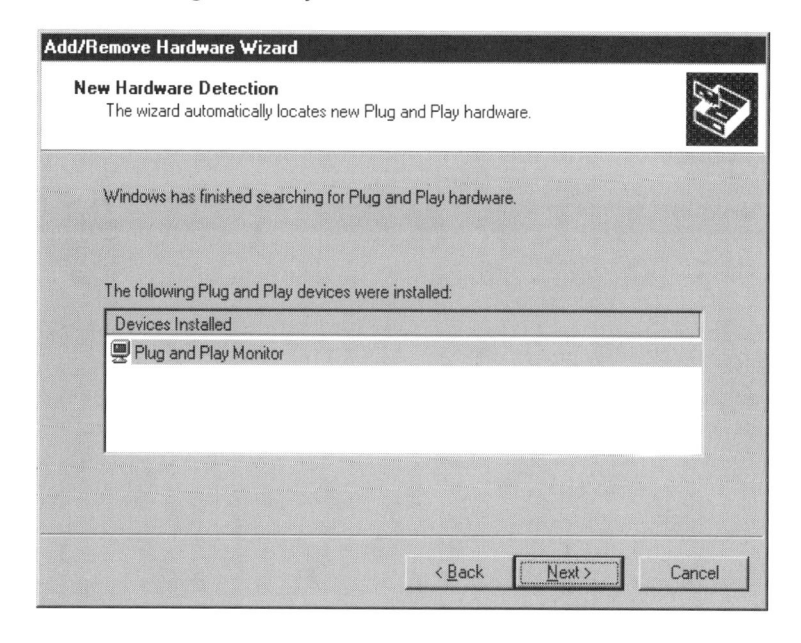

Figure 14.9 Completing the Add/Remove Hardware Wizard.

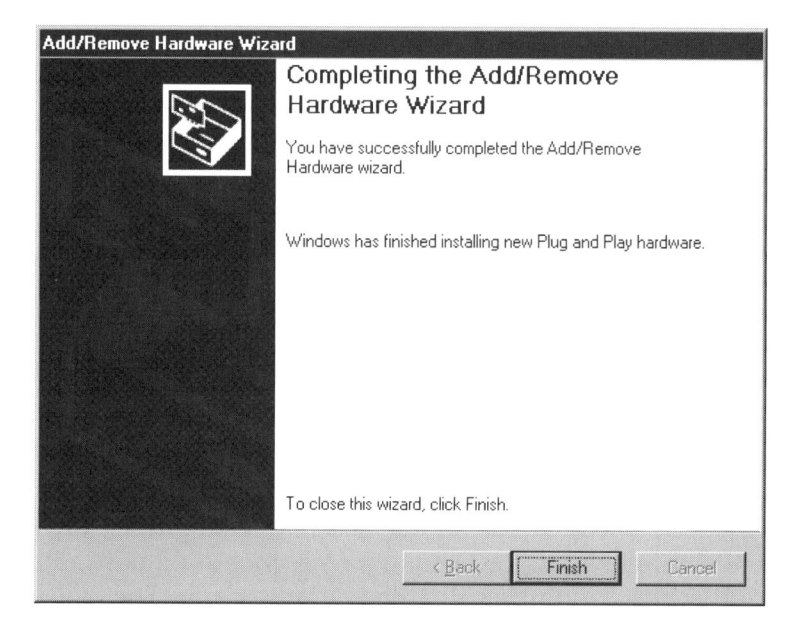

Adding a Non–Plug and Play Device

Many older devices do not support the Plug and Play specification. In order to install these devices, parameters specific to the device and its configuration must be known in advance. The following steps outline installing such a device.

> STEP 1

Launch the Add/Remove Hardware Wizard from the Control Panel (Figure 14.10).

- Click **NEXT**.

Figure 14.10 The Add/Remove Hardware Wizard welcome screen.

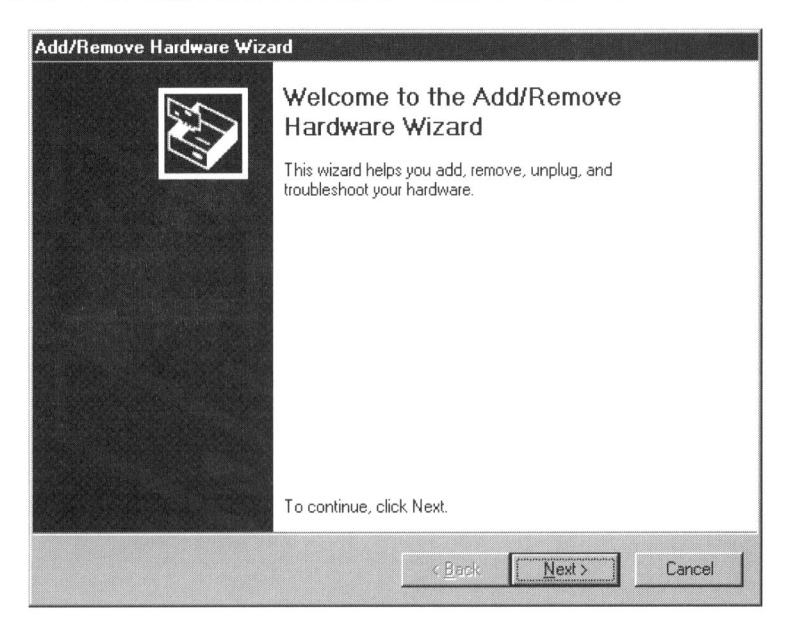

> STEP 2

Since the task here is to add a hardware device, select the **Add/Troubleshoot a device** radio button in the Choose a Hardware Task dialog box (Figure 14.11).

- Select the **Add/Troubleshoot a device** option.
- Click **NEXT**.

> STEP 3

The Add/Remove Hardware Wizard will search the system for hardware to install (Figure 14.12).

Figure 14.11 The Choose a Hardware Task dialog box.

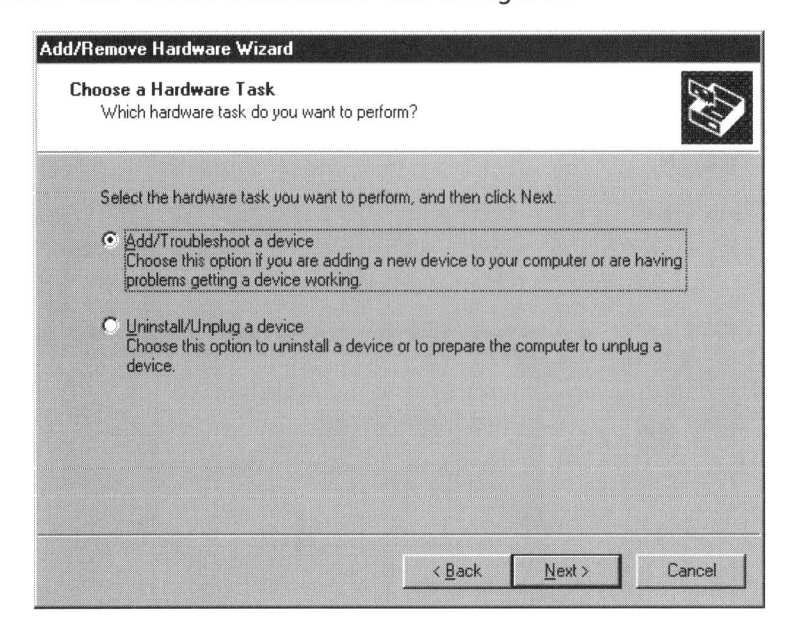

Figure 14.12 The wizard searching for hardware to install.

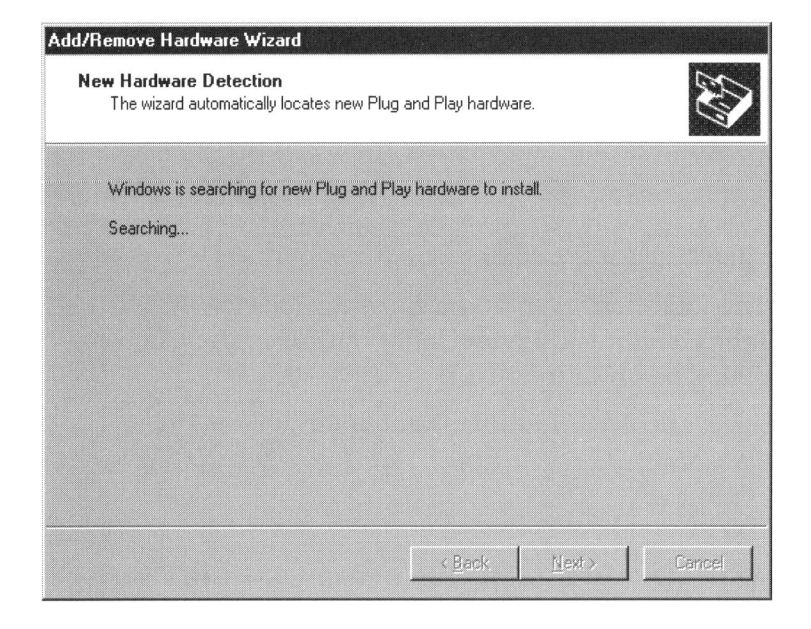

➤ STEP 4

Refer next to the Hardware Type dialog box (Figure 14.13). From the list of hardware groups shown in the dialog box, highlight the type of device that is to be installed. For this example, a 3Com 3C509 ISA Network adapter will be installed.

- Select the type of hardware that is to be installed.
- Click **NEXT**.

Figure 14.13 Selecting the type of hardware to be installed.

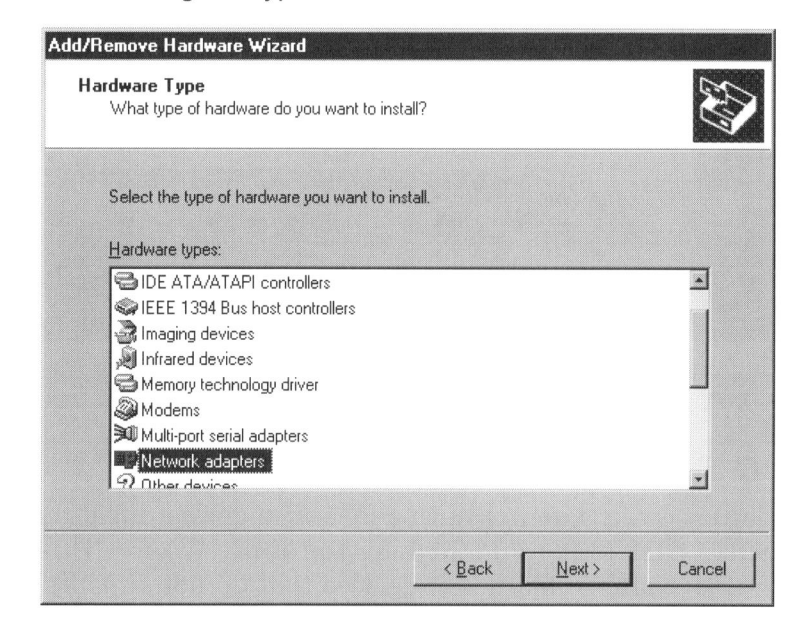

➤ STEP 5

The 3Com EtherLink III ISA card that is being installed in this example is supported by Windows 2000 (Figure 14.14). In this example, the Manufacturers list has 3Com selected, and the Network Adapter list has the new network card selected.

In the event the manufacturer or device was not listed here, HAVE DISK can be clicked. When HAVE DISK is clicked, a dialog box prompting the user for the location of the driver files is displayed.

- Select the manufacturer.
- Select the specific model hardware.
- Click **NEXT**.
- To provide a third-party or unlisted driver, click **HAVE DISK**.

Figure 14.14 Selecting the specific hardware to be installed.

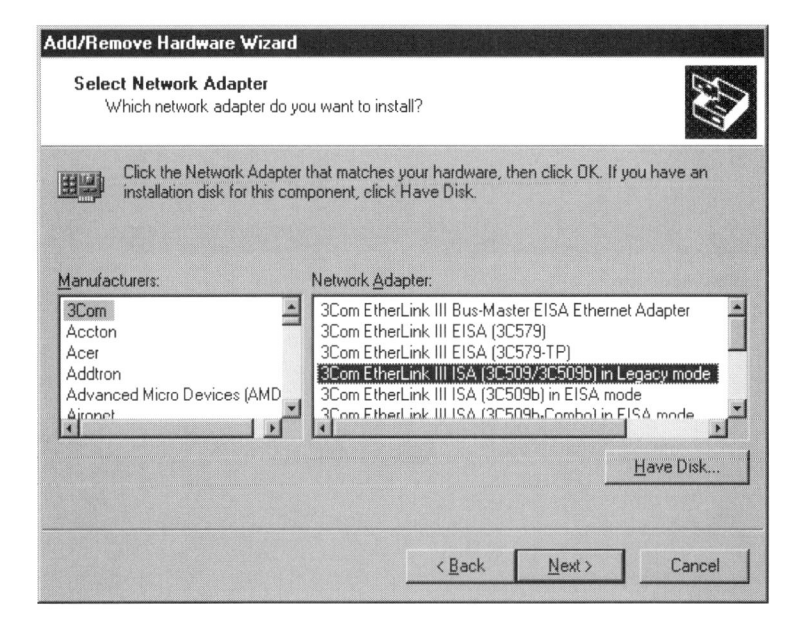

> **STEP 6**

Many legacy devices do not have a means of communicating their parameters back to the Add/Remove Hardware Wizard. This is the case in this example. Many ISA devices that do not support Plug and Play will display this behavior, as will printers, monitors, and other devices that do not support Plug and Play. In these cases, Windows 2000 displays a dialog (Figure 14.15) indicating the device will have to be manually configured. To install these devices, certain parameters will need to be provided by the user. The exact nature and values for these parameters can be located in the documentation that came with the hardware.

- Click **OK**.

NOTE

The example that follows shows the parameters needed to install this particular device. Depending on the hardware you are installing, you may see some, all, or more of these particular screens.

Figure 14.15 Dialog box indicating that the user will need to provide device information.

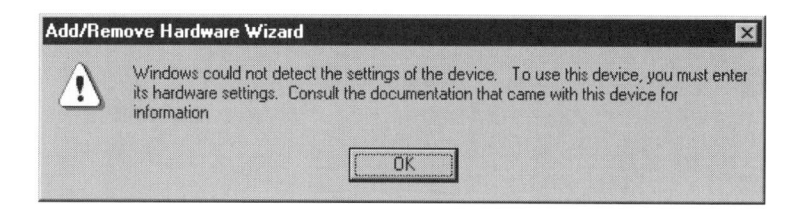

> ## STEP 7

If the device cannot communicate its parameters to the Add/Remove Hardware Wizard, the wizard will ask the user to provide this information. In this example, the I/O Port Range and Interrupt Request (IRQ) values need to be provided so the driver will be properly configured (Figure 14.16). In the dialog box that is shown, the two parameters that this particular device requires for proper configuration are Input/Output Range and Interrupt Request. The dialog box indicates the need for manual configuration of these values by displaying a "?" in the Setting field. To correctly configure any device, these settings must be filled in with valid values. The description that follows describes setting these values for this particular network adapter card and is intended as an example only (See the note following).

- Highlight the first setting that must be changed.
- Click **CHANGE SETTING**.
- Repeat this process until there are no more settings indicating a "?" value.

NOTE

The exact contents of this dialog box will vary depending on the hardware being added. For example, a multiport serial card may have different parameter requirements than a modem, which may have different parameter requirements than a SCSI adapter. Windows 2000 knows what parameters are needed to correctly configure the driver, but in the case of non-Plug and Play devices, it cannot know what the valid values might be. Consult your hardware documentation for information regarding these settings.

Figure 14.16 Resource parameter dialog box.

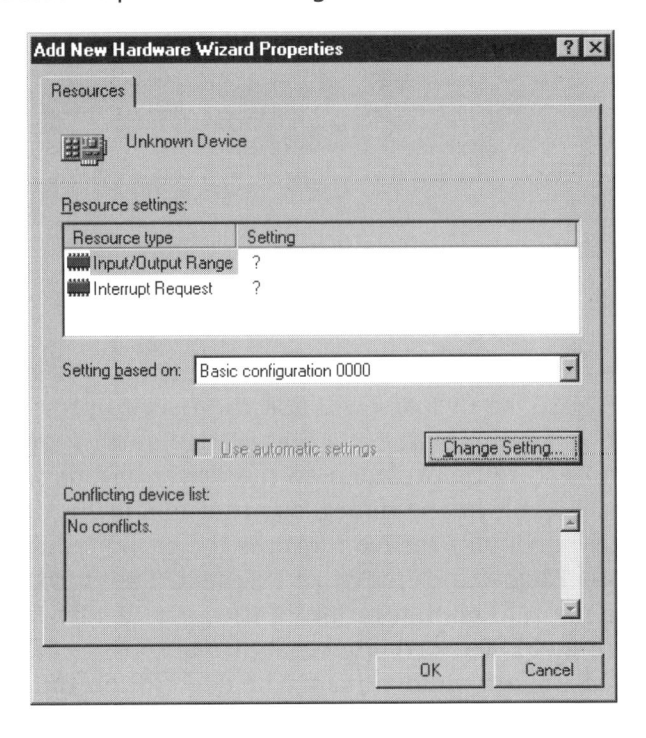

In this example, the Input/Output Range setting has been highlighted, and CHANGE SETTING clicked. This produces a dialog box similar to the one shown in Figure 14.17.

- Select a Value that is supported by the new device.
- If there are other devices already occupying this I/O Range, the Conflict information box will list the devices in conflict.
- Select a Value that shows no conflict with other devices in the Conflict information box as shown in Figure 14.18.
- Click **OK** when done, or **CANCEL** to return to the Properties dialog box.
- Select a value that does not conflict with other devices.
- Click **OK** to set the value and return to the Hardware Properties dialog.
- Click **CANCEL** to return to the Hardware Properties dialog without setting the value.

Figure 14.17 Setting the Input/Output Range for the device.

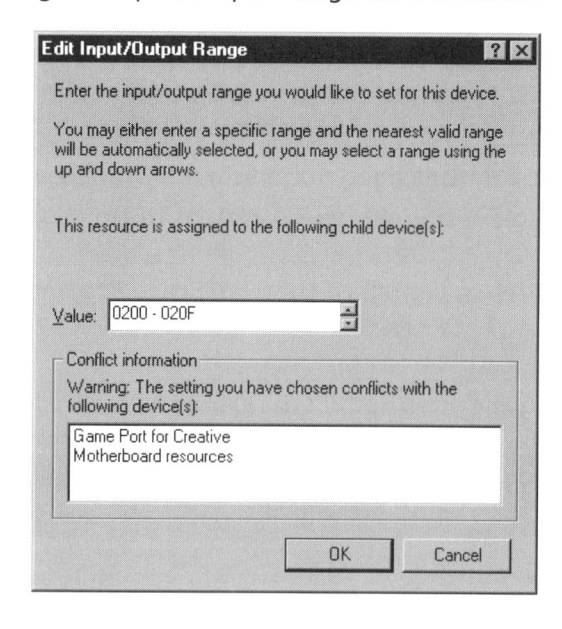

Figure 14.18 Conflict information box indicates no I/O range value conflicts.

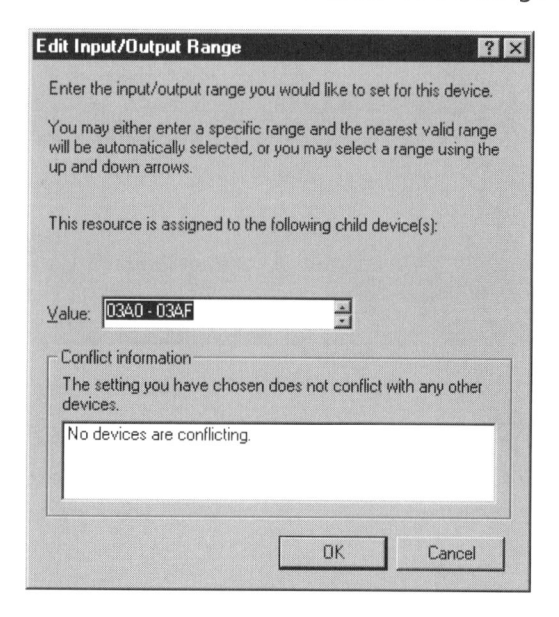

Repeat this process for any other parameters that must be set for this hardware device. In this case, the IRQ value must also be set to properly configure the network adapter. Figure 14.19 shows the dialog displayed while setting this value. Note that the Conflict information box shows no devices are currently using this IRQ value of 12.

- Select a value that does not conflict with other devices.
- Click **OK** to set the value and return to the Hardware Properties dialog.
- Click **CANCEL** to return to the Hardware Properties dialog without setting the value.

Figure 14.19 Setting the Interrupt Request value with no conflicts.

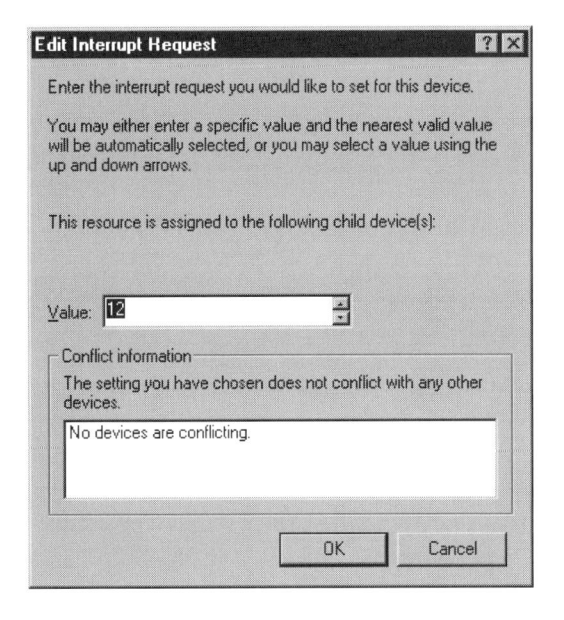

➤ STEP 8

After providing all values required by the software driver for the device, Windows will indicate that the driver is ready to be installed (Figure 14.20).

- Click **NEXT**.

➤ STEP 9

The Add/Remove Hardware Wizard will now copy the correct driver software into the system (Figure 14.21). At this point, the user may be prompted to provide a path to the Windows 2000 distribution files if they are needed by the wizard to complete the software installation.

Figure 14.20 Begin software installation.

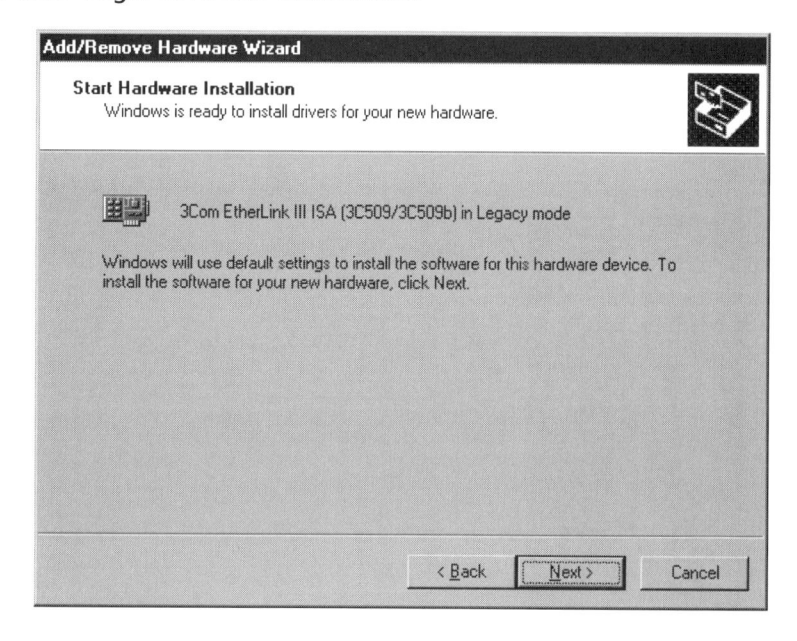

Figure 14.21 The Add/Remove Hardware Wizard installing software drivers.

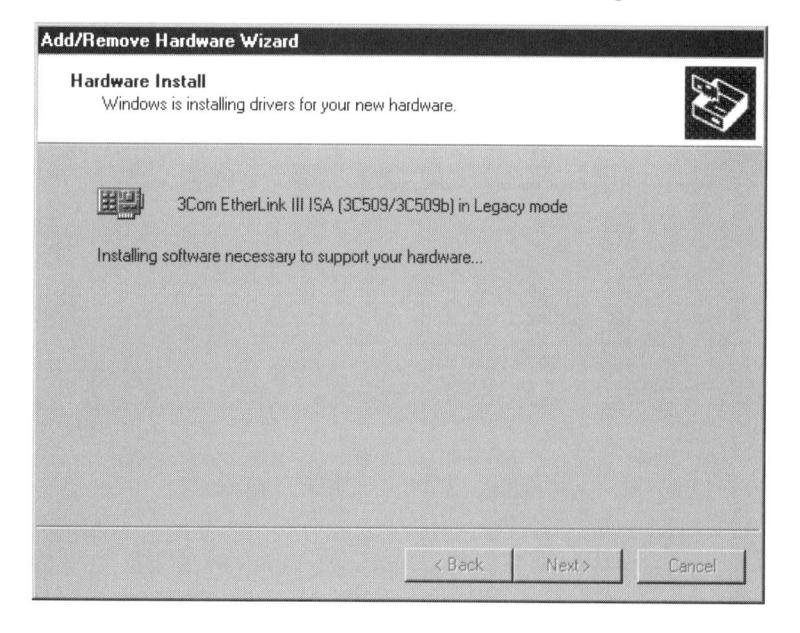

➤ STEP 10

After the software drivers have been copied into the system, the Completing Add/Remove Hardware Wizard dialog is displayed (Figure 14.22).

- Click **RESOURCES** to review or change hardware parameter settings (Figure 14.23).
- Click **FINISH** to commit changes and exit the wizard.

Figure 14.22 The Completing Add/Remove Hardware Wizard dialog.

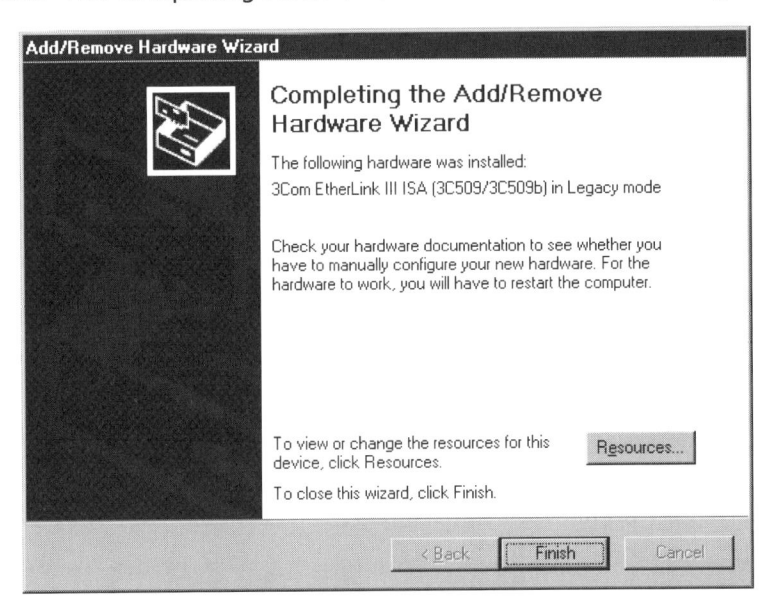

Figure 14.23 The Hardware Wizard Properties dialog run from the Finish screen.

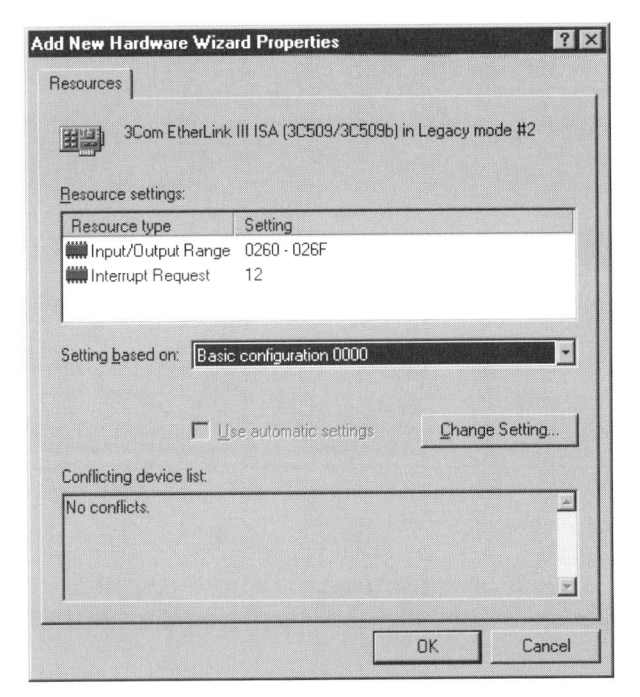

➢ STEP 11

In some cases, the computer must be restarted for the new hardware drivers to be loaded and the hardware activated (Figure 14.24).

- Click **Yes** to restart the computer and load the new driver.
- Click **No** to defer loading the driver until the next reboot.

Figure 14.24 System Setting Change restart dialog.

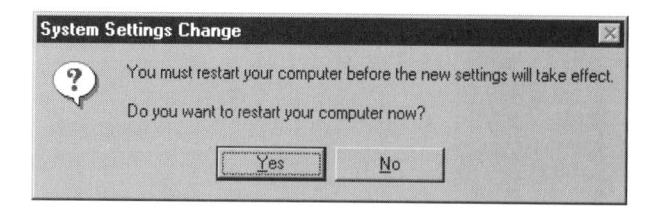

Removing Hardware

In some instances, it may be necessary to remove hardware from the system. The Add/Remove Hardware Wizard can be used for this task as well. Examples of this might be a situation where a hardware device needs to be replaced with one from a different manufacturer, or a device that has failed is to be removed. In this example, the network adapter installed in the previous example will be removed.

➢ STEP 1

Start the Add/Remove Hardware wizard from the Control Panel as shown at the beginning of this chapter. The welcome screen will be displayed (Figure 14.25).

- Click **NEXT**.

➢ STEP 2

To remove hardware from the system, the Uninstall/Unplug a device option should be selected from the Choose a Hardware Task dialog box (Figure 14.26).

- Select the **Uninstall/Unplug a device** option.
- Click **NEXT**.

Figure 14.25 The Add/Remove Hardware Wizard welcome screen.

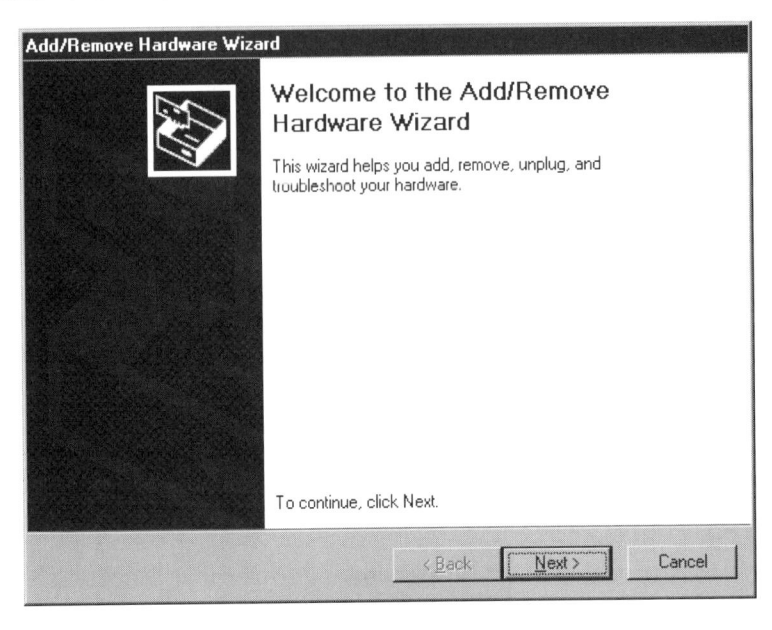

Figure 14.26 Uninstall/Unplug a device selected.

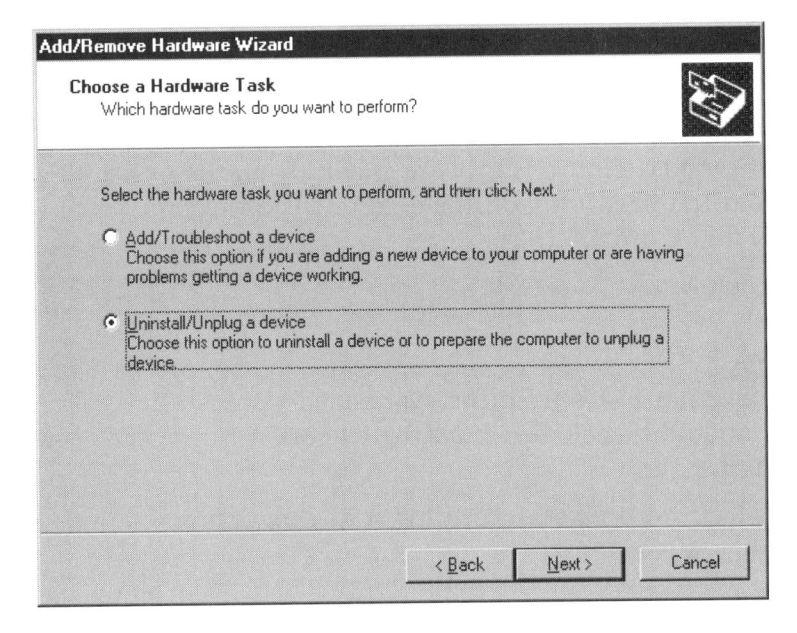

➢ STEP 3

The removal of hardware from a system may be temporary or permanent, depending on the situation. The Choose a Removal Task dialog box (Figure 14.27) allows the user to decide if the device is to be disabled or permanently removed. If the device is removed permanently, the system will free the resources used by the device. If the hardware is only temporarily removed, the system will still consider the resources used by the device as being occupied. In this example, the network adapter installed earlier will be permanently removed.

- Select **Uninstall a device** to permanently remove it from the system and free the resources that it was using.
- Select **Unplug/Eject a device** to disable the device but keep all the software and settings associated with it.
- Click **NEXT**.

Figure 14.27 Choose a Removal Task.

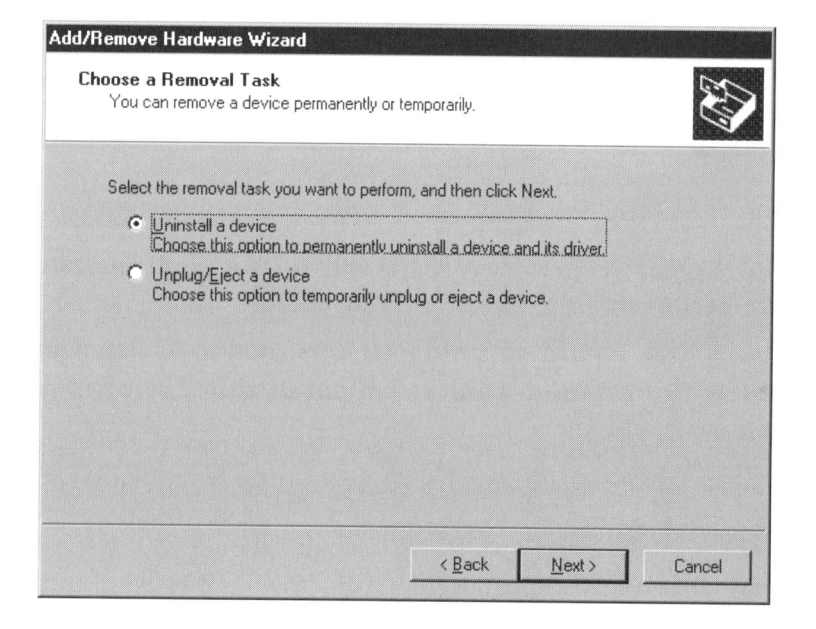

> ## STEP 4

The Add/Remove Hardware Wizard will display all the devices currently installed in the system (Figure 14.28). In this example, the network adapter that was installed previously has failed and must be removed. Note the exclamation point icon over the device's entry in the hardware list. This indicates that the device is not functioning properly.

- Select the device to be removed.
- Click **NEXT**.
- Check the **Show hidden devices** check box to display devices such as subcomponents of other devices.

Figure 14.28 The Installed Devices dialog box.

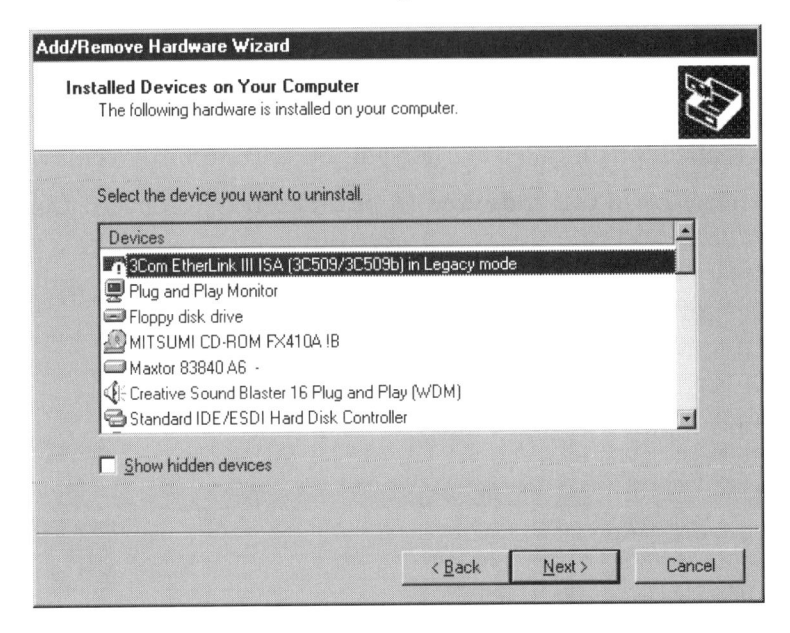

➢ STEP 5

The Add/Remove Hardware Wizard will ask for confirmation before actually performing the removal (Figure 14.29).

- Select **Yes, I want to uninstall this device** to remove it.
- Select **No, I do not want to uninstall this device** to cancel the removal.
- Click **NEXT**.

➢ STEP 6

The final screen of the Add/Remove Hardware Wizard (Figure 14.30) reports that the hardware has been successfully removed. As was the case in the previous example of installing hardware, Windows 2000 may require a reboot to complete the hardware operation.

Figure 14.29 Are you sure you want to uninstall this device?

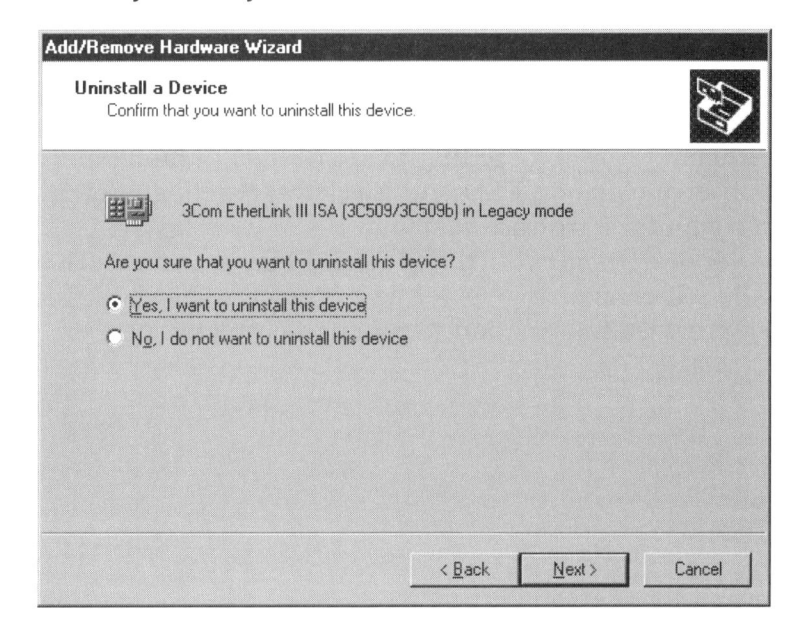

Figure 14.30 The Add/Remove Hardware Wizard finish dialog box.

Summary

The Add/Remove Hardware Wizard can be used to install new hardware, troubleshoot existing hardware, and remove or temporarily disable hardware in a Windows 2000 system. It follows a logical series of steps that eliminates human error of forgetting to set needed parameters or values.

Always observe common ESD and Electrical Safety guidelines when working on computer hardware systems.

Most newer devices support the Plug and Play standard. These devices will be largely self-configuring. Older legacy devices, however, may require critical user-provided information to function correctly.

Chapter 15
Internet Connection Wizard

Introduction

Before running Internet Explorer for the first time, Windows 2000 will run the Internet Connection Wizard. The purpose of the wizard is to ensure that Internet connectivity is configured, and to gather information for configuring Internet Explorer access to Web and e-mail servers. Most of the wizard will generally be skipped on Windows 2000 Server installations. By the end of this chapter, you will be able to configure a Windows 2000 system to access the Internet, including e-mail access.

Before You Begin

If the Internet connection is to be made via a modem and a dial-up connection, the modem should be installed first. Refer to the Chapter 14, "Add/Remove Hardware Wizard," for information on installing new devices to your Windows 2000 computer. If the modem was already in the machine when Windows 2000 was installed, chances are it was configured then. If a modem has been installed, it will be listed in Control Panel under Phone and Modem Options.

If the Internet connection is to be made via a local area network (LAN), the network interface card (NIC) should already be installed, configured, and working. Ask your Network Administrator if you have any questions regarding your computer's network configuration.

The Purpose of this Wizard

This wizard is available in all versions of Windows 2000. It will most likely be used in Windows 2000 Professional installations. This wizard configures essential Internet configuration information, including connection type, dial-up and ISP parameters, and basic e-mail options.

Information Needed to Work with this Wizard

If you are connecting via a LAN connection, you should have the following:

- Proxy configuration information from your Network Administrator

If you are connecting via a modem and a dial-up account, you should have the following:

- Your ISP's dial-up telephone number
- Your login account name and password
- ISP-specific information regarding DNS and default gateway configuration
- An IP address if using SLIP

If you will be setting up an Internet mail account, you will need the following:

- Your mail account username and password
- The type (POP3, IMAP, HTTP) and names of your Internet inbound and outbound mail servers

> **NOTE**
>
> If all this information seems overwhelming, don't be concerned. If you are connecting to the Internet through an Internet Service Provider, their setup guide or customer service department will be able to answer all of these questions for you. If you are not using an ISP, but are connecting from within your company or organization, ask your help desk or Network Administrator.

The Internet Connection Wizard

➤ STEP 1

The Internet Connection Wizard is launched automatically the first time you use Internet Explorer, or can be run at any time from the Internet Explorer Properties dialog box Connections tab. When run, the wizard displays a welcome screen (Figure 15.1).

If you do not have an existing account with an ISP and are not connecting using a company network, you might select one of the first two options as offered on the welcome screen. They can be used as follows:

- **I want to sign up for a new Internet account**. Use this option if you do not have an account with an ISP and want to subscribe to one. The wizard will call a toll-free number and get a list of ISPs offering service in your area.
- **I want to transfer my existing Internet account to this computer**. The wizard will call a toll-free number, locate ISPs in you area, and assist you in configuring your existing account for this Windows 2000 computer.
- **Tutorial**. Click this button for a brief tutorial on the Internet, Internet mail, the World Wide Web, etc.

For the purposes of this example, we will select the third of the three radio buttons that will manually configure the computer to connect to the Internet.

- Select **I want to set up my Internet connection manually, or I want to connect through a local area network (LAN)**.
- Click **NEXT**.

Figure 15.1 The Internet Connection Wizard welcome screen.

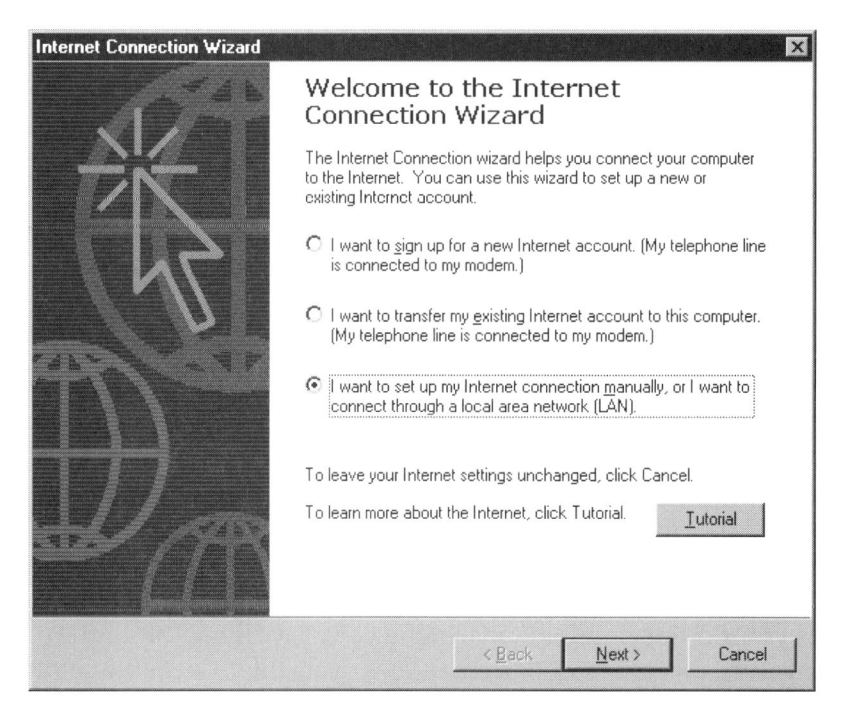

➢ STEP 2

When establishing an Internet connection, the wizard must know if the computer is to connect through dial-up modem connection, or use the LAN provided by your company or organization. The "Setting up your Internet connection" dialog box (Figure 15.2) is where this question is answered.

If you are connecting via a dial-up connection:

- Select **I connect through a phone line and a modem**.
- Click **NEXT**, and proceed to Step 4.

If you are using your company or organization's LAN:

- Select **I connect through a local area network (LAN)**.
- Click **NEXT**, and proceed to Step 3.

Figure 15.2 Determining the method used to connect to the Internet.

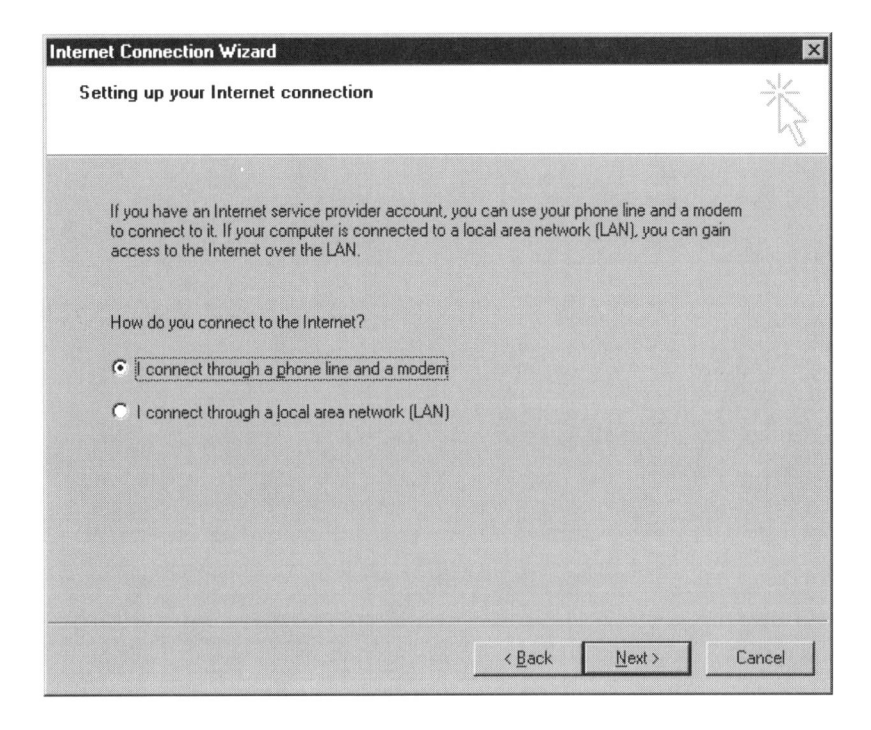

➢ STEP 3

Configuring a LAN connection is fairly simple. Since the connection to the Internet will use the existing network configuration information, the only additional configuration required is to specify proxy server information. The specifics of your network's proxy can be obtained from your Network or System Administrator. Fill in the "Local area network Internet configuration" dialog box (Figure 15.3) as follows:

- Select **Automatic discovery of proxy server** if your proxy server supports it.
- Select **Use automatic configuration script** if the proxy server is configured to support it. In this case, the Address field must be filled in with information regarding the location of the configuration script.
- Select **Manual Proxy Server** if the proxy server must be manually configured.
- Select **NEXT**, and proceed to Step 7.

Figure 15.3 Configuring a LAN connection.

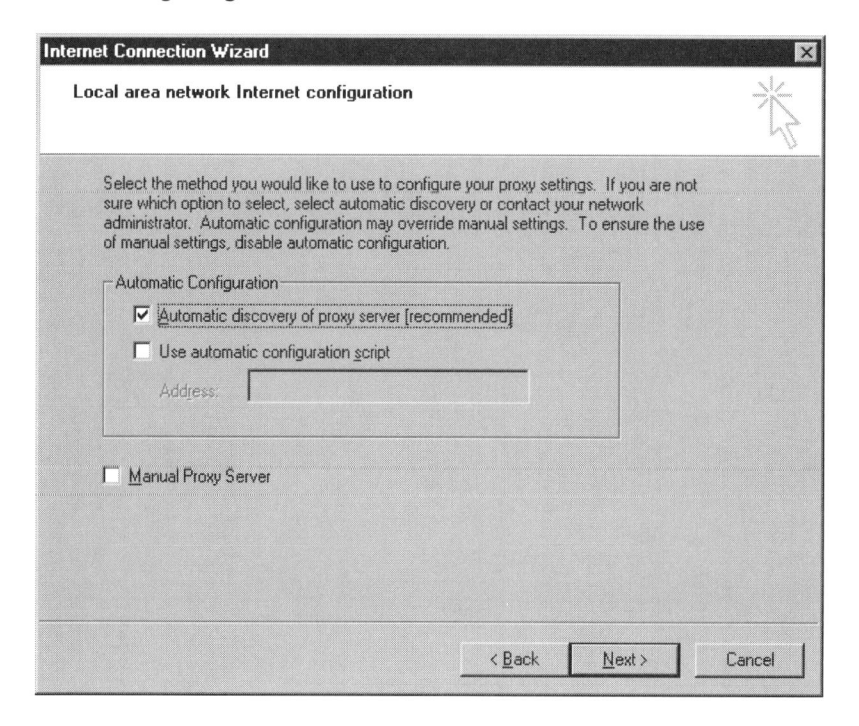

➢ STEP 4

If the computer is to dial up and connect to the Internet via an ISP, the ISP telephone number must be provided in the "Step 1 of 3: Internet account connection information" dialog box (Figure 15.4).

- Complete the **Area code and Telephone number** fields.
- Select the appropriate **Country/region name and code**.
- Select **Use area code and dialing rules**. This allows Windows 2000 to intelligently strip off area codes when calling local numbers, dial external access numbers if needed, etc.
- Click ADVANCED if advanced connection configuration is needed (optional).
- Click NEXT.

Optional Advanced Parameters

Clicking ADVANCED will present the Advanced Connection Properties dialog box. This dialog box has two tabs: Connection (Figure 15.5) and Addresses (Figure 15.6). In most cases, it will not be necessary to configure these advanced parameters. In the event it is needed, they can be configured as follows:

Figure 15.4 Entering dialing information.

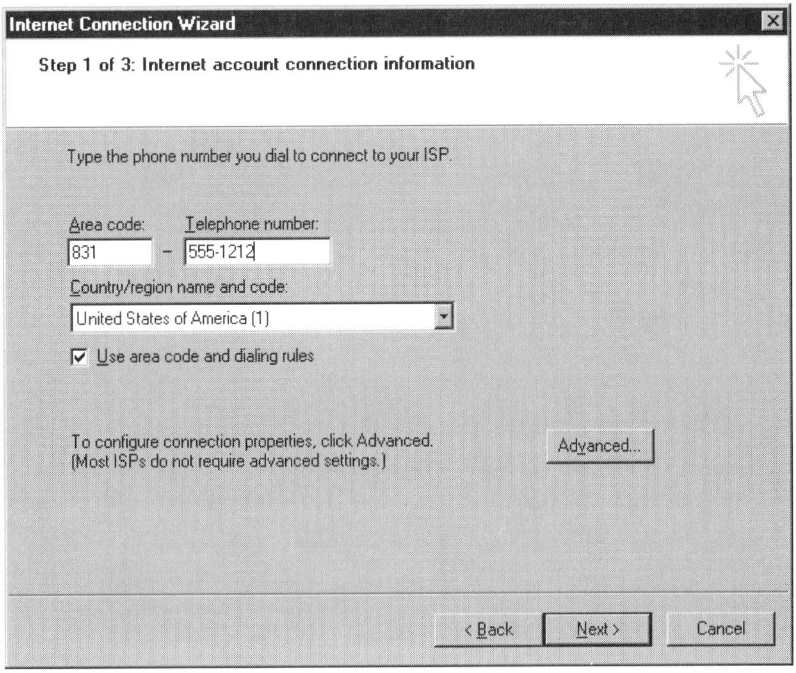

Connection type:

- **PPP (Point to Point Protocol)**. This is the default connection method for dial-up service lines and modems. It automatically configures many other parameters. Optionally, LCP extensions may be disabled.
- **SLIP (Serial Line Internet Protocol)**. This is the predecessor to PPP, and is still in use by some ISPs.
- **C-SLIP (Compressed Serial Line Internet Protocol)**. This is a compressed (faster) version of SLIP.

Logon procedure:

- **None**. Dial, connect, and do nothing further.
- **Log on manually**. After dialing, the user must enter login information such as username and password.
- **Use logon script**. If this option is selected, the Script field will become active, and a script to run after connecting must be chosen. These scripts will automate the login process for a variety of server types.

Figure 15.5 Advanced connection properties.

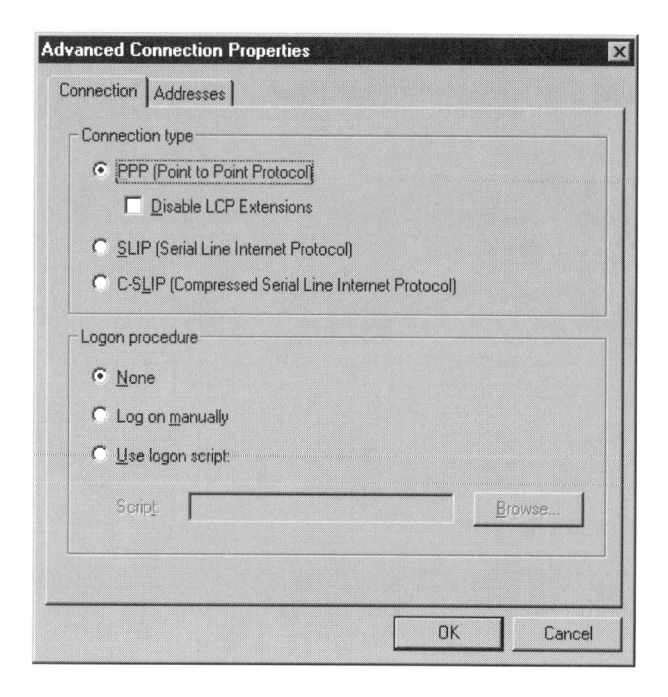

If advanced address configuration is required, the Address tab (Figure 15.6) may be filled out as follows:

IP address:

- **Internet service provider automatically provides one**. This is the default and should be used unless the ISP has specifically provided an address for this machine.
- **Always use the following:**. If the ISP has assigned a permanent (static) address for this machine, select this option and fill in the IP Address field.

DNS server address:

- **My ISP automatically provides a Domain Name Server (DNS) address**. This is the default and should be used unless the ISP has specified that DNS server addresses must be configured on the customer's machine.
- **Always use the following:**. If the ISP requires that the customer machine configure DNS server address information, select this option and fill in the Primary DNS server and Secondary DNS server fields.
- Click **OK** to save changes, or **CANCEL** to return to the wizard.

Figure 15.6 Advanced address properties.

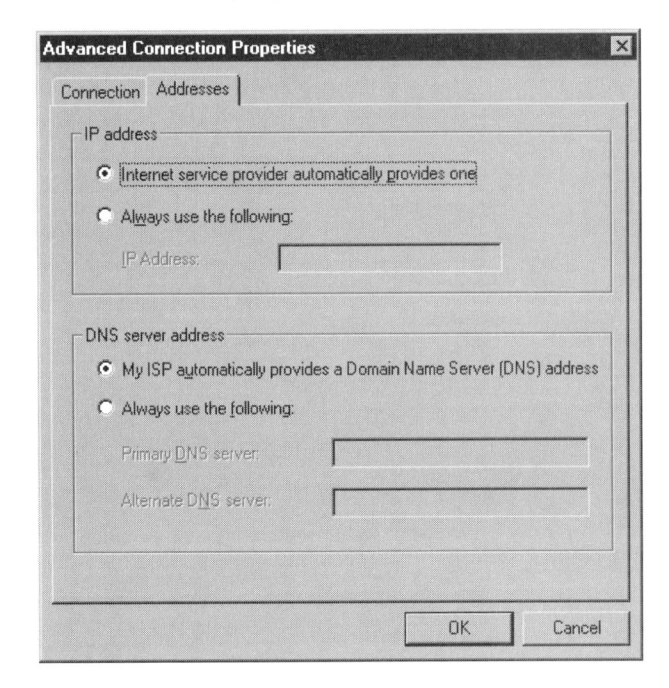

➤ STEP 5

The ISP most likely has provided a username and password to allow the owner of the account to connect to the ISP's services. This information must be filled in the "Step 2 of 3: Internet account login information" dialog box (Figure 15.7).

- Enter the ISP account username in the User name field.
- Enter the ISP account password in the Password field.
- Click **NEXT**.

➤ STEP 6

The last step in configuring the Windows 2000 computer to use a dial-up ISP account is to name and save the account information. "Step 3 of 3: Configuring your computer" (Figure 15.8) is the dialog box where this operation is performed.

- Fill out the Connection name field, or accept the default connection name.
- Click **NEXT**.

Figure 15.7 Internet account login information

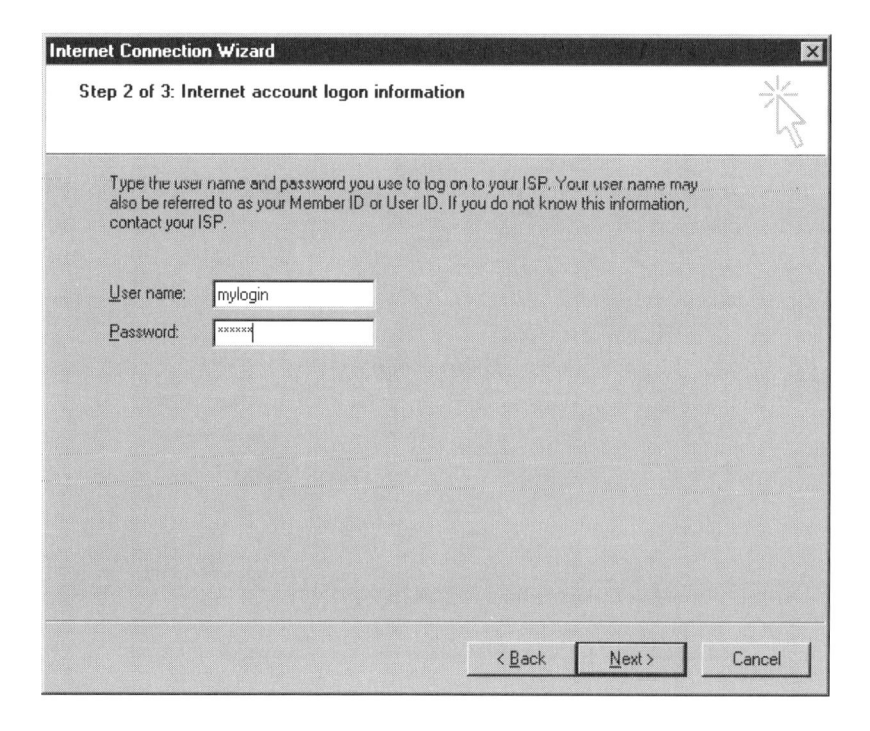

Figure 15.8 Providing and saving a connection name.

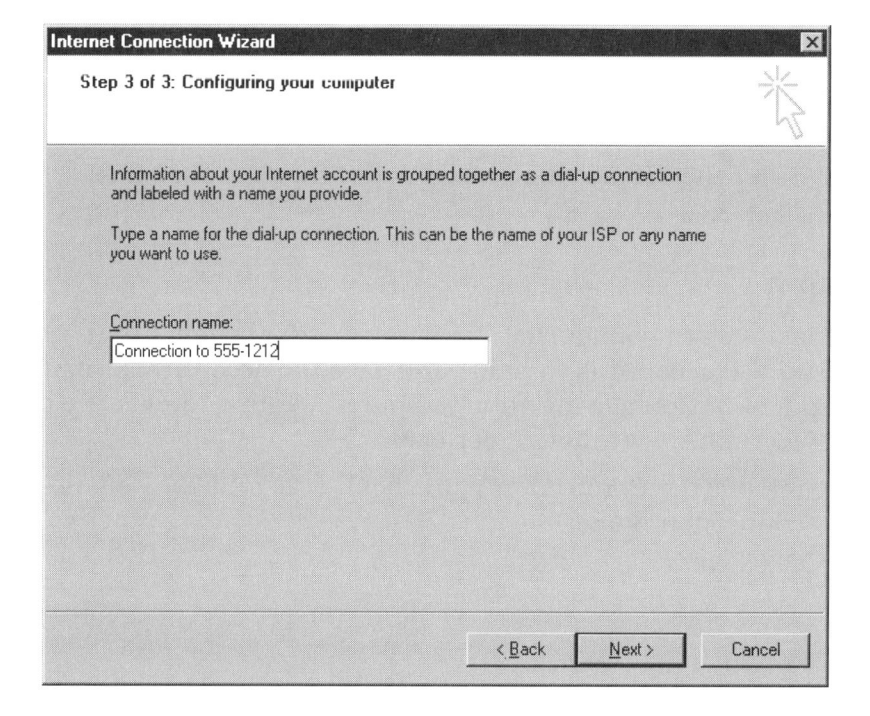

➢ STEP 7

Regardless of the connection type, the Internet Connection Wizard will ask if an Internet mail account is to be created (Figure 15.9).

- If a mail account is to be set up, select **Yes**.
- If a mail account is not to be set up, select **No**. The wizard will go to Step 12 when NEXT is clicked if this option is selected.
- Click **NEXT**.

Figure 15.9 Setting up an Internet mail account.

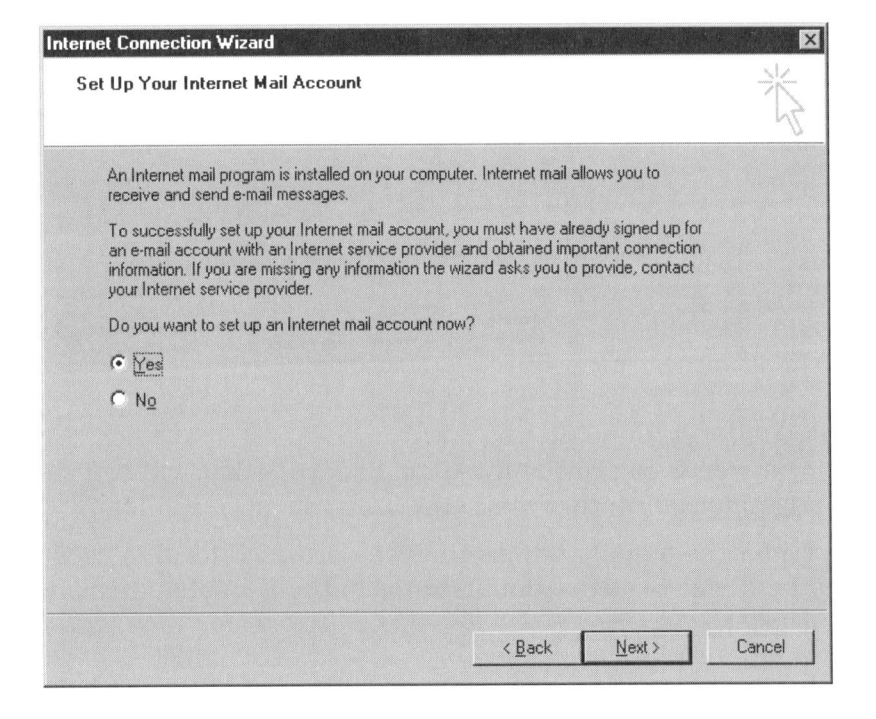

➢ STEP 8

When mail is sent from this account, the mail message will display a From name and address. The dialog box shown in Figure 15.10 sets the name that will be displayed on the From line of all e-mail sent from this account.

- Enter the name to appear as the sender of all e-mail sent from this account in the Display name field.
- Click **NEXT**.

Figure 15.10 Setting the From name.

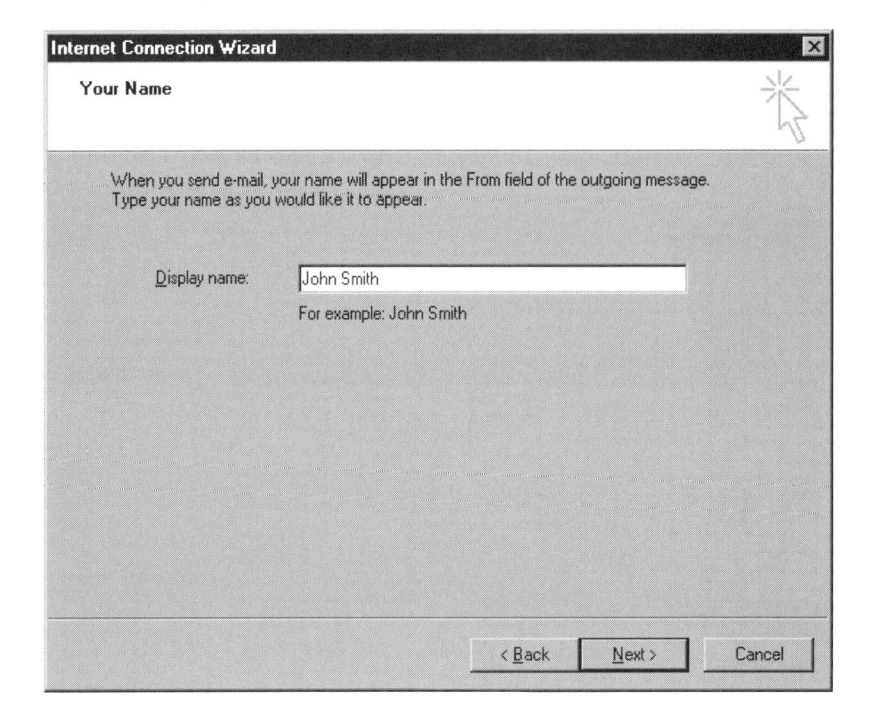

➣ STEP 9

The next step is to provide the e-mail address that will be listed as the originator of Internet mail sent from this account (Figure 15.11).

- Enter the e-mail address that was provided for this account by the ISP or System Administrator in the E-mail address field.
- Click **NEXT**.

➣ STEP 10

Windows 2000 supports POP3, IMAP, and HTTP mail servers. The next screen of the Internet Connection Wizard is where server types and their names are entered (Figure 15.12).

- Select **POP3**, **IMAP**, or **HTTP** as appropriate for the incoming mail server.
- Enter the **Incoming** and **Outgoing mail server** names in their respective fields.
- Click **NEXT**.

Figure 15.11 Specifying the account's e-mail address.

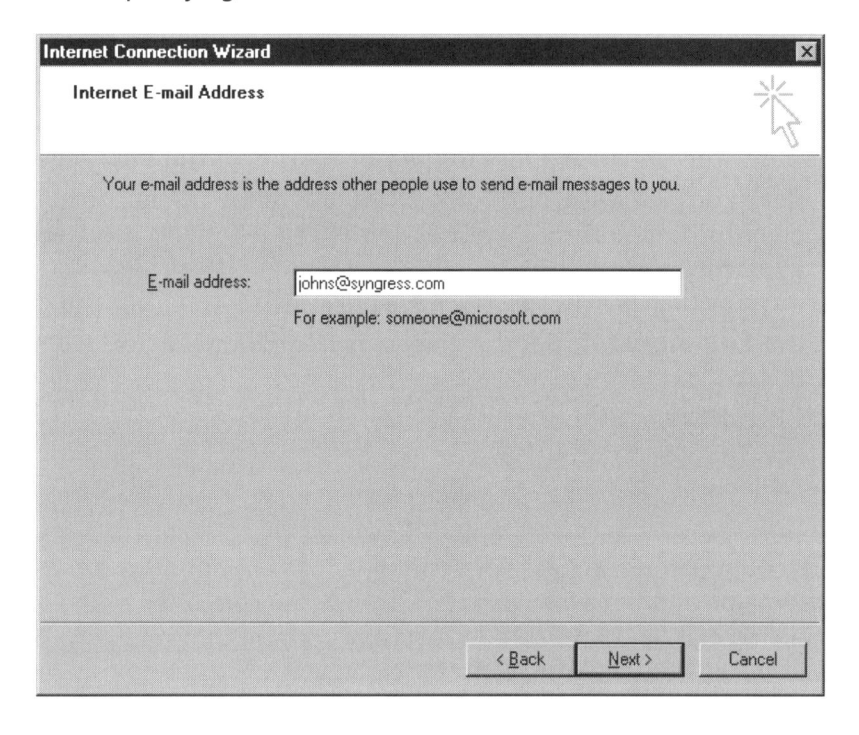

Figure 15.12 Internet mail server information.

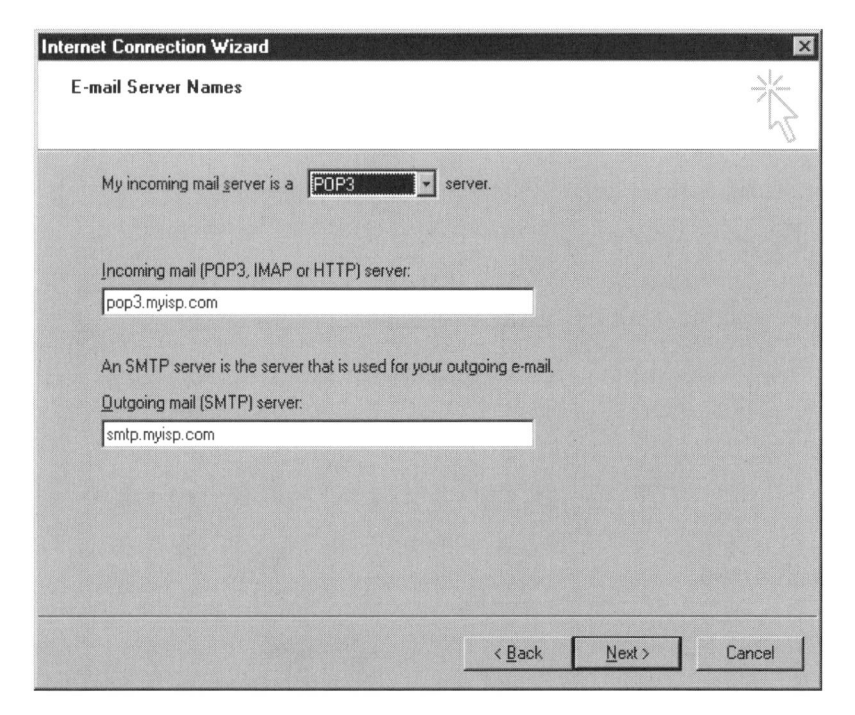

➤ STEP 11

The final screen used to configure Internet mail (Figure 15.13) prompts you to enter an Account name and password.

- Enter the **mail account name** in the Account name field.
- Enter the **password** for this mail account in the Password field.
- If you do not want Windows 2000 to ask for the account password each time a connection is made, check the **Remember password** check box.
- If the ISP supports Secure Password Authentication (SPA), select the **Log on using Secure Password Authentication (SPA)** check box.
- Click **NEXT**.

> **NOTE**
>
> Mail account name and password combinations are not always the same as the username and password used to connect the computer to the Internet when using dial-up. Make sure to read any account information provided by your ISP or Network Administrator carefully!

Figure 15.13 Entering mail account information.

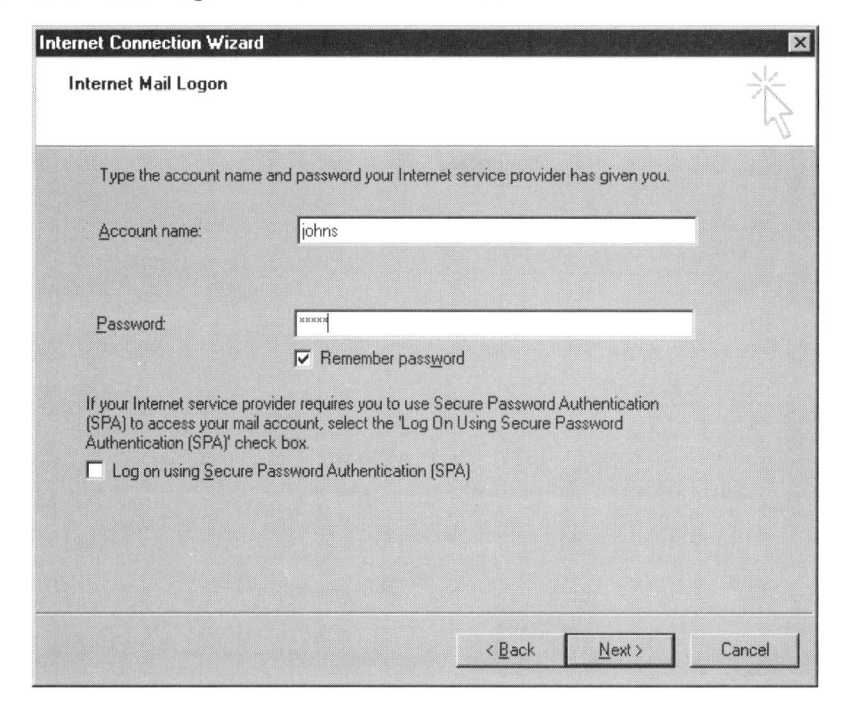

➤ STEP 12

The Internet Connection Wizard finish screen (Figure 15.14) lets you specify the action to take after the wizard exits.

- Select **To connect to the Internet immediately, select this box and then click Finish** upon exiting the wizard. If this option is selected using a dial-up connection, the Dial-up Connection dialog box will be displayed when the wizard is finished. See Step 13.
- Click **FINISH** to exit the wizard.

Figure 15.14 The Internet Connection Wizard finish screen.

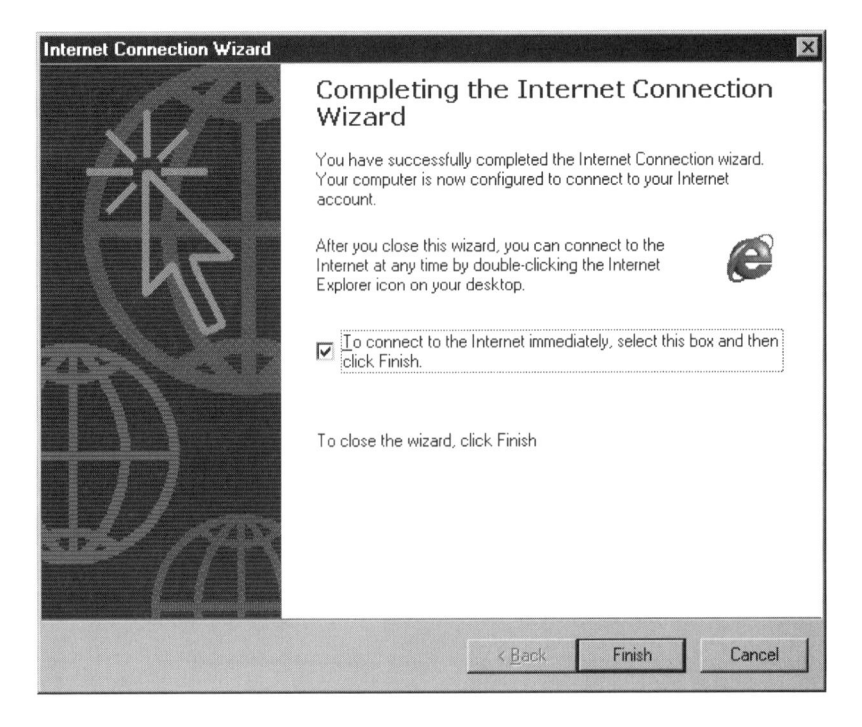

➤ STEP 13

If using a dial-up connection to the Internet, and the check box to connect to the Internet immediately was selected (the default) from the Internet Connection Wizard finish screen, the Windows 2000 computer will attempt to use the information provided to connect to the ISP. The Dial-up Connection dialog box (Figure 15.15) will be displayed.

- The Connect to, User name, and Password fields will all contain the information provided when the Internet Connection Wizard was run. There should be no need to change these.

- The Save password check box determines if the password for this connection should be saved for future logins. Clearing this will cause Windows 2000 to request a password each time a connection is made.
- The Connect automatically check box specifies whether the Windows 2000 computer should attempt to dial out automatically each time a network connection is requested.
- Click CONNECT to dial, SETTINGS to change dial-up connection settings, or WORK OFFLINE to not connect and continue.

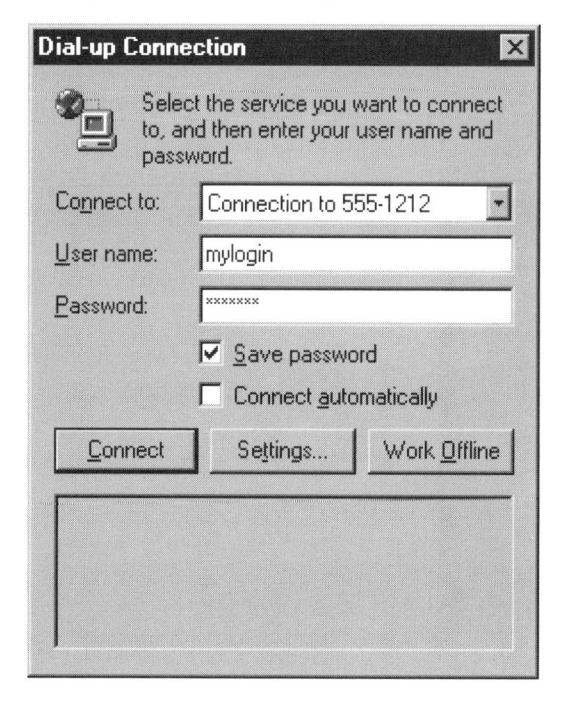

Figure 15.15 The Dial-up Connection dialog box.

Summary

Quite a bit of information is needed to successfully make a connection to the Internet. The Internet Connection Wizard makes setting all this up very easy. Make sure to have all the required information at hand before starting. This makes the whole process much more pleasant than having to look parameters up while trying to get the connection going. Your ISP or Network Administrator should have all the information needed and be able to help.

Connecting via a local area network (LAN) is straightforward and only requires proxy configuration information, which in many cases is fully or partially automatic. Establishing a dial-up connection is a bit more involved, and much more flexible. In many cases, using many of the default values provided by Windows 2000 should provide a working connection. The Advanced Connection and Advanced Addressing tabs are available for more obscure configurations.

Establishing an Internet mail account requires information regarding the names and types of mail servers, as well as account name and password information. Again, these can be obtained from the ISP or Network Administrator.

Once completed, the connection can be configured to connect automatically or manually, and remember passwords or require them at each logon.

Chapter 16

Connection Manager Administration Kit Wizard

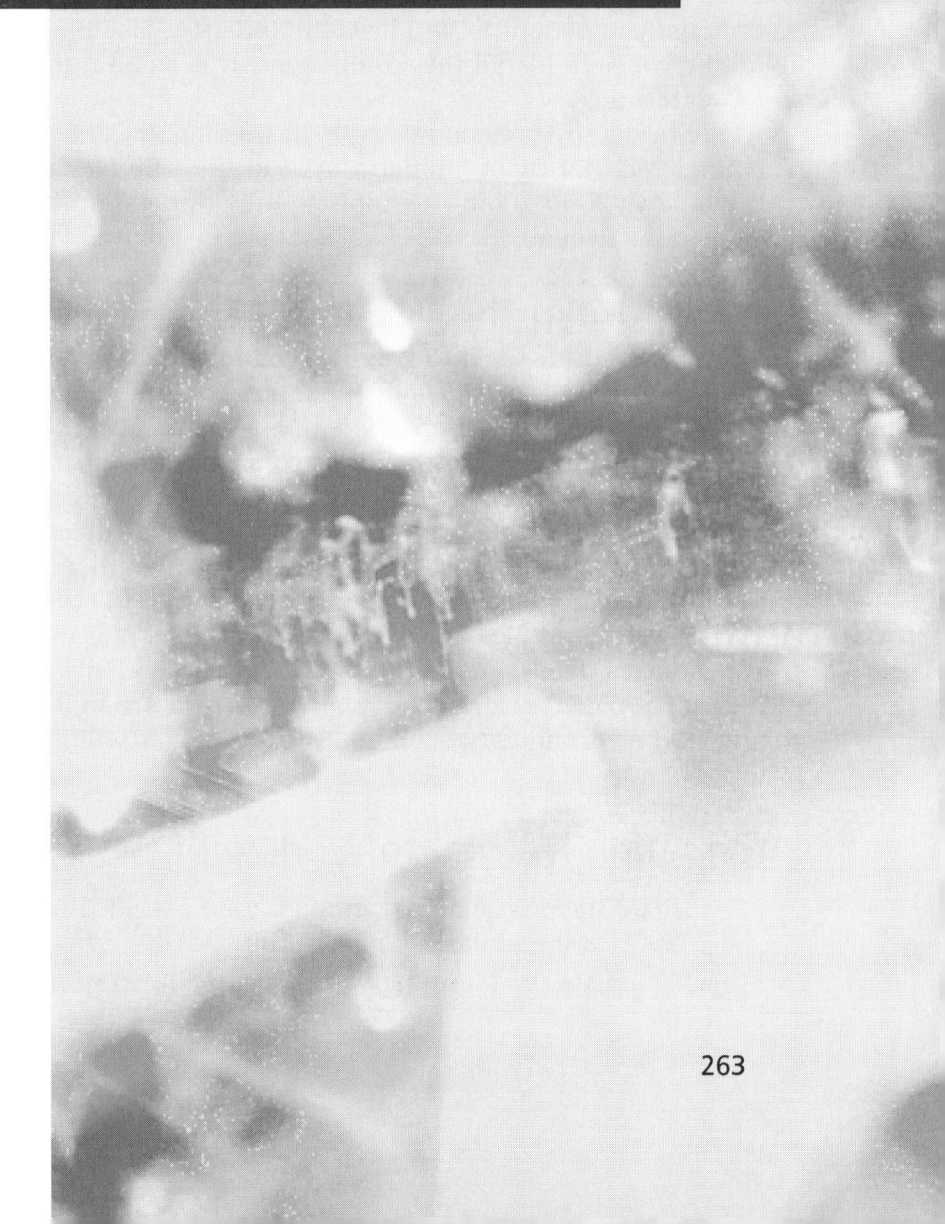

Introduction

Windows 2000 allows you to customize the connection manager for users of your remote access services. The Connection Manager kit allows you to create a profile with support information that is used for a predefined set of either dial-up or VPN connections. By the end of this chapter, you will be able to configure a profile for your remote users.

Before You Begin

The Connection Manager Administration Kit (CMAK) must be installed as an optional component to Windows 2000 Server. Use the Control Panel, Install Software to install this component. It is listed under Management and Monitoring Tools.

There are many options available in this highly configurable tool. It is recommended that the Administrator read the help files that are included with Windows 2000 about this topic to fully understand the implications of the options available.

The Purpose of this Wizard

The CMAK Wizard is used to create executable packages called *service profiles*. These service profiles define many of the options needed to allow an end user to successfully connect to a remote network service such as RAS. As most Administrators know, users can find setting up remote access difficult and confusing. By using the CMAK Wizard, an Administrator can create predefined connection packages that have been tested and are known to work, rather than asking a user to follow typed connection instructions.

These service profiles are highly customizable, and include icons, graphic images, logos, custom phone books, and other features. As such, the service profiles created by the CMAK Wizard are well suited for use in commercial environments such as ISPs, and other online service providers.

Information Needed to Work with this Wizard

- Read the online help documentation provided with Windows 2000 and installed as part of the CMAK.
- Complete the Planning Worksheet included in the online help

The Connection Manager Administration Kit Wizard

➤ STEP 1

The CMAK Wizard may be launched from the Administration Tools program group. The welcome screen (Figure 16.1) provides a brief description of the wizard.

- Click **NEXT**.

Figure 16.1 The Connection Manager Administration Kit (CMAK) Wizard welcome screen.

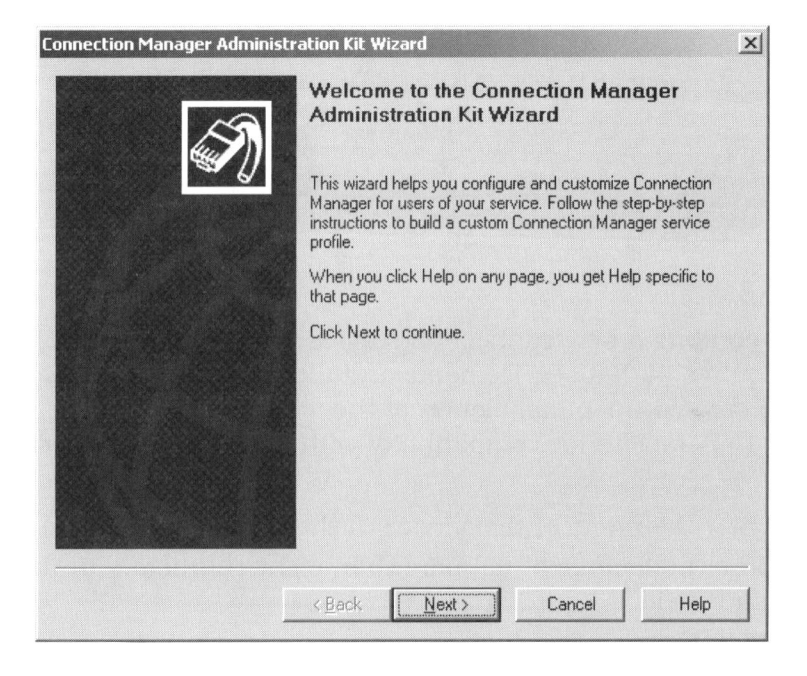

➤ STEP 2

The CMAK Wizard allows for the creation of new service profiles, as well as editing of existing profiles (Figure 16.2).

- Select **Create a new service profile** to create a new profile.
- Select **Edit this existing profile** to activate the pick list and open a previously saved service profile to edit.
- Click **NEXT**.

Figure 16.2 Create a new profile or edit an existing one.

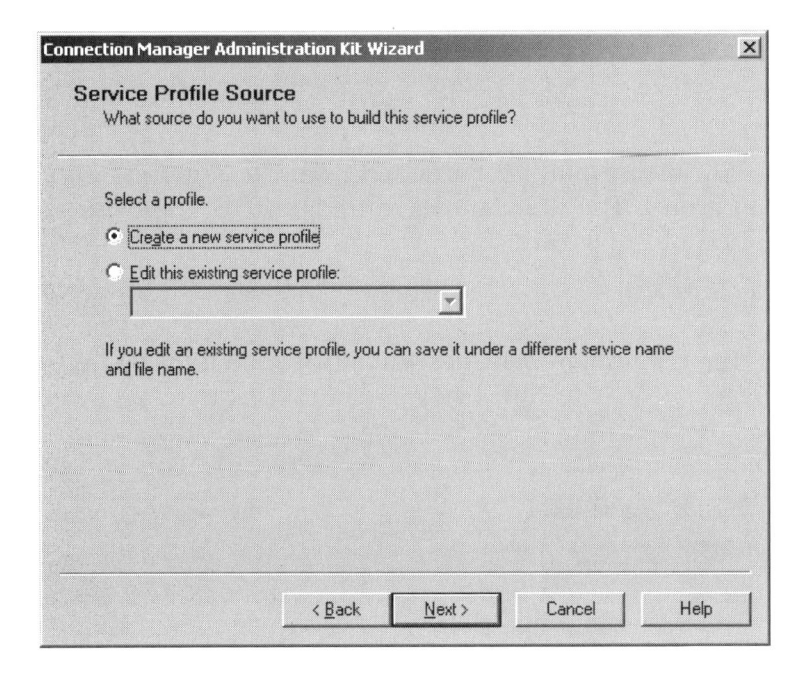

➤ STEP 3

When creating a new connection service profile (Figure 16.3), the wizard requires both a service name and filename for the .EXE file that will be created upon completion of the wizard. The filename is limited to eight characters for compatibility with non–Windows 2000 systems.

- Enter the name of the service in the Service name field.
- Enter a filename of no more than eight characters in the File name field.
- Click **NEXT**.

➤ STEP 4

If there are one or more existing profiles that should be combined with this profile to create a more comprehensive service, select them in the Merged Service Profiles dialog (Figure 16.4).

- Use the **Existing service profile** pick list to select other service profiles to be merged into this new one.
- Click **ADD** to place selected profiles into the **Service profiles to be merged** list.

- Highlight profiles in the **Service profiles to be merged** list, and click **DELETE** to remove service profiles from the list of those to be merged into this profile.
- Click **NEXT**.

Figure 16.3 Entering the new service name and filename.

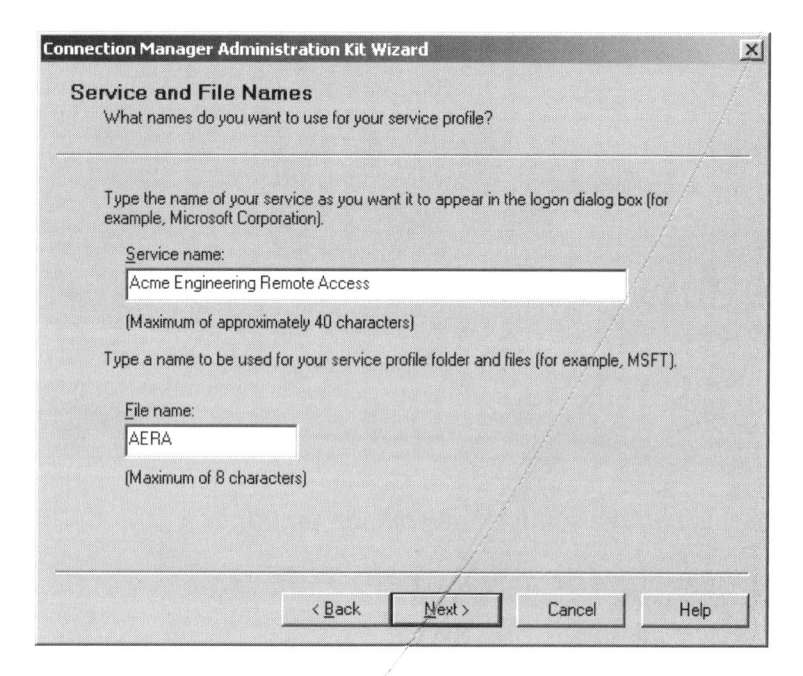

> ## STEP 5

One of the inevitable issues when supporting remote users is the need for the user to contact someone for help. The Support Information dialog (Figure 16.5) allows a short support contact message to be entered in the logon screen for the service. Later, in Step 21, there is a provision to attach a standard or custom help file that provides detailed user support information.

- Enter a short support contact note in the **Support information** field.
- Click **NEXT**.

Figure 16.4 Combining existing profiles into the new one being created.

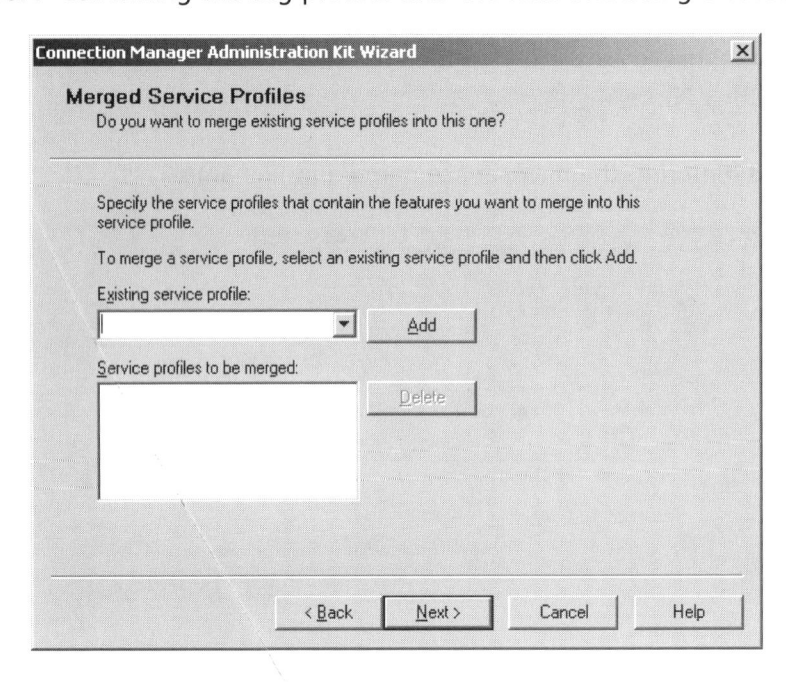

Figure 16.5 Creating the support information message.

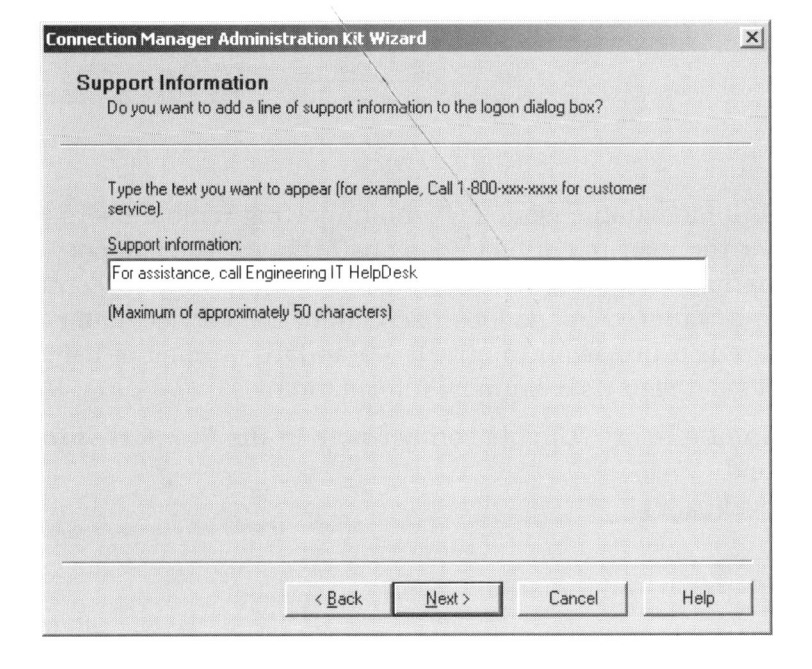

➢ STEP 6

The CMAK uses the concept of *realm names* to allow the formation of fully qualified user names. By specifying a prefix or suffix in the Realm name dialog box (Figure 16.6), the Administrator can force the modification of the login name provided by the user without requiring the user to know or understand his or her fully qualified name. This makes using the profile easier for the user, and reduces error and support calls resulting from any additional information required from the user other than a simple login name.

- Select **Do not add a realm name** if this option is not desired.
- Select **Add a realm name** to force a prefix or suffix to be added to the user-provided login name.
- Select either **Prefix** or **Suffix** as appropriate.
- Enter the text to be applied to the user login name.
- Click **NEXT**.

Figure 16.6 Entering realm information.

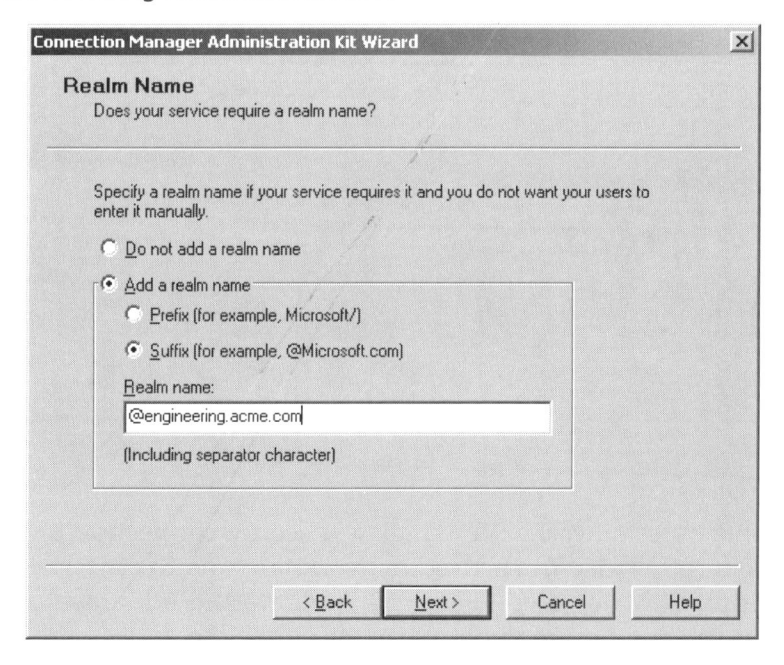

➢ STEP 7

Phone number entries are added to the service profile, allowing the end user of the profile to dial one or more specific numbers to connect to the service. The Dial-Up Networking Entries dialog box (Figure

16.7) provides the means to include these phone book entries in the service profile. Each dial-up entry may also include optional connection parameters such as DNS and WINS servers or connection scripts (Figure 16.8).

- Click **ADD** to add a phone-book entry to the list of phone-book entries to be included in the service profile (Figure 16.8).
- Highlight an entry, and use **EDIT** and **DELETE** to modify or remove an entry from the list.
- Click **NEXT**.

Figure 16.7 Managing dial-up entries packaged with the service profile.

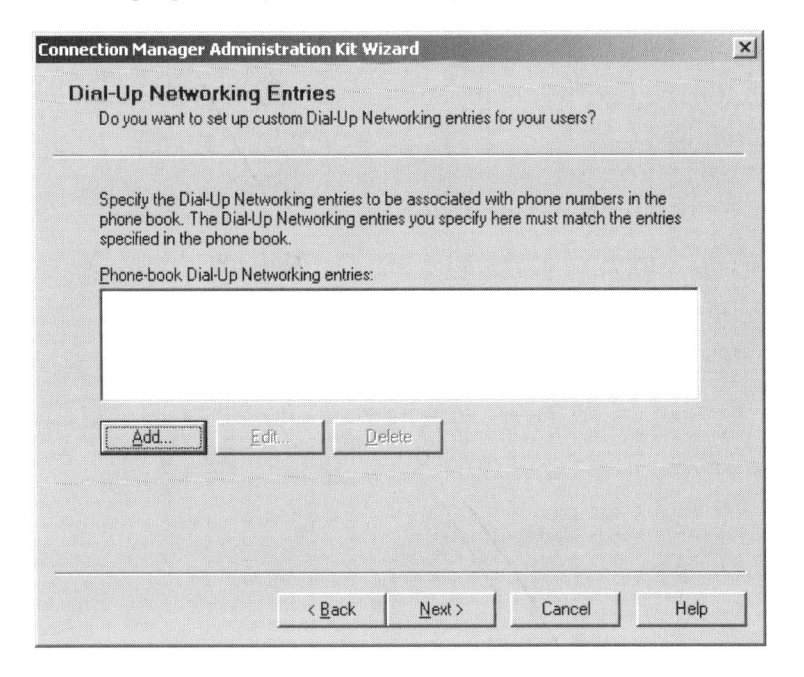

➢ STEP 8

Virtual Private Networks (VPNs) allow a secure connection to be created across an otherwise unsecured network such as the Internet. The VPN Support dialog box (Figure 16.9) allows the Administrator to request the creation of such a link for either the service profile being created, and/or the services that were combined during the Merge step.

- To create a VPN connection for the Service Profile being created, check the **This service profile** check box.

Figure 16.8 Customizing server and script information associated with a phone-book entry.

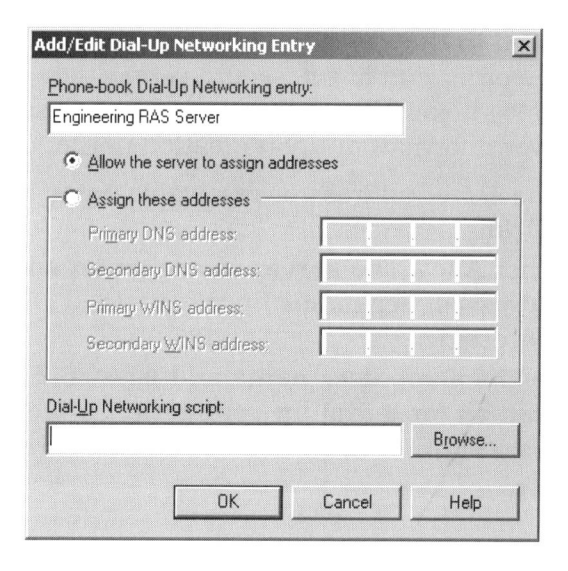

- To create a VPN connection for merged service profiles (if any), check the **Merged service profiles** check box.
- Click **NEXT**.
- If no VPN connections are to be created, skip to Step 10.

Figure 16.9 Requesting the creation of VPN connections.

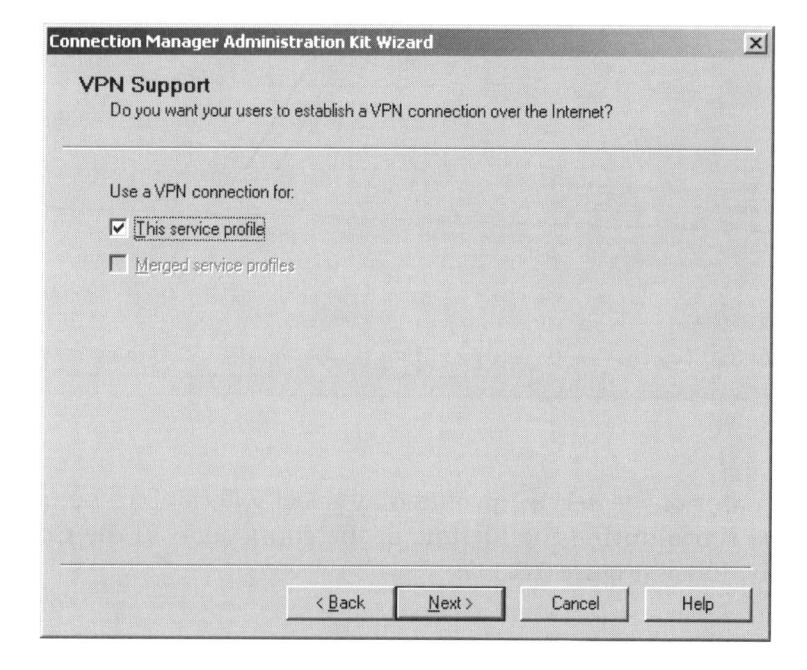

➢ STEP 9 (OPTIONAL)

If a VPN connection is to be made, the address or name of the peer must be specified in the VPN Connection dialog box (Figure 16.10). This peer is the other end of the secure connection. The VPN Connection dialog box additionally allows for the assignment of DNS and WINS server information upon creation of the VPN.

- Specify the server address or resolvable name in the **Server address** field.
- Select either **Allow the server to assign an address** or **Assign these addresses**, depending on the origin of DNS and WINS server addressing.
- Click **Use the same user name and password for a VPN connection as for a dial-up connection** if the user is not to be challenged for a VPN username and password.
- Click **NEXT**.

Figure 16.10 Configuring a VPN connection.

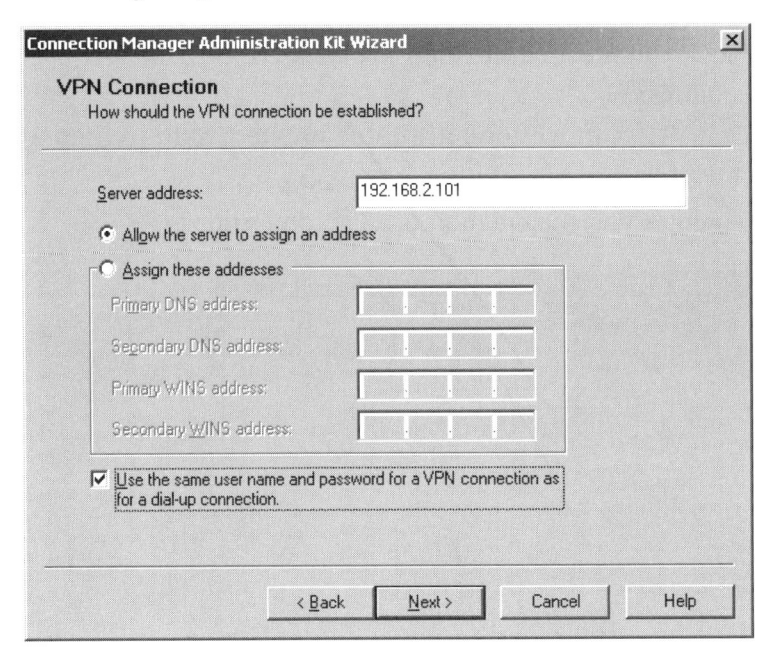

➢ STEP 10

The creator of the service profile may specify actions to be taken at various times during the lifetime of the connection in the Connect Actions dialog (Figure 16.11).

- Check **Run pre-connect actions (before connecting)** to run a program or script before the connection is attempted (see Step 11).
- Check **Run pre-tunnel actions (before establishing a VPN connection)** to execute a program or script after the connection is made, but prior to establishing the secure VPN link (see Step 12).
- Check **Run post-connect actions (after establishing a VPN connection)** to specify a program or script to run after connecting (see Step 13).
- Check **Run disconnect actions (before disconnecting)** to specify a program or script to run before the connection is terminated when the user disconnects (see Step 14).
- Click **NEXT**.
- If none of these optional actions are needed, skip to Step 15.

Figure 16.11 Specifying actions to take at various stages of the connection.

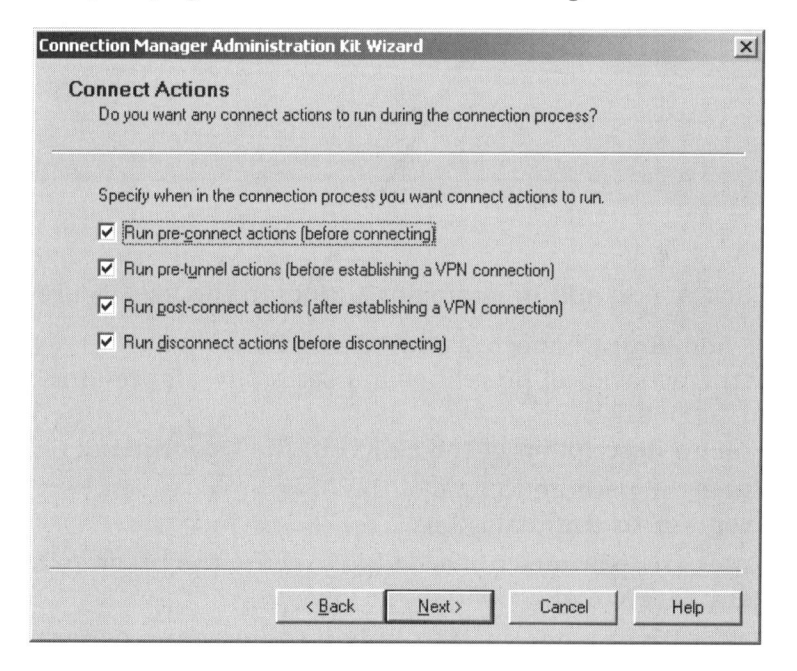

➤ STEP 11 (OPTIONAL)

The Pre-Connect Actions dialog box (Figure 16.12) allows one or more scripts or programs to be run before the connection attempt is made. This might include resetting the connection device, performing pre-dial operations, and so forth. Once programs or scripts are added via the Add/Edit Connect Actions dialog box (Figure 16.13), they may be positioned to run in a specific order by clicking MOVE UP and MOVE DOWN.

Figure 16.12 Managing the Pre-Connect Actions list.

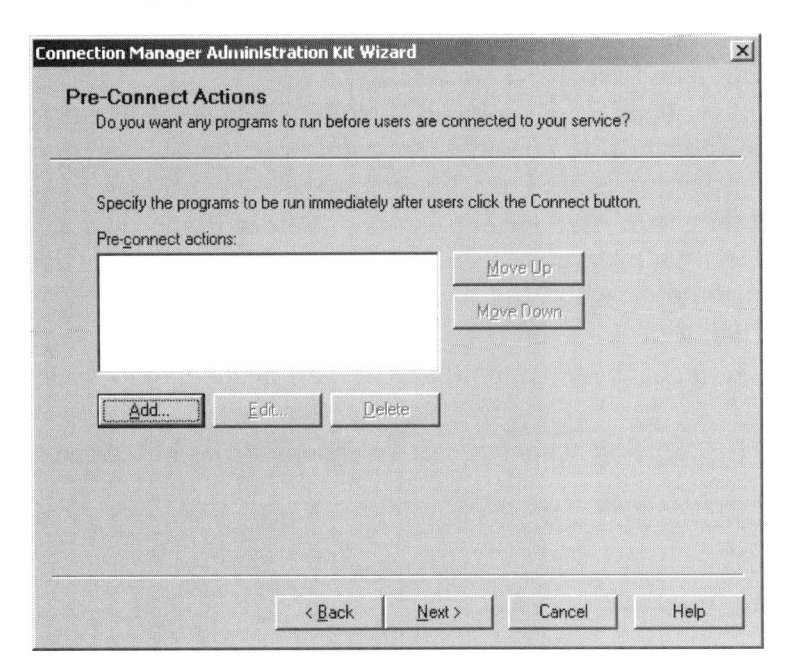

- Click **ADD** to add programs or scripts to the list (Figure 6.13).

The Add/Edit Connect Actions dialog box is used to create or modify the behavior of programs and scripts in all pre- and post-connection actions.

- Enter a description of the action in the **Description** field.
- Enter the path and name of the program or script to run in the **Program to run** dialog box.
- Enter any parameters needed to execute the program in the **Parameters** dialog box.
- Select **Dial-up connection only** if the program or script is to run only when a dial-up connection is used.
- Select **Direct connection only** if the program or script is to run only if the connection is made directly (not dial-up).
- Select **Both dial-up and direct connections** if the program or script is to be run regardless of the connection method.

- Check **Include this program in this service profile** if the program or script should be packaged with the .EXE file that is created when the wizard is completed.

After adding the entries, you can manipulate their settings or run order.

- To edit, delete, or change the execution order of an entry, highlight the entry and:
    - Click **EDIT** to edit programs or scripts in the list.
    - Click **DELETE** to remove a program or script from the list.
    - Click **MOVE UP** or **MOVE DOWN** to change the execution order of the programs or scripts.
- Click **NEXT**.

Figure 16.13 Adding or editing a connect action.

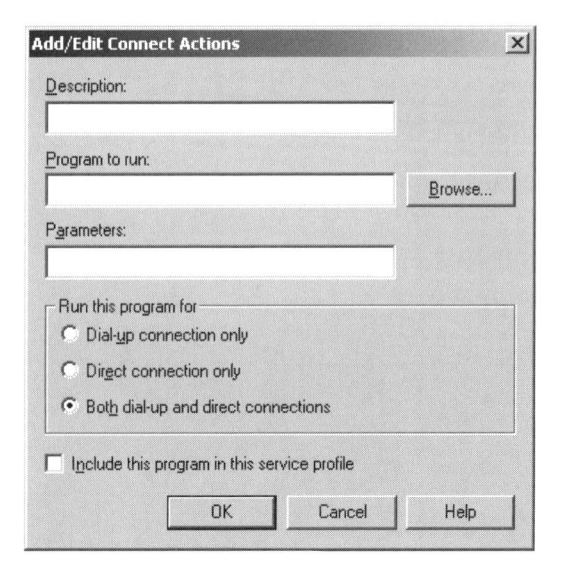

➤ STEP 12 (OPTIONAL)

The Pre-Tunnel Actions dialog box (Figure 16.14) specifies programs or scripts that should be run after the connection is made, but prior to the secure VPN tunnel being established. This might include scripts to gather user information for authentication purposes, special handshaking, or initialization of third-party security software.

- Click **ADD** to add programs or scripts to the list.

- To edit, delete, or change the execution order of an entry, highlight the entry and:
  - Click **EDIT** to edit programs or scripts in the list.
  - Click **DELETE** to remove a program or script from the list.
  - Click **Move Up** or **Move Down** to change the execution order of the programs or scripts.
- For detailed information on the Adding/Editing Connect Actions dialog box presented when selecting either ADD or EDIT, see Step 11 and Figure 16.13.
- Click **NEXT**.

Figure 16.14 Configuring programs and scripts to execute after connection, but prior to establishing the VPN tunnel.

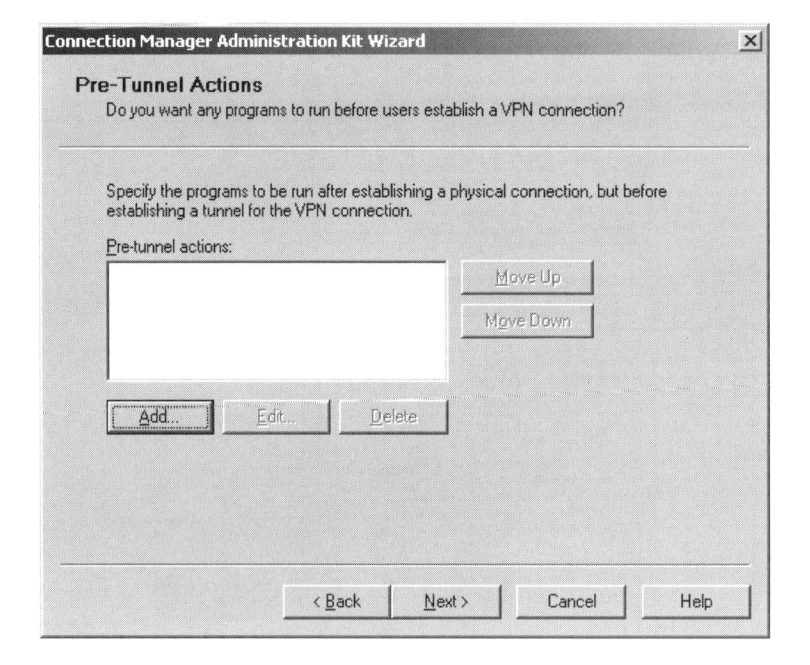

➤ STEP 13 (OPTIONAL)

Post-connection programs and scripts can be configured in the Post-Connect Actions dialog box (Figure 16.15). These programs and scripts are run as soon as the connection to the service is established. The CMAK Wizard provides options for common actions such as downloading new phone-book entries or updates, and using the Microsoft Commercial Internet System subscriber information.

- Check **Automatically download phone-book updates** to automatically update service profile phone-book entries upon connecting.
- Check **Use MCIS Membership subscribers' existing information** to obtain account information from the Microsoft Commercial Internet System upon connecting.
- Click ADD to add programs or scripts to the list of **Other post-connect actions**.
- To edit, delete, or change the execution order of an entry, highlight the entry and:
    1. Click EDIT to edit programs or scripts in the list.
    2. Click DELETE to remove a program or script from the list.
    3. Click **Move Up** or **Move Down** to change the execution order of the programs or scripts.
- For detailed information on the Adding/Editing Connect Actions dialog box presented when selecting either ADD or EDIT, see Step 11 and Figure 16.13.
- Click NEXT.

Figure 16.15 Managing post-connection activities.

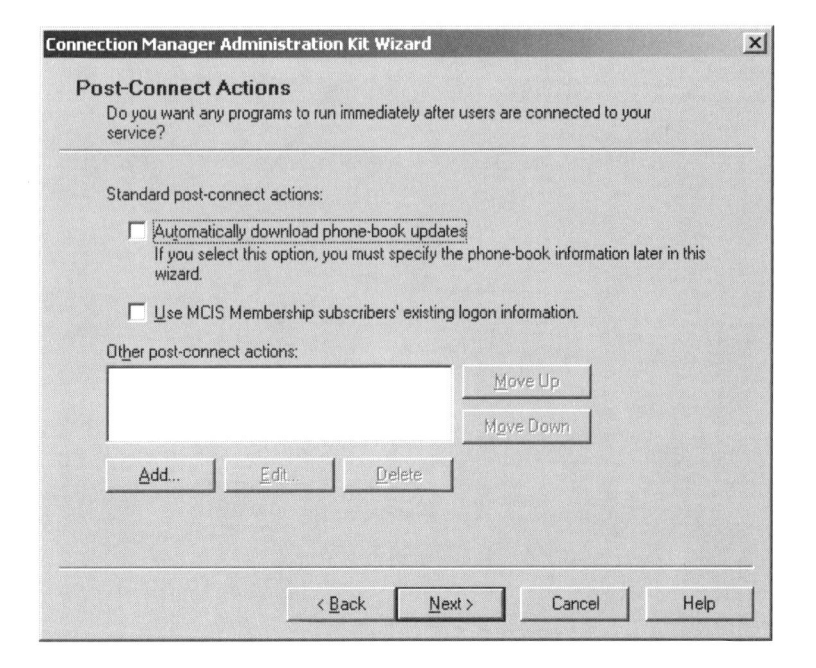

➤ STEP 14 (OPTIONAL)

Programs or scripts may be scheduled for execution when a user disconnects from the service by using the Disconnect Actions dialog box (Figure 16.16). These programs or scripts will be run when the user disconnects, but prior to the connection being terminated. Scripts that store information regarding connection details or other data regarding state information that should be persistent between connections are excellent candidates for this option.

- Click **ADD** to add programs or scripts to the list.
- To edit, delete, or change the execution order of an entry, highlight the entry and:
  1. Click **EDIT** to edit programs or scripts in the list.
  2. Click **DELETE** to remove a program or script from the list.
  3. Click **MOVE UP** or **MOVE DOWN** to change the execution order of the programs or scripts.
- For detailed information on the Adding/Editing Connect Actions dialog box presented when selecting either ADD or EDIT, see Step 11 and Figure 16.13.
- Click **NEXT**.

Figure 16.16 Configuring actions to take upon disconnection from the service.

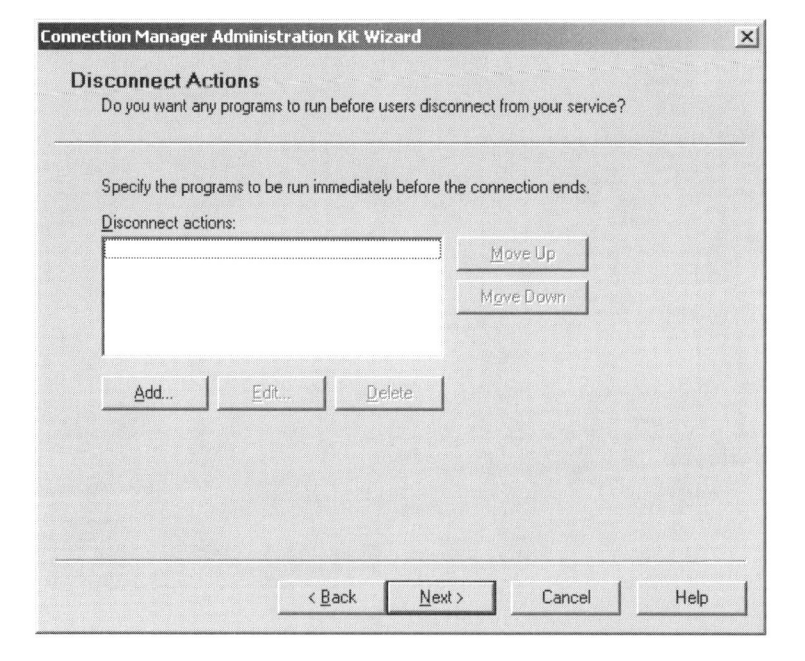

➢ STEP 15

The CMAK Wizard allows the Administrator to schedule applications to run while the connection is active. These programs might include a specific mail client, customized Web browser, or custom application such as the client portion of a client/server system. To specify such an application or script, use the Auto-Applications dialog box (Figure 16.17).

- Click **ADD** to add programs or scripts to the list.
- To edit, delete, or change the execution order of an entry, highlight the entry and:
    1. Click **EDIT** to edit programs or scripts in the list.
    2. Click **DELETE** to remove a program or script from the list.
    3. Click **MOVE UP** or **MOVE DOWN** to change the execution order of the programs or scripts.
- For detailed information on the Adding/Editing Connect Actions dialog box presented when selecting either ADD or EDIT, see Step 11 and Figure 16.13.
- Click **NEXT**.

Figure 16.17 The Auto-Applications management dialog.

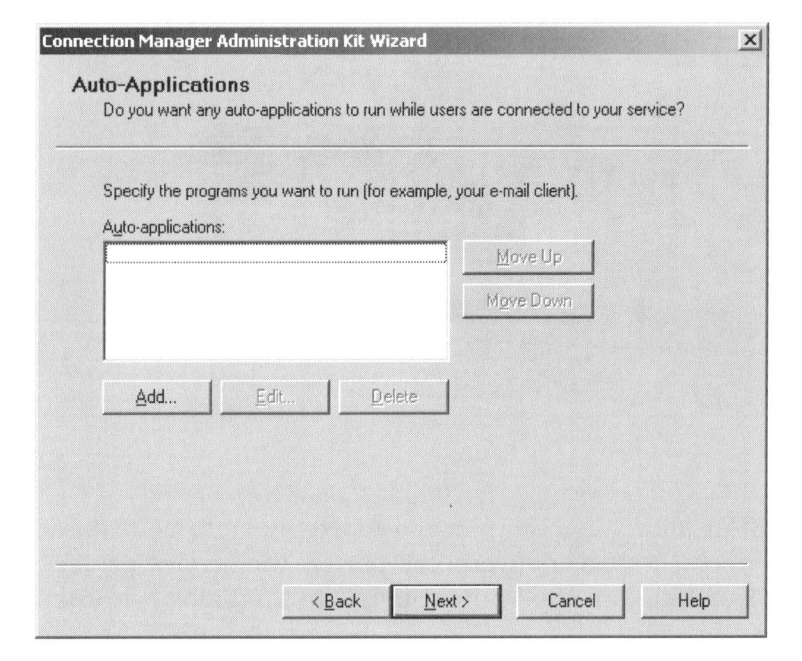

280 Chapter 16 • Connection Manager Administration Kit Wizard

➢ **STEP 16**

To further customize the appearance of the service profile, the CMAK allows the Administrator to use custom bitmap images and logos as part of the service profile. The logon graphic image can be specified in the Logon Bitmap dialog box (Figure 16.18).

- If no custom bitmap is desired, select **Use the default bitmap**.
- If a custom image is to be used, select **Use this bitmap (330x141 pixels)** and provide the path and filename of the image in the field below.
- Note that the image, custom or standard, will be displayed in the Graphic window.
- Click **NEXT**.

Figure 16.18 Specifying a custom or standard logon screen image.

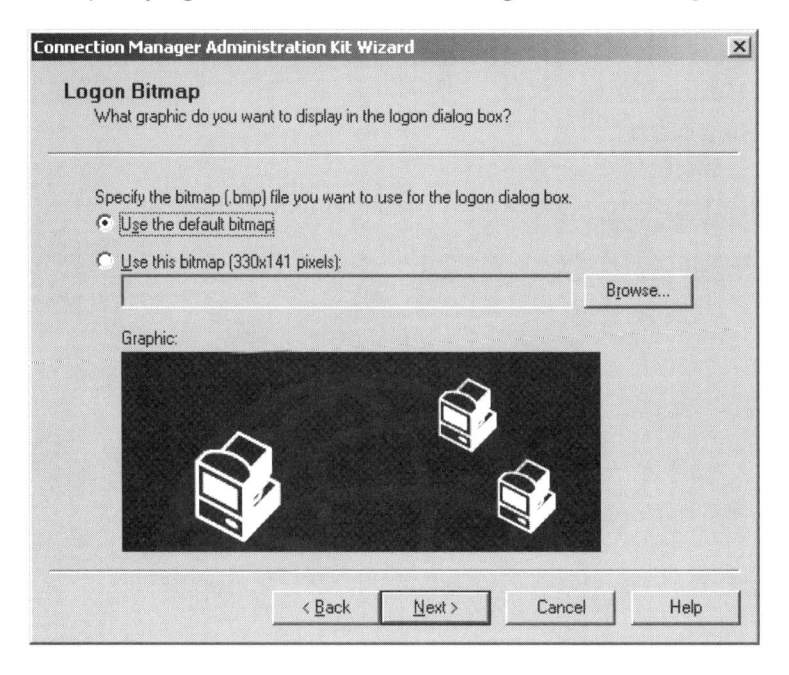

➢ **STEP 17**

The CMAK allows a custom or standard image to be displayed in the phone book that was delivered as part of the service profile. This image is selected in the Phone Book Bitmap dialog box (Figure 16.19).

- If no custom bitmap is desired, select **Use the default bitmap**.

- If a custom image is to be used, select **Use this bitmap (114x304 pixels)** and provide the path and filename of the image in the field below.
- Click **NEXT**.

Figure 16.19 Selecting a Phone Book Bitmap.

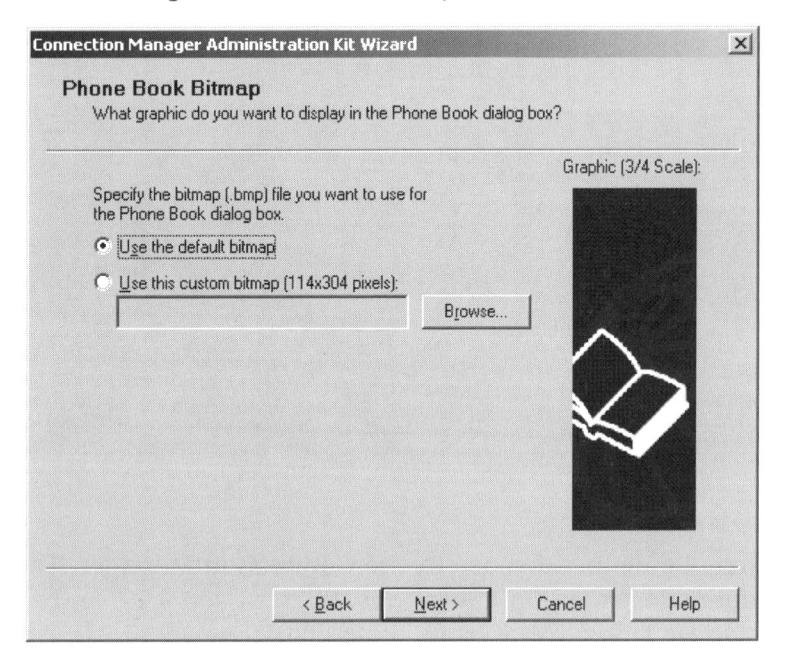

➢ STEP 18

A specific phone book may be included in the .EXE file that is created by the CMAK Wizard. If a phone book is included, it must already exist and be populated with the telephone numbers and connection information that is to be delivered to the end user. This phone book is specified in the Phone Book dialog box (Figure 16.20).

- Enter the path and name of an existing phone book (.PBK) file that is to be included in the finished service profile .EXE file in the **Phone-book file** field.
- Enter any text that is to be used to indicate that additional telephone numbers are available in the **More text** field.
- Click **NEXT**.

Figure 16.20 Specifying a phone-book file to be included in the .EXE file.

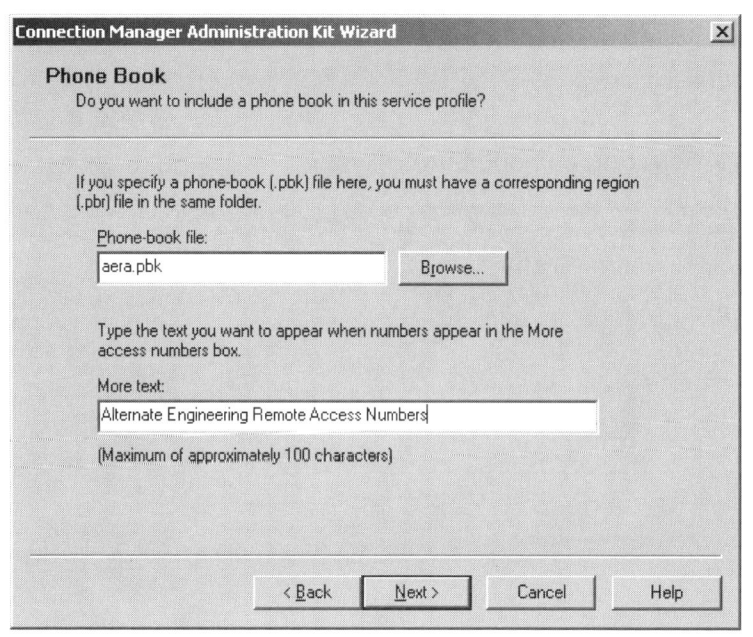

> **STEP 19**

Icons may be defined for use in the Connection Manager. These could be company logos, custom icons for different services, and so forth. Specify these icons in the Icons dialog box (Figure 16.21).

- Select **Use the default files for all icons** if no custom icons are to be used.
- Select **Use these files** to activate the custom icon fields.
- If custom icons are to be used, specify each in the appropriate field (**Program icon**, **Title-bar icon**, and **Status-area icon**). These icons will then be included as part of the final .EXE file that is distributed to end users.
- Click **NEXT**.

> **STEP 20**

The Windows 2000 taskbar runs the length of the screen, usually at the bottom of the display. This taskbar will display connection time and other status information when a user is connected to the service. In the Status-Area-Icon Menu screen (Figure 16.22), shortcuts can be defined to programs that should be available to users while they are using the service. These shortcuts will be displayed when the end user right-clicks the connection icon in the taskbar.

- Click **ADD** to add programs or scripts to the list.
- To edit, delete, or change the execution order of an entry, highlight the entry and:
    1. Click **EDIT** to edit programs or scripts in the list.
    2. Click **DELETE** to remove a program or script from the list.
    3. Click **MOVE UP** or **MOVE DOWN** to change the order of the programs or scripts.
- Click **NEXT**.

Figure 16.21 Specifying custom icons for the Connection Manager.

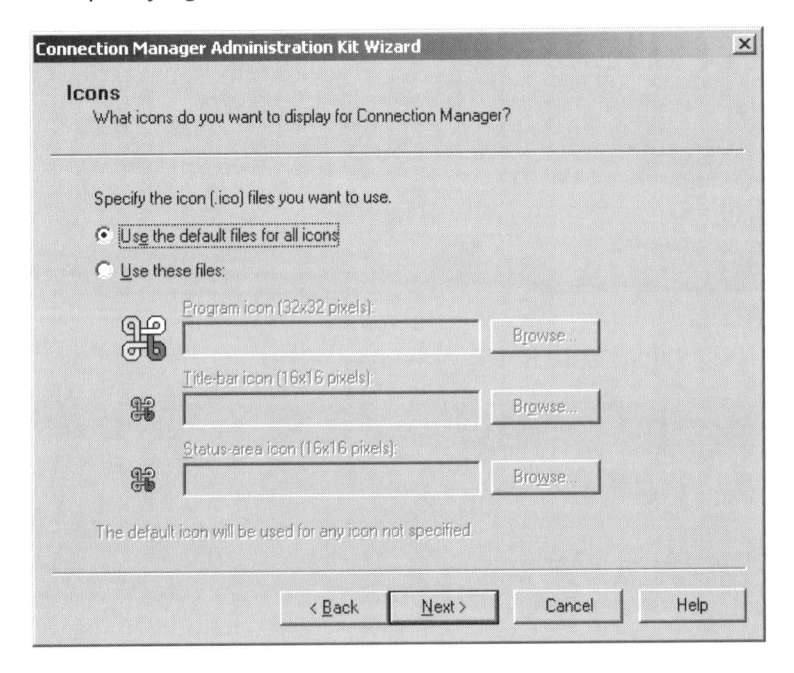

➤ STEP 21

A standard Help file may be included as part of the service profile .EXE file, or a standard Help file will be included by default. Indicate which file should be used in the Help File dialog box (Figure 16.23).

- Select **Use the default Help file** to package the default Help file.
- To use a custom Help file, select **Use this custom Help file** and enter the path and filename in the field below.
- Click **NEXT**.

Figure 16.22 Adding program shortcuts to the connection icon.

Figure 16.23 Defining the Help file to be packaged.

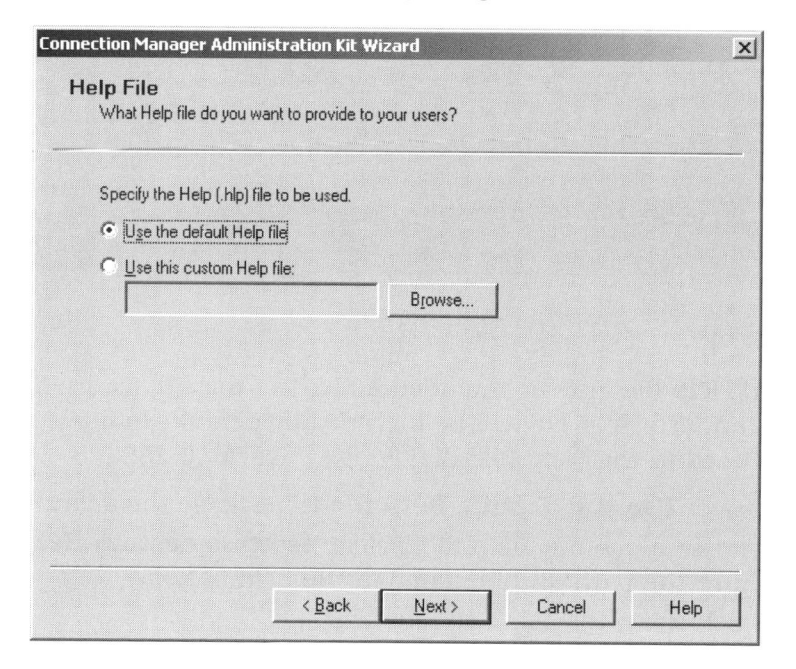

➤ STEP 22

For users to successfully use the service profile created by the CMAK, Connection Manager version 1.2 must be installed on their system. If there is any question as to whether or not it is installed, Connection Manager should be packaged as part of the service profile. If there is no question that Connection Manager is installed on the end user's machine, the size of the finished Connection Profile can be greatly reduced by not packaging Connection Manager 1.2 in the profile.

The Connection Manager Software dialog box (Figure 16.24) is used to specify the inclusion of Connection Manager version 1.2 in the package.

- If Connection Manager version 1.2 should be packaged into the final service profile file, check the box next to **Include the Connection Manager 1.2 software**. If there is no question that the end user machine already has Connection Manager version 1.2, clear the check box.
- Click **NEXT**.

Figure 16.24 Including Connection Manager 1.2 in the profile.

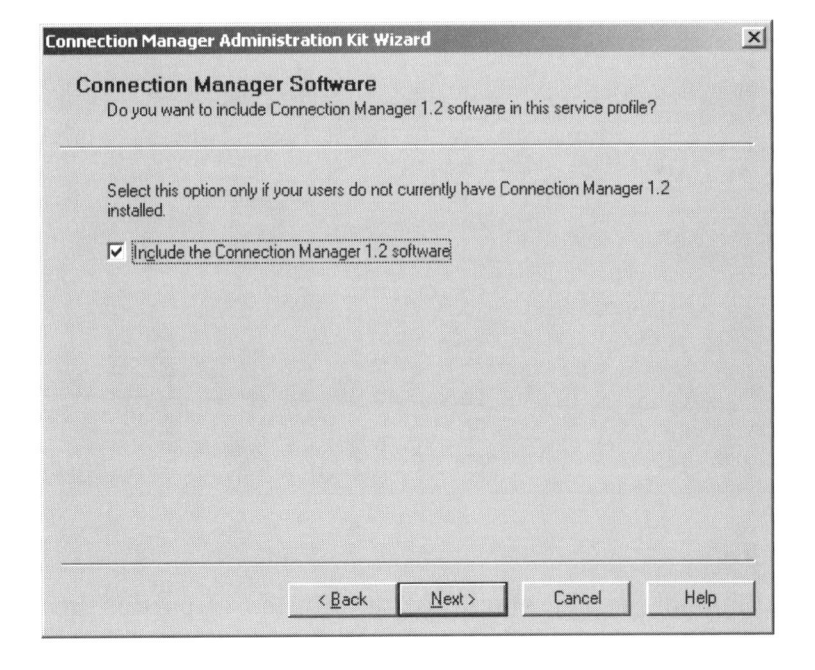

➢ STEP 23

In some cases, it may be desirable to include a licensing agreement to be displayed when the Service Package is installed. This may be a traditional licensing agreement, or a corporate-use only statement. The text file containing the agreement is specified in the License Agreement dialog box (Figure 16.25). If no agreement is to be used, the field may be left blank.

- Enter the path and filename of the .TXT file that contains the licensing agreement to be displayed prior to installing the service profile in the **License agreement file** field. Leave this field blank if no notice is desired.
- Click **NEXT**.

Figure 16.25 Entering the path and filename of the service profile license agreement.

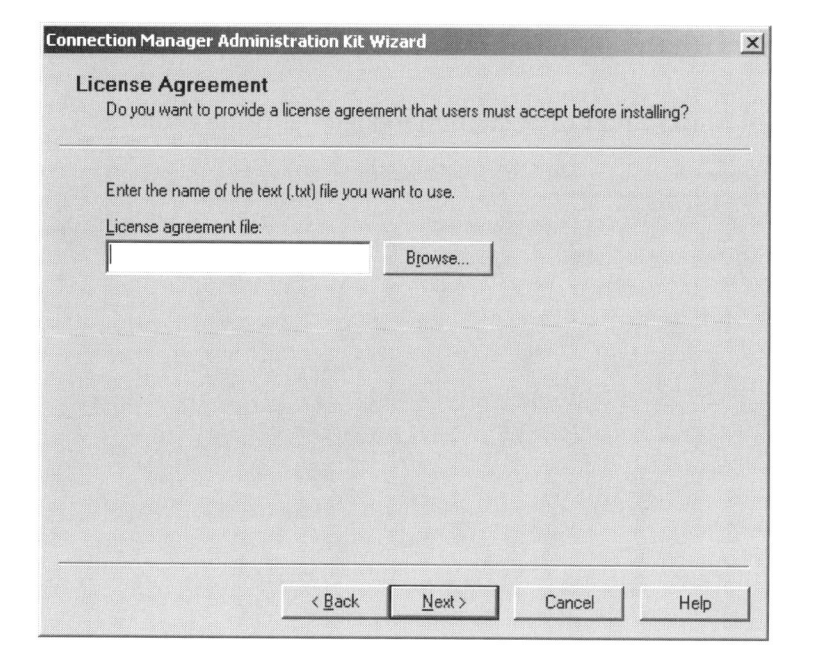

➢ STEP 24

Any additional file that should be distributed as part of the service profile package can be listed in the Additional Files dialog box (Figure 16.26). These might include support files, custom scripts, and so forth.

- Click **ADD** to add programs or scripts to the list.
- Highlight an entry, and click **DELETE** to remove a program or script from the list.
- Click **NEXT**.

Figure 16.26 Including additional files or scripts.

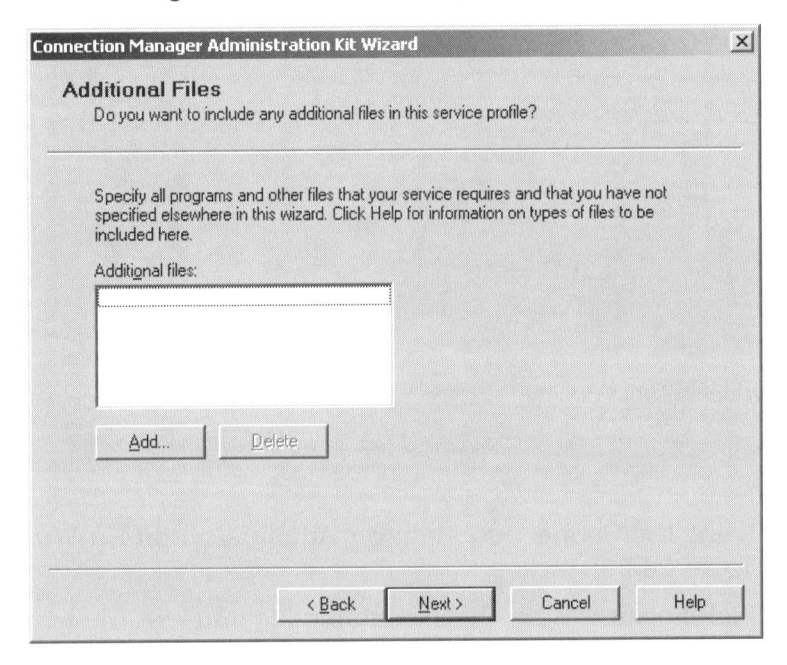

➤ STEP 25

The CMAK Wizard will ask for confirmation prior to building the distribution package. The Ready to Build the Service Profile screen is shown in Figure 16.27. If everything is satisfactory, click **NEXT** to start the package build process (Figure 16.28).

- Click **NEXT**.

➤ STEP 26

The final step in the process of creating a distributable service profile is to save the profile as a self-extracting executable file that may be given to end users. The name and location of this file is shown in the

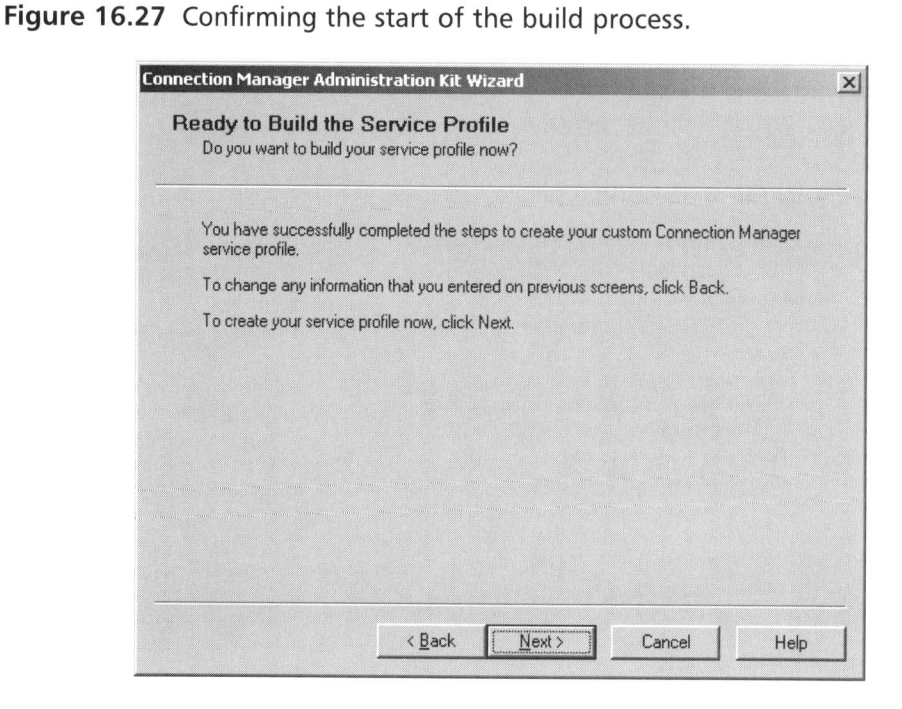

Figure 16.27 Confirming the start of the build process.

Completing the Connection Manager Administration Kit Wizard dialog box (Figure 16.29).

- Click **FINISH** to save the executable file and exit the wizard.

Figure 16.28 Command box running the service profile build.

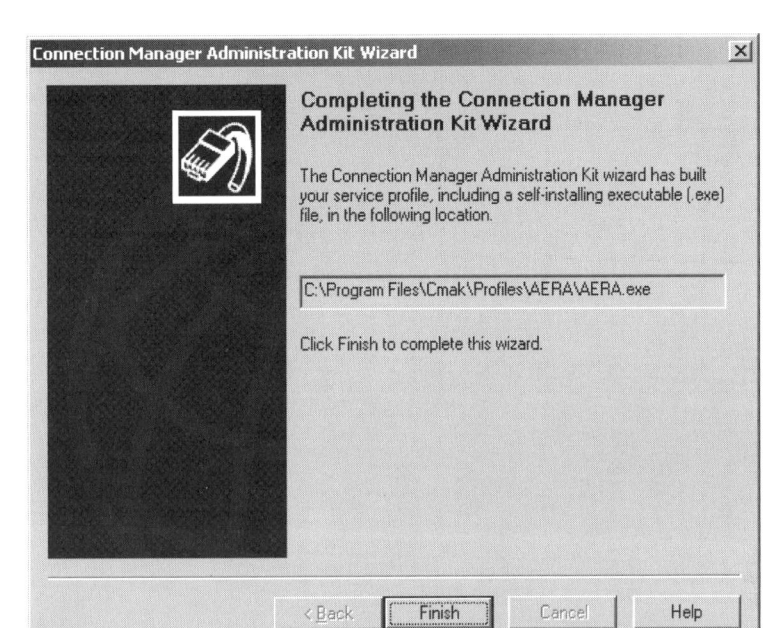

Figure 16.29 The CMAK Wizard finish screen.

Summary

The Connection Manager Administration Kit Wizard (CMAK) is a powerful tool used to create self-extracting and installing service profiles. These service profiles are used to connect end-user machines to remote networks.

The CMAK creates highly customizable packages, such as custom phone books, tailored communication parameters, icons and logos, and Administrator-defined programs and scripts. The high level of customization available makes the CMAK suitable for the creation of commercial-grade connection packages for use by ISPs and other online service providers, as well as corporate or inhouse organizational distribution.

Due to the vast number of options and choices available, it is highly recommended that the Administrator creating a service profile using the CMAK Wizard thoroughly read the online help documentation that is installed as part of the CMAK package. Prior to running the wizard, print and complete the Planning Worksheet for Connection Manager 1.2 available via the help system.

Chapter 17

Create New Dfs Root Wizard

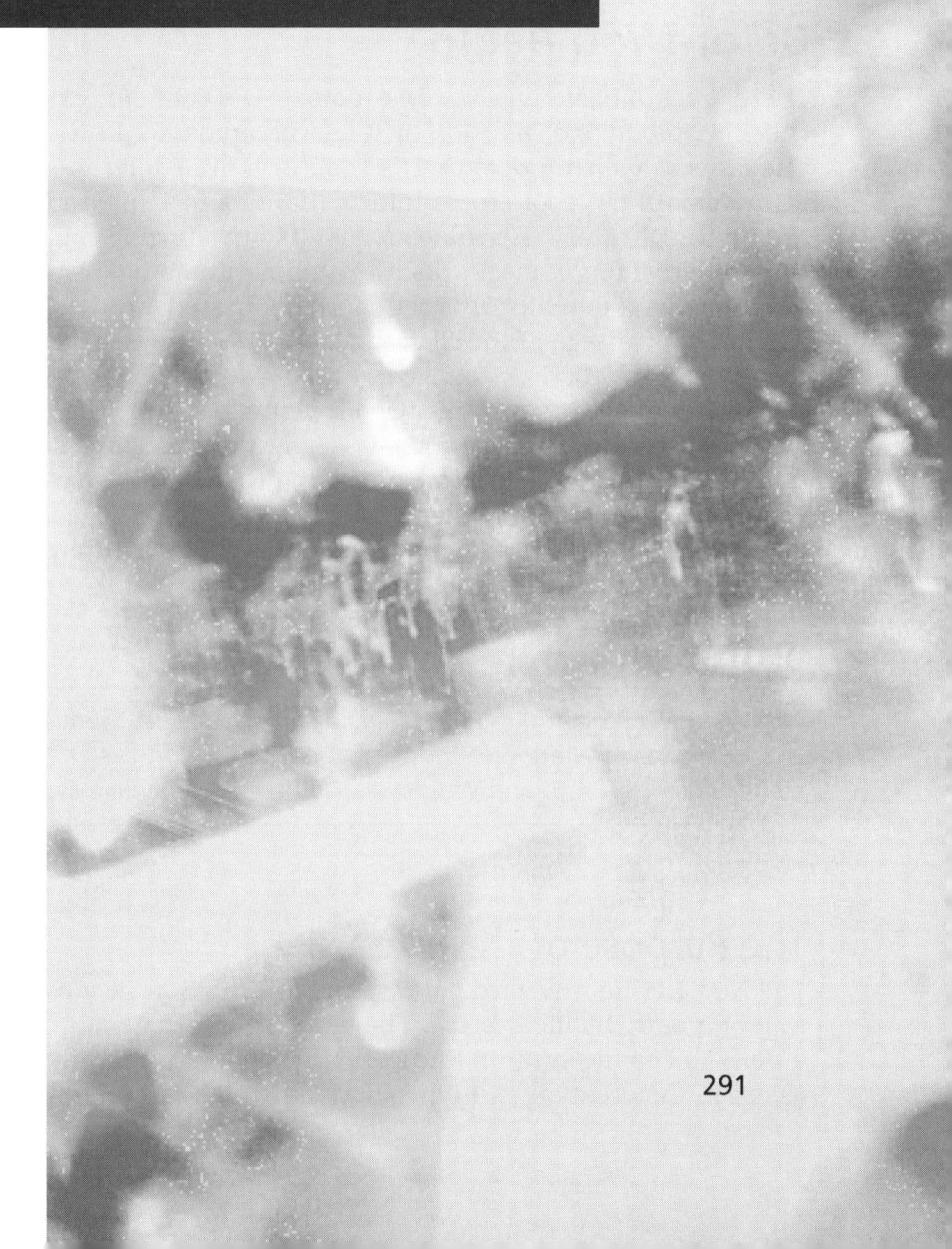

Introduction

The Distributed File System (Dfs) provides a method for enhancing the reliability and scalability of your network file services. Dfs allows you to transparently distribute file services across multiple Windows 2000 servers. Redundant paths to information can be configured in Dfs so that in case of a network or system failure, some users may be able to continue working unaffected. By the end of this chapter, you will be able to add Dfs services to your network and configure your server as a member of the Dfs hierarchy.

Before You Begin

There are two basic types of Dfs roots: a Dfs root can exist on a server, called a *standalone* Dfs root, or it can be an object in the Active Directory. The latter is called a *domain* Dfs root, or a fault-tolerant Dfs root.

A domain Dfs root stores information about itself and its topology in the Active Directory. Because of this, its structure is replicated to several servers, providing a mechanism to withstand a single-server failure. Additionally, a domain Dfs root can have nested child volumes, and they can take advantage of the file replication services that are available via the Active Directory.

A standalone Dfs root resides on a single server; the Dfs root is subject to loss in the event of a single-server failure. The loss of the server on which the Dfs root resides means losing the Dfs file structure until a server recovery can be implemented.

Windows 2000 Professional does not contain the New Dfs Root Wizard; it is a Windows 2000 Server and later feature.

> **NOTE**
> Windows 95 computers must install a Dfs support client from the Microsoft Web site, as Windows 95 does not natively recognize Dfs. Windows 98, Windows NT 4.0, and Windows 2000 computers have Dfs support built-in.

The Purpose of this Wizard

The New Dfs Root Wizard gathers the information needed to create the root of a new Dfs file system. The wizard can create either a standalone or a domain Dfs file system, and can either use an existing server share or assist in the creation of a new share on which to create the Dfs root.

Information Needed to Work with this Wizard

Before you start the New Dfs Root Wizard, you should:

- Understand the difference between a domain Dfs root and a standalone Dfs root
- Know which type of Dfs root you are going to install
- Know the server and path to the folder to be shared
- Decide on a share name
- Understand the security implications of sharing the folder.

Create New Dfs Root Wizard

➤ STEP 1

The New Dfs Root Wizard may be started from inside the Distributed File System manager tool. When run, the welcome screen is displayed (Figure 17.1).

- Click **NEXT**.

Figure 17.1 The New Dfs Root Wizard welcome screen.

➤ STEP 2

The second screen of the New Dfs Root Wizard is where the decision to make a domain Dfs Root or a standalone Dfs Root is made (Figure

17.2). Other than providing domain information, there is little difference in the behavior of the wizard based on this information, other than the specification of a domain in which the Dfs root will reside.

- Select **Create a domain Dfs root** to create a Dfs root that will be supported by Active Directory.
- Select **Create a standalone Dfs root** to create a Dfs root that does not use Active Directory (skip ahead to Step 5).
- Click **NEXT**.

Figure 17.2 Specifying a domain or standalone Dfs root.

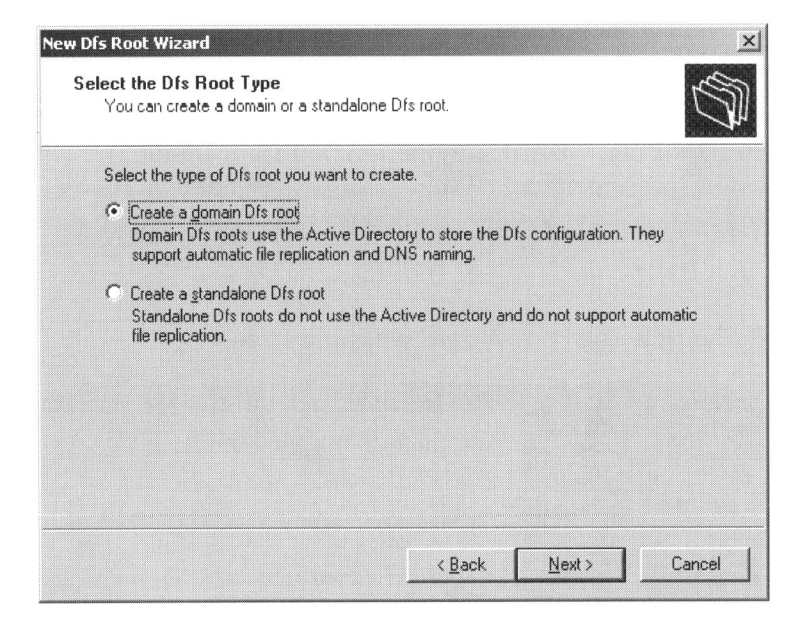

➤ STEP 3

If "create a Domain Dfs root" was selected, the next step is to specify the domain that will contain the Dfs root (Figure 17.3).

- Enter the name of the domain that will contain the Dfs root in the Domain name field (the domain may also be chosen from the list of Trusting domains).
- Click **NEXT**.

➤ STEP 4

Once the domain has been identified, the next step of the wizard is to specify the server within the domain that contains the share to be published as a Dfs root (Figure 17.4).

- Enter the server that has the folder to be shared as a Dfs root in the Server name field, or click **BROWSE** to visually locate the server on the network.
- Click **NEXT**.

Figure 17.3 Identifying the domain that will contain the Dfs root.

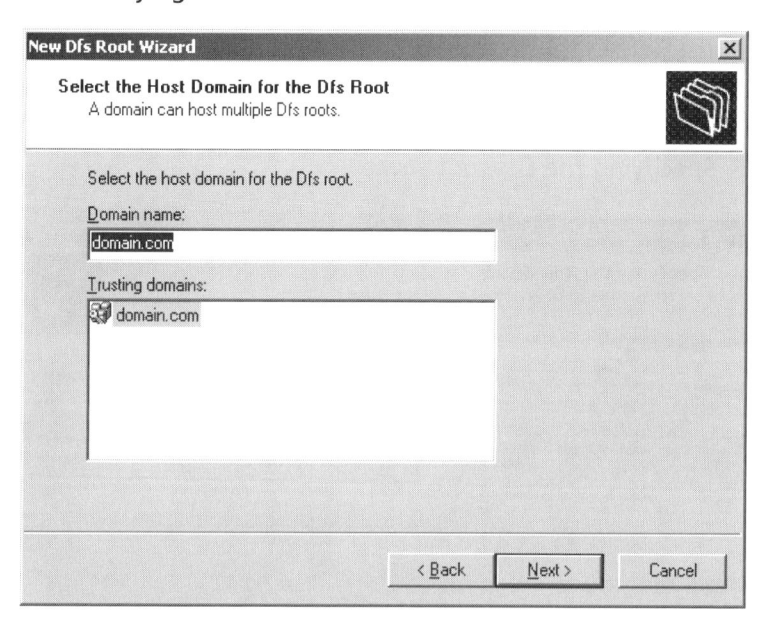

Figure 17.4 Specifying the server containing the folder to be shared.

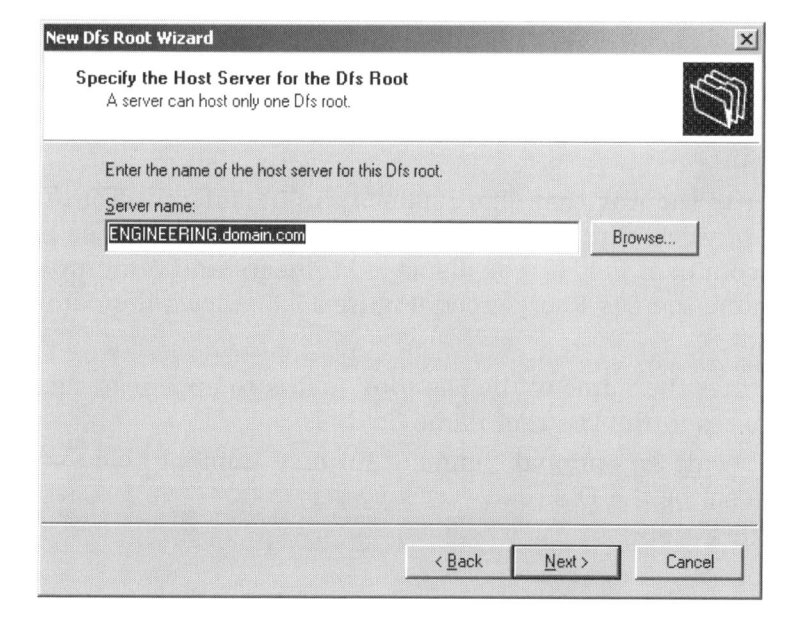

➤ STEP 5

The physical location and share name must be provided next (Figure 17.5). An existing share may be used, or a new share can be created.

- To use an existing share as the new Dfs root, select the share from the **Use an existing share** list.
- To create a new share, specify the physical path in the **Path to share** field, and provide a share name in the Share name field.
- Click **NEXT**.

Figure 17.5 Specifying the Dfs root share.

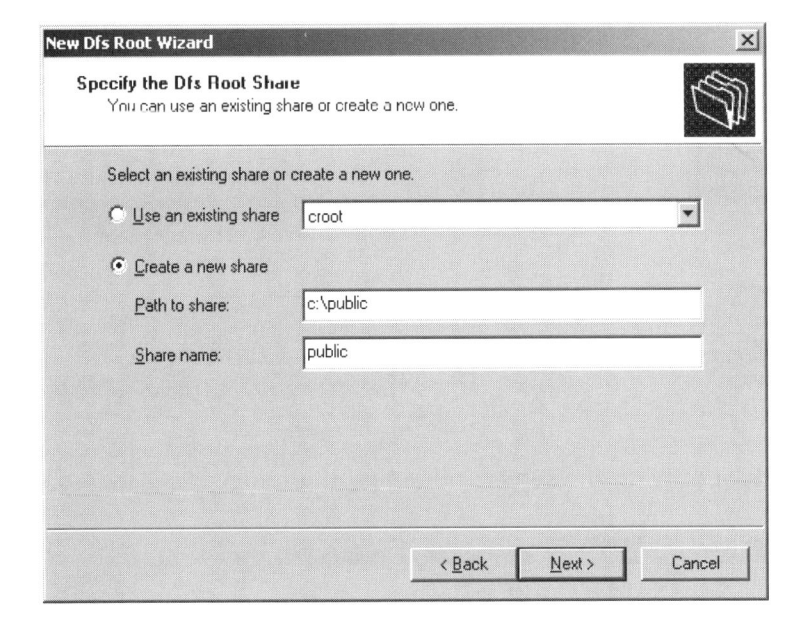

➤ STEP 6

Similar to the way that share names can be different from the name of the physical directory they represent, Dfs roots are also named and given comment fields to be displayed to users and Administrators. The Name the Dfs Root screen (Figure 17.6) allows the naming of the Dfs root.

- Enter the name of the Dfs root as it is to appear to the network users in the Dfs root name field.
- Provide an optional comment in the Comment field to further describe the Dfs root.
- Click **NEXT**.

Figure 17.6 Naming the Dfs root.

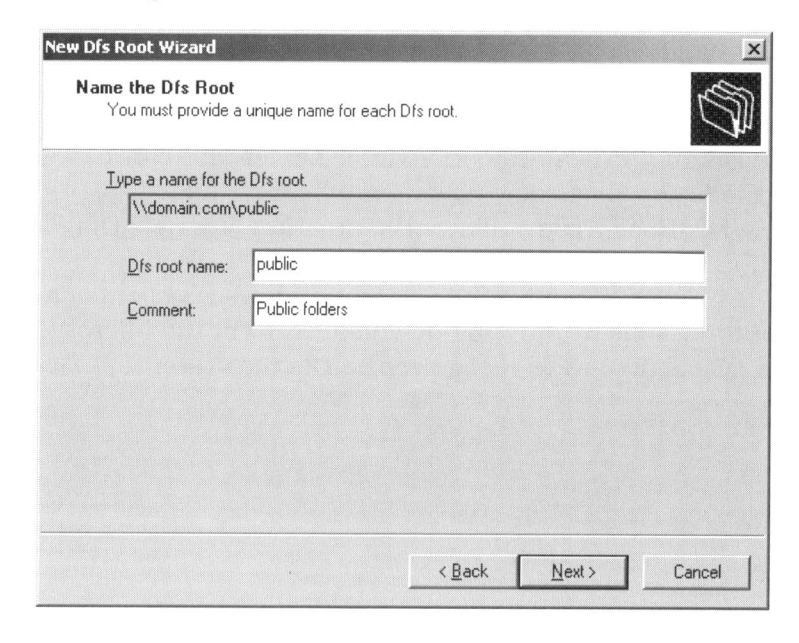

> ## STEP 7

The creation of the Dfs root is complete. The final screen of the New Dfs Root Wizard (Figure 17.7) summarizes the information that was gathered.

- Click **FINISH** to save the new Dfs root.

Figure 17.7 Summary of information gathered.

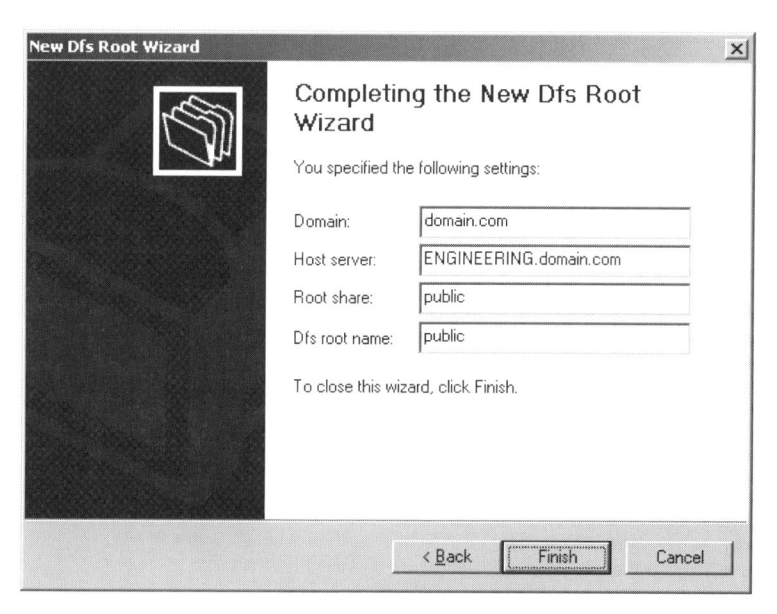

Summary

Dfs is a new Windows 2000 feature that allows directory structures to span multiple servers. A domain Dfs replicates information about itself via the Active Directory, and as such, is considered fault-tolerant. A standalone Dfs root exists only on a single server and can be lost if the host server fails.

The New Dfs Root Wizard allows the creation of a new Dfs files system root object, either a standalone or domain Dfs.

Windows NT 4.0, Windows 2000, and Windows 98 clients can use Dfs natively, but a Dfs client must be downloaded from the Microsoft Web site if Windows 95 clients are to recognize the Dfs file system.

Chapter 18

Delegation of Control Wizard

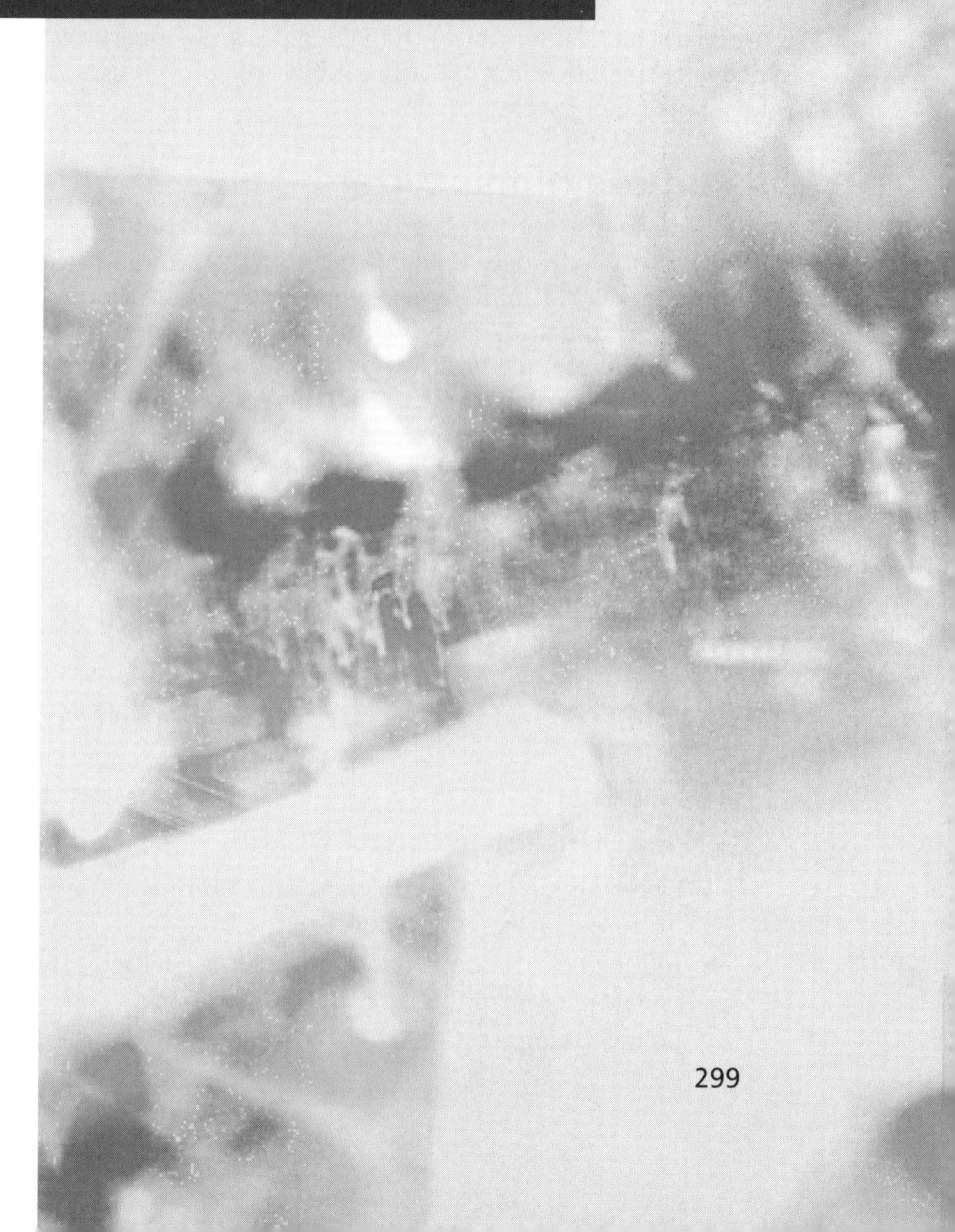

Introduction

One of the advantages of Active Directory is that everything in the directory database is treated as an independent object. An Administrator can assign rights to each object, including permissions to modify or add new objects to other users on the network. By the end of this chapter, you will know how to delegate administration of Active Directory objects to other computers and users on the network.

Before You Begin

To perform the task of using the Delegation of Control Wizard you need to ensure you use an Administrator's account and ensure Active Directory is in use on your network.

The Purpose of this Wizard

The Delegation of Control Wizard is present in Windows 2000 Server when Active Directory is in use. This wizard allows Administrators to very granularly grant specific administrative rights for organizational units, domains, and sites to groups and/or individuals. This reduces the security risk of having too many people with too much power over parts of the Active Directory structure that they do not have a need for.

Information Needed to Work with this Wizard

To use the Delegation of Control Wizard, you need the following:

- Users, Groups, or Computers you need to delegate control to
- The task(s) you plan to delegate

The Delegation of Control Wizard

➢ STEP 1

Start the Delegation of Control Wizard.

- Open Active Directory Users and Computers from the Administrative Tools menu.
- Right-click the organizational unit for which you want to delegate control (Figure 18.1).
- Select **Delegate Control…** from the pop-up menu.

Figure 18.1 Right-click on the domain you want to delegate control from.

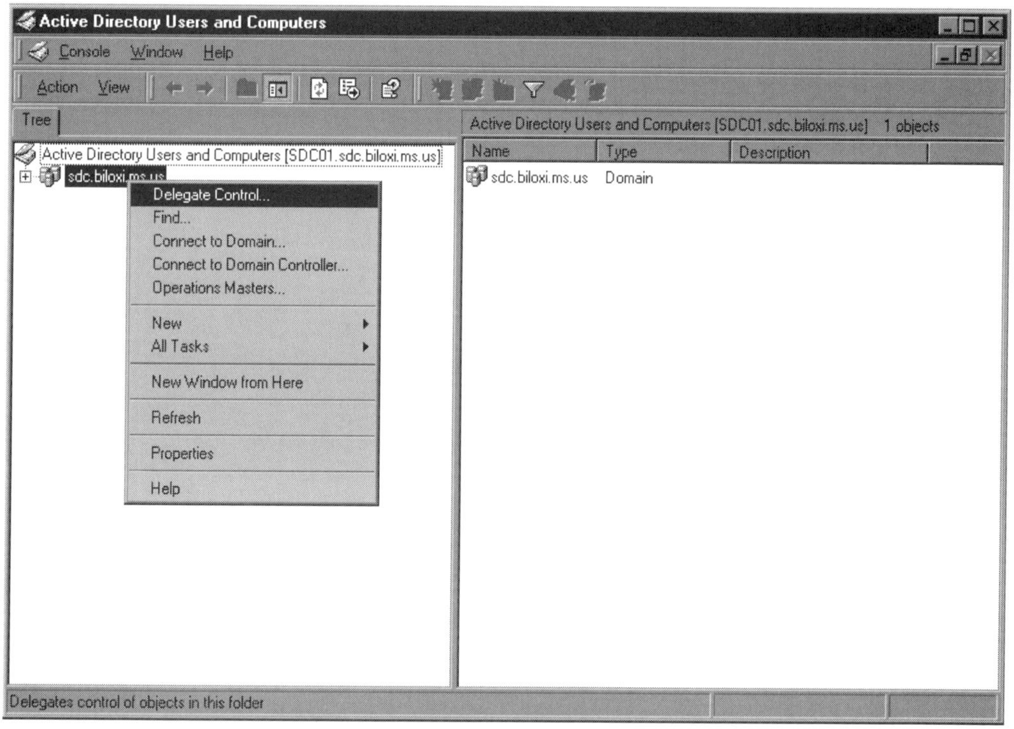

➤ STEP 2

Click **NEXT** at the Delegation of Control Wizard welcome page (Figure 18.2).

➤ STEP 3

Click **ADD...** on the Users or Groups page (Figure 18.3).

➤ STEP 4

Highlight the user and/or group you want to delegate control to, click **ADD** (Figure 18.4), and then click **OK**.

➤ STEP 5

Click **NEXT** on the Users or Groups page (Figure 18.5).

Figure 18.2 The Delegation of Control Wizard welcome page.

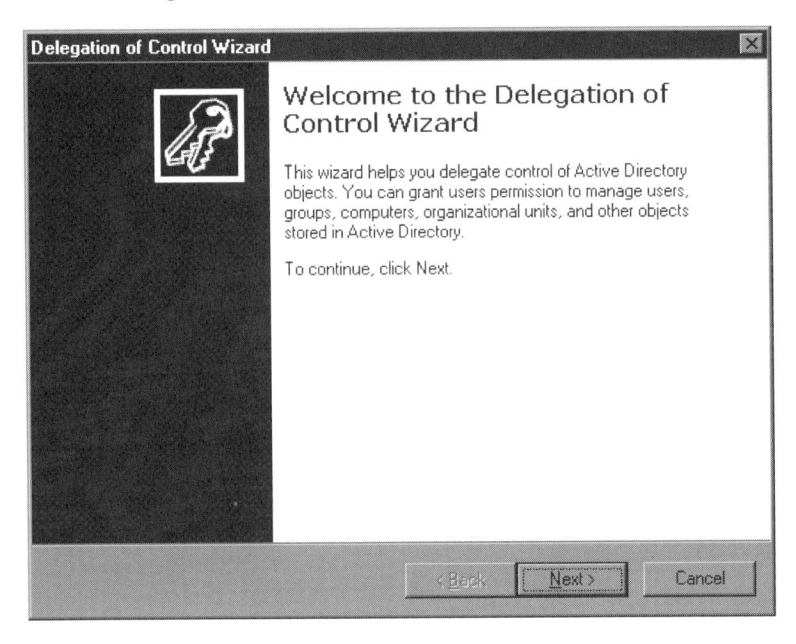

Figure 18.3 The Users or Groups page.

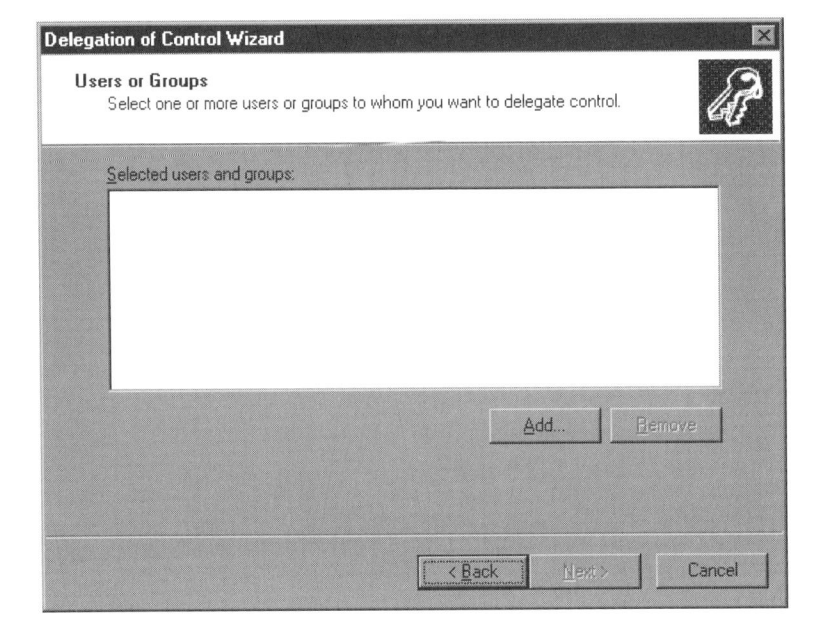

Figure 18.4 Selecting Users, Computers, or Groups to delegate control to.

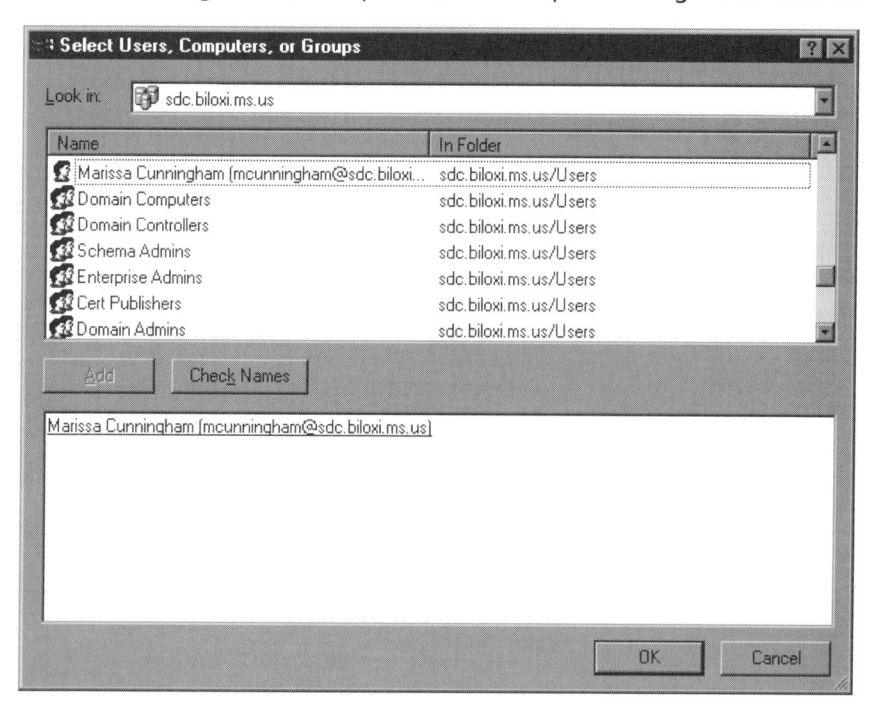

Figure 18.5 The Users or Groups page.

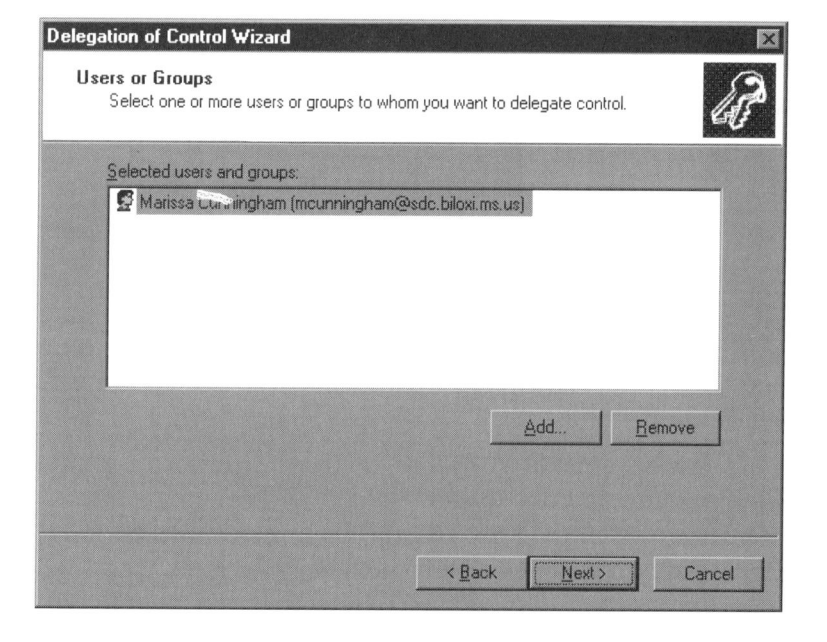

➤ STEP 6

Select from one of two types of delegation shown in Figure 18.6.

- **Delegate the following common tasks**. These two items are applied domain-wide. If you select this option, click **NEXT**, and go to Step 9.
    - Join a computer to the domain
    - Manage Group Policy links
- **Create a custom task to delegate**. If you select this option, click **NEXT**, and go to Step 7.

Figure 18.6 Selecting common tasks or custom tasks to delegate.

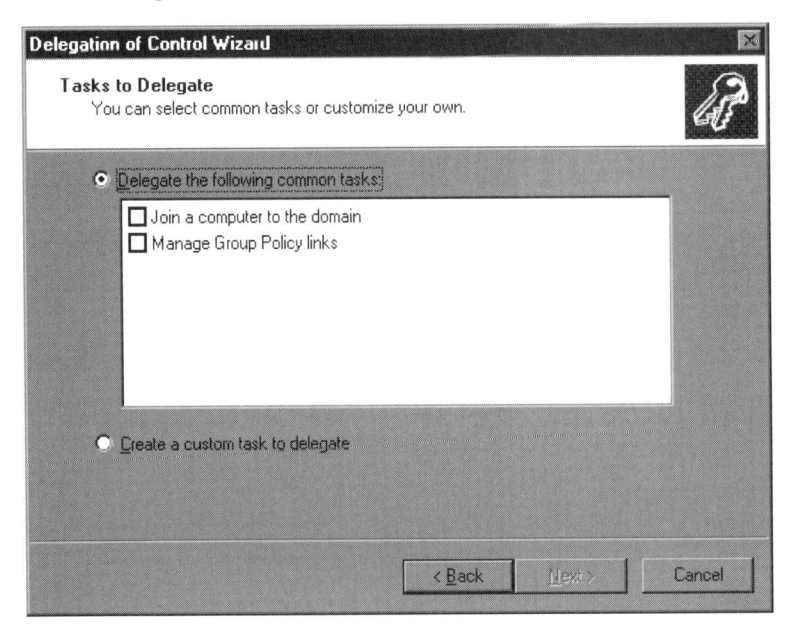

➤ STEP 7

Selecting "Create a custom task to delegate" allows you to define the task you want to delegate (Figure 18.7). There are two main choices of delegation on this page:

- **This folder, existing objects in this folder, and creation of new objects in this folder.** Selecting this choice allows delegation of control for all objects in the organizational unit. Click **NEXT** to proceed to the next step.

Figure 18.7 Custom tasks to delegate page.

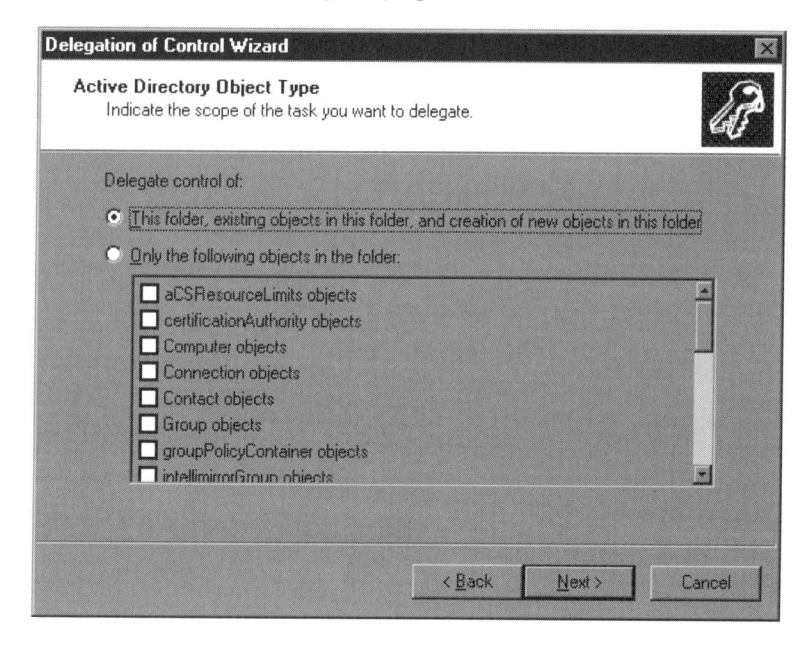

- **Only the following objects in the folder**:
  - aCSResourceLimits objects
  - Certification Authority objects
  - Computer objects
  - Connection objects
  - Contact objects
  - Group objects
  - GroupPolicyContainer objects
  - intellimirrorGroup objects
  - intellimirrorSCP objects
  - MSMQ Configuration objects
  - Organizational Unit objects
  - Printer objects
  - Shared Folder objects
  - Site objects
  - Site Link objects
  - Site Link Bridge objects
  - Site Settings objects
  - Sites Container objects
  - Subnet objects

- Subnets Container objects
- Trusted Domain objects
- User objects

This choice allows very granular delegation of only the objects you want to give another user, group, or computer. If you select this option, place a check mark next to the object(s) you want to delegate, and click **Next** to proceed to the next step.

➤ STEP 8

The Permissions page allows you to select the permissions you grant for the object(s) you have delegated (Figure 18.8). The permissions displayed for you to select from are based on which of the following three blocks you select (one or more of the blocks may be selected):

- General
- Property-specific
- Creation/deletion of specific child objects

Figure 18.8 The Permissions page.

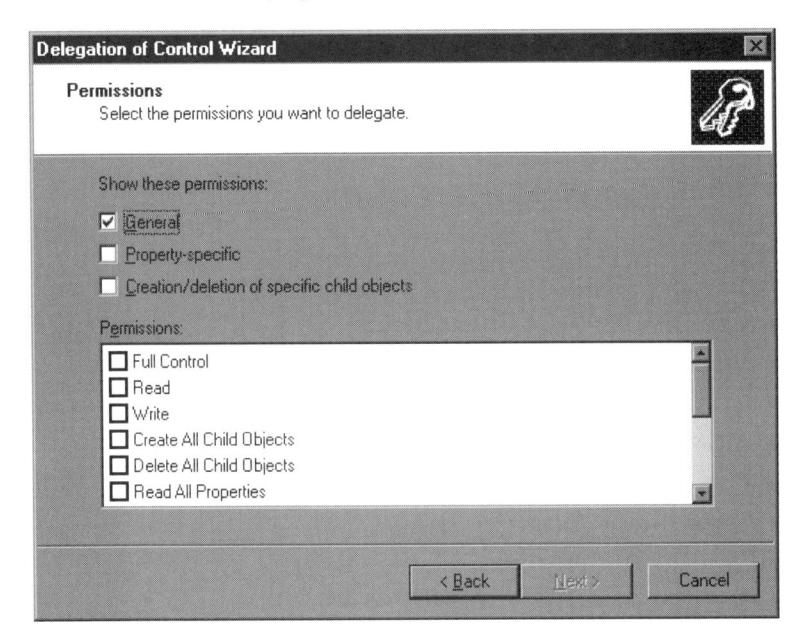

The number of permissions you can select depends not only on which of these three blocks you decide to choose, but also the object(s) you have decided to delegate. Let's look at an example of the General permissions available when the User objects have been delegated. The following are the General permissions available for User objects:

- Full Control
- Read
- Write
- Create All Child Objects
- Delete All Child Objects
- Read All Properties
- Write All Properties
- Change Password
- Reset Password
- Send As
- Receive As
- Read and Write General Information
- Read and Write Account Restrictions
- Read and Write Logon Information
- Read and Write Group Membership
- Read and Write Personal Information
- Read and Write Phone and Mail Options
- Read and Write Web Information
- Read and Write Public Information
- Read and Write Remote Access Information

While the General permissions may seem to be granular (and they are!), even more permissions are available for the User objects. Selecting General shows a choice of 20 permissions available for selection. Selecting General, Property-specific, and Creation/deletion of specific child objects boosts the number of permissions available to 150! Very granular delegation capability indeed! Click **NEXT** after selecting the permissions you want to delegate.

NOTE

The number of permissions available and the type of permission will vary, depending on the object(s) selected for delegation.

➤ STEP 9

The Completing the Delegation of Control Wizard page will display a summary of what was completed (Figure 18.9). Click **Finish** to close the Delegation of Control Wizard.

Figure 18.9 Completing the Delegation of Control Wizard.

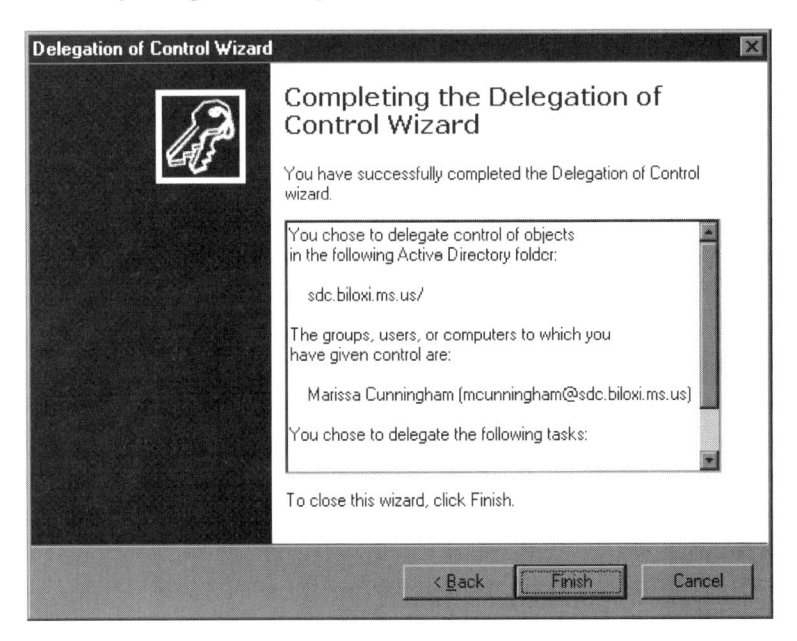

Summary

The Delegation of Control Wizard allows you to granularly control the delegation of users, groups, computers, organizational units, and other objects within Active Directory. No longer do you have to give Administrator privileges to users who do not need all of the power associated with "normal" Administrator rights.

Using the wizard, you can delegate to users, groups, or computers. After selecting whom you will delegate control to, you must decide what permissions you want them to have. You may select common tasks or custom tasks. If you select common tasks, the wizard will make the appropriate changes and the wizard finishes. If you select custom tasks, you have two choices: you may select the entire folder, or you may select one or more objects in the folder to delegate. No matter whether you select the entire folder or only certain objects from the folder, you must also select the permissions you wish to delegate. The Permissions page shows three categories of permissions: General, Property-specific, and

Creation/deletion of specific child objects. You select the permissions you wish to delegate from the list shown. The permissions shown will vary based on the choice you picked to be shown and the object(s) you have selected.

Chapter 19

Create Partition Wizard

Introduction

When configuring Windows 2000 for the first time, you were prompted to create and select a partition for the install. Once Windows 2000 is installed, you may want to add additional partitions or drives to an existing configuration. Windows 2000 offers a wizard to make the configuration of partitions easier. By the end of this chapter, you will be able to create new partitions for your Windows 2000 systems.

Before You Begin

Care should be taken using the Create Partition Wizard; data loss can occur from improper use. Administrative access is required to use this wizard.

The Purpose of this Wizard

The Create Partition Wizard is used to create partitions, and is available for both Windows 2000 Server and Windows 2000 Professional. It can be used to create NTFS, FAT, and FAT32 partitions.

Information Needed to Work with this Wizard

To use the Create Partition Wizard, you need the following:

- Free space or unallocated space on a hard drive.

The Create Partition Wizard

➢ STEP 1

Start the Create Partition Wizard.

- Open Computer Management from the Administrative Tools menu.
- Select **Disk Management** from the left pane.
- Right-click on an area of free space or unallocated space of your hard drive (Figure 19.1).
- Select **Create Partition...** or **Create Logical Drive...**, depending on the selection available to you from the pop-up menu. You will see Create Partition if the selected free space is not already assigned to an extended partition. The Create Logical Drive option is displayed if the selected free space is in an extended partition.

Figure 19.1 Right-click on the free space you want to partition.

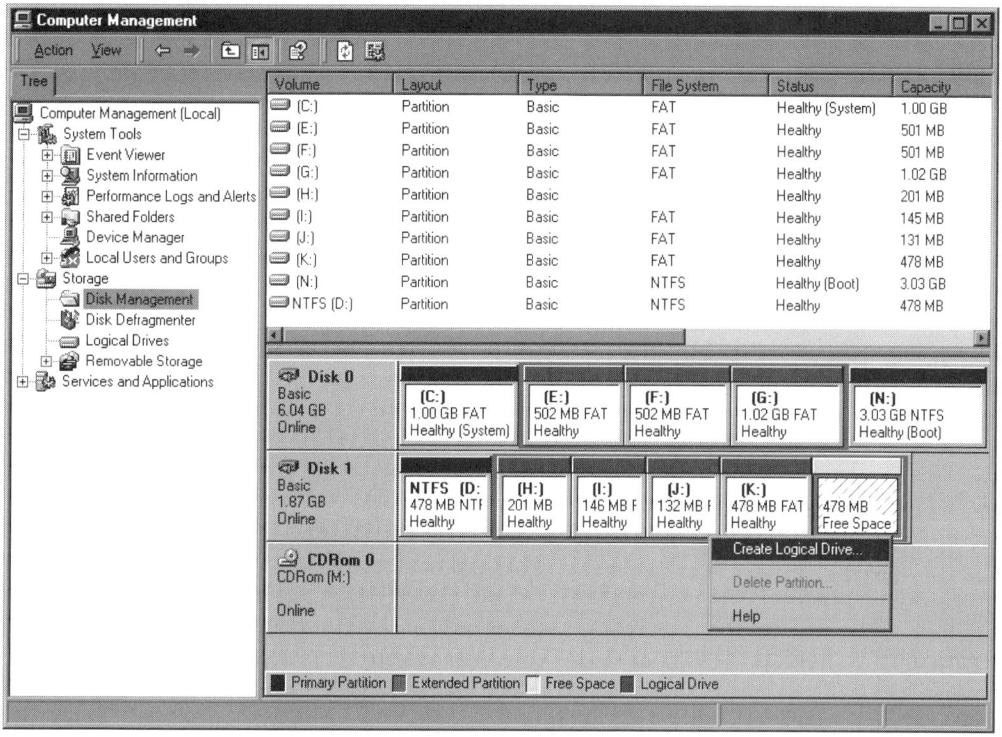

➢ STEP 2

Click **NEXT** at the Create Partition Wizard welcome page (Figure 19.2).

➢ STEP 3

Select the Partition Type you want to create, and click **NEXT** (Figure 19.3). The choices available to you depend on the existing layout of your hard drive. If you have unallocated space, you may be able to select Primary partition or Extended partition. If you chose free space in an extended partition, the only choice available to you is Logical drive (Figure 19.3). Windows 2000 starts from a primary partition and it supports up to four primary partitions on a basic disk. You can also have up to three primary partitions and one extended partition if your needs require that. Only one extended partition is allowed for each basic disk.

Figure 19.2 The Create Partition Wizard welcome page.

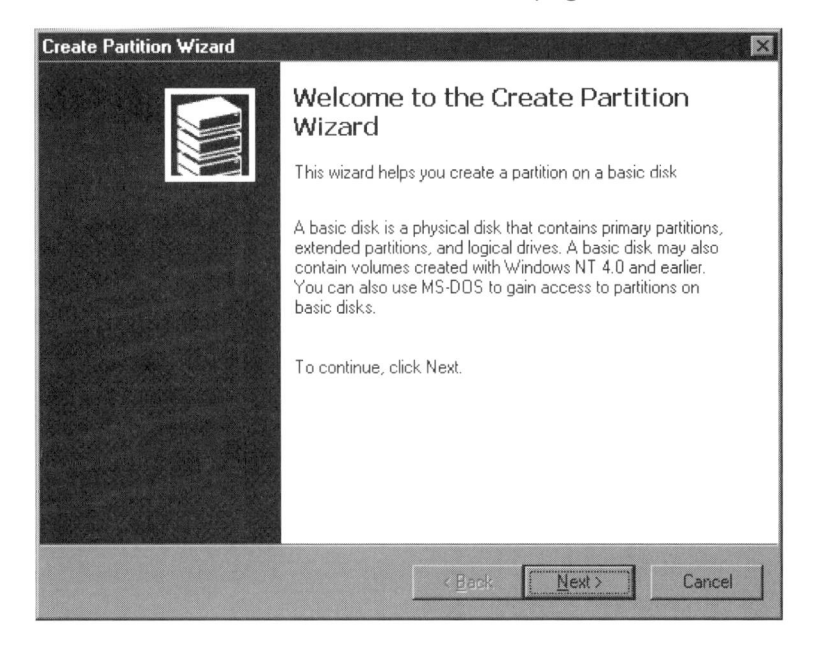

Figure 19.3 Selecting the Partition Type you want to create.

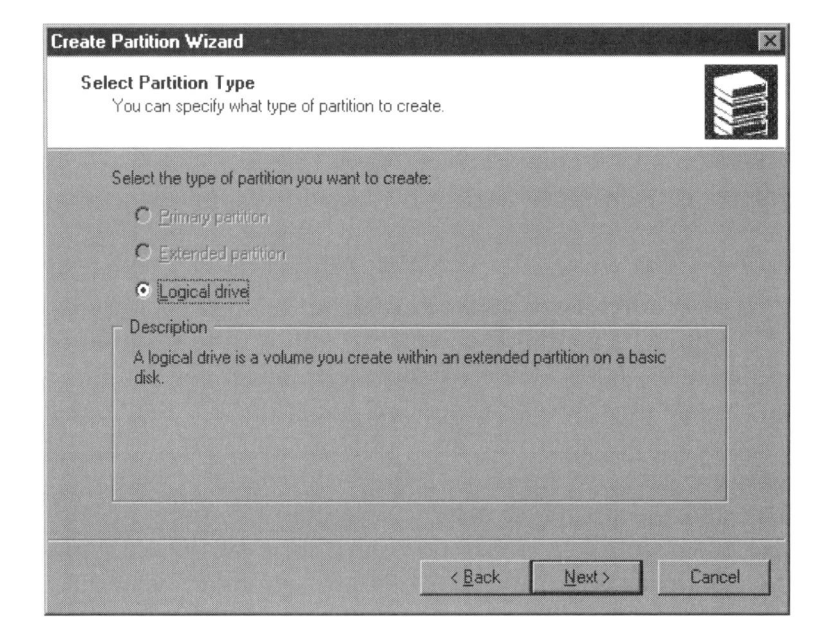

➤ STEP 4

Select the amount of disk space you want the partition to be, and click **NEXT** (Figure 19.4). The maximum size is automatically placed in the dialog box.

Figure 19.4 Selecting the amount of disk space for the new partition.

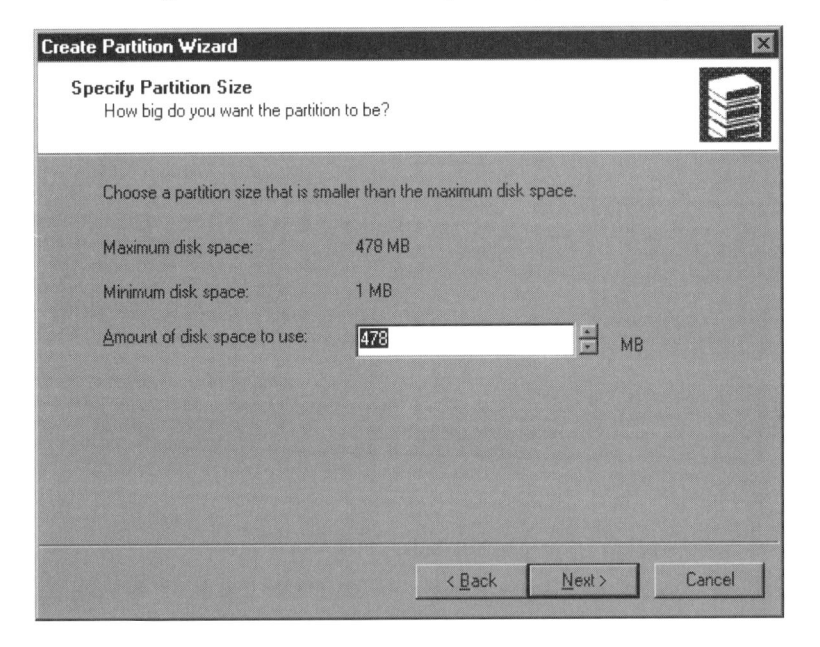

➤ STEP 5

Select one of the three assignments for the new partition (Figure 19.5).

- **Assign a drive letter**. Select from the unused drive letters shown in the drop-down box. If you select this option, click **NEXT** and proceed to Step 7.
- **Mount this volume at an empty folder that supports drive paths**. In Windows 2000, it is now possible to mount a volume to a folder. This is very handy if you are running out of drive letters! In order to use this option, you must be using NTFS. If you select this option, click **BROWSE...** and go to Step 6.
- **Do not assign a drive letter or drive path**. Select this option if you want to partition the free/unallocated space, but do not want to assign a drive letter or path. Click **NEXT**, and go to Step 7.

Figure 19.5 Selecting the drive letter, path, or neither to assign the new partition.

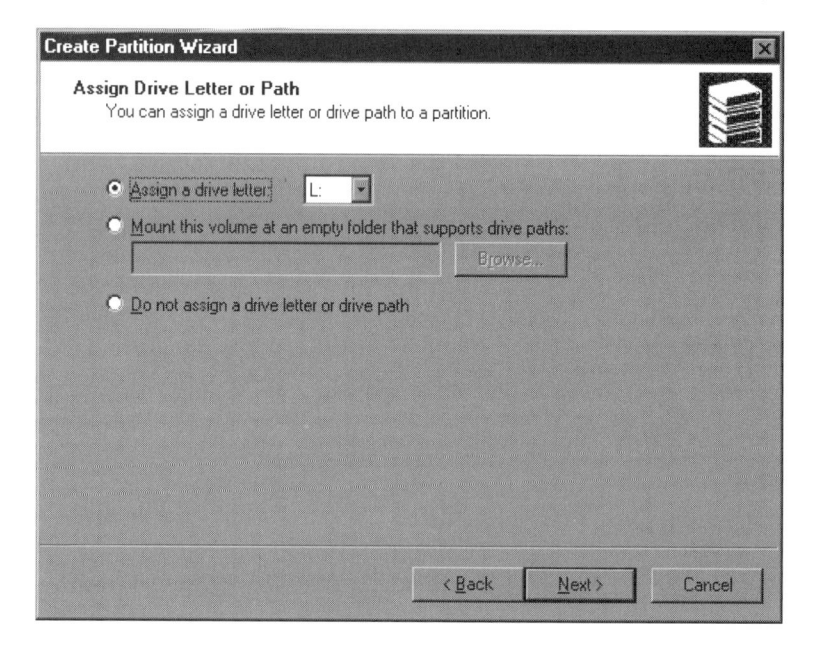

> **STEP 6**

Select the empty folder to assign to the new partition from one of your NTFS volumes (Figure 19.6). If an empty folder is not available, you may create one by clicking **NEW FOLDER**. After making the selection, click **OK**.

Figure 19.6 Selecting the folder in the drive path for the new partition.

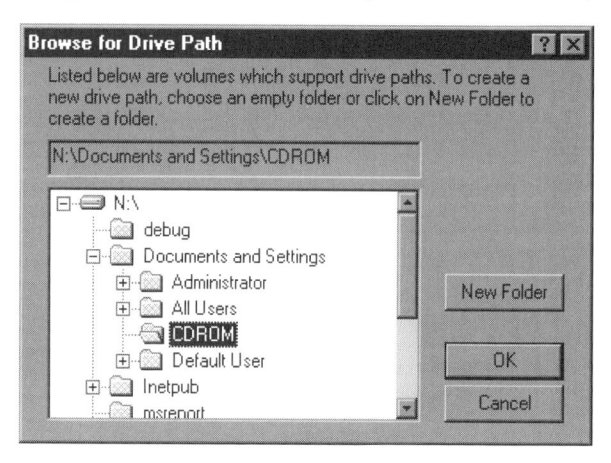

➢ STEP 7

Select from the format options for the new partition, and click **NEXT** (Figure 19.7).

- **Do not format this partition**. Select this choice if you do not want to format the new partition at this time. Remember that the new partition cannot be used until it is formatted.
- **Format this partition with the following settings**. Several choices are available for formatting the new partition.
    - **File system to use**. Windows 2000 supports three different file systems:
        NTFS
        FAT32
        FAT

Figure 19.7 Selecting the format options for the new partition.

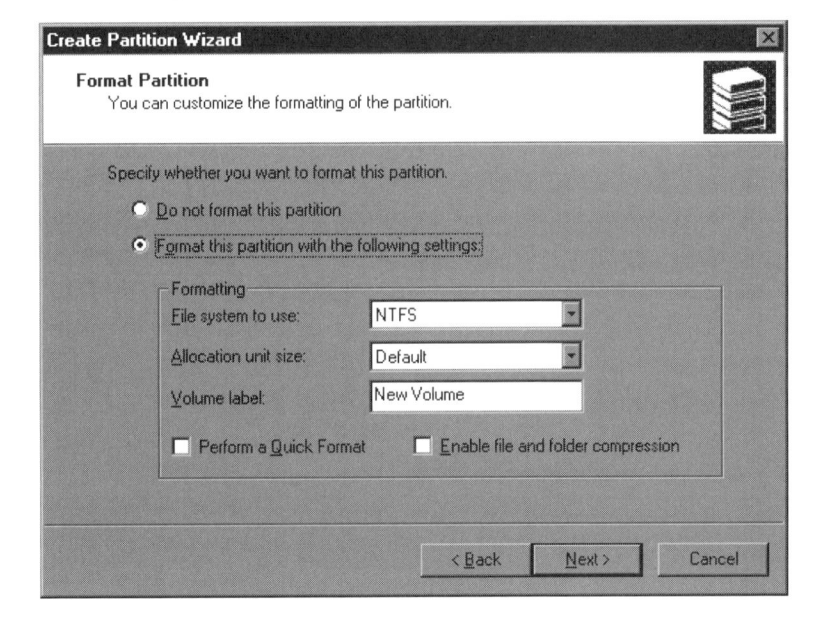

- **Allocation unit size**. The size for each unit. Leave it set to the default unless you have a very good reason to change it. The following sizes are available for selection:
    512
    1024
    2048
    4096

8192

16k

32k

64k

- **Volume label.** The name you want to give the new partition.
- **Perform a quick format.** Same as using the /q switch with the format command.
- **Enable file and folder compression.** This option is only available if you select to use the NTFS file system.

Table 19.1 illustrates the compatibility of the three different file systems available in Windows 2000 with other operating systems. The table considers only the operating systems as they are shipped by their manufacturer, not any third-party add-on products.

Table 19.1 Comparison of the Three File Systems and Various Operating Systems

FAT	FAT32	NTFS
OS/2, MS-DOS, Windows 3.x, Windows 9x, Windows NT, and Windows 2000 can access drives formatted with this file system.	Windows 95 OSR2, Windows 98, and Windows 2000 can access drives formatted with this file system.	Windows 2000 is the only operating system that can fully access all the features available in the version of NTFS that ships with Windows 2000. Windows NT 4.0 with Service Pack 4 or higher may be able to access some files as long as they do not take advantage of any of the new features of NTFS.

Table 19.2 illustrates the file and disk sizes available with the three different file systems available in Windows 2000.

There are several reasons that you will want/need to consider using the NTFS file system. A mandatory use of NTFS is for all Active Directory domain controllers. You also need to use NTFS if you plan to use file encryption, file level permissions, remote storage, recovery logging of disk activities, and disk quotas.

Table 19.2 Comparison of the File and Disk Sizes Available to Windows 2000 for Each Type of File System

FAT	FAT32	NTFS
Supports volumes ranging in size from floppy disks to 4GB	Supports volumes ranging in size from 512MB to 2TB	Cannot be used on floppy disks
Maximum file size is 2GB	Maximum file size is 4GB	Microsoft's recommended minimum volume size is 10MB
Does not support Active Directory domains	Does not support Active Directory domains	Microsoft's recommended maximum file size is 2TB, even though the file system can support bigger volumes
	FAT32 volumes in Windows 2000 are limited to 32GB	The only limitation on file size is the volume size

➢ STEP 8

The Completing the Create Partition Wizard page will display a summary of the actions completed (Figure 19.8). Click **FINISH** to close the Create Partition Wizard.

Figure 19.8 The Create Partition Wizard completion page.

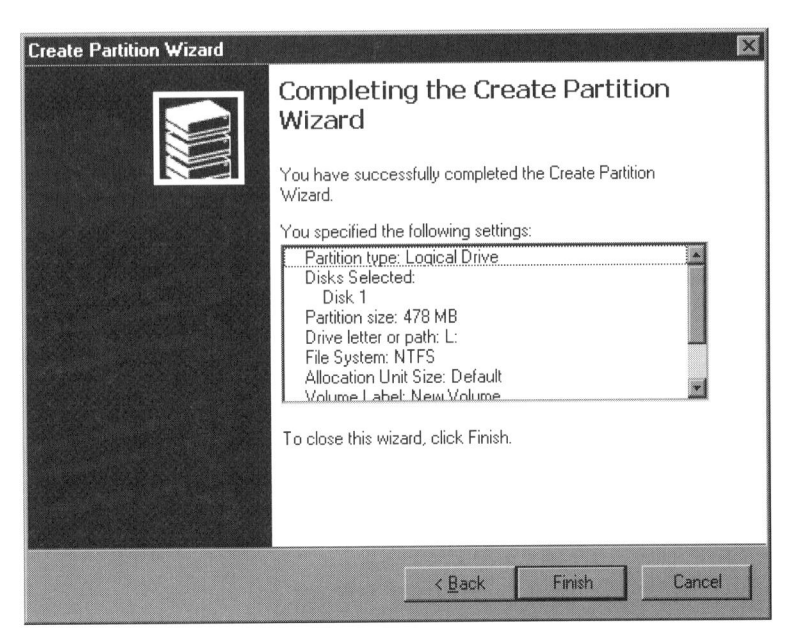

Summary

Microsoft has made the creation of adding partitions from free or unallocated space in Windows 2000 Professional and Windows 2000 Server as easy as starting a wizard, making a few selections, and clicking FINISH. The Create Partition Wizard is started by right-clicking in a free or unallocated space shown in the Disk Management section of Computer Management, and choosing Create Partition or Create Logical Drive (depending on the free/unallocated space you have selected).

The three partition choices available are primary, extended, and logical drive. Choices not available to you for the present operation are grayed out. After selecting the type of partition you want to create, you are prompted to select the size of the partition. The next choice you make is whether you want to assign a drive letter to the new partition and what the drive letter will be, or whether you want to assign the partition to a drive path. Drive paths are only available on NTFS volumes. After making the drive letter/drive path selection, you are prompted on whether you want to format the drive, and if so, what file system you want to use. The file systems supported by Windows 2000 are FAT, FAT32, and NTFS. You can also change the allocation unit size from the default to a range from 512 bytes to 64k bytes, as well as assigning a volume label if so desired. Other choices available on the Format Partition page are performing a quick format and deciding if file and folder compression is enabled. The file and folder compression option is only available if you select NTFS as the file system to use; otherwise, the choice is grayed out.

FAT, FAT32, and NTFS support a variety of operating systems, as well as different file and disk sizes. Your needs may dictate you select one file system over another of the available choices in Windows 2000. For example, if you decide you need to support file encryption on the new partition, you must format the new partition using NTFS, since FAT and FAT32 do not support file encryption.

Chapter 20

System Maintenance Wizards

Introduction

Windows 2000 includes several wizards to assist you in keeping your system running efficiently and effectively. The Scheduled Task Wizard is a scheduling tool designed to make it easy to schedule regular preventive maintenance on your Windows 2000 system, and schedule other tasks you wish to run, whether it is a script, program, or batch file. The Disk Cleanup Wizard is used to safely remove temporary files, resulting in additional resources available for use. Scheduled synchronization offers Administrators the ability to schedule the copying of files from one machine to another. This is useful for several reasons: Administrators can create backup copies of critical data on a regular basis, they can synchronize the data on several Web or FTP servers sharing the load for a large site, or they can automatically distribute files to end-user machines. Synchronizing files is also handy for the mobile users in the organization. By the end of this chapter, you will know how to schedule tasks on your system, remove temporary files from your hard drive, and schedule file and folder synchronization.

Before You Begin

The Scheduled Task Wizard and Disk Cleanup Wizard are straightforward in their use; however, scheduled synchronization of files and folders is not available unless Offline Files is enabled on your system. Offline Files is enabled automatically for Windows 2000 Professional, but is disabled for Windows 2000 Server. To enable Offline Files for Windows 2000 Server, double-click **My Computer** on the desktop, select **Folder Options** from the **Tools** menu, and ensure that **Enable Offline Files** is selected on the **Offline Files** tab.

Another requirement necessary for the Scheduled Synchronization Wizard is that the network share has to be available offline. To accomplish this, you highlight the network share from My Computer, My Network Places, or Windows Explorer, right-click the share, and select **Make Available Offline** from the context menu.

The Purposes of these Wizards

The Scheduled Task Wizard is available for both Windows 2000 Professional and Windows 2000 Server. The wizard is used to schedule a task to run daily, weekly, monthly, or at specific times. The task can be a script, program, or batch file.

The Disk Cleanup Wizard is available for both Windows 2000 Professional and Windows 2000 Server. The wizard is used to remove offline files, compress unused files, remove temporary Internet files, remove Windows 2000 temporary files, remove ActiveX and Java downloaded program files, remove unused Windows 2000 components, and remove unused programs.

The Scheduled Synchronization Wizard is available for both Windows 2000 Professional and Windows 2000 Server. The wizard is used to synchronize files and folders to maintain backup copies of critical data, as well as making files and folders available to mobile users when they are disconnected from network shares.

Information Needed to Work with these Wizards

To use the Scheduled Task Wizard, you need the following:

- The name of the script, program, or batch file you want to schedule
- The time, day, and how often you want the task to run
- The account and password the task will run under.

To use the Disk Cleanup Wizard, you need the following:

- The drive you want to clean up.

To use the Scheduled Synchronization Wizard, you need the following:

- Offline Files enabled
- Files and/or folders marked for synchronization.

The Scheduled Task Wizard

➣ STEP 1

Start the Scheduled Task Wizard.

- Click **Start**, and select **Programs/Accessories/System Tools/Scheduled Tasks**.
- Double-click **Add Scheduled Task** (Figure 20.1).

➣ STEP 2

Click **NEXT** at the Scheduled Task Wizard welcome page (Figure 20.2).

➣ STEP 3

Scroll down the list, select the application you want to schedule (Figure 20.3), and click **NEXT**. If you want to schedule a script or batch file, you may click **BROWSE...** to find the item.

Figure 20.1 Scheduled Tasks window.

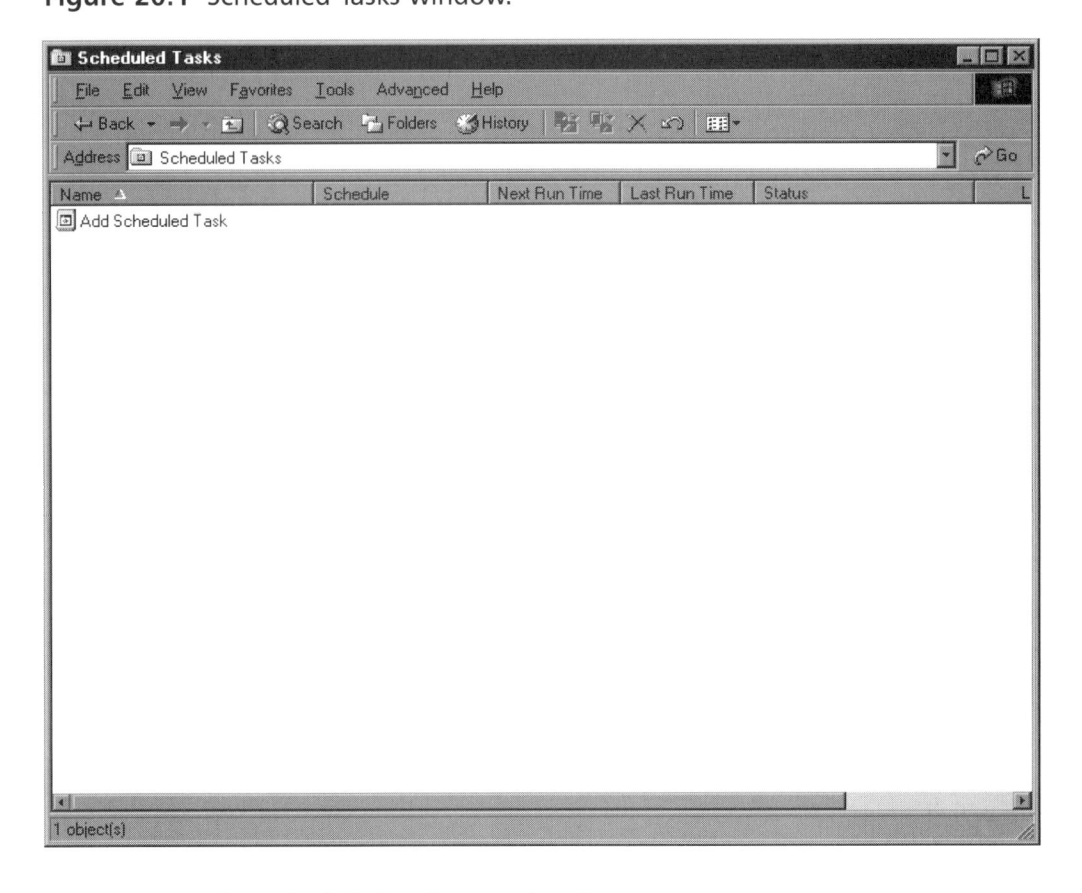

Figure 20.2 The Scheduled Task Wizard welcome page.

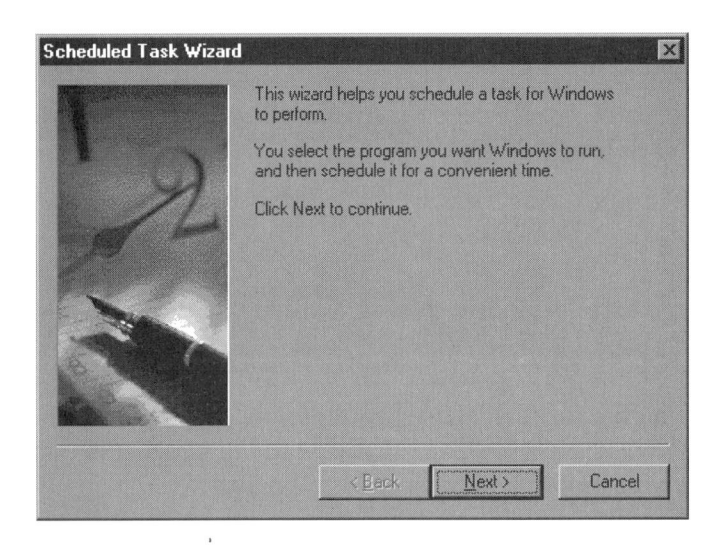

Figure 20.3 Selecting the application to schedule.

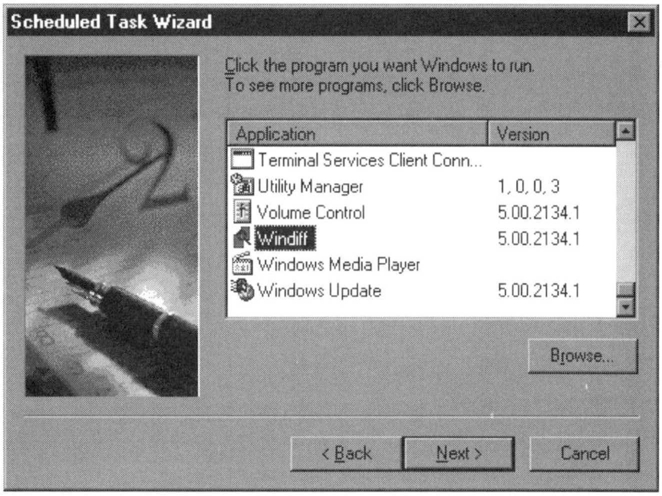

➤ STEP 4

Enter a name for the task in the dialog box, and select the timeframe for the task to be performed (Figure 20.4).

- **Daily**. If you select this option, click **NEXT**, and go to Step 5.
- **Weekly**. If you select this option, click **NEXT**, and go to Step 6.
- **Monthly**. If you select this option, click **NEXT**, and go to Step 7.
- **One time only**. If you select this option, click **NEXT**, and go to Step 8.
- **When my computer starts**. If you select this option, click **NEXT**, and go to Step 9.
- **When I log on**. If you select this option, click **NEXT**, and go to Step 9.

➤ STEP 5

Select the start time, the day(s) to perform the task, and the start date (Figure 20.5). Click **NEXT**, and proceed to Step 9.

➤ STEP 6

Select the start time, the week span, and the day(s) of the week to perform the task (Figure 20.6). Click **NEXT**, and proceed to Step 9.

Figure 20.4 Naming the task and selecting the timeframe it is performed.

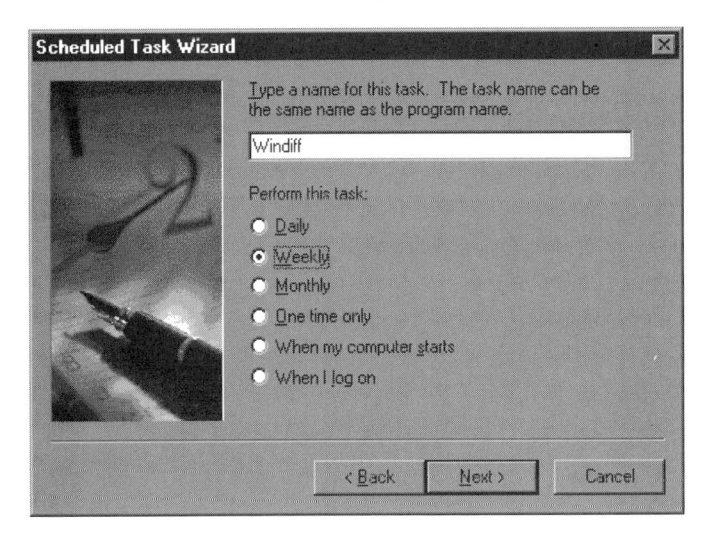

Figure 20.5 Setting the Daily options.

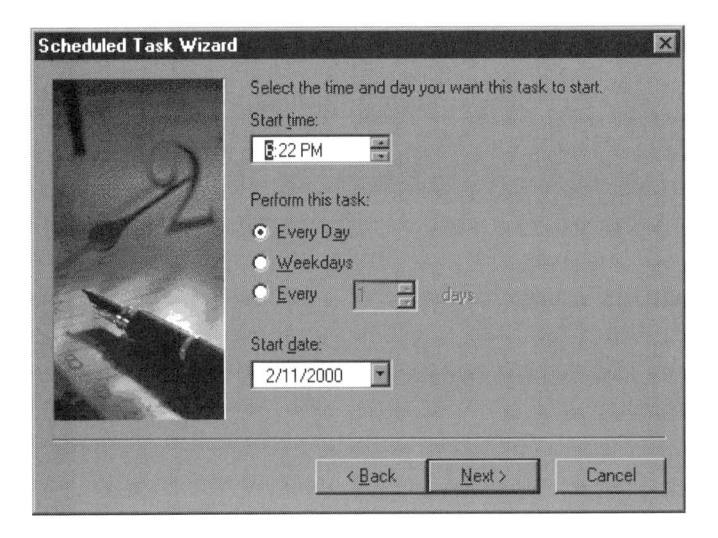

➣ STEP 7

Select the start time, the day to perform the task, and the month(s) (Figure 20.7). Click **NEXT**, and proceed to Step 9.

➣ STEP 8

Select the start time and the start date (Figure 20.8). Click **NEXT**, and proceed to Step 9.

Figure 20.6 Setting the Weekly options.

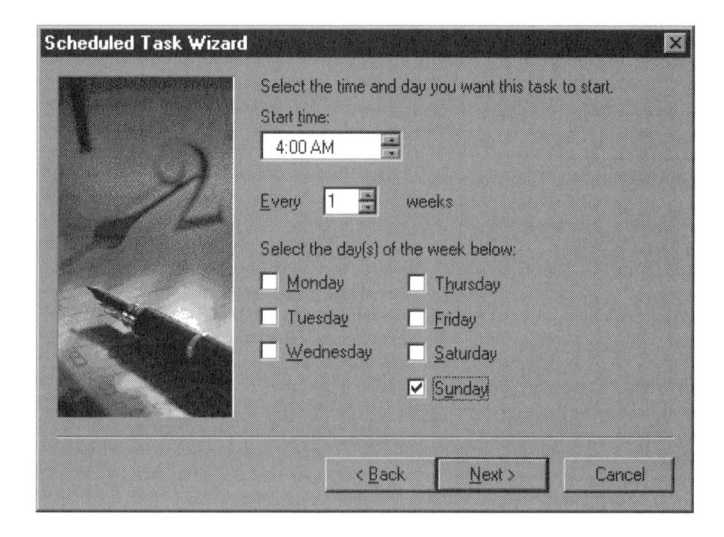

Figure 20.7 Setting the Monthly options.

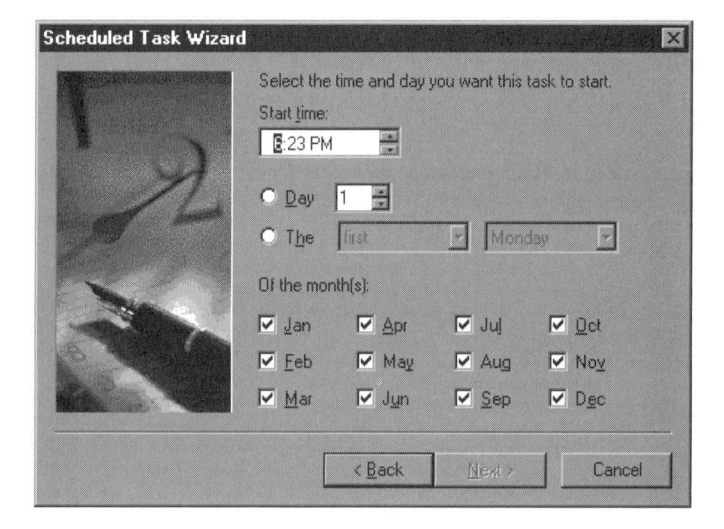

➢ STEP 9

Enter the name and password for the account that the task will run under (Figure 20.9), and click **NEXT**. Be sure the account has sufficient privileges to run the task.

Figure 20.8 Setting the One time only options.

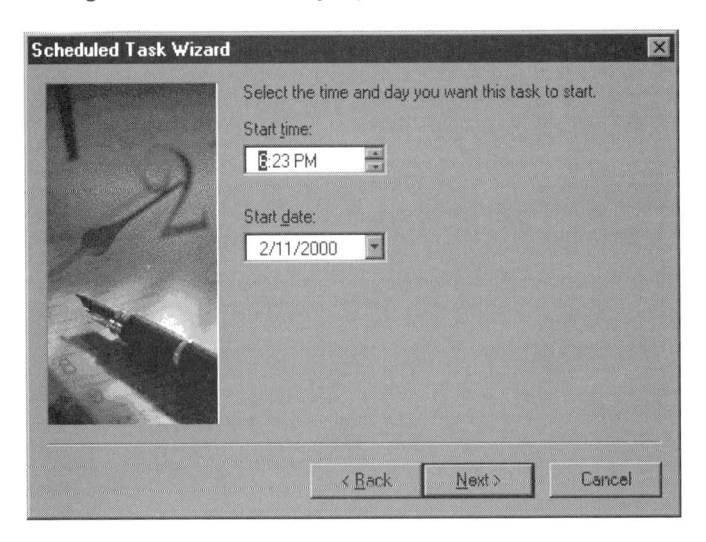

Figure 20.9 Setting the name and password of the user account.

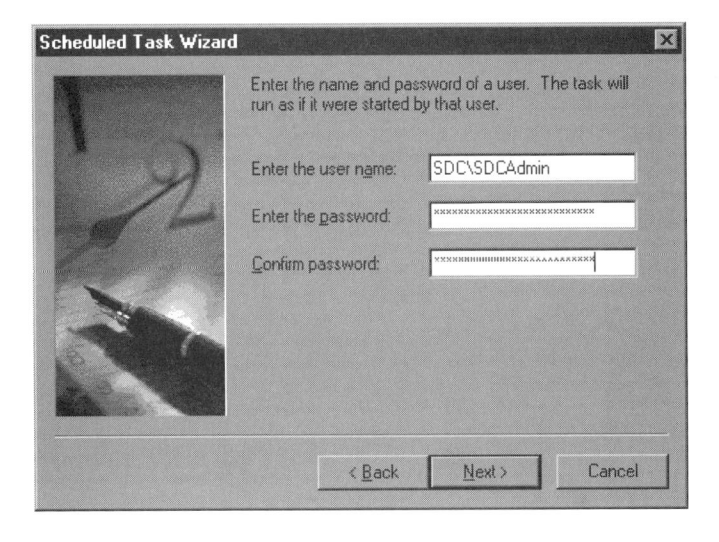

➢ STEP 10

The Completing the Scheduled Task Wizard page displays a summary of the completed task (Figure 20.10). Click **FINISH** to close the Scheduled Task Wizard, and proceed to Step 15.

Figure 20.10 Completing the Scheduled Task Wizard page.

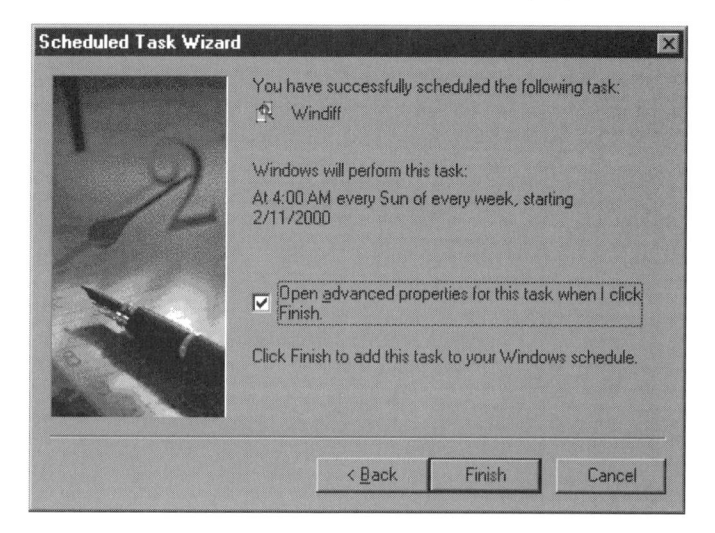

> **NOTE**
>
> If you need to set additional parameters for the task, select the check box located to the left of **Open advanced properties for this task when I click Finish**, and go to Step 11.

➤ STEP 11

The Task tab of advanced properties (Figure 20.11) allows you to modify the following parameters:

- The path of the program to run and the parameters it will use. Notice the extra parameters shown in Figure 20.11.
- The directory the program starts in
- The account the program runs under
- Enabling or disabling of the task.

➤ STEP 12

The Schedule tab of advanced properties (Figure 20.12) allows you to modify the following parameters:

- The timeframe the task is run
- The start time of the task
- Advanced settings, including end date, repeating task options, and duration.

Figure 20.11 The Task tab of advanced properties.

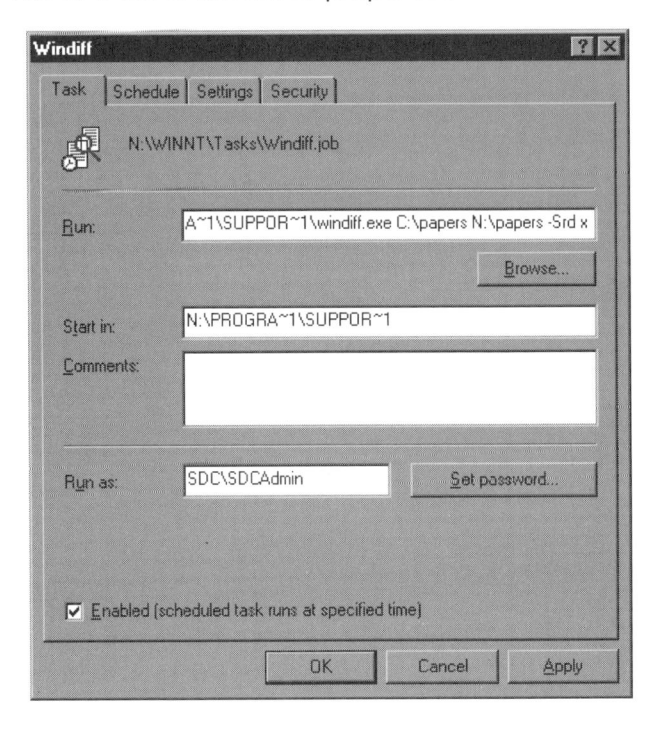

Figure 20.12 The Schedule tab of advanced properties.

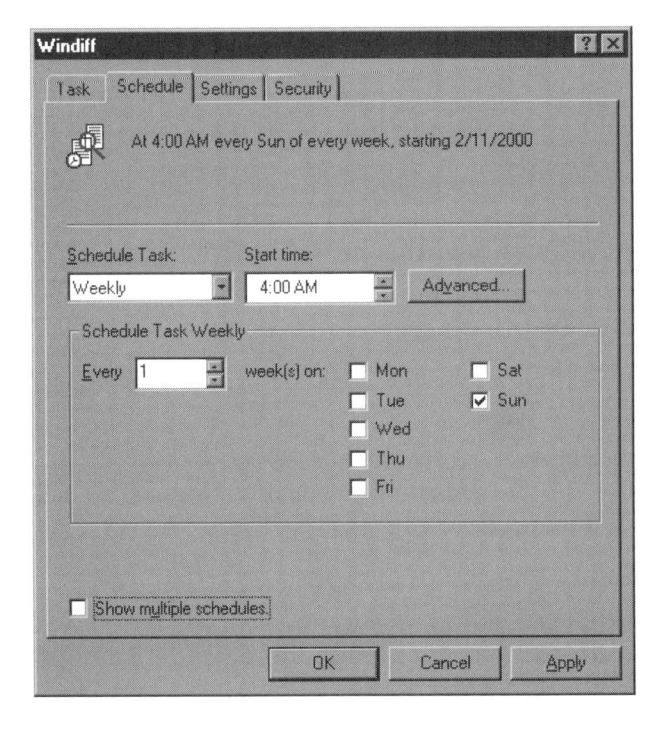

➤ STEP 13

The Settings tab of advanced properties (Figure 20.13) allows you to modify the following parameters:

- Task completion options
- Idle time options
- Power management options.

Figure 20.13 The Settings tab of advanced properties.

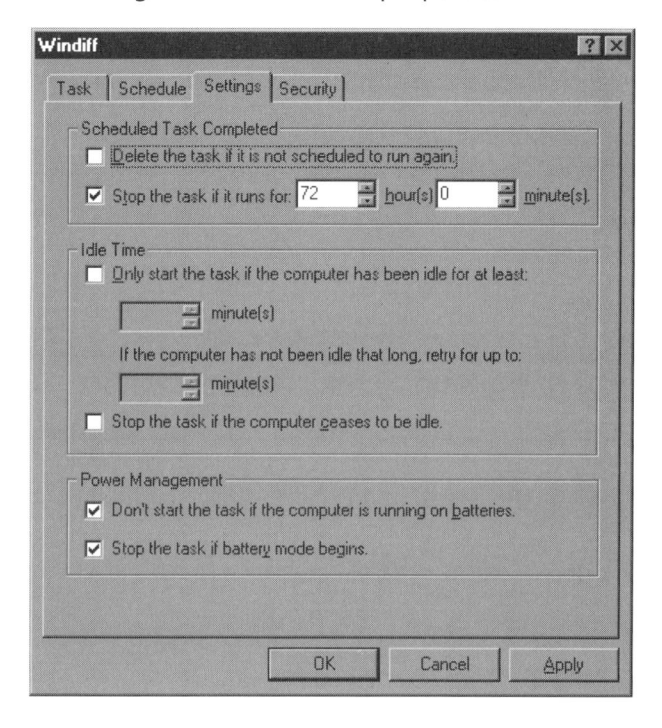

➤ STEP 14

The Security tab of advanced properties (Figure 20.14) allows you to modify the following parameters:

- Adding and removing users and groups
- Setting permissions for users and groups
- Advanced access control settings, including granular permissions, auditing, and owner options.

➤ STEP 15

Verify that the scheduled task appears in the Scheduled Tasks window (Figure 20.15).

Figure 20.14 The Security tab of advanced properties.

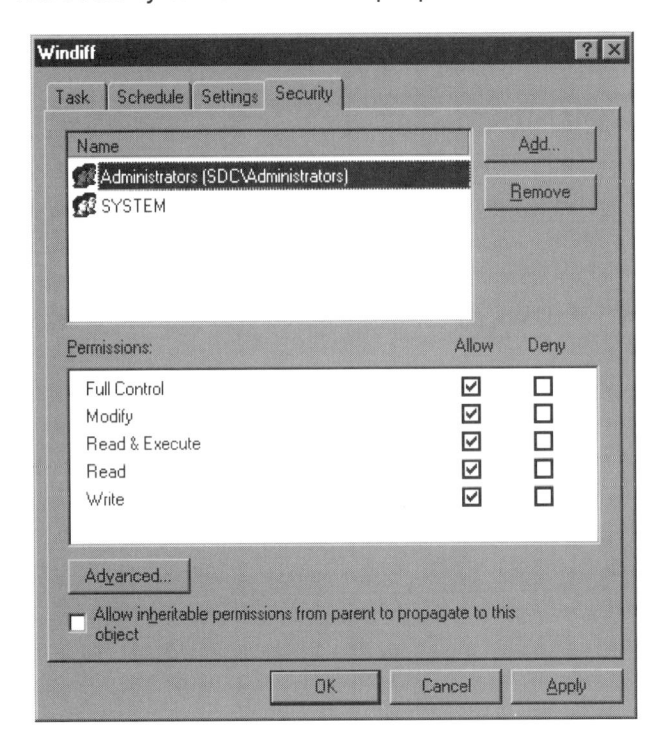

Figure 20.15 Verifying the scheduled task is added correctly.

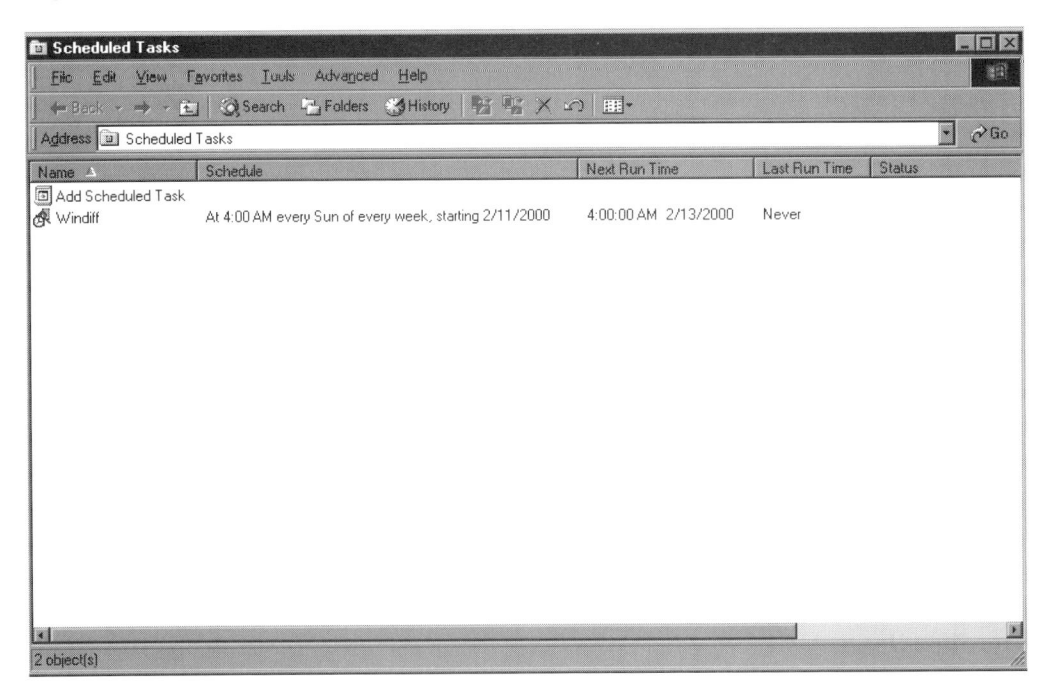

The Disk Cleanup Wizard

➤ STEP 1

Start the Disk Cleanup Wizard.

- Click **Start**, select **Programs/Accessories/System Tools/Disk Cleanup**.
- Select the drive you want to clean up (Figure 20.16), and click **OK**. The wizard will calculate the amount of free space you will be able to free up.

Figure 20.16 Selecting a drive to clean up.

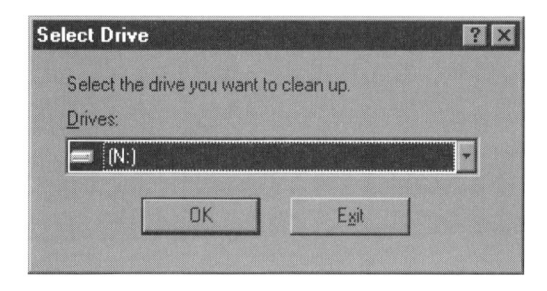

➤ STEP 2

Place a check mark in the boxes to the left of the files you want to delete (Figure 20.17), click the **More Options** tab, and proceed to Step 3. You can select to delete the following:

- **Downloaded Program Files**. ActiveX and Java applets that have been downloaded from the Internet.
- **Temporary Internet Files**. Web pages stored on your hard drive.
- **Recycle Bin Files** that have been deleted from your system.
- **Temporary files**. Temporary files left over from applications.
- **Temporary Offline Files**. Local copies of files recently used from the network.
- **Offline Files**. Local copies of files specifically made to be available while offline.
- **Compress old files**. Windows 2000 can compress files that you do not access frequently. The number of days to set compression after is an option you can set for these types of files.

Figure 20.17 The Disk Cleanup tab of the Disk Cleanup Wizard.

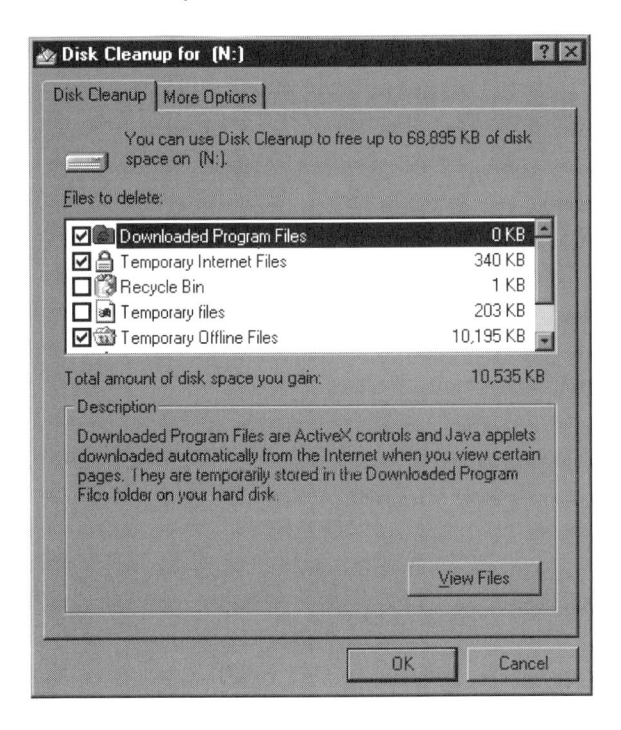

> **NOTE**
>
> Selecting **View Files** gives you the option to see the files that will be downloaded. You may want to use this button to double-check the files before deleting them to ensure you don't accidentally delete a file you want to keep.

➤ STEP 3

The **More Options** tab allows you to free up disk space by removing the following items (Figure 20.18):

- Optional Windows 2000 components
- Installed programs

Select the items you want to clean up, and click **OK**. You are prompted to continue with the file deletion or cancel the Disk Cleanup Wizard.

Figure 20.18 The More Options tab of the Disk Cleanup Wizard.

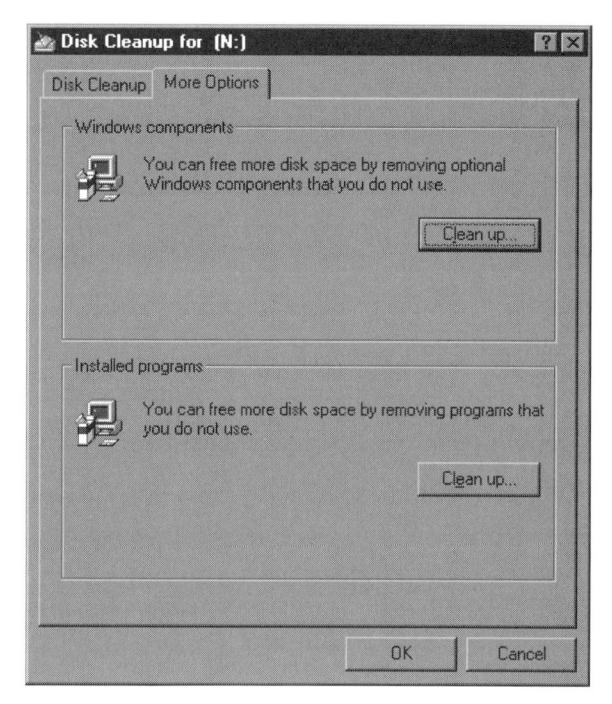

➤ **STEP 4**

The Disk Cleanup Wizard shows the status of its cleaning-up activity (Figure 20.19).

Figure 20.19 The Disk Cleanup Wizard cleaning up the hard drive.

The Scheduled Synchronization Wizard

➤ **STEP 1**

Starting the Scheduled Synchronization Wizard is slightly different from other wizards you used in earlier chapters. The first step is to double-click **My Computer** on your desktop and select **Synchronize...** from the **Tools** menu. The **Items to Synchronize** window is displayed (Figure 20.20). Click **SETUP...** to configure the Synchronization Settings.

> **NOTE**
>
> You may also select Synchronize... from the Tools menu of My Network Places, Windows Explorer, or Internet Explorer. The choice is also available from Start/Programs/Accessories/Synchronize.

Figure 20.20 The Items to Synchronize window showing no offline files to currently synchronize.

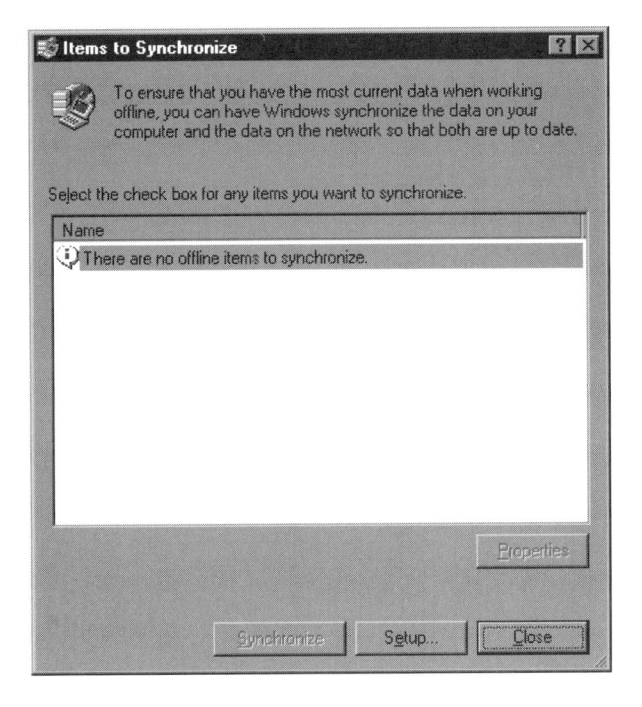

➤ STEP 2

To start the Scheduled Synchronization Wizard, select the **Scheduled** tab and click **ADD...** (Figure 20.21).

➤ STEP 3

Click **NEXT** at the Scheduled Synchronization Wizard welcome page (Figure 20.22).

Figure 20.21 The Scheduled tab of the Synchronization Settings window.

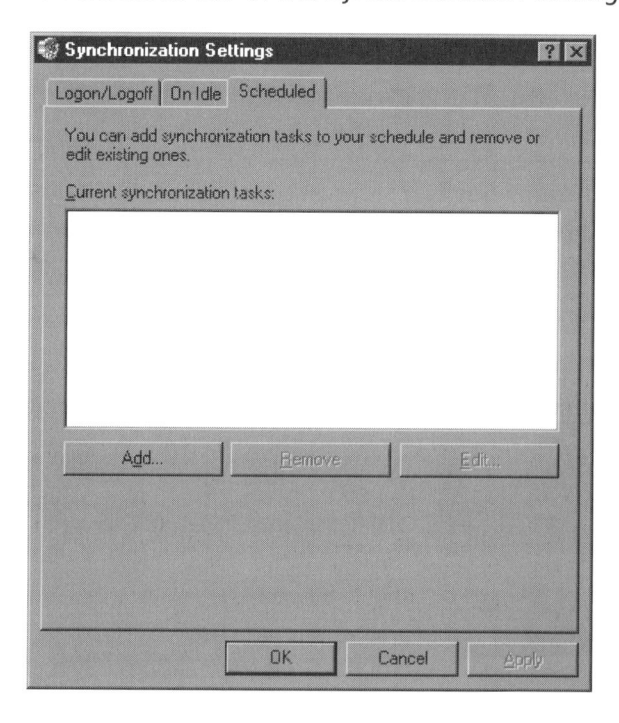

Figure 20.22 The Scheduled Synchronization Wizard welcome page.

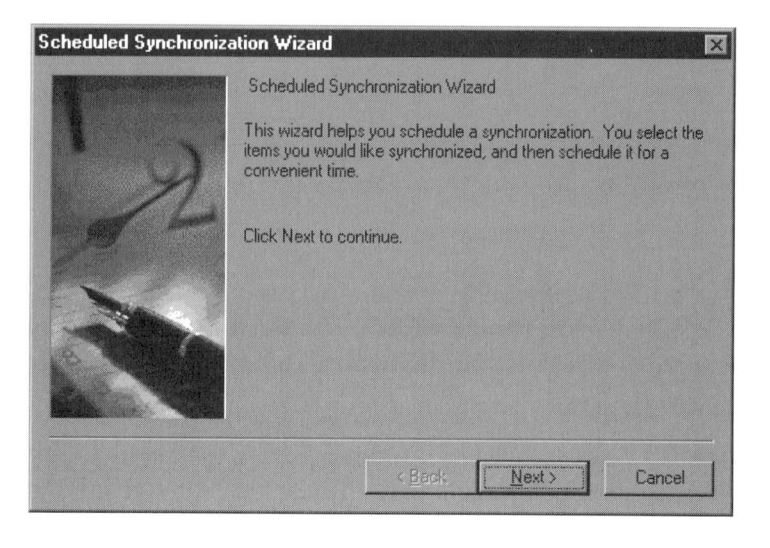

➤ STEP 4

All network shares that have been made available offline are displayed in the Scheduled Synchronization Wizard (Figure 20.23). The network connections available for selection are dependent upon the

338 Chapter 20 • System Maintenance Wizards

connections setup on your system and may include Dial-Up Networking. Select the share that you want to schedule for synchronization, and click **NEXT**.

> **NOTE**
>
> If no offline files are shown on this page, then either Offline Files is not enabled or you have not marked any network share as being available for offline use.

Figure 20.23 Selecting the offline files that are to be synchronized.

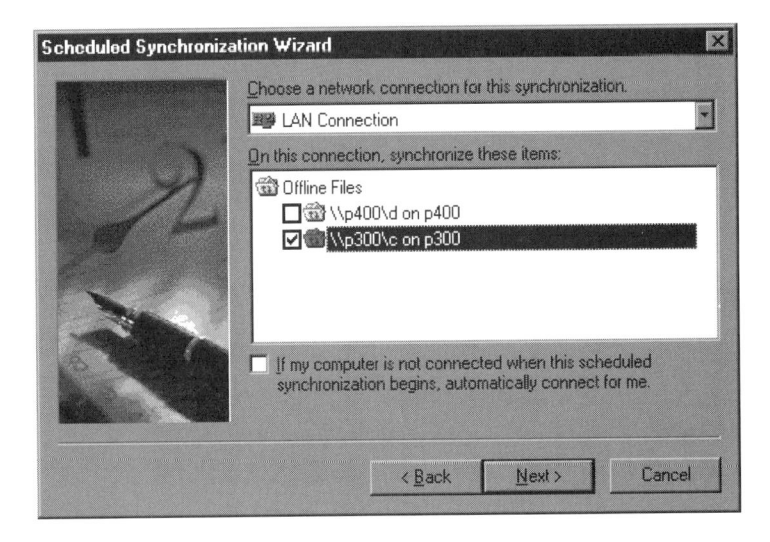

➤ STEP 5

This page allows you to select the start time for the synchronization, how often to perform the task, and the start date for the synchronization task (Figure 20.24). The following options are available:

- Every Day
- Weekdays
- Every ?, where ? can be any number ranging from 1 to 365

Make the appropriate selections, and click **NEXT**.

➤ STEP 6

Enter a name for the scheduled synchronization (Figure 20.25), and click **NEXT**.

Figure 20.24 Selecting the day, time, and reoccurrence for the synchronization task to start.

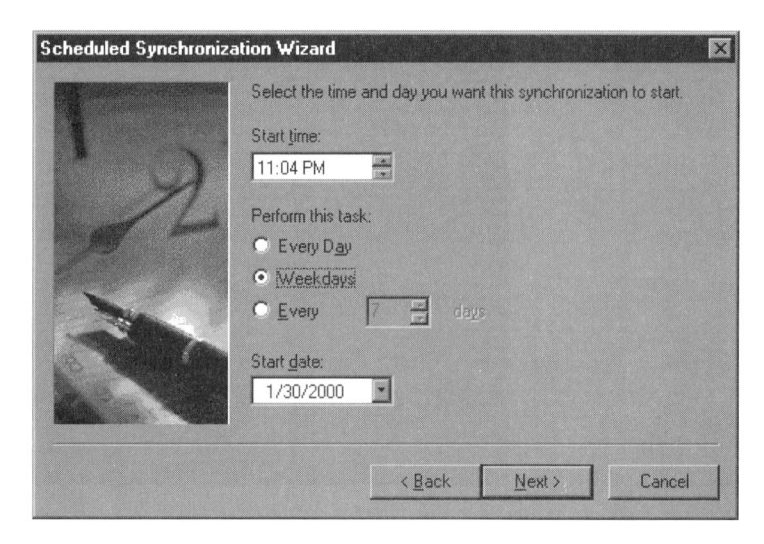

Figure 20.25 Entering a name for the scheduled synchronization.

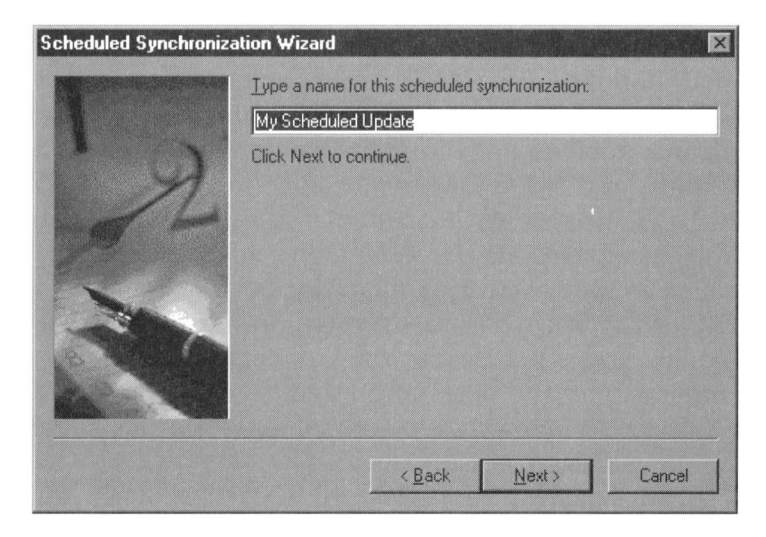

➤ STEP 7

The Completing the Scheduled Synchronization Wizard page displays a summary of the task you have scheduled to synchronize (Figure 20.26). Click **FINISH** to close the Scheduled Synchronization Wizard.

Figure 20.26 Completing the Scheduled Synchronization Wizard.

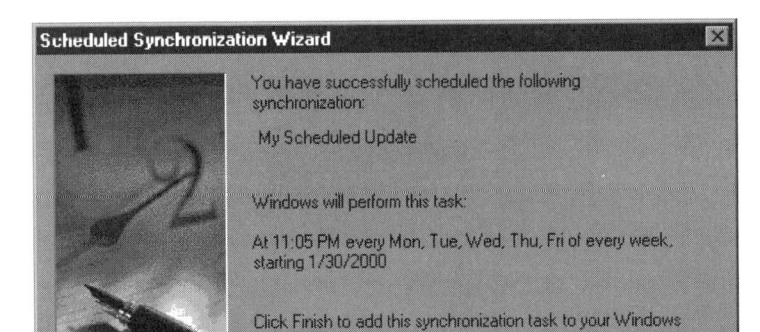

Summary

The Scheduled Task Wizard is used to schedule a task to occur at a specific time. The task can be scheduled daily, weekly, monthly, one time only, when your computer starts up, or when you log on. Depending on when the task is scheduled (weekly, monthly, etc.), you can control the timeframe it runs, such as only on Mondays or the 24th of each month. Scripts, programs, and batch files can be scheduled using the Scheduled Task Wizard. You can pass extra parameters to the task by using the advanced properties pages for the task. Other settings from the advanced properties pages include security and settings.

The Disk Cleanup Wizard is used to free up hard drive space by eliminating offline files, emptying the recycle bin, compressing unused files, removing temporary Internet files, and other items. You can use the More Options tab to select Windows 2000 components or other installed programs you no longer use.

The Scheduled Synchronization Wizard is used to synchronize files and folders to/from a Windows 2000 system. The wizard is available to both Windows 2000 Professional and Windows 2000 Server. In order to take advantage of the wizard, two criteria must be met: Offline Files must be enabled, and the network share must be marked as available offline. Windows 2000 Professional defaults to offline files being enabled, and Windows 2000 Server defaults to offline files being disabled.

The first step in starting the wizard is accomplished by choosing Synchronize... from the Tools menu from My Computer, My Network

Places, Windows Explorer, or Internet Explorer. After completing all the steps to start the wizard, you select the network share(s) you wish to synchronize, select the start time, start date, and how often the task is to run. After assigning a name to the task and clicking FINISH, the synchronization is scheduled and will occur based on the settings chosen.

Chapter 21

Environment Configuration Wizards

Introduction

Everyone likes to customize their work environment, and Windows 2000 offers several wizards to make it a little easier. This chapter includes wizards for creating new shortcuts, configuring folder views, and creating new taskpad views. By the end of this chapter, you will be able to configure your machine exactly the way you like it.

Before You Begin

The three wizards discussed in this chapter can be individually set up by several users using the same machine. Each person can customize the machine without overwriting another person's settings. Windows 2000 saves the settings for each user and activates that user's settings when the user logs on.

The Purposes of these Wizards

The purpose of the first wizard discussed, Create Shortcut Wizard, is to allow users to create shortcuts on the Programs menu. The second wizard discussed, Customize This Folder Wizard, allows users to change various parameters for folders. The third and final wizard discussed in this chapter, New Taskpad View Wizard, is used to change the view parameters for tree items in the Microsoft Management Console (MMC). All three wizards are available in Windows 2000 Professional and Windows 2000 Server.

Information Needed to Work with these Wizards

To use the Create Shortcut Wizard, you need one of the following for the shortcut you want to create:

- Network program
- File
- Folder
- Computer
- Internet address

To use the Customize This Folder Wizard, you need the following:

- Folder you wish to change the appearance of

To use the New Taskpad View Wizard, you need the following:

- Microsoft Management Console
- Tree item

The Create Shortcut Wizard

➤ STEP 1

The first step to starting the Create Shortcut Wizard is to select Start/Settings/Taskbar & Start Menu... (Figure 21.1).

Figure 21.1 Selecting Taskbar & Start Menu... from the Settings menu.

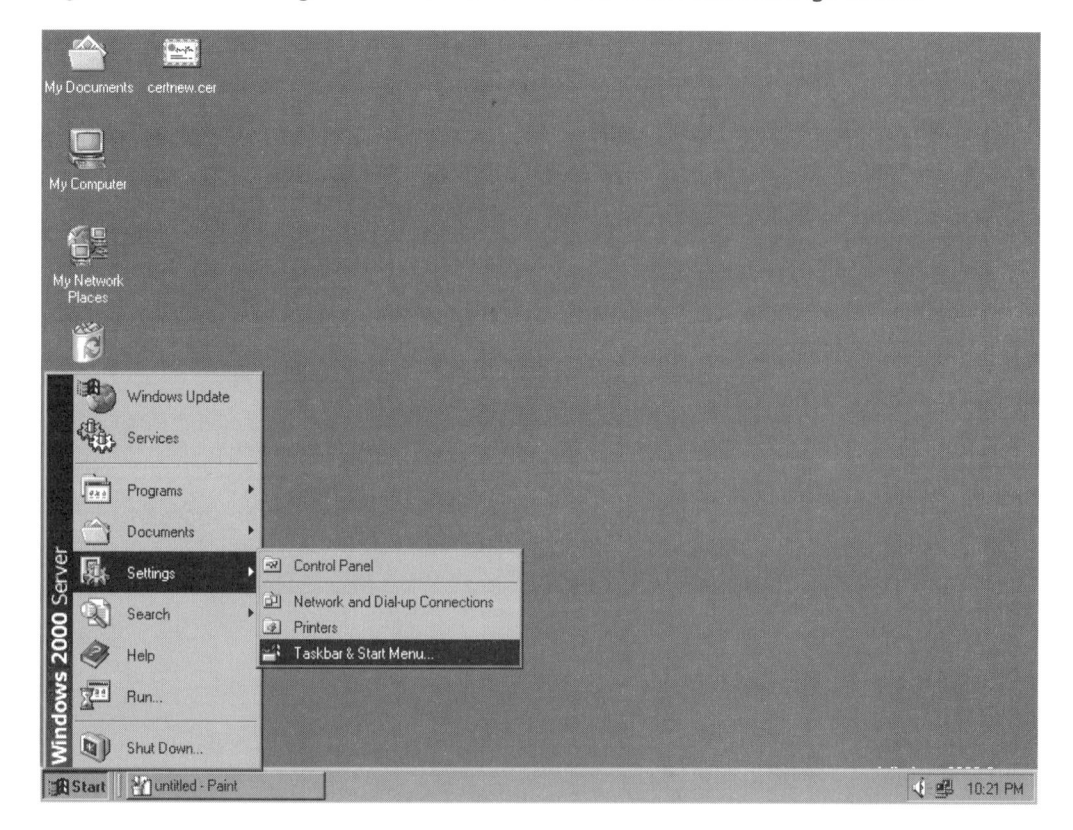

➤ STEP 2

Select the **Advanced** tab, and click **ADD...** (Figure 21.2).

➤ STEP 3

Enter the location of the item you want to create a shortcut for (Figure 21.3). If you do not know the complete path, use **BROWSE...** to find the item, and then click **NEXT**.

Figure 21.2 Starting the Create Shortcut Wizard by clicking ADD... on the Advanced tab of the Taskbar & Start Menu Properties.

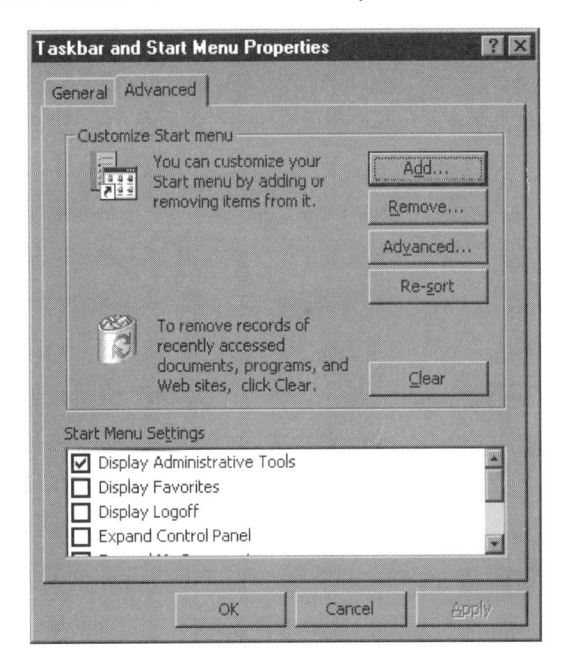

Figure 21.3 Identifying the location of the item you are creating the shortcut for.

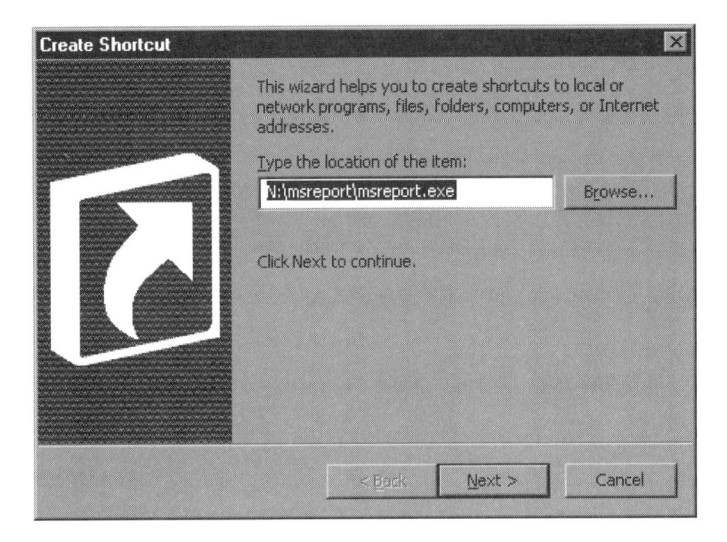

➢ STEP 4

Select the folder you want to place the shortcut in (Figure 21.4). If the folder does not already exist, proceed to Step 5. If the folder does exist, click **NEXT**, and proceed to Step 6.

Figure 21.4 Selecting the folder for the shortcut.

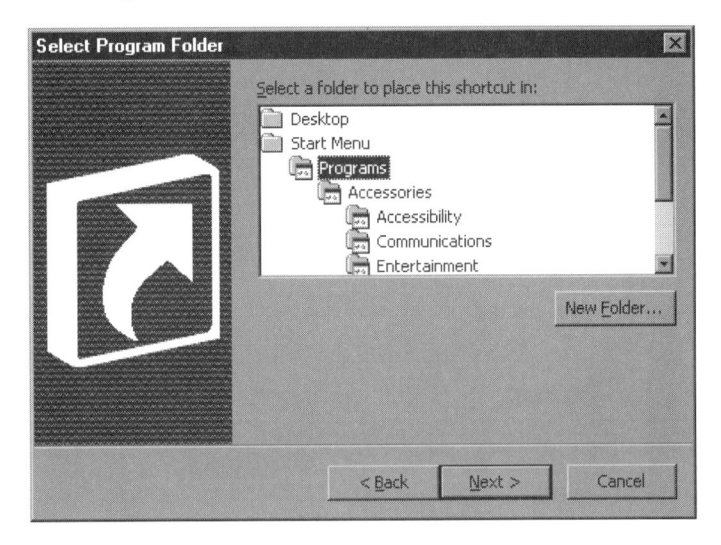

➤ STEP 5

Click **NEW FOLDER...**, and create a new folder for the shortcut (Figure 21.5). Click **NEXT** after selecting the folder.

Figure 21.5 Creating a new folder for the shortcut.

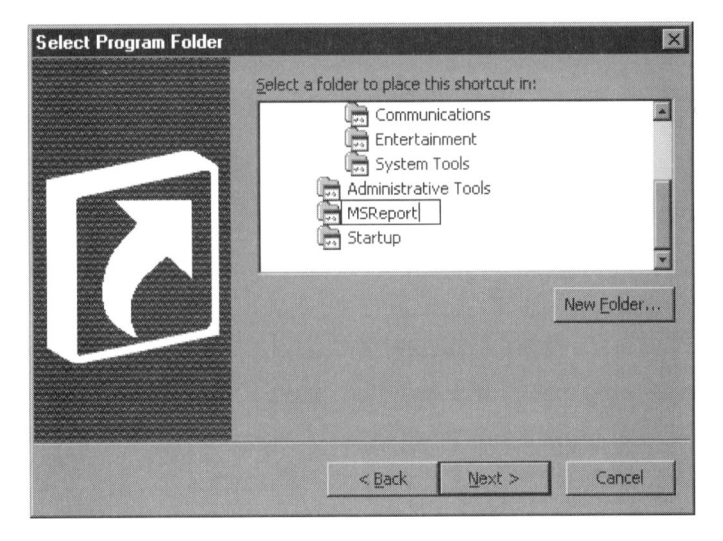

➤ STEP 6

Enter a name for the shortcut in the dialog box (Figure 21.6), and click **FINISH**.

Figure 21.6 Entering a name for the new shortcut.

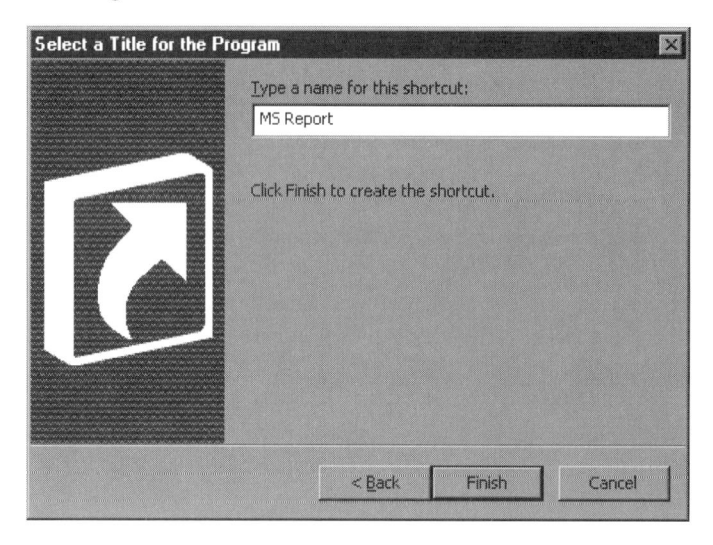

> **STEP 7**
>
> Verify that the shortcut appears on the Programs menu in the folder you intended for it to (Figure 21.7).

NOTE

If you want the shortcut to appear in the root of the Programs menu, place the shortcut in the Programs folder.

The Customize This Folders Wizard

> **STEP 1**
>
> Start the Customize This Folder Wizard.
>
> - Start Windows Explorer from Start/Programs/Accessories.
> - Select the Folder you want to customize.
> - Select **Customize This Folder...** from the View menu (Figure 21.8).

> **STEP 2**
>
> Click **NEXT** at the Customize This Folder Wizard welcome page (Figure 21.9).

Figure 21.7 Verifying the new shortcut that was just created.

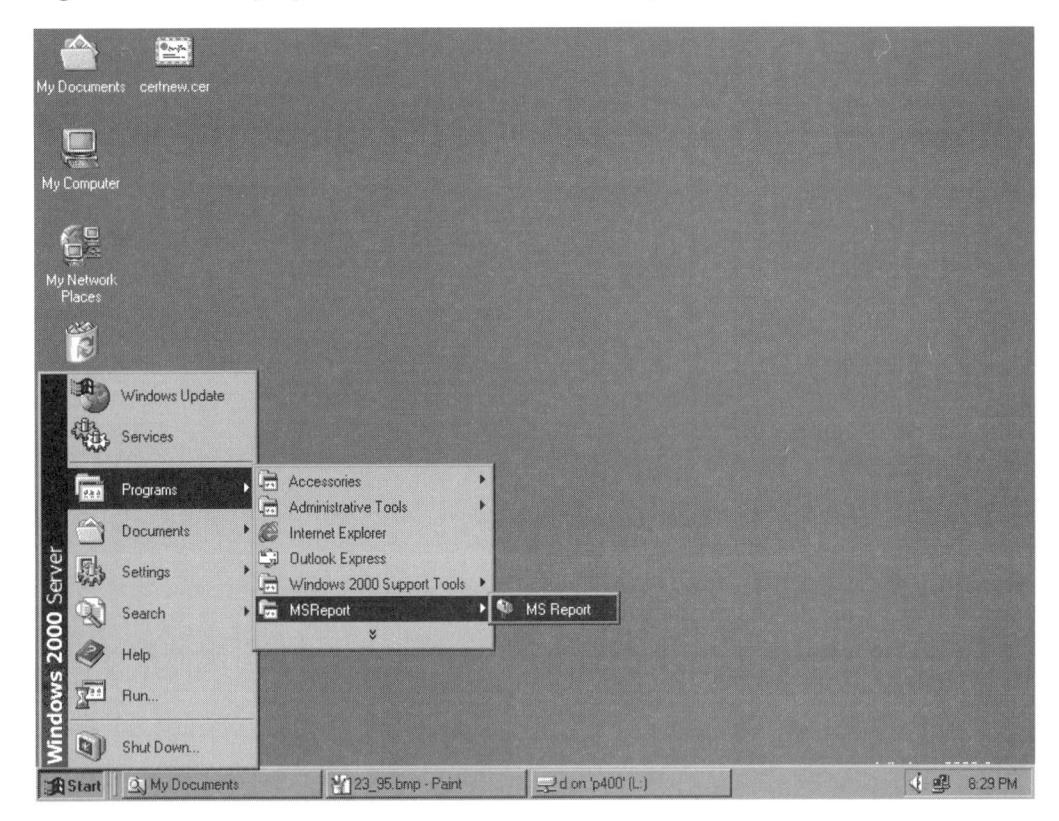

➢ STEP 3

The Customize This Folder offers the following options (Figure 21.10):

- Customize
  - Choose or edit an HTML template for this folder
  - Modify background picture and filename appearance
  - Add folder comment
- Remove customizations

When customizing a folder, you can choose to change any or all of the appearance settings.

Figure 21.8 Starting the Customize This Folder Wizard.

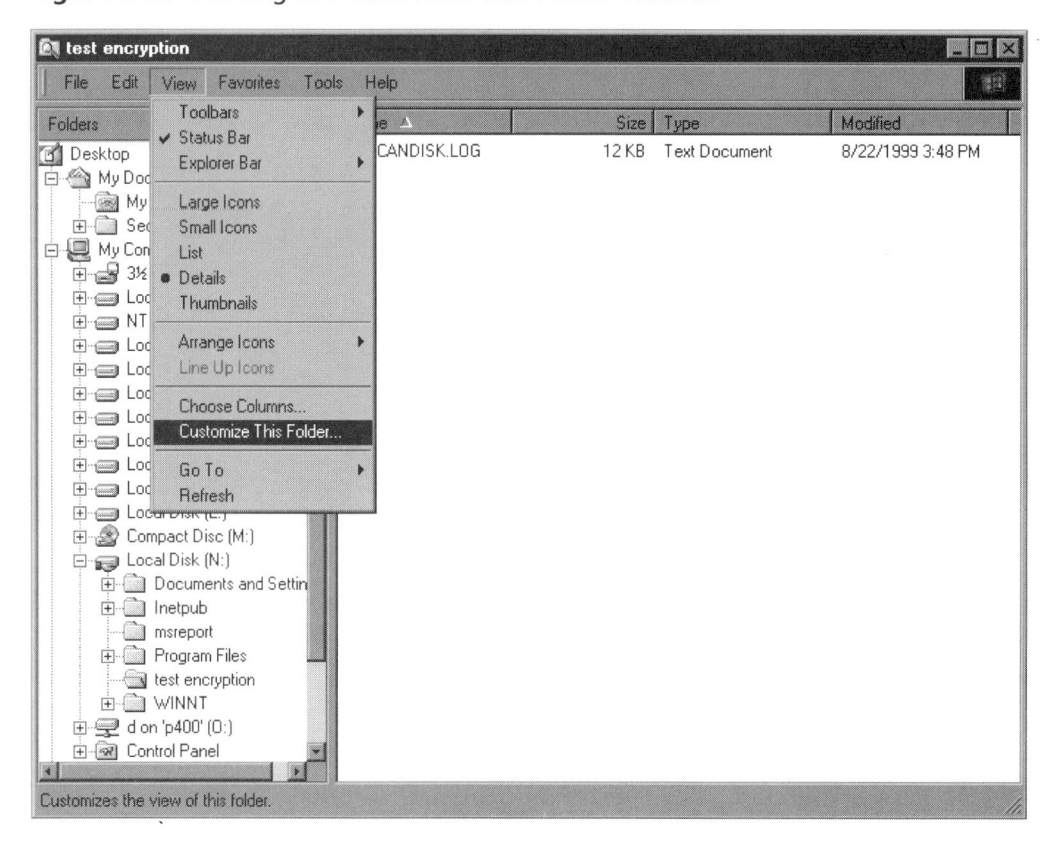

Figure 21.9 The Customize This Folder Wizard welcome page.

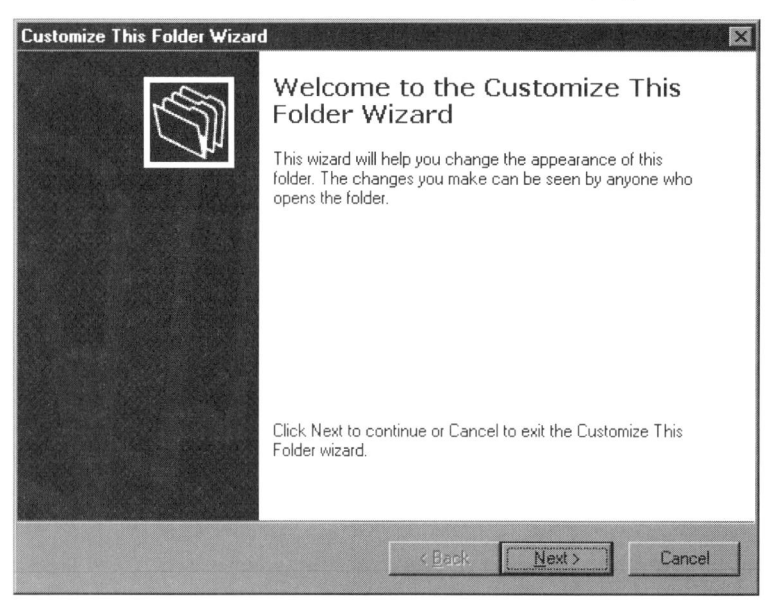

- If you select to choose or edit an HTML template, click **NEXT**, and proceed to Step 4.
- If you select to modify the background picture, click **NEXT**, and proceed to Step 5.
- If you select to add a folder comment, click **NEXT**, and proceed to Step 6.
- If you select to remove customizations (if available), proceed to Step 7.

> **NOTE**
>
> If you decide to choose or edit an HTML template, you need to ensure WebView is enabled for all folders. If it is not enabled, you will receive a dialog box prompting you to enable it before you can continue.

Figure 21.10 Selecting to add or remove folder customization.

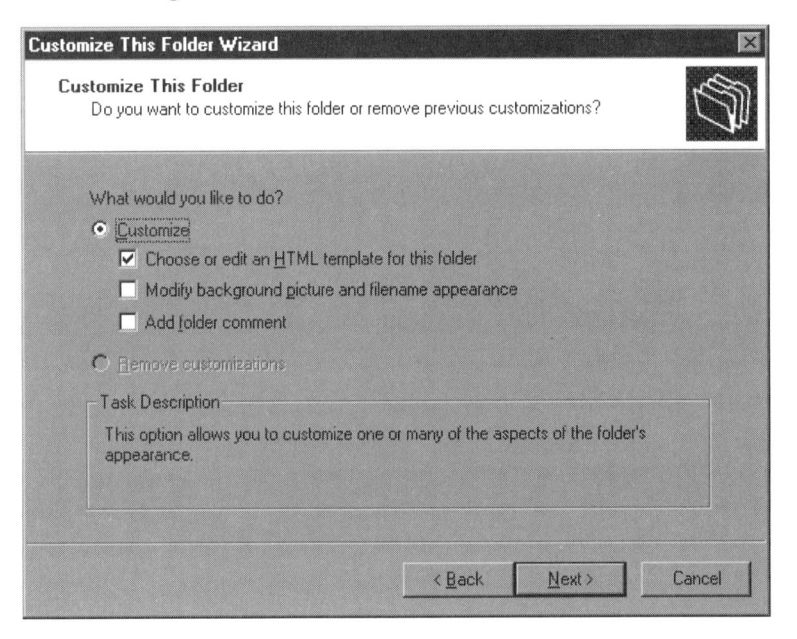

➤ STEP 4

There are four templates available for selection when you select **Choose a template** (Figure 21.11):

- **Standard**. This is the default, full-featured template for the majority of folders in Windows 2000.
- **Classic (icons only)**. This template is empty except for the icons.
- **Simple**. This template respects system colors and uses the folder icons control, but it does not contain any script.
- **Image Preview**. Mainly useful for viewing folders that contain image files. It shows a preview and specific image properties of the selected file.

You may also edit the selected template if you desire. If you choose **I want to edit this template**, Notepad will open the template file for editing when you click **NEXT**. Make your selection, click **NEXT**, and proceed to Step 8.

Figure 21.11 The four options available on the Change Folder Template page.

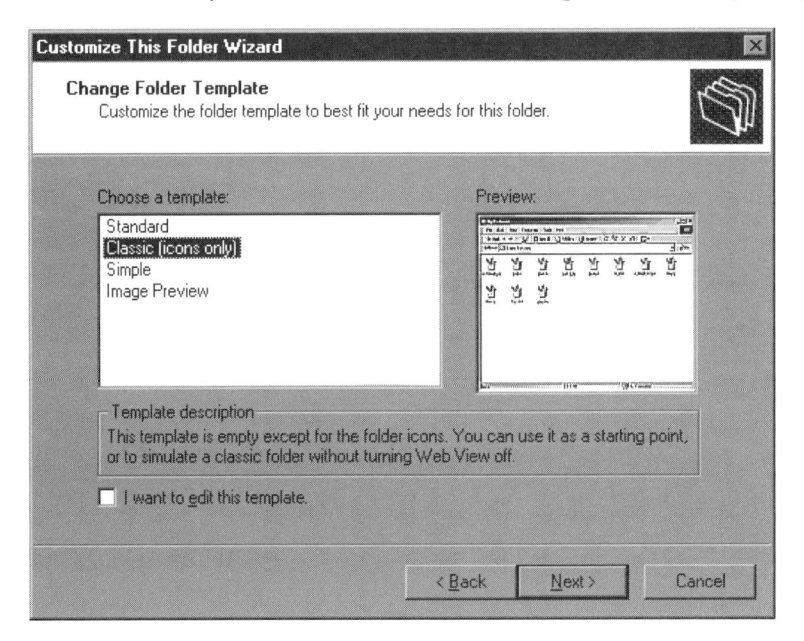

➤ STEP 5

The Modify Background and Filename Appearance page allows you to select a background picture from the list or browse your system. You can also select the color for the text and background of the filenames (Figure 21.12). Make your selections, click **NEXT**, and proceed to Step 8.

Figure 21.12 The Modify Background and Filename Appearance page.

> STEP 6

The Add folder comment page allows you to add a comment to the folder (Figure 21.13). Enter a comment, click **NEXT**, and proceed to Step 8.

Figure 21.13 The Add folder comment page.

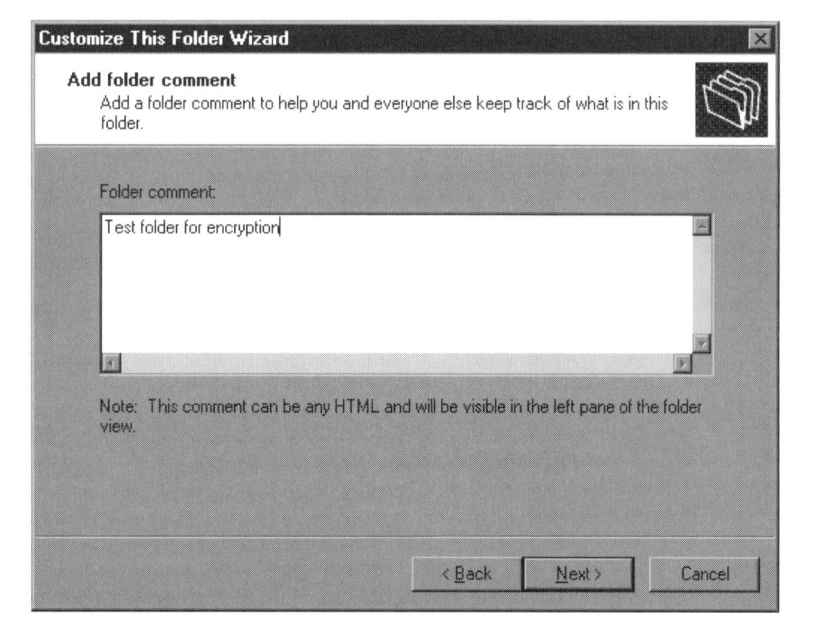

➤ STEP 7

Select the customizations you want to remove, and click **NEXT** (Figure 21.14). Only customizations applied to the folder are selectable; the other options are grayed out.

Figure 21.14 The Remove Customizations page.

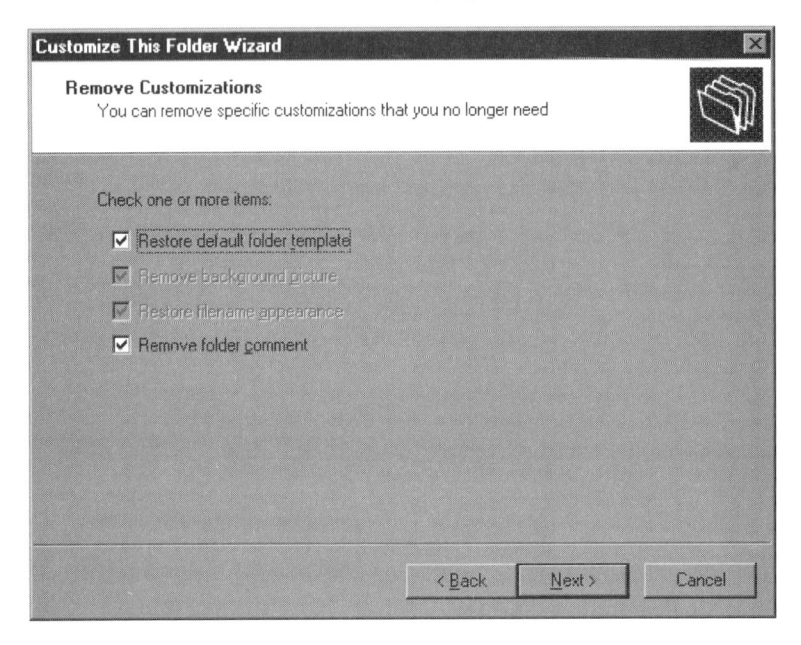

Figure 21.15 Completing the Customize This Folder Wizard page.

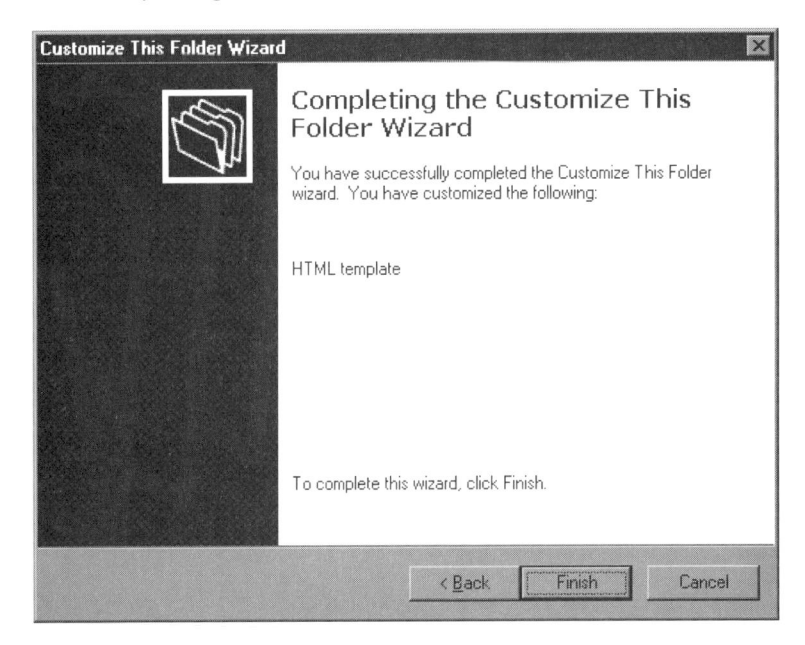

Figure 21.16 Starting the New Taskpad View Wizard for FrontPage Server Extensions.

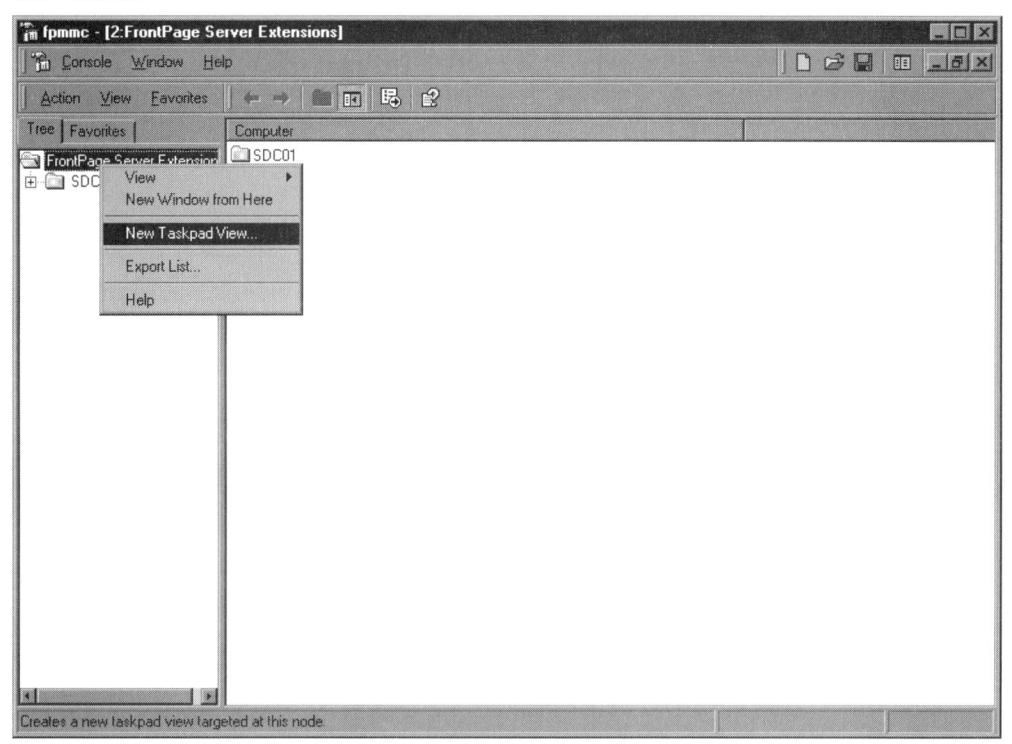

➢ STEP 8

The Completing the Customize This Folder Wizard will display a summary of what was completed (Figure 21.15). Click **Finish** to close the Customize This Folder Wizard.

New Taskpad View Wizard

➢ STEP 1

Start the New Taskpad View Wizard.

- Open Server Extensions Administrator from the Administrative Tools menu.
- Right-click FrontPage Server Extensions, and select **New Taskpad View...** from the context menu (Figure 21.16).

> **NOTE**
>
> New Taskpad Views are available for the majority of tree items in the Microsoft Management Console; FrontPage Server Extensions is just one example.

➢ STEP 2

Click **NEXT** at the New Taskpad View Wizard welcome page (Figure 21.17).

Figure 21.17 The New Taskpad View Wizard welcome page.

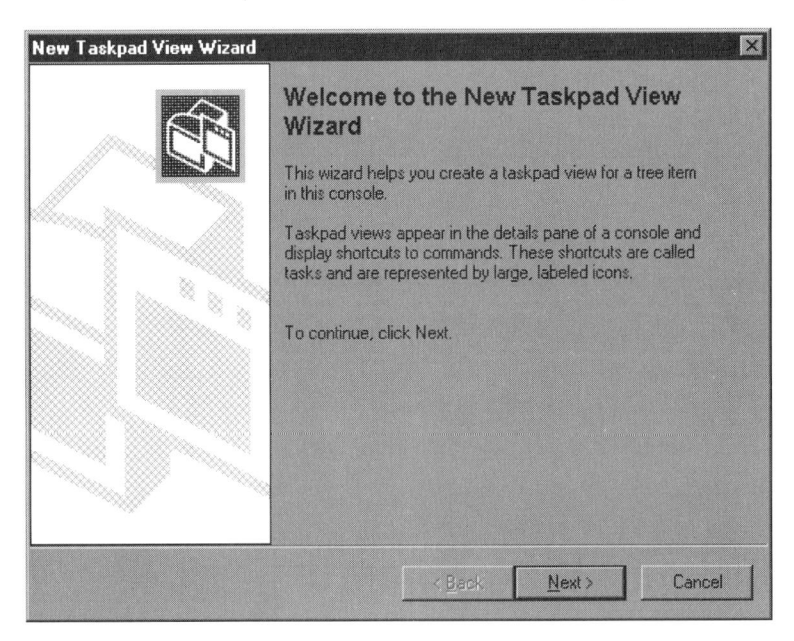

➢ STEP 3

The Taskpad Display page includes the following options (Figure 21.18):

- **Vertical list**. This option is best for long lists.
- **Horizontal list**. This option is best for multiple column lists.
- **No list**. This option is best for tasks that are not connected to list items.
- **Text**

- **InfoTip**
- **List size**. Small, Medium, Large. Option is not available if **No list** is selected.

Make your selections, and click **NEXT**.

Figure 21.18 The Taskpad Display page.

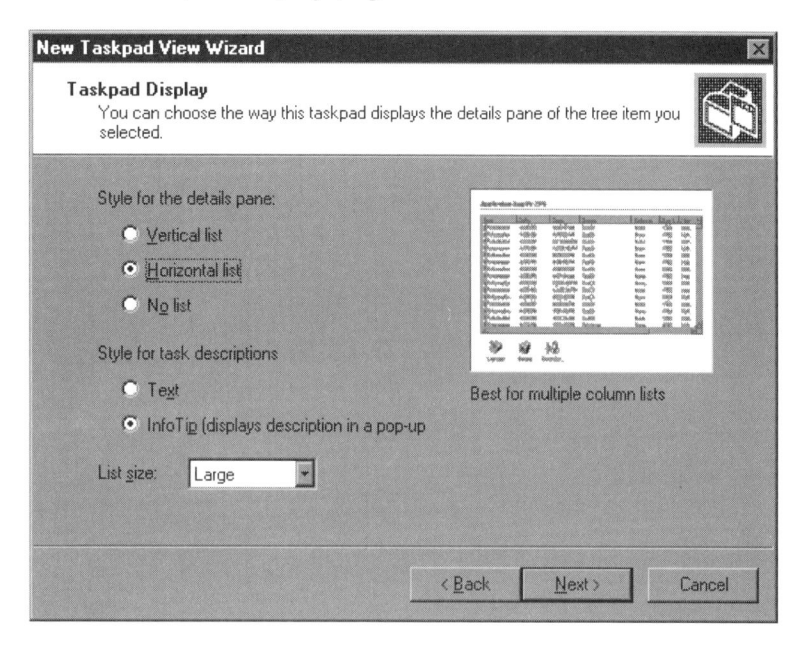

➤ STEP 4

The Taskpad Target page gives you the opportunity to apply the taskpad view to the selected tree item or all tree items of the same type (Figure 21.19). Make a selection, and click **NEXT**.

➤ STEP 5

Enter a name and description for the new taskpad in the corresponding dialog boxes (Figure 21.20), and click **NEXT**.

➤ STEP 6

The Completing the New Taskpad View Wizard page shows the successful completion of the wizard (Figure 21.21). Click **FINISH** to close the New Taskpad View Wizard.

➤ STEP 7

Verify that the new taskpad view meets your needs (Figure 21.22). Notice that you can choose the Normal tab to return to the original taskpad view.

Figure 21.19 The Taskpad Target page.

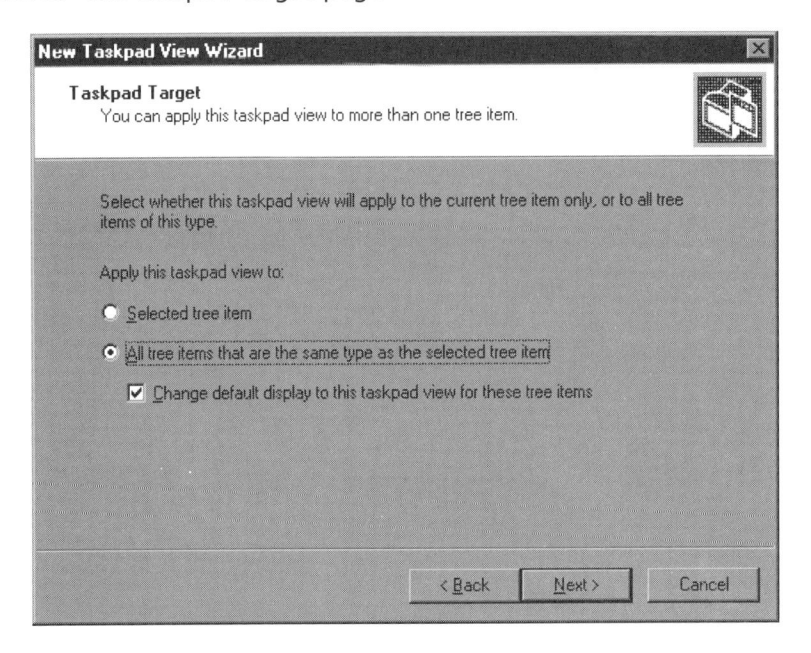

Figure 21.20 The Name and Description page.

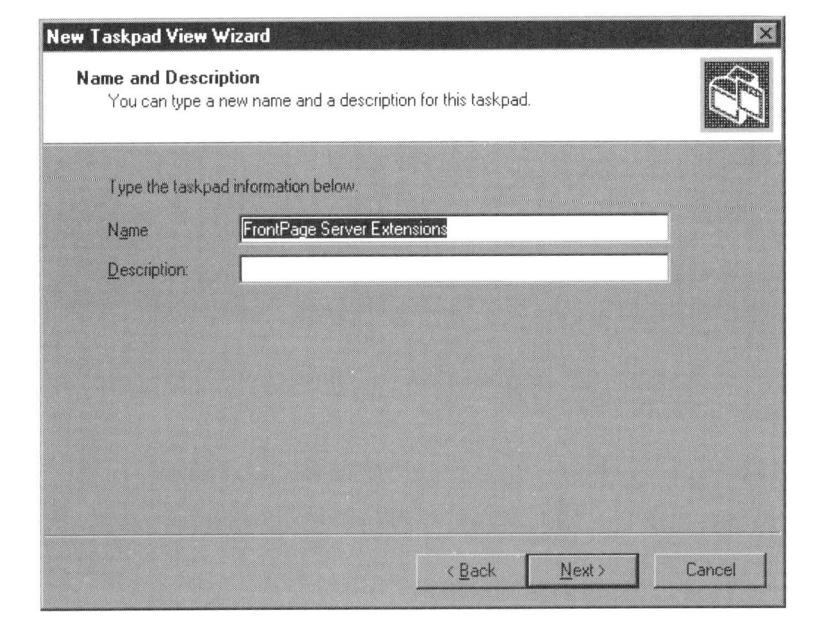

Figure 21.21 Completing the New Taskpad View Wizard page.

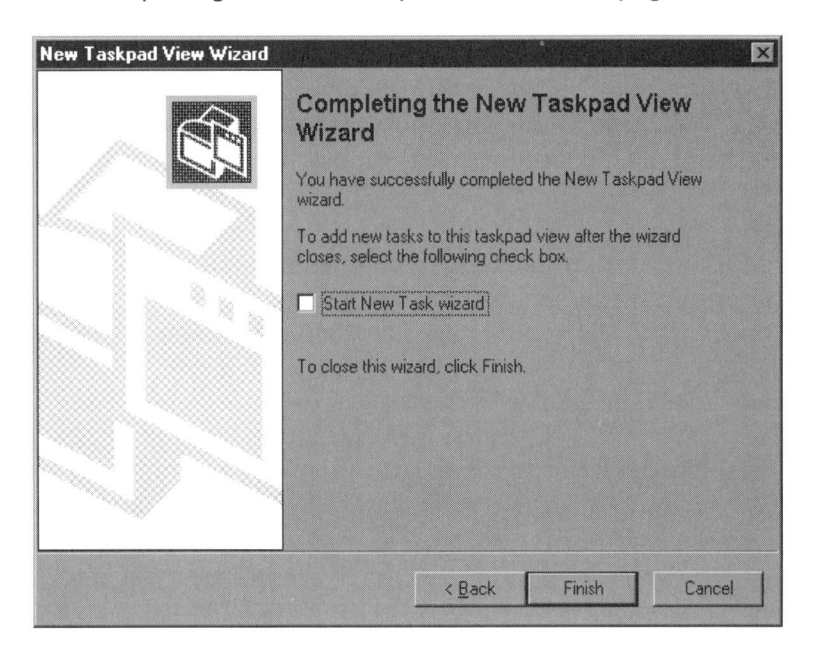

Figure 21.22 Verifying the new taskpad that was created.

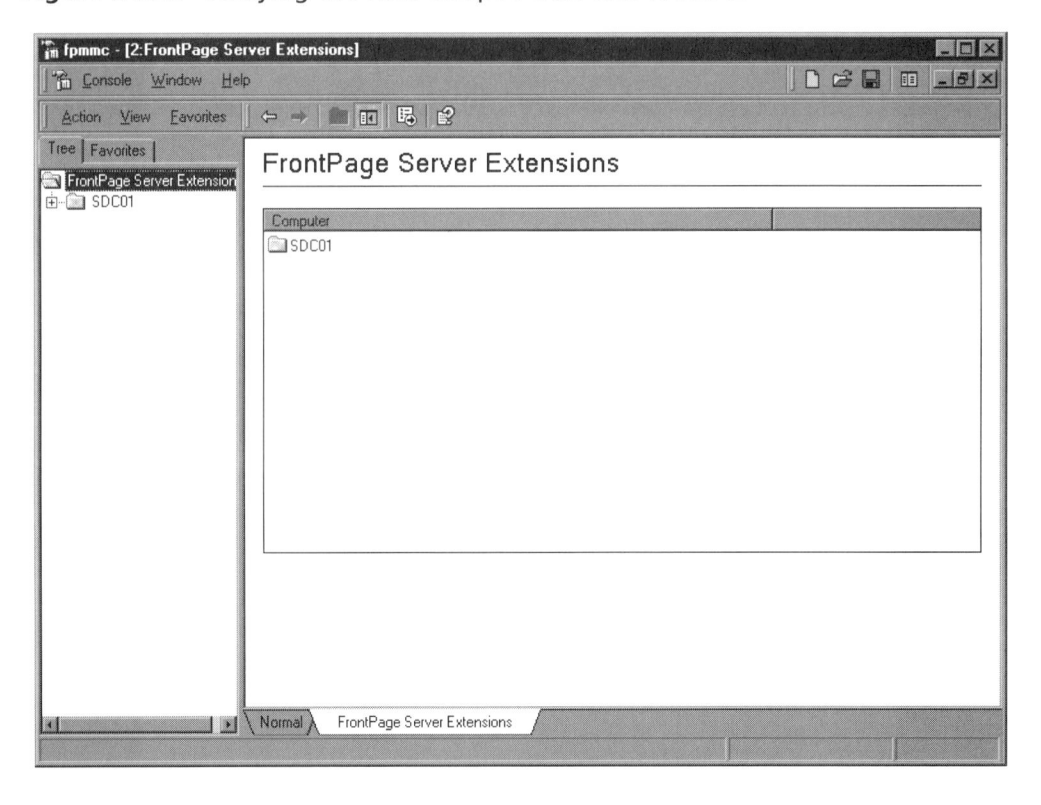

Summary

Windows 2000 offers several wizards to allow users the capability to customize their computing environment. Users of the same computer can customize the system for their likes without affecting the settings of the other system users. The three wizards discussed in this chapter are the Create Shortcut Wizard, the Customize This Folder Wizard, and the New Taskpad View Wizard.

The Create Shortcut Wizard allows users to easily add shortcuts to the Programs menu, either in an existing folder or a newly created folder. Even the Programs folder can be used to hold the shortcut if you want the item to be seen from the root of the Programs menu.

The Customize This Folder Wizard gives you the opportunity to select from several options for a folder. Those options include selecting an HTML template, modifying the background and filename appearance, and adding a folder comment. It is also possible to use the Customize This Folder Wizard to remove customizations that were previously installed on folders.

The New Taskpad View Wizard allows you to create a new view for tree items in the Microsoft Management Console (MMC). This wizard gives you choices on how the data in the right pane is displayed, including vertical list, horizontal list, and even no list. Your choice for the new taskpad view can be applied to the selected tree item or to all tree items of the same type.

Chapter 22

Accessibility Wizard

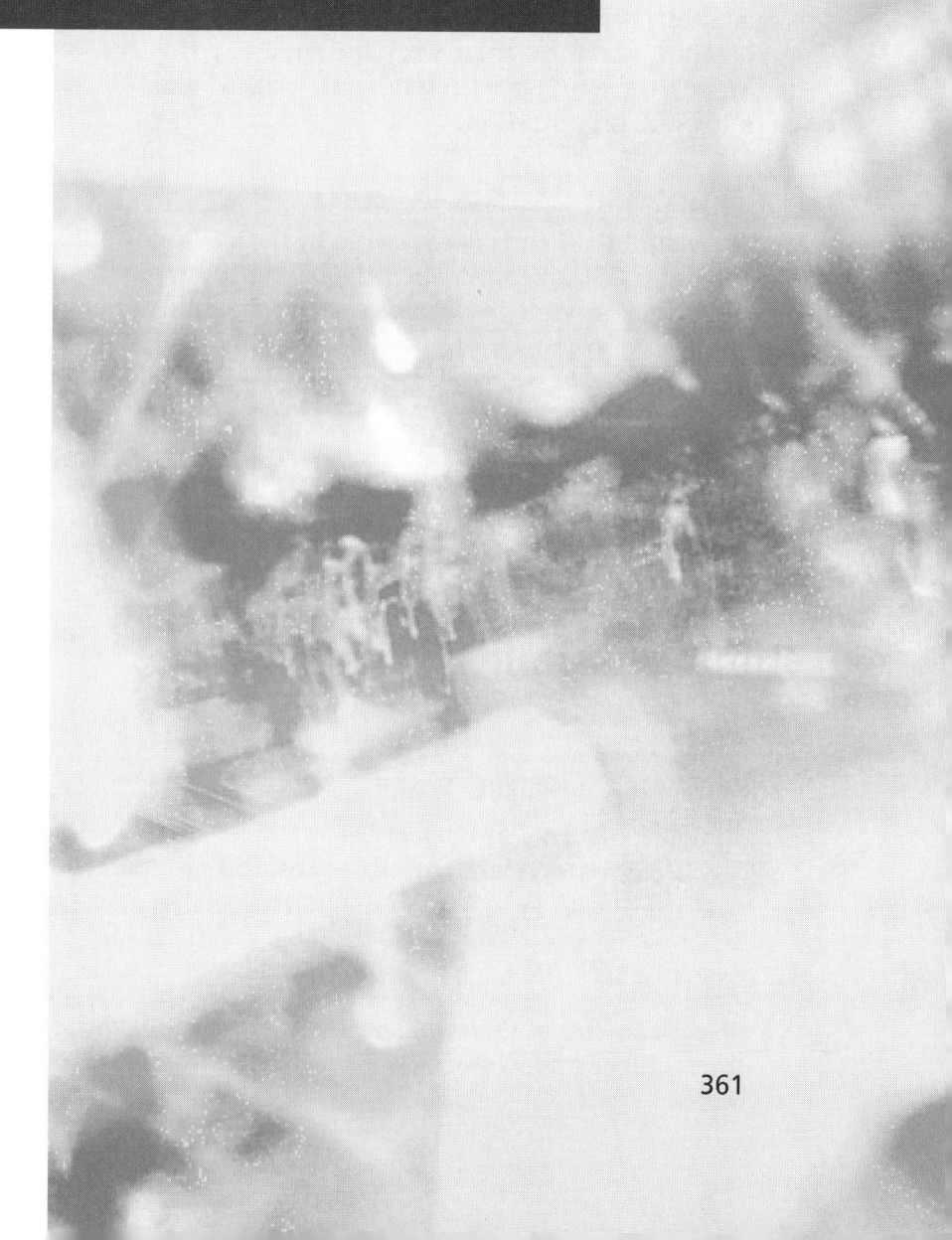

Introduction

Microsoft provides a number of configurable options to make Windows more accessible to those with disabilities or special needs. By the end of this chapter, you will be able to configure Windows 2000 to meet your needs.

Before You Begin

You may not necessarily need to use the Accessibility Wizard for your own workstation, but you may possibly need to help other users in your organization run it on their workstations. For this reason, it is a good idea to be very familiar with what the wizard can offer you and the other users in your organization.

The Purpose of this Wizard

The Accessibility Wizard is available in both Windows 2000 Professional and Windows 2000 Server. The purpose of the wizard is to make computing easier for everyone, regardless of the disability they may have.

Information Needed to Work with this Wizard

To use the Accessibility Wizard you will need to know the following:

- Does the user suffer from vision problems?
- Does the user suffer from hearing problems?
- Does the user suffer from mobility problems?

The Accessibility Wizard

➢ STEP 1

Start the Accessibility Wizard.

- Click **Start**, and select **Programs/Accessories/Accessibility/Accessibility Wizard**.
- Click **Next** on the Accessibility Wizard welcome page (Figure 22.1).

➢ STEP 2

Select the size of the smallest text you can comfortably read from the three choices shown on the Text Size page (Figure 22.2), and click **Next**.

Figure 22.1 The Accessibility Wizard welcome page.

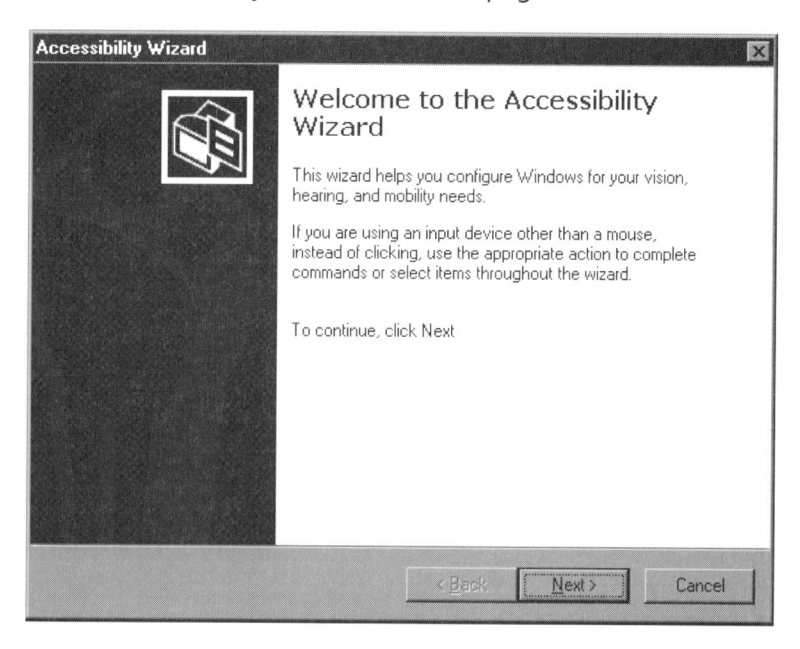

Figure 22.2 Adjusting the Text Size that Windows displays.

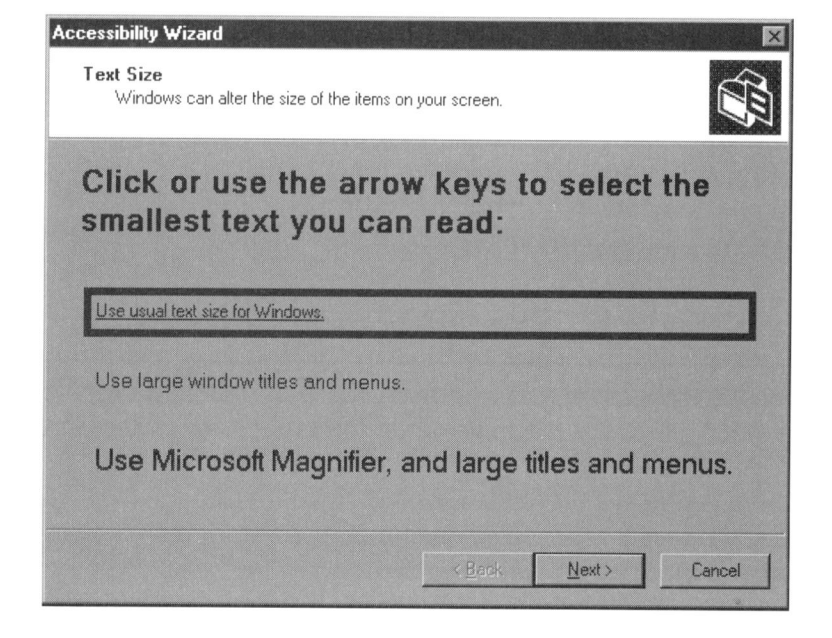

- **Use usual text size for Windows**. No change made in the text size displayed in Windows.
- **Use large window titles and menus**. Increases the size of menus and windows titles.
- **Use Microsoft Magnifier, and large titles and menus**. Starts the Microsoft Magnifier and allows the magnification level to be set, as well as other options dealing with the Microsoft Magnifier as soon as **NEXT** is clicked. The Microsoft Magnifier defaults to displaying the magnified text at the top of your monitor in a separate window. The text displayed wherever the mouse cursor is located is the text magnified.

➤ STEP 3

Select the options you want from the Display Settings page (Figure 22.3), and click **NEXT**. Some options may already be selected based upon the choice made on the previous page of the Accessibility Wizard, while other choices may not be selectable. There are four options available:

- **Change the font size**. Window title bars' and menus' font size is changed, but not the text size within windows.
- **Switch to a lower screen resolution**. Choose this option to increase the size of text inside windows, as well as all items on the screen.
- **Use Microsoft Magnifier**. As previously mentioned, the Microsoft Magnifier magnifies text at the cursor location in a separate window on your monitor.
- **Disable personalized menus**.

> **NOTE**
>
> If the only selection you make on this page is to disable personalized menus, you will receive the following information two screens later:
>
> ```
> No Options Selected
> You did not select any options.
> You did not select any areas to configure. Click Back to return to the
> options page or click Next to continue.
> ```

Even though this message is displayed, personalized menus have been turned off. For more information on this issue, please see Microsoft Knowledgebase article Q244930.

Figure 22.3 The Display Settings page.

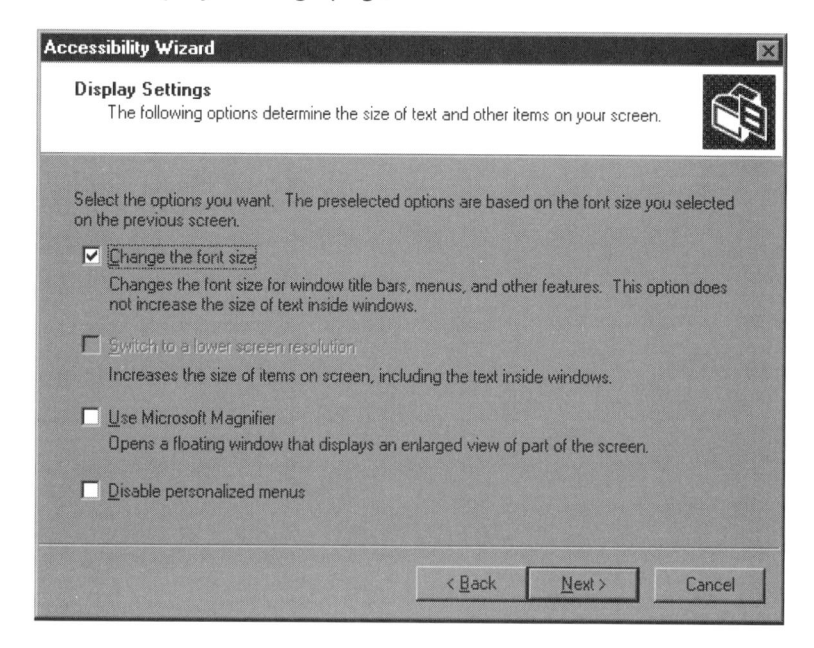

➤ STEP 4

Select the option(s) required for your circumstances on the Set Wizard Options page (Figure 22.4).

- **I am blind or have difficulty seeing things on screen.** If this option is applicable, go to Step 6.
- **I am deaf or have difficulty hearing sounds from the computer.** If this option is applicable, go to Step 11.
- **I have difficulty using the keyboard or mouse.** If this option is applicable, go to Step 14.
- **I want to set administrative option.** If this option is applicable, go to Step 25.

You may also click **RESTORE DEFAULT SETTINGS** to return the system to the default settings.

➤ STEP 5

If you fail to make any choices on the Set Wizard Options page, you will be prompted to click **BACK** (Figure 22.5).

➤ STEP 6

Select the **I am blind or have difficulty seeing things on screen** option (Figure 22.6), and click **NEXT**.

Figure 22.4 The Set Wizards Options page.

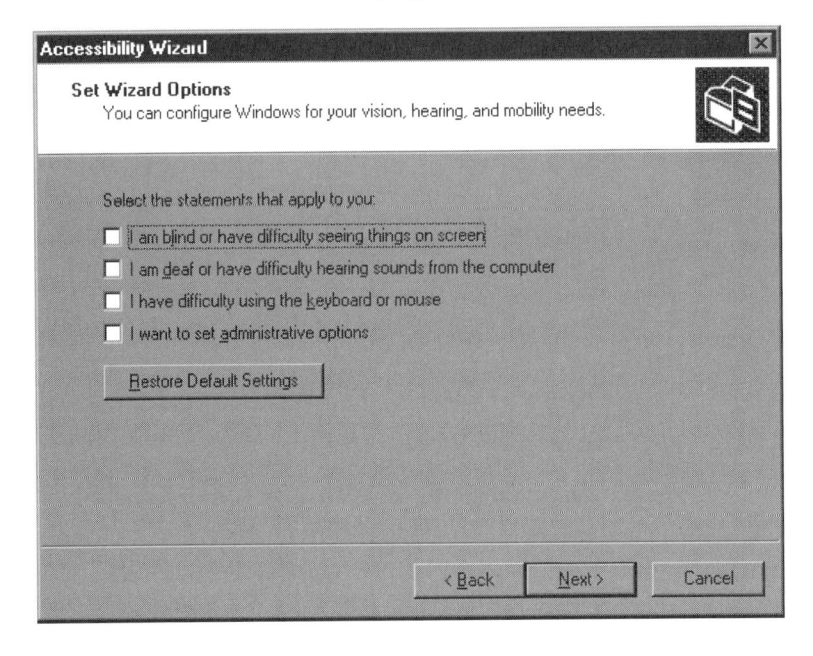

Figure 22.5 The No Options Selected page.

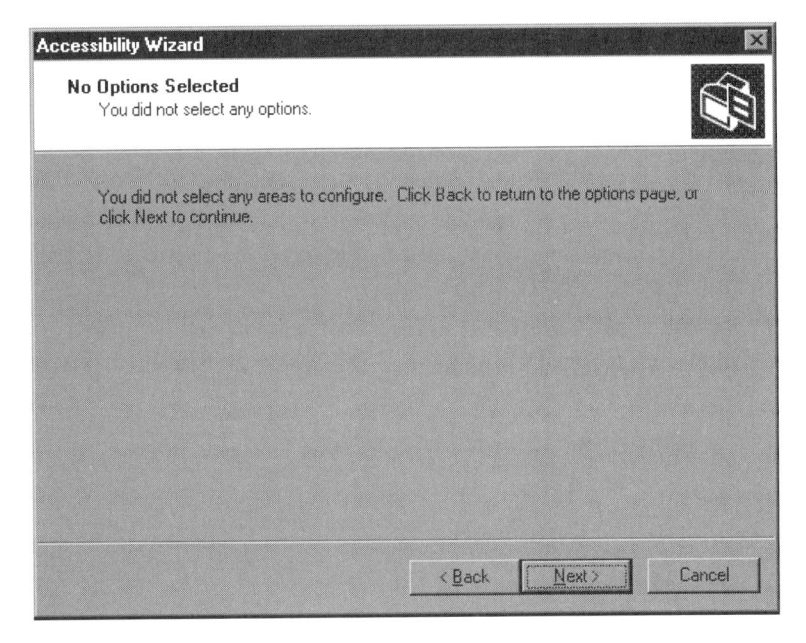

➢ STEP 7

Select the Scroll Bar and Window Border Size that best suits your needs (Figure 22.7), and click **NEXT**.

Figure 22.6 Selecting the I am blind or have difficulty seeing things on screen option.

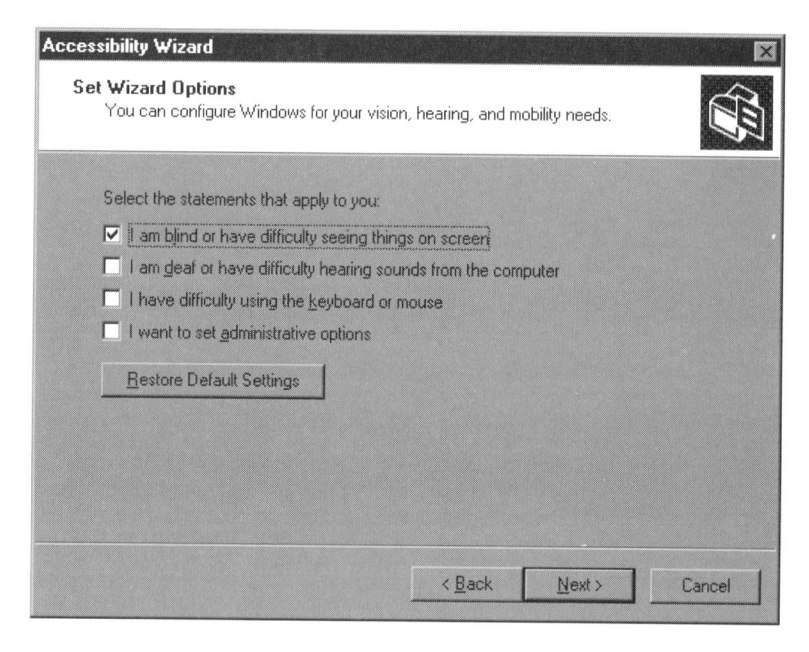

Figure 22.7 The Scroll Bar and Window Border Size page.

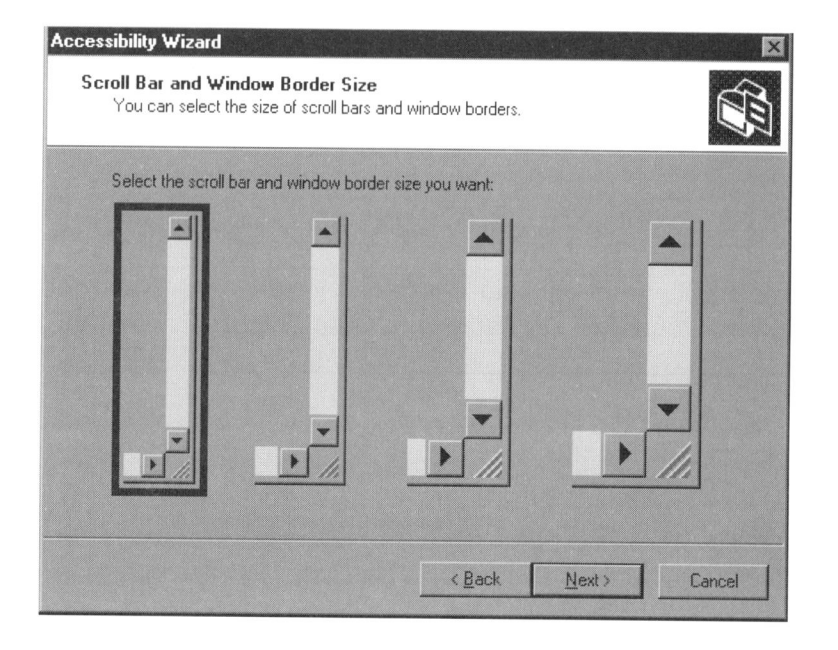

➤ STEP 8

Select the Icon Size that best suits your needs (Figure 22.8), and click **NEXT**. There are three icon sizes available:

- Normal
- Large
- Extra Large

Figure 22.8 The Icon Size page.

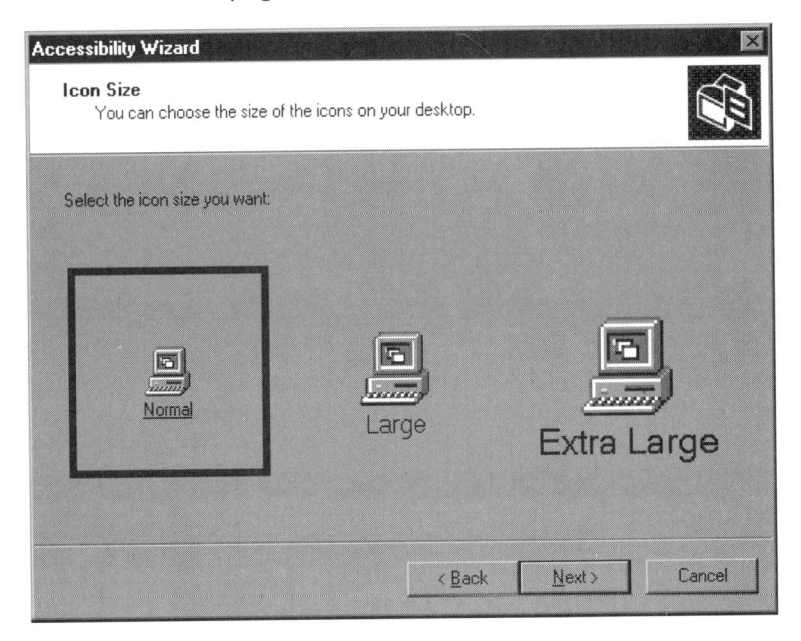

➤ STEP 9

Select the color scheme that best suits your needs (Figure 22.9), and click **NEXT**. There are six choices of color schemes available:

- Current Color Scheme
- High Contrast #1
- High Contrast #2
- High Contrast Black
- High Contrast White
- Default Windows Colors

Figure 22.9 The Display Color Settings page.

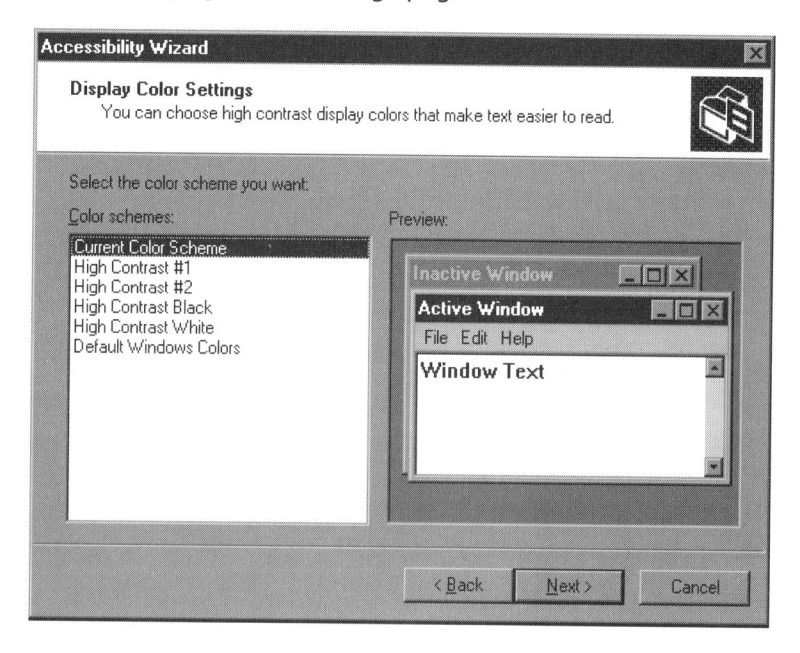

➤ STEP 10

Select the size and color of the mouse cursor that best suits your needs (Figure 22.10), click **NEXT,** and proceed to Step 28. Three size choices are available:

- Regular
- Large
- Extra Large

Three color choices are available:

- White
- Black
- Inverting

➤ STEP 11

Select **I am deaf or have difficulty hearing sounds from the computer** (Figure 22.11), and click **NEXT**.

Figure 22.10 The Mouse Cursor page.

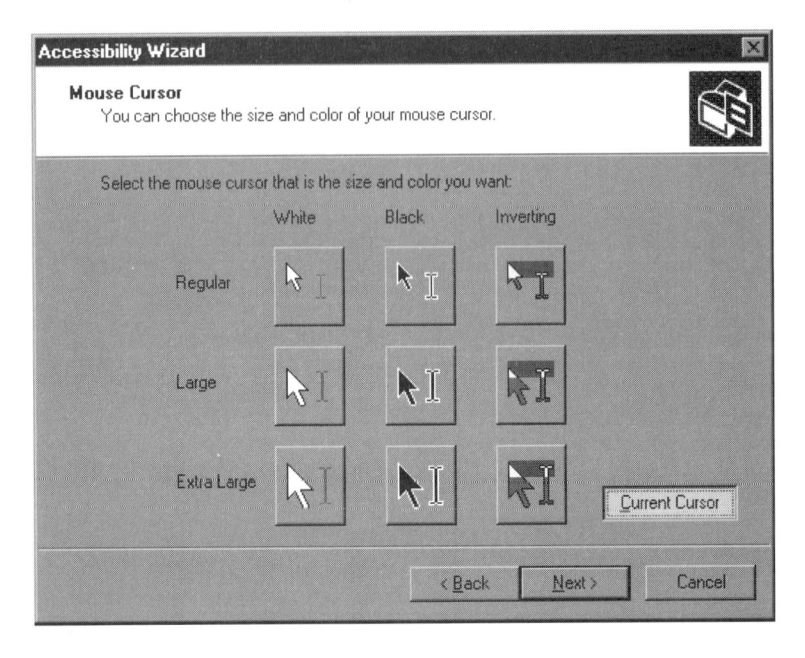

Figure 22.11 Selecting the I am deaf or have difficulty hearing sounds from the computer option.

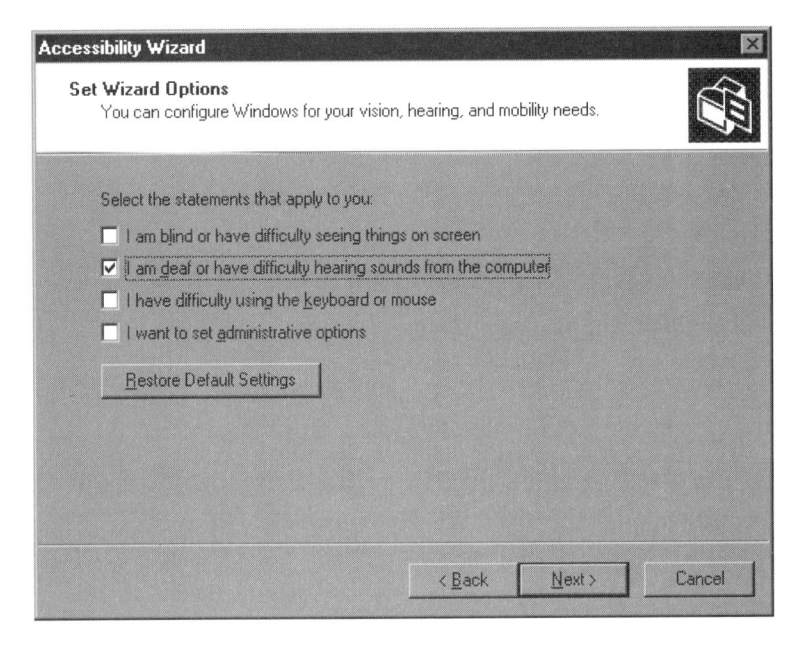

➤ STEP 12

The SoundSentry page allows you to turn on visual warnings notifying you of system events (Figure 22.12). Select either **Yes** or **No**, and click **NEXT**.

Figure 22.12 The SoundSentry page.

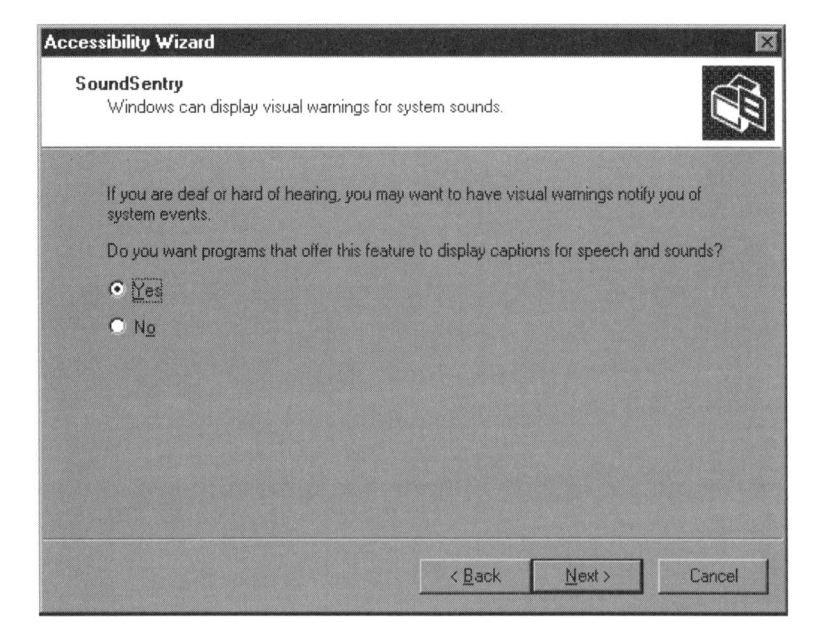

➤ STEP 13

The ShowSounds page allows you to turn on captions for speech and sounds (Figure 22.13). Select either **Yes** or **No**, click **NEXT,** and proceed to Step 28.

➤ STEP 14

Select **I have difficulty using the keyboard or mouse** (Figure 22.14), and click **NEXT**.

➤ STEP 15

If you have difficulty holding down multiple keys at the same time, you may want to enable StickyKeys. StickyKeys allows you to press one key at a time, even when multiple keys are required for the function you are performing. Select **Yes** or **No** (Figure 22.15), and click **NEXT**.

Figure 22.13 The ShowSounds page.

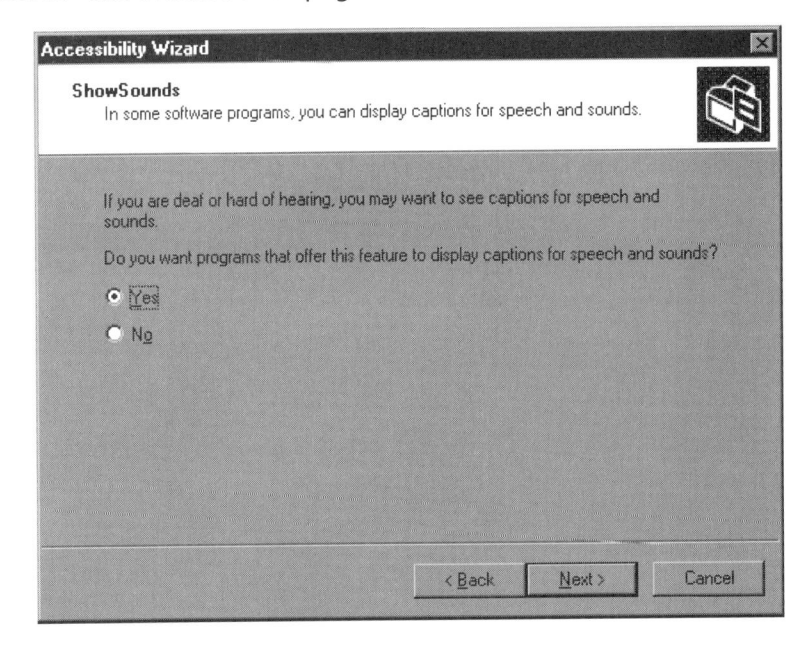

Figure 22.14 Selecting the I have difficulty using the keyboard or mouse option.

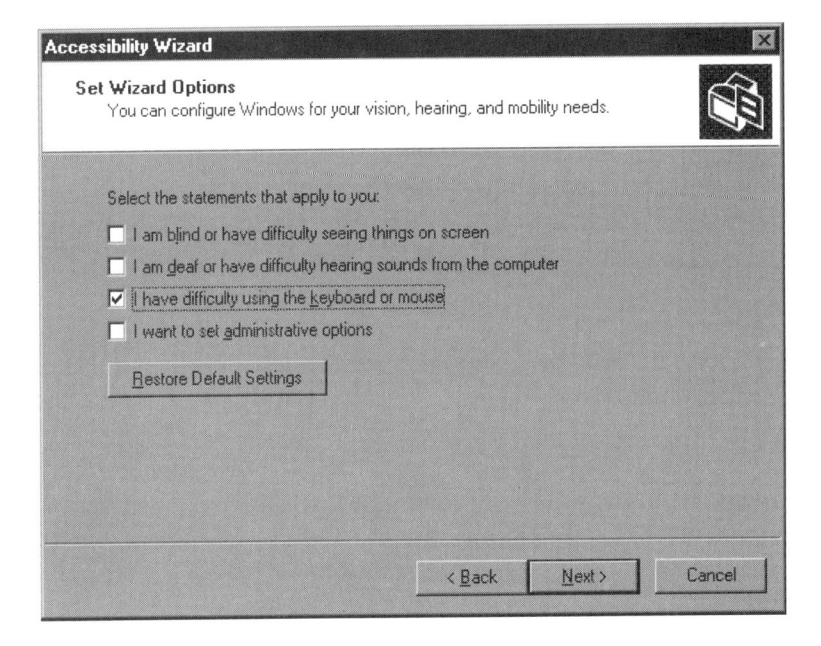

Figure 22.15 The StickyKeys page.

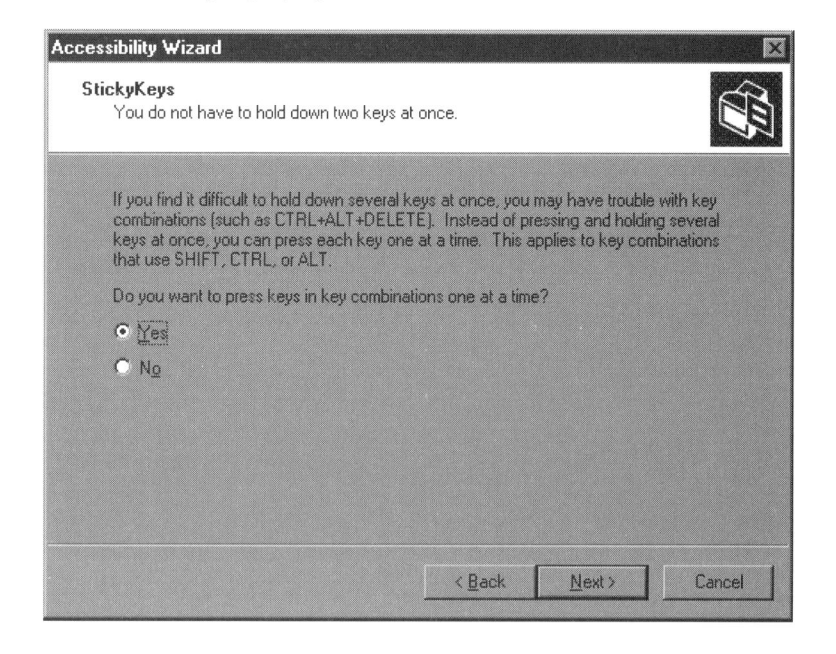

➣ STEP 16

If you suffer from motion disabilities to the point that you may unintentionally press the same key too often, you may want Windows to ignore those repeated keystrokes. This is accomplished on the BounceKeys page (Figure 22.16). If you select **Yes**, click **NEXT** and go to Step 17. If you select **No**, click **NEXT** and proceed to Step 18.

> **NOTE**
>
> Microsoft seems to use BounceKeys and FilterKeys interchangeably. If you access the same functions from Accessibility Options in Control Panel, it is called FilterKeys. On some screens of the Accessibility Wizard, it is also called FilterKeys.

➣ STEP 17

Two settings can be set when you have enabled BounceKeys (Figure 22.17). Make your selection(s), and click **NEXT**.

- **Ignore keystrokes repeated faster than:** The delay is adjusted using the slider and moving it from shorter to longer.

- **Do you want Windows to beep when it accepts a keystroke?**
  This may help you to adjust the time delay for ignoring keystrokes more accurately.

Figure 22.16 The BounceKeys page.

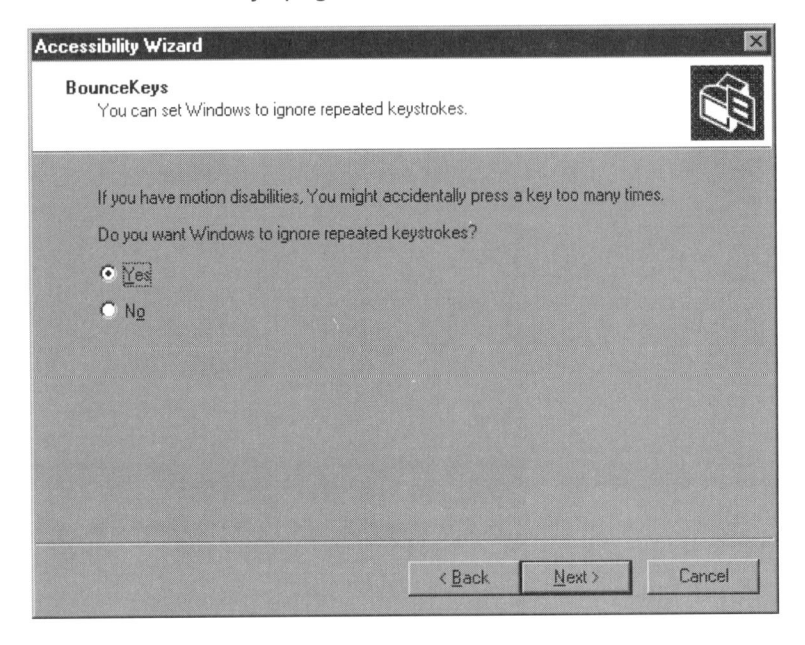

Figure 22.17 The BounceKeys Settings page.

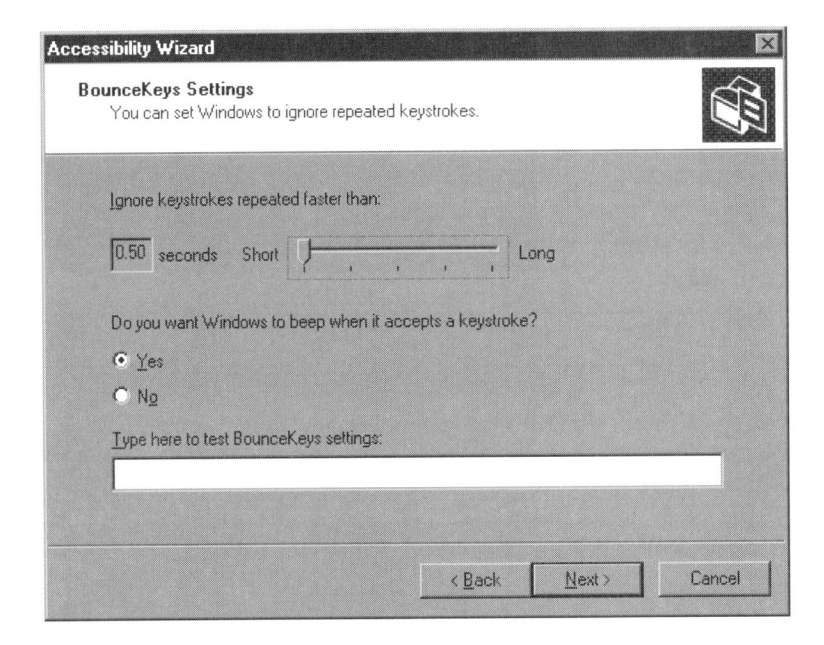

➤ STEP 18

If you want Windows to play a sound when certain keys are pressed, you can enable this functionality on the ToggleKeys page. Select **Yes** or **No** (Figure 22.18), and click **NEXT**. Three keys will initiate a sound when pressed:

- CAPS LOCK
- NUM LOCK
- SCROLL LOCK

Figure 22.18 The ToggleKeys page.

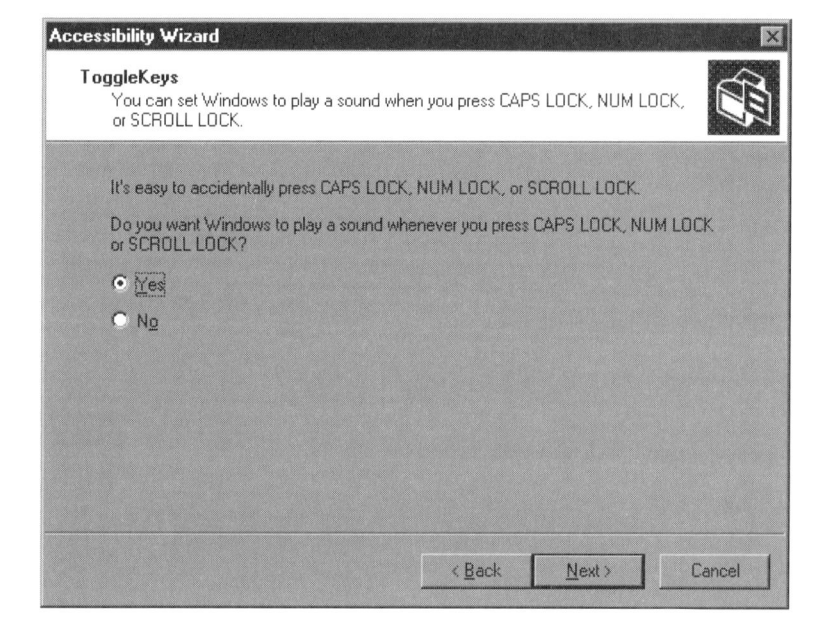

➤ STEP 19

It is possible to receive extra instructions or ToolTips for using the keyboard. To enable this functionality, you select **Yes** on the Extra Keyboard Help page (Figure 22.19). Select **Yes** or **No**, and click **NEXT**.

➤ STEP 20

If you do not like, or cannot use, a mouse, you may want to enable MouseKeys. MouseKeys allows you to use the numeric keypad on your keyboard to control the mouse pointer (Figure 22.20). If you select **Yes**, click **NEXT** and proceed to Step 21. If you select **No**, click **NEXT** and proceed to Step 22.

Figure 22.19 The Extra Keyboard Help page.

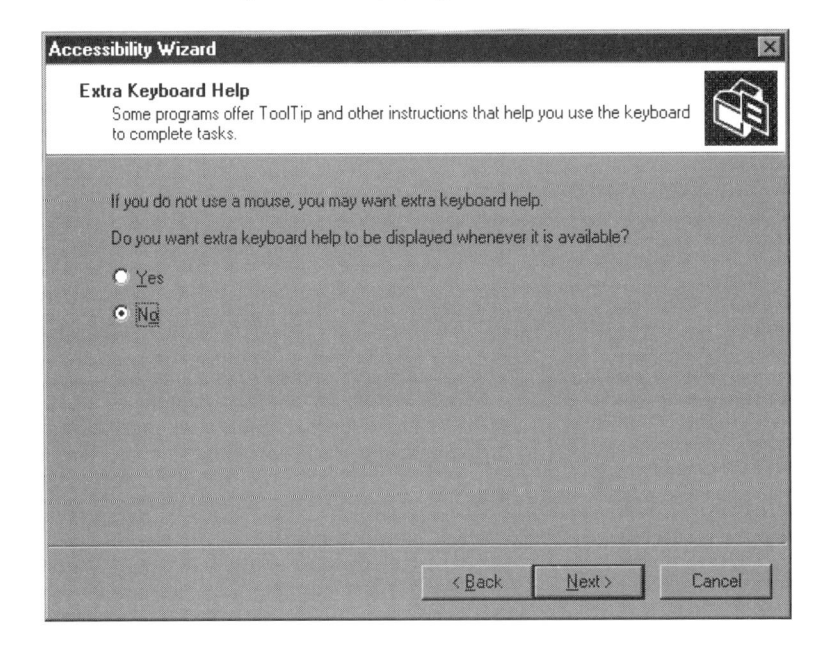

Figure 22.20 The MouseKeys page.

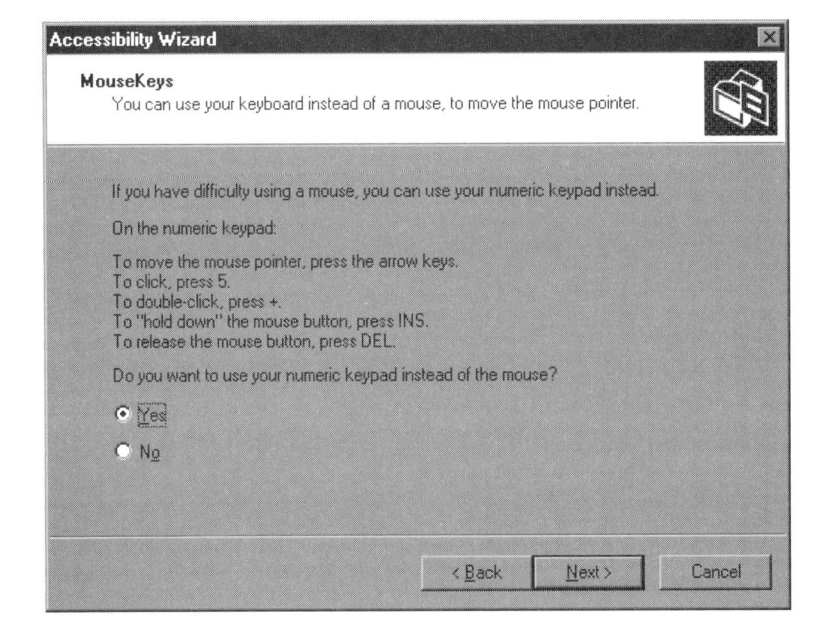

> **STEP 21**

When you enable MouseKeys, you are presented with the MouseKeys Settings page (Figure 22.21). The following options are available on this page:

- **Use MouseKeys when NUM LOCK is:** Deciding whether to use MouseKeys when NUM LOCK is on or off really comes down to how you normally use the numeric keypad. If you use it for data entry, you may want to have MouseKeys enabled when NUM LOCK is off. However, if you normally use the arrow keys, INS, and DEL, you may want to have MouseKeys enabled when NUM LOCK is on.
- **Pointer Speed**. Two options are available for the speed at which the pointer will move when controlled by MouseKeys: Top speed and Acceleration. Top speed is the setting for the fastest the cursor will move, and Acceleration is how fast the cursor will reach that speed.

Figure 22.21 The MouseKeys Settings page.

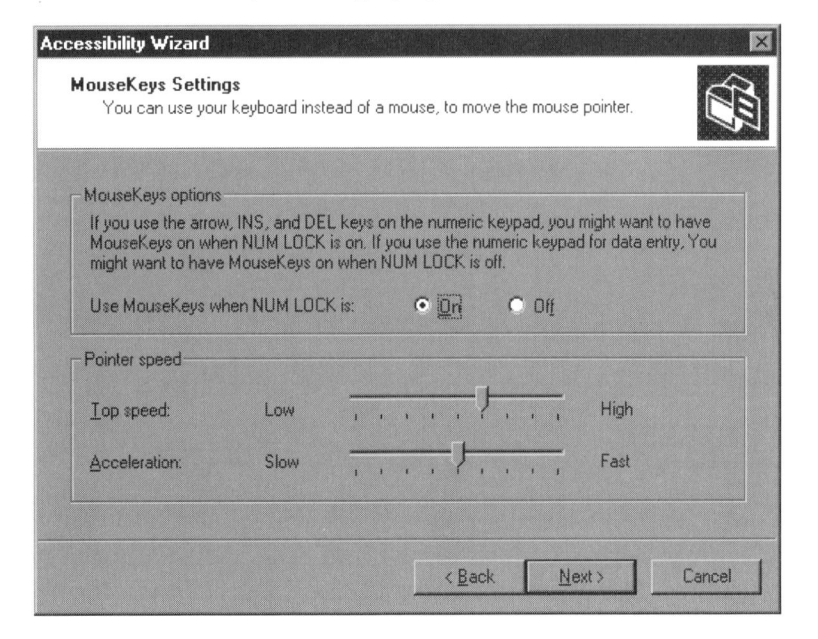

> **STEP 22**

The Mouse Cursor page should look familiar to you if you completed the steps for the **I am blind or have difficulty seeing things on screen** option. Select the size and color of the mouse cursor that best suits your needs (Figure 22.22), and click **Next**. Three size choices are available:

- Regular
- Large
- Extra Large

Three color choices are available:

- White
- Black
- Inverting

Figure 22.22 The Mouse Cursor page.

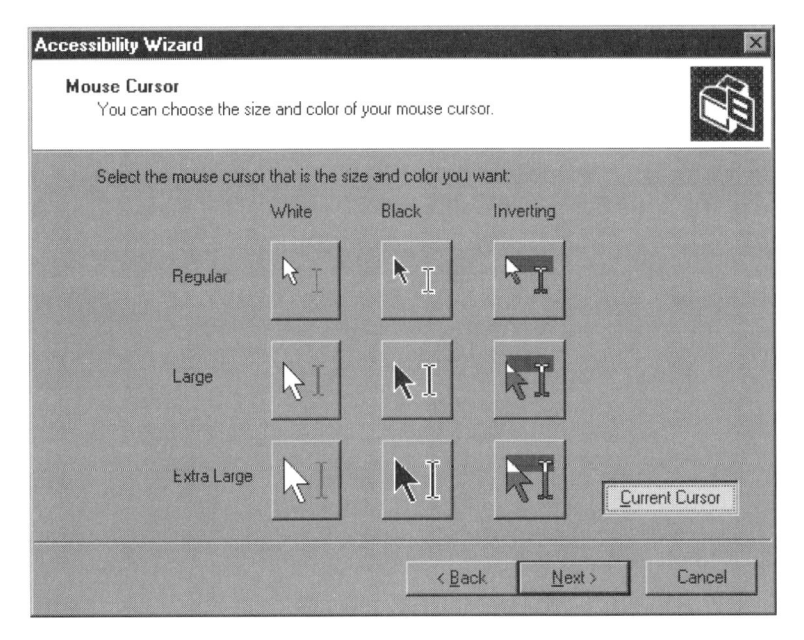

> **STEP 23**

The Mouse Button Settings page allows you to swap the functionality of the buttons depending on what hand you use the mouse with (Figure 22.23). Select an option, and click **Next**. Two options are available:

- Right-handed
    - Left button is used for normal select and normal drag
    - Right button is used for context menus and special drag.

- Left-handed
  - Left button is used for context menus and special drag
  - Right button is used for normal select and normal drag.

Figure 22.23 The Mouse Button Settings page.

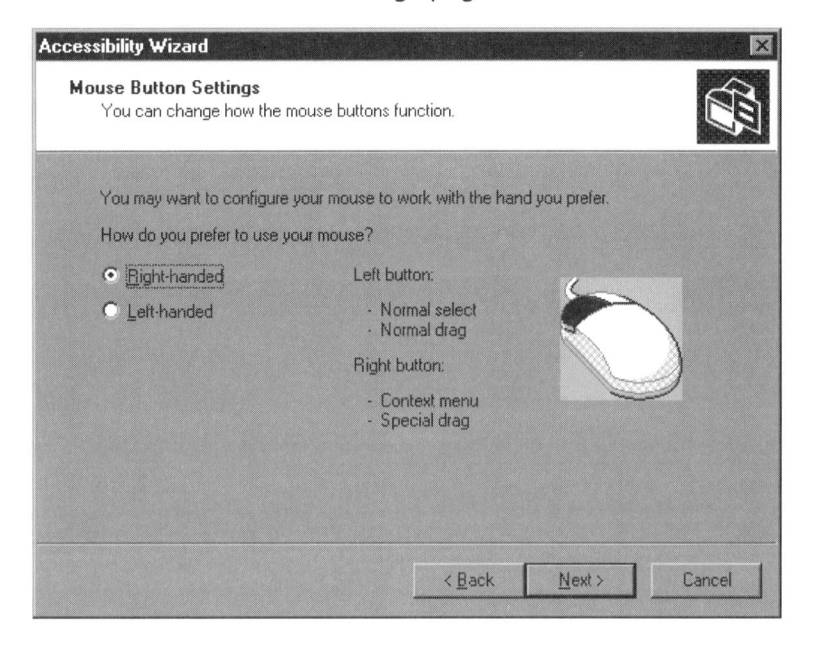

➤ STEP 24

If the mouse pointer moves too slowly or quickly for you, it can be adjusted on the Mouse Speed page (Figure 22.24). To adjust the speed, move the slider until you are comfortable with the speed, click **NEXT,** and proceed to Step 28.

➤ STEP 25

Select **I want to set administrative options** (Figure 22.25), and click **NEXT**.

➤ STEP 26

It's possible that multiple users use the same computer. Some of those users may have certain accessibility options enabled that bother other users. If this is the case, you can disable certain accessibility options after the computer has been idle for a period of time you select (Figure 22.26). Make your choice, and click **NEXT**. The following accessibility options can be turned off:

Figure 22.24 The Mouse Speed page.

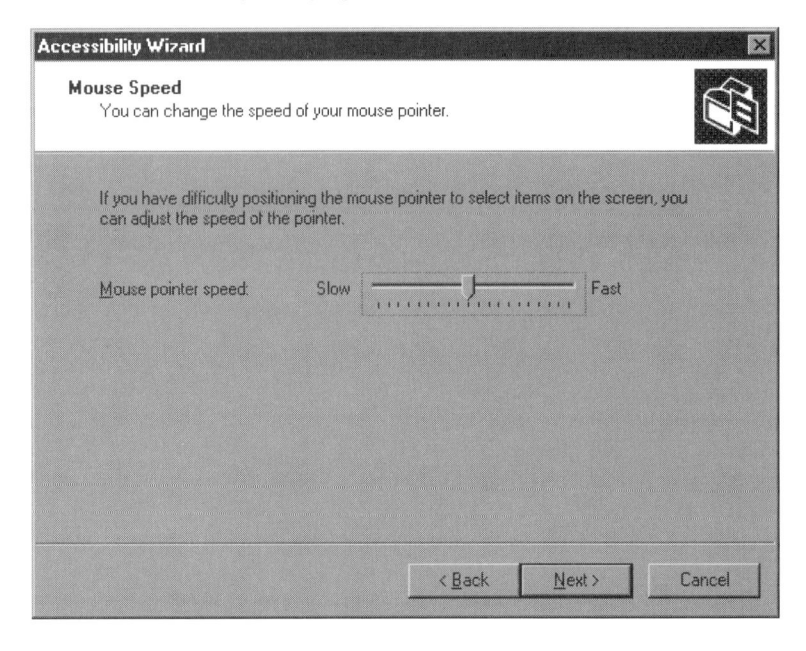

Figure 22.25 Selecting the I want to set administrative options option.

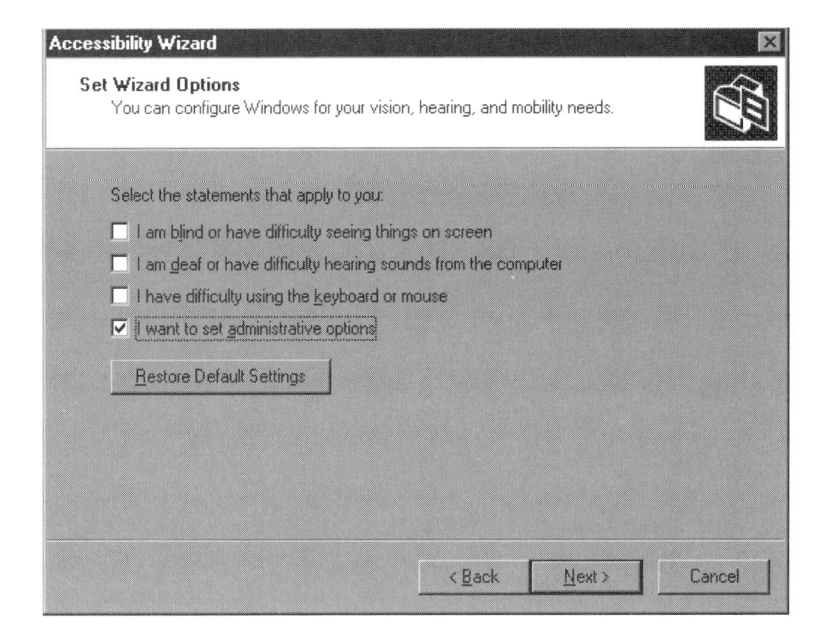

- StickyKeys
- FilterKeys (aka BounceKeys)
- ToggleKeys
- High Contrast features

Figure 22.26 The Set Automatic Timeouts page.

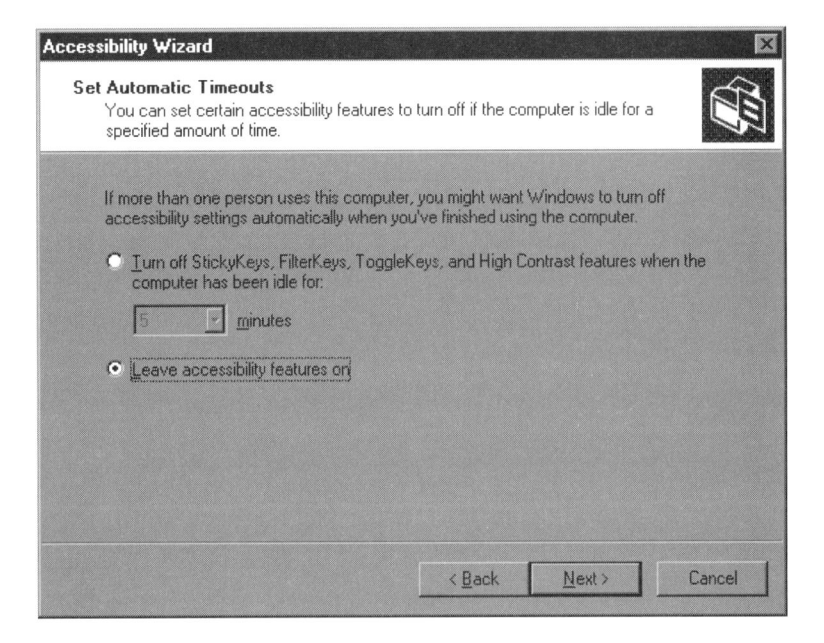

➤ STEP 27

You can also make the accessibility settings apply to all new users or only the current user profile (Figure 22.27). Select **Yes** or **No**, and click **NEXT**.

➤ STEP 28

You have the option of saving the accessibility options you have made to a file so that you can transport the file to other computers instead of having to run the wizard each time you switch computers (Figure 22.28). The file defaults to the name MySettings.acw. After making your choice, click **NEXT**. To use the file, you simply transport it to a new computer and double-click it from within Windows Explorer.

Figure 22.27 The Default Accessibility Settings page.

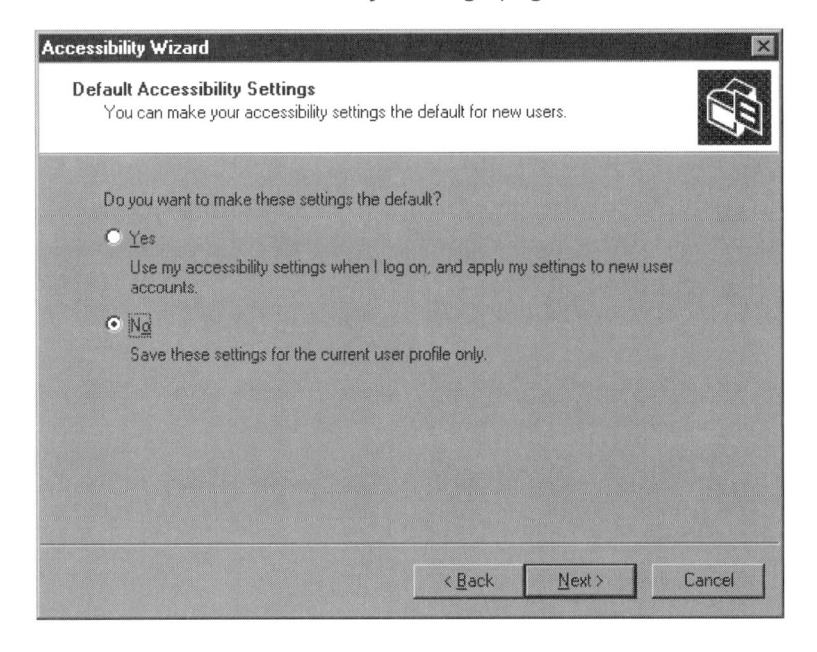

Figure 22.28 The Save Settings to File page.

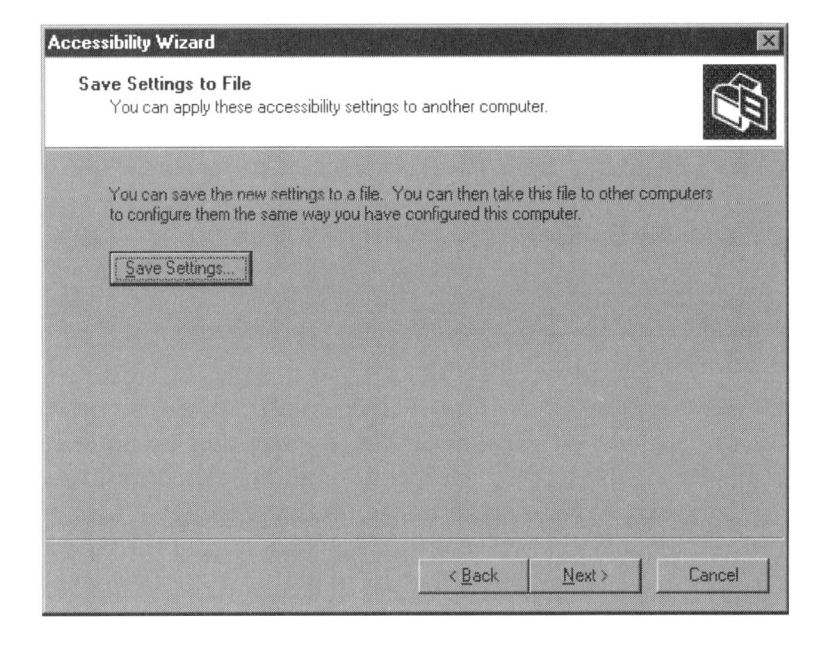

➤ **STEP 29**

The Completing the Accessibility Wizard page will display a summary of what was completed (Figure 22.29). This page is also displayed if you have double-clicked the MySettings.acw file discussed in Step 28. Click **FINISH** to close the Accessibility Wizard.

Figure 22.29 Completing the Accessibility Wizard page.

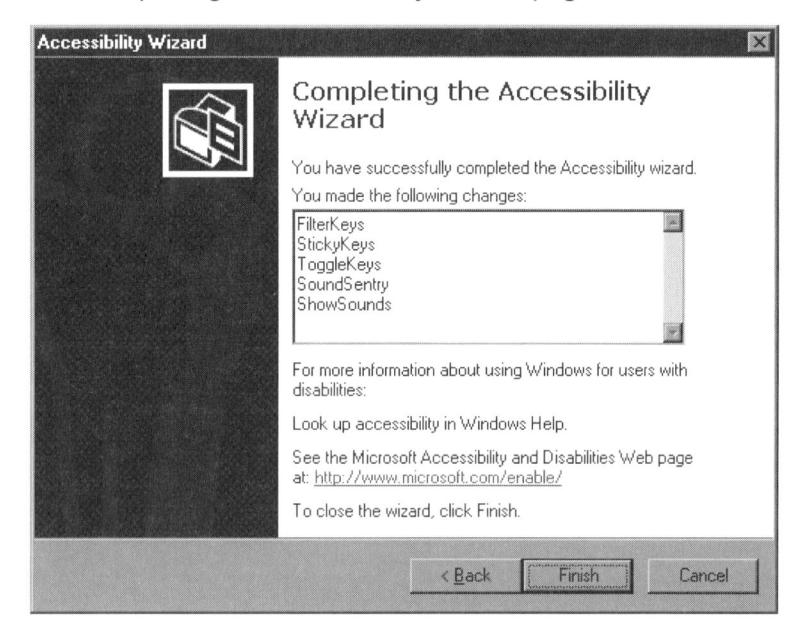

Summary

The Accessibility Wizard allows you to configure several different features in order for everyone to have a pleasant computing experience. The wizard can configure options for people who are blind or have difficulty seeing things on the computer screen, for people who are deaf or have difficulty hearing sounds from the computer, and for people who have difficulty using the keyboard or mouse. A fourth option is available for the Administrator to set limitations on accessibility options.

Depending on the option chosen (blind, deaf, or motion difficulty), the options shown in the wizard are different. For example, if a person has a hard time seeing the screen, there is no reason to adjust whether the mouse operates for a left-handed or right-handed person.

It is possible for users to save their unique settings to a file (.acw) so they can easily transport their settings to other computers they may use without having to rerun the Accessibility Wizard each time. They can simply double-click on the file to import their unique settings to the system they are using.

Chapter 23

Send Fax Wizard

Introduction

To make sending faxes easier, Windows 2000 includes the Send Fax Wizard. The feature is robust and easy to use. By the end of this chapter, you will have sent your first fax from a Windows 2000 machine.

Before You Begin

Sending a fax from Windows 2000 is not a difficult task, especially with the help of the Send Fax Wizard. Any user can use the wizard to send a text document or graphic image as a fax.

The Purpose of this Wizard

The Send Fax Wizard is available in both Windows 2000 Professional and Windows 2000 Server. The purpose of the wizard is to easily allow anyone to send a fax from any print-enabled application on his or her system.

Information Needed to Work with this Wizard

In order to be able to use the Send Fax Wizard, you will need the following:

- A fax modem
- A telephone line for the fax modem
- A fax printer device

The Send Fax Wizard

➤ STEP 1

Start the Send Fax Wizard.

- Open any Windows application that has a Print command, such as WordPad. (Start/Programs/Accessories/WordPad).
- Select **Print** from the File menu.
- Double-click the Fax printer (Figure 23.1).

NOTE

The Send Fax Wizard can also be started by selecting Start/Programs/Accessories/Communications/Fax/Send Cover Page Fax; however, it will send only a cover page and nothing else.

Figure 23.1 Selecting the Fax Printer to double-click and start the Send Fax Wizard.

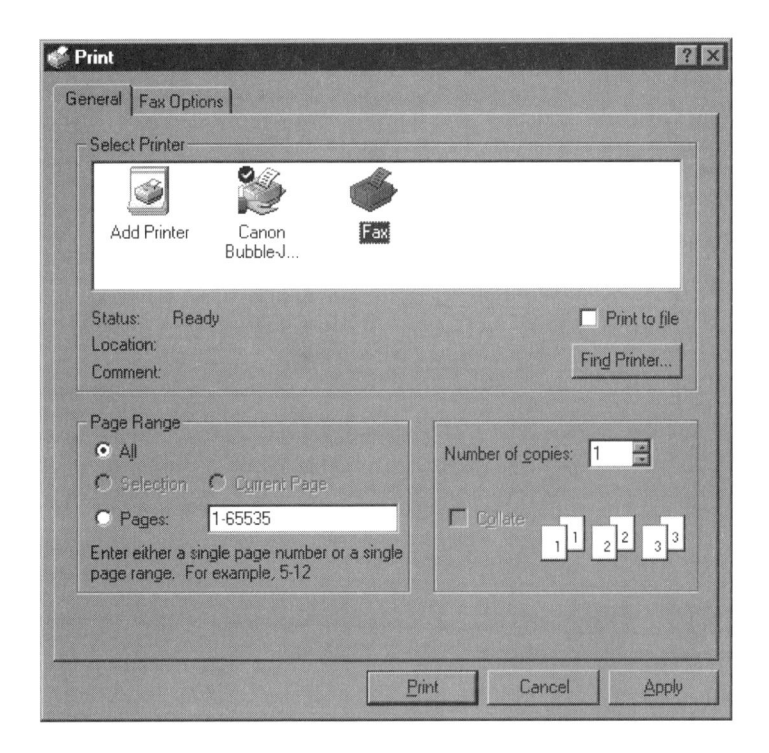

➤ STEP 2

Click **NEXT** at the Send Fax Wizard welcome page (Figure 23.2).

➤ STEP 3

The first time you use the Send Fax Wizard, you are presented with the option to edit your user information or keep the current user information (Figure 23.3). If you select **Edit the user information now**, click **OK,** and proceed to Step 4. If you select **Keep the current user information**, click **OK,** and proceed to Step 5.

➤ STEP 4

Edit the desired information presented on the User Information tab, and click **OK** (Figure 23.4).

The following selections are available on the User Information tab:

- Your full name
- Fax number
- E-mail address

- Title
- Company
- Office location
- Department
- Home phone
- Work phone
- Address
- Billing code

Figure 23.2 The Send Fax Wizard welcome page.

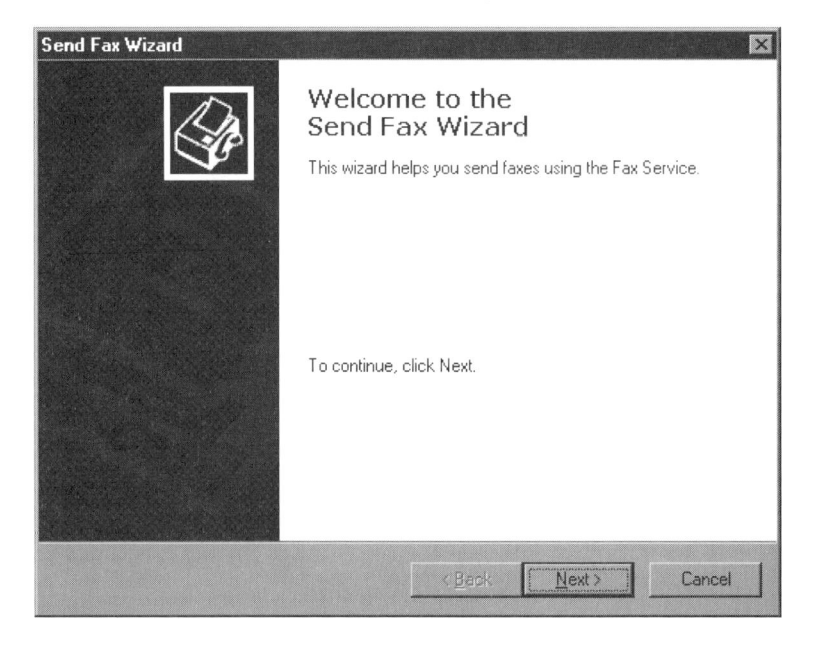

Figure 23.3 Prompt to edit or keep the current user information.

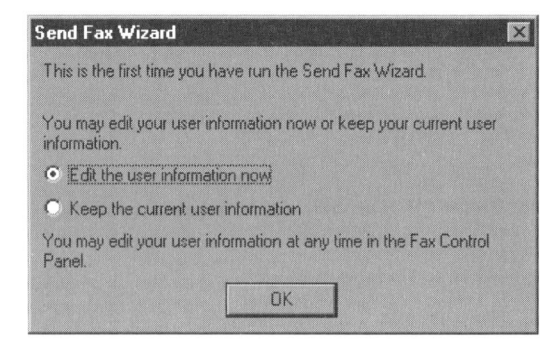

Figure 23.4 Editing data on the User Information tab of Fax Properties.

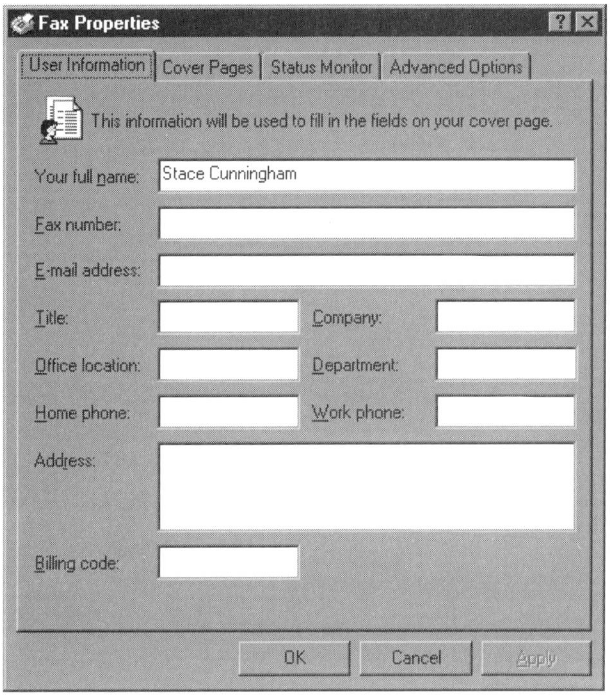

➤ STEP 5

The Recipient and Dialing Information page allows you to enter a name in the To: dialog box, or choose an entry from your Address Book by clicking ADDRESS BOOK (Figure 23.5). This page also allows you to select to use dialing rules and to pick which dialing rule to use by clicking DIALING RULES. This button is not selectable if you have not checked the "Use dialing rules:" box. Enter the name of the person you want to send the fax to, the fax number, click **ADD**, click **NEXT**, and proceed to Step 8. If you want to select an entry in your Address Book, click **ADDRESS BOOK** and proceed to Step 6.

➤ STEP 6

Select a name in the left pane and click **To** (Figure 23.6). Click **OK** to return to the Recipient and Dialing Information page where you will see the chosen recipient indicated on that page. Click **NEXT** on the Recipient and Dialing Information page, and proceed to Step 8.

If the recipient's name you want to fax is not available in your address book, you can add it by clicking **NEW CONTACT** to create the entry.

Figure 23.5 The Recipient and Dialing Information page.

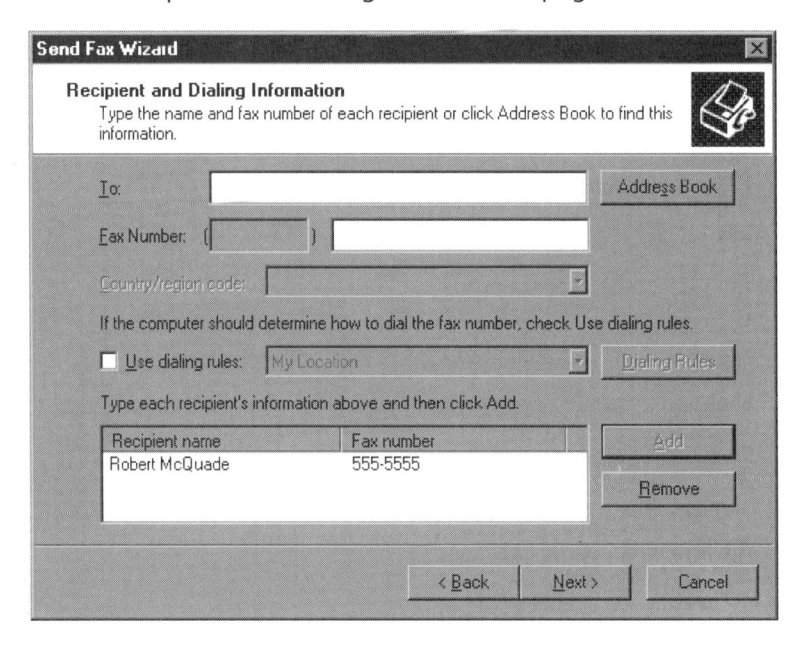

Figure 23.6 Selecting an existing name from the Address Book.

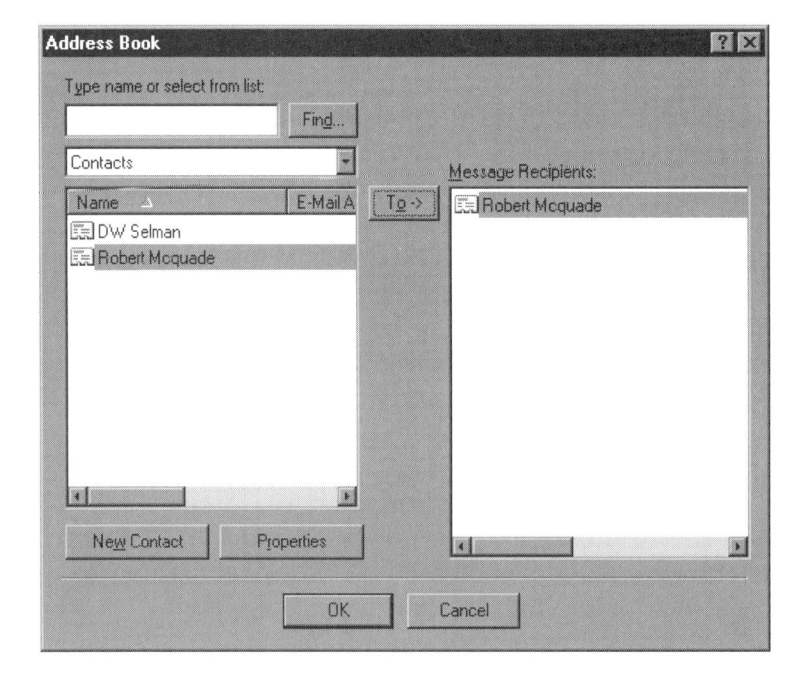

➤ STEP 7

After clicking **New Contact** in Step 6, you are offered several tabs in which to input the data for the new contact (Figure 23.7).

- Name
- Home
- Business
- Personal
- Other
- NetMeeting
- Digital IDs

Once you have completed the information you want for the new contact, click **OK** to return to the Address Book. Highlight the new name, and click **To** to add the new name to the Message Recipient list. Click **OK** to return to the Recipient and Dialing Information page. Click **Next**.

Figure 23.7 Properties page for creating a new contact in the Address Book.

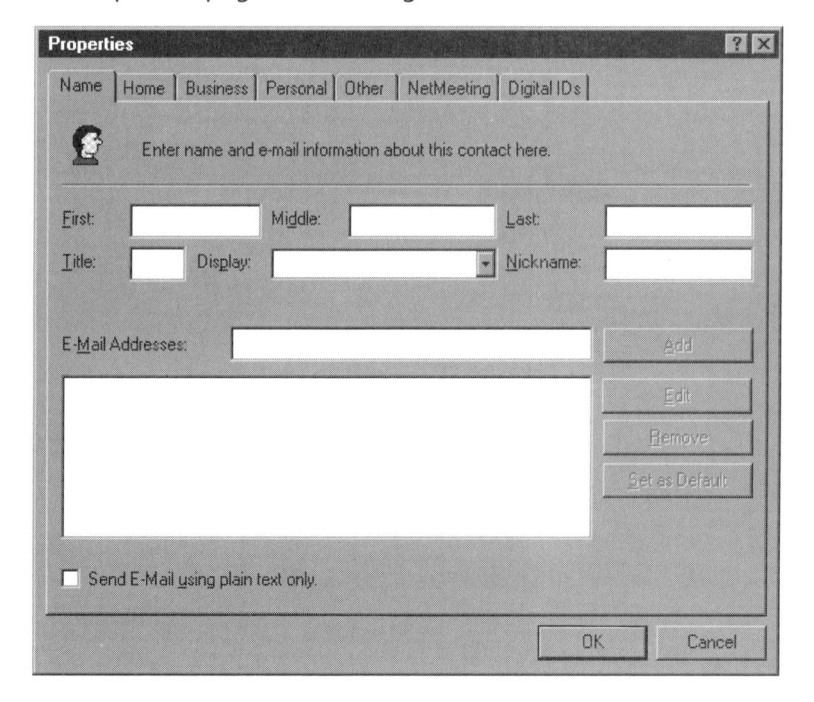

➢ STEP 8

After selecting the recipient and dialing information, the wizard prompts you to include a cover page (Figure 23.8). You do not have to add a cover page if you do not want to. To include a cover page, place a check mark in the box located to the left of **Include a cover page**. If you do decide to use a cover page, you must pick one of the available templates to use. The available templates include:

- confdent (Confidential)
- fyi (For Your Information)
- generic (Generic)
- urgent (Urgent)

You may also include a **Subject line** and **Note** to be sent on the cover page by filling in the appropriate dialog box on the Adding a Cover Page screen. Click **NEXT** after entering your choice.

Figure 23.8 The Adding a Cover Page page.

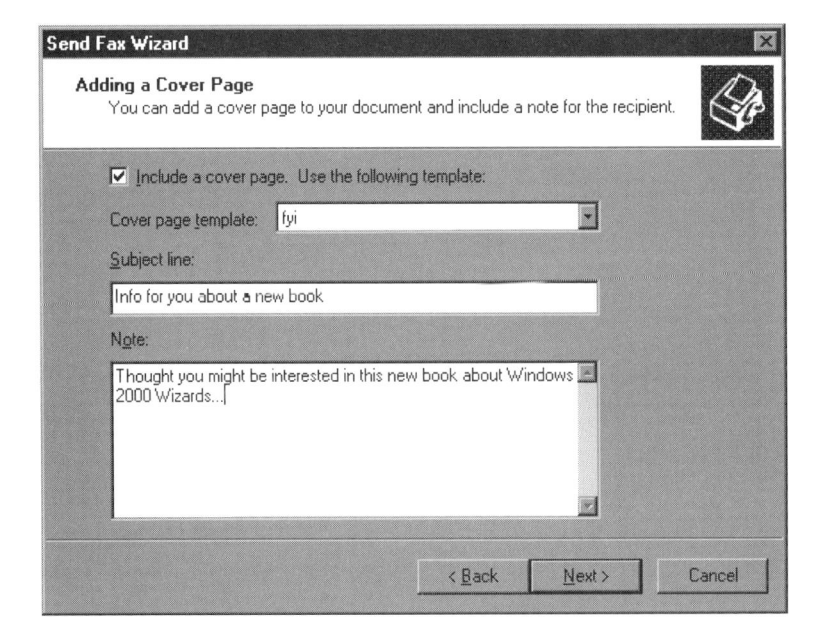

➢ STEP 9

Your fax does not have to be sent immediately if you do not want it to be. The Scheduling Transmission page allows you to specify the time to send the fax. There are three choices:

- **Now**. Send the fax as soon as the wizard is completed.

- **When discount rates apply**. A discount rate can be set from the Fax Service Management Console in Control Panel. The setting contains the start time and stop time of the discount rate period. When this choice is selected, the fax will be sent during the time period set for discount rates.
- **Specific time in the next 24 hours**. You can select a time during the next 24 hours for the fax to be sent.

You may also include a billing code on the Scheduling Transmission page (Figure 23.9). The billing code appears in the fax event log for all outbound faxes, and can be used to assign costs of faxing to a specific account for billing purposes.

Figure 23.9 The Scheduling Transmission page.

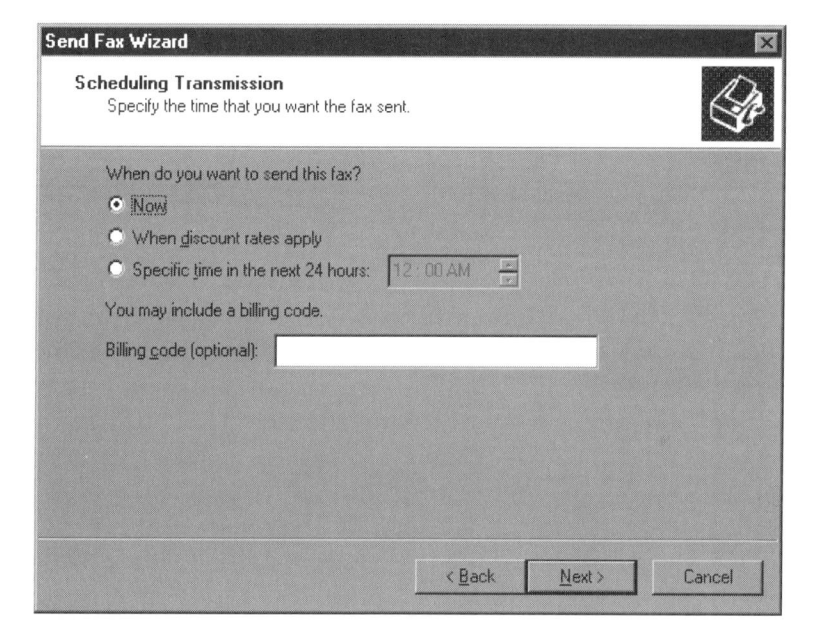

➤ STEP 10

The Completing the Send Fax Wizard page will display a summary of what was completed (Figure 23.10). Click **FINISH** to close the Send Fax Wizard. Be sure to leave your computer on if the fax is being sent from it!

Figure 23.10 Completing the Send Fax Wizard page.

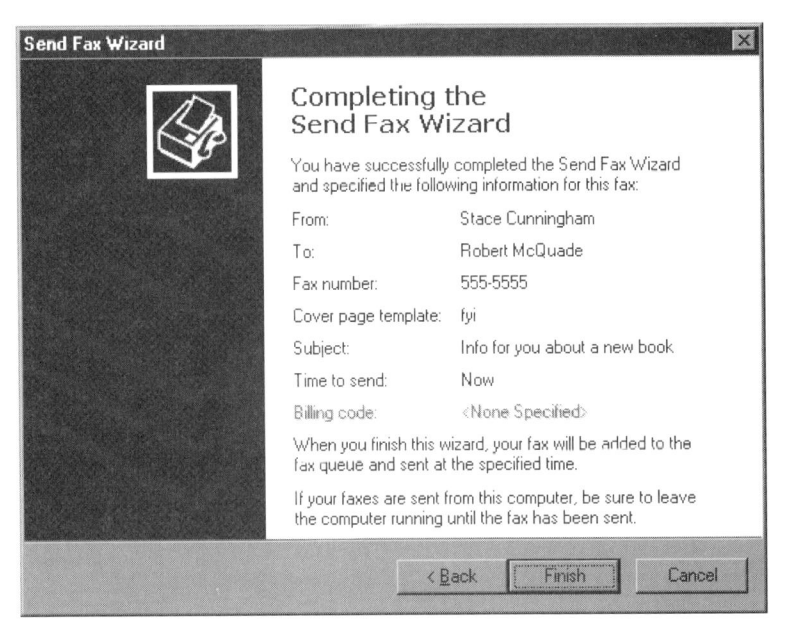

Summary

The Send Fax Wizard is available in both Windows 2000 Professional and Windows 2000 Server. It prepares a fax to be sent from any Windows application that has a Print command available. The Send Fax Wizard can also be started from the Fax menu using the Send Cover Page Fax; however, it will only send the cover page. In order to use the Send Fax Wizard, you need a fax modem, a telephone line for the fax modem, and a fax printer. Double-clicking the fax printer after selecting Print in an application starts the wizard.

The wizard allows you to pick the recipients and dialing information applicable to sending the fax. If no recipients are in your address book, you may add them from within the wizard. After selecting the recipients and dialing information, you are prompted to include a cover page. You do not have to include a cover page if you do not elect to do so; however, if you do add a cover page, you can input a subject line and note to the recipient(s). The next step in the wizard is to determine when the fax is to be sent. You can send it immediately, during a discount rate period, or some other time within the next 24 hours you select. After clicking FINISH in the wizard, the fax is queued to be sent out. Be sure to leave the computer on that has the fax modem attached to it, or the fax will not be sent.

Chapter 24

Backup and Recovery Wizards

Introduction

Systems management is a tedious and extensive task. Windows 2000 offers a number of tools and wizards to make this administrative process easier. By the end of this chapter, you will be familiar with the Windows 2000 Backup and Recovery Tools.

Before You Begin

Before beginning, you should first determine the media to which you will be backing up the data. The backup utility in Windows 2000 supports backups to various types of media, including logical drives, removable disks, and even writable CDs. In order to use a tape storage device with the backup utility, you must first ensure that you have installed Remote Storage, which is responsible for managing the storage devices and accompanying media.

Additionally, you will need to log on to the system using an account that has Administrator or Backup Operator privileges; otherwise, you will be unable to back up the Active Directory.

The Purposes of these Wizards

These wizards help protect data from accidental loss. The Backup and Restore Wizards provide a convenient method for backing up and restoring data, as well as the Distributed Services such as Active Directory, Certificate Server, and File Replication Service.

Information Needed to Work with this Wizard

Before performing the following tasks, ensure you have the following information:

- Location to store backed up data

Backup Wizard

➤ **STEP 1**

Start the Windows 2000 Backup and Recovery Tools.

- From the **Start** menu, open **Programs**, **Accessories**, and click **Backup**.

➤ Step 2

The Welcome to the Windows 2000 Backup and Recovery Tools screen (Figure 24.1) has three choices:

- **Backup Wizard.** This starts the Backup Wizard, which steps you through the backup process.
- **Restore Wizard.** This starts the Restore Wizard, which steps you through the restore process.
- **Emergency Repair Disk.** This creates an Emergency Repair Disk, which saves information about your system settings and system files. You should perform this task whenever changes are made to the system.

Figure 24.1 The Windows 2000 Backup and Recovery Tools welcome page.

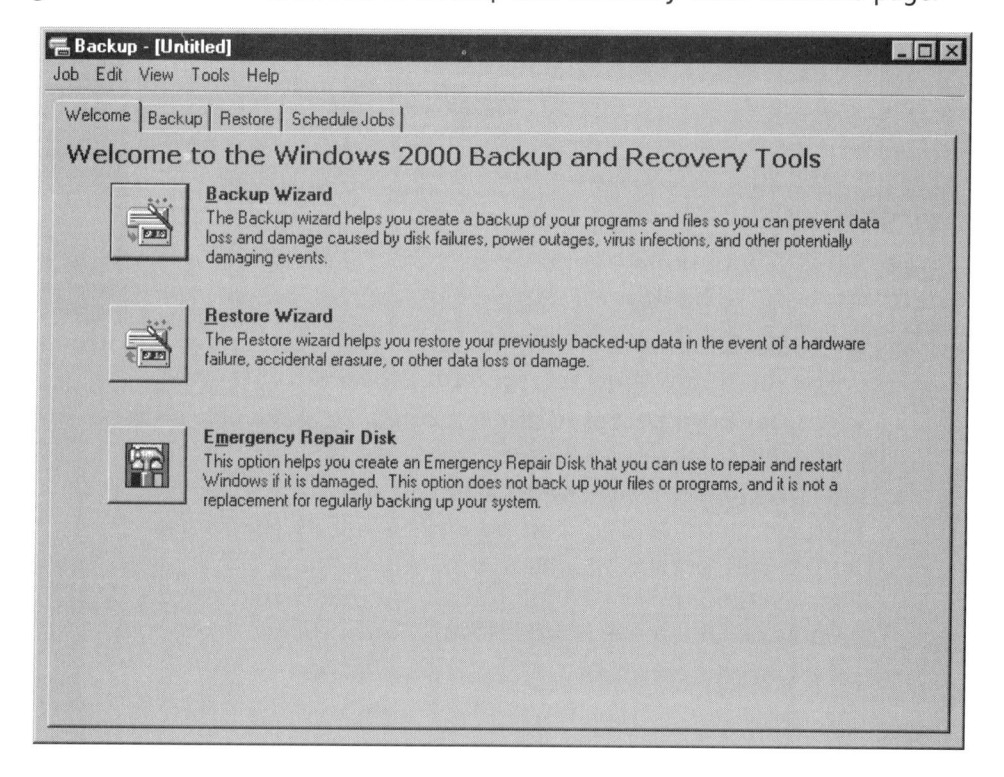

➤ STEP 3

To start the Backup Wizard (Figure 24.2), click **BACKUP WIZARD**. Click **NEXT** to continue.

Figure 24.2 The Backup Wizard welcome page.

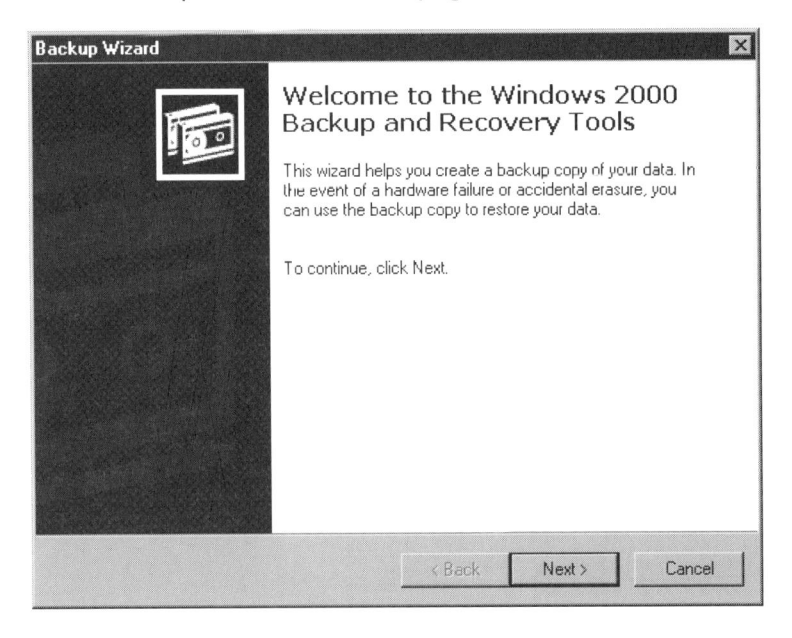

➢ STEP 4

There are a few options to choose from, depending on the specific data you want to back up (Figure 24.3).

- Select **Back up everything on my computer** to quickly archive all the data stored on the system. Proceed to Step 6.
- Select **Back up selected files, drives, or network data** to selectively choose the data to back up.
- Select **Only back up the System State data** to archive the Windows 2000 system components such as the registry, Component Services Class Registration database, system startup files, Certificate Services database, Active Directory, SYSVOL folder, and cluster service information. Proceed to Step 6.
- Click **NEXT** to continue.

➢ STEP 5

If you elected to back up selected data, the Items to Back Up page (Figure 24.4) provides a simple point-and-click method for selecting the data to back up.

- Click in the available boxes to select the data you want to back up, and click **NEXT** to continue.

Figure 24.3 What to Back Up page.

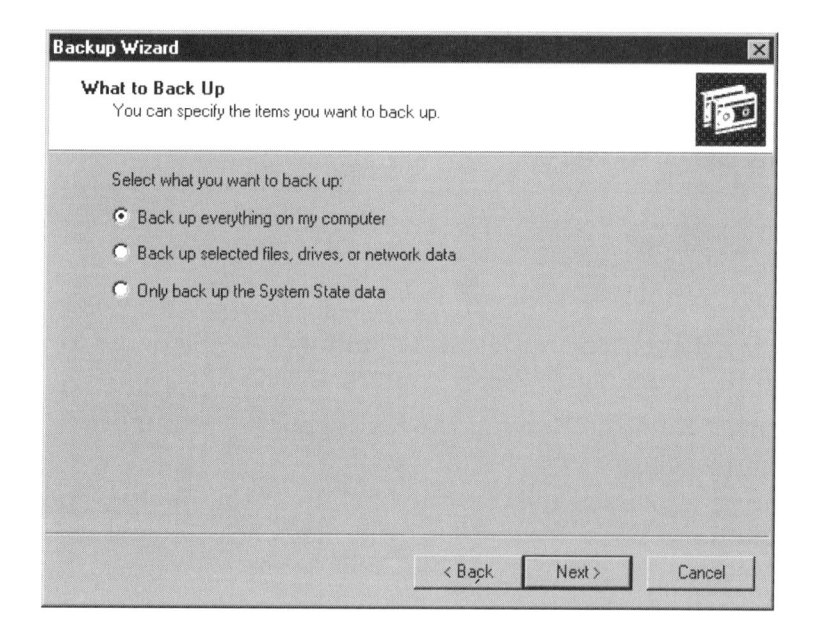

Figure 24.4 Items to Back Up page.

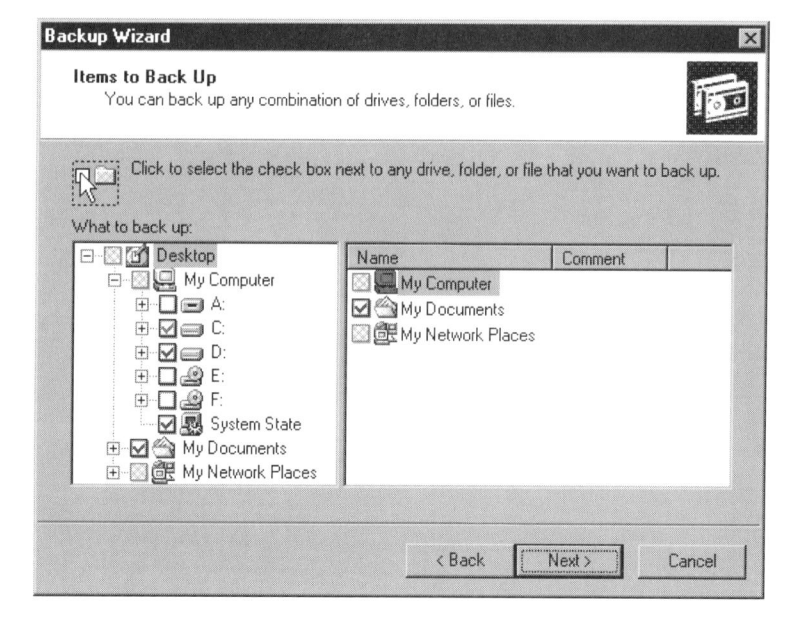

> **NOTE**
>
> A blue check mark indicates that everything within that folder or drive will be backed up; whereas a gray check mark indicates that only part of the contents will be backed up.

➢ STEP 6

Select the media type and destination media or filename to store the backed-up data (Figure 24.5).

- Select from the **Backup media type:** the destination type for your backup.
- Enter a location to store the backup in the **Backup media or file name:** box. In addition, you may click **BROWSE** to locate the destination.
- Click **NEXT** to continue.

Figure 24.5 Where to Store the Backup page.

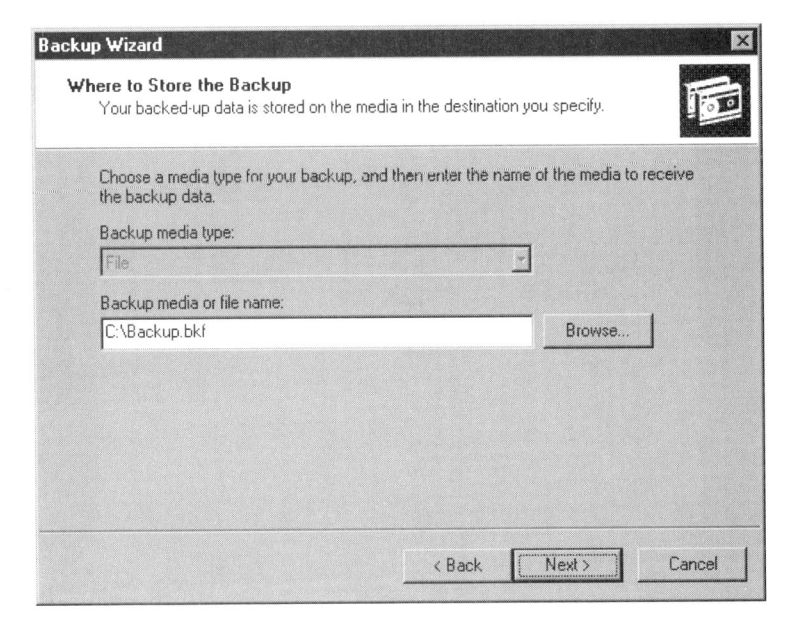

> **NOTE**
>
> Only *File* will be available from the Backup media type if no other removable storage is installed.

➤ STEP 7

You have finished setting up the system to perform a backup, and the Completing the Backup Wizard page (Figure 24.6) displays a summary of the backup settings. However, several more options can still be set. Click **ADVANCED** to specify additional backup options.

Figure 24.6 Completing the Backup Wizard page.

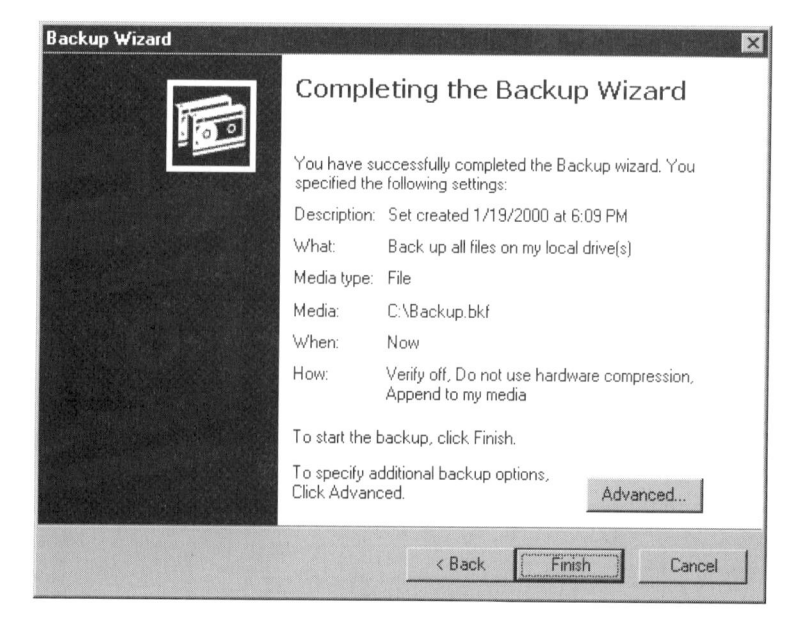

➤ STEP 8

Select the type of backup to perform from the following choices (Figure 24.7):

- **Normal**. This will copy all the selected files and clear the archive attribute.
- **Copy**. This will copy all selected files, but will not clear the archive attribute.

- **Incremental**. This will back up all selected files, but only those that have been created or changed since the last normal or incremental backup, and clears the archive attribute.
- **Differential**. This will back up all selected files created or changed since the last normal or incremental backup, but it does not clear the archive attribute.
- **Daily**. This will copy all the selected files that have changed only on the day the backup is performed, and it does not clear the archive attribute.

Check **Backup migrated Remote Storage data** to back up data migrated to Remote Storage. Remote Storage is used to extend disk space. This feature can be used to free space on your primary hard disk by copying infrequently used files on the local volumes to a tape library when the primary hard disks drop below a specified level. Click **Next** to continue.

> **NOTE**
>
> The archive attribute (also called archive bit) is associated with a file and is used to indicate whether the file has been backed up since its last change.

Figure 24.7 Type of Backup page.

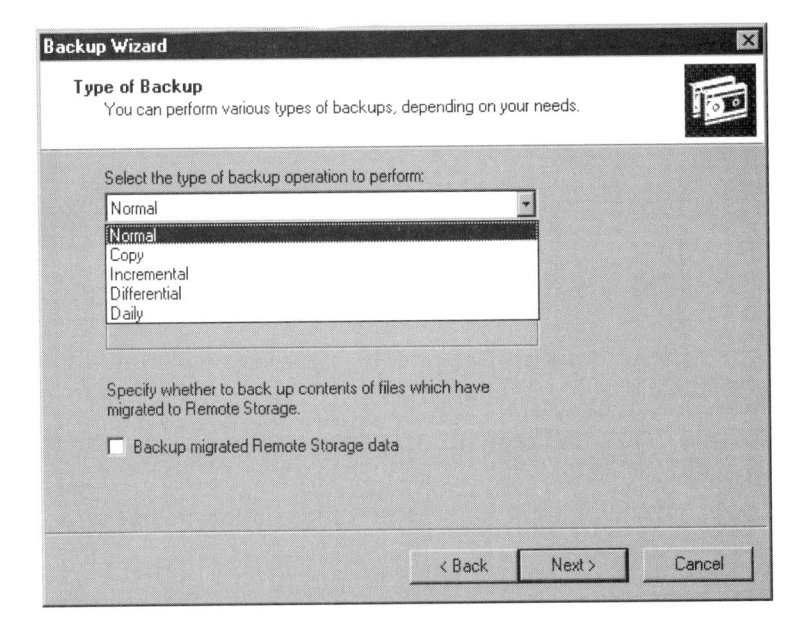

➤ STEP 9

You may optionally select verification and compression to be performed on your backup (Figure 24.8).

- Select **Verify data after backup** to have the system run a check to ensure the integrity of the backed up data. Choosing this option will cause the backup process to take longer.
- Select **Use hardware compression, if available** to increase the amount of storage on the media.
- Click **NEXT** to continue.

Figure 24.8 How to Back Up page.

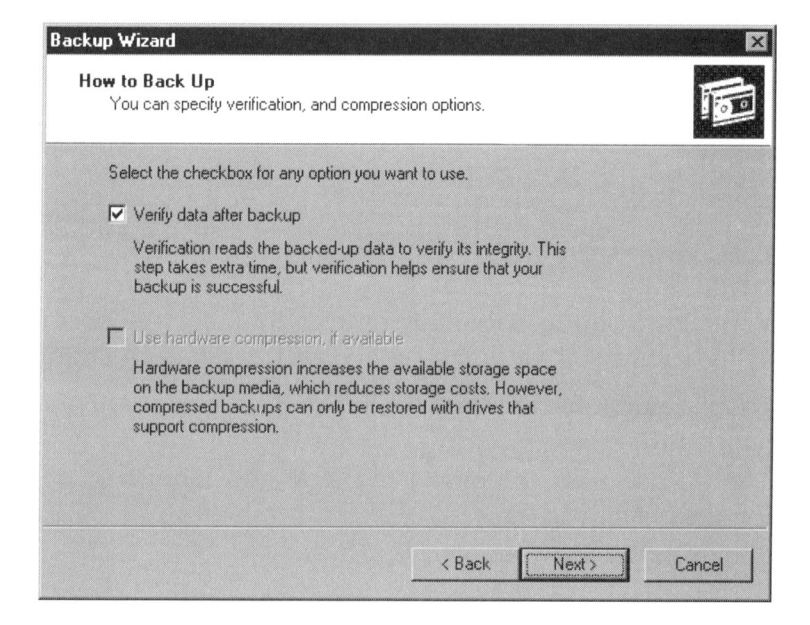

➤ STEP 10

If the media already contains data from a previous backup, select the method to apply the current backup to the media (Figure 24.9).

- Select **Append this backup to the media** to write the backup without overwriting the existing media.
- Select **Replace the data on the media with this backup** to overwrite any existing data on the media. Choosing this option will also enable the check box to allow only the owner and the Administrator the ability to access the data on the media.
- Click **NEXT** to continue.

Figure 24.9 Media Options page.

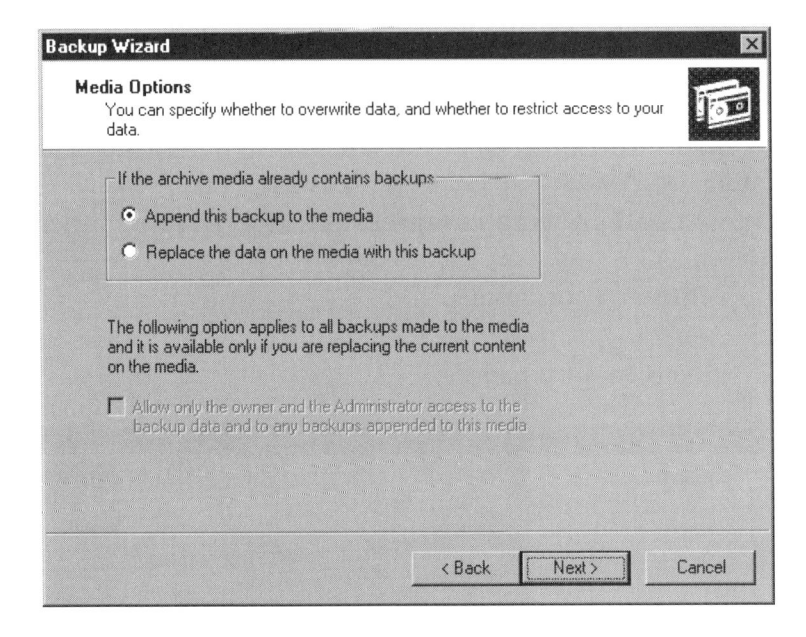

➢ STEP 11

This step allows you to optionally enter a label for the backup and the media being used, or you may accept the defaults (Figure 24.10).

- Enter a name for the backup in the **Backup label** box, or accept the default label.
- Enter a name for the media in the **Media label** box, or accept the default label.
- Click **NEXT** to continue.

➢ STEP 12

Next, select when you want to run the backup. You may run the backup immediately, or schedule a backup to run later (Figure 24.11).

- Select **Now** to run the backup immediately.
- Select **Later** to schedule the backup for a later time. Enter a name for the Job in the Job name box, and click **Set Schedule** to open the Task Scheduler, which provides you with many scheduling options. Choosing to run the backup later will prompt you to enter a password for a domain Administrator (Figure 24.12).
- Click **NEXT** to continue.

Figure 24.10 Backup Label page.

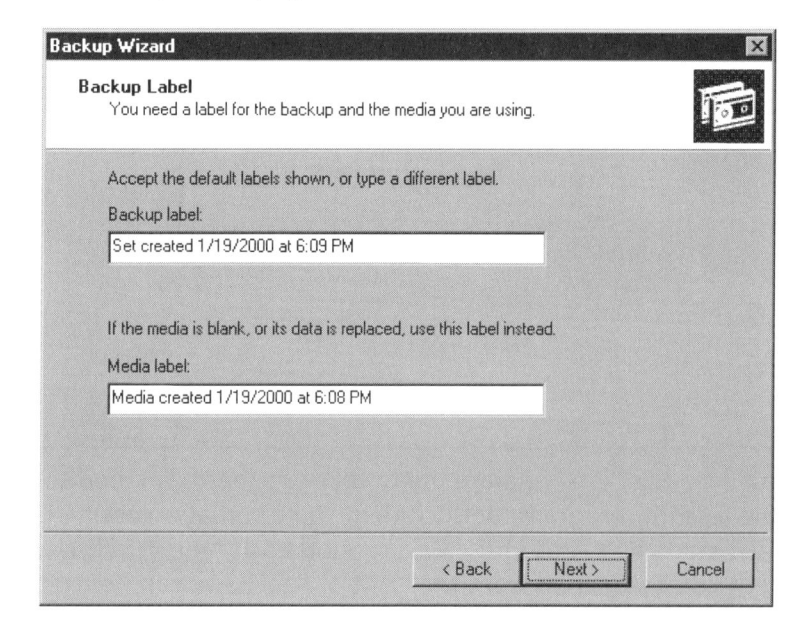

Figure 24.11 When to Back Up page.

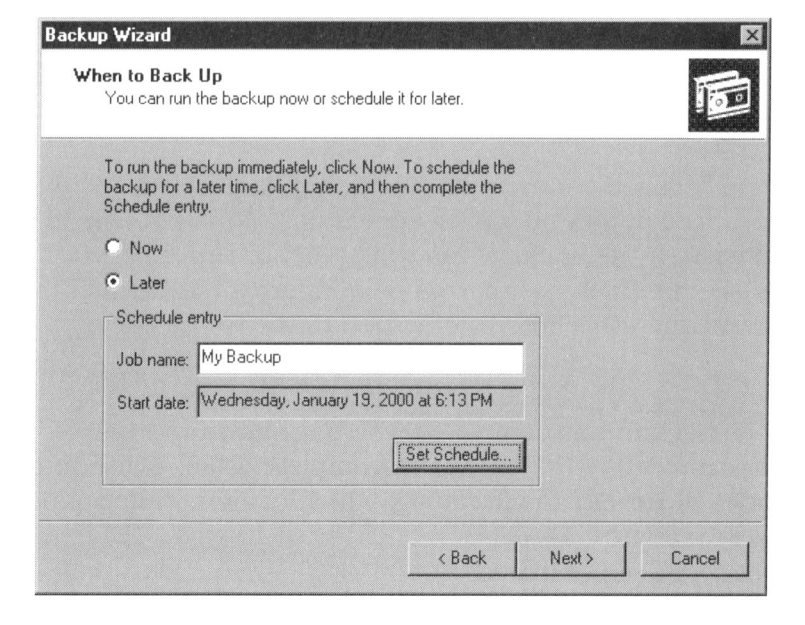

Figure 24.12 Set Account Information dialog box.

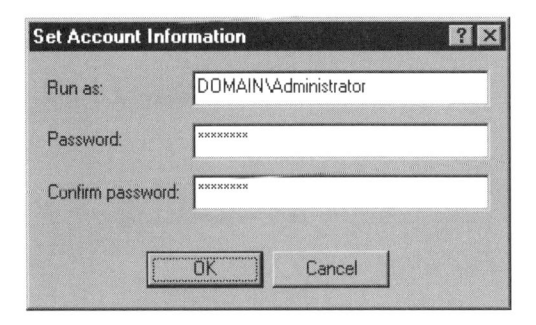

> **NOTE**
>
> The Task Scheduler is a separate utility that provides a method to easily schedule a script, program, or document to be run at a specified time. Task Scheduler starts and runs in the background each time Windows 2000 is started. It can be opened from the Control Panel and can be used to schedule a task to run daily, weekly, monthly, or at specific times; change the schedule for a task; stop a scheduled task; and customize how a task runs at a scheduled time.

➢ STEP 13

You have finished configuring the backup (Figure 24.13). Notice that the Advanced option no longer appears as did previously in Step 7. Click **FINISH**. If the backup was scheduled to run now, you will immediately see the Backup Progress box (Figure 24.14), which indicates the status and other information pertaining to the backup.

➢ STEP 14

After the backup has completed, the box shown in Figure 24.15 appears, indicating the backup is complete. Click **CLOSE** to close the box, or click **REPORT** to view a log, which contains information about the backup (Figure 24.16).

Figure 24.13 Completing the Backup Wizard page.

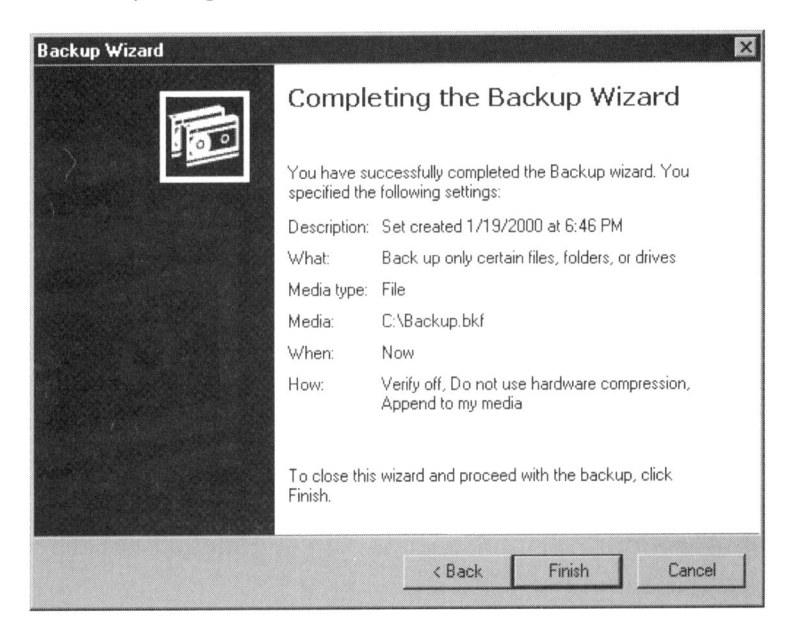

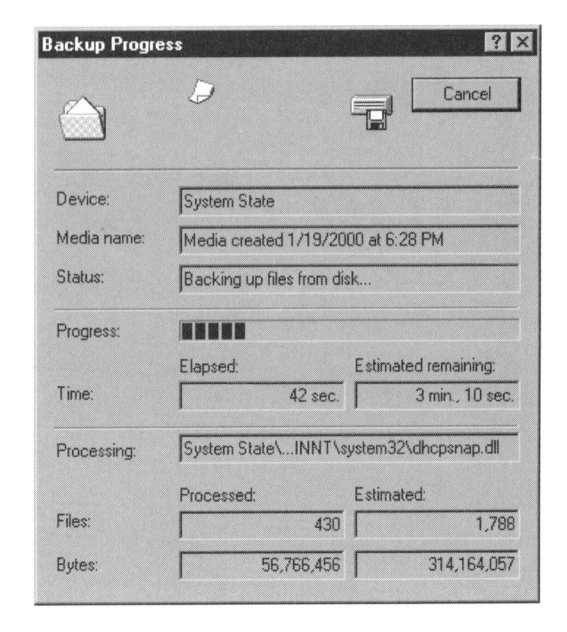

Figure 24.14 Backup Progress status box.

Figure 24.15 Backup Progress completion box.

Figure 24.16 A report is maintained containing information about each backup performed.

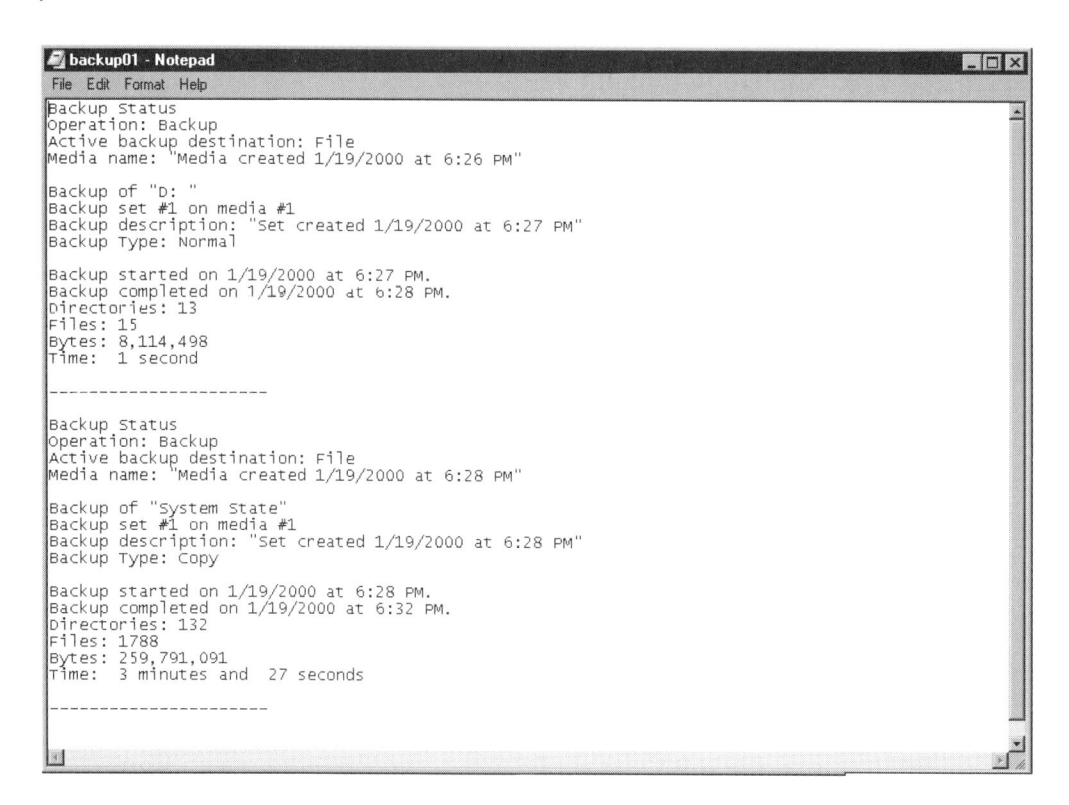

Restore Wizard

➤ STEP 1

Start the Windows 2000 Backup and Recovery Tools. From the **Start** menu, open **Programs**, **Accessories**, and click **Backup**.

➤ STEP 2

The Welcome to the Windows 2000 Backup and Recovery Tools screen, shown earlier in Figure 24.1, appears. Click **Restore Wizard** to open the Welcome to the Restore Wizard page (Figure 24.17), and click **NEXT** to continue.

Figure 24.17 The Restore Wizard welcome page.

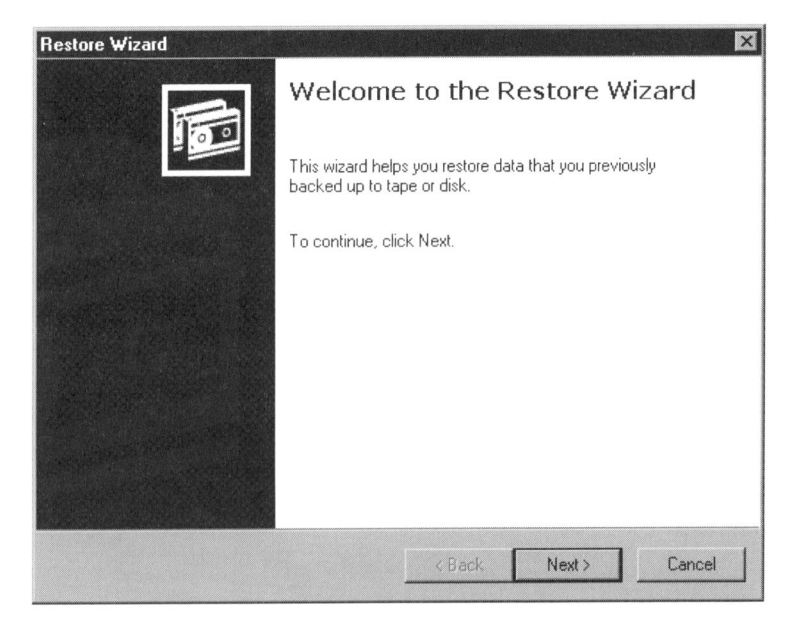

➤ STEP 3

The system catalogs and displays any backups that were previously conducted.

- Choose from the available backups, and click in the available boxes (Figure 24.18) to select the specific data you want to restore.
- To specify a media source that has not been already cataloged, select **Import File** to open the Backup File Name box (Figure 24.19), and enter the location of the media.
- Click **NEXT** to continue.

Figure 24.18 What to Restore page.

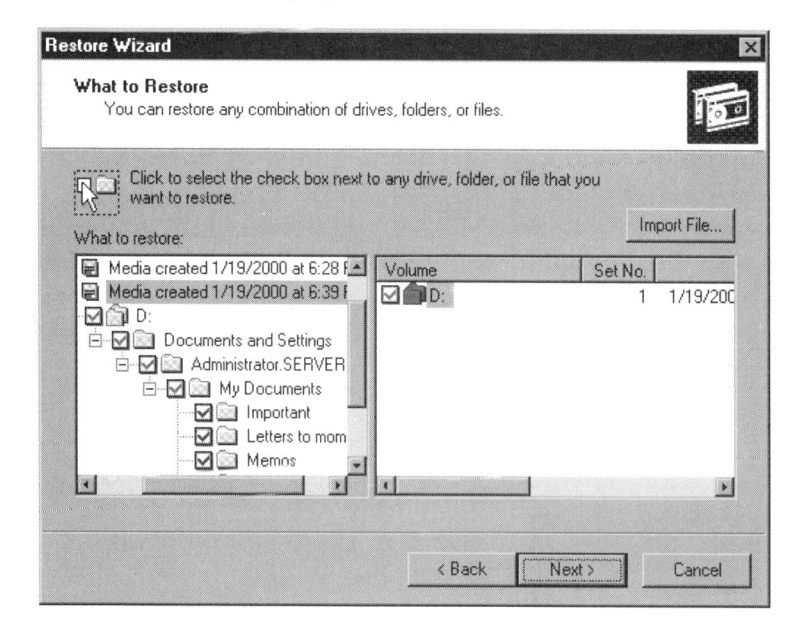

> **NOTE**
>
> To restore the System State data, see the *Getting Authoritative* sidebar.

Figure 24.19 Backup File Name dialog box.

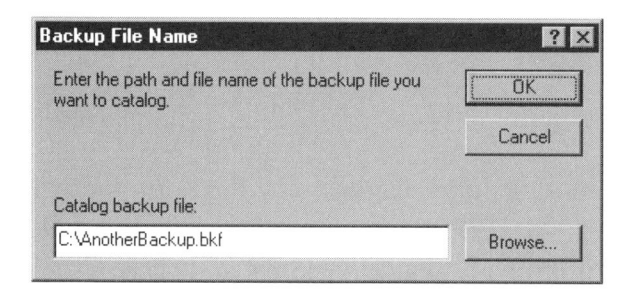

For IT Professionals

Getting Authoritative

A restore operation operates in *nonauthorativtive mode* and could possibly create the problem of the restored data being overwritten. If Active Directory is replicated across multiple domain controllers, an *authoritative restore* will need to be performed to ensure that data continues to be properly replicated.

Microsoft includes a command-line utility named *Ntdsutil*, which allows Active Directory objects to be marked for an authoritative restore. This process tags the data as being newer than any other data in the Active Directory replication system.

To authoritatively restore the distributed services, you will need to first restore the System State data from a previous backup using the following steps:

1. Restart the computer and click **F8** when the boot loader appears.
2. Select **Directory Services Restore Mode** and click ENTER twice.
3. Windows will start in safe mode after logging on.
4. Open **Backup** from the System Tools folder, and select **Restore Wizard**.
5. Select the backed up data containing the System State. (You may close and restart your computer after the restore, if you only want to nonauthoritatively restore your System State data.)
6. Once the restore is complete, enter **ntdsutil** at the command prompt.
7. Enter **authoritative restore** from the ntdsutil: prompt, and click ENTER.
8. From the authoritative restore: prompt, enter a command to restore the selected information. For example, to restore the marketing organizational unit in the domain.com domain, enter **restore subtree OU=marketing, DC=domain, DC=com**, and click ENTER.
9. Once the restore is complete, restart the computer.

➢ STEP 4

You have finished setting up the system to perform a restore, and the Completing the Restore Wizard page (Figure 24.20) displays a summary of the restore settings. However, several more options can still be set. Click **ADVANCED** to specify additional restore options.

Figure 24.20 Completing the Restore Wizard page.

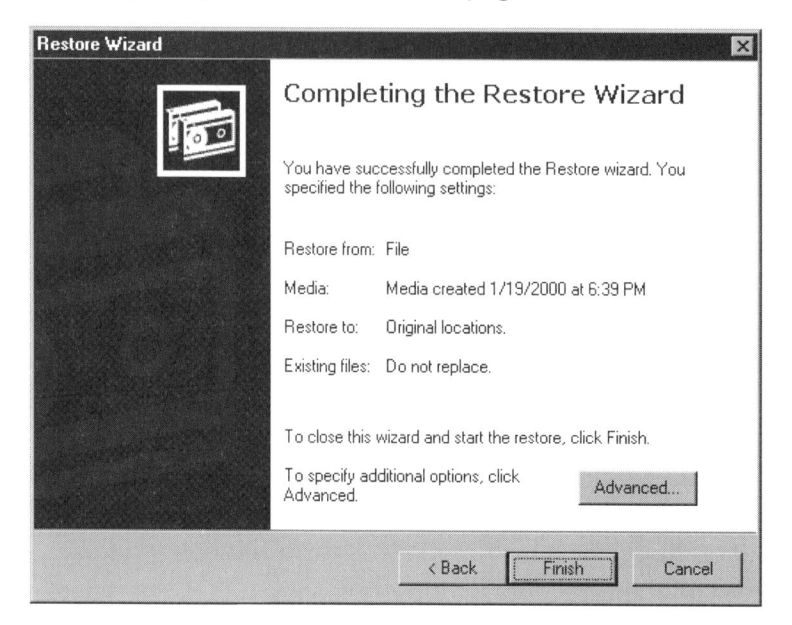

➢ STEP 5

Choose the destination for the restored data (Figure 24.21), and click **NEXT** to continue. You may choose from the following options:

- **Original location.** This choice will restore the backed-up data to the original location from where it was backed up.
- **Alternate location.** This choice allows you to browse to a different location to restore the backed-up data.
- **Single folder.** This choice allows you to restore the entire contents of a backup into a single folder.

➢ STEP 6

Select one of the available options to specify the action to be taken when restoring files that already exist on the restore destination (Figure 24.22), and click **NEXT** to continue.

Figure 24.21 Where to Restore page.

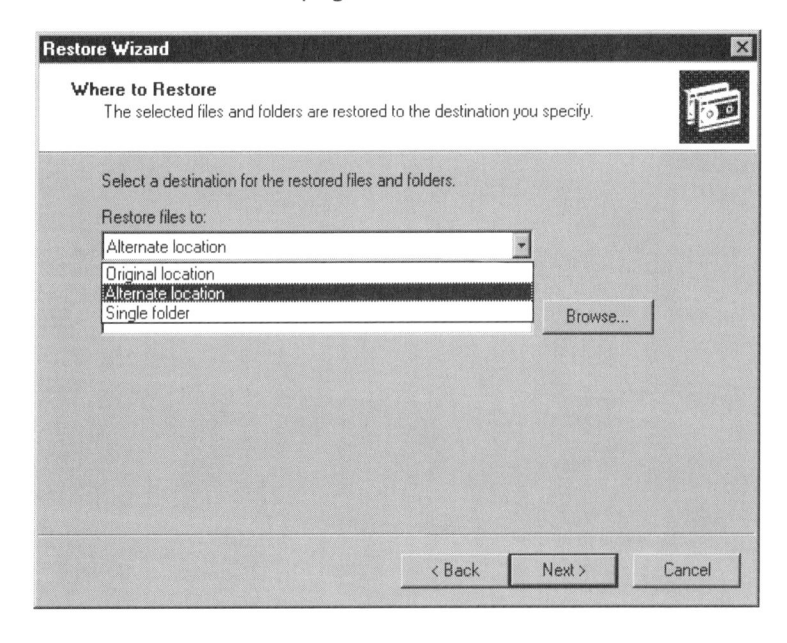

Figure 24.22 How to Restore page.

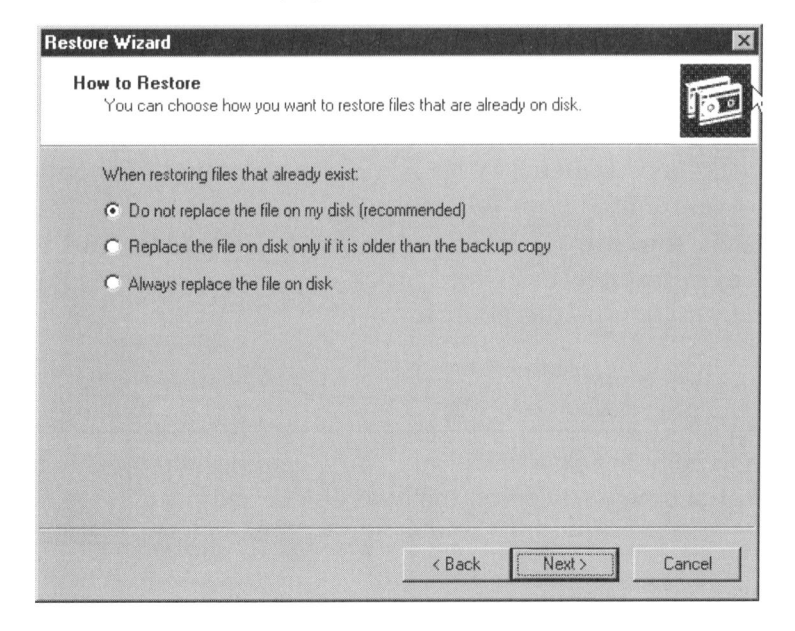

➢ STEP 7

Choose any of the available options to optionally restore security or special system files (Figure 24.23).

Figure 24.23 Advanced Restore Options page.

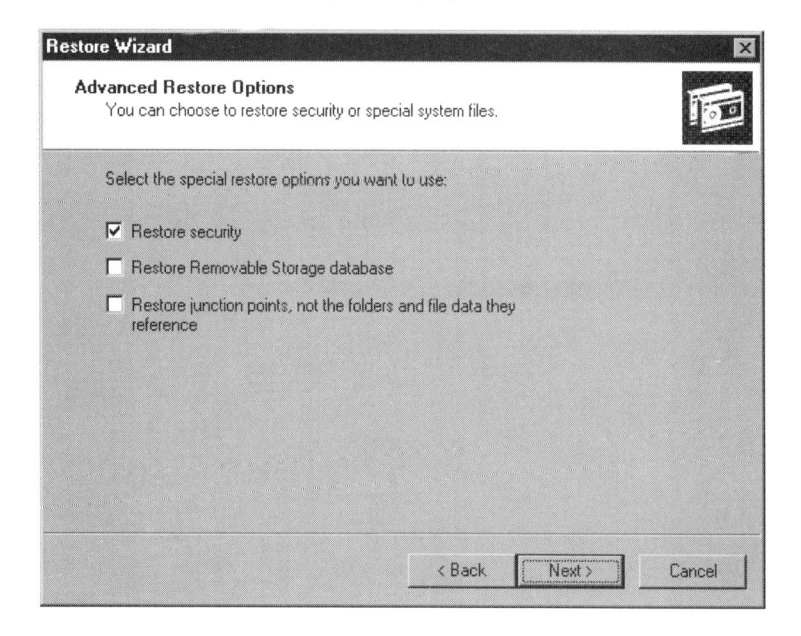

- Select **Restore security** to restore the security settings for each file and folder. This includes permissions, audit entries, and ownership information.
- Select **Restore Removable Storage database** to restore the removable storage database stored in the *systemroot*\system32\ntmsdata. Do not select this option if you are not using removable storage.
- Select **Restore junction points, not the folders and file data they reference** to restore junction points but not the data that the junction points point to.

> **NOTE**
>
> A *junction point* is a physical location on a hard disk that points to data located at another location on the hard disk or another storage device.

➢ STEP 8

You have finished configuring the restore operation (Figure 24.24). Notice that the Advanced option no longer appears as did previously in Step 4. Click **FINISH**. You will immediately see the restore progress box (Figure 24.25), which indicates the status and other information pertaining to the restore.

Figure 24.24 Completing the Restore Wizard page.

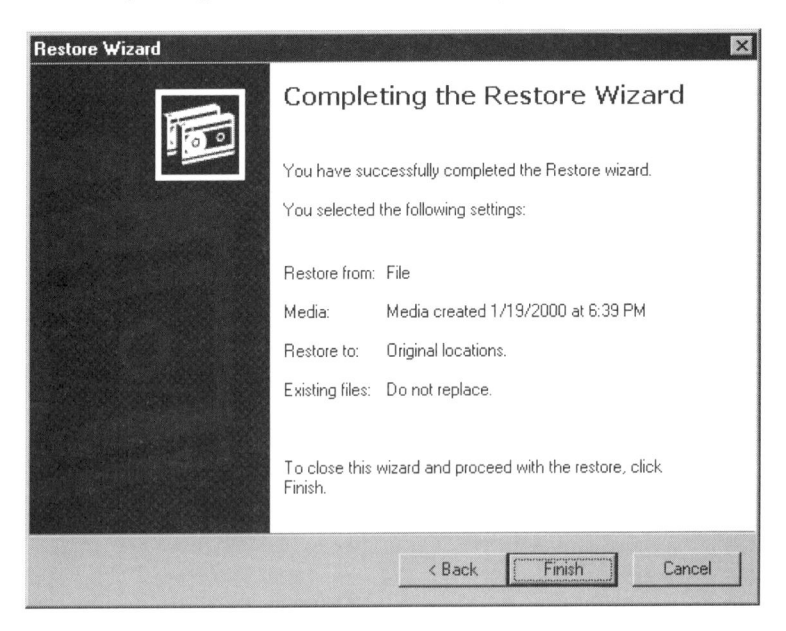

Figure 24.25 Restore Progress status box.

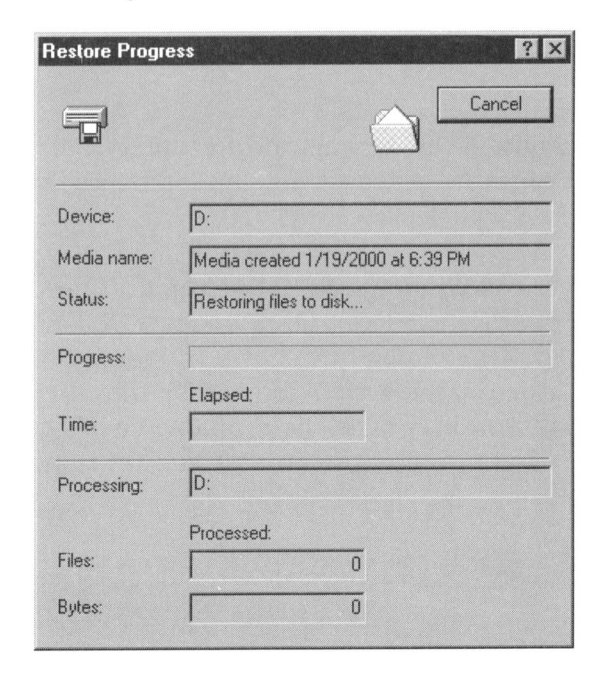

➤ STEP 9

After the restore has completed, the box shown in Figure 24.26 appears, indicating the backup is complete. Click **CLOSE** to close the box, or click **REPORT** to view a log, which contains information about the restore.

Figure 24.26 Restore Progress completion box.

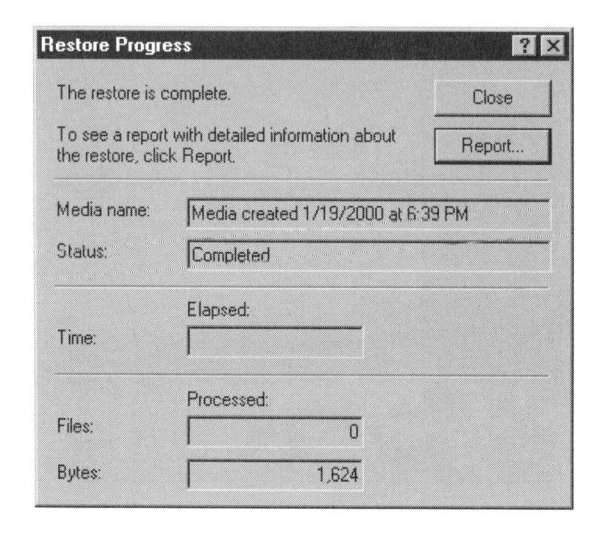

Emergency Repair Disk Wizard

➤ STEP 1

Start the Windows 2000 Backup and Recovery Tools. From the **Start** menu, open **Programs**, **Accessories**, and click **Backup**.

➤ STEP 2

The Welcome to the Windows 2000 Backup and Recovery Tools screen, shown earlier in Figure 24.1, appears. Click **Emergency Repair Disk**, and the dialog box shown in Figure 24.27 will prompt you to insert a blank, formatted floppy disk into the A drive.

Additionally, you may click the available check box to also back up the registry to the repair directory. Click **OK** to begin the process.

Figure 24.27 Emergency Repair Diskette dialog box.

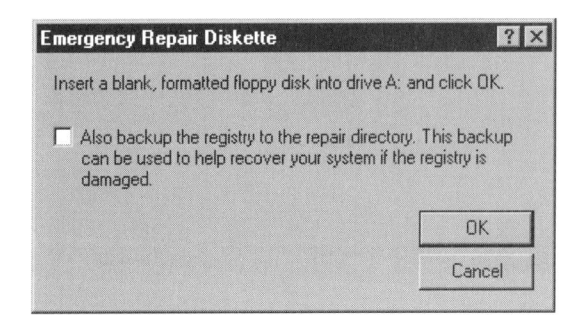

Summary

Windows 2000 finally includes a powerful and robust backup and recovery utility. Included are several wizards to assist in protecting your systems from the loss of data. From the main screen of the Windows 2000 Backup and Recovery Tools, three buttons provide access to wizards for backing up and restoring data, one of which includes an Emergency Repair Disk creation utility.

The Backup Wizard can be used to back up everything on the computer, selected data, or only the System State data. In addition, the backup utility supports backup to various types of media. The Backup Wizard can also be used to get a backup going in seconds without specifying advanced options, or additional options can easily be specified, which includes integration with the Windows 2000 Task Scheduler.

The Restore Wizard can be used to restore complete backup data files or only selected data. In addition, the Restore Wizard also supports various advanced functions such as the ability to choose the destination for the restored data other than the original location.

Finally, the ability to make an Emergency Repair Disk has been moved to this utility, providing a convenient method of keeping the repair disk up to date.

Chapter 25

Microsoft Windows 2000 Registration Wizard

Introduction

Every software vendor wants you to register the software you buy, and Microsoft is no exception. The registration wizard makes registration easy and quick. By the end of this chapter, you will have registered your copy of Windows 2000 with Microsoft.

Before You Begin

Using the Microsoft Windows 2000 Registration Wizard sends information about you and possibly your system to Microsoft. Do not use the Microsoft Windows 2000 Registration Wizard if you do not want to send information about yourself or your system to Microsoft.

> **NOTE**
>
> After registering your copy of Windows 2000, the following registry key is changed from 0 to 1:
>
> ```
> HKEY_LOCAL_MACHINE\SOFTWARE\Microsoft\
> Windows NT\CurrentVersion\RegDone
> ```
>
> This key is checked by Windows Update to ensure you are allowed to download Windows 2000 updates.

The Purpose of this Wizard

The Microsoft Windows 2000 Registration Wizard is available to Windows 2000 Professional and Windows 2000 Server. It is used to register your copy of Windows 2000 with Microsoft. Registration ensures that you receive product support, product update information, and other benefits from Microsoft.

Information Needed to Work with this Wizard

To use the Microsoft Windows 2000 Registration Wizard, you need the following:

- Modem or Internet connection
- Personal information to enter in the dialog boxes as prompted

The Microsoft Windows 2000 Registration Wizard

➤ STEP 1

Start the Microsoft Windows 2000 Registration Wizard.

- Click **Start** and choose **Run**.
- Enter **regwiz /r** (Figure 25.1), and click **OK**.

Figure 25.1 Starting the Microsoft Windows 2000 Registration Wizard from the Run dialog box.

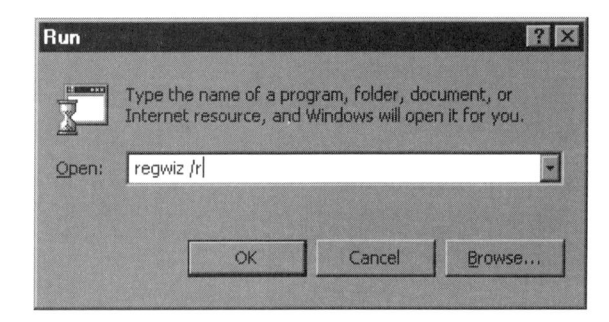

➤ STEP 2

Click **NEXT** at the Microsoft Windows 2000 Registration Wizard welcome page (Figure 25.2).

➤ STEP 3

The General Information page gives you information concerning what Microsoft will do with the information you submit, as well as where they will store the information (Figure 25.3). After reading the information, click **NEXT**.

➤ STEP 4

The Ownership Information page contains several items (Figure 25.4). Some organizations may have certain items they want in the dialog boxes located on this page, so ensure you follow local guidance. After inputting the following information, click **NEXT**.

- Home or Work (the location you are using the product)
- First name
- Middle initial

- Last name
- Company
- E-mail

Figure 25.2 The Microsoft Windows 2000 Registration Wizard welcome page.

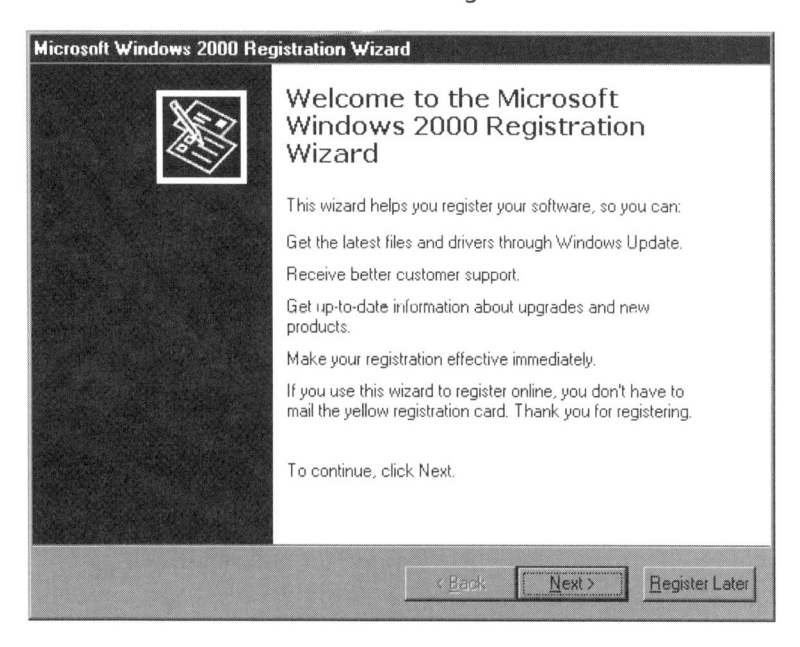

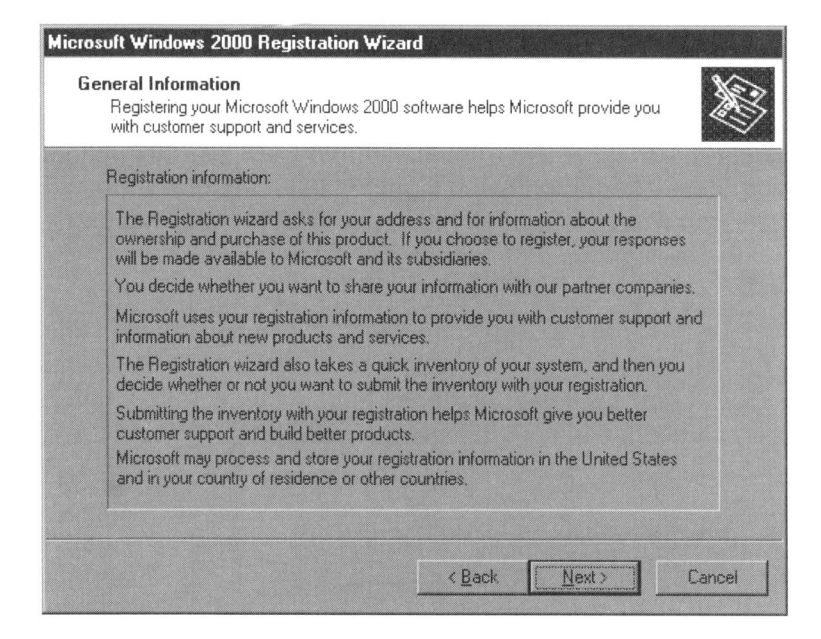

Figure 25.3 The General Information page.

Figure 25.4 The Ownership Information page.

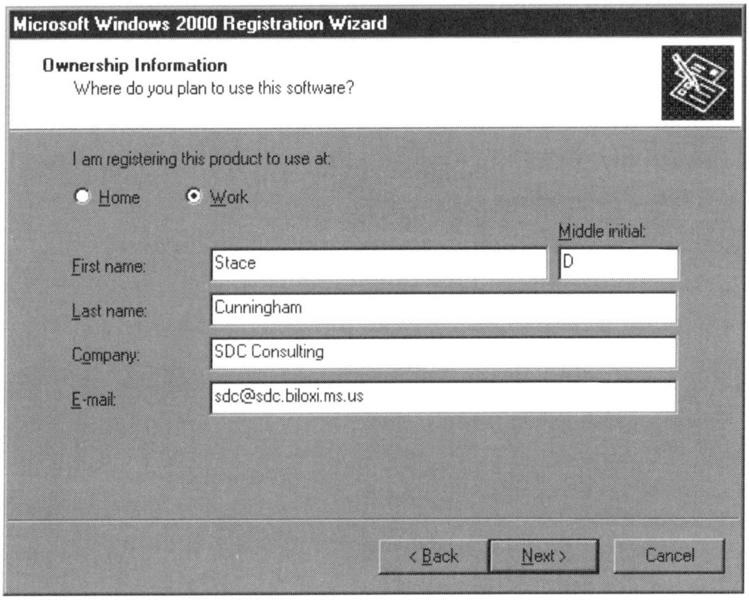

> STEP 5

The Address and Telephone Number page contains several items (Figure 25.5). Some organizations may have certain items they want in the dialog boxes located on this page, so ensure you follow local guidance. After inputting the following information, click **NEXT**.

- Country/region
- Business address
- City
- State/province
- ZIP/Postal Code
- Telephone number

> STEP 6

The Business User Role page gives you the opportunity to tell Microsoft your position in the organization, and whether you want to receive offers from Microsoft's partners (Figure 25.6). After making your selections, click **NEXT**. The following are the choices available under Role:

- Senior IT Decision-maker
- IT Decision-maker

- IT Implementer
- Professional Developer
- Web Developer
- Other Developer
- Senior Business Decision-maker
- Line-of-Business Manager
- Advanced Business user
- Computing Technology Salesperson/Consultant

Figure 25.5 The Address and Telephone Number page.

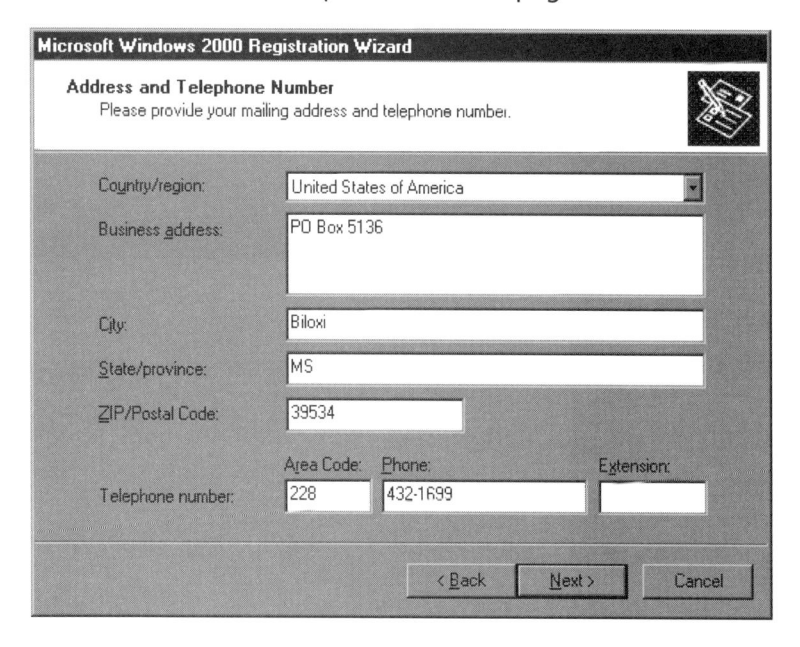

➤ STEP 7

The System Inventory page displays information the Microsoft Windows 2000 Registration Wizard has gathered about your system (Figure 25.7). After selecting **Yes** or **No** for sending the system inventory information to Microsoft, click **NEXT**.

➤ STEP 8

The Product Identification page displays the identification number assigned to your Windows 2000 system (Figure 25.8). Click **NEXT** to proceed to the next step. If you are connected to the Internet, the information will be sent to Microsoft. Proceed to Step 10.

Figure 25.6 The Business User Role page.

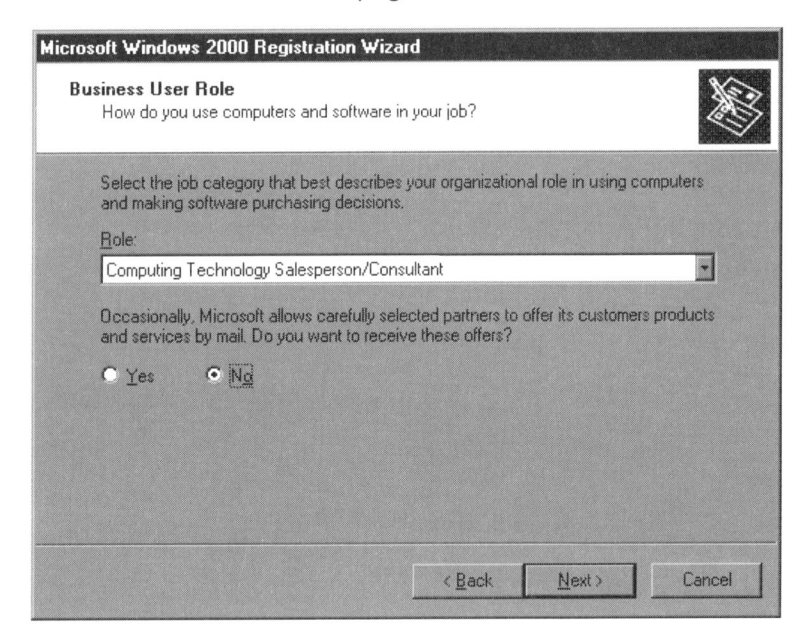

Figure 25.7 The System Inventory page.

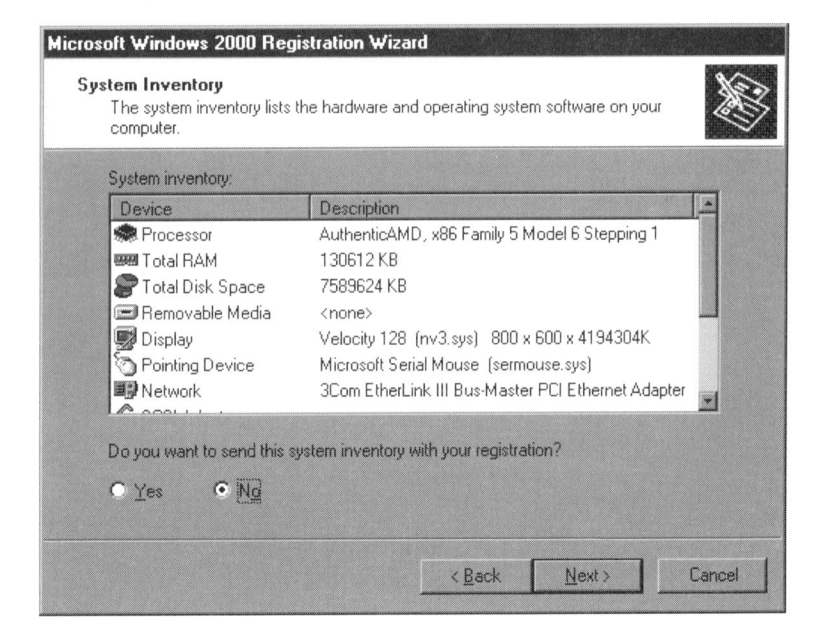

Figure 25.8 The Product Identification page.

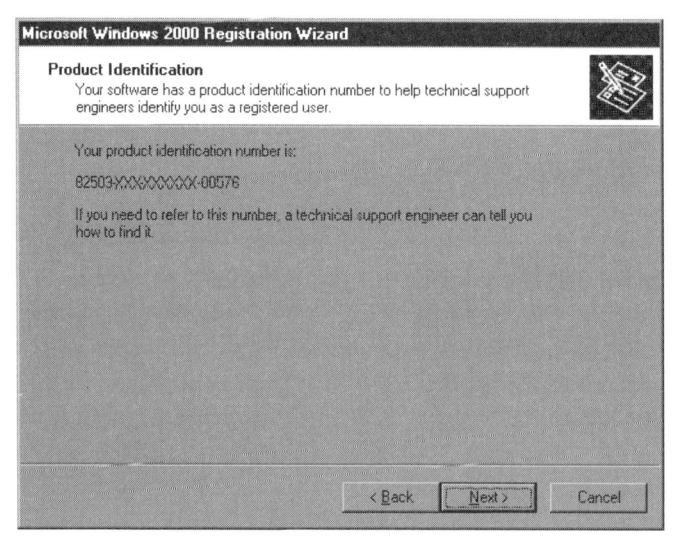

➤ STEP 9

If you are not already connected to the Internet, the Connect to Microsoft page is displayed (Figure 25.9). A toll-free number is located in the Phone number dialog box. Click **CONNECT** to connect to Microsoft's registration server at MSN. After registration is complete, click **NEXT**.

Figure 25.9 The Connect to Microsoft page.

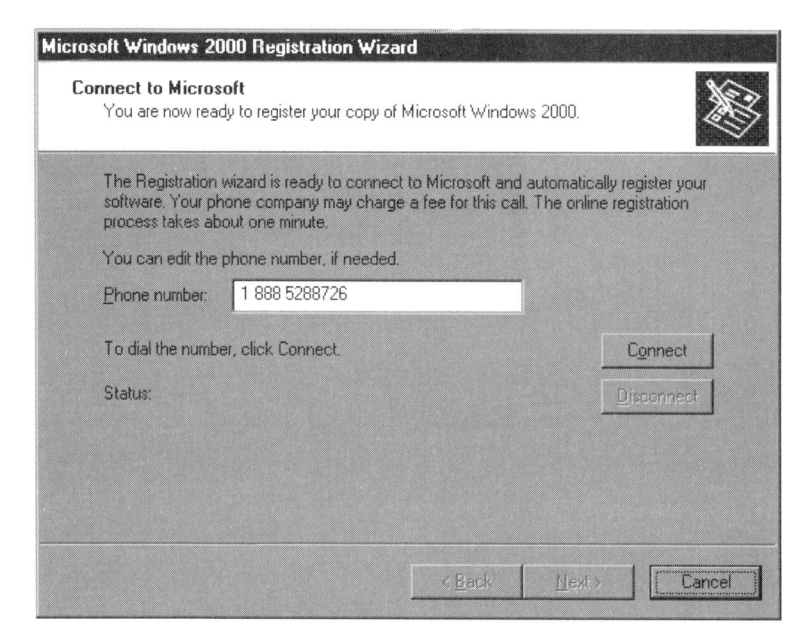

➤ Step 10

The Completing the Microsoft Windows 2000 Server Wizard page will display the registration was successful (Figure 25.10). Click **FINISH** to close the Microsoft Windows 2000 Registration Wizard.

Figure 25.10 Completing the Microsoft Windows 2000 Registration Wizard page.

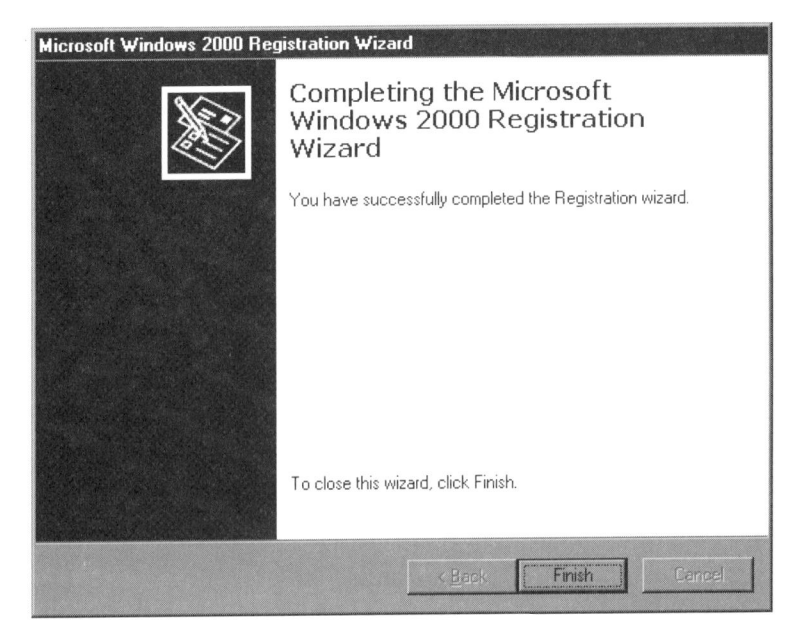

Summary

The Microsoft Windows 2000 Registration Wizard is available to both Windows 2000 Professional and Windows 2000 Server. It is used to register your copy of the operating system with Microsoft so that you can receive product support, product update information, and other benefits. Once your copy is registered, you can access the Windows Update site to retrieve operating system updates. To use the wizard, you must have a modem or Internet access. The wizard sends the requested information using either the existing Internet connection or the modem to dial a toll-free number. The information sent consists of name, address, company name, e-mail address, and the role of the registered user. Other information sent by the wizard includes system information, if you allow it, and whether you want to receive offers from Microsoft partners.

INDEX

3Com, 231

A

Access control settings, 331
Accessibility options, 373, 379, 381, 383
Accessibility wizard, 361
   information, 362
   page, 383
   preparation, 362
   purpose, 362
   steps, 362–383
Account name, 77. *See also* Login.
Active Directory, 10, 31, 292, 394, 398
   data storage, 116
   domain controller, 54
   installation, 39, 42
   link, 39
   objects, 300
   removal, demotion process, 57
   uninstallation, 54–58
   utilities, 208
Active Directory Installation Wizard, 25, 36, 41
   information requirements, 43
   preparation, 42–43
   purpose, 42
   usage, 43–53
Active Directory-integrated type, 116, 125
Active Directory-integrated zone, 117, 124
Active Directory Server, 5
ActiveX
   applets, 333
   removal, 323
Add/Edit Connect actions, 274
Add New Hardware Wizard, 30
Add Printer wizard, 155
   information requirements, 156
   preparation, 156
   purpose, 156
   steps, 157–166
Add/Remove Hardware wizard, 221
   information requirements, 222
   preparation, 222
   purpose, 222
   steps, 222–243

Address and Telephone Number page, 423
Address Book, 391
Addresses. *See* Static address.
   field, 249
   lease, 103
   pool, 86
   range, 109, 132
   static range, 141
Administrative option, setting, 365
Administrator-defined programs/scripts, 289
Administrator privileges, 394
Administrators, control, 148
Advanced link, 39
Advanced parameters. *See* Optional advanced parameters.
Advanced remote access options, configuration, 136
Allocation unit size, 317–318
Alternate location, 412
ApiMon, 208
APIPA. *See* Automatic Private IP Addressing.
AppleTalk, 25
Application Server link, 39
Applications. *See* Certified applications; Planned applications; Ready applications.
Archive attribute, 402
Archive bit, 402
ASP, 180
Auditing, 331
Authentication, 144
   configuration, 138
   methods, 139
   protocols, 139
   purposes, 275
Authentication Provider, 138
Auto-Applications, 279
Automatic IP addressing, 86
Automatic Private IP Addressing (APIPA), 15

B

Background picture
   modification, 349

430 Index

selection, 352
Backup and Restore wizard
   information, 396
   preparation, 396
   purpose, 396
Backup Domain Controller (BDC), 5
Backup File Name, 409
Backup Operator privileges, 396
Backup Progress, 406
Backup wizard
   completion, 401
   starting, 397
   steps, 396–409
Backups, 395, 398. *See also* Copy backup; Daily backup; Data; Differential backup; Incremental backup; Normal backup; Registry.
   choice, 409
   performing, 16, 17
   running, 404
   settings, 401
BACP. *See* Bandwidth Allocation Control Protocol.
Bandwidth Allocation Control Protocol (BACP), 141
Bandwidth Allocation Protocol (BAP), 141
BAP. *See* Bandwidth Allocation Protocol.
BDC. *See* Backup Domain Controller.
Bitmap images, 280
Boot disks, 22
BounceKeys, 373, 381
Browser. *See* Clients; World Wide Web.
Business User Role page, 423

C

C-SLIP. *See* Compressed Serial Line Internet Protocol.
CAL. *See* Client Access License.
Callback, 83
   number, 83
      usage, 84
Certificate Server, 396
Certificate Services, 194
   database, 398
Certified applications, 9
CGI, 180
Child domain, 42

creation, 45, 59
Child objects, 306
Classic icons, 352
Cleaning-up activity, 335
Client Access License (CAL), 11, 12, 23
Client for Microsoft Networks, installation, 25
Client/server system, 279
Clients. *See* Remote clients.
   access, denying, 74
   base, 4
   browser, 179, 184
   IP addresses, 105
   name recognition, 4–5
   subnet mask, 95
Cluster Service, 194
Cluster service information, 398
CMAK. *See* Connection Manager Administration Kit.
Color
   choices, 369
   scheme, 368
COM+, 198
Comment fields, 296
Company
   name, 427
   network, 128, 247
Component Services Class Registration database, 398
Components
   adding, 196–200
   choice, 12–13
   dependencies, 196
   installation/removal, 196
   placement, 204
   removal, 201–204
Compressed Serial Line Internet Protocol (C-SLIP), 251
Compression. *See* Disk; Files; Folders; Hardware; Software.
Computers
   direct connection, 88–90
   screen, 383
Configure Youre Server Wizard, 33
Connection Manager, 282, 285
Connection Manager Administration Kit (CMAK) wizard, 263

information requirements, 264
preparation, 264
purpose, 264
steps, 265–288
Connections, 12, 90, 91. *See also* Computers.
acceptance. *See* Incoming connections.
authentication, 139
device, 89
preference, selection, 71
service profile, 266
setup, 338
types, 255
usage, 81
Context menus, 354, 379
Copy backup, 401
Copy status, 212
Cover page, 392
addition, 394
Create A New Zone wizard, 113, 125
information requirements, 115
preparation, 114–115
purpose, 114
steps, 115–124
usage, 124
Create Multicast Scope wizard, 108–111
Create New Dfs Root wizard, 291
information requirements, 293
preparation, 292–293
purpose, 292
steps, 293–297
Create Partition wizard, 311
information requirements, 312
preparation, 312
purpose, 312
steps, 312–319
Create Scope wizard, steps, 95–105
Create Shared Folder wizard, 145
information requirements, 146–147
preparation, 146–147
purpose, 146
steps, 147–152
Create Shortcut wizard
information, 344
preparation, 344
purpose, 344
steps, 345–348

Create Superscope wizard, steps, 105–107
Customizations
removal, 349
selectoin, 354
Customize This Folder wizard
information, 344
preparation, 344
purpose, 344
steps, 348–354

D

Daily backup, 402
Data
backup, 398, 400
entry, 177
storage, 117
throughput, maximization, 87
verification, 403
Database
files, location, 48
placement, 59
storage, location, 43
dcpromo, 43
DDNS. *See* Dynamic DNS.
Default folder, 179
Default gateways, 100, 102
Default label, 404
Default name, 122
Default printer, 166
Default subnet mask, 98
Delegation capability, 307
Delegation of Control wizard, 299, 301
information requirements, 300
preparation, 300
purpose, 300
steps, 300–308
Demand-dial connections, 140
Demand-dial routers, 141
Demand dial routing, 138
Dependencies. *See* Components.
Deployment tools, 216
Destination address, 80
Destination media, 400
Developers, 424
Device driver, 156
Dfs root, 294–296

432 Index

creation, 297
DHCP. *See* Dynamic Host Configuration Protocol.
Dial-in users
  access, 84
  connection optimization, 87
Dial-up account, 246
Dial-up clients, 100
Dial-up connection, 65, 73, 81, 128, 259, 264, 274
  support, 137
Dial-up Connections folder, 66, 88, 90
Dial-up entry, 270
Dial-up modems, 62
  connection, 248
Dial-up networking, 338. *See also* Distributed dial-up networking.
Dial-up server, 84
Dial-up service lines/modems, 251
Dial-up telephone number, 246
Dial-up usage, 258
Dialing up. *See* Internet; Private network.
Differential backup, 402
Digital IDs, 391
Direct cable connection, creation, 88
Direct connection, 274. *See also* Computers.
Directory Services Restore Mode, 51
Disconnect actions, 278
  running, 273
Discount rates, 393
Disk
  activities, 318
  compression, 10
  fields, 201
  management, 319
  mirroring, disabling, 16, 17
  quotas, 10, 318
  space, 194, 196, 201, 402
    amount, 315
Disk Cleanup wizard, 340
  information, 323
  preparation, 322–323
  purpose, 322–323
  steps, 333–335
Display name, 62
Distributed dial-up networking, 134
Distributed Services, 394

Distribution
  files, 199, 236
  media, 196
DNS. *See* Domain Name System.
Domain Dfs root, creation, 294
Domain Name System (DNS), 15, 31, 113, 173. *See also* Dynamic DNS.
  address, 62, 71
  availability, 50
  installation, 39
  Manager, 122, 124
  name, 36. *See also* Full DNS name.
  opening, 115
  server, 12, 100, 102, 114, 252, 270
    information, origin, 272
    zone creation, 115
  Server address, 94
  system removal, 54
Domain NetBIOS name, 48
Domain tree, 4, 42
  creation, 45, 46, 59
  forest, creation, 46
  placement. *See* Forests.
Domain/workgroup, choice, 12
Domains, 188. *See also* Child domain; Forests; Parent domain; Users.
  availability/reliability, 44
  controller, 44, 48, 59, 117. *See also* Active Directory; Backup Domain Controller; Peer domain controller; Primary Domain Controller.
    addition, 42, 44
    creation, 58
  creation, 25
  joining, 12
  name, 170. *See also* Public domain name.
    entering, 34
    registration. *See* Internet.
  object, 189
  support, 10
Down-level server, 5
Drivers. *See* Software.
  software, 166
  support, 227
Dumpel, 208
Dynamic DNS (DDNS), 114

Dynamic Host Configuration Protocol (DHCP), 15, 31, 141. *See also* Multicast DHCP.
 client, 99, 102, 103
 definition, 95
 DHCP Locator, 208
 installation, 39
 manager, 104, 111
 usage, 86, 129
Dynamic Host Configuration Protocol (DHCP) server, 86, 132, 141
 addition, 95
 management, 93
  information requirements, 94–95
  preparation, 94–95
  wizard, purpose, 94
 running, determination, 24
Dynamic Host Configuration Protocol (DHCP) Service, 94
Dynamic updates, 124

E

E-mail. *See* Electronic mail.
Electronic mail (E-mail), 422. *See also* World Wide Web.
 account. *See* Internet.
 address, 62, 387, 427
  entering, 76
 options, 246
Electrostatic Discharge (ESD), 222, 244
Emergency Repair Disk, 397, 416–417
 creation utility, 417
Encryption. *See* Files.
End date, 329
End IP address, 94, 96, 108, 109
 inserting, 133
End-user machines, 322
 connection, 288
Environment configuration wizards, 343
ESD. *See* Electrostatic Discharge.
EtherLink III ISA card, 231
Event log, exportation, 208
Event logging, 137, 142, 144
Event Viewer, 142
External web page, 66

F

FAT, 10, 317
 partition, 11
  creation, 312
FAT32, 10, 317
 partition, 11
  creation, 312
Fault-tolerance support, 116
Fax number, 386, 387, 389
Fax Service Management Console, 393
File and Printer Sharing for Microsoft Networks, 84
 installation, 25
 property sheet, 87
File-level security, 10
File Replication Service, 394
File Server
 computer, 146
 link, 39
File servers, 99
File Transfer Protocol (FTP)
 directory, 176
 protocol, 170
 root directory, 174
 server, 170, 184–188, 191
 servers, 322
 site, 172–176
File Transfer Protocol (FTP) Site Creation wizard, 171–176
Filename, 118, 122, 400
 appearance, 349, 360
Files. *See* Distribution.
 compression, 318, 333
 configuration, 199
 copying, 199, 401
 creation, 118, 122
 deletion, 334
 encryption, 10, 318
 level permission, 318
 replication, 48
 scheduled synchronization, 322
 sharing, 87, 146
 system, 174, 317
  choice, 10–11
  conversion, 42
 usage, 118
 viewing, 334
FilterKeys, 373, 381
Folders, 400, 412. *See also* System volume.
 comment, addition, 349, 351, 353
 compression, 318

creation, 347
permissions, customization, 148
scheduled synchronization, 322
views, configuration, 344
Font size, 364
Forests, 4, 5, 42, 45
creation, 47. See also Domain tree.
domain tree placement, 46–47
root domain, 59
system removal, 54
Forward lookup zones, 117. See also Secondary forward lookup zone.
creation, 115
name, entering, 118
Found New Hardware Wizard, 26
FQDN. See Fully Qualified Domain Name.
Free space, 315
FrontPage Server Extensions, 356
FTP. See File Transfer Protocol.
Full control permission, 150
Full DNS name, entering, 43–45, 47, 58, 59
Fully Qualified Domain Name (FQDN), 184
Fully qualified name, 269

G

Gateways. See Default gateways.
General permissions, 306, 307
Granular permissions, 331
Granularity control, 308
Graphical User Interface (GUI), 23
Group Policy
links, 304
objects, 48
Guest, 88, 91
selection, 89
GUI. See Graphical User Interface.

H

Handshaking, 275
Hard disks, 402
partitioning, 10
Hardware
activation, 239
autodetection, 225
compression, 403
device, 222, 229
documentation, 232
operation, 242
properties, 234
removal, 239–243, 241
requirements. See Windows 2000.
software compatibility. See Windows 2000.
type, 230
value parameters, 222
Hardware Compatibility List (HCL), 8, 227
HCL. See Hardware Compatibility List.
Hierarchical tree structure, 42
High Contrast features, 381
HKEY_LOCAL_MACHINE, 420
Home link, 39
Horizontal list, 356, 360
Host, 91
computer, 88
ID, 98
name, 61
resolution, 114
selection, 89
Host Header field, 178
HTML. See HyperText Markup Language.
HTTP. See HyperText Transfer Protocol.
HyperText Markup Language (HTML) template, choice/edit, 349–351, 360
HyperText Transfer Protocol (HTTP), 76, 170, 247
mail servers, 256

I

I386 directory, 21, 198
Icon size, 368
ICS. See Internet Connection Sharing.
Identification packets, 142
Idle time options, 331
IIS. See Internet Information Services.
IMAP. See Internet Message Access Protocol.
Incoming connections
acceptance, 81–88
access, granting, 83
Incoming mail server, 256

Incremental backup, 402
Industry-standard protocol, 134
Information
    networking, 20
    replication, 48
Information Technology (IT)
    advice, 411
    Decision-maker, 423
    Implementer, 424
InfoTip, 357
Input/Output (I/O)
    Port Range, 233
    range, 233, 234
Installation partition, 22
Internet, 62, 164
    access, 426
    account, 77, 91, 247
        connection, 250
            signing/transfering, 68
    address, 344
    configuration page. *See* Local Area Network.
    connection, 248, 420, 424, 426
        establishing, 64
    dialing up, 68–78
    domain name registration, 34
    e-mail account, 74, 91
    files, 333, 340
    inbound/outbound mail servers, 247
    mail server, 182
    provider, 69
    services, 170
    settings, automatic configuration, 69
    standards, 50
    tutorial, 68
    usage. *See* Private network.
Internet Connection Sharing (ICS), enabling, 65, 66, 81
Internet Connection wizard, 78, 245
    information requirements, 246–247
    launching, 68
    preparation, 246–248
    purpose, 246
    steps, 247–260
Internet Explorer, 68, 336, 341
    properties, 247

Internet Information Services (IIS), 170
    component, 198
    Manager, 171, 184, 189
    services, 178, 182
    Web server, 184
Internet Information Services (IIS) wizard, 169
    information requirements, 170–171
    preparation, 170–171
    purpose, 170
Internet mail, 256
    account, 74, 255
        connection, 62
Internet Message Access Protocol (IMAP), 76, 247
    mail servers, 256
Internet Protocol (IP), 137
    addressing. *See* Automatic IP addressing.
    configurations, 140
    routing, 144
        enabling, 140
Internet Protocol (IP) addresses, 14, 33, 62, 71, 91, 114, 178, 182, 252. *See also* Client; End IP address; Numerical IP address; Server; Start IP address; Static IP address.
    assignation, 86, 94, 132, 140
    dynamic assignment, 31, 114
    entering, 87, 102, 103
    exclusion, 94
    range, 94, 95, 112
        application, 133
    selection, 172
    specification, 86, 143
Internet Server, 74
Internet Service Provider (ISP), 14, 15, 71, 247, 252, 258
    account username/password, 253
    connection, 62, 64
    listing, 69
    paramters, 246
    telephone number, 250
    usage, 134
InterNIC, 14, 15
Interoperability, 16
Interrupt Request (IRQ) values, 233, 236

Interrupt values, 227
Intranets, 164
IRQ. See Interrupt Request.
ISA
    card. See EtherLink III ISA card.
    devices, 232
    network adapter, 231
ISAPI
    applications, 180
    extensions, 180
ISDN adapter, 128
ISP. See Internet Service Provider.
IT. See Information Technology.

J

Java
    applets, 333
    downloaded program files, removal, 323
JavaScript code, 180
Junction point, 414

K

Keyboard, functionality, 375
Keystrokes
    ignoring, 373, 374
    repetition, 373
Kill, 208

L

L2TP. See Layer Two Tunneling Protocol.
LAN. See Local Area Network.
Layer Two Tunneling Protocol (L2TP), 78
LCP. See Link Control Protocol.
Lease duration, 99
Licensing, 11-12. See also Per seat licensing; Per server licensing.
    agreement, 286
Line-of-Business Manager, 424
Link Control Protocol (LCP) extensions, 142, 251
List items, 356
List size, 357
Local Area Network (LAN), 246, 248
    adapter, 128
    connection, 246, 261

configuration, 249
environments, 74, 143
Internet configuration page, 73
Manager 2.x clients, 87
routing, 138
Local Area Network (LAN) connection, 62, 69, 71
Local printer, 157
Location. See Alternate location; Original location; Physical location.
Log errors, 142
Log files
    default location, 48
    placement, 59
    storage, location, 43
Logical connectino, 141
Logical subnets, 105
Login, 260
    account name, 246
    name. See User-provided login name.
    process, 251
Logon
    graphic image, 280
    screen, 267
    script, 251
Lookup zones, creation. See Forward lookup zones; Reverse lookup zones.
Low-risk systems, upgrades, 4
LPT1, 158

M

Mail account, 77
    name, combination, 258
    username/password, 247
Mail administrator, 77
Mail message, 255
Mail server. See Incoming mail server; Internet; Internet Message Access Protocol; Outgoing mail server; Post Office Protocol.
    name, 62
    type, 62
Management and Monitoring Tools, 195, 196, 201, 264
    components, 202
MCIS membership, 277
MDHCP. See Multicast DHCP.
Media type, 400

Member server, 54
　system return, 57
Memory usage, minimization, 87
Microsoft applications, 209
Microsoft architecture, 156
Microsoft Internet Referral Service, 91
Microsoft Knowledge Base, 54, 364
Microsoft Magnifier, 364
Microsoft Management Console (MMC), 344, 356, 360
Microsoft Network (MSN), 426
Microsoft Windows 2000 Registration wizard, 419
　information, 420
　preparation, 420
　purpose, 420
　steps, 421–426
Mixed mode, 5
MMC. *See* Microsoft Management Console.
Modems, 128, 233. *See* Dial-up modems.
　access, 426
　connection, 64, 69, 246, 420
Mouse buttons settings, 378
Mouse cursor, 369
　page, 377
　size, selection, 377–378
Mouse pointers, 379
Mouse Speed page, 379
MouseKeys, 375
　enabling, 377
　usage, 377
MSN. *See* Microsoft Network.
Multicast, 108
　data, 109
Multicast DHCP (MDHCP), 108
Multicast scope, 108, 109, 111
　creation, 94
Multimaster dynamic update, 116
Multimaster replication, 50
Multiport adapter, 128
Multiprotocol Internet services server, 191

N

Name. *See* Account name; Default name; Display name; Domain Name System; Domain NetBIOS name; Host; Mail server; New Domain Name; Public domain name; Share; UNC name; User account.
　entering, 327, 347. *See also* Domain; Full DNS name.
　resolution, 103. *See also* TCP/IP.
Name Server (NS), 122
Namespace treee, 42
Naming conventions, 187
Native mode, 5
NDIS. *See* Network Driver Interface Specification.
NetBEUI, 25
NetBIOS name, 103. *See also* Domain NetBIOS name.
　configuration, 48
NetMeeting, 391
Network, 108. *See also* Company.
　adapter, 236, 241. *See also* ISA.
　applications, 87
　card, detection, 24
　configuration, 246
　　information, 249
　connection, 337. *See also* Private network.
　　type, 80, 82
　credentials, 43
　failure, 292
　ID, 98, 115, 120
　print device, 156
　printer, 162–166. *See also* Shared network printer.
　shares, 322, 323, 337, 340, 341
　traffic, 137
Network Administrator, 246, 249, 258, 260
Network Connection Type, 88
Network Connection wizard, 61, 78, 88, 91
　information requirements, 62
　launching, 63–64
　preparation, 62
　usage, 63–90
Network Connections folder, 88, 90
Network Driver Interface Specification (NDIS), 128
Network Interface Card (NIC), 62, 128, 246
Network Monitor tools, 195
Networked printer, 159
Networking, 13–15. *See also* Information.

components, configuration/selection, 84
link, 39
problems, 117
properties, 84
New Dfs Root Wizard, 292, 294
New Domain Name, 47
New Domain wizard, 188–191
New Multicast Scope wizard, 108, 111
New Scope Wizard, 96, 100
New SMTP Virtual Server wizard, 182–184, 189
New Superscope wizard, 105, 106
New Taskpad View wizard
   information, 344
   preparation, 344
   purpose, 344
   steps, 354–359
New Zone Wizard, 115, 116
   completion, 122
NIC. *See* Network Interface Card.
NNTP Service, 198
Nodes, 14, 78
Non-Microsoft DNS servers, 50
Non-Plug and Play device, adding, 228–239
Non-Plug and Play printers, 159
Non-Windows 2000 systems, 266
Normal backup, 401
Notepad, 352
NS. *See* Name Server.
Ntdsutil.exe utility, usage, 54
NTFS, 10, 11, 317, 320
   options, 152
   partition, 10, 11
      creation, 312
   permissions, 150, 152, 176
      settings, 153
   security, 148
   usage, 315, 318
   version, 42
   volumes, 316
   write permissions, 176
NTFS file system, 175
   security, 147
      models, 146
Null modem cable, 89

NUM LOCK, 377
Numerical IP address, 80

O

Offline files, 322, 333
   elimination, 340
   enabling, 323
   removal, 322–323
On-demand dialing, 66, 81
Operating system, 50
   components, 194
Optional advanced parameters, 250–260
Organizational Unit (OU), 4, 300
Original location, 412
OU. *See* Organizational Unit.
Outgoing mail server, 256
Outgoing messages, 76
Owner options, 331

P

Parameters requirements, 233
Parent domain, 42, 45
   field, 102
Partition, 43, 315. *See also* FAT; FAT32; NTFS.
   formatting, 317
   installation, 23
Partitioning. *See* Hard disks.
Password, 246. *See also* Internet Service Provider; Mail account.
   authentication, 78
   check box, 77
   choice, 24
   combination, 258
   entering, 24, 44, 46, 73, 83, 258, 327. *See also* Shared secret password.
   field, 259
PDC. *See* Primary Domain Controller.
Peer domain controller, 42
Per seat licensing, 11, 23
Per server
   licensing, 11–12, 23
   selection, 23
Permissions. *See* Full control permission; General permissions; NTFS; User-level permissions; Users.
   allowance, 152

compatibility. *See* Pre-Windows 2000 servers; Windows 2000.
customization, 149. *See also* Folders; Share.
  models, 148
  page, 306, 308
  sets, 149
  setting, 136, 180, 331
Personal information, 420
Personalized menus, disabling, 364
Phone Book Bitmap, 280
Phone-book entry, 270, 276
Phone-book file field, 281
Phone number entries, 269
Physical device, 156
Physical directory, 186, 187
  name, 187
Physical interface, 158
Physical location, 184, 296, 414
Physical name, 184
Physical network, 105
Planned applications, 9
Planning Worksheet, 264, 289
Plug and Play
  capabilities, 30
  compatibility, 227
  compliant printer, 156, 166
  detection, 157
  device, adding, 223–228
  hardware, 225, 226
  printer, 158
  specification, 228
  support, 222, 232
  technology, 30
Point-to-Point Protocol (PPP), 137, 141, 144, 251
  logging, enabling, 142
Point-to-Point Tunneling Protocol (PPTP), 78
Pointer speed, 377
POP3. *See* Post Office Protocol.
Port. *See* TCP port.
  addresses, 227
  number, 172
  settings, 178
Post-connect actions, 273
Post-connection programs, 276

Post Office Protocol, version 3 (POP3), 76, 247
  mail servers, 256
Power management options, 331
PPP. *See* Point-to-Point Protocol.
PPTP. *See* Point-to-Point Tunneling Protocol.
Pre-connect actions, 273
Pre-Windows 2000 servers, compatible permissions, 50
Primary Domain Controller (PDC), 5
Print
  device, 156
  servers, 99
  sharing, 87
Print-enabled application, 386
Print Server link, 39
Printers, 156, 161. *See also* Default printer; Network; Plug and Play.
  sharing, 159
Private network, 33
  connection, 62
    Internet usage, 78–81
  dialing up, 64–67
Privileges, 327
Product Identification page, 424
Product update information, 420
Protocols, 63
Proxy server, 74
Public domain name, 31, 34

R

RADIUS. *See* Remote Authentication Dial-In User Service.
RAID, 8
RAS. *See* Remote Access Service.
Ready applications, 9
Realm names, 269
Recipient and Dialing Information
  page, 389, 391
  selection, 392
Recovery, 395
  logging, 318
Redundancy, 42
Referral service telephone number, 69
Register Now link, 39
Registration wizard, 420

Registry (Reg), 208, 398
  backup, 416
  information, 420
  updates, 204, 212
Remote access, 130, 144
  configuration/enabling, 128
  server, 130, 133, 137
Remote Access Service (RAS), 264
  client, 64
Remote Authentication Dial-In User Service (RADIUS), 128
  accounting, 140
  authentication, 139
  client, 134
  server, 133, 138, 143
  Server address, 129
  shared secret password, 129
Remote clients, 132
Remote networks, connection, 288
Remote SMTP domain, 189
Remote storage, 318
Removable storage, 401
  restoring, 414
Replication. *See* Files; Information; Multimaster replication; Single-master replication.
  engine, 117
  performing, 54
Request For Comment (RFC)
  1034, 114
  1035, 114
  2052, 114
  2136, 114, 124
  2137, 114
  2138, 128
  2139, 128
Request For Comment (RFC) 2131, 95
Resource kit support tools
  adding, 209–218
  reinstalling, 214–218
  removal, 214–218
Resource load, 196
Resource records, 124
  types, 123
Restore wizard, 397, 417
  completion, 412
  steps, 409–416

Reverse lookup zones, 116. *See also* Secondary reverse lookup zone.
  creation, 115
  identification, 120
  name, 120
RFC. *See* Request For Comment.
Root directory, 5, 179, 185, 187. *See also* File Transfer Protocol.
Root domain. *See* Forests.
Routers, 99, 102, 137. *See also* Demand-dial routers; Windows 2000.
Routing, 144. *See also* Demand dial routing; Local Area Network.
  disabling, 130
  protocols, 129
  types, 137
Routing and Remote Access
  configuration steps, 136–143
  manager, usage, 136
  setup, 134
  snap-in, 143
Routing and Remote Access Configuration wizard, 127, 129–136
Routing and Remote Access Server (RRAS), 129
  manager, 144
  server, 140
Routing and Remote Access Server (RRAS) Setup wizard, 129, 130
Routing and Remote Access Server (RRAS) wizard
  information requirements, 129
  preparation, 128–129
  purpose, 129
Routing and Remote Access Service (RRAS), 89
RRAS. *See* Routing and Remote Access Server; Routing and Remote Access Service.
Run scripts, 180

S

Scalability, increase, 10
Scheduled synchronization, name, 338
Scheduled Synchronization Wizard
  information, 323
  preparation, 322–323
  purpose, 322–323
  steps, 335–340

Index **441**

Scheduled task
   stopping, 406
   verification, 331
Scheduled Task Wizard
   completion, 328
   information, 323
   preparation, 322–323
   purpose, 322–323
   steps, 323–332
Scheduling Transmission page, 392, 393
Scope, 95, 112. *See also* Multicast scope.
   activation, 111
   creation, 94
   selection, 105
   wizards, 94
Screen. *See* Computers.
   resolution, 364
Script Debugger, 194
SCSI, 8
   adapter, 233
Secondary reverse lookup zone, 120
Secure dynamic updates, 116
Secure Password Authentication (SPA), 258
Secure Sockets Layer (SSL), 178, 179, 191
Security, 137, 152, 340. *See also* File-level security; NTFS file system.
   files, restoring, 413
   group functionality, 5
   implications, 293
   principals, 54
   requirements, 170
   software, initialization. *See* Third-party security software.
Self-extracting executable file, 287
Send Cover Page Fax, 394
Send Fax wizard, 385
   completion, 393
   information, 386
   preparation, 386
   purpose, 386
   steps, 386–394
Senior Business Decision-maker, 424
Senior IT Decision-maker, 423

Serial Line Internet Protocol (SLIP), 251. *See also* Compressed Serial Line Internet Protocol.
   usage, 246
Serial port, 89
Server
   IP addresses, 170
   management. *See* Dynamic Host Control Protocol.
   name field, 102
   program
      configuration overview, 37–38
      running, 50
   type, 77, 251
Server Extensions Administrator, 354
Server Setup wizard, 23–26
Server wizard
   configuration, 29, 31–37
   information requirements, 31
   preparation, 30–31
   purpose, 30–31
Services, 63
   profiles, 264, 265, 270, 271, 275, 283. *See also* Connections.
   file, 285
   package, 286
   removal, 267
Setup wizard, 19. *See also* Server Setup wizard.
   information requirements, 20–21
   preparation, 20–21
   purpose, 20
Share
   description, 147
   name, 147, 296
   permissions, customization, 148
   security, 148
Shared network printer, 167
Shared secret password, entering, 134
Shared system volume, 48
Shortcuts, 344, 345
   verification, 348
ShowSounds page, 371
Simple Mail Transfer Protocol (SMTP)
   protocol, 170
   server, 77, 170, 183
   services, 188

Simple Mail Transfer Protocol (SMTP) Virtual Server, 184, 188–191
  wizard, 182, 183. *See also* New SMTP Virtual Server wizard.
Simple Network Management Protocol (SNMP), 201
  subcomponents, 202
Single-master replication, 50
Single-server failure, 292
SLIP. *See* Serial Line Internet Protocol.
Smart card. *See* X.25.
SMTP. *See* Simple Mail Transfer Protocol.
SNMP. *See* Simple Network Management Protocol.
SOA. *See* Start Of Authority.
Software. *See* Drivers.
  compatibility. *See* Windows 2000.
  compression, 142
  driver, 236
  vendor, 420
SoundSentry page, 371
SPA. *See* Secure Password Authentication.
Sparse files, 10
SSL. *See* Secure Sockets Layer.
Stand-alone server, 30, 42, 54, 59
  system return, 57
Standalone Dfs root, 292, 293
  creation, 294
Standard primary type, 116, 125
Standard secondary type, 116, 125
Start date, 326, 338
Start IP address, 94, 96, 108, 109
  inserting, 133
Start Of Authority (SOA), 122
Start time, 325, 326, 329, 338
Static address, 99, 252
Static address pool, 141
Static IP address, 15, 33, 95, 99, 112
Status-Area-Icon, 282
StickyKeys, 371, 381
Storage controllers, 8
Storage device, 414
Subcomponents, 196, 198
Subdirectories, 174
Subnet mask, 15, 94. *See also* Client; Default subnet mask.
  field, 96
Subnets, 105. *See also* Logical subnets.
Subnetting, 98
Summary page, 51, 57
Superscope, 111, 112
  creation, 94, 105
Synchronization task, 338
Sysdiff tool, 212
System
  browsing, 352
  failure, 292
  files, restoring, 413
  information, 427
  maintenance wizards, 322
  management, 396
  services, 204
  startup files, 398
System Administrator, 219, 249
System Inventory page, 424
System Log, 142
System maintenance wizards, 321
System volume (Sysvol). *See* Shared system volume.
  folder, 398
    storage, location, 43
Systemroot, 142
Sysvol. *See* System volume.

T

Task completion options, 331
Task options, repetition, 329
Task Scheduler, 404, 406, 417
Taskpad Display page, 356
Taskpad Target, 357
Taskpad views, 357
  creation, 344
TCP/IP, 13
  address
    assignment, configuration, 86
    specification, 86
  configuration, 15, 33
  connected printer, 158
  installation, 25
  name resolution, 31
  network, 14
  properties page, 84

Index 443

stack, 173
usage, 128, 132
TCP port, 172
  field, 173, 178
Telephone number, 62, 64, 281, 388, 423. *See also* Dial-up telephone number; Internet Service Provider; Referral service telephone number.
Terminal Services, 194
Test page, 167
Text file, 286
Third-party driver, 159
Third-party security software, initialization, 275
Third-party software, 8
Throughput, maximization. *See* Data.
Time-Remaining packets, 142
Time To Live (TTL), 108
Timeframe, 325, 329
Title-bar, 282
ToggleKeys, 381
  page, 375
ToolTips, 375
Tree. *See* Namespace tree.
  creation. *See* Domain tree.
  item, 344, 356, 360
  structure. *See* Hierarchical tree structure.
Trusting domains, 294
TTL. *See* Time To Live.

U

Unallocated space, 315
UNC name, 147, 164
Uninterruptible Power Supply (UPS)
  devices, 20
  disconnection, 16, 17
UPS. *See* Uninterruptible Power Supply.
User account, 24
  configuration, 136
  name, 62
User-level permissions, 174, 175
User-provided information, 244
User-provided login name, 269
Username, 44–46, 251. *See also* Internet Service Provider; Mail account.
  entering, 73
  field, 259
  graying out, 83
Users
  domain, 45, 46
  full control, 148
  information, 387
  permissions, 175, 187
  restriction, 147
  selection, 150
  support information, 267
  vision/hearing/mobility problems, 362

V

VBScript code, 180
Verification, 403. *See also* Data; Scheduled task; Shortcuts.
Vertical list, 356, 360
Virtual directory, 187
  alias, 185
  creation, 188
Virtual Directory Creation wizard, 184–188
Virtual private connections, allowing, 83
Virtual Private Network (VPN), 62, 80, 270
  connection, 138, 264, 271–273
  creation, 82
  support, 137
  destination, 91
  link, 273
  password, 272
  support, 78
  tunnel, 275
  username, 272
Virtual server, 188, 189. *See also* Simple Mail Transfer Protocol Virtual Server.
Virtual SMTP
  domain, 191
  server, 189
Visual InterDev RAD Remote Deployment Support, 198
Volume, 43
  label, 318
VPN. *See* Virtual Private Network.

W

Web/Media Server link, 39
Web Site Access Permissions. *See* World Wide Web.

Web Site Content Directory. *See* World Wide Web.
Web Site Creation wizard. *See* World Wide Web.
WebView, enabling, 351
Wide Area Network (WAN)
    adapter, 128
    environments, 143
Windows 2000
    components, 195
    configuration, 27
    directory service, 31
    hardware requirements, 7–8
    hardware/software compatibility, 8–9
    initial installation process, 21–23
    preinstallation, 3–16
    router, 129
    servers, 182
        compatible permissions, 51
    software, 219
    subcomponent, 195
    support, 103
    system, 312
    upgrading/installation, choice, 6–7
Windows 2000 Resource Kit Setup wizard, 207
    information requirements, 208
    preparation, 208
    purpose, 208
    steps, 209–218
Windows 2000 Resource Kit Support Tools Setup Wizard, 212, 214
Windows 2000 Server, 7, 94, 300
Windows accounting, 140
Windows API, 208
Windows Components wizard, 193, 204
    information requirements, 196
    preparation, 194–196
    purpose, 195
Windows Explorer, 336, 341
Windows Internet Name Service (WINS), 15
    Server address, 94
    servers, 95, 100, 103, 112, 270
Windows Update site, 426
WINS. *See* Windows Internet Name Service.
Wizards. *See* Create A New Zone wizard; Create Multicast Scope wizard; Create Scope wizard; Create Superscope wizard.
    addition, 146
    configuration. *See* Server wizard.
    post-installation behavior, 215
    usage. *See* Active Directory installation wizard; Network Connection wizard.
Workstations, 87, 204, 362
World Wide Web (WWW / Web), 184–188, 247
    browser, 74, 279
    Developer, 424
    page. *See* External web page.
    servers, 322
    sites, 173, 178, 179, 185, 188, 292
        permissions, 180
    Web-based e-mail, 76
    Web Site Access Permissions, 180
    Web Site Content Directory, 185
    Web Site Creation wizard, 176–181

X

X.25
    smart card, 128
    usage, 66

Z

Zone Type page, 116
Zones. *See* Active Directory-integrated zone.
    creation. *See* Domain Name System.
    file, 122
    name, 118

The Global Knowledge Advantage

Global Knowledge has a global delivery system for its products and services. The company has 28 subsidiaries, and offers its programs through a total of 60+ locations. No other vendor can provide consistent services across a geographic area this large. Global Knowledge is the largest independent information technology education provider, offering programs on a variety of platforms. This enables our multi-platform and multi-national customers to obtain all of their programs from a single vendor. The company has developed the unique CompetusTM Framework software tool and methodology which can quickly reconfigure courseware to the proficiency level of a student on an interactive basis. Combined with self-paced and on-line programs, this technology can reduce the time required for training by prescribing content in only the deficient skills areas. The company has fully automated every aspect of the education process, from registration and follow-up, to "just-in-time" production of courseware. Global Knowledge through its Enterprise Services Consultancy, can customize programs and products to suit the needs of an individual customer.

Global Knowledge Classroom Education Programs

The backbone of our delivery options is classroom-based education. Our modern, well-equipped facilities staffed with the finest instructors offer programs in a wide variety of information technology topics, many of which lead to professional certifications.

Custom Learning Solutions

This delivery option has been created for companies and governments that value customized learning solutions. For them, our consultancy-based approach of developing targeted education solutions is most effective at helping them meet specific objectives.

Self-Paced and Multimedia Products

This delivery option offers self-paced program titles in interactive CD-ROM, videotape and audio tape programs. In addition, we offer custom development of interactive multimedia courseware to customers and partners. Call us at 1-888-427-4228.

Electronic Delivery of Training

Our network-based training service delivers efficient competency-based, interactive training via the World Wide Web and organizational intranets. This leading-edge delivery option provides a custom learning path and "just-in-time" training for maximum convenience to students.

Global Knowledge Courses Available

Microsoft
- Windows 2000 Deployment Strategies
- Introduction to Directory Services
- Windows 2000 Client Administration
- Windows 2000 Server
- Windows 2000 Update
- MCSE Bootcamp
- Microsoft Networking Essentials
- Windows NT 4.0 Workstation
- Windows NT 4.0 Server
- Windows NT Troubleshooting
- Windows NT 4.0 Security
- Windows 2000 Security
- Introduction to Microsoft Web Tools

Management Skills
- Project Management for IT Professionals
- Microsoft Project Workshop
- Management Skills for IT Professionals

Network Fundamentals
- Understanding Computer Networks
- Telecommunications Fundamentals I
- Telecommunications Fundamentals II
- Understanding Networking Fundamentals
- Upgrading and Repairing PCs
- DOS/Windows A+ Preparation
- Network Cabling Systems

WAN Networking and Telephony
- Building Broadband Networks
- Frame Relay Internetworking
- Converging Voice and Data Networks
- Introduction to Voice Over IP
- Understanding Digital Subscriber Line (xDSL)

Internetworking
- ATM Essentials
- ATM Internetworking
- ATM Troubleshooting
- Understanding Networking Protocols
- Internetworking Routers and Switches
- Network Troubleshooting
- Internetworking with TCP/IP
- Troubleshooting TCP/IP Networks
- Network Management
- Network Security Administration
- Virtual Private Networks
- Storage Area Networks
- Cisco OSPF Design and Configuration
- Cisco Border Gateway Protocol (BGP) Configuration

Web Site Management and Development
- Advanced Web Site Design
- Introduction to XML
- Building a Web Site
- Introduction to JavaScript
- Web Development Fundamentals
- Introduction to Web Databases

PERL, UNIX, and Linux
- PERL Scripting
- PERL with CGI for the Web
- UNIX Level I
- UNIX Level II
- Introduction to Linux for New Users
- Linux Installation, Configuration, and Maintenance

Authorized Vendor Training
Red Hat
- Introduction to Red Hat Linux
- Red Hat Linux Systems Administration
- Red Hat Linux Network and Security Administration
- RHCE Rapid Track Certification

Cisco Systems
- Interconnecting Cisco Network Devices
- Advanced Cisco Router Configuration
- Installation and Maintenance of Cisco Routers
- Cisco Internetwork Troubleshooting
- Designing Cisco Networks
- Cisco Internetwork Design
- Configuring Cisco Catalyst Switches
- Cisco Campus ATM Solutions
- Cisco Voice Over Frame Relay, ATM, and IP
- Configuring for Selsius IP Phones
- Building Cisco Remote Access Networks
- Managing Cisco Network Security
- Cisco Enterprise Management Solutions

Nortel Networks
- Nortel Networks Accelerated Router Configuration
- Nortel Networks Advanced IP Routing
- Nortel Networks WAN Protocols
- Nortel Networks Frame Switching
- Nortel Networks Accelar 1000
- Comprehensive Configuration
- Nortel Networks Centillion Switching
- Network Management with Optivity for Windows

Oracle Training
- Introduction to Oracle8 and PL/SQL
- Oracle8 Database Administration

Custom Corporate Network Training

Train on Cutting Edge Technology
We can bring the best in skill-based training to your facility to create a real-world hands-on training experience. Global Knowledge has invested millions of dollars in network hardware and software to train our students on the same equipment they will work with on the job. Our relationships with vendors allow us to incorporate the latest equipment and platforms into your on-site labs.

Maximize Your Training Budget
Global Knowledge provides experienced instructors, comprehensive course materials, and all the networking equipment needed to deliver high quality training. You provide the students; we provide the knowledge.

Avoid Travel Expenses
On-site courses allow you to schedule technical training at your convenience, saving time, expense, and the opportunity cost of travel away from the workplace.

Discuss Confidential Topics
Private on-site training permits the open discussion of sensitive issues such as security, access, and network design. We can work with your existing network's proprietary files while demonstrating the latest technologies.

Customize Course Content
Global Knowledge can tailor your courses to include the technologies and the topics which have the greatest impact on your business. We can complement your internal training efforts or provide a total solution to your training needs.

Corporate Pass
The Corporate Pass Discount Program rewards our best network training customers with preferred pricing on public courses, discounts on multimedia training packages, and an array of career planning services.

Global Knowledge Training Lifecycle
Supporting the Dynamic and Specialized Training Requirements of Information Technology Professionals

- Define Profile
- Assess Skills
- Design Training
- Deliver Training
- Test Knowledge
- Update Profile
- Use New Skills

Global Knowledge

Global Knowledge programs are developed and presented by industry professionals with "real-world" experience. Designed to help professionals meet today's interconnectivity and interoperability challenges, most of our programs feature hands-on labs that incorporate state-of-the-art communication components and equipment.

ON-SITE TEAM TRAINING

Bring Global Knowledge's powerful training programs to your company. At Global Knowledge, we will custom design courses to meet your specific network requirements. Call (919)-461-8686 for more information.

YOUR GUARANTEE

Global Knowledge believes its courses offer the best possible training in this field. If during the first day you are not satisfied and wish to withdraw from the course, simply notify the instructor, return all course materials and receive a 100% refund.

REGISTRATION INFORMATION

In the US:
call: (888) 762–4442
fax: (919) 469–7070
visit our website:
www.globalknowledge.com

Get More at access.globalknowledge

The premier online information source for IT professionals

You've gained access to a Global Knowledge information portal designed to inform, educate and update visitors on issues regarding IT and IT education.

Get what you want when you want it at the access.globalknowledge site:

- **Choose personalized technology articles** related to *your* interests. Access a new article, review, or tutorial regularly throughout the week customized to what you want to see.

- **Keep learning in between Global courses** by taking advantage of chat sessions with other users or instructors. Get the tips, tricks and advice that you need today!

- **Make your point** in the Access.Globalknowledge community with threaded discussion groups related to technologies and certification.

- **Get instant course information** at your fingertips. Customized course calendars showing you the courses you want when and where you want them.

- **Get the resources you need** with online tools, trivia, skills assessment and more!

All this and more is available now on the web at access.globalknowledge. VISIT TODAY!

Access global knowledge

http://access.globalknowledge.com

SYNGRESS SOLUTIONS...

AVAILABLE
Order now at
www.syngress.com

MANAGING ACTIVE DIRECTORY FOR WINDOWS 2000 SERVER

Windows 2000's Active Directory provides a single uniform interface to all of the network's resources, including printers, documents, e-mail addresses, databases, and users. It also manages naming, querying, registration, and resolution needs. This book covers everything a system administrator needs to know about Active Directory.
ISBN: 1-928994-07-5
$49.95

AVAILABLE
Order now at
www.syngress.com

CONFIGURING WINDOWS 2000 SERVER SECURITY

Microsoft has incorporated dramatic new security changes in Windows 2000 Server, including Kerberos Server Authentication, Public Key Infrastructure (PKI), IP Security (IPSec), Encrypting File System (EFS), and Active Directory permissions. This book is an indispensable guide for anyone bearing the responsibility for the overall security of a Windows 2000 Server network.
ISBN: 1-928994-02-4
$49.95

AVAILABLE
Order now at
www.syngress.com

WINDOWS 2000 SERVER SYSTEM ADMINISTRATION HANDBOOK

As an NT System Administrator, you must quickly master Windows 2000 Server's new administration tools. Don't be left behind on Microsoft Management Console (MMC), Active Directory, IP routing, Kerberos security, and the many other new features of Windows 2000 Server. This is the one book you'll need to quickly become proficient in configuring and running a Windows 2000 network.
ISBN: 1-928994-09-1
$49.95

AVAILABLE
Order now at
www.syngress.com

IP ADDRESSING AND SUBNETTING INCLUDING IPv6

Internet Protocol (IP) is the chosen protocol for the revolutionary convergence of telephony and data. The impact of a poorly designed addressing architecture on an enterprise wide network can be catastrophic. This book provides you with complete coverage of the latest strategies, configuration scenarios, tips, techniques and warnings to successfully deploy an IP Addressing and Subnetting scheme on your network.
ISBN: 1-928994-01-6
$59.95

solutions@syngress.com

SYNGRESS®